Lord Esher

Lord Esher

Peter Fraser

A Political Biography

Hart-Davis, MacGibbon
London

Granada Publishing Limited
First published 1973 by Hart-Davis, MacGibbon Ltd
Frogmore St Albans Hertfordshire AL2 2DF and
3 Upper James Street
London W1R 4BP

ISBN 0 246 64068 5

Printed in Great Britain by
Willmer Brothers Limited, Birkenhead

Jacket and frontispiece illustrations by courtesy of
The Radio Times Hulton Picture Library

To Helena

Contents

Contents

Acknowledgments

Quotations from the Royal Archives at Windsor Castle are made by gracious permission of Her Majesty the Queen. In connection with research in the Royal Archives I am grateful for the trouble taken by the Librarian, Mr Robert Mackworth-Young, and by the Registrar, Miss Jane Langton. For access to the Esher papers, formerly at Watlington Park, and for recollections of pleasant visits there, I am beholden to the hospitality of the Hon. Christopher and Mrs Brett. For permission to make extensive quotations from these papers I am deeply indebted to the generosity of the present Viscount Esher. By kind permission of the Duke of Devonshire I have been enabled to quote from the Devonshire family papers (2nd series), and wish to express my gratitude to the Librarian at Chatsworth, Mr T. S. Wragg, for helpful assistance over the years. For access to other collections, or permission to quote from unpublished papers, I wish to make grateful acknowledgment to the following:—the Earl of Selborne: Earl Haig: Lord Primrose: Mrs Ann Arnold-Forster: the Hon. Mark Bonham Carter: Mrs Gertrude A. Morley: Major J. Maxse: Major Cyril Wilson: the trustees of the British Museum: the Passfield trustees: Her Majesty's Stationery Office: the trustees of the National Library of Scotland: the Scottish Record Office: the First Beaverbrook Foundation, and the *Spectator*: the West Sussex Record Office: the Librarian, University of Birmingham: and the Franklin D. Roosevelt Library, Hyde Park, New York.

It would be impossible to pay due acknowledgment for all the assistance received in the course of preparing this study from colleagues, librarians, archivists and persons with special information. I must mention however a considerable debt to Professor M. R. D. Foot, who kindly consented to read the original draft of the book, which has benefited from his searching scrutiny. For numerous other acts of assistance I must be content to express my gratitude here in general terms.

A*

One

The Myth
and the Man

Reginald Baliol Brett, second Viscount Esher (1852–1930) was
an enigma to his contemporaries and has remained a puzzle to
historians. He seemed to have something to do with every political
crisis and yet to avoid any official position or responsibility. It was
difficult to establish what was his principal *métier* or even to which
party he belonged. In his long career he was a private secretary to
Lord Hartington, an MP and political journalist, a man of the world
who sported his own colours at Newmarket, a fashionable associate
of the Marlborough House set and the witty loungers of Strawberry
Hill, a personal friend of Queen Victoria and an historian of her
reign; a permanent head of department in the civil service and yet a
peer, a brilliant master of ceremonials at the Jubilee of 1897, the
Queen's funeral and the coronation of Edward VII, the political
adviser of King Edward and King George V, although holding no
official position in relation to the monarchy more apposite than that
of Deputy Governor of Windsor Castle; the business associate of the
great financier Sir Ernest Cassel, and finally the master-mind behind
the organisation of the Committee of Imperial Defence. By some
strange dispensation 'Reggy' Brett seemed to remain on intimate
terms with leading politicians who were quarrelling with each other.
Lord Rosebery and Lord Curzon he knew from Eton, Arthur
Balfour and the Lyttelton brothers from his days at Cambridge.
Sir William Harcourt was his patron, but Brett was politically and
intellectually very close to Harcourt's rival John Morley. With an
acknowledged gift for charming everyone, Brett seemed attached to
both Liberals and Unionists, and was to be paid the unique compliment of being offered a secretaryship of state by each in turn.[1] But
the world called Lord Esher (as he became after 1899) a renegade
Liberal, an 'irresponsible' adviser to the Sovereign, and a member
and organiser of some 'cabal' behind the cabinet. Historians have

also viewed him as a mysterious or anomalous figure, an intermediary in cross-party intrigue and an *éminence grise* of the monarchy.

It would be silly to imagine, as some did, that Esher could have acquired and maintained his position simply as a man of personal accomplishments and a scion of the Establishment, or even as a superb courtier who could carry off such *risqué* exercises as an impromptu kissing of the royal hand in private. He was influential with three sovereigns of diverse character and on close confidential terms with three very different royal private secretaries, Sir Frederick Ponsonby, Lord Knollys and Sir Arthur Bigge (later Lord Stamford-ham). Likewise no mere intriguer, however personable, could have impressed Balfour to the extent that as Prime Minister he placed a major task of military reorganisation in his hands, and then have persuaded Campbell-Bannerman and Asquith to keep him on as military adviser to Haldane and the Liberal government. All the same, it is not easy to account for the pre-eminent authority which Esher came to enjoy in defence matters. He was never a professional soldier and had not even seen a campaign. He had however followed Lord Wolseley's expedition for the relief of Khartoum with the closest interest when, as private secretary to Hartington, the Secretary for War, he had been responsible for the receipt and dis-patch of telegrams. He had become on the best of terms with many soldiers like Wolseley and with the permanent officials of the War Office. He had in fact always been a student of military history—his mother was the adopted daughter of Colonel Gurwood, ADC to the Duke of Wellington and editor of Wellington's *Despatches*. At Eton this interest was powerfully advanced by William Johnson (alias Cory) so that in later years Esher was a very respectable military historian and an admirer of the methods of Napoleon and Wellington, Carnot and Moltke. He was abreast of the exponents of imperial development and sea power, such as Seeley and Mahan. But these amateur interests were no special qualification, even granted Esher's own strong conviction that historical and not tech-nical or theoretical knowledge was the key to strategic insight as well as to the understanding of power politics.

The role of Esher in national defence was certainly not that of the strategic 'expert' or pundit in the professional aspects of military or naval warfare. His authority in defence matters emerged from his career and achievements, and was inextricably linked with the political reputation and connexions which he had built up. Esher might be viewed sociologically as an example of the English amateur tradition in politics which always promoted the 'gentleman' over the 'specialist'. While the German Empire or the Japanese may have had consistent and scientifically progressive defence policies, thanks to their autocratic régimes, in British politics each major issue of national defence was and had to be a political football. The British system of political parties could be dreadfully ineffective or dangerously wavering and unpredictable in foreign affairs, questions of imperial concern such as the occupation of Egypt, and especially in questions of war and peace, military expenditure and retrenchment. During Esher's political career this political weakness was accentuated by the extension of democracy and the triumph of the popular press, while the commercial and military power of Britain and even its naval supremacy were open to ever more threatening challenge. A type of 'imperial statesman' emerged in response to the pressures of the new international environment, of which leading examples were Lords Rosebery, Cromer, and Milner on the Liberal side, and Joseph Chamberlain, Balfour and Lord Selborne among the Unionists. The most devoted partisans of party and economy were liable to be suddenly bitten by enthusiasm for national security and the fascination of national defence interests, as was Winston Churchill before 1914 and Lloyd George after. More generally, politicians of all shades admitted that some element of stability, immune from the swing of the electorate and the immediate exigencies of party, was desirable in the country's defence arrangements. This was the feeling which made Balfour's establishment of the Committee of Imperial Defence immediately acceptable to the majority of both parties, and kept the CID in being even under Campbell-Bannerman, one of the few survivals of the older school. Esher was associated, through the various aspects and episodes of his career, with those ideals and values of the new school which were most acceptable to both parties. He was approved by Rosebery and Morley, Balfour and Chamberlain, Harcourt and Haldane, and by many such politicians who did not approve of each other. Nor was the approval just personal. Even a brief survey of Esher's career will indicate clearly enough that he possessed the political and ideological confidence of men who from the party standpoint were poles apart.

As a political intermediary and indeed as a constitutional

3

anomaly who appeared to adopt a variety of roles which were strictly incompatible, Esher was excused and connived at by leaders of both parties because they recognised him as useful and even necessary. He was the 'caretaker' of the CID, whose structure and permanent secretariat he invented, and he was also trusted as an eminently sane and moderate custodian of national interests freed from the chances and choices of party. Able to consult persons on all sides without any ties, Esher moved freely and informally between Buckingham Palace and Downing Street, between the Committee of Imperial Defence in Whitehall Gardens and the War Office. As a former permanent secretary of the Office of Works, and also a former private secretary to the Minister for War, he understood how things were done by civil servants and the secretarial network. In the days of 'Eddie' Hamilton, secretary to Gladstone and later head of the Treasury, of Sir Francis Mowatt his successor, who concerted the political manoeuvres of his chief, C. T. Ritchie, against the tariff reform proclivities of his colleagues, or of Sir Robert Morant, who intrigued with the Webbs over London education, leading civil servants could play a decidedly political game.

It was at Esher's suggestion that Balfour, against his own instincts, created a secretariat for the CID, and the first permanent head of this 'Prime Minister's department' was Esher's nominee, Sir George Clarke. Clarke's activities soon became those of a political run-about to the Prime Minister. But in the Edwardian context the most powerful secretaries were those of the Prime Minister and the King. When these men were masterful and intriguing, like J. S. Sandars who conducted most of Balfour's political business, and his opposite number Lord Knollys, who had been King Edward's private secretary for many years before his accession and had assumed almost the character of a regent, they could engross much political power, especially when they acted in concert. Esher became Lord Knollys's principal source of information and advice, and he was always on close confidential terms with Sandars, whose chief concern was the feelings of the Unionist party rank and file as manifested in reports from the Whips' Office or the reactions of pressmen at his Sunday press conferences. The difference between Esher and all the secretaries or civil servants he dealt with was that they had a single definite function while he had a plurality of indefinite ones. They were paid officials. Esher was an unpaid and unofficial adviser, at one moment of the King, at the next of the Prime Minister.

Esher certainly stretched, if he did not violate, the Constitution. He always maintained that the Crown and the Prime Minister could take advice from any source, but his is a case of such advice being combined in the same person and under semi-official auspices, for he was the recognised military and constitutional adviser to King Edward and had among other things the exclusive custody of Queen Victoria's papers, while also being an official though unpaid member of the CID. If the doctrine of the separation of powers was ever an accepted part of the Constitution, which is doubtful, it was infringed by Esher's dual role as adviser to the King and the government. His advice was not merely military but political—as will be seen, highly political. A jealousy of the advisers to the Crown was certainly a well-established constitutional convention. It had caused Lord Liverpool to quarrel with George IV over Sir William Knighton, a physician who presumed to attempt to become an intermediary between the King and his ministers. It had caused the 'bedchamber crisis' when Peel refused to accept Whig ladies-in-waiting. It had caused Lord John Russell to refuse for years to acknowledge that General Grey was Queen Victoria's private secretary, just as it had caused Parliament to refuse to call Prince Albert anything more than the Husband of the Queen for seventeen years of his marriage.

No unofficial adviser to the King who like Esher suggested not only appointments and policies but also verbal formulations would have stood for a moment against the denunciation of ministers and Parliament, but the essential point about Esher was that he had the confidence and support of the Prime Minister as well as of the King. Under Balfour this went to the length of the Prime Minister supporting him against his own Secretary for War, who complained ineffectually about 'letters written by the King's command' insisting on alterations in his department. If therefore Esher's position was unconstitutional, it did not take the usual form of a rival source of advice to that of the King's ministers, but the extraordinary form of advice in complicity with the Prime Minister and his private secretary. On occasions Balfour and Esher could be classed as 'King's Friends' in conspiracy against the collective authority of the cabinet and the control of Parliament. This was particularly so in the case of the defeat of Arnold-Forster's scheme for army reform, which was

5

repeatedly approved by the cabinet though not by Balfour himself, who successfully killed it using Esher's influence with the King and the professional soldiers.

The British Constitution is however very flexible, and the usurpations of one age become the precedents of the next. If the establishment of Esher's position is properly considered, not in abstract terms but as an historical evolution, it will be seen that he fulfilled certain pressing needs which the party system was failing to supply. Rightly or wrongly, his own generation valued him and sustained his position. One must survey his whole career to understand what he stood for. He was, for one thing, a cross-bench peer of the kind that seemed much in demand in party deadlocks, comparable with Lord Cromer, and also like Cromer he was known as an 'imperial' statesman with a special knowledge of Egypt and South Africa. He was offered the Governorship of the Cape by Joseph Chamberlain, the Secretaryship of State for War by Balfour, and (in 1908) the Viceroyalty of India by Asquith. He was one of the oldest and closest associates of Rosebery, but he was also a lifelong friend of Balfour whose concern for the development of imperial defence he shared. Esher's supreme gift of personal address and diplomacy had indeed placed him on confidential terms with men prominent in both major parties. With Harcourt, his original political patron, he remained on fairly good terms, while becoming a confidant of his son Lewis (Loulou) Harcourt: and this in spite of his connexion with Rosebery, Harcourt's successful rival for the leadership vacated by Gladstone. Rosebery had appointed him to the Office of Works in 1895, but that did not prevent Balfour from offering him the position of Minister for War in 1903—which he declined not so much for party reasons as from the conviction that 'power and place are not often synonymous'.[2] Esher was also on the best of terms with John Morley, with whom he had been associated since the days when Morley edited the *Pall Mall Gazette*. It meant nothing that Morley was a 'little-Englander' and Esher was not, for they both shared at a deeper level the political ideals of John Stuart Mill, Morley's friend and supreme mentor.[3]

Esher's family were Conservatives. His father William Baliol Brett[4] was appointed Solicitor-General in the Derby-Disraeli ministry after distinguishing himself in the debates over the Reform Bill of 1867 for his special knowledge of urban politics in the North.

6

He became a Lord Justice in 1876 and was created a baron by Lord Salisbury in 1885. After a long career on the bench, distinguished for his confidence in the manly good sense of juries and also for some judgments that were considered reactionary, and having become Master of the Rolls, he was raised to a viscount by Lord Salisbury in 1897, when he retired. This has been hailed as the 'highest dignity yet attained by any judge...for merely judicial service since the time of Coke'.[5] Esher acquired a lasting admiration for Disraeli, whom he encountered when as a young man he attended a ministerial house party at Longleat with his father. His mother was also connected to Disraeli through slight but romantic associations. Eugénie Meyer[6] had been adopted by Colonel John Gurwood and brought up as an habituée of the salon of Mme Girardin in Paris. Emile de Girardin was Inspector of Fine Arts in the Ultra régime before 1830 and proprietor of *La Presse* which inaugurated cheap popular journalism on the Conservative side in France. Disraeli's journal *The Press* was a similar kind of venture. Delphine de Girardin was a poetess and writer of comedies and romances, and it should be no matter of surprise that when Eugénie Meyer came to England she gravitated into the circle of the Countess Blessington, and duly appeared in Heath's *Book of Beauty* drawn by the Count d'Orsay himself.[7] It was Lady Blessington who, in Esher's opinion, first discovered Disraeli and took him up before he was accepted in society, and there is a legend that Eugénie Meyer was courted by George Smythe, the mainstay of Disraeli's Young England party. Some fragments of jejune verse still exist composed by Smythe for Eugénie, and it is claimed that Disraeli took the character of Edith Millbank in *Coningsby* from her. Smythe is portrayed as flattering himself that he had 'advanced in small talk', but in spite of his 'lively observations about pets and the breeds of lap-dogs' he fails to extract a response or excite a repartee.[8] When Justice Brett aspired to marry Eugénie she was attending the London and Paris seasons and was accepted in Bonapartist circles.[9] Louis Napoleon had assigned his box at the opera to the Gurwoods before slipping away on his ill-fated expedition to Boulogne in 1840.

Young Reginald Brett, no doubt through his mother's influence, manifested an unusual maturity in outlook and manners so that when he went to Eton he was picked out by the remarkable and controversial master William Johnson,[10] who was not his tutor. Of

Johnson it has been said that 'his pupils, almost without exception, rose to the most exalted levels in every sphere of life, and all honoured [his] reverence for freedom of spirit, depth of character, and sentiment'.[11] One of Johnson's pupils was Rosebery, of whom he was severely critical and coined the apothegm, which went into general currency, that he sought 'the palm without the dust'. However, Brett claimed that it was through Johnson that he first learnt to respect Rosebery and his ideals.[12] Certainly Johnson was a great 'imperialist' before Disraeli took up the empire or was branded with the term, and was delighted to discover the word 'imperial' in the Bill of Rights. He was an authority on Pitt and on the history of England before 1830, and especially on military history. He regarded the empire as a proving ground for character, and believed in democracy so long as it was compatible with government by the gentlemen of England.[13] Curiously enough Johnson regarded himself as a Whig, which he defined as a believer in the force of reason as against authority, and he followed John Stuart Mill in holding that character was moulded largely by institutions.[14] He writes of Mill's 'most edifying, delightful, ennobling *Dissertations*. He alone did due honour to the seemingly irreconcilable philosophers S. T. Coleridge and Bentham...He alone by logic helped Liebig to go ahead in chemistry. His philosophy only is in tune with Ruskin, Wordsworth and Mozart. He was the guide of the very best and ablest academical men of the last twenty-five years—and what would England be without them? No better than France or New York.'[15] The impact of Johnson was not however so much in his ideas, strange and provoking as they were, as in his extraordinary style of teaching. He affected an emotional dependence on his favourites which was open to misconstruction, and indeed he was dismissed a year or two after Brett had left. But for Brett he remained an inspiring teacher, and the letters which Johnson (who changed his name to Cory) wrote to him over the succeeding decades made up a posthumous memoir which Brett published.[16]

From Johnson Brett imbibed Mill's cult of character and high secular ideals, and his conversion to Liberalism was completed at Cambridge through his friendship with Albert Grey, whose father recently deceased had been private secretary to the Queen. General Charles Grey was the son of Earl Grey of the Reform Bill, and had brought up his son to be a good Whig. Brett acknowledged that his political horizons were widened by Albert Grey, 'thanks to the political air he had breathed since childhood'. As the Queen's secretary his father had known 'everyone worth knowing, and all about everyone who was not'.[17] At Trinity College Brett occupied rooms in Nevile's Court lent to him by Sir William Harcourt, who had the disposal of them as Professor of International Law. It was remarkable that a Liberal politician should be so obliging to the son of Justice Brett, who that very year (1872) pronounced an over-severe sentence for 'conspiracy' on the gas-coke strikers, which Harcourt condemned as an attempt in the spirit of Tolpuddle to subvert Gladstone's recent Criminal Law Amendment Act. One suspects that Harcourt obtained more than an inkling of the way Reginald Brett's political sympathies were going. With Albert Grey Brett was attracted into the fashionable society of Grosvenor and Marlborough House, returning to Cambridge on the milk train. Visiting Howick, he listened to Albert Grey questioning his uncle about the great Whig Ministry, or Althorp and Graham, Peel and Wilberforce. With Albert Grey he was admitted, 'but only as strayed revellers', to the society of the Apostles.

At Cambridge Brett cemented the friendships that were to be the foundation of his later career. Frank, Gerald and Eustace Balfour were Apostles, but not Arthur, who was viewed pityingly as a religionist of mediocre intellect. Also in the group were Arthur and Alfred Lyttelton, Frederick and Arthur Myers, Hallam and Lionel Tennyson, Edmund Gurney and S. H. and J. G. Butcher. On one occasion Brett's rooms were commandeered by Edmund Gurney for the entertainment of George Eliot, an idol of the group, while George Henry Lewes 'buzzed round the room for no apparent reason, recalling some graceless server swinging a thurible at some pontifical High Mass'.[18] Since Brett was a proficient pianist his rooms were used occasionally, along with those of Henry Sidgwick, Frank Balfour and Henry Jackson, for musical evenings and discussions at which undergraduates encountered Henry Sidgwick and F. W. Maitland. Poetry readings by starlight and a flickering lamp, the scepticism of the new science of evolution popularised by Huxley and W. T. Clifford which so often rebounded into an interest in 'psychical research', and an impulse to better the world which found expression in the Cambridge Extension Movement—these were strong ingredients at Trinity then. James Stuart, one of the fellows in Nevile's Court,

9

persuaded Brett to take an extension class in a Bermondsey close. As Brett later recalled: 'With the pathetic enthusiasm of youth, we believed that our crude lectures...would interest and elevate...the minds of excellent mechanics whose practical knowledge of life's real values...was beyond our experiences, limited as they were by the deductions of Whig historians and the musings of John Stuart Mill.'[19]

One of Brett's exact contemporaries at Eton with whom he was on friendly terms at Cambridge was Frederick Oliver Robinson, the eldest son of the Earl de Grey (later Marquess of Ripon). Earl de Grey had been born at 10 Downing Street when his father Lord Goderich was in the course of his 'transient and embarrassed' premiership. He became a Radical Whig and an imperialist like Rosebery and remained faithful to Gladstone, which kept him in office though he became a Roman Catholic and something of a recluse. Lady de Grey was the sister of the brothers Clare, Frederick and Robert Vyner who were close friends of Rosebery. She was also by the irony of fate the political mentor of Harcourt, and brought up his son Loulou after the death of his first wife. A distinguished hostess, she competed with Lady Granville in opening her house in Carlton Gardens as a rendezvous for Whig politicians. She also happened to be first lady-in-waiting to the Princess of Wales, which provided Brett with a congenial entrée to Marlborough House.

While still an undergraduate Brett established an unusually wide range of social acquaintance which included the social citadels of both political parties. His parents had taken him in the summers to Lowther Castle, that bastion of Toryism which even Henry Brougham in his prime had been unable to crack. Curiously enough young Brett encountered the aged Brougham there, but being unable to make sense of his faltering reminiscences was only struck by his 'gargoyle features'. Since Justice Brett was still associated with Disraeli—he redrafted Bills for Cross, the Home Secretary, during Disraeli's ministry of 1874–80—Reginald Brett accompanied his father to Conservative house parties, at Knowsley, Longleat, and elsewhere. But he also accompanied his young Liberal friends to Howick, Studley Royal, and Strawberry Hill. As a much more fluent and punctilious correspondent than most undergraduates, and a consciously more politically-minded and patriotic one at that, he was already composing statesmanlike letters to Rosebery, Curzon, the

Balfours and the Lytteltons, Lady de Grey, Albert Grey and the Vyners, and numerous others. He decided he would like to be a private secretary, and on one occasion stole into the India Office, with Albert Grey, to spy out the library and see Sir Bartle Frere, Morley's 'prancing proconsul', hoping to be able to accompany the new Governor of Madras as private secretary.

When Harcourt arrived in Cambridge in November 1874 to deliver his lectures he was in open feud with Gladstone over Disraeli's suppression of ritualism in a Public Worship Bill, which Harcourt supported. Liberal party discipline had crumbled, and there was no Whip, no Whips' Office, nothing. Reginald Brett took Harcourt's side, with the comment that Gladstone's position was 'perfectly unanswerable, but perfectly unreasonable, for England is rampantly Protestant and does not need waking up'. Harcourt was soon engaged in a 'feverish' correspondence with his former colleagues to get Lord Hartington recognised as leader of the Liberals, which was accomplished when on 13 January 1875 Gladstone announced his resolve to retire. Harcourt was to claim to have 'invented Hartington', and to be sure some shrewd manoeuvres were necessary to induce that cautious character to take on the unpleasing burden. He was prodded into doing so when Harcourt succeeded in frightening the Radicals into putting up W. E. Forster against him. That did the trick, and secured for Harcourt a greater influence, for with a *roi fainéant* like Hartington, Harcourt could be the *maire du palais*. Meanwhile the renewal of the controversy over ritualism gave Disraeli an excuse to invite Harcourt to Hughenden, where the local church was about to be consecrated by a Gladstonian bishop, described by Disraeli as 'very high'.[20]

The change in the Liberal leadership made the party more attractive to Brett, who regarded Gladstone at this time as unfit to be a 'trusted leader of educated men'. But at the same time he was unsure about Harcourt. He found the tone of the weekend meetings of Harcourt's section of the party at Strawberry Hill unsatisfactory.[21] Presided over by Lady Waldegrave, daughter of the tenor singer John Braham, 'rouged to the eyes, her ever-dark and smooth head glistening beneath the chandelier', these meetings were in Brett's opinion too concerned with tactics and intrigue, where it was 'evidently *parti avant patrie*'.[22] Lady Waldegrave had inherited Horace. Walpole's Gothic folly and other estates from her second

11

husband, and at twenty-six had married Harcourt's uncle, then a widower of sixty-two, in spite of the protests of Harcourt's father who, as Archbishop of York, denounced her as a fortune-hunting Jewess.[23] However, she had restored and extended Strawberry Hill so that now, in company with her fourth husband, whom her ambition had placed in the Liberal cabinet, she reigned in opulent state yielding but little to the Duchess of Manchester, the doyenne of Conservative hostesses. Strangely enough Hartington, groomed by Harcourt for the leadership and provided by him with a private secretary in the person of Reginald Brett, spent most of his time at Kimbolton with a foot in the Conservative camp, tutored by his mistress, the Duchess of Manchester, in the arts of deportment and the ordinary rituals of tidiness.[24] Brett had serious misgivings about accepting the position of Hartington's private secretary, but was encouraged by Albert Grey and Lord Ripon to do so. Soon, as will be seen, he was busily engaged with Harcourt in an ambitious attempt to prevent Gladstone from sweeping back into the leadership after his Midlothian campaign.

Hartington represented the patriotic Liberals or 'jingoes' in the crisis over the Russian descent on Constantinople, which was at its height when in January 1878 Brett assumed his duties. Disraeli was prepared to take a large vote of credit, and war with Russia seemed imminent. Gladstone branded the vote of credit as a 'step towards violence and barbarism', but as the Russians edged towards Constantinople Disraeli countered by moving the ironclads through the Dardanelles on 13 February. Hartington thought that an attack on the government at such a juncture would be fatal to any satisfactory settlement of the Eastern question, and offered to relinquish the leadership to Gladstone. Brett was impressed by the steadiness of his chief. 'These two weeks', he noted in mid-February, 'have been anxious and troublesome ones, especially for Hartington. Not only has he had the usual responsibility of an opposition leader, but the additional difficulty of managing a refractory, undisciplined party, and soothing the furious outbursts of Mr Gladstone. A less calm, less self-controlled, less patriotic, vainer man than he would have given up long ago...'[25]

At the outset of his political career Brett was noted for two things especially, a fervent patriotism, and what Alfred Lyttelton called his 'particular genius...for influencing people'. The development of

12

a patriotic or imperialist section of the Liberal party was however impeded by Gladstone's return to the leadership, and in particular by his Home Rule policy for Ireland. This drove many of the more nationalistic Liberals over to the Unionists with Hartington himself. But Gladstone was clever enough to place Rosebery at the Foreign Office in 1886, in spite of the fact that Rosebery had already wanted to 'shelve' Home Rule by submitting the Irish question to the curious ordeal of a royal commission. Such pusillanimity was another blow to the prospects of an imperialist wing in the Liberal party. Brett, who had sat in the 1880–5 Parliament, did not attempt to find a new seat, and went neither with Hartington nor with Rosebery. His hope was for Gladstone's retirement, and a Rosebery-Chamberlain government would have been his ideal, but unfortunately Chamberlain was not available and Rosebery was not progressive enough in his social ideas. And so Brett became politically a displaced person, on the best of terms with mutual enemies like Chamberlain and Morley, Rosebery and Hartington, Harcourt and Balfour.

With his unrivalled connexions on both sides Brett became the ideal political mediator. He was prominent in the attempt to reunify the Liberals which centred on the Round Table Conference of 1887. He was used by Joseph Chamberlain in a delicate negotiation with Cecil Rhodes after the Jameson Raid. And after the South African War he seemed the ideal man to assist with the inquiries into the miscarriages of the war and the reconstitution of the War Office. He was the only man who enjoyed the complete confidence of the King, of Balfour, then Prime Minister, of Rosebery, who at that time appeared the strongest Liberal leader, of Asquith, Grey and the imperialist Liberals, and of Morley and the anti-imperial Liberals. This was a great testimony to his character, charm, moderation and sanity of outlook, and wide political experience. He had made many friends and few enemies. By 1903, when he was offered the War Office and, on declining, was made chairman of the so-called Esher committee, he was known as a man of the widest social and political connexions but not a politician, a man who had successfully stage-managed the 1897 Jubilee, Queen Victoria's funeral and the succession and coronation of King Edward. Confidence in his good sense and moderation seemed amply justified when the Esher committee published three reports in rapid succession early in 1904 whose recommendations were immediately put into effect by Balfour with spectacular results. 'I must confess,' Arnold-Forster wrote to him, 'even...with the knowledge I have lately acquired of your wonderful capacity for dealing with facts, figures and men, I stand astonished at the rapidity, the thoroughness and the correctness of your work.'[26] As an outsider, free from party commitments or responsibility to Parliament, Esher had cut the Gordian knot which had baffled politicians since Randolph Churchill had denounced the Cardwell system and called for a Ministry of Defence. With amazing rapidity he had effected a major reform of the whole bureaucracy of defence, establishing the Committee of Imperial Defence on a sound basis, creating the Army Council and abolishing the Commander-in-Chief, decentralising army administration and solving the vexed problem of dual civilian and professional control. After such an achievement there seemed a place in the political system for so successful an irresponsible politician, but as has been suggested Esher could not have maintained such a position without the support of the Prime Minister and the connivance of the opposition.

The defence reorganisation of 1904 was Esher's masterpiece, but it was also the beginning of his political career behind the scenes. It is at this point that he may be suspected of having trespassed beyond the bounds of the Constitution. In addition to becoming a member of the CID and the guiding spirit of its secretariat, he had become King Edward's adviser in military affairs and he began to assert a new meaning and force to the King's prerogatives as the 'Head of the Army'. Gradually the distinction between military and general political questions was blurred, and in any case as the authority on Victorian political precedents, the master of the voluminous files of letters and memoranda accumulated during the Queen's long reign bearing on every kind of constitutional dilemma, Esher was consulted about all kinds of constitutional conundrums by politicians as well as by the Monarch. In this way he became formally concerned with advising the Crown on general matters affecting the royal prerogatives. But more than this, he established such a close liaison with the King's private secretaries and the Prime Minister's secretaries, with the officials and soldiers at the War Office, with cabinet ministers and leading members of the opposition, that his informal activities ranged far beyond those with which he was formally credited.

14

The royal Prerogative depended on history and the correct understanding of precedents, and not on any set of definitions. The new generation of Liberal politicians, especially when like Asquith or Lloyd George they were lawyers, failed to grasp this. Hence in 1910 Asquith thought the King had no choice but to accept the advice of his existing ministers and curtly dismissed the plea that the King was entitled to consult the Leader of the Opposition. Hence also in 1917 Lloyd George, confronted for the first time with the notion that the King as Head of the Army was entitled to remonstrate about the treatment of Haig as C-in-C in the field, could only bluster about appealing to the people. But if Radicals were content to ignore the Prerogative as a significant political factor, Esher was resolved to see that it could not be ignored. From his early acquaintance with Albert Grey he understood the duties and capacities of the Sovereign's private secretary. But, more significantly, his marriage to Eleanor van de Weyer in 1879 connected him with the family of Sylvain van de Weyer, the pupil and collaborator of Baron Stockmar himself.[27]

Christian Friedrich Stockmar was originally a 'little German country doctor' who accompanied Prince Leopold of Coburg to England when he married the ill-fated Princess Charlotte, only child of King George IV. After the death of the Princess and her son in childbirth Leopold became a candidate for the throne of Greece, and then of Belgium. By this time Stockmar had become his Secretary, Keeper of the Privy Purse, and Comptroller of the Household, with the Coburg title of Baron. The Belgian venture prospered, largely through the adroitly arranged marriage of Leopold to a daughter of the King of France and the negotiations with Belgian patriots which Stockmar conducted. Prominent among the founder-fathers of the new Belgian state was Sylvain van de Weyer, who wrote of Stockmar: 'He has had for me all the love and care of a father...I shall never forget the wise counsels which I owe to his friendship.'[28] Stockmar has also been credited with arranging the marriage of the young Victoria with her cousin Prince Albert. He arrived in England as emissary and adviser from uncle Leopold on the declaration of Princess Victoria's majority, a month before her accession to the throne. The presence of a Coburg party behind the throne caused some jealousy in English political circles before and after the Queen's marriage, but it was some time before Stockmar, who knew how to hover in the wings, was identified as the true *éminence grise*. But he left the mark of his meticulous Germanic method of conducting political affairs both on the young Queen and on Prince Albert, with whose political education he was also largely concerned.

Sylvain van de Weyer came to London as the Belgian ambassador, and long after Stockmar had retired and the Queen had been widowed he remained as the representative and symbol of the expansive days of the Queen's youth. Esher's marriage brought him into the Queen's private circle. He built a house, Orchard Lea, near Windsor, close to van de Weyer's at New Lodge, and there he was occasionally visited by the Queen.[29] From the van de Weyers he probably received impressions of the Queen's powers and prerogatives which were distorted and exaggerated, for it cannot be said that Stockmar mastered the peculiarly intangible political conventions of England. The young Queen under his tuition insisted on many punctilios which ministers chivalrously conceded, and indeed it is difficult to say where ministers themselves could have acquired enough certainty in such matters to feel justified in putting up a resistance. One could hardly go back to George III for precedents, and those of George IV were not very useful. That monarch had tried to resist Canning's appointment, for example, had been defeated by his ministers, but had then found Canning extremely congenial. The King had feuded with Wellington to the extent of refusing to see him for months. He had tried to sack his ministers when they insisted on Catholic emancipation but for all his blubbering, knocking back of whiskies and threats to retire to Hanover he had been forced to give way. Lacking any skilled constitutional advisers he had scarcely ever successfully carried a point and had been constantly humiliated by his ministers, who held him in scant regard. Then, while it was supposed that the Prerogative had been somewhat eroded by the Reform Act of 1832 which among other things had, as many thought, forced the Crown to agree to coerce the House of Lords, in the early part of Victoria's reign the Prerogative had manifestly been reasserted. It was, indeed, largely as effective as the industry of the Sovereign and the judiciousness of the advice followed. Stockmar's crowning advice to the girl-Queen was 'to have every request for a decision in writing and to take time to consider'.[30] Faithful to this prescription the Queen accumulated a vast archive of ministerial submissions, and many a time a minister would give away a point to avoid a fuss. In Disraeli's case this would be an under-statement. By the end of the reign the mysteries of the Prerogative as expounded by a succession of great ministers on signal occasions were buried in the Queen's correspondence.

No doubt because of his knowledge of and interest in the early years of her reign, and his family connexion with it, Queen Victoria permitted Esher to use her journal to write a series of vignettes of her prime ministers, starting with the delicate topic of her relations with Lord Melbourne on which it would have been impossible to write without a careful regard for the Queen's own views, and including also Prince Albert. The task which must have felt like walking a tightrope was successfully concluded with general acclaim. Esher was virtually the only person to have used the Queen's archives for historical work when, now installed as Secretary of the Office of Works, and recognised as the impressario of solemn state occasions, he was deputed by King Edward on the Queen's death to search the precedents for a royal succession, the forms of which had almost faded from living memory. It seemed natural after this that he should be made Deputy-Governor of Windsor Castle (at his own request) and co-editor of a selection of the Queen's journals and letters. At his instance the publication did not extend beyond 1861, and he laid down ground rules for the use of the royal archives by scholars which were too forbidding for any but the most pertinacious to contend with. Meanwhile he enjoyed the personal privilege of browsing through them, and the unique privilege of reading certain adventitious files before they were burnt. He became the Merlin of the Prerogative, and no-one else could penetrate his book.

Yet there was a need for just such an 'expositor royal' of constitutional lore and precedent, for, as events showed, without such a functionary the King was placed at the mercy of ministers who were more conscious of their own convenience than scrupulous about constitutional exactitude, concerning which they possessed no special insight or training. While the Liberal ex-law officers of the Crown supported Asquith's idea of the Prerogative, constitutional historians like Anson or Dicey opposed it. But even the latter were hardly well-informed in Victorian conventions. Nor could the official royal secretaries, who were chosen generally from the army for outstanding personal qualities, be regarded as versed in the niceties of the Constitution. And so Esher filled the gap, compiling many memoranda on the courses of action open to the Crown, especially in the constitutional turmoil which began with the rejection of the Budget by the House of Lords in 1909 and continued unabated through the struggles over the Parliament Bill, the 1912 Irish Home Rule Bill, and the Ulster problem until August 1914. Though he began in his role of constitutional adviser as a protégé and favourite of King Edward, he was found to be equally indispensable to King George. His position was sustained by the excellence of his state papers, which remain as classical compositions today.

The successful vindication by Esher after the accession of King Edward of the Sovereign's prerogatives as Head of the Army must therefore be viewed not against any supposedly fixed or constitutionally recognised set of kingly powers which may or may not have been exceeded, but rather according to the maxim that while the royal Prerogative may dwindle by desuetude it may also expand by successful assertion. The sole test of its extent is recognised practice and propriety, and while Edwardians might have boggled at the claim that the King could personally command an army in the field they did in fact accept the King's exercise of authority over promotions and many aspects of military organisation and policy. While abolishing the Commander-in-Chief Esher accepted the argument that the King was 'virtually' in the position of that functionary and need not be given the title in order to exercise his powers: and the precedents applying to a male monarch were sufficiently distant for the argument to seem to fit them.

As a military adviser to the Sovereign Esher commenced his career during the earlier and darker months of the Boer War. He knew the War Office from the days when Hartington was Secretary for War and he knew how to handle telegrams that came in for deciphering. It had been his duty to deal with the situation when the news of the fall of Khartoum had arrived at night and ministers were out of town. He was therefore in a position to convey the latest news from South Africa to the Queen even though as Secretary of the Office of Works he had no formal connexion with the War Office. He knew the officials there and had always been on good terms with Lord Wolseley the Commander-in-Chief. When the war seemed to expose nothing but lack of foresight and preparation in the War Office and the soldiers led by Wolseley blamed the politicians, Esher assumed the task of advising the Queen on the issues which the public dispute between Wolseley and Lord Lansdowne raised. He agreed with the soldiers that the evil was civilian control which had placed economy before readiness for war. During the so-called 'khaki' election of 1900 MPs of all parties were pressed to pledge themselves to a thorough reform of the military administration and the War Office, and Esher took a watching brief for the Crown in the struggle that developed between the military reformers and the government. The Prince of Wales and the Duke of Connaught read his memoranda to the Queen with much commendation, and when he sat on the Elgin commission on the South African War Esher was confident enough of his backing to dissent from the majority and set forth his ideas in a note of his own. It was this note, and not the report, that was implemented.

The War Office had become a major political issue, and the inflated army estimates threatened ruin to the Unionist government. The solution that was evolved by Balfour as Prime Minister, with the assistance of Esher and Admiral Sir John Fisher, marks an important departure in defence policy. Fisher's 'blue water' axiom of sea power was accepted, which held that no army for home defence was needed because if sea supremacy were maintained no invasion would be possible, and if sea supremacy were once lost, invasion would become unnecessary. For then the nation would be starved into abject submission and stripped of its overseas possessions in a matter of months if not weeks. Balfour, who brought to the premiership a keen interest in such matters and a bold decisiveness, grasped the blue water principle and saw in it a political advantage. While Brodrick the Minister for War floundered his way towards dismissal the points were being set for the switch in the new direction. Esher persuaded the King that the War Office should be modelled on the Board of Admiralty, and Fisher found himself as a guest at Balmoral smothered with appreciation for his ideas. In particular his belief that spending on the army should be cut back so that more funds would be available for the navy was met with unexpected sympathy and encouragement. When Balfour was hard pressed by the unexpected resignations of Chamberlain and Devonshire in September and October 1903 the War Office was offered to Esher who by great tact succeeded in declining without permanently offending the King. The plan by which Esher and Fisher with some as yet un-named associate would effect the reform of the War Office from outside was devised with the King's approval and accepted by Balfour. From this unorthodox beginning much was to follow. In his reorganisation of the defence system Balfour enjoyed the utmost assistance from King Edward, which powerfully discouraged political and professional opposition and facilitated the sweeping dismissal of soldiers and the ruthless scrapping of obsolete ships. While Esher effected a clean sweep of the War Office Fisher, promoted to First Sea Lord, filled the Admiralty with his cronies according to his avowed motto that 'favouritism is the secret of efficiency'.

The political consequences of the new departure did not prove so prosperous for Balfour as he had hoped. His choice of H. O. Arnold-Forster as War Minister was on the face of it sound enough, for he was a 'blue water' man who had got on well with Fisher at the Admiralty and was a long-standing and respected advocate of army reform. But the appointment proved unfortunate for Balfour, who seemed never to succeed in his ministerial choices when he departed from his habit of appointing personal friends or relatives. Arnold-Forster provoked almost as disastrous a storm over the militia in 1904 as C. T. Ritchie had provoked over the corn tax a year earlier. To hold his government together Balfour needed the support of the King and the constant but secret and informal political assistance of the secretariat of the Committee of Imperial Defence. The story of the political activities of Sir George Clarke, the first Secretary of the CID who acted under the general supervision and direction of Esher in such matters, is a strange and tortuous saga. But one thing is clear, and it is that Esher and Clarke acted under the aegis of the Prime Minister in their obstruction of Arnold-Forster and their collusion with the military members of the Army Council. It was quite lawful, although very odd, for Balfour to promote an army scheme in open competition with that of his own Secretary for War. It was also perfectly constitutional for the Prime Minister to use the secretariat of the CID, which was a department under his own personal control and direction, for any purposes he chose. But in turning the secretariat to political uses Balfour was in effect employing Esher and Clarke as political associates, and Clarke was a civil servant while Esher was the King's adviser in army matters. It is in respect of this duality of roles, under which Esher acted at one moment as the known confidential adviser of the King, and at the next as the confidential adviser of the Prime Minister, that it may legitimately be questioned whether he overstepped the Constitution.

The duality of roles was certainly the secret of getting things done. Both King Edward and Balfour delegated much to their respective private secretaries, and Lord Knollys and J. S. Sandars were kept in close touch and on the best of terms with each other by Esher, who also ensured that Sir George Clarke and Colonel Sir Edward Ward, the Secretary of the Army Council, kept in step. The result was friction-free government in army and defence matters in which Arnold-Forster was the only loose part, rattling ominously but without damage to the rest of the machinery. When the Liberals came to power Esher succeeded in installing as Haldane's private secretary Colonel Sir Gerald Ellison, who had been the secretary of the Esher committee. He was also quick to reach an understanding with Captain Sinclair, Campbell-Bannerman's private secretary, while his son Oliver Brett became an additional private secretary to John Morley. The below-stairs aspect of the secretarial network, which centred on Sir George Clarke after Balfour's secretary J. S. Sandars was removed by the fall of the government, was reflected in the surreptitious manipulation of the press. Esher himself remained in close touch with Colonel C. à Court Repington, military correspondent of *The Times* and L. S. Amery, then a fellow of All Souls influential in military controversy as the historian of the Boer War, as also with J. A. Spender of the *Westminster Gazette*, on which Esher's son[31] held a position, with Garvin of the *Observer*, St. Loe Strachey of the *Spectator*, and W. T. Stead of the *Review of Reviews*. Sir George Clarke as a civil servant had been cautioned to give up his well known connexions with the press, but in fact did not do so. And so when Haldane came to the War Office he welcomed the facilities which Clarke could provide and established a kind of press bureau there.

Balfour's imbroglio with Arnold-Forster coming as it did in the formative period of the new Committee of Imperial Defence and its secretariat had the unfortunate effect of giving the committee a decisive impetus in the direction of secrecy. Most politicians then would have taken the view of Campbell-Bannerman or Arnold-Forster himself that what was really needed was a public forum where scientists, professionals and politicians would gradually evolve an agreed corpus of principles concerning the defence of the

Empire which would determine the kind of navy and army required and how they should be used. It was felt that the public ought to know the rationale of defence spending in order to accept the necessary sacrifices without the dangerous vacillations between panic and reaction, profusion and parsimony which were all too characteristic of public opinion in these matters since the days of Palmerston. It was also felt by Arnold-Forster, who had made a special study of the German Great General Staff, that in order to create an established and reliable set of doctrines concerning national defence, where the problems were so complicated as those confronting the British Empire, the findings of the experts should be made public and constantly tested by public criticism. The alternative of a committee *in camera* and defence policies shrouded in secrecy was a departure of Balfour's, and one determined largely by political reasons. Initially Balfour was as keen as anyone that his own paper on invasion should be made public, since it formed the justification for his proposal to reduce the army estimates in the confidence that no army for home defence was needed. But when a political storm blew up over Arnold-Forster's proposal to abolish the militia, the ancient constitutional force for the defence of England's shores, Balfour hesitated and finally made public only the bare conclusion of his paper. This, naturally enough, was greeted with scepticism as the dabbling of an amateur. In the same way Balfour's projects for deciding the defence needs of India and the maximum tasks to which the army might be stretched got bogged down in a dispute over Lord Kitchener's wavering figures and the bitter contest behind the scenes over Arnold-Forster's army scheme. The linen was not decent enough to display in public, and the resort to secrecy became a habit.

The Liberal opposition was perfectly aware of all this and might easily have abolished the Committee when they came to power. That they did not do so is owing to the suborning of Haldane, one of the imperialist Liberals, by Balfour and Esher. While Balfour was still in office Haldane was in conclave with him and Esher at Balmoral and agreed to support the Committee of Imperial Defence if he were placed in the government. Placed he was, and he proved as flexible and amenable a minister as his predecessor was obstinate and intractable. The Haldane army reforms owed little to Haldane. Indeed, the main principle of the scheme which Haldane proposed to Parliament was reversed by the opposition. But the final outcome bore a striking resemblance to the scheme which Esher himself championed, and Esher's part in the promotion of the so-called Haldane scheme needs to be closely followed. Haldane had been driven off-course by the resistance of the leaders of the auxiliary forces, but he was brought to harbour by skilful parliamentary tactics conducted by Balfour aided by information supplied by Esher.

The activity of the Committee of Imperial Defence and its various sub-committees down to 1914 was far more directly political than historians have as yet cared to suggest, though contemporaries had shrewd suspicions that this was so. The hypothetical number of enemy invaders which could elude the navy and be landed on British soil fluctuated between 4,000 and 100,000. It was stepped up in 1909 when for political reasons Lord Roberts and the conscriptionists were allowed to give evidence. Then in 1913 there was a lobby headed by Sir John French, then commander of the expeditionary force, to 'get rid of' the larger figure which was being used by the anti-militarists to prevent plans for 'fighting on the Meuse'. Esher formed a sub-committee in 1905 to obstruct Arnold-Forster's army scheme, and another in 1911 to help Asquith gain a tighter hold over the Board of Admiralty. In a more general way the CID served to shroud defence policies from the more pacific section of the cabinet, so that the military conversations with the French general staff initiated by the secretariat in December 1905, after Balfour's resignation but before the new Liberal government had gone to the polls, remained a secret from half the cabinet till 1911 when these ministers discovered to their dismay that a commitment to fight in France had been incurred. As the leading impresario of the Committee Esher was well versed in the political uses to which it could be put, while Asquith soon discovered that it could become a saving *deus ex machina* in the perennial drama over the naval estimates which threatened to wreck him.

But when all has been said about the incidental political uses of the CID it remains as a representative expression of the sense of imperial grandeur of the Edwardian age and of a new understanding of the scientific nature and costliness of war. Esher was in the forefront of those who sought to make it, like the monarchy itself, a symbolic imperial institution and the germ of imperial federation. The Committee also anticipated the development of secret defence planning and the withdrawal of defence organisations and budgets from the ordinary scrutiny of the public, which was to be copied by other democracies. Although Balfour claimed that the Committee was merely a 'consultative' body, as operated by Esher it transgressed on the departmental responsibility of ministers. The CID secretariat as a Prime Minister's department became the *point d'appui* of a significant trend in government which eroded away the departmental autonomy of ministers and the departmentalism of government business, while it enhanced the supra-departmental authority of the Prime Minister. This process became firmly consolidated when after December 1916 Lloyd George, casting about for a method of operating a two-tier cabinet which would free the so-called 'War Cabinet' from departmental concerns so that it could concentrate on running the war, adopted the idea of using the secretariat of the Committee of Imperial Defence as the nucleus of a cabinet secretariat.

After the defeat of Balfour over the 1911 Parliament Bill, which through his uncertain leadership caused havoc in the Unionist party, Esher lost touch with the Unionists and wished for the continuance of the Liberals in office. He preferred Asquith, Grey, Haldane and Churchill to Bonar Law, whom he held in small esteem, and the other opposition leaders. He also preferred the Liberals' Parliament Act, which at least preserved hereditary peers, to the weird devices of Lords Lansdowne and Rosebery for the reform of the second chamber. It is not therefore surprising that he counselled King George V not to depart one iota from the constitutional principle that he could only act on the advice of his responsible advisers. The Unionists claimed that the abolition of the Lords' veto as an effective check on the Liberals' Irish Home Rule Bill, introduced in 1912 supposedly without any mandate from the electorate, had revived the King's power to veto a Bill as the only remaining constitutional curb on a 'despotic' House of Commons. Certainly the question of the King's role in the bitter struggle that followed over Home Rule and the question of the inclusion or exclusion of Ulster brought the Sovereign to the forefront of the political stage. One project, broached to Esher by Colonel Repington, was the creation of some official panel of constitutional advisers to the King in place of his private secretaries, who lacked experience in great affairs of state. But Esher maintained that the persons around the King must of

24

necessity remain obscure. He was not himself among those greatly concerned for Ulster even though he sympathised with Carson. He believed that it was better to have fighting in Ireland than that the King should be dragged into the quarrel. Only when the King himself showed a determination to intervene at some point before the actual outbreak of civil war did Esher address himself seriously to the problem of what intervention was possible.

In the last months before the outbreak of the First World War Esher became somewhat estranged from Asquith and ceased to attend the CID. But when Kitchener, who happened to be in England at the outbreak of war, was placed by Asquith rather precipitantly at the War Office, Esher attached himself to him as an unofficial adviser. Soon he was in France and with Lady Esher did invaluable work for the army medical services which at first were in a scandalous condition of chaos. As practically the only English statesman who could converse with French ministers and soldiers with natural fluency Esher became Kitchener's agent in Paris where the British ambassador, Sir Francis Bertie, was conspicuously absent, having fled with the French government to Bordeaux. Before many months had passed Esher had become the linch-pin of inter-Allied liaison, for the French assumed that Kitchener was in charge of the war. Esher also became the link between the British GHQ in France and the War Office. His son Maurice Brett[32] had been ADC to Sir John French at Aldershot, and now set up an office in Paris called the *Intelligence Anglaise*. Since the relations between Sir John and Kitchener were extremely strained, such good offices obviated more than one disaster.

Esher's original mission was to collect the materials for a history of Sir John French's campaign. Only Kitchener foretold a war lasting years, and the Committee of Imperial Defence had neglected the problem of how to form a British or an inter-Allied war directorate. In a long war political considerations operate more decisively on strategic decisions, and the lack of political or military concert between Britain and France soon produced the most menacing results. As the man who went everywhere and spoke to everybody Esher became acutely aware of the scale of the problem. He came to regard the formation of an inter-Allied military council as more important than the formation of war directorates in each Allied country, and he was very near to obtaining acceptance for a scheme for such a council. Unfortunately at that juncture, in December 1915, the cabinet resolved to get rid of Kitchener by sending him on a mission to the Dardanelles and the French cried off. When Lloyd George finally helped to establish the Versailles Allied War Council for very characteristic political reasons it was too late.

In the meantime the vital tasks of Anglo-French politico-military liaison fell almost entirely to Esher himself. Although he started as a supporter of what he called 'eccentric' attacks and argued before the Committee of Imperial Defence and the War Committee for ambitious diplomatic and military policies such as an attempt to bring Holland into the war, he became a convinced 'westerner'. He did much to assist the King who, like the public, continued to support Sir William Robertson as CIGS and Douglas Haig as C-in-C in France long after Lloyd George began hunting for their scalps. One of Lloyd George's first plots as Prime Minister was to secretly agree with the French to place Haig under the command of Nivelle, who was then relatively junior and inexperienced and whose offensive proved an unmitigated disaster. Later in 1917 Lloyd George began to undermine the authority of Robertson, who as a westerner opposed his persistent requests for a Salonika offensive. Ultimately Robertson was 'outed', but Haig remained, and it was to Haig that Esher had become most attached. Having followed the Somme battles closely, Esher believed that they were far from amounting to failure, and he thought the same in the main of the Passchendaele battles. The real failure lay in his view in the bad timing of the offensives, which Haig was forced to launch at the most unprofitable times and seasons chiefly at the demand of the French. General Joffre had banged his fist on the table and shouted that the French army would have ceased to exist if the Somme battle were delayed till the arrival of the tanks. Likewise Haig was obliged to postpone his drive for the Flanders coast, which should have been launched in the early part of 1917 and combined with landings from the sea (with tanks carried in flat-bottomed barges with fronts that could be let down on to the beaches) because of the ill-advised French plan to 'break through' by Nivelle's offensive. This became sheer folly after the Germans had shortened their line and was denounced as such by Haig and even some of the French staff. Haig had to remain quiet in Flanders until the season of the rains. On the French side the imperatives were political, as Esher realised, and this was the urgent case for more effective liaison.

The political weakness of France sprang from the fragmentation of parties and German defeatist propaganda. The political wobblings and feebleness of the Asquith government and the Coalition sprang from the mistake, which the French never made, of trying to extrapolate peacetime politics into wartime. The result was a scandalous series of political crises conducted in a spirit far removed from any *union sacrée*, and without parallel in the Second World War. During these crises Esher was usually in London acting as an adviser to the King and his chief concern was to support Kitchener and later Haig. He had something to do with the suggestion of a Ministry of Munitions, which was forced on Asquith by the persistent recommendations of the King. Esher also was the guiding hand behind the Army Council and Robertson when the soldiers produced their unbeatable formula of 'every available man' which prevented Asquith from wriggling out of conscription. He did his best to educate the British in the meaning of total war by starting a movement, assisted by the Lord Provost of Glasgow, to secure the limitation of profits and wages and the discouragement of wasteful amusements, pleasure motoring and strikes. He even dared to declare in the *Glasgow Herald* that the Germans were winning the war. 'The tyrannies of the seventeenth century,' he warned the easy-going public, 'are petty compared with such a claim as Germany by her statesmen, her soldiers and her philosophers has declared her intention to substantiate.' In August 1915 the public had scarcely realised the real issue at stake, while for Esher it was an inevitable and final contest: '...we fight this war to a finish for ever, even if we stand alone.'

When Lloyd George replaced Kitchener at the War Office, and a few months later ousted Asquith from the premiership, the soldiers were in danger of falling under the tutelage of the politicians. It was largely owing to Esher that they did not. The public, indeed, remained loyal to Haig as C-in-C in France and to Robertson as CIGS at the War Office, as did also the soldiers with few exceptions. The King in such circumstances was able to exert a considerable checking influence on the volatile designs of Lloyd George. Esher's particular role lay in advising Haig in political matters. He assisted

Haig in opposing Lloyd George's policy, which originated with Pétain, of 'waiting for the Americans' and he supported the Passchendaele offensive against obstruction both from Paris and London. Though he agreed with Henry Wilson, whom Haig always distrusted, that the Flanders offensive was really too late after it had been delayed through the summer of 1917, still Esher insisted that the paramount need to keep France in the war justified it.

Suffering from war weariness and ill health, Esher decided to relinquish his ill-defined mission in Paris early in 1918. The establishment of the Supreme War Council at Versailles and the prospect that the senile ambassador at Paris might be replaced by Milner—a false hope—convinced him that his usefulness had diminished. He resigned from the CID some months later, at the age of sixty-five, and his active career was over. Though he lived until 1930 his project of a history of the Great War, for which he had collected voluminous materials, was seemingly not even begun.[33]

Two

Lord Hartington and General Gordon

At Devonshire House Hartington had a suite of rooms on the ground floor leading into the garden. Faded damask on the walls, tarnished gilding, dim lighting, fine pictures carelessly hung, and few bells, seemed to Brett to typify the 'hubristic Whig tradition'. Hartington's sister, Lady Louisa Egerton, herself one of the few surviving Whig ladies who still used the characteristic pronunciations 'goolden brasslet' or 'charrot', pointed out to Brett where the heads of powdered footmen had stained the wall in the late Duke's time when their 'yawns of boredom rang through the house'.[1] Hartington seldom rose before ten o'clock, when he would take a meagre breakfast at a small table. 'He stalked to bed in the small hours; generally after a game of bridge, which he played with vexatious deliberation and mediocre skill.' He wore the oldest tweeds, and a hat that was said to have belonged to Goethe: someone described him as 'dressed as a seedy, shady sailor'. However, he had been taken in hand by his mistress, the Duchess of Manchester, who forced him to tidy his unruly hair and helped him to overcome his naturally humble manner by overlaying it with a gravity which looked like hauteur.[2]

The austerity of Devonshire House contrasted with the splendour and brilliance of the household at Kimbolton or the town house at the corner of Great Stanhope Street where 'the Duchess' as she was called by all from the Prince of Wales down had for a generation taken 'an easy precedence in Society'. Years before, Brett himself had been among the throng which had gathered in the Park to see her drive through Stanhope Gate towards the 'ladies' mile'. Countess Louise von Alten after coming to England as the bride of the Duke of Manchester formed a liaison with Hartington which lasted thirty years until he was finally free to marry her. Brett considered her 'one

29

of the cleverest and certainly one of the best-informed women of her epoch'. Her 'ruthless beauty' and 'hardness of manner' and 'social gifts' he also noticed. The 'Tory atmosphere of Kimbolton' in his view occasionally swayed Hartington's political action, as when he refused to move a hostile resolution to the Berlin Treaty of 1878 but only what Disraeli called a 'string of congratulatory regrets'.

Hartington moved easily in both Conservative and Liberal circles. His passion for horse-racing took him also to the houses of the Rothschilds—to Palace House, Newmarket, the home of Mrs Leopold de Rothschild and her sister Mrs Arthur Sassoon, to Leopold's house at Ascot, Alfred's at Seamore Place, or Nathaniel's at Tring. It also took him, significantly for Brett, to The Durdans, Rosebery's house at Epsom.

While Hartington was politically to the right of the bulk of the Liberals, and thus exposed to the undermining of his leadership by the independent action of Gladstone on one hand and the Radicals on the other, he was not 'jingo' enough for Brett on imperial questions. Here no doubt there was a gap of generations. It was at this time that the young Liberal, Alfred Milner, spoke against Gladstone's neglect of the empire at the Oxford Union.[3] Brett had an impression of Gladstone at close quarters when in December 1878 the Liberal opposition leaders met to discuss the Queen's speech at Lord Ripon's house in Carlton Gardens. Parliament had been recalled suddenly to deal with the situation which had arisen since Lord Lytton's 'forward' policy in India had led to war with the Afghans. Harcourt thought Lytton was bent on taking Kabul, and wanted to condemn the war *in toto*. Hartington thought the Russians, whose mission to Kabul had been accepted, might have been acting defensively, and wanted more information. Brett was not so scrupulous. He thought the days of buffer states were over, and now that international politics were ruled by 'great agglomerations' (what would now be called 'power blocs') it was useless for Britain to try to form buffer states against the Russians in the Balkans or in India. Britain ought therefore, he thought, to negotiate for a Russian ex-pansion in the former sphere in exchange for our occupation of Afghanistan, or at least for what was called a 'scientific frontier'. After Lord Granville had read the Queen's speech Lord Northbrook the ex-Viceroy was in Brett's opinion 'admirably temperate', Hartington's comments were 'finely accurate', but Gladstone's were

30

quite another matter. 'I am amazed that he should be the idol of our sober people. While he was speaking I felt he was an enemy in politics and morals. He has led men by their passions rather than by their intellects.'[4]

Disraeli, of course, as the patentee of 'jingoism', could be and was accused of doing the same thing. The Conservatives, however, did not pretend to believe as Liberals did in the march of intellect or the rule of righteousness—Gladstone placing rather more stress upon the second of these two tenets of the 'party of progress'. Hartington like Brett was far too much of a realist to trust in such things as disinterestedness or righteous example in foreign policy where British strategic interests were concerned, and hence he was at a hopeless disadvantage when Gladstone launched his Midlothian tour of speeches so admirably attuned to the ears of insular Nonconformity. 'The happy conditions in which we live as an island', Gladstone declared at Loanhead, '...so long as we are believed to be disinterested in Europe, secures for us the noblest part that any Power was ever called upon to play—a part far lifted above all selfish aims and objects—a part blessed in its origin, worthy of our Christianity...for it is the work of peace and the work of goodwill among men. But how can that part be performed by a Power which pursues selfish aims in the dark?'[5] The course of European affairs during the thirty-five years to follow was a sad commentary on this text.

As a prospective Prime Minister Hartington was strangely shy and retiring, so that his private secretary had little to do. The 'shadow cabinet' had not yet quite developed in any really continuous form, and as Hartington felt the ground cut beneath him by Gladstone's role, which was quite inconsistent with that of a retired party chief, he assumed even more the attitude of a mere *locum tenens*. While Gladstone thundered on grave moral issues, Hartington only addressed social gatherings on neutral topics. Brett provided him with draft arguments for his speeches, some of which were very tiresome. Hartington was known to yawn while reading his own speeches and to apologise for their dullness. Brett could be equally uninspired, especially when covering social and industrial topics. 'I cannot imagine what you are to say to those bores on science and art,' he confessed when asked to ghost a speech for delivery at Newcastle. 'You might get rid of art by observing that science in a town like Newcastle is probably more interesting...but that neverthe-

31

less it will not do to neglect a taste for beautiful things because you live among the hideous accessories of the production of useful things...of all civilising agencies that of art...is among the most powerful.'[6] There was not much inspiration here, and in truth Brett's interests were in social matters of another sort. He was in a very listless stage of his life. He complained that the season was the thinnest on record, he spent some days with Rosebery at Mentmore, he dabbled in the acquaintance of Ellen Terry and her sister, he did the rounds of Newmarket and Ascot and spent ten days attending the theatres in Paris.

No doubt his forthcoming marriage made him restless, for he hated any fuss or limelight and planned to withdraw with his bride to Paris as soon as he could disengage himself from his duties. He found the protocol of a diplomatic wedding at Windsor most unpleasant, and before he could escape for two months to Paris he drove to his father's house at Heath Farm, Hertfordshire, to settle various matters for Hartington, who happened to be in the throes of a most unusual course of public speaking:

Brett-Hartington, 26 September 1879:[7] You will find a parcel at Devonshire House containing the Newcastle addresses...I am ready for anything else you may wish done before I leave for Paris which will be on Wednesday next.

I am pretty well considering; not feeling much the worse for the gloomy proceedings two days ago. The only pleasant thing about the day was the drive here from Windsor through a charming country. I am beginning to feel that the worst is over.

I hope the weather has redeemed Newmarket for you...You did not accept with Lady Ronald so I suppose she is unfit...

There is a general consensus of opinion that your Newcastle speech was the best you ever made;...the 'campaign' has proved a great success!

The Bretts spent October and November staying at the Hotel Brighton, Rue de Rivoli. They read George Eliot's latest novels together, and Brett kept up with the English and French papers. Once he encountered Gladstone, who was looking for ivories in an antique shop on the Quai Voltaire, and had some conversation. Reading a speech which Lord Salisbury had made at Manchester Brett thought it a 'triumphant defence of the Government policy. We deserve to be beaten at the next election.' He also took a very Tory view on Ireland—he thought Lefevre's plan for state loans to Irish small-holders would turn them all into Fenians. He had an interesting interview with Gambetta, whom he found had a high regard for Hartington's influence, yet thought it would be better for the Liberals if they lost the coming election, since they could not in his opinion conciliate the Irish Home Rulers nor gain a majority large enough to overrule them. Brett agreed.[8]

On his return to England in December Brett visited Chatsworth where he saw Harcourt but not Hartington, who hated the place. Harcourt he found 'rampant about the Midlothian demonstration', accusing Gladstone of sacrificing the 'good of the party for the sake of winning a miserable Scotch constituency'.[9] Not sharing Gambetta's view that 'a Liberal victory would be very likely disastrous to the Liberal cause', Harcourt seemed eager for office and did not like the Gladstonian recipe for party re-unification. Hartington wrote on 4 December to say that Gladstone's campaign necessitated the reopening of the question of who was leading the party. He did not feel able to demand from Gladstone a statement of his intentions, even though it was clear enough that Gladstone ought either to come forward and take the leadership, or cease to steal the thunder of the nominal Liberal chief. Brett advised him to seek an explanation at once:

Brett-Hartington, 13 December 1879:[10] I think he means to be loyal to you as the leader of the party, but I think he only remains as loyal as the people about him allow him to be... There are moments when he half-convinces himself that the national good requires that he should lead...

If Mr G[ladstone] were again formally to refuse the leader-ship he would make it impossible for him[self] a year hence to form a cabinet... Supposing on the other hand that he were to give so lukewarm a refusal that it was tantamount to an accept-ance, I do not see that you would be in a worse position than you inevitably would be in if you were asked to form a cabinet after a general election without the earnest and loyal support of Mr G[ladstone]—either within or without the cabinet.

No Liberal cabinet *half* supported by him could stand. Indeed

I think if you are not to form the next cabinet you had better give up your place *now*. The next election ought to be fought under the leadership of whomsoever is to form the Liberal cabinet.

The truth was that Harcourt hoped to be able to float a Liberal ministry with Hartington as the pledge of respectability for the moderates and with a far stronger Radical wing than Gladstone would be prepared to see in office. With Brett's help he had made out a list of peers and MPs who might be asked to subscribe to an election fund. There were 114 names on the list, and as Brett wrote to Hartington: 'An average of £500 apiece would, Harcourt thinks, enable us to win twenty county seats.'[11] A list of men who aspired to office in a Liberal government was also compiled, and Harcourt claimed for himself either the post of Chancellor of the Exchequer (the one office which Gladstone conceivably might have accepted under Hartington) or that of First Lord of the Admiralty.

In Gladstone's own eyes the contest of Midlothian county, although it involved two great campaigns of public speeches which were reported *in extenso* in the national newspapers, was rather an inquest into the iniquities of the outgoing Disraelian ministry than a programme for a new Liberal one. The fact which struck other men, and also Gladstone's party managers who so promptly published the Midlothian addresses in book form, was the tremendous public response which pulled the opposition out of the doldrums, and marked out Gladstone as the only possible leader. As in 1885–6 he went it alone without commitment to party or programme. Hartington clearly resented this method of gaining a surreptitious mandate. He arrived at Chatsworth on 15 December and said he considered his own nominal leadership to be unconstitutional in the circumstances. Gladstone was the real leader, and would be 'called upon by the general voice of the Party to form the Ministry', now that he had so signally gone back on his undertaking to retire from active political life. Only on this firm undertaking had Hartington, in his own opinion, consented to take up the lead. Once before, in moving his embarrassing pro-Russian resolutions in 1877, Gladstone had broken his pledge, though he then had the excuse that he felt a special responsibility for the Eastern question. But now at Midlothian he had 'put forward a programme on every conceivable topic'. On this ground Hartington wanted to surrender his responsibility at once.[12]

Against this course Harcourt argued 'plainly, even brutally'. He believed that Gladstone's following in the party was no larger than Hartington's and Hartington could form a stronger cabinet— Gladstone had always to pack his cabinets with Whig peers. Brett also thought that his chief 'underrates his own influence and power'. After a 'wearing interview, at which nothing was settled'[13] he compiled a memorandum pleading at least that Hartington should consult his friends:

Brett-Hartington, 15 December 1879:[14] I certainly see the force of your view that Mr G[ladstone]'s position now is not what it was understood four years ago it was to be, and further that your position is in consequence made most unpleasant. But I am not yet convinced that it would be right to relinquish it because of that alone, and because a large section of Liberals and Conservatives sneer at what they call the 'double leadership'...

I think you have a right to inquire of your late colleagues whether they will undertake to support a ministry formed by you or Lord Granville...

If next session Mr G[ladstone]'s attitude is such as to give you to understand that he is bidding for power you might reconsider the matter...

A meeting was summoned to Devonshire House on these lines and persuaded Hartington to remain quiet for the present, while Lords Granville and Cardwell sounded Gladstone about his intentions. The response came via Lord Wolverton, intimating that he would not consent to hold any subordinate position in any Liberal ministry. The question remained unanswered, whether he would come forward to head another administration.

Harcourt had long been in correspondence with the anti-Gladstonian editor of the *Daily News*, Mr Frank Hill, and whether by accident or design Hill encountered Hartington's election agent, W. J. Arnold, and delivered for Hartington's ears a disquisition on the state of the party and its press.[15] Hill deprecated the agitation being conducted by the *Spectator* and *Economist* urging Gladstone to resume the titular leadership, and supported the line of the *Pall Mall Gazette* that the opinion of the moderate Liberals was all-important. It was, said Hill, 'a great mistake to suppose that the Liberal party consists solely of Radicals, Dissenters and Ritualists', implying that these elements were the most vocal as well as the most pro-Gladstonian. Hill had also heard that Gladstone had been offended by the suggestion that he would perhaps act under Hartington as Chancellor of the Exchequer, saying that that would be putting him back thirty-five years. As for Gladstone resuming the full leadership, Hill believed that many Liberals even below the gangway would not like it, naming Dilke and Fawcett: for the Radical view was said to be that 'If Mr G[ladstone] were premier...he must collect as many dukes and great people as he can to his cabinet to show that he is not a revolutionist. On the other hand Lord G[ranville] and Lord H[artington] to prove their Radicalism must appoint many of the extreme people and so these men hope that something may fall to them.'[16] Even if Gladstone did come forward, Hill thought the public would be offended at his having abandoned the party when it was *in profundis* and then returned when the tide had turned. All these reasonings look very like what Harcourt might have thought that Hartington ought to hear.

Just before Christmas Brett heard from Lord Northbrook that there would be a parliamentary seat vacant at Falmouth, which Northbrook himself had held for some years and where he retained much influence. Brett met the borough manager at the Liberal Association Office and learnt that they were 'strong Liberals and Gladstonians' at Falmouth and that the expenses would be moderate, about £1,000 for each member. In addition 'the yearly sum drawn from each, for charities, etc, amounts to £500', which Brett thought exorbitant but reflected 'I can always give up the constituency if it is too expensive; and assuredly the new Parliament will not be a long one.'[17] Clearly he was not over-anxious to become a politician even with what was at this time an extremely cheap ticket. The elections came sooner than expected, for after a brief session Disraeli suddenly dissolved on 24 March and the results of the polls came in early in April. Brett found himself MP for Penryn and Falmouth. 'In a few weeks we shall be in office,' he notes: 'It is not a pleasant prospect.'[18] He was sincerely against the idea of a Hartington government, if only for the personal reason that he would have preferred Hartington to hold the Foreign Office where, as his private secretary, he could find just the scope for his interests that he desired.

Gladstone did not appear in London till the latter part of April, and in the meantime the charade of Hartington's prospective premiership was played out. Very possibly this procedure was the indispensable preliminary to party re-unification under Gladstone. Only Harcourt seemed to believe in the possibility of excluding Gladstone, especially after he had heard from Dilke that the Radicals would be content with Dilke at the Admiralty and a minor post for Leonard Courtney. Harcourt conveyed to Hartington through Brett that he himself would be content with being Attorney-General with a seat in the cabinet and the reversion of the Chancellorship 'from which,' as Brett explained, 'he thinks Lord Selborne should be eliminated owing to his views on land, etc.' Alternatively, Harcourt asked to be Chancellor of the Exchequer 'with the prospective lead in the House of Commons'.[19] Brett seems to have been somewhat disgusted with the manner of these demands, for he adds: 'He does not go so far as to say that if his moderate demands are not complied with he will leave the party in the lurch, but he hints that he will be seriously vexed.'[20] Another claimant on Hartington was Henry James, whom Brett reported 'would be content it appears to be Home Secretary'. The lists of aspirants to office under Hartington was at this point dispatched to him by Brett, and curiously enough it is very similar to the list of those whom Gladstone included in his ministry. Thirty-four are common to both. The difference between what Harcourt intended and what Gladstone effected lay in the selection of the cabinet, into which Gladstone placed seven Whig peers and only two Radicals, one of whom was the loyal John Bright.

Like Hartington himself, Brett was rather sick of the impasse and announced to his chief that he was off on a 'holiday', though in fact he went to Castle Ashby whence he was summoned almost daily by the 'endless intrigues and counter-intrigues' of April.[21] He was quite sure that Gladstone would not and ought not to be in any subordinate office, but he also strangely insisted that Hartington was honour bound not to withdraw prematurely from an admittedly hopeless position:

Brett-Hartington, 14 April 1880:[22] At that dinner twelve months ago at Lord Ripon's...it struck me, and must have struck everyone else, that Mr Gladstone, if he is to form part of a Ministry, could only do so in one capacity...

If you will allow me to speak frankly I think by far the wisest course would be not to see Mr G[ladstone] before you go to the Queen. After what Lord Wolverton has told you, you have nothing to learn from an interview...

Personally I would rather see Mr G[ladstone] Prime Minister and you at the Foreign Office than any other arrangement that could be made. It would satisfy the country and not impossibly the Liberal party in Parliament. It would be perfectly plain and straightforward, whereas any other combination necessitates playing a difficult game. However it is not with what anyone prefers but with what is possible that you have to deal, and all the reasons urged by you in the autumn for *then* resigning the lead or forming a government if asked to do so bind you irrevocably now to this latter course...

...in point of fact the elections have been fought under your leadership, and you are forced to take the consequences, however uninviting the prospects before you may be.

It was not an entirely perfunctory action when Hartington after his summons to Windsor on 22 April went through the motions of trying to form a government. Such things however can only be tested in the actuality of a real situation, and the ritual itself strengthened Gladstone's position. What did disappoint Brett was the relegation of Hartington to the India Office while the compliant Lord Granville, who was to prove hardly more than a puppet, took the Foreign Office. Nevertheless, the experience of Indian affairs which Brett gained thereby was highly relevant to imperial defence and gave him an orientation of interest in this direction. His involvement in Indian affairs was further consolidated when Lord Ripon, with whom he was on cordial terms, went out as Viceroy accompanied by his brother Eugène Brett[23] as his ADC and General Gordon as his private secretary.

Brett was not regarded as much of a parliamentary speaker, but in having to follow Indian frontier policy he came into close association with Sir Charles Dilke, an encyclopaedic authority on imperial questions. Dilke had first met Brett two years before, and regarded him as 'an extremely pleasant fellow' and 'the ablest secretary, except Edward Hamilton, that I ever came across'. Interestingly, Dilke adds that Brett was not a model secretary because he 'always behaved as if he held delegated authority from Hartington to represent Hartington's conscience when it would not otherwise have moved, and "Hartington's opinion" when the chief had none...But Brett in all he did had public ends in view...'[24] Brett for his part moved noticeably towards the policies of the Radical imperialists Dilke and Chamberlain during his five and odd years in the Commons, and what inspiration his electoral addresses had when he unsuccessfully contested his seat again was borrowed from the *Radical Programme.* Dilke, Chamberlain and Harcourt put forward Brett's name for an under-secretaryship with real enthusiasm, when Brett distinguished himself by his handling of Egyptian questions after the British intervention of 1882. Hartington was involved by virtue of the possible use of the Indian army and the strategic uses of the Suez Canal, but Brett delved with zest into the political and press aspects of the Egyptian imbroglio in which his efforts were commended by Chamberlain and Dilke.

He seems to have settled everything verbally with Hartington with the result that little in the way of recorded business is available as evidence of his activity as private secretary. An exception occurs when for a day or two Hartington was unable to come to the Office after the murder of his brother Lord Frederick Cavendish in Phoenix Park, Dublin. While Hartington was out of London Brett telegraphed or wrote reporting the decisions of the cabinet or the selection of officers for the new Irish Secretary's staff. He recounts how Dilke declined the Irish Secretaryship unless he had a seat in the cabinet. 'Now,' he adds, 'having left you in the lurch, I don't see that he will ever get into the cabinet...It shows also a want of feeling which I should not have expected of him. Trevelyan is sure to accept.' He is equally free in his comments on Harcourt:

Brett-Hartington, 8 May 1882:[25] Of all ministers Harcourt is the most violent. At the cabinet Mr G[ladstone] complained that Ross had told the Queen that Ireland was honeycombed with secret societies. Harcourt thereupon said 'He was quite right, and if he had not told her I should have told her so myself.' He is hoping that he will have charge of the Repression of Crime Bill. I should think it would be well if you were to suggest that it should be given to the Attorney-General. Harcourt will not conduce to its rapid passage through the House.

Hartington himself after his brother's murder took an ever-hardening line on Irish affairs and in general a reactionary stance relative to Gladstone on the questions of local government reform, the extension of the franchise and the powers of the House of Lords. His Whiggism was of the old-fashioned paternalistic kind and did not accept the belief in human rationality and goodness which Brett shared with the advanced Liberals. On a more practical level Brett was beginning to acquire a taste for surreptitious journalism and soon formed a close relationship with W. T. Stead, editor of the *Pall Mall Gazette.* Before 1883 Stead was assistant editor under John Morley who of course was in close touch with Chamberlain and Dilke. As editor from 1883 Stead, although his journal was extremely fashionable among the upper classes, also pioneered features on social problems, of which his exposure of the white slave traffic at the cost of a prison sentence was the most notorious. These associations of Brett with radicalism and imperialism spelt a drift away from Hartington, though not from Harcourt. 'You know, as well as I do, that the end must come some day,' Brett wrote to his chief in January 1884 as the prospect of another election threatened an early disclosure of their divergence. 'Harcourt thinks that if I were to resign my position with you, and take a more or less independent position in the House...it might give occasion for comment.'[26] He suggested retaining his position as private secretary for another session, after which the ministry might have fallen.

Hartington had by this time been moved from the India Office to the War Office in a reshuffle made in order to find a place for the renegade Tory, Lord Derby, in the ministry. On 26 November 1882 Gladstone intimated a desire to retire from political life the following year at Easter, meanwhile giving up the Exchequer. The leading claimants for that post were Harcourt and Hartington, and when sounded Hartington suggested that Derby should take the India Office and himself the Exchequer. Gladstone however preferred to give the Exchequer to Childers, who had been his assistant in 1865–6, on the reasoning that if Hartington were destined to succeed to the leadership in the Commons at Easter he could not shoulder such an administrative burden also. This was just one of many invocations of the Grand Old Man's retirement, which remained imminent for many years to come and was always one of his major trumps. Brett regarded this undignified shifting of the party's prospective leader as something which would disastrously weaken Hartington's position and perhaps destroy his hold over the Radical section which had been consolidated by Brett's own efforts:

Brett-Hartington, 2 December 1882:[27] I sincerely hope you will think twice before you allow yourself to be made a victim to an intrigue on the part of

1. The Court, because they think you would be more amenable to their reason than any other member of the government,

2. Childers, who for his own ends has since the government was formed been striving to get the Exchequer.

It is amazing that the offer—which I can only look upon as an impertinence—should have been made to you. From Mr G[ladstone]'s ignorance of the relative importance of other men anything might be expected...And as for Lord Granville, one can only suppose that he has some desire to weaken your influence...

From your own point of view the contemplated change would be ridiculous. You would hate the War Office with all its pettifogging questions and its perpetual conflicts with the Royal Family more than you hate this Office...

If Lord Derby, who will not be such a wonderful accession of strength to the government after all, *must* have India, then you must have the Exchequer...

For two years I have had but one object in view, and it was both in the interest of yourself and of the party to ensure that no obstacles should be raised to your succeeding Mr G[ladstone]. The main object to secure was the adherence to you personally of the Radical elements in the government and in the House of Commons. That is done, and it is well known. Were Mr G[ladstone] to retire finally...there is no-one except you who could command the undivided allegiance of the two most powerful sections of the party. Harcourt has declared that on his part he would not take office under anyone else...Dilke and Chamberlain would leave no stone unturned and their efforts along with Harcourt's are not to be despised. At this moment

they would as well as many others be disgusted to see you yield
...least of all to Lord Derby...

There seemed a real danger that Derby might supplant Hartington
as Gladstone's successor, which Brett thought would mean the
secession of the Radicals.

Strangely enough this change to the War Office proved very
opportune for Brett himself, who no doubt imagined that the occupation of Egypt having been completed, Afghanistan would continue
to hold pride of place in military and diplomatic interest in the
empire, and who was hoping for an under-secretaryship at the
Foreign Office. He could not have any idea of the tremendous drama
which would arise from the attempt to evacuate the Sudan, nor could
he have guessed that this would centre on his friend 'Chinese
Gordon' and involve Hartington at the War Office in many months
of anxious military deliberations.

Hartington's biographer suggests very credibly that the Sudan
disaster was attributable to Lord Granville's refusal to allow British
or Indian troops to be used by the Egyptian government even to
evacuate Khartoum, although the British government controlled and
in the end overruled Chérif's Ministry. Lord Granville claimed to
have no responsibility for the fate of Hicks's army which was cut to
pieces by dervishes of the Mahdi in September 1883. Yet the immediate effect of this was to imperil provinces which Egypt had
held for over sixty years and the garrisons at Khartoum, Sennar and
other places. Hartington protested to Granville in November that
'Egypt will never voluntarily give up the provinces east of the White
Nile...and I don't think she should be asked to do so.'[28] When this
proved to be just the attitude of Egypt, Sir Evelyn Baring was instructed on 4 January 1884 to deliver an ultimatum which would
force the formation of an Egyptian government agreeable to the
abandonment of Khartoum.

This British intervention in the affairs of the Sudan carried with
it a moral obligation to ensure that the enforced evacuation of
Khartoum was carried out safely. Gladstone, however, later took
the line that in sending Gordon to report on the situation, the
government had only incurred a responsibility for Gordon's person
and had no obligation to extricate the garrison of Khartoum. If this
was so, it was a strangely imprudent choice to have commissioned

Gordon. Certainly the circumstances of Gordon's appointment smack of opportunism and even conspiracy. The immediate call for 'Chinese Gordon', the quixotic adventurer who had conquered Chinese provinces on a shoestring budget, came from the public, roused to the cry by W. T. Stead. When Gordon returned to England from Palestine, *en route* for Brussels in order to accept King Leopold's commission to act as manager of the Congo Free State, Stead intercepted him as he disembarked and put before him a different proposition. This was that Gordon should go to the Sudan—he had years before surveyed the difficult route from Suakin to Khartoum—with the intention of destroying the slave trade, as it were at the Congo's back door. According to Stead's later account, Gordon at last warmed to the idea when his sister suggested that the venture would greatly assist the Congo project, which was for Gordon really an anti-slavery crusade. Stead, who was nothing if not a persuasive talker, described 'a crusading anti-slavery empire on the Equatorial Lakes'.[29] The Gordon mission to Khartoum was immediately supported by one of Stead's brilliant public appeals in the *Pall Mall Gazette*, and the government was swept along in the torrent of enthusiasm that followed.

Brett was implicated in the conspiracy, even to the extent of acting counter to Hartington who was now as Secretary for War the minister who would control the Gordon mission. He knew Gordon well and was one of those who regarded him as a genius rather than a lunatic. Gordon, in fact, had introduced Brett to Stead in 1880,[30] and from about that time Gordon's association with Brett became one of close friendship. '...he was always in and out of my home in Tilney Street,' Brett recalled after Gordon's death. 'He would generally come in the morning, with a loose comforter round his neck, and a hat—by no means a new one—set well back on his head. The eternal cigarette in his mouth...He was small—very small—and would have been unnoticed anywhere except for his eyes...of that peculiar steel-like blue...He would lounge into the library, and would stand...for hours leaning against the fireplace...His talk was always refreshing. Full of humour, as simple as the Book of Genesis.'[31] When the demand arose for Gordon to relieve Khartoum, Brett was well placed to further the design. The War Office needed to interview Gordon about his army commission and his request to serve under King Leopold. Somehow Gordon found himself being interviewed by a residue of ministers who happened to be in town—Hartington, Granville, Northbrook and Dilke—who asked him if he would be prepared to 'report on the military situation of the Sudan and return'.[32] Signs of eccentricity went unheeded. In the ante-room Gordon had asked a secretary 'Do you ever tell a lie?'. On boarding his train for the long journey he was found to have no money on him, and his official deputation had to root around to produce a gold watch and spare cash.

By this time Brett was on very confidential terms with Stead, and they both shared the idea that Gordon might 'Sarawak the Sudan' if Britain persisted in compelling Egypt to give it up, or if King Leopold declined to add it to the Congo. Hartington at this early stage of the venture adhered to the government's line that Gordon was going merely to report and not to rescue the garrisons.[33] Brett therefore found it expedient to work secretly against the official policy by leaking confidential military information to Stead and 'inspiring' him on matters of policy. He studied Gordon's telegrams on their arrival, and received occasional letters from Gordon directly. Since Gordon's communications through the months that followed were received in a different order to that in which they were written, which caused much confusion and misunderstanding, and because the cryptic style of Gordon's expressions, someone who knew Gordon well was needed as interpreter.[34] Brett saw to it that the public understood matters through his briefing of Stead, and he also succeeded in bringing his chief round to the public's view.

Gordon did not reach Khartoum till 18 February, but previously he had received instructions at Cairo and had been appointed Governor-general with executive powers by the Khedive. 'I am doing what I can to urge the government to make the Khedive supersede Hussein Pasha at Khartoum' Brett wrote to Stead on 29 January, fearing a disaster before Gordon's arrival.[35] 'The government are, I must say, behaving well to him,' he comments a little later. 'He is given *carte blanche*. His telegrams are models of cheerfulness and self-possession...By June 1st he hopes to have freed the Sudan from Egyptians.'[36] This was surely not quite his mission! On arrival at Khartoum Gordon did two things which shocked opinion at home but which were no doubt highly expedient on the spot—he authorised domestic slavery, and he asked that Zobeir, a ruthless slave trader whose son he had had shot years before, should be allowed to take over from him when he left. Needless to say, a Gladstonian government could not permit such a thing.

The military position worsened with the defeat of Baker on 4 February. British troops were now virtually besieged in Suakin and could hardly penetrate inland, whereupon General Wolseley asked for a change of policy. He wanted an announcement that the Sudan east of the White Nile would be retained and ruled not by Pashas but by Sudanese officials under British officers. The reason was military—'No army can march from Suakin to Berber if it is opposed', and when the Sudanese chiefs knew that Britain was abandoning the area, they were bound to defect.[37] This had been Hartington's line in November and it was bound to be taken up vigorously by the parliamentary opposition and also, ironically enough, by the anti-slavery lobby. As a result the Granville policy was reversed to the extent of sending Sir Gerald Graham's brigade to Suakin. Brett played his not unimportant part in this change. His personal opinion was that 'We ought to send out to *Egypt proper* at once, a reinforcement sufficient to enable a flying column to move immediately to any point on the Nile...Nobody wants them to attempt to avenge Baker or reconquer the Sudan; but they should stand, sword in hand, ready to strike if anything happens to Gordon.'[38] This was also the view of Sir Evelyn Baring in Cairo. 'I do not like being praised by the Opposition,' he wrote to Brett, '...If I get through the whole of this business without English responsibility being extended beyond Egypt proper I shall think I have been successful.'[39]

Gordon who could not fail to realise the force of psychological factors and sheer bluff in the Sudan situation was prepared to use the most theatrical methods. Gladstone was playing to the moral prejudices of Nonconformity and those sections of English opinion to which the word 'slavery' was anathema. The relationship between Gordon and the home government was full of tragic irony. 'As for Zobeir,' Gordon wrote to Brett on 3 March, 'He alone can ride the Sudan horse, and if they do not send him, I am sentenced to penal servitude for my life up here.'[40] Yet Gordon was busily undoing the powers and authorities of the Pashas and personally looked forward to an uprising of slaves. 'In a year the slaves up here will rise and will emancipate themselves. What a wonderful denouement! And how my prayers will have been then heard.'[41] He had just issued a

45

proclamation in order to avert a rising, which falsely declared that British troops were on their way to Khartoum. Gladstone supported by Hartington agreed to disavow any responsibility for Gordon's 'oriental crackers'.[42] He began to contemplate handing back the Sudan to the Sultan. Such was the gulf between theoretical and practical morality, between conscience at home and on the spot.

Brett reacted immediately against the suggestion that evacuation implied the *de jure* rule of the Sultan in the Sudan, and at once 'turned on' Stead. 'The moment has now come,' he wrote in his brief of 25 February: 'Sweep out the Turks bag and baggage from Egypt proper...Say to Europe, we make our sacrifice, you make yours. We guarantee peace and order for ten years.'[43] Once the Sultan's *de jure* authority over Egypt was repudiated, the Sudan could be dealt with on its merits by Gordon. 'A decision must be taken at once. What are the alternatives?...Gordon must decide...1. that he will stay, i.e. "Sarawak the Sudan"—2. evacuate the place, and move with the garrison to Berber...The policy would than be *a* hold the Red Sea littoral for Egypt. *No Turks. b* evacuate the Sudan, including Khartoum, and *turn the key in the lock.*'[44]

Unfortunately after March the falling of the Nile and the advent of the period of great heat effectively cut off Khartoum, especially as the government refused to approve the establishment of a channel of communication from Suakin to Berber manned by Indian troops. While Gordon's position became perilous with the advance of the Mahdi the sending of any relief expedition became militarily extremely difficult, and Wolseley who strongly favoured it acknowledged that it would have to wait the rising of the Nile. But the essential point, which was pressed by Brett on Hartington, was that although Gordon did not expect any relief force, he would 'of course, assume that the English Government would let it be known far and wide that they are prepared to support him with all the force at their disposal, if he should require and ask it; and the knowledge of this, permeating through Egypt and the Sudan, would in all probablity be sufficient for his purpose.'[45] The falseness of the fiction, which Gladstone maintained to the end, that the British responsibility was only for Gordon's personal safety and not for that of the garrisons, and the folly of the decision which Harcourt was pressing the cabinet to make against ever sending a relief expedition to Khartoum, were both clearly perceived by Brett at this early juncture and forcibly represented to Hartington. 'I wish again to say that nothing will, I am convinced, induce Gordon to leave Khartoum until all those persons who have been faithful to him can leave with him' he stressed in the same letter. Military support for Gordon should be publicly announced, and if the mere announcement failed in its purpose 'HMG would only then have to do, what, if they were by some mischance to try and leave Gordon to his fate, they would have to do notwithstanding.'[46] Prophetic words!

It was however all too apparent that Gladstone, Granville and Harcourt would regard any such announcement as far too provocative to the European powers, who were about to be summoned to London to consider Egyptian finance. That being so, Brett decided to attempt a coup of his own for Gordon's safety. The week before, Baring had sent a telegram appealing for an assurance of an autumn expedition to keep wavering tribes from becoming hostile, and Brett wrote next day:

Brett-Stead, (Sunday) 27 March 1884:[47] Unless prevented by something unforeseen I shall start on Saturday morning for Brussels. I propose to ask the King: 'Will you telegraph to Gordon on your own responsibility not to abandon Khartoum but to hold it for the African International Association?' I think no-one ought to know of my trip.

The result of this private mission, so typical of Brett, is not on record, but one may surmise that King Leopold if confronted with the proposition would have asked for some assurance as to the attitude of the British government.[48] It is therefore interesting that Lord Wolseley tried to get some kind of assurance a few days later. Wolseley was on close terms with Brett and as Hartington's chief military adviser was pressing also for at least the preparation of a military expedition. He would assuredly, also as a friend of King Leopold, have known of Brett's plan if he did not inspire it. In a memorandum to Hartington of 13 April reviewing the military position Wolseley declared: 'I know King Leopold tolerably well, and having stayed a week with him when he was incubating his African scheme, and having then talked the matter over daily with him...I think I know his aims tolerably well...it is quite possible he would allow Gordon to rule over the Eastern Sudan as an appanage

...under the protection of the African Society...I should be very glad to sound him on this subject...merely throwing it out as an idea of my own...if the idea was one that would commend itself to the Cabinet in the event of King Leopold's entering into the idea.'[49] Wolseley himself like Brett would have preferred a British expedition, and put forward the Belgian idea as the only alternative way of enabling Gordon to hold his own.

Hartington represented these views very strongly in the cabinet, which at one point looked like breaking up. Under strong pressure Gladstone conceded that the country was honour bound to extricate Gordon if need be. Meanwhile Brett was quarrelling with his political patron Harcourt, only vicariously through Stead. Harcourt took a tough line with France, and declared in public that if the Powers refused to agree to our financial proposals we ought to retire from Egypt at once. With his knowledge of French opinion on Egyptian affairs Brett thought such a policy disastrous:

Brett-Stead, 21 April 1884:[50] I hope you will *ménager* the susceptibilities of France as much as possible...At the same time...pointing out that Harcourt's speech and the policy it suggested can lead only to war between the two countries.

Before that speech France was moderate in her demands... and was prepared to accept our supremacy there [Egypt] provided: 1. We made no attempt to take sole charge of the Canal; 2. We retained Frenchmen, who were doing good work, in their employments.

After his speech, the French demands have increased, and it is now being pressed upon Ferry in very influential quarters that he should insist at least upon the renewal of the dual control.

Brett believed that the French were now, unlike two years before, ready to take Britain's place in Egypt. He disagreed with Labouchere that their interest there was purely financial, and believed it was largely political because of the impact of revolution in Egypt on Tunis and Algeria:[51]

[France] can without difficulty which is insuperable and without cost to herself administer Egypt if no Egyptian army is maintained; and she is prepared to do so. Upon this, Ferry is determined, and the Chamber will support him.

If England holds on to Egypt *and respects the just suscep-tibilities of France* the arrangement will be acquiesced in; and for this reason above all others, that England would be sup-ported by Bismarck and by Europe. If England were to evacuate, France...would occupy Egypt and defy England, in which she would be supported by Bismarck...

Gladstone regarded the French acceptance of international in place of dual control as a great concession, while he condemned as 'jingo' the demand for a permanently dominant British element in Egypt. Of the jingoes he said: 'Egypt for the Egyptians, and Egypt under Europe, are both in their view detestable ideas.'[52] He was deeply committed to the ideal of peoples 'rightly struggling to be free', which he applied grotesquely enough to the Sudan, and also to the ideal of the 'Concert of Europe'.[53] But the next few years were to show that multiple control of Egypt merely subjected Britain to diplomatic blackmail, especially by the Germans. Brett was one of those who stood out for at least a British presidency of the Caisse, and the postponement of multiple control until after evacuation. After dining with Chamberlain and Waddington, the French ambassador, whom Chamberlain questioned in his pertinacious and intelligent way, Brett learnt that the French would give way on these points, and comments to Hartington: '...what a condemnation of the F[oreign] O[ffice], that this attitude of the French Government should not have been appreciated sooner.'[54] 'Lord Granville has *failed* as a negotiator,' he wrote to Stead: 'No Foreign Secretary who knew his business would have allowed the French to make a proposal until we had made ours.'[55]

Gladstone called the French proposal one of the most liberal offers ever made in diplomatic history, but Hartington had objected to it in a 'menacing' protest. Brett advised Hartington to resign if the proposal were not modified, saying: 'I am more than convinced that the Government will be turned out if the present arrangement is made.'[56] The day before the Commons debate had revealed to Gladstone a serious Liberal split and 'more of the rot of Forsterism among us than had been supposed', as Gladstone put it.[57] Members on both sides objected to the time limit of British occupation of Egypt, and to the lack of a dominant British element in the multiple control. Granville was obliged to climb down on the latter point, partly because Hartington, having conveyed to him the revelation of the Waddington dinner, insisted on going off incognito to Paris to confirm it when Granville failed to get Waddington to do so.[58]

The Gladstone-Granville give-away of Egypt having been defeated by Hartington and the Forster group in the Commons, amongst whom Brett was one of the most active, many months of diplomatic work remained before Gladstonian utopianism came to a final crunch before the *realpolitik* of Bismarck and the French. Brett seeing the point won found himself having to strive hard to keep Stead on the Liberal side. 'I agree with you that a new departure is indispensable,' he writes on 9 June: 'I don't think, however, that I would lay too much stress upon the point.'[59] Later he was more explicit:

> *Brett-Stead, 18 June 1884:*[60] In face of accomplished fact, will you endeavour to save as much as we can out of the fire, by dropping your hostility to the government, though *not* to their policy, [and] by pointing out gravely but not threateningly the points upon which we can still advantageously insist?
> Again, 1. Will you consent to re-opening *friendly* relations with Downing Street and especially with Mr Gladstone? 2. Will you grant an armistice for a few days while we can consider and settle the right and wise course for the future?

Two days later he pleaded with Stead to call at Downing Street and get a full explanation of the Egyptian position from Hamilton, who would refer any queries to Mr Gladstone himself. 'The powers of the *Caisse* are very limited, *while we remain in Egypt*,' he stressed.[61] Evidently Brett succeeded in mollifying Stead, for he was soon feeding him again with more critical comment.

The inside knowledge of cabinet dissensions which Brett got through his official duties he used freely to inspire Stead with just the right nuance for the effect intended. When Lord Derby was 'very obstinate' in demanding that a pacific injunction should be written into Sir Charles Warren's instructions when he was sent to restore order in Bechuanaland, restraining him from operations against the Boers, Brett passed on the details to Stead adding: 'He reads the P[*all*] M[*all*] G[*azette*] diligently. Use this information discreetly if possible, but in any case effectively.'[62] Hartington himself was not immune from this kind of hidden persuasion when some great national objective was in view. One such undoubtedly in Brett's opinion was the agitation for the rebuilding of the navy.

One of the most passionate Forsterians was Hugh Oakeley Arnold-Forster,[63] grandson of Dr Thomas Arnold, Headmaster of Rugby, and the adopted son of W. E. Forster himself. A Liberal of Brett's generation (he was three years younger), Arnold-Forster was at this time political editor of the *Statist* and Liberal candidate for Devonport. Like so many younger Liberals he found Gladstone's seeming neglect of the empire and the navy incomprehensible, and threw up his candidature over the Egyptian vacillation and left the party over Home Rule. He had already become an authority on ships and armament and in 1883 and 1884 hammered away in articles in the *Nineteenth Century* on the theme that the British navy was inadequate in ships and personnel, and obsolete in construction and armament. So long as the accusations were confined to 'professional journals', 'scientific meetings' or 'private official remonstrances' they made no headway against the complaisant assurances of the Admiralty officials. They only struck home when they appeared in a 'penny newspaper'![64] No doubt realising that popular publicity was needed, Arnold-Forster had gone to see Stead and, as Stead relates, 'in his brusque, abrupt fashion asked me when I was going to take up the question of the Navy. He then set forth roughly an outline of the actual position of things, which, of course, I had often heard in a vague way before...I asked him to leave his papers...It was evident that something must be done, and done at once, unless our Imperial position was to go by the board of Germany...' Stead went to see the First Sea Lord, Sir Cooper Key, who said: 'It is no use...We have all done our best, and we have failed...Do you think that you could succeed where all the Sea Lords have failed, and move Mr Gladstone?' Another Sea Lord, Beauchamp Seymour, on being asked what would happen in the event of a war with France, replied that 'within twenty-four hours... Sir Cooper and I, and all the rest of us at the Admiralty, would be swinging by our necks from the lamp-posts in front of Whitehall... and it would serve us right too.' Such is Stead's own account of the genesis of his sensational articles on 'The Truth about the Navy' in the *Pall Mall Gazette*.[65] Even the City was roused, and W. E. Forster addressed a great meeting there which acted powerfully on the government.

In this agitation Brett played his full share. In a contribution to the *Pall Mall Gazette* on 'The Responsibility for the Navy' he argued against submitting the problem to a committee, which would mean a secret report and a victory for the Chancellor of the Exchequer while the public were distracted by other matters. 'I have no doubt the First Sea Lords for the last ten years have covered reams of official foolscap with memoranda for the waste paper baskets of the Cabinet.' But now that public opinion was 'roused, as it is now, thanks to the *Pall Mall Gazette*', the opinion of the Admiralty would at last be listened to. Did they agree with the facts that had been exposed? 'If they do not, let them say so.'[66] Brett signed this article, for MPs could still attack their own front bench and their departments openly. Behind the scenes, also, he did much to ensure that the arguments of the naval critics struck home. Here his personal knowledge of ministers and the lines they were taking in the cabinet helped:

Brett-Stead, 25 November 1884:[67] I think Egypt had better be dropped *altogether* till after next Monday, and some final shots fired into the Admiralty and War Office. The principal points as they strike me are:

1. The irreducible minimum.
2. How to get the money.
3. The responsibility of the W[ar] O[ffice] and Lord H[artington] almost as great as responsibility of Lord N[orthbrook].
4. No attempts to shuffle responsibility on to each other.
5. Personal appeal to Lord N[orthbrook] (Discount £3 million speech?) Threat of disgrace, *not* impeachment.
6. Personal appeal to Lord H[artington], possible P[rime] M[inister], all the greater responsibility. Fitness and courage for the post judged by result of this struggle with the Treasury and electioneering agents.
7. Remains to be seen whether either will shrink from his duty.
8. Blow out of water the doctrine...that putting our first line of

defence into order is [in] any degree a threat or an irritant to foreign powers.

Private This last is Lord N[orthbrook]'s pet argument... My friend's information about his state of mind has been corroborated today. Nothing however is yet settled, so there is time to deal a few hard blows.

As to German reactions to the naval re-armament or to our Egyptian policy, Brett was well informed through his correspondence with Herbert Bismarck.

Meanwhile the autumn expedition to extricate Gordon was commanded by Wolseley, who by mid-October still awaited a reply from Gordon at Wady Halfa. 'I mean to get forward the mounted infantry and Camel Corps as soon as possible' he wrote to Brett: 'and when I get to Debbeh...I hope to get in touch with Gordon and get him to formulate some practical plan for the future that will suit the views of the Cabinet.'[68] There was considerable irony in the last phrase, as Brett well knew. 'All who know the facts, and how difficult it was to get the Government to move,' he replied, 'will almost grudge them success.'[69] Brett still hankered after 'Sarawaking' the Sudan. He believed the French had recognised the African International Association, on the condition that King Leopold promised them the refusal of its property in the event of his being unable to carry it on. He also thought that Wolseley ought to be free to settle the Sudan according to circumstances, which conceivably might have included a strong recommendation from Gordon to associate it with the Congo.[70] 'With regard to our scheme for setting up a Government in the Sudan,' he wrote to Wolseley in November, 'my hope is that you will do nothing hurriedly, or give your sanction to a scheme of which you do not cordially approve...'[71]

The most illuminating information about the navigation of the Upper Nile and the terrain along the route of Wolseley's expedition was provided by the special correspondents of the London newspapers. The progress of the small force was an epic which sank into the public consciousness, so that when after all the effort Wolseley arrived at Khartoum only two days after its famished garrison had been over-run through a gap left by the falling of the Nile, the public read a lesson which was to react powerfully in the direction of imperialism and opposition among Liberals to Gladstonian policies in

Ireland. The nature of this illogical and emotional reaction may be seen in the way Brett himself reacted. The first news of the fall of Khartoum arrived in a coded telegram at the War Office at 1 a.m. on 5 February 1885, which Sir Ralph Thompson and Brett deciphered. Parliament, perhaps fortunately, was in recess, and Dilke and Chamberlain were the only ministers that could be found in town. After conferring with Dilke, Brett drafted a telegram to Wolseley: 'Until we hear certain news of Gordon's death, we are bound to assume he is alive.'[72] Wolseley was therefore to place himself in the most advantageous position to obtain his release by negotiation or force. As he explained in an accompanying letter, the main consideration was political. 'It may be that there are military reasons why we should fall back upon Debbeh,' he wrote to Hartington, 'but the political effect of such a proceeding cannot fail to be very bad.'[73] Six days later, after reading a detailed account of Khartoum in the *Daily Chronicle* Brett acknowledged: 'I have no hope that Gordon is alive.'[74] Hartington had to agree to the cancellation of a stronger expedition to recapture Khartoum, and the abandonment even of Dongola to the Mahdi, though Suakin was to be held to keep out other powers. Thus the Sudan was abandoned to its fate, which was in simple terms the reduction of its population from eight to two millions. 'When the history of the past year comes to be written,' Brett wrote to his chief, 'I doubt whether the part played by this country will be considered a very noble one.'[75] Gordon's death, he believed, was good for the nation. 'It has brought men of all classes to view their responsibilities in a different and nobler light.'[76] He composed an appreciation of Gordon for the *Pall Mall Gazette*, and a poem such as William Johnson Cory would appreciate as an epitaph.[77] Cory, a fountainhead of the patriotic spirit which moved the younger Liberals to such strange outbursts of political emotion, gave Brett the following advice as to how he should treat the 'fine catastrophe' of Gordon's death: 'You should tell them that if there were no India, no Suez Canal, still we should do right to hold Egypt for an indefinite time...we began to sink into a Holland or Spain state when we avowed that we could not afford to hold Egypt against all comers...It is now to be decided whether the gentlemen, the men of pride and of enterprise, are to hold the flag and mark out the encamping ground for the nation; or the calculators, the budget worshippers, the "majority".'[78]

54

Three

Imperial Interests

Gladstone's ministry of 1880–5 was, as his correspondence with his Foreign Secretary Lord Granville reveals, far more of an uneasy confederation of semi-hostile groups than the public appreciated at the time. The main antagonism was that between Lord Hartington's Whig section and the increasingly numerous and aggressive section of Radicals led by Sir Charles Dilke and Joseph Chamberlain. Within the Radical section, however, a significant rift was becoming manifest as the older Cobdenites represented by John Bright were superseded by younger Radicals who rejected the extreme *laissez-faire* social policies and the 'little England' attitude to empire which were associated with the Manchester school. When John Bright resigned over the occupation of Egypt he commanded little sympathy or support. Opinion in the country was moving towards a greater interest in imperial concerns as the early Victorian confidence founded on industrial supremacy and the absence of serious commercial or military menaces gave place to new anxieties. The idea that Britain's manifest destiny lay in imperial expansion gained currency with publications such as Seeley's *Expansion of England*[1] and became the inspiration of the Liberal imperialists led by Lord Rosebery. Gladstone, who increasingly referred to himself as a 'survival' from a past age, could find no sympathy either for the 'constructive' social reforms demanded by Chamberlain, or for the permanent acquisition of Egypt, Uganda or other such territories which Rosebery was largely instrumental in securing. Yet Gladstone was radical enough when it came to the drastic curtailment of the powers of the House of Lords or the disestablishment of the Anglican Church in the Celtic fringe, on which questions he quarrelled with Hartington and the Whigs.

As Hartington's private secretary Brett found his position increasingly intolerable. In questions of social reform he sympathised with Chamberlain and in imperial and foreign affairs he followed

55

Rosebery who had kept aloof from Gladstone's ministry. He decided to break with Hartington even at the expense of his seat in Parliament. 'I do not care to ally myself again closely to the family,' he notes, 'so I shall not fix up a constituency till November, and I shall then take my chance.'² Meanwhile in the summer of 1885 the feud between Chamberlain and Hartington over the 'unauthorised programme' of the former threatened to spilt the Liberals as the election approached. Many turned to Gladstone to provide the customary compromise which would hold the party together. Brett on the other hand protested at the idea that Gladstone should give up his proposed retirement in order to repeat the balancing act of his late premiership. In a scathing letter to *The Times* he declared that Gladstone could not 'head a crusade of which the end and the watchword is simply and solely himself. And apart from their leader, the Liberal party have no central idea, no single object of supreme importance and general interest...The "old cause" is pure claptrap.' This was reported by his friend W. T. Stead in the *Pall Mall Gazette* under the caption 'The Old Umbrella Worn Out'.³ It was in this journal, which under Stead had pioneered the personal interview and the investigation *in situ* of slums, prostitution and suchlike matters of general taboo, that Brett adumbrated his political programme. This was a leaf from Chamberlain's book. He 'deplored the misery of the people who lived in crowded and unhealthy dwellings, and said this evil was in great part referable to the accumulation of land in the hands of a few persons. The land laws must be amended or repealed.'⁴ These sentiments did not go unnoticed by Chamberlain, who took a benevolent interest in Brett's attempt to win a popular parliamentary seat at Plymouth in the November election.

It was not until after the polls that Gladstone's former ministerial colleagues had cause to suspect that he was in negotiation with Parnell and the Irish Nationalists about the form of a Home Rule Bill. Brett was among those who later objected to the Gladstonian Bill, but like many other younger Liberals his opposition to Gladstone stemmed from other causes, and especially the lack of constructive leadership. As he put it, writing in August: 'Government by a Liberal cabinet without a policy is inevitably government by intrigue. And if we are to be governed after that fashion, personally I should prefer to be governed by the Conservatives which would, at any rate, leave individual members of the Liberal party...unfettered by the necessity of yielding their convictions and their interest in particular reforms to the primary object of keeping their leaders in office.'[5] As an admirer of Chamberlain, a friend and literary associate of John Morley, and a protégé of Dilke, who had wanted him as an under-secretary, Brett shared the hope of the Radical section that they were about to lose Gladstone and seize the preponderance of strength in the party from the Whigs. But misfortune wrecked the carefully laid plans of the Radicals. Before the election Dilke was struck down by the divorce scandal which proved fatal to his ministerial ambitions, and the electoral verdict was a severe disappointment. The Liberal majority over the Conservatives was exactly balanced by Parnell's eighty-six Home Rulers, so that as Brett observed, writing to Chamberlain, the solution of the question of 'the form under which Ireland is to govern itself' would have to depend on the 'co-operation of *three* parties'.[6] Rather than accept dictation from Parnell, Chamberlain would have preferred to stand aloof from another Gladstonian government, and as Brett learnt from Dilke, Chamberlain was also 'full of fury against Parnell for having sold him' and 'very angry with Mr Gladstone for having "negotiated"— which he says he has done—with the Irish and the Tories...'[7] But the shrewdest blow of all for Chamberlain still remained. Brett had advised him 'that you and Morley...be content to bide your time'. Morley, however, discovered a real affinity with Gladstone's new Irish policy, and, of all men, he was chosen to be Gladstone's Irish Secretary. Brett dined with Chamberlain, at the end of January 1886, when Morley was present having just been offered the Irish appointment, and observed that Chamberlain was 'in good spirits, but indifferent temper'.[8] Soon Morley had diverged hopelessly from Chamberlain, and their alliance was broken for ever.

For Brett the disruption of the Radicals was the obliteration of his political bearings. He found himself attached to individuals and absolved from party. He was on good terms with the more progressive Conservatives like Balfour and Lord Randolph Churchill. Balfour, indeed, regretted his losing his seat with the observation that the new Parliament would have a short life but a merry one, adding: '...in the general imbroglio which I foresee your peculiar gifts would I think have found a great sphere.'[9] As a decided opponent of Gladstone's Home Rule measure, Brett must be classed as a Liberal Unionist, and he certainly remained in close confidential relations with Hartington who led the dissentient Liberals. But at the same time he continued to cultivate Rosebery and Morley. Rosebery had been wished on Gladstone as Foreign Secretary by the Queen, and might perhaps be classed as an opponent. He intended to implement a foreign policy very different from Lord Granville's, and had Brett retained his seat in the Commons he would probably have been his under-secretary. With Morley Brett shared some political sympathies and also a close personal relationship. Differences of importance there certainly were. Brett admired Disraeli while Morley as editor of the *Fortnightly Review* had done as much as anyone to damn him. Disraeli's imperial grandiloquence struck Morley as mere bombast, or worse, as virulent jingoism. More immediately, Morley's Irish policy which amounted to conceding all of Parnell's demands was publicly labelled by Brett as an 'anti-national conspiracy'.[10] But the two men were close and articulate enough to realise that they shared the ideals of John Stuart Mill, whom Morley had known personally and fervently admired. As Brett later admitted to Stead, 'Morley...represents, to me, the moral element in our party. No one else has the conception of it; and he will bear onward that torch when it falls from Mr G[ladstone]'s hands.'[11]

Brett's friendships with Balfour, Rosebery and Morley were to last and to be the basis of much political confidence. Rosebery became his political patron, Balfour entrusted him with the most important project of his premiership, and Morley confided to him and thereby to the King the secret dealings of Asquith with the Irish. Yet while Morley was the real author of the Home Rule Bill of 1886, Rosebery as Prime Minister was to 'shelve' it, while Balfour was a leading opponent and as Irish Secretary the perpetrator of the counter-policy of coercion which has been described as 'light railways and heavy punishments'.[12] The Home Rule shibboleth did not mar Brett's relations with these protagonists, largely because he deliberately remained out of the Commons while Gladstone held the leadership, and by 1895 he had become a civil servant. In the meantime his freedom from political responsibility and his inter-party associations made him an ideal intermediary in the negotiations for Liberal re-unification.

It is not quite the right image, therefore, to see Brett as sitting on 'the top of one of the most carefully constructed fences ever known in our history' as a recent history of the Round Table Conference describes him.[13] True enough, he could be all things to all men, but he was also very definitely *hors de combat*. His personal views on Home Rule were definitely hostile to those of Gladstone and Morley. He believed that the English had shown themselves historically as unfit to govern Ireland, but he also held that the English were not half so unfit to govern Catholics as the Catholics of Dublin were to govern the Protestants of the North. He therefore advocated the end of the Dublin Castle régime and a scheme of local self-government which looked much like a hybrid between Chamberlain's National Council scheme and the project of county councils for Ireland which he knew the Conservatives were contemplating. This appeared in the new year number of the *Pall Mall Gazette* under the heading 'General Gordon's Plan of Home Rule,' purporting to be what Gordon had thought practicable in 1883. Forty Irish county councils would each send a deputy to a national Council, and the Irish Chief Secretary would be one of these and also president of an Irish Local Government Board. It was asserted that the sentiments of Britons all over the world were against the restoration of a Dublin parliament. Some days later, and still before it was apparent that Gladstone meant to topple Lord Salisbury's Conservative government, Brett proposed in *The Times* a cross-party solution to the Irish problem, to be discovered by a team of nine delegates, three from each party, investigating the crucial difficulties of landlords' rights, the sovereignty of the imperial parliament, and the apportionment of the financial burdens. The examples of Austria-Hungary, north and south Germany and the USA were to be studied.[14] It is safe to assume that Brett was trying to counteract the Gladstonian scheme which although not officially evolved was sufficiently foreshadowed in press leaks and gossip. He had just after the election hinted at 'an alliance offensive and defensive' against the 'anti-national conspiracy' which was feared, but at the same time had thought any such compact impracticable because of Salisbury's 'prudence and reserve'.[15] When in March 1886 the Gladstonian measure, with its critical provision which removed Irish representation from Westminster, was finally made public, Brett delivered a most outspoken attack on it. It was, he declared in *The Times*, 'political cynicism... gravely to maintain that a people are fit for uncontrolled self-government, while at the same time providing for a numerous section of them means of escape from tyrannical oppression admitted to be probable.'[16] For the landlords were to be bought out by a Land Bill. This policy of 'shirk and surrender' would turn an 'educated influential class of Irish landlords...into émigrés by Act of Parliament'.[17] At this early date in the session Brett was able to add the dark hint that in 'quarters not generally ill-informed' the measure was rightly regarded as unacceptable to Parliament or to the people.

With the resignations of Chamberlain and Trevelyan the prospect of a serious Liberal party split over the Gladstonian Home Rule Bill became imminent. To Brett as to Chamberlain it was a question of whether a complete sell-out to Parnell and to Spencer, the representative of the Irish landlords, was justifiable at the cost of gross political apostasy and the wreck of the party:

Brett in The Times, 21 April 1866: Mr Gladstone's speech has made the government of Ireland by any one except Mr Parnell or Mr Gladstone himself impossible...

Mr Jesse Collings, in his letter today, unanswerably shows how impossible it would be for any Radical to vote with a clear conscience for a Bill containing principles against which the Liberal party has spent its lifetime in protesting.

Taxation without representation, the abrogation of the sovereignty of Parliament, the creation of 'fundamental laws', the limitation of the power of the House of Commons, the institution of a hybrid convention to override Parliament...'inseparably connected' with a measure which involves pledging the unlimited credit of the state in the interests of a class...

To Lord Spencer's inability last June to accept the very moderate Irish policy agreed upon by Mr Chamberlain and Mr Parnell we were indebted for the defeat of the Government and the unvictorious issue of the general election. To him we are apparently still further to be indebted for the total disruption of the Liberal party.

To avoid disaster Brett appealed to Gladstone to dissolve Parliament without pressing a second reading. It was common knowledge that the Bill had not been shaped or even criticised by the cabinet, and significantly enough Rosebery, talking with Brett some weeks earlier, had complained that Gladstone had assumed a task beyond his powers. He had five years before told Rosebery that he was losing his constructive power and ought to retire, and yet now he was 'revelling in a constructive problem bristling with difficulties; plunging about in it, like a child in its tub'.[18] By retaining the Irish at Westminster, which Parnell had wanted, Gladstone might have saved his party. He even admitted that a new Bill with this amendment was needed, and that the second reading was therefore merely a token vote after which the Bill would be dropped. It was therefore a purely political motive, and no matter of principle or legislative requirement that drove him to insist on the second reading. Brett had found that his leading ministers, Harcourt, Rosebery, and even Morley, recognised that defeat was certain. The monomania of the old man had reached the point at which he actually wanted a party split in order to annihilate the Unionist Liberals, as Arnold Morley and Francis Schnadhorst had advised him could be done.

The reaction of the younger Liberals to the prospect of the 'dismemberment of the empire' was epitomised by the frenzied activity of Alfred Milner and his associates in promoting the organisation and propaganda of the Liberal Unionist Association. Milner had worked under Morley on the *Pall Mall Gazette* and had remained when Stead took over the editorship, approving of Stead's fervent appeals for leadership in foreign and imperial affairs and even for a time of his sensationalism.[19] Then in 1885 Milner had become private secretary to Goschen, Hartington's right-hand man in the promotion of the cause of the Liberal Unionists. It is difficult to see how Brett contrived to avoid being caught up in the same cause, which he had already conspicuously assisted in *The Times* and which Milner, in association with Brett's close political friend Albert Grey, was so involved in. It is possible that Brett did not wish to compromise his relations with Rosebery and so kept in the background. Certainly in June 1886 he was approached by Albert Grey who told him 'that an individual had some information for sale, which would connect the Parnellite members with the "physical force" party in America', and suggesting that Hartington might be interested. Brett referred Grey to Stead, who duly met the anonymous vendor at Dorchester House.[20] But whatever active part Brett took, he certainly shared exactly the same view of Gladstone's political conduct as did Milner, who prided himself on delivering a hundred speeches at this time without mentioning the Grand Old Man.

Rosebery had already become the most eligible model of an imperial statesman for Brett and Milner, who were both at Mentmore just before Rosebery rather impulsively joined Gladstone's government early in 1885. The occasion of joining was Gordon's death, the motive, no doubt, a hope that Gladstone might after all be persuaded to remain in Egypt. The famous speech, in which Rosebery had referred to the empire as a 'commonwealth of nations', had been delivered. He had declared that 'it is on the British race, whether in Great Britain, or the United States, or the Colonies,....that rest the highest hopes of those who try to penetrate the dark future, or who seek to raise and better the patient masses of mankind.'[21] The movement for Imperial Federation had been launched with Rosebery's approval, and when speaking immediately after the news of Gordon's death Rosebery had envisaged possible colonial contributions to imperial defence, raised either 'by a protectionist tariff, or on free trade principles'.[22] Having assumed this general position in imperial affairs, Rosebery's acquiescence in Gladstone's Home Rule policy a year later is puzzling. True, he did little to defend it: and the most charitable interpretation, in view of his later apostasy, is that he was too engrossed in his duties as Foreign Secretary, and too attached to that prized office, to contemplate an early resignation. He did not seem to notice the crucial difference made by the removal of Irish representatives from Westminster. And, to be sure, he did not for a moment wish to sever the connexion between the two countries. As he had admitted, writing to Brett before Gladstone resumed office: 'I detest separation, and feel that nothing could make me agree to it. Home Rule, however, is a necessity both for us and for the Irish. They will have it within two years at the latest, Scotland will follow, and then England. When that is accomplished Imperial Federation will cease to be a dream.'[23] Gladstone spared him any discussion of the details of his measure: and later, during the election of 1886, designated Rosebery, the youngest member of his cabinet, as 'the man of the future'.

Brett, like Rosebery himself, no doubt thought that the consolidation of British rule in Egypt was a far more important consideration than a detail of a Home Rule Bill which seemed doomed in any case. There was also the consideration that Rosebery as Gladstone's likely successor ought not lightly to follow Chamberlain and throw away his inheritance. No-one after July 1886 expected Gladstone to head another government, or thought that Hartington and the Unionist Liberals would form a lasting junction with the Conservatives. When therefore at the end of 1886 the alliance of Chamberlain and Hartington with the Conservatives seemed to be shaken by the sudden resignation of their closest associate in the Conservative cabinet, Lord Randolph Churchill, the re-union of the Liberal leaders seemed very feasible. Even John Morley conveyed to Hartington through Brett the wish that he would not take office in any reconstituted Conservative government, for this, said Morley, 'would leave the Liberal Party, and consequently the destinies of the country' in the hands of those in whom he had no confidence. Morley declared that he looked upon Hartington as the 'strongest bulwark we have against all the strong socialist doctrine I hate'.[24] Brett added his own opinion, addressing Hartington as if he were still an influential Liberal: '...you would be wrong to abandon your strong position in the Liberal party for the sake of temporarily strengthening the Tories. If a coalition could last twenty or even ten years there might be some advantage in it...but the old party prejudices and habits are too strong, and with you in the Tory camp your followers would gradually drift over to Rosebery or somebody else not strong enough to hold their own against Chamberlain and Churchill when they are wrong...'[25] The main preoccupation of both Morley and Brett seems at this juncture to have been the danger of socialism, not Ireland, and indeed Brett assured Hartington that: 'When Mr Gladstone or Parnell dies or disappears the Irish question will solve itself by a common understanding.'[26]

Rosebery was away on a visit to India and Egypt during the complicated criss-cross negotiations which were known to the public as the Round Table Conference. In these Brett was the chief intermediary, being on confidential terms with all the principals. Morley, who loathed the idea of Harcourt as Prime Minister and was aware of Rosebery's strange diffidence as well as disliking his imperial foibles, would have liked to secure Hartington as the new Liberal umbrella. But as things shaped he was in danger of acquiring Chamberlain without Hartington. Chamberlain made a genuine attempt to reach some compromise on Ireland, which gave priority to the land problem. He certainly received encouragement from Brett, whom he knew to be deep in the counsels of Morley, Harcourt and his

63

actively intriguing son Loulou, and the absent Rosebery. Brett stressed to him that it was desirable 'as quickly as possible to create the "cadre" of an alternative administration which is not separatist', adding that 'the more violent partners of Mr G[ladstone]—more Gladstonian than himself—fear that you may be successful'.[27]

Here indeed was the snag, for a compromise in face of Mr Gladstone's own uncompromising attitude would necessarily have meant his supersession, and the party managers—Arnold Morley of the *Daily News* and Francis Schnadhorst the Secretary of the National Liberal Federation—regarded the name and authority of the Grand Old Man as the Liberal party's chief asset. The *prétendants* for the succession to the leadership could not afford to antagonise Gladstone and were in the event obliged to follow him to the last extremity and then to fight a triangular duel with each other. Great historical figures leave no growing space for a successor, and rarely designate one. Brett probably underestimated the sentimental attachment to Gladstone in the country. He had, oddly enough, been offered the editorship of the *Daily News* by Labouchere just after Gladstone had assumed office in 1886, but declined, commenting to Rosebery that while *The Times* ought to be kept well in hand, the *Daily News*, 'uninfluential and foolish, can be left to Arnold Morley and the small fry'.[28] During the Round Table Conference he was in close touch with G. E. Buckle, the Unionist editor of *The Times*, which was hardly the right medium to gauge the strength of Liberal feeling about Gladstone. An appraisal of the chances of Liberal re-union which Brett contributed to the *Ninenteenth Century* as the Conference foundered showed him to be over-optimistic.[29] The Conference proved to have embittered the relations of the leaders and to have exasperated the country. It helped to estrange Brett himself from his earliest political patron, Harcourt, and it appeared to confirm Rosebery in the wisdom of his remaining in opposition to Chamberlain.

Since Brett was not in the Commons, his vacillating course over Home Rule, first opposing it and then settling down to become a close associate of Rosebery, did not much matter, though there were some who gave him a black mark for it. Once Rosebery came to insist on the retention of the Irish at Westminster the view he had expressed in 1885 that Home Rule would be a step in the direction of Imperial Federation became more intelligible. It is perhaps significant that Cecil Rhodes held exactly this view, and in 1888 donated £10,000 to the Parnellite party, while in 1891 he contributed £5,000 to the Liberal party with a warning to Schnadhorst that: 'If the exigencies of party necessitate a Home Rule Bill without representation at Westminster, your association must return my cheque.' Rhodes also made the significant remark in the same letter: 'The future of England must be Liberal, perhaps to fight Socialism.'[30]

There was a link between Rhodes and Rosebery, through W. T. Stead, in which Brett to some extent participated. Stead's *tête à tête*'s with Rosebery could last seven hours, and he was noted for his insidious directness and unquenchable enthusiasm. Rhodes also was clearly impressed by Stead, for in his fifth will made in 1891 he left the bulk of his estate in trust to him as the most fitting person within his acquaintance to carry out his ideas. One must assume that Stead shared Rhodes's visionary and, in the light of later experience, ludicrous ideas, such as 'the bringing of the whole civilised world under British rule', 'the recovery of the United States' and 'the making of the Anglo-Saxon race into one empire'.[31] Rhodes wrote to Stead of 'union with America and universal peace' to be promoted by a 'secret society organised like Loyola's supported by the accumulated wealth of those whose aspiration is a desire to do something'.[32] Brett was familiar with these enthusiasms of Rhodes's. He was at Stead's house when Rhodes called on his arrival from South Africa in February 1891 to talk about 'all his great schemes'. His impression was that Rhodes was 'a splendid enthusiast. But he looks upon men as "machines".' Shortly after, having had a long talk with Rhodes at Tring, Brett noted: 'He has vast ideas. Imperial notions. He seems disinterested. But he is very *rusé* and, I suspect, quite unscrupulous as to the means he employs.'[33] However, Rhodes's policies and practice conformed with Rosebery's, with the stresses on the diffusion of the language and values of England, the mystique of an 'imperial race', and the importance of territorial acquisition and trade in undeveloped areas. Thus Schnadhorst was able to assure Rhodes before the election of 1892 that Rosebery, who would be Foreign Minister, would not agree to abandon Egypt. By sending out Sir Gerald Portal to survey the affairs of Uganda Rosebery stole a trick from his colleagues and ensured that the British flag would be planted at Kampala. Rhodes's fears for his telegraph line from the south to Egypt were thereby relieved.

The prospect of another Liberal government did not enchant Brett, who in 1887 had declined to consider standing again for his old seat of Penryn and Falmouth 'until I am assured of the support of the united Liberal party in the Borough, upon a platform including large measures of domestic reform—and a foreign policy imperial and at the same time peaceful'.[34] He could not stand as a Liberal without being taunted for his attacks on Gladstone. His hopes of a Rosebery ministry receded as the anti-imperial section under Harcourt and Morley consolidated their position while Gladstone still declined to retire. 'Charming as Harcourt is in private,' he wrote to Rosebery, '...his talk always brings home the difficulties of our political prospects.'[35] He confessed to dreading a Liberal victory at the approaching election on account of 'the fundamental divergence of views upon so many important questions between Harcourt, Morley and yourself'.[36] The worst of it was that Rosebery would not fight for himself. His strange streak of self-depreciation, so uncommon in a politician, and his tendency to withdraw when his voice was eagerly expected, did not become less pronounced with his political advancement. After the death of his wife in 1890 he suffered dreadful bouts of depression and somewhat later an almost fatal spell of insomnia. He had few friends and no confidants. Brett became almost his sole companion, and his journal provides one of the most penetrating assessments of Rosebery's enigmatic character.[37] When Lord Granville's death left the Liberal leadership of the House of Lords vacant, Rosebery shrank from assuming it and also disclaimed any wish to be Prime Minister. 'Place Harcourt in a position where it becomes his great endeavour to keep the Ministry together,' he said. Brett did not dislike the idea of Rosebery being 'an unfettered Foreign Secretary' as he would be in such a government. But Morley had just told him he doubted 'whether he could ever serve with Harcourt'. Such was the state of dissension among Gladstone's lieutenants when he formed his final ministry in 1892. Rosebery resolutely declined office, but his protestations were simply ignored and he was informed that his name would be submitted to the Queen.[38] Morley, of all the ministers, had insisted on Rosebery's inclusion: while Rosebery, brought in in this manner, became absolute at the Foreign Office, doing what he pleased.

The final disruption of Gladstone's ministry came not from foreign affairs but from Lord Spencer's navy estimates. Gladstone was basically out of sympathy with the European trend away from the high-minded Concert of Christian Powers and towards what he called 'militarism', the naked rivalry of force, fed by conscript armies and competitive armaments. The unlooked for escalation of defence expenditure also destroyed the system of finance which represented much of his life's work, while higher taxation undid the work of Cobden, and consolidated the income tax which he hated. In this last contest even Morley did not go with him. Meanwhile Harcourt had made himself insufferable to Gladstone as to Morley, and so in spite of Loulou Harcourt's strenuous and ubiquitous efforts on his father's behalf there was little prospect of Harcourt succeeding to Gladstone. The objections to Rosebery as a peer and an imperialist weighed little in the circumstances, and the Queen's choice of Rosebery as Prime Minister seemed reasonable enough.[39] Gladstone, had he been asked to suggest a successor, would have named another peer, Lord Spencer.

The Home Rule Bill which Gladstone had carried through the Commons in 1893 had depended on Irish votes, the Liberals of the United Kingdom being in a minority. Though the Bill proposed to retain Irish representation at Westminster, it was doubtful whether the Irish Nationalists, now torn into factions over the Parnell divorce and its sequel, would have been able to accept or work a Dublin parliament. The passing of the Bill through the Commons was a pious exercise, and its rejection by the Lords was an example of how useful the reviled Upper House could be to a Liberal party embarrassed by old pledges or exigent allies. To launch a crusade against the House of Lords for rejecting the Bill, as Gladstone wanted to do, would merely have exposed the ambivalence of English Liberals. Hence when Rosebery omitted any mention of Home Rule in the first Queen's Speech of his premiership, he was not out of line with his colleagues. He overreached himself, however, when he was drawn into the declaration that before Home Rule could be conceded: 'England as the predominant partner would have to be convinced of its justice.' This, as Morley admitted, was what he had privately agreed with Rosebery, but it was 'not to be said at this delicate moment'.[40] Coming by surprise from a Prime Minister in the Lords, it gave a handle to those Liberals who resented the leadership of a peer like Rosebery.

In his strange way Rosebery agreed with his critics that the composition and powers of the Lords were unjustifiable. His critics looked forward expectantly to his honours list to see what peerages he would create, but he dodged the difficulty by claiming them as Gladstone's recommendations. But his other appointments gave scope for censure. A recent biographer refers to 'some appointments so bizarre as to arouse merited suspicions of frivolity', one of which was that of Frederick York Powell, a law tutor when Rosebery was at Oxford, as Regius professor of history in succession to Froude. His inaugural lecture was described as 'almost a scandal'.[41] Reginald Brett's appointment by Rosebery to the position of Secretary to the Office of Works, which was a brilliantly successful inspiration of Rosebery himself (Brett had asked for something different), was greeted with the same kind of scepticism. Rosebery's Chief Whip, Tom Ellis, commented: 'Brett's appointment is simply *execrable*... a man with about £6,000 a year with five houses in town and country who has "always left his party in the lurch"... It will be looked upon as Whiggery with a vengeance. Ugh!'[42] Brett himself was not unaware of the hostility in the party to his appointment, but told Rosebery that 'whatever views may now be taken of your choice, I shall justify your selection'.[43]

The duty of the Office of Works was to supervise all public buildings, palaces, royal parks, etc. in England and Scotland, and also to exercise a certain initiative in the erection of new public buildings or in civic improvements. The Secretary was a permanent civil servant and also an official in close relations with the Sovereign. Rosebery judged rightly that Brett would be more than *persona grata* to the Queen. As the son-in-law of one of the Queen's most long-standing friends, the Belgian ambassador Sylvain van de Weyer, Brett was already admitted to the private circle of the Queen, who 'often visited Orchard Lea informally'. Brett had done much to foster the informal connexions between Eton and Windsor Castle, the Queen's normal 'London' residence. His daughters attended a dancing class there with those of Princess Beatrice which the Queen occasionally attended,[44] and like Rosebery he had recently become a frequent guest at the Castle. Already he had manifested a love of pageantry and ceremonial and had no doubt helped to encourage the occasional performances of opera and formal dinner parties which marked a less reclusive phase of the Queen's widowhood. Like Brett's other contemporaries Rosebery was impressed by his tact and charm. He also appreciated his historical sense which was almost an indispensable qualification to an office dealing with ancient monuments and works of art, ceremonies of state, tombs, collections, furniture and decor, historical archives and all the precedents governing the royal establishments.

Rosebery's great success in the publication of a short study of Pitt was closely followed by a similar study of eighteenth-century statesmen by Brett. The coincidence of subject and publication suggests an interest shared when as a widower Rosebery plunged into historical study. Brett followed up his *Footprints of Statesmen* with a series of studies of Queen Victoria's prime ministers, commencing with the still somewhat delicate subject of Lord Melbourne's relationship with the girl-Queen, and including rather audaciously the sacred subject of Prince Albert. These were serialised in the *Nineteenth Century* and were obviously written from the 'inside' and drew on the Queen's own journal.[45] The confidence reposed in Brett's discretion and sympathetic treatment was fully justified. The studies are amusing and far from trivial, while being also, as a friend pointed out to him, 'courtier-like'. Since the living subjects of the contemporary historian must always feel that truth has been outraged in some particulars, and granted the Queen's special feelings about Disraeli and Gladstone not to mention the more personal relationships, it is almost inconceivable that Brett could have produced these vignettes without detailed discussions with the Queen. To have treated them to the satisfaction of the public while also remaining on the best of terms with the Queen argues no mean literary skill, and extraordinary tact. This success must have weighed much with Rosebery in deciding on Brett's appointment. Brett had asked for the Woods and Forests, and had shown some hesitation in complying with Rosebery's decided opinion that the Office of Works was much more suitable. He soon completely agreed.

As Secretary of the Office of Works from 1895 to 1902 Brett was involved in the management of an extraordinary series of state occasions: the Diamond Jubilee of 1897, the funeral of Gladstone, the opening of the Victoria and Albert Museum, the funeral of Queen Victoria and the coronation of King Edward. Even more significant, perhaps, he was responsible for the sweeping changes in the royal palaces made by the new King, the re-establishment of

Buckingham Palace, the disposal of Osborne, and the reorganisation of Windsor and Hampton Court. He also chaired the committee which chose the Memorial to Queen Victoria, and succeeded in persuading this inter-party body, on which Rosebery squabbled with Chamberlain, to adopt his own plan. This resulted in the modern layout of the Mall and the open space before Buckingham Palace, and the building of Admiralty Arch.

State ceremonial was not a strong point of British administration when Brett assumed his office, in spite of the enormous expenditure of the services on a colourful range of uniforms unequalled abroad, and the dedication of army and navy to ancient drills and exercises. To leave a ceremony to the College of Heralds was to invite disaster, marching columns that concertina'd, coffins borne in the wrong way and unforeseen snags of all kinds. The offices of Master of the Horse, Lord Steward, Lord Chamberlain and Earl Marshal which were traditionally intended to deal with state ceremonials had become virtual sinecures, and under their management the Queen's reception of the members of the House of Commons at the 1897 jubilee seemed 'like a crowd being let onto the ground after a football match'.[46] However, the important ceremonies and functions of the Jubilee were well organised, thanks to the efforts of Brett in association with a small committee under the Prince of Wales.

The original idea was to invite royalty, but the problem of resolving precedence and accommodating the astonishing number of 'royals' and their suites before the advent of César Ritz made this less attractive than Chamberlain's suggested alternative. This was a great military display, with Colonial premiers instead of crowned heads, which the Queen accepted with alacrity. Brett's own contributions were a children's fête in the Park, at which the Queen presented Jubilee medals, and some 'beautiful pageants' in London and at Eton. His duties ranged from preventing landlords from clearing tenants from properties along the route of the procession, to dealing with imminent perils on the occasion. The Queen's secretary recounts how when people were fainting in an over-heated tent in the grounds of Buckingham Palace everyone turned to Brett, who was present in court dress. Impulsively drawing his sword, he began to demonstrate how holes could be cut for ventilation. He thrust his blade through the canvas, whereupon a piercing scream came from outside. Luckily the person escaped injury.[47] The problems of organisation were made all too apparent in the fiasco of Chamberlain's ball for the Colonial premiers, when it was almost impossible to get through the crowd into the house. Brett instinctively did not go to this 'fearful bear-fight', but noted: 'Princess Maud nearly got torn to pieces. The foot-men were...ragging all the guests and using most filthy language—especially to respectable elderly ladies. The Princess of Wales drove up and had to drive away.'[48] Yet the great procession to St Paul's, where the Queen sat in her coach attending a brief thanksgiving service conducted on the steps, was universally acclaimed as a success, thanks to Brett's arrangements and even more to his way of dealing with others.

Some months later John Morley, who was literary adviser to Macmillan's, approached Brett with a commission to write the Life of Disraeli. Brett said his whole time was absorbed, and was unwilling to leave his office. One of those who pressed him not to leave the civil service was Chamberlain, who the following year offered him the Under-Secretaryship of State for the Colonies, and later the Governorship of the Cape. Chamberlain seems to have regarded Brett as still his man, in spite of his attachment to Rosebery. Of Rosebery Chamberlain said to Brett, when they were dining alone: 'I shall never forgive him for having known, when he became Prime Minister, how to revive the old Liberal party, having tried to do it, in the right way, by his "predominant partner" speech, then having funked, and destroyed his own handiwork and the party for ever.'[49] It would have been reasonable for Chamberlain to have supposed that Brett was in sympathy with his South African policy, then being energetically pushed to the conclusion of war with the Transvaal by Sir Alfred Milner. For he knew that Brett had approved Milner's appointment as High Commissioner, while Milner had never been taken up by Rosebery. Had Rosebery, one wonders, forgotten the bright young man pressed on him by Jowett in 1885, when six years later Brett wrote to him: 'I want you to see Alfred Milner... Such a charming fellow, with a *culte* for you...'?[50] There was in reality little affinity between the ideals of Rosebery and Milner. Milner despised democracy and his ideals could be easily extrapolated into national socialism. Rosebery for all his talk of an 'imperial race' remained a Whig and something of a Millite Liberal. Brett never resolved his own position in this antagonism, remaining more of a socialist than Rosebery and more of a democrat than Milner. When the crisis of the South African diplomatic struggle between Kruger and Milner came in the summer of 1899 he was sufficiently out of touch with the latter to deplore his brinkmanship. A Boer war, he thought, would be 'such a horror—and a crime too'.[51]

In May 1899 Brett succeeded to his father's title and became Viscount Esher. Normally his assumption of a seat in the House of Lords would have terminated his office in the civil service. But the Queen and Prince of Wales were 'most anxious' that he should remain, and Balfour pressed Sir Francis Mowatt, the permanent head of the Treasury, to acquiesce. It seems to have been agreed that Esher should take no active part in debates, and he was all too pleased to take his position on the cross benches, leaving his party allegiance uncertain. He was now eligible for a political appointment, and was soon to achieve the unique position of being able to decline the War Office proffered by the Unionists and the Viceroyalty of India proffered by the Liberals,[52] while possessing more actual power than these offices would have conferred. Initially his position depended on the fact that after the Duke of Cambridge relinquished the post of Commander-in-Chief of the Army no convenient intermediary existed between the War Office and the Sovereign. When the Boer War with its early defeats, casualties and anxieties swept over the peace-orientated Victorian society the Queen became at once the resort of soldiers and their relatives not only for news but for every kind of representation and complaint. Lord Esher stepped effortlessly into the niche which this situation created. He knew the War Office from the inside and had kept up his relations with the officials there. As the permanent head of a department he was on confidential terms with other officials and had become accepted as the Queen's plenipotentiary. He was therefore given access to the secret telegrams as they were received at the War Office, and indeed very soon he was offered the post of permanent secretary there.[53] Prudently he did not wish to be involved with the War Office administration, whose gross oversights and incompetencies were being exposed. Instead he became the Queen's personal adviser in military affairs on a purely informal basis until, after the Secretary for War Lord Lansdowne had quarrelled publicly with Lord Wolseley the Commander-in-Chief, Esher set down his views on the question of their respective functions. He thus began to exercise power without responsibility.

Esher had by this time very distinct ideas of his own about the War

Office and the duality of the Secretary of State and the Commander-in-Chief. He took Wellington and his system as a model, and believed that the Commander-in-Chief should be an executive officer freed from all concern with administration and dealing directly with his staff officers—the Quartermaster-General who oddly enough dealt with intelligence and operations, the Adjutant-General who dealt with organisation, and the Commissary-General responsible for supply. Such he supposed had been the system during the Peninsular War. But from the time of the Crimean War the Quartermaster-General had gradually lost his responsibility for operations and had from 1868 been officially subordinated to the Adjutant-General. From 1888 the QMG's department ceased to be an integral part of the staff, and indeed the duties of an operations staff ceased to be assigned to any branch of the Army. The removal of the Commander-in-Chief from the Horse Guards to the War Office involved his staff more and more in questions of finance and peace administration, so that the Adjutant-General's department ceased to reserve any staff officers for the special purposes of a general staff. When the Boer War broke out, no trained general staff existed, nor was there any real understanding in the War Office of the purpose and functions of such a body of officers. Hence the opinion of Esher was also that of the public, that 'the splendour of our fighting is beyond compare, but the tactical errors have been awful'.[54]

The British army had been allowed to become what Sir Charles Dilke described as 'an army to which peace is necessary'.[55] Lord Wolseley, who was Adjutant-General in the 1880s and Commander-in-Chief from 1895, was a leading exponent of the idea of a war-orientated army and so aroused the hostility of the anti-militarists, who said he should be put in a glass case in peacetime. According to Wolseley the army of the 1880s was 'clumsily and badly organised, drilled on an obsolete system, and dressed in ridiculous and theatrical costumes'. Its tactical instruction was bad and 'a large proportion of the superior officers' were 'not fully competent to command in modern war'.[56] The anti-militarists no doubt imagined the army as being always in a defensive role. To be anything more it needed both a striking force, and masses of second line troops to follow and secure lines of communication. Dilke, one of the foremost advocates of an efficient army, pointed to two experiences which showed the anti-militarists to be unrealistic. In 1870 Britain had guaranteed the inviolability of

Belgium only to discover that there would be no troops available to enforce it. Even after the Franco-Prussian War the Belgians did not follow their neighbours in having conscription but had what was virtually a mercenary army. In Dilke's well-informed estimation they were not strong enough to hold Liège and the line of the Meuse, their official plan against invasion, and that therefore 'all that Belgium really does is to hold the fortress of Antwerp for us, as a port of disembarkation', a prophetic insight.[57] But had Britain, after Cardwell's army reforms, the will and even the capacity to land a force at Antwerp, or anywhere else?

Dilke's second example was the Wolseley expedition for the relief of Khartoum. As such a force moved deeper into a hostile territory it shed more and more of its fighting strength in establishing supply lines and protecting them. It could easily dwindle into a mere skeleton force by the time it reached its main opponent. The European armies understood this problem well, and reckoned to use millions of trained but older ex-conscripts to maintain their lines of communication. Britain then could not be held to possess a striking force unless there were also in readiness large numbers of secondary troops available for service abroad.

The naval scare of 1884 worked up by Arnold-Forster and Stead, with Brett in a minor part, led to the Naval Defence Act of the following year which appropriated £5,500,000 to ship construction and fortifying coaling stations.[58] This was bound to bring the level of defence expenditure into question, and Lord Randolph Churchill as Chancellor of the Exchequer seized the opportunity to criticise the high cost of the army. In a public speech he declared that the British empire spent £51 million on war establishments, as compared with £20 million of the German empire and the £31 million of the Russian, and yet Britain 'is, as compared with these two Powers, in a state of utter and hopeless military and naval defencelessness...'[59] Before his resignation Lord Randolph attempted to get the Salisbury cabinet to abandon Britain's traditional commitment to defend Constantinople against Russia. After resigning he threw himself into the arena of defence policy, chairing a controversial parliamentary select committee. Brett, who was on close terms with Churchill (Lord Randolph showed him all the correspondence bearing on his resignation) seems to have attempted to support the same policy, that is, the abandonment of the anti-Russian emphasis on diplomacy and the axiom of

Constantinople, while switching the preoccupation of defence to the protection of the route to India and the colonies. He told his former constituents he would require: 'Enquiry to be followed by energetic action into the administration of the great departments of State, especially the War Office and Admiralty.'[60] When Churchill was trying to persuade the cabinet to abandon Constantinople, Brett wrote two letters to *The Times* arguing that the Palmerstonian policy with regard to Constantinople had become obsolete after the battle of Sedan.[61] France had 'ceased to count in the combinations of European policy', while Russia had become 'the natural friend, under existing conditions, of England all over the world'. Russia could therefore be allowed to take Constantinople, Britain's route to the East having been secured by the possession of Alexandria and Cairo. When Churchill had resigned and Liberal re-union was on the cards Brett published an appeal which would have given a motif to a Hartington-Churchill Liberal ministry. He also attacked Rosebery's conservative foreign policy, which he dared not do openly and so adopted the pseudonym 'XIII' which escapes even the indexer:

Brett in Pall Mall Gazette, 19 January 1887: What is Bismarck's mysterious secret? It is, after all, nothing more than a bold business-like way of stating to the world the problem he wishes to solve...Yet how many English statesmen are there who would dare...to adopt an attitude at once so popular and so bold? Lord Hartington, perhaps...or Lord Randolph Churchill...

But would Lord Granville, or would Lord Rosebery...have had the courage to say what the vast majority of their countrymen feel,...that Bulgaria...must work out its own salvation?

The English Foreign Office is a close borough—absolutely unrepresentative of anything save the most indifferent provincial traditions...Frankness...is the quality which democracy should require from its Foreign Secretary—Bismarckian frankness.

If Churchill commenced as an advocate of mere economy he soon became an advocate of efficiency and value for money, heartened in this cause by the startling facts and figures which his committee unearthed. Sir Henry Brackenbury revealed that while the German army cost £19 million and could put nineteen army corps into the field, the British army (not including the Indian) cost £14 million and at most could field two army corps.[62] It was easy to blame this state of affairs on the soldiers, but Churchill came round to accepting that it was the fault of the politicians. By 1888 he had been converted to the programme of Wolseley and the soldiers. He claimed that the War Office had 'civilian management' but not 'Parliamentary control'.[63] Readiness for war was sacrificed to the interests of economy and peacetime management. The characteristic British response to the kind of colonial war for which the system was best suited was to improvise the stores for a campaign, which would be paid for by a special parliamentary vote, according to the needs of the occasion. In his Afghan expedition Lord Roberts had 'practically killed all the camels which could be procured in Asia'.[64] Likewise mules, khaki uniforms, or special equipment or provisions were not normally provided for in advance of the occasion. The armies of the Continent knew exactly what their wartime campaigns would involve, but the British army had to deal with anything anywhere.

Lord Wolseley became the champion of the soldiers' demand for a unified responsibility centred in his own office of Commander-in-Chief, while Lord Lansdowne as Secretary for War favoured the alternative conception of a plurality of military advisers to the Secretary of State. Wolseley thought in terms of appeal to the cabinet and even Parliament, while the politicians insisted that the minister was ultimately responsible and should be the sole channel of military advice. The soldiers complained that military efficiency and preparedness was constantly sacrificed to economy, and that the party system only responded to the needs of the army in some scare or crisis. This charge was more or less admitted by Lord Salisbury during the Boer War. It was, he suggested, inherent in the British system of government. Lord Wolseley and his backers were not prepared to take so supine a view of the situation, and argued that public opinion could be educated to military needs. There was however, in opposition to the soldiers and to the demand for a general staff, a strong body of opinion headed by Campbell-Bannerman that dreaded military efficiency as the precursor of 'militarism'. Once the nation possessed a powerful striking force the temptation to use it could not be resisted.

The military reverses which quickly followed the outbreak of the Boer War brought these issues into debate. The Intelligence Department was found to have given quite accurate warnings of the Transvaal's military capacity, but the government countered the charge of neglecting these with the argument that military preparation of large reinforcements to South Africa would have been provocative. To be sure, the want of preparation was explicable largely in terms of the failure of the politicians to emphasise the imminence of danger. Chamberlain's diplomatic pressure on Kruger had seemed to be succeeding and perhaps did succeed momentarily, until by a sudden impulse the militant section of the burghers opted for war. Normally in a game of brinkmanship the party being squeezed utters some cry of exasperation before resolving to fight, and had Smuts the Attorney-General given an indication that he was being pushed too far it is very likely that Chamberlain would have taken a step backwards. As it was, the Boers secretly prepared an attack and struck only a few weeks after the tension had seemed to have relaxed. They fought to win, which the politicians and most of the soldiers had not foreseen. However, the leading soldiers and politicians were foremost in launching public accusations against the system and against each other. Relieved of his position as Commander-in-Chief, Wolseley led the way, and Lansdowne followed suit after relinquishing the War Office in September 1900. The Queen seems to have taken the soldiers' side in the dispute even before Mr St John Brodrick, Lansdowne's former under-secretary, took over the War Office. She questioned whether even Mr Balfour might be inclined to take 'an extreme civilian view of the War Office arrangements', whereupon Brodrick retorted that he thought Balfour and Salisbury were disappointed at the unreliability of 'the advice the cabinet had received from Lord Wolseley on military matters'. The position of a Commander-in-Chief, already condemned by the Hartington Commission, was again in question, and the Queen made some effort to justify its maintenance, requesting Wolseley to state his side of the case.[65] Lord Esher was also given the same task, and in a letter to Sir Arthur Bigge of 22 October 1900 he provided a rejoinder to the common notion that the Commander-in-Chief's office had been condemned *per se*. The Hartington Commission, he asserted, had not condemned the Commander-in-Chief's 'personal responsibility' when the post was held by the 'ablest military officer obtainable'.[66] 'The proper organisation is for the Commander-in-Chief to be responsible for the "efficiency" of the army and responsible to the Secretary of State only...But ...I think heads of the various departments *under him*...should be appointed *not* for five years but for one year renewable...'[67]

On the face of it the advice that Esher gave to the Queen at this juncture was diametrically opposed to the recommendations of the so-called 'Esher committee' of 1903–4. Instead of advocating the abolition of the Commander-in-Chief, the subordination of the War Office to the Defence Committee, and the formation of an Army Council, he did the reverse. After seeing Wolseley's memorandum of 12 November Esher referred to Martin's *Life of the Prince Consort*[68] as a source of the principles which should govern army organisation, not, one might guess, entirely to flatter the Queen with the authority of Prince Albert, but in reference also to the heyday of the Wellington system. These principles, he thought, condemned the idea of a shared responsibility of the soldiers as expressed in the existing Army Board:[69] 'They dispose to my mind of the idea of a *Board*: and strengthen the argument in favour of a Commander-in-Chief *responsible personally* for the efficiency of the army to the Secretary of State and to the Queen.'[70] As for the Defence Committee, an inter-service committee of the cabinet which Salisbury had instituted and which had continued on a very sporadic career under the Unionist government, Esher did not at this stage see that it ought in any degree to qualify the personal responsibility of the Secretary for War or the Commander-in-Chief for 'great questions' of army administration:

Memorandum by Esher, 10 December 1900:[71] Few members of the majority of the present Parliament have contrived to avoid a pledge to their constituents that they will see a large measure of reform applied to the War Department...

Who is to decide on the measure of reform to be applied, and what is the reform to be?...No elaborate mechanism, no substitution of 'Boards' for personal authority, can obviate the necessity of leaving in the hands of the responsible cabinet minister the final decisions upon great questions of military administration...It is useless to enquire whether a Defence Committee acting without the knowledge of the Commander-in-Chief and the Secretary of State, consulting with subordinate officers... can fulfil these conditions...

Faced with the prospect of a reorganisation of the military system by political pressures which might in all probability institute the dominance of the military by the politicians, Esher advocated the creation of

a general staff under the Commander-in-Chief who should become
the authority in matters of army organisation and reform.

> *Ibid:* The General Staff should take over the work of the Intelli-
> gence branch subject to the control of the Commander-in-Chief
> but widening their functions so as to include the consideration
> of defence by sea and land of the whole Empire.
>
> It is to a General Staff composed of the most experienced and
> skilled officers who have seen service in India and Africa that
> the two questions as to the purposes for which the British Army
> is required should be referred, and it is to them that the Crown
> and Parliament should look for advice as to the principles which
> should govern the constitution of the Army...

These views are a strange contradiction of those that Esher put forward so vigorously and successfully three years later. Had he been a
politician he would have been accused of inconsistency and opportunism. As it was, he enjoyed the privilege of formulating two solutions in different sets of circumstances. At this time he was defending
the soldiers from the threat of the kind of multiple system of Boards
that had been devised in 1895 with little success or permanence. He
also considered the Defence Committee as a mere cabinet sub-committee. By 1903 he had greatly extended his knowledge of military
affairs by chairing a committee on the engineers and taking a very
active part in the Elgin royal commission on the South African War.
Also he became more familiar with Balfour's ideas, and in particular
his vision of a revivified Committee of Imperial Defence. But above
all by 1903 Esher himself had arrived at what was to be the master
conception of the whole defence bureaucracy, a secretariat for the
Committee of Imperial Defence which would among other things
engraft the function of a combined services general staff on to a
cabinet committee. This enabled him to resolve the hitherto insoluble
conundrums of dual responsibility. Hence the inconsistency of the
scheme of the Esher committee with the earlier memorandum is a
testimony to the extraordinary speed with which he developed his
ideas, from the time he first took up military reform seriously.

For his services in the matter of the Commander-in-Chief, whose
office was enlarged by Order in Council, Esher received an order
within the Queen's personal gift, the KCVO. This was one of the

Queen's last formal acts, for in January after a sudden illness she died. The demise of a sovereign after so long a reign, which had almost removed the formalities of a succession from living memory, presented Esher with a challenge which he took up with alacrity. He found that no particular preparations had been made in anticipation of the event. 'The ignorance of historical precedent in men whose business it is to know is wonderful,' he observed.[72] The Lord Mayor of London had to be refused admission to the special Council where the act of homage was done and the King's speech given. While most of those concerned shared Lord Salisbury's wish to escape the 'gruesomeness' of the traditional rituals, Esher lovingly resurrected the details from historical records and from those who like the Duke of Cambridge remembered two previous royal funerals and coronations. He was put in charge of the ceremonies at Windsor, where the funeral service was held in St George's chapel, and had leisure to enjoy the 'brilliant success' of his own arrangements. 'The ceremonial was lovely today,' he recounted without any false modesty to his son: 'and perfectly arranged from start to finish. I had to receive everybody at the Mausoleum. It was beautiful, interesting and pathetic...The procession down the Long Walk was most striking...Keep always in your heart the memory of the Queen whom your immediate forefathers served so closely and faithfully and well.'[73]

The suggestion of an official *Life of Queen Victoria* based on the Queen's journal and the enormous correspondence of her reign seems to have been made originally by Sir Arthur Bigge. It envisaged a narrative biography, but Esher when consulted thought this would be 'impossible during the life-time of certain persons, and until the shadow of events grows longer'.[74] Instead he proposed that the Queen's papers should be collected and arranged, and the journal printed up to a certain date with a very full supporting selection from the correspondence. This he believed would be far more interesting than an expurgated biography. Though other authors had been named for the task, it gravitated to Esher himself,[75] chiefly because he had begun to consult the Queen's papers for precedents concerning the royal succession and funeral, the new Civil List on which he reported to the King, and the host of questions concerning the coronation. Also, no doubt, the extensive rearrangements which Esher made under King Edward's direction in the royal apartments at Windsor and at Buckingham Palace involved searches in the Queen's papers.

Antiques from Brighton Pavilion which had lain neglected were restored to prominence and a wealth of pictures hung lovingly by the King. Enormous hoards of bric-à-brac were cleared out, including as legend has it a great quantity of elephant tusks, the annual tribute of some African chief. Esher discovered through the questioning of an old workman the statue of the Queen done by Marochetti in 1865, which had been walled up, and placed it over the Queen's tomb. King Edward found his Secretary of the Office of Works so full of assiduity and resource that he pressed him: 'For God's sake don't give up your appointment.' 'He talked over some very private affairs with me,' Esher noted along with the former remark, 'and I shall not venture to write down the conversation.'[76] In April the King asked him to arrange Queen Victoria's papers, and at the same time appointed him Lieutenant and Deputy Governor of Windsor Castle.[77] In this manner Esher came to have charge of the royal archives, and since he did not advise their open access to scholars he came to enjoy the exclusive command of much constitutional lore and precedent. His position as a political *éminence grise* to Edward VII and George V in successive crises involving the powers and prerogatives of the Sovereign rested on this basis.[78]

The coronation was postponed to 1902 when it was hoped that peace with the Transvaal would be concluded, and Esher decided to leave the Office of Works after playing his part in the arranging of the many functions associated with the coronation service. This would free him to play a political role, though his ideas were more in the direction of journalism or finance. In October, shortly after coming to the decision to resign his office, he lunched with Alfred Harmsworth, later Lord Northcliffe, but found him a 'clever, vain man—not very intelligent about anything except organisation and money-making; but full of aspirations for power.'[79] In December 1901 he was offered a business association with the great financier, Sir Ernest Cassel, which he decided to accept and to take up when free to do so. Meanwhile there was much to occupy him. The scheme for a public memorial to Queen Victoria took the form of the present spacious lay-out of the Mall and the Brock Memorial before Buckingham Palace. Esher carried this scheme through the inter-party committee in March only to encounter resistance from the royal family. Princess Louise feared the Memorial might replace Trafalgar Square and the plinth of Nelson's column as a rallying-point for demonstrators, and that there might be 'mobs in front of the Palace'. Esher, knowing that an appeal would be made to Balfour, explained that 'Princess Louise, furious because she was neither consulted nor employed, has been worrying the King to death about the site for the Memorial. She wants it in Green Park...The King shows, in this as in other matters, a slight tendency to yield to the pessimistic attacks of his sisters.'[80] Balfour was requested to 'help him to be firm', with evident success.

Esher was asked by the King 'to "stage-manage" the ceremonial in the Abbey' for the coronation, but refused 'very politely, on the ground that the little Duke of Norfolk would be horribly hurt!'[81] However, he agreed to help, and set up a special office at 1 Chapel Place. He proposed that the royal procession to the Abbey should be as short as possible, while a long route should be followed by the King and Queen when crowned. It was settled that the Queen should have four tall duchesses beside her, and that the princesses should put their crowns on when the Queen did so. The invitations for the procession had been sent off, and the final rehearsals with the Knights of the Garter and the four duchesses were in progress, when the sudden illness of the King caused an indefinite postponement. The Ritz was already crowded with foreign royalty and Americans when the announcement was made. According to Sir Almeric FitzRoy, Clerk of the Council, the postponement to 9 August, when the King had recovered from his appendicitis, saved the proceedings from being a fiasco. Even so, this sharp critic of the proceedings found much to cause anxiety and even alarm. Sir R. Paget was seized with a fit 'ushered in by gutteral sounds of most ominous significance'.[82] A worrying queue formed outside the ladies' lavatory which is explained in one account as caused by a peeress who had disappeared inside carrying a pair of forceps, and who finally emerged triumphantly having recovered her diadem from the pan.[83] The conduct of the service by the Archbishop, who proved to be as blind as he was obstinate, was a nerve-racking ordeal for the officials responsible. The Archbishop had had his liturgical and ceremonial utterances copied in large type on a series of scrolls, but the light in the Abbey dimmed. The scrolls were 'not held with any remarkable steadiness, and their succession was not observed with punctuality'.[84] A blunder occurred when the King was adjured to give his special protection to 'widowers' instead of 'widows', the irony of which was only emphasised by the Archbishop's correction. After the Enthronement and Homage the

Archbishop had to be raised from his knees by two bishops, who pulled opposite ways and nearly upturned him. FitzRoy felt that it was a 'striking tribute to the impressiveness of the ceremonial that its effect was not marred by these disquieting accompaniments'.[85]

Few who witnessed the scene will ever lose their recollection of four of the loveliest women in England, with their trailing purple robes and sumptuous *appareil*, supporting the canopy beneath which the stately figure of England's Queen received the holy oils, and when the group dissolved it seemed like the passing of a dream that might have haunted the imagination of Vathek or De Quincey...

But even here, in the annointing, 'the infirmities of the Archbishop, assisted by the greater feebleness of the Dean of Westminster, who insisted upon his privilege of administering the Cup to the Queen, were allowed to distract', particularly when the Dean 'narrowly escaped emptying the contents of the chalice upon the Queen'.[86] The 'extreme tact, authority and exactness' of the King covered up these flaws, and also the Queen's self-control when, if one account is to be believed, a spot of oil fell on her nose which had to be borne without any grimace or movement.

After the King had proceeded, bearing the sceptre and orb, down to the west door, the Duchess of Devonshire attempted to leave the choir, 'engaged in some discussion with the officer-in-command, and then, pressing her way through, missed her footing, fell heavily forward, and rolled over on her back at the feet of Sir Michael Hicks Beach'.[87] Her coronet 'flew off and struck the stalls' while willing hands, directed by Soveral (the Portuguese ambassador and special friend of the King) at last restored her to her legs. Such were the ordeals dreaded by those who have to manage the solemn national rituals which can in a moment turn to farce. Esher no doubt shared all the anxiety and suspense, and there is a legend that he himself contributed to the alarms of the occasion. Before the Abbey had quite emptied after the occasion was over some cavernous reports were heard and the alarmed attendants rushed down to the vaults only to break in on a champagne luncheon at which Esher was presiding, attended by his family.[88] He was celebrating not only the success of the day but his own release from the responsibilities of office.

Four

The Committee of Imperial Defence

The problem of defence was largely one of educating public opinion, which as the military reformers saw it had got dangerously out of step with the times. The military requirements of the Empire in face of the increasingly hostile and effectively armed European powers and the extension of British territorial commitments overseas had greatly outstripped the capacities of the army, as was only too painfully emphasised when in the crisis of the Boer War the country had been denuded of troops. Yet the public was demanding drastic reductions in the army estimates and was as vigorously opposed to the idea of conscription as ever. An army which needed to recruit men in competition with civil employments was bound to be expensive, the more so since social trends had rendered service in the army relatively less eligible than it had been. The British army was one of foreign service, an additional reason why conscription was unsuitable to recruit it, but the public had scarcely begun to resolve the questions of how or even whether their imperial possessions should be defended. While the navy's role of defending the homeland and protecting the nation's commerce was well understood, the army's functions were obscure and the fact that its cost had soared above that of the navy caused widespread resentment. The professional soldiers led by the Commander-in-Chief, Lord Roberts, were in general advocates of conscription, so that while the reforms of 1901 which consolidated the powers of the office of Commander-in-Chief and absolved the soldiers from the incubus of the 'red-tape bureaucrats' of Pall Mall were beneficial in themselves, they did nothing to ameliorate the political problem of the army's unpopularity.

The Defence Committee of the cabinet when instituted by Lord Salisbury was intended to reconcile the competing claims of the navy and army and also to match the demands of the professionals against the policies of the politicians.[1] Campbell-Bannerman, an early supporter who was later to condemn the Committee of Imperial Defence as an 'aulic council', viewed it as a means of bringing the extravagances of the experts under political control. It might well have become a kind of 'estimates' committee of the cabinet conducting a more or less public inquest into the technical and strategic factors affecting defence expenditure. The secrecy which shrouded the Committee of Imperial Defence as it evolved in the hands of Lord Esher and Balfour represented an altogether different conception. At first, Balfour's reorganisation of the Defence Committee was prompted by a demand from Arnold-Forster for a committee of professionals, scientists and politicians acting as a public forum with the prime purpose of creating a publicly accepted corpus of beliefs concerning defence spending and policy.

As Secretary to the Board of Admiralty Arnold-Forster presented the naval estimates in the Commons, the First Lord being Lord Selborne. When meeting a criticism from Haldane in February 1902 about the superiority of the German Naval Intelligence department he declared: 'I am still unregenerate in regard to the broader aspect of this question...there is need in this country for a more general organisation, not only of the Naval or the Military Branch, for war, but of both services together.' When in the summer Balfour succeeded his uncle Lord Salisbury as Prime Minister he encouraged Arnold-Forster to formulate his ideas along these lines, and the result was an important memorandum on 'The Need for Organisation for War' dated 20 October 1902, which was circulated to the cabinet.[2] Viewing the existing Defence Committee as a useful 'link between the Naval and Military Departments and the Executive Authority vested in the Prime Minister and the cabinet', Arnold-Forster nevertheless did not feel that its members, who were 'not specialists', were 'really capable' of supervising and directing the defence of the Empire. What was needed was something on the lines of the Great General Staff at Berlin, a body of experts keeping continuous records and training up specialists so as in time to acquire 'sufficient prestige and authority to ensure its recognition in the Services and by the public'. At present, he declared, 'no true professional opinion exists', only a medley of untested individual opinions. He therefore asked for the creation of a 'special body, whose duties shall be different from, and additional to, those now assigned to the Intelligence Departments of the two Services'. Never a party man, Arnold-Forster had consulted Sir Charles

Dilke,[3] and he clearly envisaged that the new 'special body' should be non-political and, equally important, that its findings should be made public.

As First Lord of the Admiralty Lord Selborne read this project with uneasiness.[4] He congratulated Arnold-Forster on his 'very able paper' and added that he agreed in spirit but not with every word of it.[5] Moreover, Arnold-Forster had presented a loophole. He had seen plainly enough that only the Prime Minister could set up his 'special body' and had therefore called for a 'preliminary committee' formed by the direct authority of the Prime Minister, who would preside to give it 'status and independence' while the naval, military and civil secretaries and their staffs and the ordinary members of the 'special body' were being selected. Selborne and Brodrick, the Service chiefs, seized on this preliminary committee but suggested, in their well-known memorandum, that the secretariat should come from their own departments, the very last thing that Arnold-Forster envisaged and also an unnecessary addition unless they thought of it as being permanent. Yet this was denied. 'Pray understand,' Selborne assured Arnold-Forster, 'that the reformed Defence Committee is not a substitute for the machine you advocate, but the first present possible step towards it.'[6] Accordingly, the first meeting of the Committee of Imperial Defence was held on 18 December at the Privy Council Office with the Duke of Devonshire in the chair and the Directors of Naval and Military Intelligence responsible for minutes, records and papers to be kept by a civilian secretary. The Service chiefs sat on the CID *ex officio* and also their Directors of Intelligence, who had right of speech. Against this patent dominance by the Service heads Arnold-Forster protested:

Arnold-Forster to Selborne, 28 December 1902:[7] I confess your letter had cheered me more than the document itself.

I cannot help feeling that nothing would be better calculated to put an end to all my hopes than a reference of my paper to the Joint Committee...Is it conceivable that those whose whole policy is under review should ever admit that their policy has been quite inadequate, or that they have failed to such an extent that a new organisation, such as they have never proposed...should be created?

It is the Prime Minister, and not the professional Heads of the two Departments, who ought to initiate the required reform.

The first act of the 'Joint Committee' (it was not yet known as the CID) was to constitute itself according to the Selborne-Brodrick memorandum. Moreover, the King's approval was conveyed in a manner which guarded even more pointedly the position of the Services. 'He hopes,' Lord Knollys wrote to Devonshire, '...that the reconstituted Committee will not have too much power, and thus decrease the proper responsibility of the Secretary of State for War and the First Lord...'[8]

In the preceding months Esher had altered his standpoint on defence questions. He had taken up his association with Sir Ernest Cassel, which was to be for three years with a stipend of £5,000 a year and 10 per cent of profits. Cassel must have valued Esher's widespread connexions and influence, and also his knowledge of political and strategic matters. Cassel was interested in the political questions raised by the American shipping combine and also in steel works in India, about which he dealt with Chamberlain and Curzon respectively. Early in 1903 he planned a mission to Berlin about the Baghdad railway, and Esher knew that the CID was strongly in favour of the line on strategical grounds. One may guess that through his friendship with Balfour, who on assuming the premiership gave a new push to defence matters, Esher was quite *au fait* with the thinking behind the reform of the CID, and he claimed that Balfour had been jogged into it by the incompetencies being uncovered by the Elgin commission. 'Lord Esher believes,' he wrote to the King, 'that the change in the constitution of the Defence Committee is directly due to the questions put by the South African War commission to every witness of importance, as to the work and sphere of action of that body. Mr Balfour's attention was drawn by Lord Esher to the responsibility which must attach to the Defence Committee for the neglect of proper precautions before the war...'[9]

Esher's own views had certainly been modified by the interrogations of the commission, which interviewed every soldier of importance. As the King's special informant on these matters he composed summary and opinionated reports on the soldiers and their evidence in courtly language sure to engage the King's interest. He also made sure that the War Office administrators always had the worst of it. Lord Kitchener, he reported, made the 'astonishing assertion' that the 'military authorities' had not questioned him on his experiences.[10] 'The evidence again shows,' went another letter, 'that the War Department had neglected the lessons of former campaigns.' 'The gist of his [Sir E. Wood's] evidence...was that...it is Your Majesty's civil servants, and not the military officers, who are to blame.'[11] Sir John Ardagh's sensible proposals had been 'scoffed at by the Financial Authorities of the War Office...'[12] Reading these racy reports, the King was soon 'full of interest in the army'. It is interesting that Esher attributed to Rosebery a proposal that the King himself should be C-in-C of the army. 'Lord Wolseley,' he reports, '...suggested that Lord Rosebery's plan should be adopted, and that Your Majesty should be the sole Commander-in-Chief, and that the Secretary of State for War should always be a soldier.'[13] This represented Esher's own view as well, for he had come round to believe that the post should be abolished and the title conferred on the Crown. Later however, finding that the King was virtually Commander-in-Chief and would gain no new powers from the title, he was content to let it disappear.

Once it had been decided by Balfour to change the Defence Committee from a mere cabinet committee to the inter-Service planning body suggested by Selborne and Brodrick, Esher seems at once to have viewed the CID as the proper authority to control a general staff, so that the Commander-in-Chief was no longer needed for this purpose. Also the position of the Secretary for War, which he had wished to keep distinct from that of the soldiers, could now safely be merged into a predominantly military board. This was the principle of the Board of Admiralty, which unlike the Army had not seemed to need a war staff. After December 1902, therefore, Esher boldly advocated an Army Council, 'somewhat on the lines of the Board of Admiralty' as he described it to Lord Knollys.[14] That such a body, presided over by the Secretary for War, would be under the control of the CID in matters of general military planning in Esher's scheme of things is clear from his letter to the King a month later. It remained, he wrote, to awaken in the CID 'a sense of the absolute necessity of settling the *main lines* of imperial military policy' and also 'a full appreciation of the importance of constant and serious deliberation'.[15] He noted that 'the Prime Minister is a member, but not the President of the Defence Committee', which should 'not be taken as a precedent'.[16] Esher found that Brodrick, the Secretary for War, was resisting his ideas, and so worked to cut the ground from under him. 'Your Majesty will have noticed,' he writes on 11 March 1903, 'that Mr Brodrick in his speeches in Parliament has unfolded schemes of reform, based on the lines of cross-examination before the Commission...Lord Esher hopes that the Report will press for the conversion of the War Office Council into a highly efficient Army Board on the lines approved by Your Majesty.'[17] In case the King had forgotten what these lines were Esher composed a memorandum for him after a long talk with Balfour on 16 March, who was 'not unfavourably inclined' to the scheme, including the daring proposal to 'let the King be the nominal Commander of the Land Forces of the Crown'.[18] This memorandum of 19 March[19] anticipated Esher's minority report on the Commission, and proposed the abolition of the position of Commander-in-Chief, to be resumed by the Sovereign, an independent Inspector-General, an Army Council or Board on the lines of the Board of Admiralty, and the decentralisation of the War Department. The King seemed to approve: 'He is more appreciative than you are,' Esher told his son, 'and attaches more importance to my humble views.'[20]

For Balfour the 'seeling point' of the plan was the idea of the Sovereign at the head of all imperial forces including those of the Dominions. But Esher whose delvings into the royal archives at Windsor revealed how incessant was Queen Victoria's intervention in army affairs, meant to make more of it than that. He also knew how to get support for the plan from inside the War Office and indeed from the navy. The Adjutant-General, T. Kelly Kenny, went so far as to say that the Sovereign already possessed the powers of a C-in-C. He controlled promotions, rewards and appointments, and could review and drill troops.[21] Who could tell what the limits of his feudal and prerogative powers were? Kelly Kenny had obviously had the idea of a special committee of Esher and Admiral Fisher mentioned to him, for he agreed it would be a good thing. Armed with his written approval, Esher approached Admiral Fisher and Prince Louis of Battenberg (the Director of Naval Intelligence). Their approval rested chiefly on a promise to cut down the army estimates and abolish the Secretary for War! Fisher obligingly suggested that the Secretary of State's office should be put in commission, like that of the Lord High Admiral.[22] Battenberg agreed that the Secretary for War should be 'abolished'. 'He is too great a man to sit on the Board like our First

Lord.' As for the army estimates: 'Why not disband the superfluous line battalions,' he added, 'put the men into the reserve and the officers into the auxiliary forces.'[23]

Against this kind of subversion Brodrick could only have contended if he had been supported by Balfour, which he was not. Enforcing ministerial solidarity was not one of Balfour's strong points, and he was about to be pitched into the great tariff reform squabble with Chamberlain and Devonshire through failing this very month to prevent his Chancellor of the Exchequer, Ritchie, from overturning a cabinet decision. His government was about to experience, and surprisingly survive, the most massive series of ministerial resignations in memory. In the reshuffle he removed Brodrick and tried to put Esher in his place, but Esher refused. We may deduce from this glimpse ahead, from March to September 1903, that Brodrick, floundering in the failure of his army scheme (it was of course his and not the government's) was a doomed man.

The 'Esher committee' was on the cards long before the reconstitution of Balfour's government in the autumn. The idea that Esher as an 'irresponsible adviser' should chair an informal committee unknown to the Constitution and indeed contrary to its spirit was attributed by Balfour to the King. It could hardly with decency have been said to come from Esher himself, but it probably did. The theoretical justification for empowering a peer, a journalist and an admiral to turn the War Office upside down was that some impartial authority 'outside' the professional soldiers and politicians was needed to effect a 'clean sweep' of the abuses and inefficiencies that had been exposed in the South African War and were made voluminously public in the Elgin commission's report of August. But was Esher really free from a political bias, and did he choose impartial assistants? The answer must be, as so often with Esher, that he was clear as to where he was going and ruthless in getting there: that he saw his way clearly in this case, and simply used the myth of the clean sweep to implement a plan of reform of his own. An 'impartial' outsider, trying to enforce a fair compromise, he would have viewed as a recipe for disaster.

He had changed his mind, and instead of wanting to uphold the personal responsibility of the C-in-C, as he had done when Wolseley filled the post, he now wanted to abolish it. For one thing, there was now a king as Sovereign and not an aged queen, and, a cynic might add, Esher was his adviser. But the real difference was that Esher now saw that a reformed Defence Committee could fulfil the functions of the C-in-C at home (though not of course in the field) in so far as they were administrative, while much could be delegated to the commands, and much of the dignified functions assumed by the Crown. What he had always abominated was the departmentalism and the red tape of the War Office and what Henry Wilson on reading the Elgin report called 'our rotten system of having our army run by politicians'.[24] He had therefore favoured the personal authority of the C-in-C as against a War Office Board. But now he had decided on an Army Board (the later Army Council) which would be the Secretary of State in council, expressly because he intended to subordinate the Board to the Defence Committee as he intended to make it, and as the Esher committee did make it. 'Your Majesty is the natural Head of the Army all over the world,' he wrote in a disquisition proving that the post of C-in-C was not a great historic office, and that of GOC of troops in Great Britain was the natural and proper position for the senior general of the army. Only the King could be the 'focus of all imperial military forces' and the 'centre of civil loyalty' in the dominions.[25]

Having mooted his plan to Brodrick and Lord Roberts, the C-in-C, Esher knew that they would put up a strong opposition. Brodrick might not have liked the system of 'dual control' but he seemed to Esher 'too timid to tackle the C-in-C'.[26] Also the Elgin Commission dragged its feet over the War Office Board and Esher with two supporters had to append a supplementary note to see that his plan was not lost.[27] The report certainly made a great splash in the press, but since the government seemed about to break up on the fiscal question, it lost a lot of its reality. Would the King, who was away in Marienbad, *force* Brodrick or his successor to carry through the reform? Lord Knollys assured Esher on the King's return that he was determined to insist on it, and Esher replied: 'If at the commencement of the next war...we are better prepared than last time England will owe it to the King.'[28]

On 18 September the resignations of Chamberlain, C. T. Ritchie and Lord George Hamilton were announced, to be followed by those of Balfour of Burleigh and Arthur Elliot on the 21st. Esher was summoned to Balmoral for what he thought was the customary deer-stalking, but: 'Directly I got there the King sent for me, and I had no sooner kissed his hand, than he asked me to be one of his ministers, and spoke of the W[ar] O[ffice].'²⁹ Taken aback, Esher stalled for time. 'I am purely selfish in the matter,' he commented privately, 'and I really do not think that I can bring myself to sacrifice all independence, all liberty of action, all my *intime* life, for a position which adds nothing to that which I now occupy.'³⁰ Balfour, Lansdowne and Akers Douglas (the Conservative Whip) were at Balmoral, and it had been settled that Brodrick should go to the India Office. Esher suggested that Selborne should transfer to the War Office. He protested that he was not a politician and could not ally himself to a party. He also proposed that Akers Douglas should take the War Office as a man of straw, while he himself assisted by Fisher and a third partner should carry out the reforms. Letters from his son and Harcourt arrived and fortified him in his determination to refuse office in spite of a 'pathetic and entreating' interview with the King. It was lucky that he had the 'Esher committee' idea up his sleeve, and even so Balfour must have been determined on army reform to have swallowed it. It needed all Esher's talents for conciliation to come away without disgrace, though he promised to serve the King in a position of 'less honour and dignity, but of greater practical effect'.³¹

Balfour had set his heart on a great success in the realm of military reorganisation and army reform as the chief justification for his remaining in office. The political benefit of his plan would be a large saving in the army estimates arising from his espousal of the 'blue water' axiom that no army was needed for home defence—that invasion was impossible—which he was about to set forth in a paper he would present to the Defence Committee. Dilke and Arnold-Forster, among others, had long argued the 'blue water' theory, and Balfour was therefore quite ready to have Arnold-Forster at the War Office. He knew that Esher and Fisher were also strong 'blue water' men, and so he could expect to gratify the public, which was clamouring for an end of the inflated wartime estimates and taxes, while also redeeming his pledges to make the Defence Committee really effective, and the War Office efficient. Esher was careful to brief Balfour on 27 September for a speech he was about to make, giving the reason why the War Office should be reformed by someone other than the Secretary of State—who had still to be chosen. This was that there was needed a 'special commission under the supervision of the Prime Minister and the Secretary of State' to implement the recommendations of the Hartington commission of 1889–90 and of the Elgin

92

and Dawkins reports. Esher adds: 'If...I am chairman of such a body, I shall propose to take the War Office administration right through, from top to bottom, and endeavour to make it a first-class business machine.'[32]

At first the King declined to accept Arnold-Forster: 'The King has frequently told Mr Balfour the reasons why he does not approve Mr Arnold-Forster's appointment as Secretary of State for War.'[33] He might be Under-Secretary, and 'in that case the King strongly urges Lord Selborne being appointed, who would make also an admirable chairman of the committee of which Lord Esher and Admiral Fisher are to form part.'[34] If the King objected to Arnold-Forster because he thought he was opposed to royal influence, to the amateurism and social pull of what Esher called the officer 'caste', or to the redundancy of the auxiliary forces, he was well advised to do so; and in these matters Selborne was the natural opponent. Arnold-Forster however was clamoured for by the press because he combined a long-standing reputation in both army and navy matters with the required knowledge of the Board of Admiralty on which the War Office was to be modelled. Balfour had to take him as the obvious man, although he admitted that his 'manner is not his strong point'. Still, he had 'immense knowledge, untiring industry, and a burning zeal for reform'—at which King Edward must have shuddered.[35]

While Arnold-Forster was in the offing the King became most doubtful about any Esher committee, and Esher was obliged to write to Knollys: 'The King is quite right I am sure about the proposed War Office committee. My suggestion involves too wide a departure from precedent and from constitutional practice...the experiment would be too dangerous...'[36] But Knollys induced the ebullient Jackie Fisher, then Second Sea Lord and Commander-in-Chief at Portsmouth, to come to Balmoral early in October. 'It was curious how he and Esher seemed to hit it off together,' observed Sir Frederick Ponsonby: 'Both were very clever; both preferred to come in at the back door instead of the front; both had the early Italian type of mind.'[37] Fisher succeeded in impressing the King with the epoch-making importance of War Office reform if implemented by the 'blue water' school: [38]

...the organisation of the War Office is intimately associated with

93

our naval strength. Who has yet stated exactly what we want the British army to do? *No one*...

For instance, what would be the good of a British army as big as that of Germany if the navy were insufficient to keep command of the sea?...In the month of March England has three days' food in the country...

Let the army's needs be stated publicly, and then let them be weighed, said Fisher, against 'the naval necessity which makes £34 million sterling insufficient to ensure not the *safety* but the *very existence* of the Empire!'[39]

The War Office must be reorganised on such lines as will ensure most intimate joint naval and military action, and the natural question that arises [is] 'Can this imperative requirement be met by any other method than a single Cabinet chief as in Austria?'

Here Fisher was pleading for the need to end the 'autonomy' of the War Office by placing it under the overall control of the Defence Committee. These arguments convinced the King that his scruples about departmental autonomy were outmoded, and by 8 October the Esher committee was again in play. The King had just been 're-assured on certain points' by Selborne as to the choice of Arnold-Forster, and had 'reluctantly' agreed to him. Informed by Knollys, Esher admitted that Arnold-Forster was 'a very clever man and exceedingly hard-working, but he is of the same "class"—intellectually—as Brodrick, and (to use your own expression) I prefer a more "commonplace and practical" type of politician.'[40] When Esher saw the King on 12 October he found that there was now no resistance to the original plan for the committee, which Balfour had agreed to in September. The only modification, imposed because of the prejudice against Arnold-Forster, was that the King 'sees that Arnold-Forster had better *not* be upon it—that Fisher, a soldier and I could do the job'.[41] This agreed, Esher saw Balfour's secretary, J. S. Sandars, the next day and arranged for Balfour to be informed. The committee's terms of reference, drafted by Esher, stated the principles on which the reorganisation of the War Office was to be based.[42]

Balfour had been somewhat out of touch with these developments, and absorbed in a rather ill-humoured correspondence with

Devonshire over the latter's sudden resignation. He had assured
Arnold-Forster that the Esher committee 'would act as a buffer' to
absorb the shocks which 'such official revolutions involve'.[43] In his
reply the new Secretary for War said outright: 'The War Office I am
convinced cannot be worked on the principle Lord Esher suggests...
there must be a head.'[44] Balfour realised that a Secretary of State could
not be pushed around by an irresponsible peer, and warned the King:
'We must be careful in appointing the committee to have regard to
the *status* of the Secretary of State. It would seem proper therefore
that the committee should be appointed either by him or by the Prime
Minister and him...'[45] Esher on the other hand was thinking of some
extra-constitutional mandate. 'Personally,' he had just written to
Knollys, 'I incline to commissioners having royal authority rather
than a committee: a "new departure", but the case requires abnormal
treatment...'[46] On receipt of Balfour's letter the King was 'strongly of
opinion that the committee should be appointed by the P[rime]
M[inister] and not by the Secretary of State for War...he should
not form part of it...'[47] Balfour accepted this, but he did not accept
the request to announce that the Esher committee had the King's
'special' approval.

The choice of the third member of the Esher committee caused
considerable dissension and delay, but in the end Fisher got his way
and Sir George Sydenham Clarke, then Governor of Victoria, was
brought over. Since his recall was not decided till 2 November, and
he did not arrive till 28 December, all the important decisions of the
Esher committee were made before he could participate in them. On
reading of the public response to the Elgin report Clarke had written
to Fisher in his self-vaunting style: 'I have over and over again
pointed out the great danger of our War Office and army system. I
would give anything to have the chance of participating in reorganising both, and especially to bring the army into harmony with our
maritime position...The real point (as I have often tried to explain)
is to take the Naval Basis for the organisation of the army.'[48] As Clarke
observed, the army was costing £52 million and the navy only £34
million. He wanted like Fisher to cut army estimates to £25 million
and spend more on the navy accordingly. Here was a 'blue water' man
after Fisher's heart. 'Humbly submit he is absolutely indispensable,
so please press his inclusion in the committee, which of no use without him' he wired to Knollys.[49] Clarke was a bouncing crude fellow,

D*

who quarrelled with everyone in the end, and a journalist who would never give up his leaky confidences to the press, but he was just the man for the purpose.

Meanwhile Esher proceeded on his own lines more or less unimpeded by Fisher, whose ideas on army reform were stimulating but remote from the details of reorganisation. Fisher's idea that the Army Council members should be 'lords' as in the Admiralty was quickly trodden on, and his scheme brushed aside.[50] By mid-November Fisher had read the proofs of three papers by Esher and admitted '...you are absolutely convincing on the main lines'. 'The regular army...should be regarded as a projectile to be fired by the navy,' was one of his memorable pronouncements in the same letter.[51] He also pressed that Balfour should lay down 'how the Army should be constituted'. Arnold-Forster was hard at work on his own scheme for infantry reorganisation, but Esher did not intend to allow him to proceed before the reformed Defence Committee had surveyed the purposes and global commitments of the army as a whole. '...do not let Arnold-Forster be in a hurry,' he cautioned Balfour: 'Brodrick created six beautiful Army Corps *on paper*. Let his younger colleague beware...I can imagine the fate of these memoranda if they come before the Cabinet. They will be riddled with criticism by Brodrick and Lansdowne, whose administration they largely condemn...And when all is said, we shall not be much nearer the only real solution, to which your Defence Committee Draft Report of the 11 November so powerfully and lucidly points.'[52]

Balfour had committed himself to the 'blue water' departure, which implied the scrapping of all the aspects of the post-Cardwell army system that were aimed at producing an army for home defence, and substituting an organisation which would supply the most effective 'striking force' and the reserves for a reinforcement of the Indian army. Arnold-Forster, seemingly with Balfour's backing, was proceeding on the assumption that army reorganisation would be a problem for the general staff which he wished to create, somewhat on the German model. Esher was determined not to encourage the War Office to have anything like an independent staff which he equated with too 'professional' an army. But the real issue between them was not departmental autonomy—for Arnold-Forster was a leading exponent of an independent and supra-departmental Defence Committee —but whether the amateurs and politicians, or the professionals and lay experts, should dominate defence planning. For Esher the essential 'amateurism' of the British army officer 'caste' was a matter of history and social tradition. A scientific and professional army would be both too expensive for a naval power and unnecessary so long as the navy was supreme. His ideas were elaborated in a printed paper on the general principles of the Esher committee which he sent to Balfour:

'First Note' by Esher, 2 December 1903:[53] There is no *tabula rasa*, and the constitution of this country, and the political habits of our people, are main factors of the problem...

The Defence Committee is a case in point. Originating in Imperial needs...it has already developed capabilities beyond the expectations of its founders. Does it not contain the germs of a growth more in accord with British institutions than a general staff on the German model?...

The Defence Committee is not...formally a Committee of the Privy Council, but would there not be advantage in giving it...the guarantee of a Privy Councillor's oath?...the Committee could be strengthened by including representatives of the Dominion and Australia...Sub-committees might have to be appointed for the purpose of working upon specific points of detail, in connexion with the world-wide problem of defence and offence.

Would not such a body require a permanent staff? A clerk or secretary, to keep minutes and to preserve records, already exists. He should be established and located.

Would it not be of great advantage if one or two specially qualified naval and military officers were attached to the Committee, in order to work out military and naval problems in concert, and to obtain information from the intelligence branches of both services, from India and the colonies?

Thus would come into existence a Department of Scientific or Theoretical War Problems, wholly distinct from the Admiralty or the War Office, and subject to the authority of the Prime Minister himself...

For a Great General Staff on the German model, i.e. independent of the War Office, material in the shape of a number of highly trained staff officers does not exist, and even if such a department were desirable or possible for Imperial purposes

97

under our *present* institutions it could only be the growth of years...

After Devonshire's resignation Balfour had presided over the Defence Committee himself, and on 4 December he got cabinet approval to change its rigid membership into those chosen by the Prime Minister for each sitting, which might include representatives from the colonies. Thus far Balfour was in step with Esher, but he took a lot of convincing that the Defence Committee needed a secretariat.

Hitherto Esher's conception of the Defence Committee was close to what Selborne's had been when he forestalled Arnold-Forster a year before. It was simply a kind of clearing house where the service staffs and intelligence departments could bring their expertise and trained knowledge before the scrutiny of the cabinet ministers most involved, though Balfour had broadened the political purview by the idea of colonial representatives. But in December he came to think of the secretariat as being a 'Prime Minister's department'. This would open up possibilities for expert staff both independent of the service departments, and not independent of political control. The Prime Minister would become virtually Minister of Defence, in charge of an inter-service 'general staff', while the new Army Council that Esher was proposing to set up would be essentially an executive authority. 'If Arnold-Forster is wise,' he wrote to Balfour, 'he will bury his memorandum for the present, and will throw all his energy into the creating of a "Department" for the Defence Committee (we will call it a General Staff) and a War Office Council, as an executive authority.'[54] The conception of a secretariat which Esher had arrived at was speedily embodied in another printed paper:

'Second Note' by Esher, 20 December 1903:[55] The progressive work of the Defence Committee makes it more evident every day that the primary act of military reorganisation should be to establish a department under the Prime Minister, as Chairman of the Defence Committee, which in fact, although not in name, would constitute in time a 'Great General Staff' suited to our imperial requirements...I am still of opinion that no material exists for creating such a department on a very ambitious scale— but, on seeing the rapidly developing scope of the work of the Defence Committee, I doubt whether the appointment of a

private secretary and one or two officers from the Army and Navy respectively would meet the needs of the Prime Minister.

A 'Permanent Secretary', with a trained strategical mind and, if possible, a man who has given attention to the great historical and practical problem of Imperial Defence, seems an essential requirement...

Under this official might at first be grouped two soldiers, two naval officers...and two Indian officers...with, if possible, a Canadian officer...

I would not propose to interfere with the branch of the Director of Naval Intelligence...nor with the QMG's branch which it is contemplated to form at the War Office.

Before sending this off to Balfour Esher awaited the arrival of Sir George Clarke, whom he met at the station on 28 December and took to the War Office. He had been anxious lest Clarke should prove a 'difficulty', for a letter which arrived ahead of Clarke had mentioned as 'quite essential' for the new Defence Committee a 'good civilian non-ministerial element'—something it was never to have while Esher had anything to do with it. However, Clarke proved to be 'amiable and conciliatory' as well as appearing '*fat* and comfortable', and accompanied Esher to Portsmouth for the first meeting of the 'triumvirate'.[56] There and then the Esher programme was endorsed and forthwith sent off to Balfour: a department for the Defence Committee under the Prime Minister, and an Army Council of four military and three civilian members, to be set up before Parliament assembled in February. 'I see that Clarke himself will have to be your permanent secretary to the Defence Committee,' Esher added: 'He is cut out for the place.'[57]

Balfour ruminated over the two *Notes* at Whittinghame, and did not reply till 14 January, when he questioned the idea of an independent secretariat. 'Will not the creation of a *third* expert body, different from both and in the closest relation with the Defence Committee, be very difficult to work...? Under the present system the Naval and Military heads of the "thinking" departments, with the Prime Minister and the parliamentary heads of the Military and Naval Departments, discuss problems of defence together.'[58] Balfour therefore wanted the secretariat chosen from the staff of the intelligence branches of the War Office and Admiralty, so that: 'They would be under no temptation to assume the role either of the First Military Member or the First Sea Lord, or of the Committee of Defence itself.'[59] Esher countered this by arguing that the Secretary would collect material for the Prime Minister not only from the service departments but from others, and that the service heads with the heads of their intelligence branches attended the Defence Committee as *members*. He gave way by agreeing that the subordinate staff of the secretariat should be drawn from the intelligence branches on temporary secondments but insisted that the secretary himself be independent and that he should have a special collative function. His subordinates became 'orderlies', and hence the conception of an independent 'general staff' under the Prime Minister dwindled into a department for collation and briefing.[60] It was a big surrender, but Esher could content himself that at least a nucleus had been established which might develop. He frequently referred after this to the 'nucleus crew' of the Defence Committee. In practice, the absence of independent experts and professionals in the secretariat exposed it to the political jobbery of the Prime Minister and Esher himself. Amateurism and political opportunism tainted its sub-committees under Balfour, as will be seen. It became as much a political as a defence department.

The proper scope of the Esher committee was War Office 'reconstitution', and in his swingeing way Esher got the King to agree 'to get rid of *all* the W[ar] O[ffice] officials, without exception'.[61] This gave him almost unchecked patronage over the whole range of the department, and it cannot be said that he exercised this patronage fairly. His appointments were politically biased, and were a sad example of the abuse which creeps in when power is unchecked. The only extenuation is that he acted with an important end in view, and was dealing with soldiers who were themselves steeped in political intrigue. The worst case, perhaps, was that of Sir William Nicholson, whom Esher himself had recently described as: 'The cleverest soldier I have yet seen... Most clear and determined and explicit.'[62] As Director of Military Intelligence under Arnold-Forster, Nicholson had the temerity to criticise Esher's *Notes*. He failed for example to understand how the Defence Committee could be a 'general staff', whom he defined as officers with war experience, who can tell if paper schemes will work.[63] The fact that Arnold-Forster made a fight to retain him[64] only made him more obnoxious, and he was sent to gain more war experience in the Russo-Japanese conflict. 'Nicholson must

go. He doesn't get on well with the Admiralty and he is too "grasping" ',
Esher commented to Knollys: '*Not* an original mind, and by no means
indispensable.'[65] Arnold-Forster wanted to make Nicholson the Chief
of the General Staff, and he was in fact appointed CIGS later. But
Esher preferred to him a nominee of Balfour's and the least able of
the Lyttelton brothers, Sir Neville Lyttelton, who was perfectly incompetent as First Military Member of the new Army Council and
could only have been placed there to render the body compliant.
Arnold-Forster could not begin to form a central general staff
while Lyttelton remained the titular head of the non-existent body,
and in spite of his admitted incompetence Balfour would not remove
him. In this ruthless way Esher cut the ground from under Arnold-
Forster's intention to form a real general staff.

Another appointment which was politically inspired was that of a
royal duke, the Duke of Connaught, to the critical post of Inspector-
General, which the Esher committee insisted, in the teeth of strong
objections in the cabinet, on making tenable with the presidency of
the Appointments Board. 'Lord Esher would venture to say,' went the
submission to the King, 'that if the Duke were simply a general officer
in Your Majesty's service unconnected with your Majesty he would
easily hold his own and prove an efficient administrator...'[66] The
battle over this appointment culminated on 29 January when Clarke
went over the whole Esher scheme with Balfour, and assured him
rather rashly that the Inspector-General would be subject to the
Army Council. Balfour threatened to forbid publication of the
scheme, but Clarke retorted that it could be issued to the House of
Commons.[67] It was a curious situation, for Esher had recommended
the Duke of Connaught to the King, and when Lord Roberts who
was about to be 'abolished' as C-in-C showed an unhealthy interest
in becoming Inspector-General he was put off with the argument that
he was too important for the post. The King was 'very kind but very
firm in telling Lord Roberts that he ought not to accept the IG...
From what I saw of Lord R[oberts], afterwards, I don't think that
he made much impression. The little man is very tenacious. The D.
of Connaught called here and I drove with him to Paddington.' 'Our
torpedo has exploded and the little C-in-C has left the W[ar]
O[ffice] for good in a devil of a temper.'[68] Clarke witnessed these
manoeuvres admiringly. But for Esher's 'admirable diplomacy', he
told him, 'we should have been shipwrecked.'[69]

Little diplomacy was wasted on the subordinates at the War Office, who were ejected from their offices with careless indifference. 'Do you think the victims of the "clean sweep" have been informed?' Clarke inquired of Esher on 30 January, a day or two before the Esher committee report was due to appear.[70] Seemingly Esher was too busy, with the scandalous results which Henry Wilson happened to note in his diary:[71]

(3 February 1904) ...the Chief came into my room while I was having a cup of tea and told me all sorts of gossip. Lyttelton, Douglas, Plumer and Wolf Murray replace Nick, K-K, Johnnie and Brackenbury. This is a *sweeping* change. During the day I saw Nick, who is very sore, and I must say justly so...

(10 February.) The 'Triumvirate' are appointing officers to billets here, there and everywhere, quite regardless of anyone... The King has signed the Patent...abolishing C-in-C, AG, etc, and when I went up to see the Chief before dinner I found that he knew nothing about it...

(11 February) Our days pass like nightmares... This morning I was in Nick's room talking over things...when in walked Jimmy Grierson and said *Esher* had ordered him up from Salisbury to take over Nick's office. Nick himself had not been informed... and he called me to witness that he gave over the keys of secret boxes etc to Grierson simply on the latter's word...

(12 February) This morning I was summoned before the Esher-Fisher-Clarke Committee, and Esher asked me if I would undertake the new office which dealt with Staff College...I said I would if I might have three DAAG's and other officers. He said there would be no difficulty about that...

Perhaps Nicholson who had offended Esher personally was singled out for special discourtesy: but Wilson, a beneficiary of the clean sweep, still deplored the 'kicking out and appointing, destroying and constructing at a pace and with a lack of knowledge which quite takes one's breath away'. There was a certain amount of pure jobbery. Clarke himself in consenting to accept the position of Secretary of the Defence Committee for a 'short time' (less than five years) wanted an understanding that he should then succeed Lord Cromer in Egypt or have an Indian Governorship. In the same letter he mentions the

King's wish to 'find something for his dear Lane, who has excellent qualities but a marked lack of brains'.[72] The new appointments to the Army Council were undistinguished and proved to be lacking in any conspicuous talents except those for political subservience and intrigue. Esher had no intention of allowing a budding Moltke to stray into the War Office, and it was one of his principles that if the machinery of military administration were good the men could be indifferent. As for Lord Roberts, he was a loose gun of too heavy a calibre to be allowed to career about the ship, and he was made the first salaried member of the Defence Committee.

As has been seen, Clarke's appointment as Secretary of the Defence Committee established a principle, the supra-departmental responsibility of the Prime Minister for concerting all aspects of imperial defence. Esher had been forced to reduce the Prime Minister's secretariat to one really independent element, Clarke himself, after Balfour's objection, and now again Balfour hesitated at enforcing even this irreducible minimum before the strong objection of a section of the cabinet led by Selborne. Selborne had grave doubts, which proved to be perfectly justified, whether Clarke could be trusted to give up his journalistic associations, and tried to have him excluded even from attending as a witness the meetings of the Defence Committee, remarking that it would be 'quite intolerable if the Secretary or his department were allowed to become in any sense or degree a rival authority to the Board of Admiralty on naval questions'.[73] Balfour had assured him that the Defence Committee's function was 'consultative, not executive', but this meant little when in practice Balfour used Clarke to draw up army schemes in opposition to those of his Secretary for War.

Personal objections were made against Clarke not only as a journalist but as an ex-civil servant who had been sacked and was consequently prejudiced against the financial section of the War Office, which did indeed come under the most damning castigation in the Esher report. Esher had told the King that Sir Redvers Buller was the 'high official who was unable to tolerate Sir George Clarke's opinions and who removed him'.[74] Clarke himself felt he had some secret enemy: 'Of course I have been a trenchant reviewer in my time, and I may have stamped heavily...on some personage who had written or spoken rubbish.' His chief recommendation as Clarke himself saw it was that: 'The sailors trust me, and it would not be easy to find anyone whom they would all welcome in this position.'[75] True enough, at this point Fisher and Prince Louis of Battenberg were acting strenuously behind the scenes for the man they knew would carve up the army estimates. Prince Louis urged that no time be lost in forming the secretariat,[76] and Fisher explained to Lord Knollys that the second part of the Esher report was due for the King's approval on 7 March by which time also the appointments of Clarke and his 'selected satellites' as the 'nucleus crew' of the Defence Committee should be made. The King, he suggested, should press Balfour to ask Clarke to attend the 'very next meeting' of the Defence Committee. 'Clarke is the man and 7 March is the hour! PS 7 March is a Monday which is always a good strategical day for the newspapers, as our friend Sandars has them all separately in 10 Downing Street all Sunday.'[77]

The publication of the second part of the Esher committee's report which contained 'a bitter attack on the Finance Department, which was unsupported by any evidence',[78] caused the government considerable embarrassment. Sandars was blamed for letting it go to the printer without vetting it, and Arnold-Forster stated from the front bench that the criticisms of the civil branch of the War Office were 'to say the least exaggerated'. Pressed on all sides, Sandars asked Esher: 'Were you and your two colleagues...prepared to discuss it with the Prime Minister, and *if he had asked you* would you have amended it? ...I have received nothing but blame...for my share in securing that prompt publication to which you all attached so much importance.' Esher's reply was unyielding: '...we had determined under no circumstances to alter a line' he replied.[79]

The criticisms of the civil branch were attributed to Clarke although Esher covered up by saying that he had composed the text. Among the defenders of the branch was Lord Haliburton, permanent Under-Secretary at the War Office from 1895–7 and friend of Campbell-Bannerman and Haldane, who delivered what Clarke called 'an elaborate personal attack' on him in *The Times* on 16 March. 'I have told Buckle [*The Times* editor] that I am glad of it,' wrote Clarke to Esher, 'because it gives an opening for a powerful reply... Amery must be turned on, and I will see that he has notes of all the points.'[80] As for Lord Haliburton,[81]

he was a temporary clerk in the old commissariat department in

1855...He was permanent Under-Secretary of State for *two* years only, 1895–7, and he was made a peer and a GCB!

His attack on the 'nucleus', which he says can have very few questions to deal with, discloses the readiness with which the Civil side deliver their opinions on matters quite outside the province of a commissariat clerk or an assistant under-secretary.

A week later Haliburton returned to the charge with another telling point, that the Secretariat would interfere with the War Office. This proved as well-informed as the earlier attack, for sufficient evidence had already come to light to show that the reformed War Office was thoroughly disloyal to the Secretary of State and was acting *ex parte* of the Esher committee.

Arnold-Forster had already had cause to complain of the clumsy interference of Clarke and his factotum, Colonel Sir Edward W. D. Ward, who was the new Secretary of the War Office and Army Council. When Arnold-Forster objected to appointments being made without his knowledge, so that he had heard of dismissals only through his wife's social connexions, Clarke had replied disingenuously that 'we had merely discussed certain persons as possibilities for certain places', and when he was pinned down to two irrefutable cases he passed the blame to Ward. 'You know how impossible it is to discuss things with Arnold-Forster' he wrote to Esher: 'I hope you won't take [his] letter seriously.' He added: 'I confess I don't trust Ward's discretion. He brings in lists of people he proposes to fit into places, and they think they emanate from us...I am not sure that he would not do better as Governor of Natal than as Secretary of the War Office.'[82] One might be tempted to wonder why the Triumvirate had chosen Ward in the first place for such a key position. The answer is simply that he was thoroughly disloyal to Arnold-Forster and acted as Esher's source of information about army orders and Army Council business before these were officially minuted, when they reached him as the King's adviser. Funnily enough Ward had been offered a post in South Africa, but at present he was more useful where he was. A specimen of his manner, attitude and method can be seen in his letter to Esher of 25 March: 'I fear that Arnold-Forster is again going to trouble you. He now for some weird reason, probably a desire to increase my difficulties, is fighting against the grant to me of an assistant secretary which you recommended.'[83] The War Office was suffering from a new kind of 'dual control'!

This interference by Esher and Clarke in the internal business of the War Office was by no means confined to appointments. Indeed the Triumvirate, although it was not officially wound up till mid-May some weeks after it had delivered the third and last report, had virtually ceased to exist in March. And before the 'secretariat' was established or Clarke officially installed, Esher and Clarke were actively preparing to supplant Arnold-Forster in the formulation of a scheme of army reform. '...we could never agree to it as it stands,' Clarke wrote on 28 March to Esher about Arnold-Forster's infantry scheme, enclosing a sketch of his own scheme, which at this stage was based on a territorial militia of 200,000 men.[84] The day before, when Haliburton's second attack appeared, Clarke had commented to Esher that his contention that the Secretary of the Defence Committee would interfere with the War Office was 'absolutely preposterous'.[85] He clearly had remarkable powers of self-deception, for when he became Secretary, his interference became an all-absorbing obsession, a daily concern to counteract Arnold-Forster's every move.

Clarke however was merely an instrument, and a fairly blunt one, nominally of the Prime Minister, really of Lord Esher. It was by the manipulation of less intelligent men that Esher forged his way through the shoals of petty ambitions, jobbery and inefficiency. He knew that the value of his work depended on its being carried into effect whole, and that it would be wrecked if its swift momentum were checked and it got bogged down in any parliamentary controversy. He enjoyed enormous advantages. He had the complete confidence of the King, and was fortunate in the opportunity, which Balfour was clear-sighted and daring enough to grasp with him, of the universal feeling in favour of a shake-up at the War Office and a reform of the defence bureaucracy. Even so, it needed every ounce of his extraordinary diplomacy to make headway. He had the influence of the Sovereign at one elbow—an influence which his historical knowledge and imagination did much to enhance, for it was an extremely variable and uncertain quantity—and the authority of the Prime Minister at the other, which again meant steering Balfour's moves through his private secretary Sandars. He was constantly informing and being informed through the secretarial network of which Lord Knollys was at one pole and Sandars at the other. Recognising a powerful and dedicated enemy in Arnold-Forster, he staffed the War Office with men who would work against him and removed those like Nicholson who were his supports. He knew that the personnel would change but the system had to last.

Sadly enough Arnold-Forster did not realise that his name was taken in vain by Esher and Clarke until late in 1904, when he had the first glimmerings, or later still in February 1905, when he realised he had been deceived. Before then he remained pathetically willing to oblige, and he was one of those whose determined pleading clinched Clarke's appointment. Balfour finally took the cabinet over the hurdle on 14 April when it agreed 'with misgiving', some still feeling that his 'well-known connection with the press was a serious objection'.[86] Arnold-Forster was also among those who really understood and appreciated the scope and completeness of the Esher committee's reorganisation. 'I must confess,' he wrote to Esher, 'even...with the knowledge I have lately acquired of your wonderful capacity for dealing with facts, figures and men, I stand astonished at the rapidity, the thoroughness and the correctness of your work.'[87]

Five

The Militia and the Voluntary Principle

Arnold-Forster had come to the War Office to implement a scheme of army reform. As Secretary of the Board of Admiralty he had drawn up some of the essential papers on which the Selborne-Fisher reforms were based, and in army organisation he was an even more confident 'expert' who had deliberated on the problem of reform for twenty years. Balfour was well aware of this when he appointed him to succeed Brodrick. He had invited Arnold-Forster to set down his views on army reform in 1897 and he knew that his basic idea was to create two armies: a long-service one for abroad, and a short-service one at home whose purpose would be to create a large reserve. He would abandon all idea of an army for home defence, and from this a substantial saving on the army estimates might be expected.

The work of the Esher committee was supposed to help the project by supplying Arnold-Forster with an Army Council whose members had to agree with the Secretary of State or resign. 'The members of the Board of Admiralty are not all equal in authority' Arnold-Forster had plainly insisted when he assumed the War Office: 'The First Lord is supreme. Decisions do not depend upon a vote.'[1] The Triumvirate had agreed, and Sir George Clarke thought it should be laid down as a 'fundamental principle' that a member of the Army Council should resign if he disagreed with the Secretary of State on a matter of importance, although he admitted that the soldiers did not understand this. When the Army Council came into existence the four 'Military Members' began almost from the outset to act in concert, while the two civilian members under Arnold-Forster, the Financial Secretary and Parliamentary Under-Secretary, lacked authority in military questions. The balance between the majority opinion of the Military Members and the overruling authority of the Secretary of State was obviously a very delicate matter especially in the case of army reorganisation where political policy merged into considerations

108

of military efficiency. What one would not expect would be that the Military Members should be motivated politically or that the Secretary of State should overrule them on grounds of military efficiency. But under Arnold-Forster's troubled presidency the Army Council decidedly did not follow its prescribed courses.

Admittedly the question of army reform was highly political, while the soldiers rarely agreed about even elementary consequences such as the effect on recruiting of altering the period of service. Also Arnold-Forster was a far abler man and in many respects a greater military expert than his colleagues. He knew every European army at first hand, and spent his summers attending their manoeuvres. He was acutely aware that these professional troops would 'eat up' the raw country lads and portly civil gentlemen who made up the Militia and Volunteers. The Continental armies conscripted all strata of society and had a good level of intelligence and physique in the ranks, while recruitment into the British regular army, which creamed off the Militia, was admitted to be no longer attracting the best type of soldier. While the public in a mood of post-war retrenchment clamoured for the disbanding of forty-five line battalions, Arnold-Forster found himself so short of drafts for India that he had to send men with only a few months of service left. Any scheme for army reform faced two political stumbling blocks. The public in general and the Liberal opposition in particular were emphatically against what was called 'Continental militarism', and preferred to place their reliance on a strong navy and the auxiliary forces for home defence. The professional soldiers on the other hand, soon to be led by Lord Roberts, were coming out for conscription and raising alarmist notes about the peril of invasion. To espouse the 'voluntary principle' and pay lip-service to the 'old constitutional force' of the Militia or the 'patriotic spirit' of the Volunteers might be popular but militarily disastrous: while to advocate conscription, which the Military Members secretly believed to be inevitable, would spell certain political defeat.

It was reasonable, therefore, for Arnold-Forster to attempt what was often spoken of as the 'last chance' of the voluntary system. His basic idea was to extend the catchment area of recruiting by creating a short-service army stationed at home which would, especially if territorialised so as to appeal to local patriotism and gain local support, attract a more intelligent class than that which was being recruited for long service abroad. Like the Continental conscripts the short-service recruits would serve for two years with the colours and be trained by professional soldiers. They would then go into the reserve, and as trained soldiers could be rapidly embodied in wartime for overseas service where they would be a match for European troops. This the auxiliary forces were admitted not to be, even by their supporters. In the South African War militia battalions officered by squires had presented a sorry performance of raw heroism and amateurism upon which modern weapons levied a terrible cost. The Militia had no artillery or organisation above the brigade and it was not supposed to go abroad. Yet the 'militia ballot' was still cherished by the anti-conscriptionists as a counter to conscription, and members of the 'classes' like Esher himself found a commission in the militia a congenial form of military service. The force had powerful friends in the cabinet, notably Wyndham, Selborne and Salisbury. The last named became its champion against Arnold-Forster and Haldane, and no wonder. 'There he was,' Esher notes admiringly, 'under the shade of his perfect Elizabethan place...drilling and training seven or eight hundred fine young Englishmen, quite as stalwart as any who fought for the Tudors.'[2] Could such 'heart-whole voluntary service to the state' be seen in any other country? The snag with Arnold-Forster's scheme was that it proposed to abolish the Militia. He proposed to 'absorb' the best militia battalions into his short-service army and sweep away the rest. The Militia were 'useless', 'chaff': and he meant to have grain for the money.

The army scheme which Arnold-Forster embodied in his first 'blue paper' and subsequent 'white paper' with later modifications was militarily impeccable. No-one could put a better one in its place. The objections to it were political. It did not provide a quick cut-back of expenditure, and if it gave greater value for money at a higher price, no-one felt the need for a large reserve to be urgent enough. It was thought that the Indian army could hold its own against Russia for a year, during which time the half-trained horde of militia men could be embodied and brought up to par. The idea of sending an expeditionary force to France was not seriously entertained by the government and would have been scouted by the public, in spite of the negotiation of the Entente and the military 'conversations' which were to come shortly after. John Bull was in no humour to pay for or countenance schemes for the rapid expansion of the small but highly efficient regular army he grudgingly supported.

110

Yet at first Arnold-Forster's scheme went forward without much trouble. He was indeed surprised when his old chief Selborne counselled delay, especially as Arnold-Forster had supported him when he had provided a sudden reform. Had he not produced a plan on Christmas Day 'practically revolutionising the organisation of the navy from top to bottom' and aided by the Secretary put it into immediate operation?[3] 'If Parliament lasts,' he told Lyttelton, 'I intend to put forward my army scheme, or go.'[4] Subsequently Selborne, after thoroughly perusing the scheme, took a 'very favourable view' of it, while Balfour's secretary, Sandars, said his chief was 'most anxious the matter should not be "hung-up" '.[5] The only delay that Balfour imposed was a cabinet committee to ascertain the financial result of the scheme. The crucial time approached when the debates on the army estimates would disclose the government's intentions. The Army Council after somewhat amending the scheme approved it on 25 March, when Lyttelton the first Military Member declared himself 'fully in agreement' and another thought it 'quite admirable'.[6] Hence Balfour was able to herald in the Commons four days later 'at least one other great reform which may compare with any of them—the reform of our Army system'.[7]

Astonishing as it may seem, Sir George Clarke at this point not only was preparing a rival army scheme which would preserve the Militia, but was quite confident that he would carry it. When Clarke sent Esher his paper on the 'Basis for our Military Organisation' on 28 March he was only a member of the Esher committee which was winding up its work. It seems hardly credible that Balfour encouraged him to draw up a rival scheme at this point, for Balfour had still to plead for Clarke's appointment as Secretary of the Committee of Imperial Defence with the assurance that he would not interfere in the military department. Clarke wrote as if he were the responsible minister. 'I see no other way of bringing the estimates down to a reasonable figure,' he tells Esher: 'Some such basis as this seems essential... As regards the blue paper, we could never agree to it as it stands, and he has evolved another skeleton scheme which I don't like. He does not realise that £4 or £5 millions must come off his estimates.'[8] Rumour had it that Clarke was a Liberal, which Esher certainly was, and this plan for a territorial militia of 200,000 men was exactly what the opposition would have approved. One must presume that Esher did not discourage Clarke, who now got the officials inside the War Office to supply him with the facts and figures needed to overturn the Secretary of State's scheme. 'I am getting the numbers of recruits required and also the numbers of reserves created...' he reports on 4 April. Reckoning that recruiting for what Clarke regarded as the proper period of service for the regular army could be sufficient on 10s. 6d. pay a week, he concluded that the Militia could be 'regenerated'.[9] The Army Council committee on the army scheme was not allowed by Arnold-Forster to meet again till the debates on the army estimates were over, but as the Secretary, Ward, informed Esher: 'I am having an informal conference tomorrow which will be as good as a committee meeting without its dangers.'[10] A cabal among the Military Members was being encouraged.

On 14 April the cabinet approved Clarke's appointment as Secretary of the CID which Arnold-Forster warmly supported, noting that the meeting was: 'Very satisfactory from my point of view, both with regard to my army proposals, and new appointments to the Committee of Defence.'[11] Little did he realise that the two were incompatible. No sooner was Clarke safely installed than he came into the open:

Clarke-Esher, 15 April 1904:[12] [The] Secretary of State has modified to some extent his army scheme...

Unless the latter has been most materially changed it is in my opinion wrong and reactionary. I believe the only sound lines to go upon are those I sketched out in the papers I sent to you. On this basis I see my way clear to working out the reorganisation of the army. The Secretary of State's plan I fear reconsecrates many of the evils of the past...

The virtual destruction of the Militia is a grave mistake. All my information is to the effect that the Militia can be regenerated...

From this day things began to go wrong with Arnold-Forster's scheme. Newspaper reports sowed strange dissensions among ministers. Brodrick came to the War Office and expressed annoyance at press comments on a statement that his army corps scheme was coming to an end. Lord Salisbury came to see Arnold-Forster and asked him to supply facts and figures for an army scheme of his own which was, as the latter recorded, intended to preserve 'the fourteen line battalions which I proposed to abolish, and all the militia intact ...it would mean the sacrifice of every advantage I hope to attain. I cannot help wishing that everyone else would not try and run my department for me.'[13] Then Lyttelton, the Chief of the General Staff, brought a document from the Military Members asking him not to state in Parliament that his blue paper had 'their entire approval', in spite of the fact, as Arnold-Forster remarked, that 'I had asked for and obtained their advice at every stage, and...when I received it I had adopted it'.[14] At the cabinet of 26 April Balfour began to hedge, for he reported to the King that he feared that 'although Mr Forster's scheme appears...a great improvement on the linked battalion system, it does not seem likely to be very much cheaper'.[15]

Arnold-Forster got wind of real trouble when on 4 May he discovered that the Service Members Committee of Parliament had met without consulting him and passed a resolution for the retention of the Militia which they sent to Balfour with a request for an interview. He then found that the War Office had leaked information about his scheme to two MPs who were prominent champions of the Militia, Sir C. E. Howard Vincent and J. E. B. Seely (a Liberal). The blue paper had been transcribed at the War Office and a copy given to a journalist MP, the Hon. J. W. E. D. Scott-Montagu. But as yet Arnold-Forster did not know whom to suspect, though he complained that he had to work with 'men who are evidently dishonourable and untrustworthy'.[16]

The backbench revolt encouraged Arnold-Forster's opponents in the cabinet, who concentrated on the financial aspect of his scheme and persuaded their colleagues that this was 'so unsatisfactory' that at a 'largely attended' cabinet held late at night on 14th–15th 'it was decided to defer till a later day the statement intended to have been made tomorrow' by Arnold-Forster in the Commons (i.e. on 16 May).[17] The Secretary for War was obliged to embody his scheme in a series of propositions to be passed one by one in the cabinet. This he managed to do, for he was extremely persistent and no-one could match him for expertise and erudition in army matters. The result was therefore that on 19 May the cabinet were reluctantly taken on a tight rein over the hurdles, and Balfour's report to the King reveals incidentally that the real worry was not so much expense as the sacred cow of the Militia. He describes the discussion as 'most amicable' (the King was concerned about the squabble) although the decisions were 'not in all cases unanimous': 'his scheme was adopted in its entirety—a few very subsidiary points being reserved for the consideration of the Army Council. The cabinet do not conceal from themselves that considerable parliamentary difficulty will arise in connection with the Volunteers and Militia.'[18] After all the shilly-shallying here was a decision: but unfortunately Balfour was not the man to stick to it.

The CID had been corresponding with Lord Kitchener in India about the size and nature of the reinforcement that would be needed in the event of a war with Russia. Kitchener's demand was large, and was to become larger. Hence Balfour was squeezed between the political pressure to reduce the regular army, and the Indian requirement of the capability of a rapid expansion. Arnold-Forster had agreed to reduce by 30,000 men and to budget for estimates of £29 million reducing to £27 million in four years. In the short term while the reserve was small the needs of India could only be met by the Militia unless much more were spent on the army, and Arnold-Forster had been instructed to absorb only thirty militia battalions while retaining sixty until it could be seen whether they could have 'enough vitality to be effective for war'. Arnold-Forster himself was horrified at the idea of using the Militia for overseas service, which it had never been intended for: '...the possibility of a battalion of militia boys, as I have seen them, being sent out within four months of the commencement of a war to keep the peace in an Indian city in midsummer, or to protect communications against Afridis or Pathan tribes' he dismissed as madness—'these battalions will be destroyed.'[19]

In his dilemma Balfour naturally turned to Clarke, who was working on his scheme for regenerating the Militia and reducing the army estimates to £24 million. Clarke called it an 'Imperial Militia' while Balfour more realistically termed it a 'glorified militia'. The justification for overruling Arnold-Forster would be the supreme authority in defence matters of the CID whose secret methods almost disguised from the public—but not quite—the fact that the leading papers on imperial defence were written by Balfour himself while the 'Prime Minister's scheme' for the Militia was evolved single-handed (except for surreptitious incursions into the War Office for statistical help from subordinate officials) by the head of his secretariat. On 14 June Balfour interrupted a meeting at the War Office to hand Arnold-

Forster Clarke's scheme, which, he notes, he had already seen.

Esher was solidly behind Balfour—he had written a paper on national strategy which eulogised Balfour's papers written for the CID and was printed for private circulation outside the CID membership.[20] Now he pressed Balfour to publish his main paper on national defence as a counter to Arnold-Forster: while Balfour had begun to confer with Clarke about an alternative army scheme;

> *Clarke-Esher, 17 June 1904*:[21] I hope you had a satisfactory talk with the Prime Minister and his Secretary of State, and I hope the latter gave you a hearing and did not speak continuously...
>
> The Secretary of State's scheme is really hopeless and always was. It would have been difficult to devise anything which would so completely revolutionise the army, so intensely aggravate the soldiers, or so greatly increase the difficulties in the way of real reform.
>
> The only way to proceed now is to get the cabinet to decide certain points—the duties of the military forces, the necessary strength..., the maximum sum which we ought to devote to the army, having due regard to the inexorable requirements of the navy...
>
> The Prime Minister thinks I have cut down the figure too low. I do not admit this...
>
> I will try and get the Prime Minister to read a paper on his Swiss militia...Our longer training is some set-off against our lower intellectual average, but I believe that my 'Imperial Militia', if the king would give them this title, would be very much superior in all ways to the present force.

It should not be supposed that Clarke's modesty restricted itself to overthrowing the decisions of the cabinet in order to substitute his militia scheme, for he sent Balfour the next day papers concerned with the reorganisation of the regular army. A 'table showing the strength of the Regular Army as I propose to constitute it' allowed a 'striking force' of two divisions or 25,000 men backed by a 'second line' army of eighteen militia divisions. Balfour had clearly not quite made up his mind, and as a make-weight Clarke pleaded the political incentive, observing that 'the regeneration of the Militia would be exceedingly well-received in this country'.[22]

As Clarke was aware, Esher had decided to try to resolve the deadlock on the army question, though he was no more committed to Clarke's scheme than Balfour was. He had been busy organising an Eton regatta and some royal festivities, and he had arranged for Balfour to accompany him to Windsor for the weekend. Calling on Balfour at 11 a.m. on 17 June he found him just out of his bath and hurrying on his clothes for a meeting of the CID—for Balfour was never an early riser and actually forgot to attend one of the meetings.[23] There was only time to talk 'very rapidly about the abandonment, *sine die*, of Arnold-Forster's army scheme', and in his casual way Balfour asked Esher to go and see him. No doubt there was no need for elaboration, for they were in perfect agreement and the task had to be played by ear. Arnold-Forster was ill in bed, no doubt a better place to tackle him than openly over the table of the CID. Esher found him being 'dosed every half-hour by his excellent but rather harassed wife', and 'feeble'. 'But I think I managed to cheer him up. Encouragement is the only method with him, as he has the weakness of a child...I was with him for an hour and a half, and he said at the end that he thought he saw daylight!'[24] Esher had not in fact told him that his scheme was abandoned, but instead had gone through it in detail and encouraged him!

Arnold-Forster's own account of what happened is in curious contrast. He had strained his heart some years before in riding, and was medically a doomed man—he died in fact five years later. Hence when his pulse became 'jumpy' and he felt 'rather overtired by anxiety and work' his doctor ordered him to bed. Even so his day was not exactly a holiday, as his diary records:

17 June 1904:[25] Kept in bed by doctor's orders, but got through much work. My principal task being to recast my scheme...I had calls during the day from A. H. Lyttelton, Shute, General Plumer, Esher, Gibson, Donoughmore...

Got up at half-past seven and went to the dinner in my honour at the Savile Club...I made a speech, which really expressed what I felt, and which I think gave pleasure...

Been much better during the day, and have got through my work splendidly.

It is puzzling to see how Arnold-Forster needed encouraging or

why Esher, who wanted to check him, should be the man to do it!
The truth was that nothing would deflect him. He was re-casting his
scheme for a cabinet on 25 June, 'a big piece of work': while Balfour
was intending to submit a counter-proposal.

At Windsor after viewing the quaint ceremony of Waterloo Day
Esher and Balfour retired for a comfortable chat. They enjoyed reminiscences of the Disraeli ministry, and commented on the serialisa-
tion of Disraeli's *Life* in *The Times*, which Balfour thought 'rather
degrading'.[26] Esher had just been handed Disraeli's letters to the Queen
during these years, but Balfour wanted his co-operation for the more
pressing purpose of searching Queen Victoria's letters and papers for
precedents concerning his possible Liberal successor. He thought the
King should call on Campbell-Bannerman rather than Lord Spencer.
Rosebery, they both agreed, was 'hopeless' though he was far pre-
ferable for imperial reasons.[27] Balfour's mind was brooding on a parliamentary defeat. His party, already riven by the tariff reform dispute, could easily founder on the convenient pretext of the Militia.
Esher persuaded him to circulate Clarke's paper with the expanded
title of 'Army Reform and the Military Needs of the Empire' which
duly appeared approved by the CID on 22 June.[28] He also stressed
that the military needs of India should be settled before any army
scheme could be approved. Kitchener wanted a reinforcement of
100,000 men in the first three months of a war, and reckoned these to
be sufficient with the army already in India for the first year's campaign. Arnold-Forster was given a Memorandum 'written at Windsor',
as he pointedly observed.

The strange drama of the Secretary for War being opposed by the
Prime Minister was beginning to be dimly perceived by the intelligent
public. 'What on earth is happening in the world of military affairs?'
L. S. Amery asked Esher, writing from All Souls. 'Arnold-Forster's
scheme, which seemed to me on the right lines on the whole, has
suffered a sudden eclipse. Vague rumours and vague moans and
laments float to me from the War Office...'[29] Well might one ask why
Balfour, if he did not approve Arnold-Forster's scheme, did not
let him resign. The responsibility for allowing Arnold-Forster to
drift into a thoroughly false position was Balfour's alone. Clarke
could not have stood for a moment without his support. The truth
was that Arnold-Forster's resignation, which came to be proffered
with regularity, would have brought down the government. Everyone

admitted it. And so this conscientious, able but politically tactless minister was subjected to the most persistent and discreditable deception practised by a prime minister against a secretary of state in recent times.

Hence so long as he carried the cabinet with him, Arnold-Forster could not be openly opposed, and the scenes which followed are instances of the free-for-all manner in which Balfour managed the government, much as a head boy would deal with his fellow prefects, which indeed some of them were. On the eve of a cabinet meeting fixed for 29 June Balfour and Wyndham got at Arnold-Forster privately. 'Both of them tried to persuade me that my scheme is wrong, which it is not; that we have too many men, and should remedy the evil by retaining the Militia instead of the thirty-five line battalions, a plan which would give us chaff for grain... Then they suggested that we should only retain a portion of the Militia...by retaining some fragments they will conciliate opinion. This is rubbish.'[30] Balfour impressed Arnold-Forster as one of the 'cleverest and most delightful people', but he 'really knows nothing whatever about the Army, and treats it as he does a good many other questions, as the subject matter of the most charming dialectical exercises... He keeps talking about the Militia and the Line as if they were interchangeable counters.'[31] Arnold-Forster still refused to be party to 'shipping thousands of immature boys to India' and he regarded Balfour's estimate of fifty-two battalions of regulars as the requirement for a serious war as far too low, pointing out that the Japanese had 225,000 men (five hundred battalions) in one of their field armies alone.[32] When the cabinet demurred at the modified scheme of 29 June based upon reductions in the home service battalions alone, which did not produce enough saving, Arnold-Forster reverted to his original scheme which did yield a saving. He proposed to convert forty-five line battalions augmented by militia battalions into his short-service territorial army, and abolish the whole remaining Militia. He justified this bold retreat to his original position on grounds of simplicity. 'I believe the public will never understand the creation of four different armies... they will easily understand...the division of the army into General Service, Territorial and Volunteers...I am confident that the Lord Lieutenants and Deputy Lieutenants of the counties are the proper persons to take the lead in this organisation of the Territorial Army...'[33]

Arnold-Forster had come out boldly against the Balfour alternative which he called 'an inconsistent plan which is obviously a concession to a supposed public sentiment, and not a measure taken in the interests of the Army'.[34] He carried the Army Council and nine-tenths of the cabinet, which on 5 July supported him, 'the Prime Minister and one or two others dissenting as to certain portions, but all agreed to let me go forward'.[35] Balfour's own report of this decision reveals that he retained substantial doubts:

Balfour-King Edward, 5 July 1904:[36] Mr Balfour has some doubts whether it is necessary to have quite so many infantry units as Mr Arnold-Forster proposes, and whether it is necessary wholly to abolish the Militia, but the matter has been fully discussed...

His general scheme is sound, and has the approval of the Army Board. Mr Balfour therefore though not wholly convinced did not press his objections, and proposes to give Mr Arnold-Forster his hearty support.

Whether the support was ever hearty is doubtful, but its duration is certain. It lasted exactly a week.

Although resolute in the face of Fenians, and steady against the hostility of foreign powers, Balfour vacillated in the face of certain manifestations of public opinion. As the major policy speech due on 14 July in which Arnold-Forster would unfold the long-awaited scheme for army reform approached, he became nervous, and there were those in the War Office who knew how to play on his nerves. The plan agreed to was leaked to the press, and a backbench revolt fanned by the partisans of the Militia flared up again. Hastily a cabinet was summoned on 12 July and sat all day trying to find some compromise. 'The government are so frightened!' Esher observed.[37] Another Prime Minister might have stood to his guns, but Balfour was in his heart on the side of the mutineers. His report of the climbdown makes sorry reading:

Balfour-King Edward, 13 July 1904:[38] The indiscretion (or worse) which enabled the *Daily Express* and the *Standard* to obtain a version of Mr Arnold-Forster's plan last Friday has aroused the suspicion and hostility of the auxiliary forces.

In the circumstances the cabinet strongly urged the Secretary

119

E

of War to make his statement in *general terms*...in a way which might make retreat possible without discredit.

In the Commons debate the next day the opposition, who were well apprised of these developments, noticed that Arnold-Forster claimed that his scheme had the support of the Army Council while saying nothing about the support of the government. Consequently Lord Spencer asked if this meant that the Army Council were independent of the government, and mentioned rumours of 'serious opposition on the part of the Secretary of State's colleagues to what he wanted'. The details of the scheme were kept obscure according to the cabinet instruction. 'He made it all appear big, dramatic and vague,' Clarke commented: 'Nobody understood it.'[39]

The demoralising effect of the government's failure to support their own War Minister now appeared on all sides. Henry Wilson advised the Military Members to draw up a statement of their 'exact wishes and thoughts', on the ground that 'if Arnold-Forster's scheme of the abolition of the Militia...is hissed off the stage, the careers of the Military Members will be ruined at the same time'.[40] Wilson and Sir Gerald Ellison (the recent Secretary of the Esher committee) discussed with L. S. Amery an army scheme of their own which appeared in *The Times*. The idea was to reduce all battalions to four companies and use the officers and men thus available as a backbone for the Militia. Amery wrote to Esher drawing his attention to this plan: 'You could create a new territorial army out of the existing militia, and the officers and men left over... Do press the idea in all quarters where you have influence. I believe it will make all the difference between a successful scheme and an unpopular abortion.'[41] The soldiers were looking to their careers, and searching for a frankly political conveyance in which to withdraw from Arnold-Forster's position, now so patently abandoned by the government to its fate.

The government had not in fact gone back on the army scheme, but had simply refused for the time being to associate themselves with its details in public. There was nothing therefore to prevent Arnold-Forster from proceeding to implement it on an experimental scale, and this he determined to do forthwith. He circulated a defiant paper to his colleagues which asserted that although 'requested not to give precise figures', and forbidden to 'pledge the government with regard to the Militia', he had been empowered to lay his scheme before

Parliament and had done so. 'I therefore assume that the Army Council is at liberty to act in accordance with the policy I have announced,'[42] he concluded, and set about converting a number of battalions into his short-service army on the basis of four home service soldiers to every one general service soldier in the ranks.

Sir George Clarke regarded this compromise as a disaster. It would, he wrote to Esher, 'create absolute chaos in our military arrangements' and 'turn the army upside down'.[43] Esher was more immediately concerned with the creation of the Aldershot striking force of two divisions of long-service infantry, and did not mind if one division of short-service infantry was added. He regarded the one successful coup of Brodrick to have been the initiation of a striking force, which was an elementary lesson from the South African War, and he dreaded a collapse of Arnold-Forster's project. Hearing that Arnold-Forster was 'breaking down' he wrote to Sandars: 'This would be awful, for everything turns on keeping him on the saddle for a while. No-one else can pull his scheme through, and a great part of it *must* go through...You *must* keep him going...'[44] In August he pressed Arnold-Forster to make a start with the Aldershot force, and pleaded with Balfour not to allow it to be a brigade short. Early in October he found himself at Balmoral in company with Arnold-Forster, who made a good impression on the King. 'So it was a score all round for our little friend' he reported to Balfour: '...he has plucked up courage, and got his Army Council by the beard. I was so mortally afraid that his administrative capacity was like his shooting. He knows all about guns, but can't hit a haystack.'[45]

121

Six

The Secret Esher Committee

The Esher committee, having published its three reports in the spring of 1904, lingered on indeterminably. Esher and Fisher did not attend the CID in the ensuing months, but Esher continued to advise Balfour on military matters and to receive CID papers from him and confidential information from Sir George Clarke. Both in his capacity as chief author of the Esher reports which became a kind of holy writ and as the founder of the CID secretariat Esher enjoyed a special kind of authority, while politically as the King's adviser he was consulted by Lord Knollys and Sandars. He was certainly in a position of vantage. He exercised a general surveillance over the War Office and the policies of its nominal head, his prime concern being to see that these were subordinated to the CID which was groping towards the formulation of a permanent plan of imperial defence. It seemed more important to him to settle the whole structure of defence administration than to embark on an army scheme which was so unpopular it might bring about a reaction against the whole new departure. The Liberal opposition were divided over the question of the CID but it seemed a fair calculation that if Campbell-Bannerman had his way this new 'aulic council' would be swept away.

Clarke certainly continued to treat Esher as his patron while with the rather *distrait* Balfour he was at an unsure distance—but then, Balfour rarely answered letters himself and access to him had to be through his factotum Sandars. It was as a 'triumvir' of the Esher committee rather than as Secretary of the CID that Clarke continued to inform Esher:

Clarke-Esher, 29 July 1904:[1] I will keep you informed of what goes on... The Admiralty of course plays up perfectly. I think the War Office will be all right when I can get a change of scene for Altham. He has been at the bottom of much friction and obstruc-

tion. I am going quietly; but I let nothing pass, and I write freely
to the Prime Minister which he does not seem to mind...

I wish he could let me re-write 'Invasion' as a state paper...
and publish it. We could then have a chapter to which we could
refer, and many economies would be possible...

It will be obvious from Clarke's letters that he was not keeping within
his brief as Secretary of the CID. Journalism, political activity, interference with the War Office, and attempts to manipulate Balfour
himself, continued to be his daily concerns, and in his strangely un-
self-critical way his letters display the very characteristics he disavows
in them. From Esher's point of view the important thing was to
develop the scope and importance of the secretariat so as to pass on
to the next government a going concern too embedded in the Constitution to be uprooted. But Clarke was too restlessly pushing to be
content with his real secretarial functions, and he never appreciated
the purely advisory, non-executive role of the CID as Balfour had
represented it to Parliament. Even less did he accept his own subordinate position as a supposedly neutral aide to the premier. When
the Liberal journalist J. A. Spender criticised the CID as a sort of
rival cabinet which might develop policies of its own Clarke retorted:
'He does not seem to realise that the Committee for most of its purposes *is* the cabinet, supplemented by professional opinion, and that
it can do nothing except as ministers decide after a round table discussion.'[2] This caballing of ministers outside the cabinet room, settling
executive matters between them, was exactly what Spender objected
to: and in practice many of the executive decisions were settled by
Balfour in consultation with Clarke behind Arnold-Forster's back.
Even so, Clarke felt frustrated. 'I need more power and position,' he
complains to Esher: 'It is unsatisfactory when dealing with matters on
which one feels oneself an authority to be restricted to the gentle
pulling of strings instead of being able to speak with power.' He
wished he could 'get at Mr Balfour more often'.[3]

One of Arnold-Forster's chief administrative acts was to get back
to the full nine-year period of enlistment for general service, which
was an integral part of his scheme. When Clarke got wind of this he
objected on political and personal grounds and at once interfered
behind the scenes:

Clarke-Esher, 28 September 1904:[4] The Secretary of State has
decided to issue an army order that *all* enlistments for the line are
to be for nine years with the colours and three with the reserve.
This step should *not* be taken. To change abruptly from three
years (Brodrick) to nine years will cause a general howl, and it
would fail...

I have this privately from Douglas this morning, and I have
told him to take his stand on the Army Council, and to say that a
question so important *must* be there discussed before action is
taken...

As a first step A[rnold]-F[orster] should revert to seven
and five years, and he should have done this months ago, as I
told him...

When Esher got back to London from Scotland he was curious to
get hold of the Army Order, and after a conversation with Sir
E. W. D. Ward, the Secretary of the Army Council, the latter obliged
him, sending him next day 'a proof of the proposed Army Order for
your *secret* information, as I am not supposed yet to have seen it'.
Ward incidentally thanked Esher for the opportunity 'to let you know
my views about myself, and a job in which one could do some work
such as South Africa'.[5] He was not however destined to get there. Esher
got Clarke to traverse the Army Order, which implemented the plan
of army decentralisation recommended by the Esher committee, and
the two found it not to their liking. It failed to make the Aldershot
force independent of the commands, and it cut down the number of
its cadres.

The situation presented Esher with an opportunity to enlarge the
King's powers with regard to the Army Council, which were still un-
defined. He sent Lord Knollys the provisional Army Order with
Clarke's comments, and also a printed list of officers in the CGS's
department, and commented:

Esher-Lord Knollys, 19 October 1904:[6] As the King is going to
see Lyttelton today, I should like to draw your attention to a
point which affects the old prerogatives of the Crown...a large
number of officers have been appointed and many posts created.
Formerly nothing of this kind would have been done...without
the fullest information being laid *beforehand* before the
124

Sovereign. The King as *de jure* C-in-C has even greater right to know *early* of prospective changes...

The fact is that the information laid before the King as to matters connected with the Army is not nearly full enough... Under the new system it was always intended by my committee that it should be *more* fully imposed than hitherto...

I am sure that it would do good if the King were to say to Lyttelton today...that HM is 'most surprised' to find that important steps are taken by the military authorities without reference to the sovereign... Are the 'proceedings' of the Army Council sent to the King?

While Arnold-Forster was prepared to send the final decisions of the Army Council to the King for approval, he had not thought of sending proposals while they were being formulated. When he discovered that the provisional Army Order had been seen by Esher he was most annoyed, and Esher learnt that the Adjutant-General, Sir C. Douglas, was intending to bring the matter up at the Army Council. Warning him of this, Ward added that if he were asked: 'I shall say that I showed it to you *in my room*', which would cover up the fact that Esher actually possessed a copy.[7] Esher walked into the War Office the same day (7 November) and confronted Arnold-Forster, who laboured under the misapprehension that Esher had merely examined a copy in the A-G's office; and who 'told him quite frankly that I was greatly concerned...and that I was astonished that he [Esher] after what he had said to me about Clarke's action, should think it right to take such a step...' He still, however, regarded Esher as 'one of our best friends,' and he said 'should at all times be glad to see him and tell him anything...'[8]

Esher was certainly not candid with Arnold-Forster and instead of warning him about the trouble that might be caused by the non-submission of the Army Order, simply prepared the King's brief on the question. No doubt his objection was a very uncertain one, for when Sandars, who wanted to prevent a political row, inquired at the War Office about the preparation of the Army Order he only asked for an assurance that it would not be actually published before submission to the King. However, in a memorandum of 16 November Esher claimed that it had been the general practice in Queen Victoria's reign for 'all proposals for important administrative changes' and 'suggested nominations for important posts' to be laid before the Sovereign *before* formal submission, and that this applied particularly to the Church (of which she was the constitutional head) and the Army (of which she was the supreme commander). These prior notices were given in writing, he claimed, and 'over and over again the minister gave way to the arguments used by the Queen'.[9] What he failed to emphasise was that the Queen's criticisms were her own: while the criticisms of the Army Order which were typed out, with pencilled captions of 'The King thinks that' or 'The King would not object to', were those of himself.

In due time the Army Order, as approved by the Army Council, was sent to the King, and the storm broke. Arnold-Forster refused to accept the objections to his Army Order as coming from the King, and wrote of 'letters written by His Majesty's command'. He made his grievance plain enough to Clarke:

> *Clarke-Esher, 26 November 1904:*[10] His grievance is that you did not tell him your objections earlier, that the Army Council gave much consideration to the matter, and that it is discountenancing for them to be met with opposition now...he would resign at once if it did not wreck the government... I was quite unable to get from him what the criticisms (of which you had told me) were.
>
> All he would insist upon was that the King did not know, and had probably not read, the Order, and that it was hard upon him to have to deal with objections which you had inspired...

'Of course I knew nothing and I asked him to let me see the Order,' Clarke writes in the same letter, while adding: 'The points to which we object are really not matters on which the Army Council need offer obstruction.' On receipt of this letter Esher sent it to Lord Knollys, with the comment that Arnold-Forster had omitted to consult either himself or Clarke on the decentralisation question:

> *Esher-Lord Knollys, 27 November 1904:*[11] He contents himself with being 'petulant' and 'injured'. As you will also note, Clarke, to whom I had stated my objections to the proposed plan of the Army Council, agrees with every word...
>
> As I have often told you...Arnold-Forster takes every criticism

126

to be either opposition or personal affront. The Prime Minister
will have to take the matter into his own hands...

But the issue was being rather side-tracked from the original objection to the way Arnold-Forster ignored the convention of timely
notice, to the personal objections of Esher and Clarke to his Order.
'He does not really understand the great principles for which we
contend,' Clarke complains: '...Now the only hope seems to be...if
the cabinet have to look into the matter they will send for us.'[12] Clarke
advanced a whole string of criticisms against the administration of
the War Office, but they hardly amount to anything substantial, and
he and Esher were certainly wrong in blaming Arnold-Forster for
neglecting the re-arming of the artillery. They could hardly expect to
be really *au fait* with what the Secretary of War was doing, and their
criticisms amount to no more than the usual semi-informed and
politically motivated opposition to a minister. The only novelty was
that they claimed to be colleagues.

Esher had been deeply incensed by Arnold-Forster. Perhaps his
pride had been wounded by being caught out filching in the War
Office, or challenged by Arnold-Forster's refusal to accept his objections as coming from the King. Whatever the reason, he certainly lost
his usual composure in damning the rejoinders that the Secretary of
State was making. 'He is a very odd type,' he writes to Knollys. 'I am
pretty sure he will get the government into serious difficulties unless
he is looked after sharply by the Prime Minister... They are wonderful exhibitions of 1. ignorance 2. conceit 3. disingenuousness (I
fear).'[13] Those who read the excellent diaries which Arnold-Forster
kept at the War Office will no doubt agree that these are the very last
qualities to be found there. What he suffered from was a lack of due
deference to royal influence and perhaps too much self-sufficiency. His
only real fault was that he refused to allow two ex-members of the
Esher 'Triumvirate', who treated him outrageously, to run his
department for him. And that was just what they were about to do.

Balfour was becoming seriously worried about the failure to
economise on the army, so that in the coming session the estimates
would have to be considerably above £29 million. Short-service
recruiting would have saved money, but Arnold-Forster's nine years
recruitment was going well and he had decided to postpone his short-
service recruiting while the desperate shortages of trained men and

drafts created by Brodrick's three-year enlistments were remedied. The re-arming of the artillery with the new field gun also added to the short-term estimates. When therefore Balfour and the Chancellor of the Exchequer, Austen Chamberlain, summoned him to Downing Street on 7 December they pressed two suggestions on him: either he should cut down the regular army still further, or agree to a 'glorified militia' (Austen thought one year's training would be enough). Arnold-Forster was doing various things to improve the Militia, but he would not accept it as a 'second-line' army for foreign service. If economy were wanted, he said: 'It could be effected by authorising me to absorb the Militia, which is useless and costs £2 million.'[14] After this interview Balfour should certainly have given way, or accepted Arnold-Forster's resignation. But instead, he encouraged Sandars to think of some expedient such as another Esher committee to dictate an army scheme to the War Minister, and he allowed Clarke to probe the costing of Arnold-Forster's scheme behind his back in the War Office.

Clarke was quick off the mark, and while the Minister was away visiting Edinburgh and Newcastle he slipped into his office. 'By the Prime Minister's order,' he reported to Esher, 'I have extracted from the War Office a statement of the estimated output of the scheme, which he has long wished to get hold of... I begin to doubt if it can ever be carried out, and perhaps in that case my plan might secure a chance.'[15] Four days later Esher called on the Adjutant-General at the War Office and learnt (as he immediately informed Balfour) that he and two other Military Members 'were on the point of presenting an ultimatum to Arnold-Forster,... (a) "The Army Scheme, as regards the short-service battalions, *cannot* be introduced piecemeal." (b) "It will involve a large extra cost" (c) "We must have an undertaking that the Government are resolved to go through with it..." '[16] Balfour sent Esher and Clarke to take a statement from the Adjutant-General, which was duly read out to him, dated 15 December, in which Douglas asserted that the Arnold-Forster scheme as a whole had not been discussed by the Army Council, although the Military Members had agreed individually to its principles. 'Hence it follows that the Council will not approve of any change being inserted in the estimates of 1905–6 based on this compromise between the two systems.'[17] This was just what was wanted, as also was the paper which Clarke got from Lyttelton, the CGS, claiming that 'Arnold-Forster's scheme leaves a *deficiency* of 100,000 regulars relatively to "actual requirements",' which Clarke sent to the Chancellor of the Exchequer with remarks.[18] More men with less money? Clarke was the man for that!

Balfour may well have been perplexed by this sudden shortage of men when there was supposed to be too many, and he asked Esher to draw up a note on how the navy estimated its requirements, as a guide, and received the following;

Note by Esher, 16 December 1904:[19]

The way in which the Board of Admiralty have approached the question of estimates is roughly as follows:-

1. The standard of requirements = Two Power Standard.
2. Cut off every item which does not minister to the fighting efficiency of the Navy.

The fighting force is divided

    (a) Fleets in commission,

    (b) Fleets in reserve.

In practice (a) are kept in fighting trim,

            (b) manned with 'nucleus crews' to be supplemented from the reserve.

Query. Would it not be possible to approach the Army estimates on very similar lines?

1. The standard of requirements

    (a) 75,000 men for India

    + minimum number required in Colonies

    + Aldershot Field Force of one Army Corps

    + force required in this country to find drafts for India and the Colonies

    (b) Cut down ruthlessly all expenditure which does not minister to the fighting efficiency of the Army.

2. (c) The forces under (a) can be reckoned as the 'Army in commission', and should be fully equipped for war.

    (d) The 'Army in reserve' would consist of 'cadres' both of officers and NCOs and only a sufficient number of men to keep the 'cadres' efficient.

    (e) The real reserve should be the *Militia*, enlisted and main-
        tained for service at home in peace, but liable for foreign
        service in war...
    (f) All 'Third-class cruisers' in the shape of militia artillery
        with obsolete guns, submarine mines, inefficient battalions
        of Militia and Volunteers to be abolished...

This was exactly the political formula that Balfour wanted, but it was
not an army scheme. The Militia were not a reserve and the whole
dispute was about the minimum training needed to make a reservist.
It was also probably a false analogy between the nucleus crew of an
expensive ship, and a nucleus 'cadre' of officers and NCOs, which, if
it was not training its full complement of men, would be cheaper on
the reserve itself. Esher believed that so long as the cadres had
trained together and were thoroughly efficient they could be filled up
with half-trained men.

    The key man in the preparation of the army estimates was Sir Guy
Fleetwood Wilson, the director-general of army finance whom
Arnold-Forster had put in charge of reorganising the financial section.
He was one of the civilians most criticised in the Esher report, but
when Clarke went over to talk to him about his troubles he got good
results. Wilson was still awaiting answers from his chief on which to
frame the estimates, and after 'many adjections' agreed he was 'quite
impossible'. 'I reached the point,' Clarke continued, 'which is that
Fleetwood Wilson wants his salary raised to £1,800 p.a....I also think
it would be good policy to give it to him. Will you have this in mind if
you have a chance to say a word?'[20] With Arnold-Forster's financial
assistant thus squared the way was clear for the subversion of his
army scheme from inside. That Sandars had broached this idea to Esher
with Balfour's approval is clear from what followed:

Esher-Sandars, 28 December 1904:[21] There *is* something further
to consider about a committee such as you hinted at, over
which I should preside (preferably the old committee revived),
i.e. it would be a bold and complete reply to those who may try
to show that the War Office reforms have failed. There is nothing
like a well-delivered counter stroke in the art of defence.
    On reflection, I *think* we could:
(a) Take Arnold-Forster's scheme as the basis of reform;

(b) Reduce the estimates by £3 million when the new scheme is in operation;

(c) Cut down the estimates *this* year to £28 million inclusive of the gun.

But, drastic measures would be necessary. I can tell you more after a 'fishing' talk with F[leetwood] Wilson.

Esher had already written to Knollys mentioning Arnold-Forster's 'abortive scheme' and suggesting a new Triumvirate, but in a novel form. He thought that 'a sub-committee of the CID is the only practicable method', and 'If the Prime Minister would appoint Roberts, Brackenbury and myself to see what portion of Arnold-Forster's scheme could be adopted' it might cost £27 million or less. 'Clarke of course would be invaluable. I do *not* believe that Arnold-Forster would object. By a side wind the Defence Committee would be more permanently established.'[22]

If the King or Balfour knew about the plan for an Esher sub-committee, which they surely must have done, neither cared to be the first to broach it openly. Balfour wrote darkly to the King on 29 December saying that the Secretary of State must reduce if he was to avoid a large growth of expenditure because of the guns, the new pay rates and capital works. 'Such a growth would be fatal to the government (which is a small matter); but it would never be tolerated by the country, and might lead to a dangerous reaction, and *this* is of imperial importance.'[23] The reply was equally brooding over the uncertain outlook:

King Edward-Balfour, 30 December 1904:[24] Unfortunately Mr Arnold-Forster's scheme, at which he has been working for a year, has been abandoned owing to his military advisers having proved to him that it was not practicable owing to its great expense—with this the cabinet agreed.

What is to take its place? What will satisfy the country when the matter is discussed in Parliament? The latter would probably not grudge the cost if it were convinced that a scheme for the efficiency of the army was a really good one.

In addition Lord Kitchener's demands gave rise for 'serious reflection'. The King's appreciation of the situation was hardly correct, and he was clearly not being properly informed. Arnold-Forster began to sense that he was being hemmed in. 'I suppose soon I shan't be able to ask my private secretary to tea without consulting the King, the Cabinet, Lord Esher and the Committee of Defence, Sir George Clarke, the Army Council collectively, and Sir J. W. Murray individually,' he recorded.[25]

Sir George Clarke had no intention of being a mere amanuensis on any sub-committee, and when Esher suggested Lord Roberts as a possible chairman of the body Clarke replied: 'I am sure that his ideas would not in the least agree with mine... Unfortunately the man in the street and the least intelligent...peers might probably howl for his inclusion.'[26] Meanwhile Esher was persuading Sandars that another 'Esher committee' would not do now that the CID was a going concern, while the Army Council 'would be totally unable to deal with the problem in view of the political considerations involved in a far-reaching scheme of organic army reform'.[27] One might pause to wonder why in that case Arnold-Forster's scheme was so assiduously referred back to the Military Members by Esher, were the answer not obvious. But now, when Esher wanted swift action, constitutional forms went to the wind. 'I would venture to suggest that, avoiding publicity, he [Balfour] should summon *ad hoc* and for the special purpose meetings of the Defence Committee, which surely need not for this purpose be regularly presided over by himself nor constituted in the usual way, but specially summoned.'[28] The terms of reference of the secret inquiry would be to see how 'Arnold-Forster's scheme can be practically applied to the needs of the Empire, subject to...(a) the desire of Parliament not to abolish the old historic force of the militia, and (b) the reduction of the estimates to £25 million.'[29] Shortly after, Esher dined with Balfour and Austen Chamberlain to talk of army matters, and he must have got their general approval. But how would Arnold-Forster be managed?

On 12 January Esher walked into the War Office and actually persuaded Arnold-Forster to accept the sub-committee. But in order to do so, he had to stress some aspects of the inquiry, and suppress others. The formulation of the permanent military needs of the empire and consequent purposes of the army was something the CID was supposed to be undertaking, and even reducing the estimates was, in the long term, a thing Arnold-Forster approved of. What Arnold-Forster did not realise was that the reduction was intended to be immediate, and, as Esher had already expressed it to Sandars, 'by the abandonment for the present of Arnold-Forster's scheme':

> *Arnold-Forster's diary, 12 January 1905:*[30] Esher called...and I had a long talk. He is I think really friendly, and wishes to help me, though of course he very much likes to gossip and to know as much as he can of other people's business. I think he is to a large extent 'all things to all men'...
>
> He then made his suggestion, which was that I should ask A. J. B[alfour] to form a committee in connexion with the Committee of Defence to examine into the question of what forces are really required for Indian and Home defence, and what reduction is necessary to bring the expenditure down to £25 million, and where that reduction can best be effected...
>
> I am quite favourable to the idea of such a committee if it were worked quickly and with adequate knowledge...

Arnold-Forster naturally got an assurance that he himself would be able to attend the committee when he pleased, and it is likely judging from his later protests that he stipulated that Clarke should not be a member. Needless to say, he was not told that the terms of reference should be the preservation of the Militia! Hence he gladly composed a formal letter to Balfour which he showed to Esher before he sent it off:

> *Arnold-Forster to Balfour, 13 January 1905:*[31] I told you the difficulty I felt in attempting to deal with the army problem without any exact knowledge of what the army was for, or what ought to be its true dimensions.
>
> As you know, despite our hard work on the Committee of Defence, I and my colleagues are still quite in the dark on this subject.
>
> ...we shall never touch £25 million without an entire change in our conceptions of what is essential.

He therefore asked Balfour as chairman of the Defence Committee and 'for all practical purposes the Defence Committee itself' to appoint a small committee to discuss and report on the best means of employing an expenditure of £25 million, and suggested eight names.

The letter was to go that evening, and Esher wanted to write a commentary on it for Sandars but did not care to do so from the War Office. He drove to Buckingham Palace after the last collection had gone, to get the special late post, and wrote to Sandars pointing out that Arnold-Forster had not suggested that the committee should be a sub-committee of the CID but that: 'This...is in my opinion essential for the reasons I gave you. Please rub this in...in that case Clarke would be the Secretary of the Committee...' As for the names, he suggested Lord Roberts, Sir John French and himself with George Murray (one of Balfour's officials from the Treasury). 'I am sure that *four* names are sufficient...'[32]

In due course Esher received from Balfour the Arnold-Forster letter with Balfour's draft reply which he considered in consultation with Sandars and Clarke. He then returned them with two letters of reply to Balfour both dated 17 January, one[33] mentioning a *secret* committee and paying a mild compliment to Arnold-Forster, the other much more businesslike:

Esher-Balfour, 17 January 1905:[34] Please remember that your association with the work of this committee would be more nominal than real...

It seems to us that if you should approve of the nomination of this limb of the Defence Committee, the meetings should take place in Sir George Clarke's room and that he should be authorised by you to place his invaluable knowledge at the disposal of the committee...Sir George might also be empowered to summon any assistance from the War Office which might be required...

Balfour's reply was awaited by Clarke with eager expectation. He thought that Esher should preside in Balfour's absence, and 'that I act, if at all, on equal terms with Murray and Co... I do not think I could do such secretarial work as Ellison did for us.' As for Lord Roberts: 'He will be of no use practically but his co-operation is desirable—perhaps essential—for reasons of policy.' Lord Roberts wrote frequently to Clarke about 'all sorts of things' and seemed safe enough although he had 'no ideas of his own on these questions'. If anyone influenced him, thought Clarke, it was Henry Wilson, 'and his mind is now running on my lines'.[35] The two 'triumvirs' were in short fixing up the Esher committee again but dressing it up as an extension of the CID.

Balfour's reply to Arnold-Forster was dated 21 January and to the initiated must have made amusing reading. He began by rejecting the contention that there remained doubt about the purposes for which the army existed, indicating his own papers of June and December on the subject. 'Our real difficulties lie elsewhere. You have been embarrassed by the obvious reluctance, both of some of the members of the cabinet and of a considerable number of members in the House of Commons, wholly to abolish the Militia.' He therefore suggested that the proposed committee should consider a means of combining Arnold-Forster's home-service army with a portion of the Militia, the expansion of the 'peace' army in war, and economy.[36] Disappointing as this must have been to Arnold-Forster, it still did not make clear to him what was in store. Hence he was easily persuaded to accept it:

Arnold-Forster's diary, 25 January 1905:[37] Esher called, and I showed him a letter which I had just received from A. J. B[alfour]... We agreed that it was only part of what I had asked, but also that it would be a good thing to accept the committee, even for the purposes of the limited inquiry proposed.

The next day Arnold-Forster wrote to Balfour accepting his offer of a committee, and expecting further consultation as to its nature and composition, terms of reference, etc. He did not realise that the Adjutant-General, Douglas, was busily preparing the way for Clarke to probe the War Office finance department in order to frame new estimates for the coming session: nor, of course, did he guess that Clarke who was so inveterate against his scheme would have anything to do with the proposed committee. Clarke for his part was already sharpening his knife for the *coup de grâce*. Well might he wonder how on earth Esher had got Arnold-Forster to agree, and as soon as he heard of it he commented: 'The extraordinary thing is that Arnold-Forster seems to think that his blue paper still holds the field. It has virtually become waste paper.'[38] It should not be thought that Clarke was playing the part of a military expert advising the CID on the technical side of army reform and defence. He was playing a purely political role as a personal aide to the Prime Minister:

135

Clarke-Esher, 28 January 1905:[39] The difficulty for the Prime Minister is very great. The cabinet did in a way accept the blue paper: though I plainly warned the Prime Minister many months ago that it was hopeless...

I think the Prime Minister now realises that the blue paper is hopeless, and this and the estimates are being framed on a basis which excludes all Arnold-Forster's proposals. The situation therefore is that the government must face Parliament under the disadvantage that there is no scheme at all...

When two days later Balfour presided over the first meeting of the secret sub-committee, Arnold-Forster had merely been informed by Sandars that it would commence the day after. In his absence his scheme was expounded, and as Esher observed, Balfour did not really understand it. More significant is Esher's comment on its rival: 'Clarke expounded *his* scheme. But it is a *paper* affair, like A.–F.'s, and would not stand a puff of criticism.'[40]

From its first informal session on 31 January the secret sub-committee was chaired by Esher except for the rare moments when Balfour appeared. Members of the cabinet did not know of its existence, and its sessions were held clandestinely at 10 Downing Street, whither War Office officials and soldiers from the commands were summoned by telephone. The object of the prolonged interrogation lasting three or four weeks was to find the total of regular troops which Arnold-Forster's plan would produce in peacetime, and then to ask Balfour whether it needed to be increased or diminished: and to consider the expansion of this force in war. Esher's personal preference seems to have been for the Arnold-Forster plan so far as cadres were concerned, but also for utilising the Militia for their expansion. He did not support Clarke's plan for sending the Militia abroad in large formations. He was therefore not entirely a party to Clarke's crude machinations against the Secretary of State though he was certainly implicated in the interference with War Office officials when he held no government position except that of irresponsible adviser to Balfour. That he was personally antagonised by Arnold-Forster is clear from what he wrote to Knollys, and by posing as his friend he had tricked him into a false position.

Even after the secret sub-committee had been created, Arnold-Forster thought that its conception was Balfour's and not Esher's.

After the sitting on 31 January Esher came to see him and told him what had happened:

Arnold-Forster's diary, 31 January 1905:[41] Of course the whole proceeding is rather ridiculous, settling or trying to settle the whole future of the British army by means of a committee, of which not one single member knows the facts, and without reference...to the responsible minister...

However, Esher was exceedingly friendly and my talk was most useful. He is one of the very few people who has ever tried to understand my proposals and for the most part he does... and is in agreement with them.

Finding that Clarke was on the sub-committee, Arnold-Forster wrote at once protesting to Balfour. Clarke he said was prejudiced, having a scheme of his own which 'would ruin any party that proposed it'. 'I can imagine ministers taking a strong objection to a public servant ...being called into consultation with the Prime Minister to deal with the affairs of at least two of the great Departments of the State.'[42] Balfour did nothing to redress this complaint, but in writing to the King gave a wholly misleading impression two days later. 'With Mr Arnold-Forster's full consent Mr Balfour has appointed a small and *quite informal* sub-committee of the Defence Committee to get to the bottom of the matter.' He mentioned the sub-committee's composition and that it was 'very secret', so that the King would naturally assume that these details had also been approved by the War Minister.[43] Hence the King's reply reflected what must have been the general reaction of those who were informed simply that Arnold-Forster had allowed his scheme to be scrutinised by a committee:

King Edward-Balfour, 3 February 1905:[44] The King highly approves of the composition of the proposed committee, and although he is glad that Mr Arnold-Forster gives his full consent, he is much surprised that the latter does so, as it is virtually putting his important office 'into commission'.

Arnold-Forster had already discovered that Balfour had abandoned the sub-committee while Roberts had not yet arrived, so that the proceedings had resolved into 'the cross-examination of two uninformed and not too well-affected subordinates from the War Office'[45] by a new triumvirate composed of Esher, 'who really is friendly and I believe honestly tries to understand the problem', Clarke, who 'as Esher says, has all the time no other object than to put forward a scheme of his own', and George Murray, a 'friendly, rather sleepy, moderately interested amateur, who sees everything from a purely Treasury point of view'.[46] The Secretary of State found from hearsay that his plans were being misrepresented by ignorant subordinates, and after he had declined to allow the Adjutant-General to return for another cross-examination in office hours in response to a request by telephone, he found to his annoyance that Douglas had already set out.[47] By 3 February, when Balfour received the King's letter, he received in the same post Arnold-Forster's complete rejection of the committee:

Arnold-Forster to Balfour, 3 February 1905:[48] You will remember that you were unable to accept the form of reference which I originally proposed, and that you substituted another...

I gather that the committee has become a sort of tribunal engaged in criticising me and my work with a very imperfect knowledge of my objects and intentions...three absolutely irresponsible persons...catechising the War Office staff, without any reference to its chief...

I am told, but...I depend on hearsay only, that the Committee requires secrecy from those of my colleagues and subordinates whom it summons before it, and that when it has arrived at a conclusion, it will make known that conclusion as a decision or recommendation of the Committee of Defence. To any such action I should altogether demur...

I consider that a body...on which neither the Prime Minister, the First Lord...the Secretary of State for War, the principal Naval and Military Officers, nor the representatives of either Intelligence department are represented or heard, cannot reasonably be taken to be the Defence Committee of this country. I certainly do not so regard it.

Balfour ignored this protest as he had the last. Having embarked on an operation on what he regarded as a vile body he was not going to put away his scalpels just because the patient was manifesting signs of animation. However, he felt constrained to attend the sub-committee that day, for five hours according to Esher.

The suborning of Arnold-Forster's officials was conducted in an eighteenth-century manner. Fleetwood Wilson's salary increase had been turned down when advocated by the Secretary of State, but he had more success when he mentioned the matter to Esher. Writing on 4 February he had supplied some useful advice about the 'Campbell-Bannerman returns' which were the true basis of the Arnold-Forster scheme as it had been proposed in the Commons. As a postscript he added: 'If you can give my £300 a push I will be *very* grateful to you. It is a great matter for me.'[49] The salary increment came through in five days! Another useful subordinate was Colonel Lake, head of the mobilisation branch, whose promotion Arnold-Forster opposed. On 9 February he was handed a note signed by Balfour, Sandars and Lyttelton ordering him 'in the name of the cabinet' to promote Lake—the CGS had actually brought the case before the cabinet rather than before the Selection Board.[50] By 17 February the Secretary of State learnt from Fleetwood Wilson, who was playing a double game, that 'the Committee now consider that they have captured all the military members'.[51] There was, as Esher told Sandars, 'no concealment of the Prime Minister's ideas' from the Military Members:[52] they were told to be loyal to Balfour by being disloyal to the Secretary for War.

At long last Arnold-Forster began to have doubts about the genuineness of Esher's protestations of friendship but they could only be doubts:

Arnold-Forster to Esher, 5 February 1905:[53] You told me that your idea of the committee was that, of course, I should be free to go in and out of it when I pleased; and yet I have not yet received a single notice of its meeting...

If I am to be thrown over, it must be done openly and squarely...

I have an absolute faith in your good will and sincerity, of which I have received so many proofs. If I were wrong in my trust, I don't think I should care to remain in politics; they would be too depressing.

Balfour, who at the cabinet on the 6th spoke to Arnold-Forster about the matter, assured him that 'they were very friendly to me, that they were trying to improve my scheme, and so on'. When challenged about the 'sordid intrigue' among the officials at the War Office Balfour shrugged his shoulders and exclaimed: 'Oh, your soldiers, of course!', but did not explain why they needed to be consulted.[54] Esher's protestations were no doubt written under the inspiration of his maxim that Arnold-Forster must be humoured:

Esher to Arnold-Forster, 5 February 1905:[55] The Prime Minister and all of us are striving *not* to upset your scheme, but to harmonise it in every important particular with the retention of the Militia...

For God's sake don't try to retract now from the position you took up as regards the formation of this sub-committee of the Defence Committee. I am *sure* that it will lead to a result far better than you hoped for. You can rely always on my thorough friendliness and sympathy with the absolutely sound principles of your scheme, and upon my sole wish to help you.

[2nd letter] ...We are getting at some fixed numbers for the establishment of the Regular Army, in view of eventualities in India and elsewhere...

Was Esher really on Arnold-Forster's side? And was Clarke deluded in thinking otherwise when he wrote the next day: 'I hope you flattened out the Secretary of State; he is really like a fractious child'?[56] Clarke was certainly deluded in thinking that Esher was backing *his* scheme. 'I am getting my five divisions scheme into shape,' he had reported: 'I require about 27,600 recruits only.' He had got Repington of *The Times* to support his militia plan and thought he was succeeding. 'The regeneration of the Militia as I conceive it is a big thing with ramifications into the social structure of the country.'[57] While Esher took alternative opinions concerning the organisation of the Militia, Clarke damned these ferociously. 'I cannot regard [Sir John] French's opinions of Militia seriously...he has quite failed to see that the Arnold-Forster scheme tears the army to pieces.' Lord Selborne's proposals would 'go far to destroy the Militia'.[58] Yet much evidence hostile to Clarke's scheme was taken, and as will be seen the committee came out in the end against it.

Balfour seems to have imagined that the sub-committee's scheme which was spoken of as the 'Prime Minister's scheme' as it evolved could be forced through the cabinet and the Army Council in competition with the Arnold-Forster scheme, which would thereby lapse. At the cabinet dinner on 13 February at 10 Downing Street the King's Speech for the coming session was read, and Arnold-Forster found that the reference to his proposed Militia Bill had been omitted. In undisguised anger he demanded the reason from Sandars, who blandly replied: 'Our people would not have it'. Tackled later and privately, Sandars made other excuses, saying it was a blunder, but then adding that the Chief Whip had objected to it.[59] The following day Arnold-Forster spoke to Balfour who broached to him his alternative militia plan. The proposal was for a militia trained for six months on enlistment and then for a six-week period annually. Arnold-Forster made it clear he would never agree, but still it was evident that Balfour was contemplating a Militia Bill of his own design. Clarke was quite happy in being plagiarised by Balfour, just as he was very flexible and accommodating about the actual details of any scheme. 'Surely the safest course,' he advised Esher on 15 February, 'is for the Prime Minister to make the *first* announcement...by saying that HMG have decided to improve the Militia, but giving no details. This would be exceedingly popular...The Prime Minister's military scheme should save about £3¾ million.'[60]

Esher's own military preferences, which were truly inimical to the central part of Arnold-Forster's scheme, may be guessed from a letter to the King reporting on the sub-committee:

Esher-King Edward, 16 February 1905:[61] Mr Arnold-Forster's scheme has been found unsuitable to the requirements of India both in peace and war. It is also impracticable in some of its most important particulars...especially...[the] plan of splitting the army into two portions, and largely reducing the 'cadres' of the regular army.

Construed in the light of Esher's other opinions, military, social and political, this criticism stands on two strong beliefs. First, that the army would be demoralised and the *esprit de corps* which kept up the recruiting of its officers shattered if it were divided into a regular long-service army mostly abroad, and a territorialised short-service army at home merged into a body of semi-amateur ex-militia officers. And secondly, that under the voluntary system the country could not afford to train a large reserve but could afford a semi-trained reserve for the reinforcement of India. The inspiration of Esher's position was really not a military but a political or social conviction. Like Balfour himself, he was unashamedly willing to admit that defence policy was a matter of political judgment much more than of military science. With conscription it might have been otherwise.

By 21 February Esher had established to his own satisfaction what were the military needs of the Empire after working from 11 a.m. to 5-30 p.m. on a paper which was printed that night. 'Tell the Prime Minister,' he scribbled hurriedly to Sandars, 'I want him to submit [it] through A.-F. for the comments of the Army Council—military members.'[62] The 'exordium' of this paper, which he thought was 'Fisheresque', stated that the army was not organised for home defence, but 'to take the field, at any threatened point, where the interests of the Empire are imperilled, and especially on the NW frontier of India.' Had not Balfour pronounced that the problem of imperial defence was expressed in one word—'Afghanistan'? Kitchener's demands for British troops in addition to those already in India amounted to eight divisions or 71,014 men, and adding the additional drafts needed to keep these in the field (32,454 men) and also three battalions to complete the ninth division of the Indian army, Esher reckoned on fifty-two battalions as the minimum number for reinforcing India in war. He took the 'cadre' as the battalion, and reckoned another thirty-five for the colonies. Nothing was said as to the quality of these battalions, which could not all be of the regular army, for the Esher sub-committee was still debating the character of the Militia which would have to supply a proportion of them. The soldiers, represented by Lord Roberts and General Mackinnon, were trying to persuade Lord Selborne that a year's training was needed for the Militia, and General Douglas was asking for the whole question to be referred to the military members of the Army Council. This struck Esher as opportune, for so long as the home-service army idea was killed and reorganisation was based on the existing forces, he felt the actual plan for the Militia could be allowed to ride. All that remained of Arnold-Forster's scheme were the pickings—'large depots', 'grouping of regiments', the shrinking of numbers in home-based battalions, and the 'territorialisation of line regiments' (not quite what Arnold-Forster wanted).[63]

After Balfour had received the sub-committee's printed paper, at first called 'Principles of Army Organisation', he tackled Arnold-Forster as they sat on the Treasury bench, saying it was time they had a talk. Arnold-Forster replied with his characteristic bluntness that the time had arrived long ago, and went on to repeat that he took 'the gravest exception to the proceedings and the procedure' of the secret sub-committee. Equally characteristically Balfour reacted 'as if he had heard this for the first time' although he was in fact thoroughly acquainted with Arnold-Forster's objections. He claimed that they knew he was 'very busy' and 'wished to help', but Arnold-Forster thought this 'bosh'. 'It is not the way to help any man to undermine all his work and all his authority behind his back.'[64] By this time Arnold-Forster had discovered that his scheme had been thrown over. Esher was now behaving with marked coolness to him, and had told Raymond Marker, Arnold-Forster's private secretary, that he 'knew' Arnold-Forster was 'angry with him'. When Arnold-Forster bumped into Esher coming out of a gathering he took the opportunity to deny this, and got the impression that 'his conscience smote him, for he really has behaved very ill'. Esher had apparently told Marker that his chief's scheme was 'gone', and after the unsatisfactory conversation with Balfour the War Minister wrote another long formal protest ending with the declaration that he would not provide any more facilities in the form of advice or returns from War Office staff for the secret sub-committee, or accept its report. He got the next day (28 February) a note from Balfour enclosing the sub-committee's report, with an amendment to its title. Balfour had crossed out 'Principles of' and substituted 'Suggestions for'![65]

At the meeting of the CID on 1 March the doctrine was accepted that the maximum strength of any 'raid' against which home defence was needed could not exceed 5,000 men. No larger force could get past the navy. Arnold-Forster 'immediately raised again the whole question of the policy of maintaining an absolutely useless force of 375,000 men in peace time...and all tied to this country'. Balfour replied that there was nothing new about the doctrine of 'raids'—they had both spoken of it in their speeches. Arnold-Forster thought however that it was important that the CID should make its finding public. 'It was the object of forming the CID to enable the public to obtain the considered opinions of professional men and responsible Ministers combined.'[66] Balfour would only agree to a statement drawn

143

up for the cabinet. And as if to emphasise his own conception of the CID as an adjunct of the Prime Minister's person, available for political purposes but muzzled for public ones, Balfour sent Arnold-Forster the next day a revised copy of 'Suggestions for Army Organisation' which had the caption 'Printed for the Committee of Imperial Defence'. This Arnold-Forster regarded as a device 'in order that Clarke and Esher may force it into circulation', and wrote protesting to Balfour that he trusted he could assume the paper 'neither has been, nor will be, circulated to the Committee'.[67]

So far as Esher was concerned the paper had already passed the CID and he wanted it circulated to the cabinet to be referred to the Army Council:

Esher-Sandars, 3 March 1905:[68] I think it essential that it should be circulated to the Cabinet at once.

Remember, Part 1 is vital.

Part 2 is only 'suggestions'. The Prime Minister commits himself to Part 1 but not to Part 2.

Arnold-Forster should not be *humoured* but driven. He deserves no consideration at the hands of any friend of the Prime Minister. Besides, this memorandum *must* go to the Army Council at once. They expect it, and we are stultified, if it does not appear immediately...

Will you see to it? Do not let the Prime Minister's work be thrown away.

The army estimates were due to come on within ten days or a fortnight, and unless some government pronouncement were agreed on by then, the *status quo* would have to remain for another session. An army reform had been promised, and an announcement was being anticipated in the press. The *Irish Times* had got on to the story that Arnold-Forster was being badly treated, and the *Daily Express* (Dublin) guessed some alternative scheme was on the cards. But this time Esher did not get his way, and at the cabinet on 10 March Balfour was obliged to expound his militia scheme without the advantage of having circulated a preliminary paper. Indeed he was badly briefed on the details, and from what he told Clarke after the meeting, his performance was hopeless. He admitted he 'could not remember anything of importance except as regards reserves'.[69] Arnold-Forster notes that at the cabinet Balfour 'expounded his scheme, then I examined it and I think blew it to pieces'.[70] But Balfour's real object now was obstruction, and he persisted in getting the cabinet's consent to circulate his scheme even though it would be too late to implement it. He reported to the King that the cabinet was anxious that Arnold-Forster should not use 'unnecessarily precise language as to his future plans'[71] in presenting the estimates, but it is clear that the cabinet had not been impressed with his own scheme:

> *Balfour-King Edward, 10 March 1905:*[72] Mr Balfour has laid before Mr Arnold-Forster an alternative scheme of his own which would preserve a much larger number of the existing battalions available for foreign service and would to a great extent substitute the militia in an improved state for the proposed short service army.
>
> Mr Arnold-Forster does not like this scheme. And Mr Balfour does not doubt that there are serious objections...but he is anxious that it should not be ruled out of court before being subjected to a closer examination...
>
> The cabinet of course were hardly in a position to express an opinion on the merits of complicated plans put before them orally...

The significant part of this letter is the final opinion that 'nothing can be done in the near future to carry the one plan or the other into practical effect.'

Looking back over the work of the secret sub-committee, which he persisted in regarding as a sub-committee of the CID, Esher thought that its great achievement was 'to lay down quite clearly the principles upon which an Army should be maintained, and what size that Army should be'.[73] This had been 'placed on record in a very solemn document signed by the Prime Minister and left behind with the Defence Committee', so that there would be very little doubt that 'the new Government will accept our conclusions'. Who would notice that he did not say 'approved', or even 'discussed', by the CID? Who would care that the 'size' of the army was based on sending eight divisions to India, and that the government soon went back on that assumption? Or that a respectable school of opinion, supported by Dilke, believed that the Russians who had not even completed their strategic railways could not possibly mount a major attack on India even if they wished to do so? Or that the commitment to send an expeditionary force to France would soon throw everything again into the melting pot? The legend was launched that the CID had pronounced on the military needs of the Empire.

What Esher had really done was to divert the CID from the sort of role which it might have had in helping to create an 'accepted' military opinion, into a secret and politically orientated body. His secretariat had stymied the proper work of the intelligence branches, and by putting Sir George Clarke at the head of it for his compliance, and encouraging his blatant political intrigue, Esher reduced his own brilliant theoretical conception to a nullity. A comparison of Clarke with his able successors, Sir Charles Ottley and Sir Maurice Hankey, throws into relief his egotism, prating foolishness and indecent methods. It is difficult to imagine Clarke retaining any influence for more than a week had he been elected, as he wished, to the House of Commons. Yet he was eager to become a minister and indeed to take the place of Arnold-Forster, whose work he did so much to wreck by underhand methods. If he were offered the War Office, he wrote to Esher in March 1905, he would not hesitate. 'This is what I have always wished...I am in such close accord with the Prime Minister's own views on nearly all military questions that he himself would probably wish that I should take it.'[74]

The responsibility for Clarke's misbehaviour as a civil servant rested squarely on Balfour, by whose authority he acted. Ottley and especially Hankey became political runabouts in moments of crisis for Prime Ministers, but there is not the same evidence of their manipulating the press or suborning officials in order to advance the presidential power of the Prime Minister against the cabinet or heads of departments. Also, Balfour left questions of patronage and political (as distinct from party) management to his private secretary, J. S. Sandars, who conducted his political strategy against the tariff-reform schismatics and had become hardened to what might be regarded as counter-espionage against dissident ministers. Brodrick, Ritchie and his associates, Devonshire and Joseph Chamberlain, had undergone a semi-hostile surveillance before they resigned, and Chamberlain's actions and motives were still closely scrutinised by Sandars. The network of private secretaries headed by Sandars, Clarke and Lord Knollys, which included Esher as a lay figure, was habitually preoccupied with saving Balfour from imagined disaster which threatened to arise from the seemingly uncontrolled initiatives of his colleagues in or recently out of the government. Nor was the 'network' politically impartial, but strongly against the tariff reformers. One of Clarke's advantages which Esher mentioned to Knollys was that he was 'altogether of *your* way of thinking on the fiscal question and will furnish you with some arguments from the Colonial side which will be new to you!'[75] Arnold-Forster was an active tariff reformer, and the pro-Chamberlain pamphlet he published in 1903, 'The Case for Enquiry', would have placed him outside the pale so far as the 'network' was concerned. Ideologically there were obvious affinities between the state socialism to which the Tariff Reform League seemed to be heading, and demands for conscription or a professional army.

Politically, therefore, the Arnold-Forster army scheme was not merely an annoyance to a few militia enthusiasts. It threatened a deeply divisive split among the Unionists, many of whom regarded the auxiliary forces as the sheet anchor of the voluntary principle, just as 'free food' was the mainstay of free trade. There does not seem to have been any conviction so important as this one in inspiring Esher, somewhat earlier than Balfour, to oppose the Arnold-Forster scheme. For Esher the historic position of the King at the head of one army, drawing in war on the voluntary spirit of the auxiliaries, was at stake, for the new short-service army would be composed of career soldiers, not civilian militiamen. For Balfour, who was congenitally out of touch with popular feeling and for whom the furore over the Militia was an unpleasant surprise, the incipient party split in 1904 seemed ominously like the split over food taxes in 1903, and he quietly determined at all costs to avoid it. How opportune, therefore, that Esher had pressed for the CID secretariat and designated as Secretary an ex-Liberal like himself who had a scheme for the regeneration of the militia prepared before Balfour saw the need for it!

Such was the background to the secret Esher sub-committee which Balfour called a *'quite informal* sub-committee' of the CID, but which amounted in practice to putting the War Office into commission under Lord Esher, who was not even a member of the CID at the time. It was a political manoeuvre of an underhand kind which reflects little credit on any of those who supported it.[76]

Seven

Esher and the
General Staff

In suggesting that the Defence Committee could be a 'general staff' Esher was making the point that a political control over strategic planning was unavoidable. In the German Empire the Great General Staff was directed by the Military Cabinet of the Emperor. In England the supreme direction of defence and strategic planning could only be placed in the hands of the Prime Minister, and the Defence Committee would become his military cabinet, only with the complication that the defence policy of a maritime empire would necessarily be more complex. It would also, in the context of a more democratic constitution and of self-governing dependencies overseas, have to be more 'political'. To allow the army to set up a powerful and professionally independent general staff on the German model seemed in Esher's view to be a mistake based on two un-noticed conditions which were absent in England's case—a gigantic army and a military autocracy.

Even so, the proposal to call the Defence Committee a general staff was odd, and was quickly opposed as a solecism by Sir William Nicholson the Director of Military Intelligence, in a long memorandum of 4 February 1904.[1] He claimed that the army and Indian army already possessed 'very able and experienced staff officers' who were accustomed to preparing the papers for the Defence Committee: especially in the strategical branch of the War Office under Colonel Altham, and in the mobilisation branch under Colonel Lake. How could the Defence Committee produce an 'expert' staff, he asked, or adjudicate between the military and naval departments. Such adjudication was one of the responsibilities of the Committee itself, and should 'not be delegated to its secretarial staff'. How could the secretarial staff be a 'general staff', for in Nicholson's view war experience was necessary. It would become an *imperium in imperio* and result in 'confusion, friction and ultimate failure'.

148

Esher's retorts to this memorandum were made seriatim for the information of the King, and are interesting in the light of later developments already described. He claimed that the officers of the Defence Committee should not *prepare* anything but act as 'orderlies' and simply arrange and communicate papers from the War Office, Admiralty and other departments. To the objection that the secretariat would tend to 'adjudicate' he replied specifically that the *'Defence Committee* alone would advise', while the 'expert staff' would 'merely prepare information'.

As for the army's general staff, the Esher committee had at first made no provision for it in composing the Army Council, for originally the first 'Military Member' had been the Quartermaster-General.[2] Finding that the proposal to call the third Military Member the 'Commissary-General' was opposed because it was too reminiscent of the blunders of the Crimea, that post became the QMG and there was a blank. At this point it was decided to call Sir Neville Lyttelton the 'Chief of the General Staff' even though there was no such staff for him. When the King's consent to this was obtained Esher minuted that in spite of Lyttelton's new title he would not interfere with the Chief Staff Officer attached to the GOC in peace or with a Chief of the Staff in war.[3] Esher was thus enabled, a week later, to claim in his reply to Sir William Nicholson that: 'We have now got a general staff for the army' under Lyttelton.[4] Lyttelton's promotion was an answer to Nicholson in more than one sense, and the latter (who with the advent of the Liberals became a Field-Marshal, Baron and CIGS) was sent as chief military attaché to the Japanese army in Manchuria.

Sir Neville Lyttelton was an establishment figure. His brother Alfred Lyttelton had been a companion of Balfour and Esher at Cambridge and enjoyed a sudden elevation into the office of Colonial Secretary in 1903. Of Alfred Lyttelton the King had asked: 'What real experience has he, and will he give strength to the government?',[5] to which Balfour could have answered that he was a most popular cricketer. Had the same question been posed about Sir Neville, it would have been said that he was a very gallant soldier of considerable war experience, but he was hardly distinguished for administrative and strategic capacity. Rightly or wrongly he was accused of being involved in the incompetence of the commissariat during the late war, and as Chief of the General Staff he voluntarily suspended his duties while the Commission on War Stores was deliberating. He was chosen as a safe man, a quiescent and compliant man, who would create a general staff of the right kind.

The crucial questions to be decided in the formation of the general staff were: 'Should the general staff be a specially qualified and specially trained élite?' 'Should it have an accelerated scale of promotion to attract brains into the army and give responsibility to able young men?' 'Should staff college entry be possible on purely scientific or technical subjects?' 'Should staff officers retain their distinctiveness when seconded for the sake of gaining experience to ordinary duties?' Men like Arnold-Forster or Sir William Nicholson might be suspected of being ready to entertain answers in the affirmative to these questions, and the original Military Members were chosen on the opposite supposition. A representative of the anti-élitist view was the CGS's brother, Canon Edward Lyttelton, who as Head Master of Eton took Arnold-Forster to task for a new regulation on army qualifying certificates which sought to abolish compulsory Latin. Arnold-Forster regarded the Classics shibboleth as conferring an unfair advantage on certain schools, while Canon Lyttelton took the older view that Classics taught one how to 'think', even as a soldier. '...the Army is, as it has for thirty years been, staffed with stupid men, who have never had the chance of being taught to think' he wrote to the War Minister, who wryly commented: 'His brother is Chief of the General Staff—and an Etonian.'[6] The ideal of the well-educated gentleman, the man of all-round ability, lofty character and good sense, of which the Duke of Wellington presented the best example, still stood in the way of the scientific training and professional specialisation demanded by the élitists.

If the Military Members were chosen for what they would not do, they succeeded beyond expectation, and the Esher 'Triumvirate' became worried lest their total lack of progress in forming the right kind of staff might leave a vacuum in which a new government might form the wrong kind. Hence Clarke complained:

Clarke-Esher, 29 November 1904:[7] The General Staff business also worries me much. It is going very badly. Lyttelton does nothing, so that power tends to centre in the AG's branch. Grierson is lazy and conceited. He has no idea how to work the large staff which we have obtained for him. He has done some very indifferent work already in regard to the subjects referred to the General Staff...

Meanwhile instead of doing its proper business, which should afford ample scope for our best brains, the General Staff is trying to get hold of 'ceremonials' and of 'camps'...

A special army order, published in January 1905, divided the United Kingdom into seven commands following the recommendation of the Esher committee, and defined the duties of the general staffs so 'decentralised'. But the structure, selection, promotions, or status of the central general staff remained undecided, largely because Arnold-Forster resisted the kind of solutions which his Military Members would have imposed. When therefore Sir Neville Lyttelton made a public fool of himself Arnold-Forster pounced on the opportunity and tried to get rid of him.

In a fatuous and imprudent speech Sir Neville declared that he 'did not know much about the Army Council' of which he was First Military Member, except that it worked in 'water-tight compartments'.[8] Even his backers thought this a fatal blunder. 'Fancy a Sea Lord making a speech of this character,' Sir George Clarke commented to Esher,[9] who assumed that Lyttelton would have to resign. Esher wrote to Sandars calling the speech 'foolish and undignified', adding: 'He is *supposed* to be a Jackie Fisher!'[10] In the list of possible successors to Lyttelton which Esher enclosed the name of Sir William Nicholson stood last, with the comment: 'Very good; if the time has come to bring him back.'[11] The Prince of Wales drew the King's attention to the speech, and he instructed Lord Knollys to write to Sandars about it. Could Sir Neville survive such a general condemnation?

One is tempted to imagine that he survived because among the voices raised against him was that of Arnold-Forster, who informed Balfour: 'I regard the speech as an outrage which makes the continued association of Sir Neville and myself on the Army Council quite out of the question.'[12] Did Balfour entertain for a moment the tempting idea of shunting Arnold-Forster on so convenient an issue to avoid a terrible public collision on army reform? It is certainly true that Balfour and Alfred Lyttelton both persuaded Sir Neville to hang on and refuse to be outed. They encouraged him to make an abject apology, and Sir Neville confessed: 'I began public speaking too late in life to become a safe speaker, and I blunder into things...and in future

151

F

I shall do as little of it as I possibly can.'[13] Alfred Lyttelton came to see Arnold-Forster and admitted that his brother's speech was 'indefensible', but he added the warning that if he were forced to resign 'people would never believe his accusations were not serious and true'.[14] The Secretary of State was made to feel the full import of trying conclusions with a man who had 'all sorts of fashionable relations', and was left reflecting: 'I wonder how many people would bother themselves to the same extent to get me out of a hole?'[15] Balfour was luckily out of town when the matter blew up, and returned when it had spent its first force. He backed Sir Neville to the full, and when repeatedly challenged by Arnold-Forster would only mutter: 'It is hard on poor Neville.'[16]

Yet Sir Neville was supposed to be the 'Brain of the Army', and even his brother had to admit that he was not 'intellectually up to the post'.[17] Arnold-Forster hoped that Alfred would obligingly promote Sir Neville to the Gibraltar command, which was a Colonial Office appointment soon to become vacant. Privately the Secretary for War thought Sir Neville was 'becoming a scandal,...the Army laughs at him,...the Office despises him, and...the work of the department is getting into a hopeless mess.'[18] 'I could not face the creation of the new General Staff under the present auspices.'[19] That however was the trouble. Esher had found out that Arnold-Forster wanted to install Sir William Nicholson in Lyttelton's place, and he was apprehensive about his intentions concerning the nature of the general staff, details of which he had tried to elicit through Knollys. But in general Esher and Clarke were confident that they could 'press' their General Staff plan on Arnold-Forster. Hence in May 1905 Esher supported the project of Lyttelton's 'promotion':

Esher-Sandars, 15 May 1905:[20] I saw the King today, and he asked me to see the Prime Minister about Lyttelton and Nicholson. I want to see you first...

The King thinks that Lyttelton *ought* to accept Arnold-Forster's proposal, and I am sure in his own interest it would be the best thing he could do; for I am *sure* that if there were a change of government, there would be a new Army Council and no such good billet as Gibraltar might then be available.

I feel very strongly that in the Chief of the general staff *competence*, i.e. a strong character and the most recent and wide

152

theoretical experience are necessary. Amiability and gentlemanly qualities take a second place...

The position was becoming very complex because of the uncertainty about whether the government would hold on for a parliamentary session in 1906, or whether it was in fact concluding its last session. It seems that Balfour at this stage reckoned on a dissolution in the spring of 1906, and it was mooted in the secretarial 'network' that if Arnold-Forster could be induced to resign in the summer recess, Esher might take the War Office in order to constitute the new general staff as his final task in the work of military reform. This project was discussed in the summer, but as early as 28 May Clarke suggested to Esher that 'the best solution for the country' would be 'that Arnold-Forster should go at the end of the session, and that you should take the War Office till the dissolution'.[21] Such a plan would render post-ponement of action on the general staff question desirable: whereas if Campbell-Bannerman took office in 1905, as he did, Esher would prefer to complete the general staff at once as an outwork of the CID.

The Military Members had shown themselves hostile to the élitist conception of a general staff, and were therefore all that Esher could desire if he became Secretary for War. The only significant supporter of the other side was Henry Wilson, the moving spirit behind the 'staff ride' in January which became an annual convention of the general staff. Soon after this conference the Military Members discussed the principles of a general staff and 'by ruling that no brevets no accelerated promotion, and no half-pay lieutenant-colonelcies were to be given, they gave the death blow to the whole idea'.[22] After that Arnold-Forster preferred to take no step, rather than one in the wrong direction. But when the prospect of Lyttelton's removal seemed near the War Minister wrote to Wilson asking him to set down his views on the general staff question. The following week, on 5 June, Arnold-Forster invited Sir William Nicholson to dinner and had 'an interesting talk over the question of the General Staff and its proper organisation'.[23] Still Lyttelton showed no signs of obliging. He was busily engaged in preparing his defence before the Commission on War Stores, and he made the excuse that to leave his post at this time would be an admission of weakness. Arnold-Forster appealed to Balfour, who admitted that he could not suffer 'permanently, or for any very great length of time' the absence of an active CGS.[24]

Although he had been actually asked formally to resign by the War Minister, Lyttelton refused to go saying 'everyone had advised him not to do so'.[25]

While Henry Wilson was deliberating on a scheme which threatened to be unpalatably élitist, the Esher 'Triumvirate' set about formulating a rival one. 'We could do it in a week,' Clarke agreed with Esher, and in hardly more time he had one prepared.[26] After a few days the 'psychological moment' arrived for its presentation to Arnold-Forster, and on the day when Arnold-Forster spoke to Henry Wilson about his 'excellent paper' on the general staff he received a 'curious' letter:

> *Esher to Arnold-Forster, 9 July 1905:*[27] Should you mind if your old co-adjutors were *privately* and *secretly* to present you with the enclosed...
>
> It has been prepared, after a good many talks, by Fisher, Clarke and myself...

Arnold-Forster was sure he meant well, but thought it 'odd how he likes to have a finger in every pie'. He was grateful but saw 'no reason whatever why I should receive a round robin...printed at the public expense'.[28] Strangely enough the two schemes were remarkably similar, so that when a day or two later the director of recruiting and organisation, Sir Herbert S. G. Miles, went to Whitehall Gardens to read the Wilson paper to Clarke the latter thought it 'on quite sound lines', a rare tribute: 'but I must try and see the warrant or Army Order before it issues,' he wrote to Esher: 'You will get hold of the copy sent to the King if I fail.'[29]

Meanwhile Arnold-Forster had sought an audience with the King to press for the appointment of Nicholson as CGS. According to his characteristic form of diary entry, King Edward 'trots out that Sir N. Lyttelton can't go while the Commission is pending. Of course someone has said this.' Arnold-Forster suggested his replacement by Nicholson. 'At this he seemed aghast...here again I recognise another hand. I reminded him that he had himself approved of and agreed to Nicholson a few weeks ago.' The King later said that he would think it over—that it was true that it was hard to find an alternative.[30] Well might the War Minister imagine that Esher had advised against Nicholson, who was said not to be popular in the army. But Esher

154

received at this point two letters from Clarke, the one of 12 July informing him that the Wilson scheme was 'on quite sound lines', and the other of 13 July reporting a conversation with Lord Roberts, who said that Nicholson was 'absolutely opposed to Arnold-Forster's fatal scheme' of army reform but 'would dissemble his opinions in order to get into office'.[31] Esher saw Arnold-Forster 'by appointment' on 15 July and asked him about his personal views concerning the general staff, which were explained, whereupon Esher declared: 'we were so entirely in agreement that there was no more to be said.'[32] Some conversation followed about Nicholson in which Esher repeated the opinion that he did not 'get on with the army'.

Esher's account of this puzzling interview does not tally at all with Arnold-Forster's. Writing the same day to the King he stated that Arnold-Forster had 'asked' him to call and after 'a very lengthy preamble which extended over the whole field of army matters came to this point':

Esher-King Edward, 15 July 1905:[33] Mr Arnold-Forster wishes to get rid of General Lyttelton (a fact well-known to Your Majesty) and proposes to offer the general a command, but previous to taking this step he desires to be sure that he will be allowed to appoint Sir William Nicholson as his successor.

Two possible obstacles have occurred to him, the one being a disinclination on the part of Your Majesty, and the other a refusal of the Prime Minister to agree...

In reply to a direct question Lord Esher found that Mr Arnold-Forster was asking him to undertake to find out whether these obstacles were insuperable. Lord Esher thought it his duty to state his strong conviction that whatever personal opinions Your Majesty might entertain...Your Majesty in such a matter would leave the responsibility to Your Majesty's ministers...Lord Esher felt sure Your Majesty would not anticipate this advice...

With regard to the Prime Minister, Lord Esher said that he would repeat to Mr Balfour the conversation, and would convey to Mr Arnold-Forster any reply.

This looks very much like 'telling tales' and was admirably calculated to suit the image which had been so unfairly planted on the Secretary for War. But it was also using him as a stalking horse to broach an unfamiliar idea, namely that the King should not express his own opinions in a military appointment but defer to the Prime Minister, whom Esher now authorised himself to approach on the King's behalf. The most rational interpretation of the whole manoeuvre is that Esher had decided to support Nicholson after all as CGS and felt unable himself to undo the unfavourable judgment of Nicholson which he had impressed on the King.

This is corroborated by a remark of Esher's later, after the Nicholson suggestion had fallen through and been supplanted by the offer of the post of CGS to Lord Kitchener. 'Sorry about Tokyo. Let us try Simla... Our hopes are not yet wrecked', he wrote to Sandars on 3 August.[34] Much had happened in the intervening two and a half weeks. Balfour had sustained a parliamentary defeat on 20 July, all the more humiliating since it followed immediately upon an appeal for better attendance. Instead of resigning Balfour chose to hang on, at least until the conclusion of the Japanese treaty. Esher, enlightened by his delvings into Queen Victoria's correspondence which he was editing, supplied Sandars with precedents to show that a Prime Minister need not resign on an adverse vote in the Commons even on a material point. Had not Mr Gladstone in April 1872 been twice defeated? And then in trying to get one of these votes rescinded because it 'very gravely' affected the Ballot Act, had he not been beaten by twenty-eight and yet showed no sign of resignation?[35] Fortified by such historical lore, Balfour braved the vituperation of Churchill and Lloyd George and the more dignified contempt of Lord Grey, and carried on. It was no doubt during this crisis that Balfour mentioned to Esher the plan which Sandars had been maturing for some time, of letting Arnold-Forster resign in the recess to be succeeded by Esher, and taking a defeat in Parliament in February 1906. And Esher felt that if he himself were presiding over the Army Council, the Chief of the General Staff would have to be someone big. He therefore wrote an extraordinary letter to Simla:

Esher-Lord Kitchener, 26 July 1905:[36] I should think the future full of hope for the Army, if you would accept the office of Chief of the Staff to the King, and establish yourself here to undertake the great work of reorganisation which would grow rapidly under your hand.

156

The position—if you were to accept it—would have to be
enhanced in importance...
(a) By an increase in the emoluments of the post.
(b) By giving you at once a Field-Marshal's baton...
If I were Secretary of State, I would make an appeal to your
patriotism...
...the Defence Committee increases in power and authority
every day, and upon that body a Chief of the General Staff,
whose mind is clear, and whose determination was obvious, must
wield an authority, which has never been exercised in this
country since the death of the Duke of Wellington...
I have written this unknown to anyone, and it is for your eyes
alone...

A naive reader might well ask how Lord Esher could so confidently
dispose of the highest patronage in the army in this secret and private
manner. Kitchener, who was far from being naive, declined the offer
with a polite suggestion that it was outside his sphere.

While Esher was awaiting Kitchener's reply he tried to install
Douglas Haig in the position which was peculiarly important in the
formation of a general staff, that of Director of Staff Duties. This post
was held by General H. D. Hutchinson who might have been regarded
as of the Henry Wilson persuasion in general staff matters, and Esher
wanted him removed. Feelings ran high on these questions so intimately connected with the careers of soldiers, and Henry Wilson's
own quick promotion seemed to some as indecent as his élitist ideas.
From Repington of *The Times* Esher had just received a rabid letter
along these lines: 'Wilson is an arch-intriguer and a second-rate place
hunter: if this imposter is to train our future general staff it will never
be trained.' Repington was recommending the appointment of Colonel
H. Lawson as successor to Rawlinson (Commandant of the Staff
College at Camberley) but feared that Wilson would beat him 'because he has "boomed" his fool of a general, old Hutchinson, in the
press, and has made friends of every unrighteousness'.[37] Hutchinson
was obviously in the key position, and needed replacing.

By chance Douglas Haig, then Inspector-General of Cavalry in
India, happened to be on leave. He had been an acquaintance of the
King as Prince of Wales, and was invited to stay at Windsor for the

Ascot races. There he happened to meet Miss Dorothy Vivian, a Maid of Honour, and after an expeditious courtship he married her in the private chapel at Buckingham Palace on 11 July. Haig had long been regarded by the King as one of his most promising young officers. He impressed Esher as a fine specimen of the officer 'caste' and shared the dislike of Arnold-Forster and all his works. Haig's marriage might have seemed to present a reason for an immediate re-appointment, and Esher decided to get him placed as Director of Staff Duties. He asked Sandars to drop a hint to the War Minister, and no doubt inspired the mission of Sir John French who called on Arnold-Forster the next day:

Arnold-Forster's diary, 4 August 1905:[38] He pressed me very strongly to replace General Hutchinson by General Haig. I told him that I really could not make such a change 'off my own bat' and apropos of nothing... I spoke of the added difficulty of appearing to favour—or rather of favouring—an officer who was recommended by the King directly he had married a Maid of Honour. Two officers had done this, and within a week they were both recommended for purely exceptional treatment.

This rebuff must have been conveyed immediately to Esher, who produced a 'suggested draft' of a letter from the King to Balfour the same day, expressing 'much concern' at the scare about the shortage of officers which Lord Roberts had just raised by a public speech, and continuing:

Suggested draft by Esher, 4 August 1905:[39] ...and finally the King notices with much regret that no steps have yet been taken to organise a General Staff as recommended by the Esher Committee and as approved by the Government...
    The C[hief of the] G[eneral] S[taff] is not, the King believes, properly supported by General Hutchinson, whose experience is mainly Indian and whose knowledge of the English army is not sufficient... The King wishes Mr Balfour to look into the matter himself, and to recommend the Secretary of State for War to replace General Hutchinson, for whom some more congenial post can doubtless be found... The King thinks that General Douglas Haig is an officer whose experience of staff work...and whose high abilities should be utilised in this particular branch...

The matter is of such urgent importance that the King must press Mr Balfour to see the Secretary of State for War...

Balfour was however himself hard pressed at this juncture by Lord Roberts's condemnation of his administration of the War Office. After his Mansion House speech of 1 August Lord Roberts had been asked by Lord Newton to become president of the National Service League which was supposed to be working covertly for conscription. After accepting, Roberts was chaffed by Rosebery for making a fool of himself by espousing so unpopular a cause, and the word 'compulsion' in the League's programme was brought to his notice.[40] It was certainly highly anomalous that Roberts, the sole salaried member of the CID at this time, should thus throw over the main axiom of the defence policy which that body had formally approved, and Balfour was met with demands for his removal. Arnold-Forster got Balfour's consent to circulate a condemnatory letter and his agreement that the speech was 'lamentable', but Balfour had added: 'Of course, we cannot get rid of the old man.'[41] Four months later Balfour was forced to get rid of him, but meanwhile he contented himself with a public speech stating the counter-proposition that the army was in an improved condition and ready for war. But even this gentle rejoinder brought Roberts storming into Sandar's office with a complaint.

While Balfour was thus quarrelling publicly with his chief independent military adviser his Indian Viceroy Lord Curzon was conducting an intemperate feud with Lord Kitchener, which was so far mercifully concealed from the public in the secret telegrams. Clearly this was no moment to open up dissensions in the General Staff, and so Hutchinson remained undisturbed for two more years before Haig succeeded him. All Balfour could do was to urge Arnold-Forster to go ahead with the formation of the general staff. The subject came before the Army Council on 9 August when the Secretary for War pleaded for the formation of a separate Corps 'in conformity with the practice of all other nations', but in vain.[42] It was decided otherwise, for fear that, as Arnold-Forster put it, 'An infantry officer might find...that a better man whose commission dated two days later than his own, was actually put over his head'. Nor was any special qualification, such as the Staff College certificate, to be a *sine qua non* for the general staff. The distinction between staff and other officers was to be minimal, and the effects of accelerated promotion almost nullified.

159

Arnold-Forster drew up a minute along these lines but delayed implementing it for two more months while he tried to get rid of Lyttelton. Balfour continued to urge the immediate implementation of the scheme while refusing to consent to a new CGS. He had forwarded the War Minister's scheme to Clarke, who thought it 'generally sound'. But the deadlock remained with the well-known result that the general staff minute was released to the press by Arnold-Forster after consulting Henry Wilson just before Balfour resigned. Lyttelton was at that point still holding up progress but the press release was arranged while he was absent on one of his frequent sporting parties.[43] The press reception was favourable, and goaded Clarke into commenting that it was based on 'our memorandum' and yet was 'an amateur production' sent to the press 'to enable him to pose as the creator of the General Staff'.[44]

Clarke was quite right to claim himself and Esher as the real authors of the scheme as it was handed on to the incoming Liberal government. The élitist school of opinion on the question had been thwarted through the manipulation of the Army Council and the retention of Lyttelton with his crucial casting vote. The result of this critical decision made itself felt at the outbreak of the Great War, which through lack of new talent was initially fought by Boer War generals acting without any central general staff in London or any specialised civilian assistance. As Esher himself later had to admit, the 'general staff' in London set out for France in 1914 to see the fighting leaving old Ewart of the Scottish Command as a lone voice pleading for an attack on Zeebrugge.[45] There was no-one to support him, and staff officers had to refer to maps to see where Zeebrugge— the key to the safety of the English Channel—was situated. Neither Kitchener in London nor Sir John French in Flanders had the faintest understanding of or use for a modern general staff. They thought they could run a war or direct a campaign single-handed.

It is quite clear that Esher likewise did not anticipate the need for the kind of general staff which a protracted land war demanded. He thought in terms of quick campaigns or joint naval and military operations, previously studied by the CID but confided to the direction of one commander. When he had advocated the creation of the CID secretariat for 'imperial staff work' he had laid it down that 'imperial staff work and local staff work should be kept as far as possible distinct. You cannot at present without hopeless friction, divorce the staff work of the army, whether imperial or local, from the executive authority of the Secretary of State in Council. This is an axiom.'[46] There is nothing like an axiom to disguise a blind spot, and if Esher was considering 'organisation for war' he was overlooking the fact that having proposed to abolish the Commander-in-Chief to avoid 'dual control' he had confided the strategic control of the army in war to a civilian. The anomaly was cured in 1914 by making a soldier who had no experience in Parliament a Secretary of State, and later by the extraordinary compact with Kitchener which Robertson struck when he became CIGS. As has been seen, Esher only gave the first Military Member of the Army Council the title of 'Chief of the General Staff' as an after-thought. Fisher had wanted the 'First Military Lord' to have charge of the Adjutant-General's department controlling organisation and discipline and, only incidentally, the directorate of military intelligence.[47] The simple truth was that the 'Triumvirate' had at first conceived of all real general staff work being confided to the Defence Committee under the rubric of 'combined operations', while the army's staff work was seen as concerned with administration and local operations. Hence the directorates which the Esher committee prescribed for the general staff (Military Operations, Staff Duties and Military Training) were adapted to administrative and peacetime requirements.

When therefore in August 1905 the Army Council discussed the general staff Esher did not intervene to extend the Directorate of Military Operations. Instead he seems to have been concerned to ensure that the nascent general staff was properly decentralised by giving staff officers in the commands equivalent rank to administrative officers. In this matter his influence was effective enough:

Sir Edward Ward-Esher, 9 August 1905:[48] I am amused at your remarks that these are proofs of my 'power and influence'. The two proofs are:-

1. That by telling each member of the Council privately and individually of the King's wish regarding this rank question, I have been able to turn their minds collectively towards a proper decision, and

2. That by secretly informing Lyttelton of the proposition to make these three appointments of brigadier-general for the General Staff at the three principal commands, I have been able to get him to take it up as his own...

161

>   A condition of our compact is that Lyttelton should adopt the
> plan, not divulging the fact of my interest in it...

Esher was indeed highly satisfied with the non-progress which Arnold-
Forster was experiencing in trying to form a corps d'élite. In 1904
and again in 1905 the Secretary of State had tried to get a positive
decision. All he could report in the way of progress was the institution of a ten-day lecture course at Camberley ending with a 'staff
ride', and the institution of a 'Staff List' on which Douglas Haig's
name was duly enrolled.[49]

Esher's attitude is largely explained by the political situation. He
had been invited to go to the War Office himself to complete the
general staff during Balfour's last months of office, but he preferred
to retain his unofficial position and let the task hang over until the
Liberal government took office. His immediate concern was to keep
the Army Council amenable to his influence, and he wished to keep
Douglas and Wolfe Murray as Military Members while dismissing
Plumer, whose fault as Clarke expressed it was that 'he has acted on
the idea that it is his duty to support any rubbishy notion emanating
from the Secretary of State'.[50] Esher discussed the question with
Knollys, to whom he wrote on 20 August: 'I should deprecate a clean
sweep, and hope the King will make this one of the conditions of a
C[ampbell]-B[annerman] summons. If Lyttelton goes, which he
ought to do, and if the King thinks Nicholson's unpopularity with
the army is a bar, then I should hope to see the following arrangements: Hildyard CGS, Douglas = AG, Tucker = QMG, Wolfe
Murray = MGO'[51] Lyttelton was recommended for the Scottish command, but Esher significantly omitted to press this on Balfour.

It was a tall order to dictate the composition of the Army Council
to the incoming Prime Minister, but Esher had discovered from his
editing of Queen Victoria's correspondence that 'the monarchical
system changed materially under the influence of the Prince Consort',
and that 'the present ministers, mainly through defective training and
carelessness, do not adhere...to the old practice of writing fully to
the Sovereign upon important questions *before* Cabinet decisions are
finally taken'. This principle applied with especial force to army
appointments, and 'no promotion to the rank of Major-General, nor
reward nor appointment of any kind of an officer over the rank of
Colonel, was made without a long written explanation to the
Sovereign...in the handwriting of the Minister...'[52]

Esher-Knollys, 1 September 1905:[53] The Army Council are much too fond of exercising *command*...The executive commands of the army *must* assert themselves...And of course there is always to be developed as time goes on the authority of the King as Commander-in-Chief. I mean in all personal questions. The King should adhere tenaciously to his right to veto any appointment. Gradually it will become clear to everyone that under a *King* a C-in-C was an anomaly. Under a female sovereign it was another matter, although the Duke of Wellington (as you know) thought no-one but the Prince Consort ought to hold that office.

The royal powers and prerogatives in army appointments were extremely uncertain, depending on constitutional practice, and Esher meant to regard as an aberration the practice which had crept in under a widowed queen. If the assertion were successful, it would legitimise itself.

While the general staff problem could be postponed, the consolidation of the CID so that it could weather the unfavourable treatment it was expected to receive at the hands of Campbell-Bannerman seemed very urgent. 'We *might* under C-B get another type of Arnold-Forster,' Esher wrote to Knollys just after he had decided it was 'too late' to take the War Office himself: 'The solution is to widen the functions of the Defence Committee and then we shall be to a great extent independent of any Secretary of State's vagaries.' And so to 'render possible the future sound organisation of the army' the CID should be 'enlarged' at once by Balfour, who should appoint 'a certain number of persons to act as a permanent sub-committee on the lines we have so often discussed'.[54] Writing to Balfour the same day, Esher recommended the sub-committee as a means of escape from the embarrassment of the dispute with Lord Roberts, and suggested as its membership Lord Milner, Admiral Sir Arthur Wilson (a Fisherite), Sir John French and himself! '...all questions of *organisation* both for Army and Navy will have to be the work of the Defence Committee. *Administration* will take all the time of the Admiralty and Army Council.'[55] What he meant by 'organisation' was indicated in an explanatory letter to Sandars: 'As to duties, there is no doubt that we shall speedily come to this, i.e. *organisation* whether Naval, Military, or Indian, the policy of sea or land fighting, cannot be left to the old Departments.'[56] He was suggesting that organisational reforms as well as strategic planning should be the concern of the CID, while

163

by shrinking the scope of the Army Council to 'administration' he was cutting away its potentiality as the matrix of a real general staff, that is a staff that could plan as well as command a campaign. He arrived quite explicitly at this conclusion a month later, after Balfour had appointed the CID sub-committee, when he assured Balfour that it 'will fulfil the highest functions of a General Staff, the only sort of General Staff suited to our requirements, i.e. a joint Naval and Military Staff'.[57]

This sub-committee and its revived version under Asquith was the precursor of the Joint Chiefs of Staff Committee and established the excellent principle of 'combined operations'. But it failed to bear fruit in the form of inter-service co-operation during the Great War not simply because the CID became semi-defunct in the war, nor because of Fisher's suspicions at the Admiralty, but chiefly because it was never based on the conception of a 'war directorate'. Esher was sufficiently 'élitist' to see the necessity of a general staff of trained commanders, and sufficiently aware of the need for inter-service strategic planning. Where his reforms proved inadequate to the conditions of the Great War was in the deliberate rejection of strategic 'direction' as distinct from strategic 'planning', leaving a vacuum only tardily and partially filled by Lloyd George's War Cabinet. He was quite aware of the role which strategic direction could play in modern war, but thought it inappropriate to British circumstances. 'I have always said that the German system was unworkable,' he wrote to Sandars on 1 October 1905, '...Now you see the Japs find a Moltke is not workable except under *German* conditions, i.e. Royal Princes as Figureheads. If you have a *real* Commander, Napoleon, Wellington or Roberts, he won't stand a Moltke.'[58] During the Great War Esher and others of his way of thinking expected the war to throw up some great leader, and even after the advantages of the Kaiser's war directorate had been abundantly demonstrated Esher remained more a champion of Haig than a keen supporter of Henry Wilson's directorate at Versailles. Britain could hardly be said to have evolved any real military directorate during the War, while her war directorate in default of effective service staffs was run by the politicians.

Eight

Caretaker
of the C I D

Although the CID was perhaps the greatest of Balfour's constructive measures as Prime Minister, he had good reason to anticipate that the Liberal government would allow it to atrophy after he quitted office. Its creation and its uses were so mixed up with political causes in ways which might seem to fulfil Campbell-Bannerman's prophecies, that people expected the Liberal leader to give it short shrift, and the sympathies of the Liberal 'imperialists' seemed its only hope. Balfour had not been over-hasty in making public the work and findings of the CID, and when he did the reception was somewhat sceptical. When the 'blue water' axiom was proclaimed, with its corollary that no army was needed for home defence, it aroused an unpleasant controversy. Even Repington, who usually yielded to Clarke's persuasions, attacked it in *The Times* and followed this up with a letter reflecting on the competence of the CID:

Repington-Esher, 18 May 1905:[1] ...the announcement of the Defence Committee's opinions should be unassailable in point of fact and argument...and they can only be this when they are based on a complete examination of the facts...

If the argument put forward by Mr Balfour is an argument for anything at all it is an argument for a weak navy and a weak army...

I do not think that the political bias and training predisposes even a great statesman like Mr Balfour to discuss strategical problems with the necessary precision and detachment.

It seemed altogether too opportune that the defence power of the submarine and the torpedo boat or the fleet control made possible by wireless telegraphy should have been so dramatically discovered by a Prime Minister embarrassed by inflated army estimates. Contemporaries were also too perspicacious to be bamboozled by the formal composition and secrecy of the CID and correctly identified the guiding hand of its political chairman. They could not fail to notice how Fisher had packed the Admiralty with his own creatures of the 'torpedo' school of thought and discouraged the freedom of opinion which had formerly prevailed at the Board. Fisher's obsession with the submarine was by no means commonly shared by all or even most leading naval officers, and while he may have been right he never publicly gave reasoned arguments for his opinions. The 'blue water' axiom was still controversial and was espoused by Balfour as an amateur before he began to chair the CID. Reformers like J. R. Colomb in close touch with such matters knew this well enough:

> *John R. Colomb-Clarke, 25 May 1905:*[2] It offered an excuse for the reversal of a policy to which Parliament was wedded by long habit, and indeed offered to Balfour himself a door of escape from the false views he had so often before defended. In fact the introduction of the submarine offered a colourable pretext to present to Parliament a reason for a reversal of opinion. His speech in reply to me on Brodrick's army scheme made it very difficult for him to explain away his complete change of front.

Instead of being the public forum of professional and scientific opinion in defence matters which Arnold-Forster had wanted it to be, the CID had been turned into a secret conclave corrupted to political purposes and practically useless either for consulting or leading expert military or naval opinion. Its chief formal function had become that of a supra-departmental extension of the cabinet exploring the legal, economic and political aspects of a general war, which were beyond the purview of individual departments.

The failure of the CID to develop as a focus of military opinion and expertise was emphasised by the continuing feud over army reform. The Military Members were encouraged to oppose Arnold-Forster's scheme but they were quite unable to suggest any alternative plans of their own. Significantly enough Balfour did not attempt to resolve his differences with Arnold-Forster before the CID itself but instead allowed Sandars, Esher and Clarke to encourage the Military Members to appeal to the cabinet. The cabinet was so out of touch that it had to ask Arnold-Forster on the eve of his speech on the army estimates what he intended to announce as his plan. As in the previous session the War Minister was told to speak for no-one but himself, while Balfour lamely reported to the King: 'The Military Members of the Army Council, or rather a majority of them, are understood to be now opposed to the plan; but they have no alternative to offer.' Unfortunately for Balfour the Unionist leader of the House of Lords, Lord Lansdowne, failed to grasp the political importance of not seeming to approve of the Arnold-Forster scheme even as a long-term project, and 'practically committed' the government to it. This brought a protest from Lord Roberts, who, as Clarke feared, might attack the government and 'having been invoked for the purposes of our sub-committee is in a strong position for so doing'. In a hurried effort to prevent a disastrous public squabble between the Secretary for War and Lord Roberts, the two leading military authorities of the CID, Balfour got out yet another memorandum on the Militia which now offered a six-month period of training. In conversation with Arnold-Forster he gathered that the latter would accept twelve month enlistments for his short-service army. To this however Clarke would not agree, rightly seeing six months as the limit of training which citizens, as opposed to professionals, would accept. The Balfour militia scheme was 'hawked about the clubs' by Esher to prove that it was still in the running, while the King was invited to lend his support to what Esher had represented as a CID paper:

Esher-Lord Knollys, 3 April 1905:[3] Before the King sees Arnold-Forster it may be desirable that HM should see Clarke's letter enclosed.

The two things which I would venture to suggest that the King should say to Arnold-Forster are:

(a) that about a fortnight ago Mr Balfour sent the King a copy of his memorandum upon the reorganisation of the army, and that the King would like to know whether the *military members* of the Army Council have seen it, and if so HM would be glad to see their views upon it in writing.

(b) that HM notes that Lord Lansdowne refers to a proposal to cut down the number of regular long-service battalions of the line from 156 to 104, and that the King cannot, *under present circumstances and until a great deal more explanation has been submitted to him*, agree to this proposal.

167

The 'present circumstances' referred to the moribund course of the government, which could not hope for another full legislative session and might therefore destroy battalions without being able to reconstruct the army.

The rival schemes were now common knowledge. 'All the world knows by this time,' Arnold-Forster wrote to Balfour on 5 April, 'that the Prime Minister has propounded a plan of army reform which differs fundamentally from that of the Secretary of State for War.'[4] Liberals who were strong believers in departmental and ministerial responsibility might well object that the CID had in practice subverted the parliamentary responsibility which the War Secretary supposedly shouldered and transferred the control of his important department into the hands of Sir George Clarke, a salaried civil servant absolved from all parliamentary scrutiny. The only redeeming feature of Clarke's situation from the Liberals' point of view was that he was on their side.[5] Had his political role been different there would no doubt have been a great outcry for his removal.

In the absence of any firm direction from the CID the problem of army reform became the sport of political and professional factions. Arnold-Forster's scheme had the political object of forestalling the known intention of the Liberals to abolish fourteen third and fourth battalions and possibly more, by 'converting' these and others at home into his territorialised short-service battalions which would retain long-service cadres. The Clarke scheme reduced the army to 149 battalions on a low establishment and a shorter enlistment (seven and five years) which saved money and rendered an improved Militia necessary for reserves. It was popular with the politicians but Clarke was over-hasty when he assumed the Military Members would accept it. For professional reasons they got cold feet, not wanting to be associated with reduction. In desperation Clarke recommended his scheme, the supposed product of the CID, as only a 'suggestion for them to work on'! His mind then turned to the idea of carrying it over to the next government, while dispensing with the recalcitrant Military Members sooner.

Clarke-Esher, 11 June 1905:[6] Mr Balfour came to my office on Thursday and Friday and spoke most freely about everything. Arnold-Forster is to bring out a modified scheme, which I gather is only the conversion of 7 and 14 battalions into his patent short-service force.

This must not be; and its acceptance would break up the present Army Council. You I know would advocate the resignation of the three Military Members in this event...

...I rather think he contemplates the application of the curb [i.e. A.-F.'s dismissal] when the session ends. If he does not, there is no hope of any military progress until there is a change of government.

Esher however did not regard Arnold-Forster's token scheme as being anything but a surrender. His original scheme involved the conversion of fifty-two battalions and a 'huge unestimated expenditure for barrack accommodation' to territorialise them; also the creation of 'two castes of officers'. Now he would merely 'play' with fourteen battalions. 'If it is desired to retain him as Secretary of State his retreat can be allowed to proceed unharassed, without doing material harm to the regular army, while the benefit of an improved militia will be an asset of great value.'[7] Balfour acted on this advice when on 22 June the cabinet met at 10 p.m. for the second time to consider a dossier of printed papers which had been circulated by the rival army reformers.[8] Arnold-Forster carried all before him and got Austen Chamberlain to note down the eight decisions he obtained, a precaution he had learnt from the aptitude of his colleagues to forget his projects. Balfour reported to the King that 'Mr Arnold-Forster, to end two or three competing schemes, proposed a compromise which will at least tide over the present difficulty'.[9] The next day the Prime Minister conferred with Clarke, who decided, with the vague concurrence of his chief, to obstruct the cabinet's decision:

Clarke-Esher, 23 June 1905:[10] Most interesting talk with the PM today. The cabinet seems to have decided to let Arnold-Forster go on with his modified scheme without asking for military opinion upon it from the Army Council...

The PM said frankly that it was a case of political exigency, and that he could not just now shed Arnold-Forster or find anyone to take his place. I sympathise with him most fully, and can see how terribly Arnold-Forster has tried him; but one must think of the army. If therefore Arnold-Forster begins to operate on these fourteen battalions, I think the three Army Councillors ought most certainly to go, and I told the PM I believed they would. For Lyttelton this would be providential...

...our scheme in any other hands would have proved an unqualified success.

The immediate problem was to delay any action on Arnold-Forster's part while the session lasted, after which, at this stage, it was thought that he would be allowed to resign. Sandars recommended this tactic.

Arnold-Forster took the correct constitutional view that having obtained cabinet approval he was free to announce his plan in the Commons, and that the Army Council must support it or resign. He told them that he intended to say that he had their support, and he also asked the War Office directors if they supported him. Hearing of this, Clarke supposed that he was intending to represent the token plan as an authorised beginning of the whole scheme. To this he raised a frankly political objection. '...even from the political point of view it would be best for the cabinet to shed Arnold-Forster,' he wrote to Esher on 29 June.[11] Esher lent his support in drafting a rebellious round robin for the Military Members to present, which called the plan 'purely experimental' and declared that since it was associated with an energetic attempt to improve the Militia, they would 'refrain from dissent' though they 'cannot approve' of it.[12] By 5 July Clarke was able to report that the 'Military Trio' had signed and delivered the 'reply we drafted', adding: 'If Arnold-Forster says in the House that he is going on with his *scheme* it will be necessary to have a question asked.'[13] Meanwhile Esher had also drafted a letter which he wished to circulate to Balfour, Arnold-Forster and the Army Council as the King's reply to Balfour's report of the cabinet decision:

Draft by Esher, post 23 June 1905:[14] I am desired by the King to say that your letter giving an account of Mr Arnold-Forster's latest scheme affecting the army which was laid before the cabinet and agreed to, gives His Majesty much concern. The King is strongly of opinion that what the army, especially the officers throughout the army, requires at the present time, is a period free from disturbance and constant change.

...the King must view with great regret proposals which are admittedly 'half-measures' of a tentative character...which are

170

not calculated to reassure the officers and men of the army, who have been disturbed by the uncertain prospects held out to them under the various projects which the Secretary of State has foreshadowed from time to time...

In presenting these proposals to the House of Commons the King hopes that Mr Arnold-Forster will not once more depreciate the private soldier and the army in the eyes of the country.

There can be no doubt that the Military Members if they could not accept the policy of the government and Secretary of State ought to have resigned. As Arnold-Forster facetiously remarked to Sir Neville Lyttelton, he could hardly announce in the Commons that 'the CGS of the Army is actively engaged in carrying out proposals which he believes to be to the detriment of the Army'.[15] He believed that Lyttelton was opposed to remedial army reform: '...you told me,' he added, 'that you had a preference for conscription, but that that would not come without a smash...'[16] Not surprisingly, therefore, Lord Roberts also intervened to oppose the plan.

It is a fair conclusion that the whole conception of the CID and the reformed War Office had broken down under the pressure of political interests allowed by the Prime Minister to assert themselves unchecked. On one side the Secretary for War exercised his traditional rights of formulating proposals urgently needed to maintain the running of the army and especially the supply of drafts for abroad, of gaining the consent of the cabinet and announcing the results as the policy of the government. But on the other side the Prime Minister, who hardly seemed to appreciate the principle of ministerial solidarity, readily exploited the supra-departmental authority of the CID to obstruct the decisions of the War Office and the cabinet. Gradually with Balfour's connivance and the active assistance of his private secretary a system of obstruction had subverted the whole system of official responsibility. The Army Council was played off against the Secretary of State in contradiction to its basic charter. The CID was played off against the cabinet although its role was supposed to be purely consultative. And finally Clarke, aided by Esher, Sandars and Lord Knollys, operated a secret political bureau by which Balfour obstructed the workings of his own government. Even a Prime Minister's power can be exercised irresponsibly when it is delegated secretly to agents who have the power to corrupt officials and to misinform the Sovereign, to dismiss or appoint soldiers, and to manipulate political processes and the commentary of the press. In justice to Balfour it must be admitted that he sinned largely through a wilful negligence, allowing himself to be managed by the secretarial network.

The final demise of Arnold-Forster's scheme was brought about by the indefatigable machinations of the Secretary of the CID. Four days before it was to be announced in the Commons he had the 'Military Trio' round at Whitehall Gardens for a 'preliminary discussion' before Esher saw them at the same place the next day.[17] Then Clarke proceeded to the House of Commons 'in the hope of seeing Mr Balfour' but was obliged to communicate with Sandars instead:

Clarke-Sandars, 10 July 1905:[18] The point I wanted to speak about to Mr Balfour is that unless an absolute understanding, which should be in writing, has been arrived at, there is a real danger that Arnold-Forster will intimate that his 'policy' holds the field.

He tells everybody that he has beaten the cabinet, and in his *tête montée* condition he might easily say something in which the cabinet would have to acquiesce, unless the PM disavowed it promptly.

No-one knew what Arnold-Forster would say, and it was hoped that Balfour might challenge him at the CID meeting on the 13th just before his speech. In preparation for this encounter, as Clarke informed Esher: 'The military members wrote as we arranged and Sandars has the whole correspondence,' adding, 'I don't want them to have to go now'.[19] Perhaps they had seen the merits of Clarke's scheme. Arnold-Forster failed to appear at the CID which he cried off to prepare his speech, but even Clarke could not find serious fault with his speech the next day. He did not try to commit the government to more than the experiment, and the approaching end of the parliamentary session would mark the termination of his ambitious hopes. 'I suppose we can now assume that there is not the faintest chance for any part of Arnold-Forster's scheme,' Clarke wrote to Esher: 'This you always said.'[20] What Clarke did not realise, however, was that his own scheme was in Esher's eyes merely an instrument of obstruction.

Balfour was thinking of resigning as soon as the Japanese treaty was signed, but Clarke assumed that he would remain in his key position as Secretary of the CID even though he had turned it into a secret agency of Unionist party interests. He spoke of Balfour as 'the chief' and claimed to be acting as a devoted Unionist. He had made the secretariat and the CID itself extremely vulnerable. The 'Triumvirate' were well aware of this, and their answer was to devise a permanent sub-committee so that regardless of what Liberal ministers did or whether Clarke himself remained the CID should be a going concern. The plan for a sub-committee 'to consider joint naval and military operations' was submitted by Clarke to the CID of 13 July.[21] 'There are many plans in existence both at the Admiralty and the War Office which require to be co-ordinated', he explained. It was an excellent idea, but Admiral Fisher's agreement to it was hesitant and politically motivated. He never agreed to divulge his plans. As for Sir Neville Lyttelton, it is doubtful whether he had any. However, the establishment of the principle had the important consequence of enabling Esher and Clarke to initiate the Anglo-French military conversations in December while Liberal ministers were away electioneering. Clarke was to be Secretary and the senior officer present could chair the sub-committee in the absence of the Prime Minister. It was authorised to 'call to its counsels such officers as it requires', and its composition was, apart from the Prime Minister, entirely professional, consisting of the First Sea Lord and Chief of the General Staff, the Directors of Military and Naval Operations, and officers from the strategic sections of the Intelligence Departments. The CID chaired by Lord Roberts approved the scheme and stipulated that the sub-committee's proceedings should not be printed or circulated.[22]

Lord Roberts was the sole salaried member of the CID, a kind of anomaly that had arisen through his being dismissed as C-in-C when his salary could not be immediately terminated. As an advocate of compulsory military training and a believer in conscription he was out of line with the declared public policy of the Unionist government and CID and an anathema to Liberals. Nor was he content to remain quiet, but as has been seen came out in his Mansion House speech for national service and became president of the National Service League. He followed this up by stumping the country uttering heresies which completely nullified the doctrines proclaimed by the CID. Esher saw his defection as peculiarly embarrassing in view of the fact that he had been the chief independent member of the secret sub-committee:

Esher-Balfour, 3 September 1905:[23] **What he forgets...is the fact** that he was a member of the sub-committee of the CID that approved what is known as the 'Prime Minister's scheme' of army organisation...

The basis of that paper was the maintenance of voluntary enlistment...Also, no 'universal training' short of conscription in its most concrete form, can add to the organised military fighting machine of the nation...

Lord Roberts would not say clearly whether by national service he meant school training, which Esher had approved when he signed a rider to the Elgin report, or something more drastic. He demanded an official inquiry and wrote to the King asking for permission to conduct his propaganda. If his association with the government continued he bade fair to become a major vote-loser in the coming election.

Esher presented Balfour with a solution which was to have important consequences for himself. In his best manner he suggested that the newly proposed sub-committee for combined operations should be enlarged in scope to cover 'Organisation for Imperial Defence', i.e. 'what provision can be made for naval and military expansion in the event of war...I need not emphasise, as you always understand. Add to the Committee, Milner, Arthur Wilson, French, and if I may venture to suggest myself...*Then*, say that...no-one acting on the Defence Committee can...take part in any public discussion of matters which come within the purview of that committee.'[24] Was reform always to wait upon political exigency? Or was there intrinsic merit in the idea? It amounted to placing the formulation of the most delicate and politically sensitive aspect of defence policy over which all the trouble with Arnold-Forster had arisen in the hands of four unrepresentative and irresponsible men with the professionals of the service departments. How accountable the 'sub-committee' would have been to the CID itself may be judged by the conduct of the previous Esher subcommittee. That this kind of sub-committee was in his mind is made clear by another letter of the same day:

Esher-Lord Knollys, 16 September 1905:[25] As a member of the Defence Committee, *and upon Defence Committee subjects* to take part in a propaganda is deplorable. If the PM wants to stop it and also render possible the future sound organisation of the army, he *must* enlarge the scope of the Defence Committee, and appoint a certain number of persons to act as a permanent sub-committee on the lines we have so often discussed. *Army organisation* is the proper function of the Defence Committee. 'Administration' of course rests with the Army Council.

It was at this juncture that Esher abandoned the idea of taking Arnold-Forster's place at the War Office. That was not the kind of position he relished, and he did not mean to prejudice his influence under the next government. 'I should sacrifice my independence for ever, neutralise all good which otherwise I might do under a change of Government, and yet not be in office long enough to carry out the reforms,' he confided to his son.[26] He had decided that to become a permanent associate of the CID would serve better.

Early in October the King summoned Lord Roberts and Haldane to Balmoral to confer with Balfour and Esher about the future of the CID. Roberts disclosed his scheme, which in Esher's view boiled down to nothing, but if he resigned as the sole permanent member of the Committee its continuance under the new government would obviously be greatly jeopardised. In Haldane's presence Esher's proposal was discussed and drawn up in a formal memorandum to Balfour. It envisaged two permanent sub-committees of the CID, one being to consider combined naval and military operations, which had been more or less approved though as yet without any 'outside' members, the other a new sub-committee to consider 'Certain scheduled recommendations made by the Elgin Commission', a phrase suggestive of another Esher committee.[27] From Esher's accompanying observations it is clear that he was really arguing for the addition of outside members like himself to the CID. He thought the CID could conduct many of the inquiries hitherto delegated to royal commissions which might be beyond the scope of the cabinet or individual departments. The cabinet's function was to 'arrive at decisions upon facts or theories carefully presented in concrete form', and with its increasing burden of work it 'cannot...enquire into, nor ...construct elaborate schemes involving much technical consideration'.[28] This reasoning was very plausible but did not cover the real character of the activity of the sub-committees of the CID in Esher's hands. This was not technical so much as political, secret and irresponsible. Even the military 'conversations' with France which remained for several years a secret for the majority of the Liberal cabinet were in

175

essence a political decision. Churchill and Lloyd George rightly felt that the cabinet was never called into 'genuine consultation' on these matters.

As a prospective minister, angling for the post of Lord Chancellor, Haldane's presence at Balmoral was questionable. His revelations about Campbell-Bannerman alarmed Esher, for the prospective Liberal premier was said to have as his only intimate friends the arch-enemies of the Esher committee, Lord Haliburton and Sir Ralph Knox. It seemed doubtful whether he would consent to chair the CID. The imperialist Liberals were perhaps favourably disposed to the continuance of the Committee, but it seemed that something had to be done to strengthen its position. Of this the King had been persuaded, and he had taken up the suggestion that Esher and Milner should be appointed as permanent members. Balfour however left Balmoral without agreeing either to this proposition or to the establishment of such outsiders in a special sub-committee. Esher pursued him with another letter a week later, but without effect. Only the sub-committee for combined naval and military operations had been approved, and Balfour was inclined to leave things as they were. But Sandars might persuade him:

Esher-Sandars, 7 October 1905:[29] Haldane says Campbell-Bannerman...is secretly hostile to the Committee. Asquith, Grey and he are strongly in favour of it, only they want to give it a more 'scientific' and less 'political' complexion.

The King wants to strengthen *while you are in office* the permanent element. He thinks Lord Roberts and one or two others should be appointed 'permanent' members for three years...

My fear is that Campbell-Bannerman will let it die of *inertia*: that Clarke will be disgusted, and accept a governorship: and that *then* Spenser Wilkinson will take his place, or the committee will revert to what it was, a spasmodic meeting of cabinet ministers..

We drive over the 'Devil's Elbow' (sounds like Arnold-Forster).

Esher was working with Sir George Clarke on a paper which would explain and justify the CID, and the weakness of the 'expert' element was all too apparent in the very restricted list of such men who had actually attended meetings. In a marginal note Esher suggested as

176

'experts' who might constitute a strengthened permanent element of the CID Lord Roberts, Admiral Fisher, Milner, Curzon and Cromer, the last being justified as 'not disqualified' by belonging to neither political party. Such people were strange substitutes for the best scientific and military opinion of the country.

What Esher assumed, rightly or wrongly, to be the reason behind Haldane's demand for a more expert and less political CID (he did not for a moment take this as a reflection on Clarke or himself) was their fear of being pushed by an anti-imperialist majority of the next Liberal cabinet into too pacific defence policies. Hence the common factors in his list of the 'expert' or 'permanent' element were proconsular imperialism and militancy. This appears plainly in his confidential response to Clarke's paper:

> *Esher-Clarke, 12 October 1905:*[30] I have read your note upon the Defence Committee with great interest. May it not be possible that Haldane and Asquith have been influenced by a feeling that their views will not find adequate expression in the next Defence Committee. Suppose Campbell-Bannerman is Prime Minister, and neither Grey, Asquith nor Haldane are at the War Office or Admiralty, the 'radical' section of the cabinet might dominate the Committee of Defence.
>
> Although I think you are probably right, and that possibly the lesser evil is to retain the *political* complexion of the Defence Committee unaltered, still the evil must be admitted, and faced. It is too soon to expect that men of all parties will agree to allow defence questions to remain outside the arena of party politics...
>
> I shall show your memorandum to the King.

Against the original Campbell-Bannerman idea of the Defence Committee, as a public forum for the justification of the army and navy estimates, Esher put forward the idea of the CID as the germ of a body that 'will represent the *Empire* for purposes of defence'.[31] This was always his justification for the candid admission of its predominantly political role:

> *Esher-Clarke, 10 October 1905:*[32] Lansdowne...said that you are, at present, holding the most important post in the Empire, and to desire *anything* else, is to show want of true perspective...

What we have got to do is to *fight* Campbell-Bannerman, Knox and Haliburton: and *not to be disheartened.*

The CID is far more powerful than I hoped to see it within two years of our first committee meeting! We shall, I hope, live to see it, under your auspices, eclipsing the cabinet in questions of defence...While you are in Whitehall Gardens we hold the fort. Nothing can remove you, for the King would back us up...

The suggestion which Esher made for a new Esher committee constituted as a sub-committee of the CID had a curious sequel, but one all too typical of Balfour's methods. Lord Roberts had in August asked Balfour to refer his scheme for compulsory military training to a sub-committee of the CID composed of 'representatives of the various state departments, one or two of the largest employers of labour, and some soldiers'.[33] Later at Balmoral Balfour had agreed to refer Roberts's scheme to a sub-committee, but Roberts soon found that this was to be the sub-committee conceived by Esher. No one knew better than he what that meant, and he promptly refused it. Balfour then offered that representatives from the Board of Education should attend the next CID meeting to comment on Roberts's proposal for rifle drill in schools, but again Roberts refused, knowing that the Board had already found the idea objectionable. He now asked to give his reasons to the CID for resigning his place and appealing to the public. This request was to be conveyed by Esher, who flashed a warning to Sandars asking to confer with him the next day (Monday).[34] One might well detect the tactics of the secretarial net in what happened at the CID's eightieth meeting that Tuesday.[35] Balfour was absent, and Roberts himself took the chair. He was met by several objections from members who had only received their copies of his scheme that morning, and who demanded time to consider it. His resignation was not accepted, but nevertheless Roberts tendered it to the King and to Balfour by letter. Balfour replied ten days later, with a manifesto carefully composed in case of publication:

Balfour-Roberts, 20 November 1905:[36]...you have used phrases which to the careless reader seemed to indicate that in your view the regular army was less prepared for war than at other periods of our history...

This of course is conscription, indistinguishable from the con-

scription which prevails on the Continent except by the fact that
it is less efficient because the training is for ten months...and
more onerous because it requires every citizen in case of need to
serve oversea...

I am...quite ready to admit that our army is wholly insufficient
in point of numbers to carry on a great continental war, unaided
by Continental forces...The case of India is different...

Balfour was now within a few days of resignation, and he managed to
delay the announcement of Roberts's resignation until it seemed to
form part of the dissolution of his government.[37]

Esher had been called in to the series of conferences which Balfour
held to decide when and how to quit office. As soon as an immediate
resignation was decided on, Balfour mentioned Roberts's resignation
from the CID and Esher's going on to it, whereupon Esher made his
acceptance conditional on Sir John French being appointed also.[38] In
this way he avoided being sole caretaker, and established something
like a permanent element. He was already busily involved in the
Liberals' cabinet making, through his close association with John
Morley and J. A. Spender, with whom he lunched the same day. As
an important anti-imperialist Morley held a key position, and by
refusing to serve under Asquith as Leader of the Commons, he obliged
the Liberal imperialists to consent to the retention of Campbell-
Bannerman in the Lower House. In Spender's presence Morley asked
Esher if he would accept the War Office. Esher was flattered but
unmoved. 'To have an offer by one PM and a feeler from the other
side is an adventure almost unparalleled. And how silly these politicians are.'[39] As the newly appointed caretaker and umpire of the CID he
no doubt felt as he had in 1903 that: 'Power and Place are not often
synonymous.'[40]

The change of government, in which Esher played an important
role behind the scenes, hardly disturbed the continuity of the CID
and its policies. After Balfour had tendered his resignation to the
King Esher accompanied him back to Downing Street for his last
informal conference. He declined a GCB on the ground that to appear
on a Unionist honours list would brand him as a 'spy left behind by
Arthur',[41] and he explained to Campbell-Bannerman that while he
had been 'most intimate' with Balfour he would work as loyally with
the Liberal government. His eldest son, Oliver Brett, had worked on

the *Westminster Gazette* under Spender, and Esher now placed him as an additional private secretary under Morley (when Morley took the India Office). This was to prove an invaluable connection with India, hitherto the key to CID policy.

Even more vital a concern was the establishment of a new secretarial nexus to replace the loss of Sandars. Esher found that Captain Sinclair, Campbell-Bannerman's private secretary, was a man of 'good easy manners, and excellent sense' who readily confided the problems of cabinet formation, and these were discussed freely when Esher took him to confer with Lord Knollys.[42] The distribution of offices which had been proposed included Haldane as Attorney-General or Home Secretary and Herbert Gladstone was Secretary for War, which Esher condemned as 'thoroughly bad'. Haldane only got the War Office by asking for it with the King's support.[43] Once this had been settled Esher had a 'long and most satisfactory talk' with Haldane who professed to be 'willing to be nobbled' by the Esher committee, whereupon Esher summoned the former secretary of the Committee, Sir Gerald Ellison, and asked him if he would like to be Haldane's private secretary. 'This would be a great stroke,' he observed, and it succeeded.[44] Haldane liked Ellison and promised that he would rely on Esher and Clarke, having been given a free hand in regard to the CID by the Prime Minister. He even seemed ready to implement Balfour's army scheme:

Clarke-Esher, 10 December 1905:[45] Haldane had been here some time when Mr Balfour arrived. Both were pleased and the situation was very interesting. Mr Balfour in his charming manner told Haldane where the difficulties lay, spoke fully of his scheme, and explained why it was not carried out, and...indicated the direction in which he had wished to move.

Will it not be strange if we got Mr Balfour's policy carried out by C.-B.? He had read our report carefully and was much impressed by it...I believe he will work in with it as we should wish, more especially if he has Ellison at his elbow...

I have urged on Haldane to take the military members into his confidence from the first...

The next day, when Esher brought Ellison along, he also suggested a programme for Haldane, which included 'estimates and the Militia' in

1907. More immediately he suggested the general staff, and a 'striking force'.[46]

Apart from Haldane, the two important members of the CID in army concerns were now Morley and Sir John French, C-in-C at Aldershot. With his son Oliver Brett as Morley's private secretary and his son Maurice Brett as French's ADC, Esher could keep these men, neither of whom was particularly adept in military politics, well in hand. French was already beholden to Esher for getting him made a permanent member of the CID, and he was destined for the highest appointments—Inspector-General with the presidency of the Selection Board, CIGS and C-in-C of the British expeditionary force. Another protégé of Esher's was Douglas Haig, and he immediately got Haldane's consent for him to come home and replace Hutchinson. Out in India Lord Kitchener might have seemed a dangerous and enigmatic figure, who had just worsted Curzon and toppled his career as Viceroy. In that dispute Esher, writing to Kitchener, claimed to take his side, though he had recently discussed with Curzon as his old friend 'Kitchener's character and methods...showing the unscrupulous use which he makes of any means to an end', and had agreed that he was the 'type of man' who caused others' downfall and would fall himself.[47] Even so, Esher offered Kitchener advice as to how to avoid unfavourable publicity, and encouraged him to write 'full and privately' to Morley. His letter contained a significant sentence: 'I hope that now, the scheme for the army, which I have had much at heart, will have a fair trial.'[48] He had certainly created the right 'set-up' for that.

Before the new government had gone to the polls and while ministers were scattered on electioneering tours the sudden invasion of France remained in prospect. The Moroccan crisis seemed to be being worked up by Germany to exploit the discomfiture of Russia at the hands of the Japanese. The French were worried lest Grey should prove less staunch to the Entente than Lord Lansdowne had been, and in any case it was uncertain whether the Entente implied military aid to France in the case of a German invasion. In this atmosphere *The Times* military correspondent, Repington, published an article on 27 December 1905 intended as a warning to Germany. Dining with the French military attaché the following day, Repington found that Huguet expected a German attack, possibly through

Belgium, but did not realise that a violation of Belgian neutrality would sway British opinion in favour of war.[49]

The initiation of the Anglo-French military and naval 'conversations' at this time has been described as 'one of the most obscure, as well as one of the most important, episodes in the recent history of British foreign policy'.[50] The first intimation of British interest in such talks occurs in Esher's letter to King Edward of 14 December, relating a remark made by Clemenceau the previous day.[51] Accordingly Esher convened an extraordinary 'conference' of the permanent element of the CID on 19th to which Clarke brought various 'Fisheresque' projects having failed to elicit much interest from the Admiralty. It is notable that at this stage the idea of concerting Anglo-French plans before the outbreak of war was rejected. A prearranged naval plan was regarded as 'at present impracticable'. Also it was reasoned, in marked contrast with the view shortly to be adopted, that unless Belgium were involved, there would be little point either in sending the Channel fleet to effect landings in the Baltic (one of Clarke's ideas) or transporting the Aldershot force to France. 'Neither course would be likely to confer any real advantage upon our allies in the great battles which would be fought on the frontier, while the second…might be unpopular in this country.' The conclusion of the conference was simply that more discussion between the British War Office and the Admiralty was needed.[52]

How exactly Repington and his friend Huguet, the French military attaché in London, got drawn into close and secret discussions with Esher and Clarke during the ensuing weeks is still open to surmise. Repington was ideally placed, as a leading military journalist, to make tentative and unofficial overtures. He was well qualified to attempt to gauge the military implications of the British treaty obligation to Belgium, having been both a military attaché in that country and an officer in British military intelligence who still retained personal connections with officials in the War Office. Huguet was pressing for assurances from Grey and it was reasonable to assume that if the French could be assured that the violation of Belgium would almost certainly bring Britain into the war, their general staff would be able to undertake that they would not be the first to invade Belgium. It is highly probable that Esher, having won Haldane's confidence, was anxious to test Grey's views, about which he would have received second-hand accounts through Ellison, who accompanied Haldane on his election tour. What is known is that Repington presumed to send an express letter to Grey on 29 December reporting Huguet's ideas, and on the following day he lunched with Esher and 'discussed the whole situation'.[53] Clarke, who was in Bournemouth, was now involved at Esher's suggestion, and his reply to Repington received on 1 January approved an approach to the French embassy while disapproving of 'the idea of our joining the French Army in case of war, and also of our supporting the Belgian Army unless Germany violated Belgium'.[54] Repington's mission was to muster ideas for a questionnaire which Huguet would take to Paris and place before the Conseil Supérieure de la Guerre. 'I do believe we can trust him absolutely,' Clarke wrote to Esher on 2 January: 'Except we three, however, it is best *no one* should know anything.'[55] The final paper was completed when the three met on the 5th at Whitehall Gardens. It was daringly simple and inquisitive and diplomatically indiscreet, touching on the disposal of captured shipping and colonies, the allocation of command, and the expected German line of advance. On the following day Esher presided over a second CID conference which was now concerned with the immediate despatch of the Aldershot force, even to the extent of mobilising it in France to save time. The conference dismissed the Baltic foible as 'impracticable' and laid down that: 'Any military co-operation on the part of the British army, if undertaken at the outset of the war, *must* take the form of either an expedition to Belgium or of direct participation in the defence of the French frontier.'[56]

Esher was no doubt complying with the thinking of Grey and Haldane. Grey inclined to support war in the event of a German attack on France, while Haldane shared his conviction that Anglo-French military talks should proceed on an official footing immediately, subject to the consideration that the Prime Minister opposed them and the government was dispersed. Esher must have known this, and it enabled him to overrule his fellow CID member, Sir John French, and also Clarke, who in any case had no vote. Hence at its final meeting on 12 January the CID conference considered the French replies brought back by Huguet, and directed that Grierson, who was present as Director of Military Operations, should prepare plans of the 'utmost completeness' for sending the Aldershot force to France, where it would entrain 'on the twelfth day'. If employed on the French frontier the force would be placed 'under the general control of the

G

French C-in-C'.[57] There are indications that both Clarke and Sir John French disliked these decisions,[58] though not for the reasons which would have caused a public furore, had they been known.

It is puzzling how Grey and Haldane induced Campbell-Bannerman to accept the need for military and naval 'conversations', and even more surprising that they managed to involve him in their high-handed presumption in not bringing the question before the cabinet. In agreeing to make the secret talks official, Campbell-Bannerman did indeed insist that there should be a written understanding that no obligation to France was incurred. But the matter was not so simple as that, as time showed, and the fact remains that Esher on his own responsibility had promoted or allowed one of the most fateful departures of the age. It was a triumph for his conception of the CID as a body which could place strategic interests above politics and boldly follow the logic of a situation.

Nine

The Creation of the Expeditionary Force

The very idea of a 'striking force' was abhorrent to certain sections of the Radicals and even of the 'blue water' school, so that these with Churchill's support were credited in 1908 with a plan to reduce what Haldane himself had been obliged to call the 'Imperial police' to a mere 10,000 men, the scale of so many small expeditions sent out in Victorian times. The public at large had no more idea of the import of the Anglo-French military 'conversations' than had the bulk of the Liberal cabinet, and so the term 'expeditionary force' which Repington claimed to have coined had comforting associations with the army's traditional police actions. It was therefore something of a surprise that Haldane's army reorganisation, embodied in an army order of January 1907[1] and in the final form of his Territorial and Reserve Forces Bill of the same year, should have yielded the huge force of 170,000 men able to take the field in a matter of days. The creation of such a force by Haldane, a flourishing lawyer who was not even entitled to wear a Volunteer uniform, was also a surprise. For it is only by following the secret aspects of strategic planning that one sees this outcome as natural.

Haldane has been criticised in his own lifetime and after as somewhat tricky. He struck Esher as being rather managing. In army matters he might easily have been a plagiarist of the German methods, about which he knew something, or a simple enthusiast for economy. But like Asquith he had the lawyer's habit of taking other men's ideas and making the best of a case as it stood. He succeeded because success was his chief aim and because he did not mind implementing other people's ideas and bowing to circumstances. He was the very antithesis of Arnold-Forster, and when the Military Members asked him what scheme he proposed he told them he 'was a young and

blushing virgin united to a bronzed warrior and that it was not expected by the public that any result of the union should appear until
at least nine months had passed'.[2] Esher was apprehensive at first that
Haldane would undo the general staff scheme which he had forced
on the previous War Minister: he reminded Haldane that his own
memorandum, a copy of which he gave him to study, was designed
for 'our peculiar island race' with an army officered in the voluntary
system 'by a caste, with caste prejudices'.[3] He need not have bothered,
for Haldane's general staff order of September 1906 was substantially
the same as the plan published by Arnold-Forster.

Haldane's immediate task was to effect a reduction in the army
estimates, which Clarke proposed to do by a large reduction in the
regular army. Haldane himself proposed to follow Clarke's scheme
and the general definition of the purposes of the army as it had
emerged under Balfour, and he swallowed Clarke's plan for territorialising the Militia. This would have meant that large formations
of a second-line army for foreign service would be provided fully
officered and equipped by the new local associations. Esher flatly
rejected both these proposals:

Esher-Haldane, 4 February 1906:[4] I have now read your memorandum and Sir George Clarke's...With the exordium...I entirely
concur...but with his conclusions I do not agree.

The gist of his memorandum[5]...is a considerable reduction in
that portion of the regular army which requires the highest
degree of training...

I hope that on re-consideration he will agree that until you
have not only prepared a definite scheme for galvanising the
militia into life, and for providing for expansion of the military
forces of the Crown, to meet the exigencies of a great war...the
regular army should not be reduced in numbers...

Your second memorandum contains a suggestion...which if you
will allow me to say so...requires careful consideration. As I
understand it, you propose to create a territorial army which
would be raised largely by the efforts of local associations on the
Cromwellian type. This military force would as I understand be
paid and trained and possibly commanded through the medium of
these local associations. This is indeed a 'new model' according
to our modern ideas...

You must not suppose that I am hostile to the idea, for I think your suggestion may contain the germs of what may prove to be a perfectly healthy growth...

...expansion to meet the exigencies of a great war must be governed by the possible necessity of sending abroad a force of not less than 250,000 men within the first year...

Esher conceded that 'some reduction' in the fourteen redundant battalions of the line might be made provided the money saved was 're-appropriated to the strengthening of the first and second line armies, i.e. the regular forces and the Militia, by adding to the number of regular trained officers'.

In further conferences at Whitehall Gardens Haldane met Esher's objections by agreeing that the territorial army should be commanded by regulars and financed by Treasury grants:

Esher-Haldane, 14 February 1906:[6] What you said to us at our last meeting removed the objections which I ventured to point out to the idea of a second line army under local command and control.

As I understand, your suggestion now is that the territorial army should be an amalgamation of yeomanry and volunteers administered by local associations, formed partly by nomination and partly by elected members, but commanded and trained by the regular officers of the big commands...Your expectation is that under a system of this kind the volunteers would increase in numbers...They would be available primarily to man the coast defences and resist raids, but they might also in a great national emergency provide men—even if they could not provide cadres —for re-inforcing an army...oversea.

Haldane was obviously completely in the hands of his advisers, and the only question was which of these would come out on top. Esher had let Clarke have his say and expound the Balfour scheme which Clarke wished to develop in the direction of local autonomy while expecting his 'citizen militia' to be capable of fighting overseas in complete formations. Now in a long paper Esher at last played his own hand and revealed his own ideas which had been all along incompatible with those of Clarke:

Esher-Haldane, same date:[7] ...we should no longer think of a regular army plus the auxiliary forces...[but] a regular army composed of the first and second line for service oversea, and a territorial army for the purpose of manning the defences of our great ports at home, and of providing the largest possible imperial reserve... Behind these...we should have physical and simple military training in schools...

...you will find a very obvious 'caste' distinction between the regulars and militia on the one hand and the volunteers on the other... Men of the line and of the militia are drawn mainly from the poorer inhabitants of the great towns... Volunteers and yeomanry...are recruited from the comparatively well-to-do classes... It is a piece of good fortune that this natural grouping of the army...should correspond with the artificial grouping which you desire to bring about...

The territorial army was thus to be the preserve of the 'classes' who would come forward in large numbers if local patriotism and the lieutenancies of the counties or the public schools were appealed to. The OTCs would be the recruiting ground for officers, while the transport, medical, engineering, electrical, and other specialised services which would need rapid expansion in war would be represented more strongly among the skilled and professional classes of the territorial army than among the Militia or regulars. With conscription this consideration would not matter, but under the voluntary system the regular army did not attract skilled men.

The Militia in Esher's view was needed not for 'expansion' but for the immediate support of the regular army. He claimed that the 'tendency of the Cardwell-Wolseley' reforms was to 'draw the militia battalions of the territorial unit into closer connexion with the battalions of the line...in regimental *esprit de corps*, in training and even in dress'. This should be taken further towards the 'ideal' of 'complete interchangeability of officers and men in war, and as complete unification in peace as the different terms of service...shall permit'. Militia battalions should be brigaded with battalions of the line for manoeuvres. They should be soldiers, admittedly only partially disciplined and trained, rather than 'civilians trained to bear arms'. 'Thus,' he told Haldane, 'they should not form part of your territorial army, and the line which bisects the armed forces...according to your general

188

idea should be drawn below and not above the Militia.' This brought Esher into direct conflict with Clarke's most cherished idea of a territorial Militia:

Esher-Haldane, same date:[8] As a second line you would have an improved Militia, stiffened by...trained regular officers interchangeable and interchanged with the officers of the affiliated first line battalions. In peace these second line battalions... would not be liable to be sent abroad, but in war they would after embodiment... The purposes for which they would be primarily utilised would be to provide drafts and repair losses...[or]...as battalion units...

Sir George Clarke, I am aware, believes such a plan as this to be fatal to the efficiency of the Militia. He holds the opinion most strongly that the Militia should not be closely associated with the first line army, but that it should be a county force raised and nurtured under county auspices, as far as possible, removed from the central military authorities. He is in favour of militia brigades under distinct staffs, trained and commanded as large and distinct units... I venture to think that such a policy would be retrograde, and would have the fatal defect of drying up one of the most fruitful springs of recruiting the first line...and would leave the field army without a reserve in war from which its losses can be made good.

It was the ambitious size of the 'field army' and the intention of keeping it in the field for a year and 'making good the losses of a campaign' which demanded a supporting militia of the first line. Esher reminded Haldane of their recent decision to 'keep nine divisions of infantry and two cavalry brigades trained, staffed and equipped with the proper proportion of artillery, which can be sent from this country...at the shortest possible notice, without calling Parliament together, and without considerable delay and economic disturbance... That this can be done you have satisfied yourself is the case.'[9] The expeditionary force was later announced in Parliament as consisting of six of the larger Continental-style divisions and one cavalry brigade.

The dimensions of the expeditionary force had been determined by the CID after long consultations with Kitchener as to the needs of

India. But the defeat of Russia by Japan, the reassurance to the position in the East afforded by the renewed Japanese treaty, and the isolation and danger of France emphasised by the Moroccan crisis, had entirely altered the strategic scene. The undertaking to send Kitchener eight divisions now seemed an embarrassingly useless commitment, while the capacity to give immediate assistance to France and Belgium in the critical first weeks after a German attack seemed much more valuable. The military 'conversations', and the informal contacts of the general staff—notably Henry Wilson's with Foch or Repington and Esher's with Huguet—acquainted British military thinking with the startling fact that a new Franco-German land war would be lost and won in the first month if not the first fortnight. But the British public would not have accepted an expeditionary force maintained solely for this purpose, and so Haldane, who from his close association with Grey knew very well what the French liability might be, represented the force as an impartial police. The soldiers in general believed in conscription or other forms of compulsory military training while Henry Wilson at the Staff College set up anti-German war games and disseminated the French view that sea power would be largely irrelevant and that only massive British assistance on land would be of any use in a war against Germany. Esher himself believed that the voluntary system was failing but he was determined to make the best of the existing political opportunities. He regarded the territorial volunteers as potentially having a 'moral effect out of all proportion to their real value as a military instrument'. He knew that Douglas Haig shared the same idea of sympathetically 'rooting' the army in the people, and he persuaded Haldane to bring him back from India. 'If *you* get back here in that [Hutchinson's] place for two years the whole tone of army officers and their education will have undergone a change which will recast the army.'[10]

Haig was introduced to Haldane in June and his first position was Director of Military Training. He became a valuable assistant to Esher, who had been appointed by Haldane as chairman of an informal inquiry into the territorial aspect of the army scheme. The terms of reference of this 'duma' were described by Esher to the King as 'the substitution of County Associations for the Commanding Officers of Yeomanry and Volunteer units' as the administering authority, and 'The endeavour to mobilise and support certain units of the Regular army, especially Army Service Corps, Engineer and

Medical units, which cannot under existing circumstances be mobilised at all, by means of half-trained men'.[11] Esher had got his way, and he made sure his plan was not upset by packing the Committee with regular officers. His only difficulty was 'to keep Clarke from making a flank attack'.[12] The Committee's report kept command and inspection in the hands of the General Officers of the Commands, and excluded the Militia. The function of the Territorial Army was defined as 'expanding' the regular army in a great national war. The Militia were to be for the 'support' of the regular army in lesser wars, or while the nation was being enlisted and trained in arms.[13]

The value of Esher's conception of the Militia was demonstrated to Haldane when it saved him from the necessity to cut down the artillery and gained him a minor parliamentary triumph. As Arnold-Forster's new field guns were delivered in large batches it would have been necessary either to have largely increased their supporting ammunition columns—for they consumed ammunition more quickly—or to admit that they could not be mobilised. By using militia garrison artillerymen Haldane was able to claim in July that he was increasing the batteries available by twenty-one while effecting a saving.[14] The same kind of economy was possible in the case of the line battalions, and so Haldane in the end only reduced eight of these, and one battalion of guards, largely through Esher's tact and resourcefulness. In June Haldane had proposed the reduction of thirty batteries of artillery to a two-gun basis but by 10 July Esher was able to report to the King that eighteen of these and two horse-artillery batteries were reprieved.[15]

It was obvious that Esher's plan for the Militia would be fiercely contested by the partisans who wished to preserve the auxiliary forces in their historical role. In June the CID discovered a 'radical difference of opinion' between the Army Council and the officers of the Militia 'as to the proper functions of this force'.[16] When the 'duma' reported the next month Esher commended as a beneficial political effect of his territorial scheme the breaking up of the Volunteer forces. But the Militia and Volunteers could be expected to make common cause in resisting the whole army reorganisation. When another committee composed of Militia officers, with Lord Roberts, Haig and Ellison as members and Esher in the chair, considered the territorial scheme, it failed to reach agreement about how the Militia might support the expeditionary force. Haldane tried to gain support for the territorial plan in Lancashire, but failed. He decided to abolish the Militia and create a 'Special Reserve' out of the best battalions. At the same time he shrank from the task of trying to bring the Volunteers—a far more influential political force than the Militia—under elected County Associations. Esher did not allow him to slide out of the territorial scheme merely because he feared the charge of being undemocratic, and urged him to make the County Associations, if necessary, the particular preserve of the Volunteers:

Esher-Haldane, 19 October 1906:[17] What we 'agreed on when we met' was that there was imminent danger of the country getting hold of the idea that you had 'gone back' on your original idea...

What is wanted is a plan which seizes hold of the imagination of the public...

It is over-sanguine to suppose that the GOCs of the big commands and the Volunteer COs...are going to produce for you the Douglas Haig TA.

He wants to be able...at the end of twelve months to place an army of 900,000 men in the field, and keep it there for five years...

Competition between counties, as you originally suggested, might have a chance.

However, this is my swan-song. If you decide to make the Associations 'advisory bodies' with no real powers...I have no more to say.

Haldane was advised to brave parliamentary criticism and place the Associations in the hands of the Volunteers and Yeomanry and other nominated members.

For a brief period the political opposition of the Volunteers and Haldane's hesitation made Esher despair of the voluntary system. 'As you know,' he wrote to Knollys, 'I am a confirmed believer in *compulsion*; but until a final experiment has been tried...there is not much hope of getting Parliament or the Country to agree...'[18] It could only be implemented, he believed, through local institutions, as compulsory education had been. But he was oppressed by a sense of urgency, seeing in the course of international affairs the certainty of a war with Germany:

192

Esher-Duchess of Sutherland, 7 September 1906:[19] There is a bad time coming for soldiers; for the laws of historical and ethnographic evolution...require that we shall fight one of the most powerful military empires that has ever existed.

This is *certain*, and we have a very short period of preparation. I fear that proficiency in games, or in the hunting field, will not help our poor lads much when they have to face the carefully trained and highly educated German officers.

Esher therefore decided at this point to attempt to gather by private appeals to wealthy men a fund to pay lecturers and propagandists who would retain the appearance of independence while advocating compulsion. He told Lord Roberts of his plan, but the method was to be that of the hidden persuader, not the open orator. One of the men to whom he appealed was W. W. Astor,[20] to whom he wrote with his usual panache: 'I want £100,000—and I want it unconditionally...The object is to secure compulsory military training of the youth of the empire...We have now arrived at the critical stage, when the voluntary system has finally broken down...I am no believer in politicians or platform oratory. But there are methods in which I believe, and it is in order to try them that I want you to throw away...a sum which for you is almost negligible. I want five years and absolute secrecy.'[21] If the 'act of folly' achieved no result, it need never be known. But the King would be told of it, and if it succeeded it might be publicly acknowledged as 'one of the most romantic episodes of history'. As a further inducement, Esher undertook to send Astor 'all the recent private and official papers' on army expansion. But the appeal failed in this case, because Astor would not support the cause until the Unionists took it up. Almost a year later the project was still afoot, and although the Haldane scheme had by that time emerged from the Commons in the shape that Esher had wanted, it did not seem to him enough:

Esher-Lord Roberts, 28 August 1907:[22] I have been doing everything possible to raise secretly—which is our sole chance—a fund for the purpose we have so often discussed...

Although under a voluntary system Mr Haldane may achieve a partial success, and obtain very much what he asks for, no one knows better than you...that in the event of a great war, which is bound to come and in which the stake is the British empire, the numbers he aims at are quite inadequate...

I pointed out that we require writers and lecturers not 'labelled as paid agents', but with an appearance of independence...

So long as he remained an official member of the CID Esher was more or less precluded from advocating compulsion himself, and his public writings on the question remained mild and uncommitted.

Meanwhile the Haldane scheme was being embodied in one great Territorial and Reserve Forces Bill, which was scrutinised by a sub-committee of the CID in November 1906 with Esher in the chair, before which Haldane himself was examined. In explaining the report of this committee to Campbell-Bannerman, Esher found that the Prime Minister had not been able to understand Haldane's 'rhetorical rendering' of the scheme.[23] Considered in its political aspect the scheme presented the same kind of hazard that Balfour had experienced in the Commons, for Haldane had failed to placate either the Militia or the Volunteers. It was not certain that the government would stand behind it for, like Balfour, Campbell-Bannerman manifested the older style of leadership with limited liability for the measures of his own ministers. Esher found that he 'put his finger, in that quiet way he has, upon the weak points' but nevertheless got the impression that he would back Haldane. 'If that is so, our fat friend stands a good chance.'[24] But while Haldane might get round Howard Vincent's opposition in the Commons, he might easily be overturned in the House of Lords, where the Duke of Bedford might command a majority. The decision would probably rest with Balfour and Lord Lansdowne, who took their cue from Esher.

The scheme as it was finally approved by the CID and cabinet for presentation to Parliament embodied an important modification to Esher's original outline. Finding that the militia officers objected to providing drafts as opposed to complete units to supply the wastage of the line, Haldane had 'abolished' them, in their own estimation, by converting the best Militia into 'third battalions' forming a 'Special Contingent', while relegating the worst of the Militia and most of the former officers of the Militia to the Territorial Force. As the *Westminster Gazette* put it, the 'existing Militia material must be organised with the Regular Army and the Militia cadres handed back to their officers, to be filled up with a new force and organised with the

194

Territorial Army.'[25] The Territorial Army or 'second line' was to be a fusion of Militia and Volunteers receiving the same training, annual camps and occasional drills and exercises. The Volunteers objected that this 'National Militia' would become a 'County Council Militia' since Haldane proposed to place the County Associations more or less under the local authority. The militia officers objected that they would not recruit men under the new conditions. Haldane had in fact given way under two pressures, one from the militia officers who wanted complete units without being affiliated to the regular army, the other from his party which would not stomach a new non-elective *ad hoc* authority.

Neither Clarke nor Esher was pleased by this compromise. 'My faith in Haldane has been rudely shaken,' Clarke declared, 'and I believe he will get the army into a hopeless tangle from which someone else will have to extricate it. In that case the little that is good in his schemes will probably go overboard.'[26] Esher naturally welcomed the use of the best Militia as a special reserve in the first line, the main point he had pressed on Haldane, but he felt strongly that to make the County Associations the sport of local politics like the former School Boards, or even to hand them over to the Auxiliary Forces without War Office control, was to spoil much of the value of the territorial plan. However, the more stringent requirements of training and the statutory penalties were an advantage. The increased obligations which those citizens who came forward under the voluntary system incurred effectually cleared the way for making such obligations universal and compulsory.

There are indications that Esher hoped and even expected that the Bill as introduced to Parliament would be amended into the form he favoured. The *Westminster Gazette* where his son had held an important position positively invited the Militia to propose their alternative scheme while supporting Haldane personally.[27] The two basic principles which Haldane stuck to were derived from Esher, one being his historical interpretation of what the Cardwell plan for associating the Militia with the line had been, the other being the axiom that there must be only two armies and not three. Haldane was quite glad to enlist the active support of the opposition, and Esher saw to it that he got it. He kept Balfour fully informed of evolution of the plan, with Haldane's approval, and gave him his cue as to what to oppose:

195

Esher-Balfour, 9 January 1907:[28] This document will never see the light, but Haldane has allowed me to send it to you.

You will gather from it that the 'scheme' has two positions:

(a) To organise the *regular* forces of the Crown into six divisions with a *'reserve'* behind, i.e. one infantry battalion partly under *regular* officers, for every two battalions of the line.

This was the A.J.B. scheme of two years ago. This part of the scheme will succeed, I am convinced.

(b) A Territorial Army being a converted Volunteer force, under conditions which make it more than doubtful whether it will ever come into existence.

You will perhaps think the Report not over-enthusiastic.

Haldane will meet with a good deal of opposition. But, he will this year effect a large reduction in the cost of the army.

Was Haldane assuming that Balfour would treat this information as part of his watching brief on the CID or did he expect that it might be used to keep Balfour in control of the political opposition to the Bill? Certainly Balfour conducted an obligingly restrained opposition which concluded in a drastic amendment to the Bill which Haldane gladly accepted, for the result neatly forced the acquiescence of the Volunteer and Militia spokesmen. As opposite partners Esher and Balfour played a superb game.

The opponents of the Haldane scheme were quick to identify Esher as its real author, and in March the *Standard* in its leading article asserted that there was 'throughout the higher ranks of the army, a growing resentment of the influence which he is exercising at the War Office' and spoke of actions 'which do not originate with the Army Council or the Secretary of State'. The paper mentioned a correspondent who complained that Esher had 'considerable influence, and even, to some extent, an executive power without any sort of responsibility', specifying cases of promotion in which Esher had 'himself promised advancement'.[29] Haldane, it was said, was under his influence. The attack was not supported by any specific information but it alarmed Repington and disturbed the King. Repington guessed that it was inspired by Arnold-Forster, but it was no doubt welcome to the champions of the auxiliary forces also whom Arnold-Forster had castigated. What must have perplexed these exponents of the voluntary system was the strange way in which Lord Roberts came out openly

196

for the Bill, for they did not know of his secret understanding with Esher. The Bill's opponents rightly sensed that they were isolated. Arnold-Forster's bitter acerbity stood out in stark exception to the general tone of the Unionist benches.

Haldane himself was a good stage manager. He set up a special department at the War Office which dealt with publicity, while he gave privileged facilities to Repington, whose regular visits to the War Office and Whitehall Gardens were commented on. In return Repington undertook to become the informal editor of the *Army Review* and kept *The Times* on the side of the Haldane scheme. Never did a reforming War Minister have such a favourable press. Even in the Commons the criticism of the Bill was muted and helpful, thanks largely to Haldane's readiness to entertain any constructive amendments. A serious objection was put forward by Ramsay MacDonald against placing labour representatives on the County Associations who would find themselves becoming involuntary recruiting agents. Balfour seized on this point to agree that the County Associations could not be run locally without producing social discord, and in any case the 'leisured classes' in the counties already had their hands full.

Opinion was thus prepared to accept the final provision of the Bill, which greatly increased the control of the Army Council over the Associations. The Militia officers were brought to heel by the threat of county council control in the original Bill and of amalgamation with the Volunteers who would, under the equal conditions proposed, attract better recruits and consequently enjoy better prospects of establishing 'service units'. Hence at the report stage the Bill underwent a dramatic modification. Haldane agreed to allow twelve Irish and fifteen English Militia battalions to become fourth battalions of the line and supply 'relief units', and to absorb all the efficient bat-the British Navy, and that "Two Keels to One" was the basis of naval 124 would, he declared, 'arise phoenix-like in the form of the third and fourth battalions'.[30] The Bill as it went up to the Lords was very much in conformity with Esher's original scheme, and Haldane's aberrations from it had accidentally served to educate its potential opponents as to its advantages. To round off this very satisfactory episode Esher himself moved a final amendment to the Bill in the Lords which had the effect of permitting the County Associations to give financial aid to cadet corps out of non-parliamentary funds. This made sure that the OTCs were in a position to build up a reserve of officers, corresponding to the reserve of men. These numbered in 1914 over 20,000 drawn almost entirely from the universities and public schools.

The success of Haldane's Bill in the Commons coincided with Clarke's departure from the CID. He left the secretariat with a deep sense of grievance against Haldane and Repington and possibly Esher. Haldane he described as 'a visionary talker with a rooted belief in his power of manipulating men by petty diplomacy'.[31] Repington was 'a clever but not a fair controversialist. He has not really met his opponents at all but he may have dazzled the readers of the paper. He has done great harm and I feel keenly that he has gone very far to destroy my work of many years.'[32] He regarded Fisher's regime at the Admiralty as 'demoralising' through the abuse of patronage. His comments on his other fellow-Triumvir have not been encountered. Esher felt that Clarke would be a loss 'in many ways'.[33]

The passing of the Haldane scheme was the final consummation of Balfour's 'Invasion' paper presented to the CID, for it subordinated to the purposes of the expeditionary force the auxiliary forces at home which were officially declared to have been useless for repelling an invader. But Balfour had declared that there ought to be a sufficient number of troops at home to repel 'raids' and even to force an enemy to invade in strength. Even the 'blue water' school supported this basic minimum of home defence. But the 'bolt from the blue' school led by Roberts and Repington had been assiduously collecting information to prove that a large German invasion by eluding the navy was not by any means impossible. The question had really been prejudged by Balfour, and now a full CID inquiry into the chances of invasion was successfully demanded. There were those who claimed that the expeditionary force could only leave the country at an extreme risk, and it was certainly necessary to know how far the country could be safely denuded of troops and what was the largest enemy force that could hope to get past the navy.

The Admiralty's assessment was obviously the key to the question, but the Admiralty had no War Staff and Fisher as First Sea Lord proved quite unco-operative. He regarded the sub-committees on Indian defence and invasion as 'irresponsible' and invasion as a purely Admiralty concern until sharply reproved by Esher. Luckily the new Secretary of the CID, Sir Charles Ottley, had just been the Director of Naval Intelligence, and his knowledge must have done much to redeem Fisher's reticence and the First Lord's 'inconsequential and petulant asides' before the Invasion sub-committee chaired by Asquith. The inquiry was pursued until July 1908, but early that year its political import, already emphatic enough through the prominence of Roberts and Repington at its deliberations, was given even more point by a public storm over Fisher and the naval estimates.

The Radicals in the government and Liberal party demanded social reforms and a reduction of naval expenditure. Churchill had not yet taken alarm at the German peril, and Lloyd George viewed Fisher's escalation of naval competition by laying down the dreadnought class in 1904 as 'a piece of wanton and profligate ostentation'.[34] The First Lord, Tweedmouth, conscious of the German naval programme which was overtaking Fisher and which was to cause a sudden panic at the Admiralty at the end of the year, wanted an increase in the navy estimates, but the government decided against this. They were obliged to go further and dictate a reduction after being forced to accept an amendment to the Address. Lloyd George, L. Harcourt and McKenna formed a cabinet committee to effect the reduction, and while Harcourt threatened Fisher with dismissal and replacement by his arch-enemy Admiral Beresford, Lloyd George tried to get Fisher to accept the reduction as temporary.

Campbell-Bannerman had seemed to Esher to have already thrown away the margin of dreadnought superiority which Fisher had gained, building only two against Germany's four in 1907. The Prime Minister's strange and equivocal declarations and tolerant attitude to the Hague Conference's jugglings with naval disarmament were not reassuring.[35] On being fully informed by Fisher of this latest squeeze on the navy, Esher sent off an indiscreet letter to the Imperial Maritime League in reply to a request to join its council. The letter appeared in *The Times* as an attempt to justify Fisher:[36]

...on November 12 1903, nearly twelve months before Sir John Fisher went to the Admiralty as First Sea Lord, I went as his guest to Admiralty House at Portsmouth, and on this occasion he unfolded his plans for increasing the efficiency of the fighting fleet, for a redistribution of the fleet on strategic grounds, for a complete change in the *personnel* of the Navy...and generally for a scheme of naval reform [embodied in]...a series of memo-

randa in my possession...dated September and October 1903...
types of fighting ships, strategical problems, tactical ideas—
everything is dealt with and everything discussed...

There is not a man in Germany from the Emperor downwards,
who would not welcome the fall of Sir John Fisher...

The public was left wondering how Esher, then in no official
position, and Fisher the C-in-C at Portsmouth, could have been in a
position to deliberate so confidently on the future of the navy. Among
those who took notice of Esher's letter was the German Emperor
himself, who took the extraordinary step of writing personally to
Lord Tweedmouth, as First Lord: [37]

Now I am at a loss to tell whether the supervision of the founda-
tions and drains of the Royal Palaces is apt to qualify somebody
for the judgment of naval affairs in general. As far as regards
German affairs naval the phrase is a piece of unmitigated balder-
dash, and has created immense merriment in the circles of those
'who know' here...

Tweedmouth at first was flattered as the recipient of this undiplo-
matic missive with its Germanic humour and ambivalent tone, and
talked about it. At a levée Fisher came up to Esher in an excited
manner and exclaimed that Esher had 'the greatest compliment' paid
to him, nine pages full of abuse with corrections in the Kaiser's own
hand![38] But King Edward was annoyed and embarrassed by Esher's
indiscretion. Worse, the affair was splashed in *The Times* by
Repington as a German plot to influence the minister responsible for
the naval estimates.[39] Tweedmouth was compromised. But the incident, trivial in itself, strengthened the navalists by revealing the
force of public feeling. The naval estimates were perhaps never in
real danger, but Campbell-Bannerman and Asquith who succeeded
him in April were under strong pressure to switch the demand for
economy from the navy to the army. Lloyd George did not think it incompatible with his new position as Chancellor of the Exchequer to
threaten Esher that 'no reduction in army estimates next year means
no dreadnoughts'.[40] Churchill was machinating against Haldane, who
decided to hang on to the War Office rather than see his reorganised
army pared down further.[41] For Haldane was the one minister apart

from Grey who accepted the doctrine of 'two keels to one' *and* a 'second line of defence' in a good army.[42] Other Liberals and Radicals were apt to place their reliance in a strong navy alone and they were nearer the truth than they knew when they suggested that an army for offence would probably land the country in Continental entanglements. Only those who were following German affairs closely could realise the strategic reasons which were forcing Britain into military alignment with France, or the certainty of a German challenge.

Haldane had come to accept Esher's view that Germany presented Europe with a menace more formidable than had existed in the times of Louis XIV or Napoleon. 'She has a geographical "grievance" which *must* be remedied if she is to find expansion for her increasing population and it can only be remedied at our expense or at our risk, in the Low Countries or the Colonies.' Grey, Haldane and Asquith had therefore secretly resolved to come to the immediate military aid of France if Germany attacked.[43] But they could not advertise this resolve publicly. Instead Haldane encouraged the CID to revise its 'invasion' doctrine under the obliging pressure of Lord Roberts and Repington.

Earlier, in January 1908, the 'Invasion' sub-committee discovered that Napoleon had said that four auxiliaries were needed to match one professional soldier, while the navy put at 100,000 men the figure of the invading force they could guarantee to intercept. It was deduced that an invading force of less number would need to be opposed by some 300,000 auxiliaries at least.[44] By July 1908 after the threat to the army estimates had clearly emerged, the CID discovered that in the opinion of Roberts, Sir John French and indeed 'all soldiers' an invasion of 33,000 men would 'probably be successful'.[45] They had not seen this under Balfour. General Murray, who was in charge of home defence, showed that after Balfour's pronouncement all home defence against an invading force of over 5,000 men was put aside as unnecessary.

Curiously enough the Invasion sub-committee had been instituted at Balfour's request in order to consider 'new facts' supplied by Lord Roberts and others. In May Balfour himself gave evidence before it in the form of a speech traversing the whole area of home defence, a dazzling performance which left no room for questions or discussion. By November, in time for the planning of the estimates for 1909, the CID arrived at its final verdict. It endorsed Balfour's opinion that assuming the navy was kept at the two-power standard the country was safe from invasion, but with the novel condition that the forces kept for home defence should be sufficient to force an invader to come 70,000 strong. Only four of the six divisions of the expeditionary force could therefore be safely allowed to go abroad until the territorials had been embodied for six months.[46] The political implications of this new doctrine were pointed out by Esher to the King: that is, that Haldane's hand would be strengthened against those who would reduce the army, and that 'at least six' dreadnoughts should be laid down in each of the next four years.[47]

The real dimensions of the German naval programme were becoming clear. By a massive investment in plant, and by the rapidity with which the guns and essential parts of her ships were being completed, Germany appeared to be about to achieve a naval equality. McKenna, now First Lord, found that: 'If by any spurt Germany can once catch us up we have no longer any such superior building capacity as would ensure our superiority.'[48] He found that while Britain could lay down almost any number of dreadnoughts, she could only complete six a year, which was also Germany's capacity. By secrecy and financial juggling the German programme was being accelerated, so that they would have thirteen big ships in commission in 1911 and would 'probably have twenty-one big ships in commission in the spring of 1912'.[49] The position as explained by McKenna to Asquith on 3 January 1909 was 'most alarming' and 'would give the public a rude awakening should it become known'.[50] As a result of the revelation McKenna demanded six dreadnoughts in his estimates while Churchill and Lloyd George threatened to resign if more than four were included. The 'compromise' of eight dreadnoughts was really only a postponement, for it meant accepting four only while Lloyd George launched his ambitious budget, leaving the question of the other four in suspense.

McKenna had done his best to champion the Board of Admiralty, whose willingness to resign was however tempered by the consideration that Beresford, the protégé of the 'economists', had just been ordered ashore when the Channel Fleet was absorbed in the new Home Fleet. Beresford's long and disgraceful public feud with Fisher again came to a head and McKenna, like Haldane, was obliged to have recourse to Balfour for assistance through the mediation of Esher:

Memorandum by Sandars, 15 March 1909:[51] At 10 p.m. Esher came to see me. He had come straight from Fisher. It had been so arranged.

They are both deeply concerned in the line of your [Balfour's] speech tomorrow.

But first McKenna has written out a very good speech... But it may be toned down because he is to show it to some of his colleagues. He will *probably* admit the acceleration of the German programme.

Now Esher is *very* anxious that you should give prominence to the following inquiries in your speech...

1. Did the Germans anticipate this programme last November to the extent of four ships?

2. When did the Admiralty first become aware of this fact?

3. Are the government aware of the tonnage and speed of the four...German dreadnoughts; and if so, how do they compare with the most modern British ships of this type?

4. Is it not the fact that if *this year* we lay down eight dread-noughts, twenty is the margin we shall have in 1912: and if Germany lays down eight more this year they will have twenty-five...

I gather that the Admiralty *desire* that these questions be pressed and answered...[and] are determined to have sanction *forthwith* to place *immediately* orders for eight dreadnoughts. The government dare not refuse this demand or else McKenna and Co will resign...

The government...*want* to be forced—even Lloyd George—to surrender their virtue and be committed to eight ships at once...

Esher and Fisher are not anxious about the December 1910 comparison... But they are *really* anxious about 1912...

Balfour had exacted a pledge from Asquith the previous March, which Esher attributed to the beneficial effect of the Kaiser's letter to Lord Tweedmouth, that in the three years following they would en-sure British naval superiority, and he now had him in a trap. It was really a matter of exerting the pressure of public opinion on the 'economists', and Esher addressed himself to this task with alacrity. He created a society called the Islanders which was launched in March 1909 to propagate the 'idea that the British Empire floated on the British Navy, and that "Two Keels to One" was the basis of naval supremacy'.[52] The method was to reach the most influential men in the constituencies. It was to be 'perfectly secret and perfectly democratic' and as regenerative as the Jesuits, for Esher believed it wanted 'something like that, if we are not to go downhill as a nation'.[53] He was confident that his society would 'do more for a big navy than the Government bill and all the Admiralty bounce'. And certainly the Islanders became a power to be reckoned with in elections.

But the torpedo which Beresford had fired at Fisher was not without effect and might even be claimed to have sunk him. The specific charge against the First Sea Lord was that the country had 'never been prepared for war' during Beresford's command of the Channel Fleet. It seemed reasonable to McKenna that this should be submitted to a secret investigation by a sub-committee of the CID in order to silence public controversy while the matter was *sub judice*, and carry conviction when the result was announced. Accordingly Asquith summoned Crewe, Morley, Grey and Haldane, with McKenna and Fisher in attendance, to the inquiry's first meeting on 27 April. He had a week previously asked Esher to draw up a reference for the committee and suggested that he and Sir Arthur Wilson, a new 'permanent' member of the CID, should attend. But the two nonministers were not in fact invited. 'The queer thing...is that I have never had a line from Asquith to tell me of his change of mind, Esher wrote to Sandars. '...You can imagine how pleased I am *not* to have to adjudicate.'[54] Esher's absence did not do Fisher any good, and when the report appeared in August it criticised the Board of Admiralty for an 'absence of cordial relations' with Beresford and for not taking him 'sufficiently into their confidence as to the reasons for dispositions to which he took exception'. Beresford was more severely condemned for disobedience, but Fisher had been compromised. Esher had in fact come to believe that Fisher ought to resign in time to save his reputation. 'I agree that at the end of the year Jackie ought to go' he had observed to Sandars before the committee had convened.[55] But the report was a painful blow to Fisher:

Esher-Sandars, 24 August 1909:[56] I have just read a letter from poor Jackie to the King. He is frightfully sore! And I am not surprised. The government have not shown conspicuous courage! Haldane—whom I saw on Sunday—thinks the report a model of ingenuity. Other people—more blunt—would call it cowardice.

A month later Esher wrote 'very strongly' to Fisher urging him to retire quietly at the end of the year, while McKenna was pressing him to stay. Fisher at the last moment took Esher's advice.

Fisher's departure would hasten decisions as to the creation of an Admiralty War Staff, and the nature of the expeditionary force which would go immediately to France. In March 1909 Esher thought that he had made progress on both these problems. He was pleased with the talks on a naval War Staff which he had with Fisher and McKenna, and he had even got from Fisher an approving comment on a paper for the CID in which the question had been posed: 'Are we or are we not going to send a British Army to fight on the Continent as quite distinct and apart from Coastal raids and seizures of Islands etc. which the Navy dominate?'[57] Fisher thought that question was still an open one. But his failure to develop and expound the naval side of it before the CID while the army side progressed meant that his case went by default.

Meanwhile Esher had very reluctantly taken the chairmanship of the London County Territorial Association and was doing much to stimulate recruiting. He won the confidence of Northcliffe and the active support of the *Daily Mail* and was quick to exploit Du Maurier's play *An Englishman's Home*. 'You have shown in this matter of the Territorials that you understand the handling of that most delicate machine, the Press'[58] was a handsome compliment, coming from Northcliffe. Even so the recruiting was only somewhat over 60 per cent of the desired level. Lord Roberts had some ground for claiming that without compulsion the scheme would fail. But Esher like the good Liberal he was would not admit that compulsion would mark an advance in 'civilisation', for the voluntary system was the Roman ideal at the zenith of the republic. 'I should—in view of the great awakening during the past few years, so largely due to your efforts—prefer to give that system a little longer trial.' He might have added his own name also, for he had done as much as anyone to make the best of the military resources which a grudging democracy afforded, and to awaken the country to its approaching ordeal. 'You are a wonderful man, everything you touch succeeds,' the King had said to Esher after the success of the Territorial recruiting drive and the launching of the Islanders.[59] But the very success of the military and naval policies which he had helped to promote was inflating the costs of defence. Lloyd George was determined to see that these fell on the 'classes'. He was dressing up his Budget in scarifying clothes, and he was about to defend it in language offensive to dukes and landowners. The Unionists were provoked into the imprudent course of rejecting the Budget, an act that Esher condemned in advance. Its consequences were to involve him deeply in the kind of constitutional lore and conundrums that he loved, while it distracted the country from its external peril with dangerous results.

Ten

The Royal Prerogative

Lloyd George's great Budget of 1909 was revolutionary only if measured against the scales of fiscal proportion which vanished after 1914, or if viewed through the colourful distortions created by the partisans of tariff reform or free trade. It added only £14 million to taxation to meet the needs of defence as well as the unforeseen costs of existing old age pensions. Its modest land taxes on the unearned increment of urban land values were accepted by Radicals of the previous generation and were not so socialistic in principle as Harcourt's death duties or Asquith's special levy on unearned income. Its levy of a half-penny in the pound on undeveloped land was only of token significance. Yet it was forty-two days in committee in the Commons. The Lords threw it out on second reading without even considering its details. Asquith's biographer reasonably claims that if the former Chancellor of the Exchequer and not Lloyd George had had charge of it, it would have been ultimately passed.[1] One has therefore to ask why Lloyd George went out of his way to provoke the peers into rejection by his 'Limehouse' speeches. The answer is that he was pursuing a wider political strategy, aimed at securing one of two objectives. Either he would vindicate the fiscal priority of social reforms, which had been subordinated to the needs of defence and economy, and do so by a fiscal departure in a positively free trade direction: or he would provoke serious amendments or even the rejection of a budget by the House of Lords, and so place the peers manifestly in the wrong in the settlement of scores with them which was coming in the next election. He probably expected the Budget to pass, but there was plenty of time between April and November to appreciate and exploit the alternative possibility.

The curtailment of the powers of veto of the House of Lords was part of the Liberal programme in any case. Campbell-Bannerman's resolutions of 1907 were substantially similar to the ones which

Asquith introduced in 1910 before the Parliament Bill. By exploiting their large majority in the Upper House, using it to reject any important Liberal measure which they thought the public would not actively support, the Unionists had laid themselves open to retaliation. Lloyd George was as keen as anyone to place Mr Balfour's 'poodle' on a short leash. It was obvious that this would form a useful electoral cry, and Liberal governments had used the Lords' restriction of their measures as a motive for dissolving often enough. The difficulty in 1909 was that in the very likely event of the huge Liberal majority being cut down to moderate size in the coming election, and the Irish Nationalists consequently gaining the casting vote between parties, any project to curtail the peers' veto would look like an expedient to facilitate the passing of an Irish Home Rule Bill. By quarrelling with the peers on the Budget Lloyd George diverted the issue.

The 1909 Budget was therefore a trap, however inadvertently laid. Those who proposed to reject it knew that in so doing they forced an immediate election on the unfavourable ground of the violation of the Constitution by a House of Lords then in a trough of unpopularity. A Parliament Bill and sequential Home Rule Bill were also clearly foreseen as bound to follow a Liberal victory. To understand how the Unionists could risk such an outcome, one must be acquainted with J. L. Garvin's journalism and the rationale of the militant tariff reformers, with the free-food Unionists' fixation about 'socialism' and with the exigencies of Balfour's uncertain leadership. To Esher, who had never been a tariff reformer, the idea of rejecting the Budget seemed like madness. In September he thought 'the whole situation too perilously resembles that of 1640 for my taste.[2] The idea is that the General Election will practically destroy the Liberal majority. The whole thing is a political gamble. It may turn out a political blunder...I still think the end will be, not perhaps yet, a complete constitutional change—at the expense of the House of Lords.'[3]

The King proved to be 'strongly opposed to the Lords' throwing out the Bill' when Esher who was at Balmoral sat next to him at dinner,[4] and Esher suggested that it would be in keeping with Victorian precedents for him to consult Balfour and Lansdowne as to their intended course of action.[5] Asquith appeared two days later and agreed, and accordingly the King saw Balfour and Lansdowne at Buckingham Palace on 12 October. Sandars had seemed to disapprove of this interview, and indeed the Unionist leaders could not say anything positive at it for fear of encouraging Asquith:

> *Sandars-Esher, 13 October 1909:*[6] My sole point was to call attention to the inevitable publicity attending the step... If there had been a scintilla of doubt upon the constitutional question, I should not have ventured to write... But your letter, now that this grave matter has taken its place in constitutional history, leads me to make some respectful observations upon it...
>
> On previous occasions, I believe, a deadlock or impasse has actually occurred... There may be indications that the trend of political opinion upon our side is in the direction of momentous action, but the case is not ripe for decision...therefore...there is some danger lest the public mind should see in the audience which has been commanded, an effort to influence political action in the future...
>
> The ex-ministers were well aware that, when summoned to the Palace, they would be there with the approval of the Prime Minister. They were equally aware that every word they said would, in accordance with constitutional rule, be communicated to the Prime Minister...

Sandars would have preferred 'some discreet ambassador' to act as informal intermediary, a method which also had its dangers, as will be seen.

The Budget went to the Lords early in November, by which time its rejection was regarded as a certainty. Lunching with Balfour, Esher discussed the danger of this course to the Monarchy, but Balfour confidently rejected the idea. 'Hands laid on the Sovereign would mean the disruption of the Empire.'[7] On 30 November, the day the Bill was rejected, Haldane approached Esher to sound him on a plan which the cabinet were already considering for the King's intervention. They proposed to offer the King an alternative, either to surrender his right to create peers to the Prime Minister of the day, or to pledge publicly his support for a Parliament Bill by 'a promise to create a sufficient number of Peers to pass the measure'.[8] Esher told Haldane the former would be 'an abdication by the Sovereign of his Prerogative' and 'an outrage'. The latter proposal of threatening to swamp the recalcitrant peers was in Esher's opinion unprecedented. Queen Anne had created only twelve peers, and 'The case of 1832 is no precedent, as no peers were created, and it is by no means certain that the King would in the last resort have made them'. But what seemed most objectionable was the idea of a pledge before an election. 'In other words,' as Esher reported to Knollys, 'the Government wish to make the King a party to their dissolution programme. I cannot conceive a more monstrous proposal... The Sovereign's freedom of action should be unimpaired; and HM's ultimate decision will, of course, be guided largely by the result of the appeal to the country.'[9] Asquith was content to dissolve Parliament three days later, after passing a resolution condemning the action of the Lords as 'a breach of the Constitution and a usurpation of the rights of the Commons'.

The election was not to be held till 14 January, but Esher anticipated its result by three articles in *The Times* on the theme: 'If we are to substitute a written for an unwritten Constitution, the draft cannot be prepared by the caucus of any political party, or amid the dust of a general election.'[10] 'Personally' he declared, 'I do not believe that we can escape from the present political deadlock without a political revolution', which would transfer from unwritten usage to statutory regulation the relations of the two Houses of Parliament and 'possibly the Prerogative of the Crown'. But he argued that such a revolution would have to be approved by 'all classes...whose interests have hitherto been safeguarded by the habit of compromise and the practice of reasonable give and take which have characterised the nation'. He repudiated both the Liberals' contention that the Lords acted in a selfish class interest, and the Unionists' equally mechanistic notion that deadlocks could be resolved by the referendum. During the coming year the two main parties were to continue their dispute as to what should be the 'reserve power' in the Constitution, the Liberals wanting joint sittings of Lords and Commons contrived to ensure the majority rule of the party in office, the Unionists wanting to submit major constitutional or financial reforms to a referendum. Both parties seemed to be bent on subordinating the permanent interests of constitutional reform to the immediate demands of their political situation. What the controversialists called 'single chamber despotism' was necessary for the Liberals if they were to oblige their Irish Nationalist allies with Home Rule, while the referendum appealed to Balfour as the only available counter. In this factionary struggle the historical role of the Upper House was in Esher's opinion being overlooked, as were the defects of the Commons:

'Historicus'[11] *in Times, 6 December 1909:* [The House of Lords] represents, far more accurately than any great Liberal majority of the House of Commons, the fundamental conservatism of the English people, their wariness, their love of tradition, their adhesiveness to precedent, their denseness to 'ideas', their habitual preference for the evils they understand...their shrewd belief that the man who has something to keep is a safer guide than the man who has something to gain...

...the constitution of the House of Commons, its unwieldy size, its mis-representative character, its ludicrous over-representation of Ireland, its dangerous under-representation of the great centres of population, including London, its antiquated and unsystematic grouping, its fantastic rules of procedure, and its unbusinesslike habits, render a thorough examination of the House of Commons an imperative condition of any constitutional change in the House of Lords.

He claimed that the Lords were 'man for man...more than the equal' of the elected representatives of the people, and 'responded as a rule more surely to the changing temper of the nation'. The basis of such a claim could not be rational, of course, but Esher was the first to admit that such assertions rested on an understanding of history. 'The test of ideas,' he asserted, 'is not their originality but their weight. Novel ideas, like cleverness, are becoming a drug in the market.' Was not his old chief, Devonshire, more acceptable to his countrymen than the most brilliant of his contemporaries?

The polling lasted for a fortnight from 14 January, and reduced the Liberal majority from 146 to 42, thus rendering Asquith dependent on the goodwill of the 82 Irish Nationalists whose adverse vote would put him in a minority. Was the electoral verdict sufficiently plain to justify proceeding with a Parliament Bill which would enable the new government to force through a Home Rule Bill? It was not sufficient to enable Asquith to carry through the full reform of the House of Lords, which his Radical section preferred to 'end' rather than 'mend', or to reduce the number of Irish parliamentary seats, without destroying the basis of his working majority. A 'Veto' Bill and a Home Rule Bill would be a partial and partisan programme. It would curb the Lords as a historical anomaly by exploiting historical anomalies.

No 'guarantees' had been taken by Asquith as to the King's consent to the creation of peers needed to force through a Veto Bill, but he did not make this fact public until 21 February. Before the polls Lord Knollys had made it clear to Asquith's private secretary that before a large creation of peers was 'embarked upon or threatened' the actual measure should have been produced, and that a further election would be necessary.[12] Asquith fulfilled this requirement. But in January when Esher discussed the situation with Balfour at Whittinghame, they both assumed that Asquith would require a guarantee as soon as Parliament met. Balfour was prepared to assume office if the King refused the guarantee, and was confident the King would be supported by the country.[13] When the election result showed the large decrease of the Liberal majority Esher felt that affairs could not 'take altogether the turn we discussed at Whittinghame'.[14] Asquith could not 'bully' the King, who was now 'less depressed than he was'.[15] At the King's request Esher wrote a memorandum on the political situation, and when discussing it with the King on 25 January Esher found: 'He is quite clear that he will not assent to any request to make peers.'[16] This resolve was based on Esher's rejection of 1832 as a valid precedent, and on his assurance that Balfour would 'come to the King's assistance'. It was an outright resolve not to agree to a massive creation in any circumstances, and to make this plain Esher wrote another 'excellent little lecture for the King...urging him not to agree to any reform of the Constitution which did not deprive him of the power of creating more than a fixed number of peers in any year'.[17] The Queen Anne precedent was to hold the field.

The rejected Budget of 1909 was assured of passing in the Lords, but its passage in the Commons was delayed by the Irish Nationalists, ostensibly because they wanted the spirit duties altered but really because they refused to allow it to pass before they had assurances as to the success of the Veto Bill. Asquith proceeded by resolutions so that the essential form of the Veto Bill had been approved by the time it secured its first reading on 14 April. The Budget Bill did not appear till 20 April, after an accommodation with the Nationalists had been reached. Esher received a urgent request from Morley just before the cabinet's momentous decision of 11 April on this problem, and called on him at Wimbledon on the 10th to find him contemplating resignation.[18] Morley had pangs of doubt concerning a plan which Churchill and Lloyd George were pressing on Asquith with a threat of resignation. This involved conveying a secret pledge to the Nationalist and Labour leaders that in the event of the Lords' rejecting the Veto Bill Asquith would 'warn' the King that if in the ensuing election he got a majority, he would not remain in office without an assurance that the King would create peers enough to carry the Bill. This 'political procedure' would be made known to the country before the election. Meanwhile the pledge would ensure that the Nationalists accepted the Budget Bill. Esher wrote at once directly to the King informing him of this plan, which he described as intended 'to purchase the assent of the Irish representatives to a Budget of which they disapprove, and the price given is to threaten Your Majesty, with a view ultimately of inducing Your Majesty to assist in a *coup d'état*.' Morley was told plainly by Esher that it would be a lamentable outcome of his long career to 'lend his name and authority to a policy of menace to the Crown, and of parliamentary corruption.' In the upshot, Morley did not resign and Asquith seems to have rejected the plan, for on 13 April he thought it probable that he would be defeated by an adverse Irish vote on the Budget.

In preference Asquith chose the open course of announcing in the Commons on 14 April that failing a means to carry the Veto Bill in the present Parliament, which he did not specify but which may have included a referendum, he would not recommend a dissolution 'except under such conditions as will secure that in the new Parliament the judgement of the people...will be carried into law'.[19] The implications of this announcement were secretly discussed, at the instance of Lord Knollys, by Balfour and the Archbishop of Canterbury, Esher and Knollys being present, with a view to the Archbishop acting as mediator in a deadlock involving the King.[20] It was assumed in the discussion that Asquith would first ask the King to create five hundred peers to force the Bill through the present Parliament, in which case the King's course 'seemed clear'. Asquith would then ask for a dissolution 'coupled with a promise to create peers', and 'much would depend—indeed the future of the Monarchy itself might depend' on the answer. Balfour proposed that the King, if he determined to refuse, should do so in a carefully worded document, preserving impartiality between the two parties; whereupon

Asquith would resign and Balfour would form a government for the purposes of dissolving. He thought he could get over the difficulty of the refusal of Supply.

Esher then made a counter-proposal, which was that the King should follow the example of 1884 and try to arrange a compromise. This had seemed impossible in 1884, but Salisbury's unexpected suggestion on behalf of the opposition of single-member constituencies had commended itself to public opinion and Gladstone had been constrained to accept it. In like manner Esher thought a compromise would emerge on the Veto Bill, such as a referendum whenever the two Houses disagreed. This idea of a royal intervention to promote a compromise commended itself to all present. Lord Knollys thought the preamble to the Veto Bill might offer an excuse for doing so, for it announced the intention to constitute the Upper House on a 'popular instead of hereditary basis' and define its powers in another Bill which had not been produced. He summed up to the effect that Balfour would 'come to the King's assistance', and that 'there was no objection to the King proposing a compromise'.

King Edward's death early in May imposed a truce in party warfare, while a secret 'Constitutional Conference' sincerely promoted by Lloyd George and Balfour undertook an ambitious review of the national problems which seemed incapable of resolution by the normal processes of party strife. However, Lloyd George's faith in the possibility of a National Government was not shared by Asquith, and most of the discussion in the meetings which were held between 17 June and 10 November turned on the distinction between ordinary, financial and constitutional legislation and the method of resolving deadlocks on the last. The Unionist representatives were inclined to accept the proposed 'joint sittings' of both Houses for most purposes, but they came to insist on the referendum for such measures as Home Rule, which the Liberals could not accept. It has been said that the Conference was attempting nothing less than 'to convert the immemorial unwritten into a written constitution', a task impossible for politicians who were 'deeply committed' to current policies.

Esher's part in the Conference was minimal. He conferred with Balfour at Whittinghame in October about its progress, or more accurately its lack of progress, and composed a memorandum pleading for the 'Joint Committee' of both Houses as 'the nucleus of an Imperial Senate'.[21] But the Liberals would hardly have surrendered

214

their party majority to the decisions of the small and impartial body which Esher envisaged. Balfour therefore moved towards accepting the plan of a referendum, which Asquith was considering when he made his pronouncement of 14 April, and which he was about to embody in a Bill shortly before King Edward's death.

The idea of a referendum on Home Rule, the Veto Bill or anything else was obnoxious to Esher. He had condemned it in *The Times* in December. Equally emphatically he condemned the solution of using the Prerogative to create peers. 'There was no essential difference and no moral distinction between swamping the majority of one of the Houses of Parliament by men in black coats or in red. Force was the essence of both.' The only true precedent for swamping had been Pride's purge of the Commons in 1648. The only 'act of violence' since 1688 had been the sudden creation of twelve peers at the instance of Lord Oxford in 1711. In 1832, he argued, the King had only given his undertaking to create peers if necessary after Wellington and the other opposition peers had assured him confidentially that they would withdraw their opposition. The real 'reserve force' in 1832 had been the overwhelming will of the people. 'The only rational reserve force in the Constitution is the common sense of the nation, which, at certain moments, insists upon accommodation and compromise between party leaders.' This was a plea for the working-out of conflicts by a historical process. 'An unwritten Constitution rests upon precedent and reasonableness.' If it was intended to effect a revolution by transferring the Constitution to a written basis, this would have to be done by the assent of the nation as a whole and not by a bare majority of votes. Otherwise, 'politicians who embark on revolutionary courses must always remember that behind revolution lurk insurrection and civil war.' Though he did not mention it, Esher no doubt had Ulster in mind, and the prophecy proved correct.

Esher's own remedy was the historical process of the passage of a Bill, a crisis and the intervention of the Crown to promote a settlement which public opinion would understand and endorse in an actual situation. This had for centuries been the normal course of legislation. The contrary idea of an electoral mandate and a prearranged parliamentary programme carried by a party majority had not been pushed very far by earlier Radicals nor publicly endorsed by Asquith. The true model for Liberals as Esher pointed out was Gladstone's action against an unyielding House of Lords in 1884. At the time the Tories

215

were demanding safeguards against a Franchise Bill which was to be
followed by an undisclosed Redistribution Bill—just as the Veto Bill
was supposed to be followed by a Bill to reform the House of Lords—
and in the crisis an unexpected and acceptable provision was found.

The secret 'Constitutional Conference' was of course no substitute
for the democratic process. The politicians, who were only really
concerned about the immediate interests of their parties, had got
seriously out of touch with the public. Two days before the final
break-up Esher had a long talk with Balfour, who was depressed
about his own prospects as leader, and feared that another election
would not produce a change. He preferred 'a compromise on the
lines almost agreed to', but had been overruled by his militants.[22] To
Esher it was no surprise that a compromise had not emerged. He confessed: 'I think the situation is not one susceptible of a compromise,
except on the Bill itself in Parliament.'[23] Unfortunately Asquith was
determined to treat the Conference as the one and only attempt at
accommodation, and if it failed he would appeal to the country without more ado. But he would insist on 'guarantees' before allowing a
dissolution, and since his secret deliberations had shown that the
referendum was unacceptable to his party the guarantee could only
take the form of a royal promise to overcome the resistance of the
Lords.

Lord Knollys was well apprised of this likely sequel to the Conference. At the Lambeth consultation in April, as has been seen, he
summed up the discussion himself as concluding 'that Mr Balfour
would come to the King's assistance if His Majesty refused the
"advice" of his present Ministers to dissolve Parliament, and that there
was no objection to the King proposing a compromise...' In October
Esher had sent him another note dictated by Balfour at Whittinghame
on the Sovereign's prospective position, suggesting that to avoid
seeming to favour the opposition by calling on Balfour to dissolve,
the King might summon some neutral statesman like Rosebery to
'keep the ground' between parties.[24] Yet Lord Knollys did not inform
King George of the existence of the papers drawn up by Balfour and
Esher on the question of guarantees, or acquaint him with the substance of the Lambeth Conference. The King only discovered them
when Esher asked Lord Stamfordham to look them out from Knollys's
papers in December 1913, whereupon the King minuted: 'The knowledge of their contents would, undoubtedly, have had an important

bearing and influence with regard to Mr Asquith's request for guarantees on November 16, 1910.'[25]

The new King was undoubtedly hustled into the position of having to accept the guarantees, and he rightly resented it. When Asquith went to Sandringham to report the failure of the Conference on 11 November and to ask for a dissolution, he did not mention them.[26] On Monday 14 November Lord Knollys went to London and found a change in Asquith's overt attitude: 'What he *now* advocates,' he reported to the King, 'is that you should give guarantees *at once* for the next Parliament.'[27] The King instructed Sir Arthur Bigge (later Lord Stamfordham) to send a telegram on the 15th to say that 'it would be impossible for him to give contingent guarantees' and reminding Asquith 'of his promise not to seek for any during the present Parliament'. Asquith had indeed promised not to seek guarantees *for* the present Parliament, but he had not precluded himself from seeking, indeed he had promised to exact, guarantees of some kind for the next Parliament before dissolving the current one.[28] He convened a cabinet the same day and got approval for what the King's biographer rightly describes as a 'somewhat peremptory minute', which was sent at once to the King. The minute was exactly what had been expected since April, a refusal to advise a dissolution unless 'in the event of the policy of the Government being approved by an adequate majority in the new House of Commons, His Majesty will be ready to exercise his constitutional powers (which may involve the Prerogative of creating peers), if needed, to secure that effect should be given to the decision of the country'. What, perhaps, had not been foreseen so certainly was the additional provision that the 'intentions of the Crown' should remain secret 'unless and until the actual occasion should arise'.[29]

By every canon of constitutional propriety the King should have been given adequate time and opportunity to deliberate on this novel demand with its extraordinary proviso, to seek advice from those who could assess its legal and practical effects, and to argue with or warn his ministers from a position of knowledge. The cabinet's demands were obscure and ambiguous. What was an 'adequate majority' and when was the 'actual occasion'? Was the 'policy of the Government' the actual Veto Bill or the general principles behind it? Did the guarantee mean that no amendments could be made to the Veto Bill? The only point of the guarantee was to overawe opposition. In the event, the Unionists behaved as if the government might in the end invoke the Prerogative to create peers subject to the natural reluctance of the King to agree. They had to be told of the secret guarantees weeks before the 'actual occasion': and even so they could not be sure that it was not a bluff, for no authentic documents were presented to them. They had assumed that the King was a free agent and that the drama would be played out historically. The secrecy of the guarantee was represented by Lord Knollys as a 'great compromise', but it proved to be a most mischievous and unfair deception of the opposition and of Parliament. To it, more than to anything else, Balfour owed his political downfall.

According to Bigge, Lord Knollys was 'adamant' against the guarantees, but 'in less than 48 hours' completely changed his mind. He was in London on 14 and 15 November and manifested this change of front in a letter accompanying the cabinet's minute on the latter day. It is by no means unlikely that he was swayed by Esher, who on the 14th composed a memorandum for the King arguing that 'Now that there is a probability of the Veto Bill becoming law', it was worthwhile to consider how its effects compared with the Unionists' projects. Esher had decided, after seeing how the Unionists were going for the referendum, that the Veto Bill was relatively innocuous:

Memorandum for King George, 14 November 1910:[30] I do not think that the new proposals will be likely to shock the feelings of the country. Although the Bill materially affects the existing powers of the House of Lords it does not strike a deadly blow at the influence of the House itself, or the influence wielded by its individual members...In any case, the composition of the House remains what it has been for centuries, and the hereditary principle is not...in any way infringed...

It seems to me ludicrous to suppose that measures of secondary importance opposed in the House of Lords will stand any chance of becoming law under the Government scheme, while the number of measures of first-class importance which are likely to pass through the ordeal instituted by this novel machinery must be rare and few...

When we come on the other hand to consider the ingenious proposals which are said to have been under discussion at the conference involving apparently joint sessions of both Houses, an expedient strange to our institutions...The effect of this must, I think, inevitably have been to increase the radical legislative output of the House of Commons, in a degree far in excess of that which they will obtain under the Veto Bill.

Esher knew what was going on, for he noted on the 19th that: 'All through the crisis of the past week Asquith has shown great firmness but perfect temper...When the king came up to town, he sent for Asquith and Crewe and agreed to what Asquith asked. It was clearly understood that if the country returns the Government again with a good working majority, the King will support his Prime Minister in passing the Veto Bill through the House of Lords.'[31] Esher therefore knew of the 'guarantee' in general terms, while Balfour did not. Why did he not tell Balfour? Why did he acquiesce in the project of swamping which he had publicly condemned as a resort to force? Why did he put aside the idea of a compromise promoted by the King, and a possible resort to Balfour's assistance? One reason was the recent Constitutional Conference, which had exhausted every attempt at accommodation and queered the pitch for any public parley. Another reason, which Esher actually alludes to, was the novel and uncertain public position of the new King, who could not intervene with the same certainty of being understood as King Edward at the end of his reign. But the main reason was probably the condition of secrecy. This was certainly Lord Knollys's reason. 'What is now recommended,' he wrote to the King, 'is altogether different in every way from any request to be allowed publicly to announce that you have consented to give guarantees.'[32] Knollys was emphatic that King Edward would have seen it that way, and this testimony above everything else persuaded King George to accept.

But the condition of secrecy did nothing to remove the objection to 'contingent guarantees' which Knollys had agreed with Balfour to be unacceptable. For this reason Balfour was not told of them. When, many months later, he learnt the full story, his anger against Knollys knew no bounds and for the first time in his serene and affable career he lost his temper. Balfour would certainly have formed a government had the King appealed to him:

Balfour-Stamfordham, 1 August 1911:[33] Had I been asked to
219

form a government in order to protect His Majesty from giving a promise not merely that a Parliament Bill should be passed over the heads of the Lords, but that it should be passed in a form which by implication carried Home Rule with it, I should not only have formed a government but I should have had great hopes of carrying the country with me.

Yet Lord Knollys assured the King that Balfour would 'in any event decline to form an administration'.[34] He grasped at the chance to keep the King's name out of the coming electoral struggle. He must have realised that if Balfour had been told the full circumstances by the King he would have advised a dissolution with the King's predicament in the forefront of his appeal. Esher also seems to have supported the reasoning that since Balfour could not have remained in office but would have had to dissolve immediately it would have placed the King in the invidious position of 'according to a Tory Prime Minister what a few days before he had refused to a Radical'.[35] This had not worried him in April, but as he also noted: 'There was only one possible and prudent course for a young Monarch i.e. to abide strictly within the Constitution and to take the official advice of his responsible Ministers.'[36] The defect of an irresponsible adviser, as Esher was, is that at critical moments he will tend to slide out of tacit engagements or dodge hard choices. Esher preferred personally the Veto Bill to Balfour's referendum or Lansdowne's new-fangled peerages. Did the pledges really matter? After all, they were secret, and perhaps their secrecy absolved him from any obligation to consult Balfour.

The country and the opposition knew that Asquith would not have dissolved Parliament so suddenly, before the Veto Bill had had more than its first reading, unless he meant to get the necessary mandate for the Veto Bill. They might have guessed that he had got some assurance from the King, in conformity with his declaration of 14 April. But that declaration belonged to the previous reign and to a situation which had been altered by the Constitutional Conference. Asquith had manifestly failed to comply with it, for he had dropped his promised attempt to pass the Bill in the current Parliament. It was therefore thought to have lapsed, and it is possible that Asquith was pushed back into it by a section of his cabinet between 11 and 15 November. After seeing the King at Sandringham he certainly mentions guarantees in his note of the conversation, but only *after* the election. There is every appearance of his having been carried along into demanding an explicit and immediate guarantee by the argument that his honour was involved. It is difficult to conceive, otherwise, why he failed to explain so vital a matter to the King and his secretaries at Sandringham. His next interview with the King, five days later, was the most important in his life, and his political career was at stake.

As should have been foreseen, the guarantee became embarrassingly ambiguous when the election result was known. The voters behaved much as they had done in the January election and much as was expected. But it was uncertain whether they had given a sufficiently clear mandate for the guarantee to operate. Esher tried to reassure Knollys, however:

> *Esher-Knollys, 28 December 1910:*[37] the creation of five hundred peers is a revolutionary proceeding, and a revolution pushed through upon a majority of the electorate not exceeding 350,000 is an act hardly justified... If you take a simple population basis ...the Government majority would possibly not amount to more than ten...
> The whole responsibility must be thrown upon the Ministers. At the right moment, that is to say when the Bill with reasonable amendment proposed by the Opposition is before Parliament... the King can ask Asquith to say how far the Government will go towards meeting the suggestion of the Opposition, and ... induce the Ministers to accept a reasonable compromise which would leave them in office and in power.

But if the guarantee meant anything, it meant the Bill in its original shape, and this was just what Asquith exacted. Was it fair to allow the opposition to go through the charade of discussion and amendment when these were known to be futile? Or to allow them to advance fundamental alterations on the assumption that there would be a day of compromise, only to use these as an excuse for rejection *en bloc*? Esher and Knollys failed to see that the King had surrendered his power to effect a compromise, and for this reason the secrecy of the pledge was particularly pernicious.

This soon became apparent. Lord Knollys was anxious to give the King some assurance that he had acted correctly, and so he took the

opportunity to question Balfour at a private dinner at the Marlborough Club on 10 January.[38] Esher was present, and produced a
résumé of what was said. Balfour was allowed to expatiate at length
on the assumption that the King might be asked 'in the near future to
promise the creation of peers'. He declared that he would not feel able
to come to the King's assistance because: 'A third General Election
in January is quite out of the question.' Therefore the King 'could
not well ultimately refuse to comply with Mr Asquith's demand,
should it be made, for a promise to create peers'. Balfour then went
in detail into the question of how the King should reply to the
demand, and how he should give Asquith a written protest to be
read to the cabinet. He even promised not to question the government,
so that 'no public disclosure would be made of the so-called
guarantee'. Knollys then asked him if he would have taken office 'in
December last' if summoned, and got an affirmative answer. 'When
asked further what advice he would have given to the King had he
been privately sounded...he replied that he would have strongly
advised the King to act as he did and agree to a dissolution...in the
interests of the King and of the Monarchy, he thinks it would have
been imprudent and unwise if the King had dismissed his Ministers...'

The only conclusion to be drawn from a close study of this
document is that both Esher and Knollys had conspired to produce
trumped-up evidence that the November pledges were justified to
satisfy the King's misgivings. One would not know from reading it
that Esher had any inkling of the pledge, and hence, curiously enough,
when the document later fell into Balfour's hands he did not accuse
Esher of lack of candour. He was annoyed at the time, for in his own
words: 'Shortly before the company separated I learned to my surprise that the dinner had been held with the knowledge and approval
of the Prime Minister and that presumably, therefore, everything I
said in the freedom of friendly conversation was to be repeated to him.
I told Lord Knollys at the time that if these were to be regarded as
the only conditions under which HM's Private Secretary could see
politicians...HM would be parting with a valuable right...'[39] Knollys
was really collecting the 'unbuttoned' observations of Balfour in an
attempt to reassure the King. As he explained months later:
'The King was so unhappy...at the idea that he might have
acted differently...that I determined to ascertain from you whether
you could have [taken office] for HM's information only.'[40] But

222

Knollys could not explain why he extracted statements which were worthless and misleading because he had deceived Balfour. As soon as Balfour heard of the pledges his wrath fell on Knollys: '*I* had not an inkling that in November anything of importance on this subject had been arranged between the King and his Ministers. Lord Knollys seems, therefore, to have endeavoured to extract from me general statements of policy to be used as the occasion arose, whilst studiously concealing the most important elements and the actual concrete problem that had to be solved...It seems to me, looking back on this transaction with the full knowledge which I now possess, to have been one of the most singular examples of domestic diplomacy of which I ever heard.'[41]

It is significant that Balfour was thinking of another election as a possibility in January 1911 and again in July, after the coronation. He did not realise that another election was absolutely ruled out by the November pledge. Even so, he was secretly contemplating surrender to the Veto Bill which he thought might take the form of forcing a 'token' creation of new peers to brand the Bill as carried by force and therefore morally worthy of being repealed. Only the extremists in his party, led by J. L. Garvin of the *Observer* and Leo Maxse of the *National Review* and composed chiefly of tariff reformers and Halsburyites, positively wanted to force a massive creation of peers. The Unionist leaders expected that guarantees would be obtained at some point during the passage of the Bill, but they could not believe in any sudden and massive creation of peers, for there was no known sanction which could be put on the King. Were the King a free agent, as they thought he was, there would have been some indication of a crisis before he agreed to what was widely believed to be an illegality, and was certainly a most unpalatable extremity. By July the Unionist leadership was on such a dangerous collision course with the secret guarantees that the secrecy had to be broken. The task fell to Esher, who reported to the King:

Esher-King George, 5 July 1911:[42] It was with some surprise that Viscount Esher heard from Mr Balfour, that while suspecting the facts of the political situation, he was not sure of them.

The main point, Mr Balfour said, which has been exercising all the powers of his judgment...is what answer he should give

223

Your Majesty if he were called upon at this juncture to accept office...

Mr Balfour told Viscount Esher that he and Lord Lansdowne had never quite agreed upon the probable creation of peers.

Lord Lansdowne has refused to believe that this step could ever actually be taken...

Mr Balfour now realises the true state of affairs...

But this was altogether too simple. The enigma of the guarantees had not been made clear. In particular, it was never clearly spelt out, until Morley's statement at the final debate on 10 August, that the creation of peers would be so large as to overcome all possible combinations against the Bill. Up to that moment it was thought by Balfour that a token creation of peers could be forced, a natural assumption when Asquith did not discourage but rather seemed to be encouraging through Alfred Rothschild and others, the efforts of the 'Judas' group and the compilation of a list of Unionist abstainers by Curzon. Even Sandars, who was seldom in the dark as to what was secretly going on, was completely deceived, as his diary reveals:

> *Sandars's diary, 2 August 1911:*[43] In the afternoon, Lord Lansdowne reported that Cromer had informed him on the authority of Crewe, that the Government were most anxious to encourage the support from Unionist peers, mentioning as an inducement for this support, that if they did not receive promise of it they would undoubtedly begin to create peers to the number of three hundred. I pointed out to Lord Lansdowne that this was mere bluff.

Balfour advocated a 'token' creation as late as 7 August, and although Lansdowne had been finally convinced of the real truth by Crewe, he was not believed. On 10 August, before Morley's statement, Lansdowne again warned Sandars that the government had 'permission to make enough peers to swamp the House of Lords'; but Sandars notes: 'I told him I did not agree with him.'[44] If the guarantee had been exacted at the time expected, and Asquith's interpretation of it made clear, the Unionists may have split but they need not have been broken up.

Esher's responsibility in the affair was considerable. He might have checked Knollys and he might have seen that Balfour was consulted. Instead, and in spite of his public assertion that guarantees to swamp the Lords were illegal and revolutionary, he aided and abetted Knollys and may have actually inspired his course of action. He expressed his sympathy with the King plainly enough. 'When the history of the past year comes to be written,' he wrote to the King on the day after the Bill had passed, 'the procedure of Your Majesty's Ministers in November last will be very justly criticised...But, no one ...can ever do otherwise than praise the wisdom of your Majesty's action in not swerving by an inch from the role of a constitutional Sovereign.'[45] He had consistently viewed the problem as pre-eminently one of keeping the King out of the dispute. The price was paid by the Unionists. 'The Bill will go through' he had told Fisher in April. 'Nothing can prevent it... I prefer the Bill to the opposition plan. It is less revolutionary, and involves fewer breaches with the historical past.'[46] In the list of new peers which Asquith had prepared for the swamping the name of Esher's eldest son was included. Esher and Knollys were of course Liberals, but they were becoming partisans. When Balfour's leadership of the Unionists had become untenable owing to the demoralisation which followed his enforced 'surrender' which the "Die-Hard" section of his party had refused to accept, he quietly resigned it in November to be replaced, unexpectedly, by Bonar Law. Esher made it clear that his loyalty had been to Balfour rather than to his party:

Memo. by J. S. Sandars, 9 November 1911:[47] Lord Esher spoke angrily about the conduct of the men who had treated their leader in the way Mr Balfour had been treated. He dwelt upon the impossibility of finding anybody to take his place. He said that he should not further interest himself in the affairs of the Unionist Party, that he would never vote for them; on the contrary, he would work to keep them out of office.

I vainly urged that this was paying Mr Balfour but a poor compliment. He said nothing would arrest his determination.

Esher had expected Balfour to return to office after the Liberals failed to satisfy the Irish over Home Rule. He now felt that 'there is not a man on the other side fit to carry on the work of Winston or Asquith or Lloyd George'.

It might be said of the Veto Bill as of the 1832 Reform Bill that the most important thing about it was the manner of its passing. Asquith was fond of quoting Lord Grey's conduct in the 1832 situation but he left out the most important consideration, which was that in 1832 the nation was aroused and almost unanimous in its expressions at meetings. In 1911 the nation was neither aroused nor unanimous, and the use of the Prerogative marked a victory for the Commons and not for opinion out-of-doors, especially since the intervention of the King was invoked secretly in advance. In 1832 the Crown and the people had played a principal role in the final drama. In 1911 their roles were played for them by Mr Asquith. They had surrendered to that astute lawyer their powers of attorney. And so the precedent of 1911 was a great departure from the practice of resolving party conflicts and contentious political issues which had prevailed through the nineteenth century. This had involved the participation of public opinion directly in the shaping of momentous decisions through the power of the press and the relative independence of MPs, through meetings, petitions and demonstrations, and the conventions which party discipline and the 'mandate' were to make obsolete. The passing of the Veto Bill was a legal foreclosure against public opinion and the Prerogative as they had acted historically.

The Unionists' chief objection to the Veto Bill was that it enabled a Home Rule Bill to be passed at the dictation of a House of Commons in which Redmond held the balance of parties. They claimed that the 'veto' of the House of Lords was only effective when public opinion upheld it, and was therefore a means of 'referring' to the people. This need not have taken the form of a dissolution of Parliament, which the Liberals rightly claimed to amount to control over policy. It had traditionally taken the form of a deadlock between the two Houses, a royal intervention to promote an accommodation, and the endorsement of the settlement by public opinion. By removing the 'veto' of the Lords, therefore, Asquith had also removed the traditional cue and occasion for the intervention of the Crown as a mediator between parties. There was now no means of invoking public opinion as a check on the Commons which fancied it had a mandate to pass an undisclosed Home Rule Bill. Should the public not wish Ulster to be subjected to this Bill, it had now no means of intervention except those of insurrection and civil war. The three lawyers most prominent in promoting the Home Rule Bill—Asquith, Lloyd

George and Haldane—now set to work on a bigger foreclosure than the Veto Bill itself. Their sense of constitutional law was more acute than their sense of history.

The thwarting of the normal expressions of opinion in realistic political situations led to two characteristic features of the politics of 1910–14, public apathy and party violence. In their sense of impotence the Unionist leaders invented devices of strange and ominous import. They claimed that the royal veto had been restored by the obscure wording of the Veto Bill, they abetted 'mutiny' in the army and insurrection in Ulster, they thought of obstructing the Army Annual Bill and even of persuading the Speaker to 'lose' a Bill. As the nemesis of the Veto Bill, the Home Rule Bill ground on mechanically to its conclusion of civil war which, in the nick of time, was forestalled by the Great War itself.

The King's position in this situation was extremely important. As head of the army, and as having a legal power, however obsolete, of legislative veto, the King was looked to as the one hope for reconciliation. The competence of his private advisers was being questioned. Chief of these was Esher, who since King Edward's death was being increasingly criticised as an irresponsible *éminence grise*. *The World* ran a series of articles which attacked him along with Sir George Clarke and Repington under the title 'the Cabal'.[48] These concluded with a demand that Esher's position should be defined in a white paper. After Esher's seeming defection to the Liberals even Repington himself began to question his influence. In February 1913 he came by appointment to see Esher and broached the delicate question of 'whether the King has about him men competent to advise at a constitutional crisis'.[49] Some leading newspaper editors had discussed 'whether public attention should be drawn to the fact and suggestions made which might lead to placing about the King persons competent by their abilities and experience to advise him'. He meant men like Rosebery, St Aldwyn, the Archbishop of Canterbury, etc. Esher made two points in reply. He thought the people about the King were 'bound to remain obscure' or else there would be 'strong jealousies': and he claimed that 'only two men in England' could safely and constitutionally advise the King, the Prime Minister and the Leader of the Opposition, 'should he feel himself strong enough to carry on the King's Government'.[50]

This reply to Repington was of course an evasion. But it did reflect

Esher's firm resolve to keep the name of King George out of the raging political controversy at all costs.[51] When he went to Balmoral in September 1913 he found the King much concerned by the responsibility he might incur by consenting to the Home Rule Bill. He composed a memorandum for the King very similar in purport to that which Asquith presented at the same time, completely absolving the King from responsibility for actions he could not prevent. 'At a given moment...when he is forced to choose between acquiescence and the loss of his Ministers, the Sovereign automatically...ceases to have any opinion...If the constitutional doctrines of ministerial responsibility mean anything at all, the King would have to sign his own death-warrant, if it was presented to him for signature by a minister commanding a majority in Parliament.'[52] The most that Esher would concede was that the King could insist on getting categorical answers from the cabinet to carefully framed questions, about the risk of civil war in Ireland, the possibility of the use of troops, and the advisability of a general election.

At this stage the government was proposing to pass the Home Rule Bill without any reprieve for Ulster, and they threatened that if the King vetoed the Bill 'every minister, from Asquith downwards, including Grey, would attack the King personally'.[53] As soon as Esher had completed his memorandum the King sent for him and 'recapitulated the whole argument for exercising his veto and for insisting upon an appeal to the country even if it involved the loss of his ministers'. Esher advised him to 'build up his case and not rely on one remonstrance' and admitted that 'the trouble over the Parliament Bill two years ago would have been mitigated and perhaps avoided if King Edward had taken action in December 1909 when he first heard of "guarantees".'[54] The King was still not acquainted with the story of the events of 1909–10, and so Esher gave him a volume of his letters to read. On returning this later the King 'blamed Francis Knollys for not having laid before him, long before November 1910, the whole story...since the idea was first mooted of..."guarantees".'[55] He soon came to the conclusion that all his troubles stemmed from that disastrous omission.

The King's case for dismissing his ministers was stronger than it had been in November 1910. Under cover of the Veto Bill, whose preamble declared that the Upper House would be reformed, a Home Rule Bill whose provisions had never been before the electorate was being applied to Ulster at the manifest risk of civil war. This was the kind of major constitutional change which the Liberals had agreed at the Constitutional Conference required something more than the unilateral approval of the Commons alone. From his wide contacts with the army the King knew that his officers would throw up their commissions and refuse to coerce Ulster. 'There is Hamilton in my own household,' he said, 'who has signed the Covenant, and will leave me the moment the Bill is passed and go to his people in Ireland. The Government pretend not to believe these things...' Esher's reply was consistent with his attitude to the guarantees. 'I said that it was far better there should be fighting in Ireland than that they should involve the Monarchy in this quarrel.'[56]

The suggestion that the King should develop the case for conciliation, between the two extremes of coercing Ulster, and using the 'Ulster card' to scupper Home Rule altogether which had become the Unionist policy, bore fruit in a long and carefully argued statement which the King sent to Asquith on 22 September.[57] This placed the Crown clearly in an impartial position while advancing all the doubts and questions that could fairly be put to Asquith. It asked for a reply before Asquith's next audience with the King, and it elicited what was to be the key concession—Asquith offered 'some special arrangement' with regard to Ulster.[58] But it was now too late to conciliate Carson, flushed with the success of his preparations for a provisional government, nor could Bonar Law easily persuade his followers to accept partial Home Rule without an election.

Esher like Curzon and others thought that the issue which had been so aggravated could only now be settled by fighting on the soil of Ireland. 'Those who hate Home Rule sufficiently should be ready to risk their skins, but they should not skulk behind the Throne.' He was convinced that the danger of civil war was very real, and he impressed on Morley and Haldane that they could not bank on the King's shrinking from any action, however detrimental to himself, which might save the misery of civil war. Also 'the disaster may not be limited to Ireland, but may precipitate a struggle on far wider issues'.[59] This latter conviction had been borne in on Esher by the developments of the autumn. By the end of the year he had completely changed his mind, and now advocated the use of the royal Prerogative to dismiss the government. 'I doubt whether the Sovereign would now be thought to have done his duty,' he wrote to Stamfordham, 'if he were to permit the opposing forces, not only in Ireland but in this country, to rush into conflict until every step had been taken to ensure that the nation should have a preliminary say in the matter.' It might be the Sovereign's duty 'at any risk to himself, to insist upon a dissolution, and if it is refused by Asquith, to send for a neutral statesman... Rosebery for instance.'[60]

But unforeseen complications were emerging from the mechanistic Veto Bill. While its passing would be the signal for an Ulster convention, an election prior to this would lose the Home Rule Bill and prolong the crisis for years even if the Liberals won. The amendments to the Home Rule Bill that were being considered could only get past the Lords quickly by the old procedure, and if the Amending Bill did not get the agreement of both Houses before the Home Rule Bill passed automatically the latter would go in its simple form for the royal assent. The Unionist extremists thus had every motive for preventing the Amending Bill from passing. Stamfordham was perplexed by these complications and had hoped for some manifestation of public opinion, but Asquith's *démarche* towards a written constitution had made politics comprehensible only to lawyers and interesting only to soldiers and politicians:

Stamfordham-Esher, 29 December 1913:[61] I confess to being somewhat surprised at your changed views as to the action to be adopted by the King in the event of negotiations breaking down. The situation changes so rapidly...

One had hoped that by now the whole country would have been roused—mass meetings held condemning the policy of the government towards Ulster, urging upon the Crown to interfere...

If the King *does* dissolve he is establishing a precedent... Again, unless the General Election takes place before Parliament meets the PM would inevitably say something to this effect... 'Whatever results, Home Rule is put off for another three years' ...or 'But why dissolve now? The Bill has not yet passed. We may be turned out on some other issue before it ever gets to Your Majesty'.

The worst of the situation was that the government might welcome an enforced dissolution so that they could escape from their difficulties and blame the King for the chaos that would ensue.

Some intimations of what ministers were intending appeared in a letter from Morley:

> *Morley-Esher, 1 January 1914:*[62] Your whisper of a hint disquiets though it does not surprise me. Lord Knollys is to lunch with me at the Carlton on Monday...
>
> You know that conversations have ended in smoke...All now depends on the PM...It is all very well to keep saying with Grey that 'the door is open'. The diabolic truth is that all the doors, windows and chimneys are shut—not by the will of anybody here—but by the inexorable circumstances of the Irish case. Our policy is at the mercy of a series of Irish faction fights...due to England's selfishness, negligence and ignorance which has prevented the Irish from having any chance of learning *responsibility* for two or three centuries past.

Esher was shocked at the 'moral cowardice' and 'want of common honesty' revealed in this letter's admission that while the public believed the door was open, it was really bolted. It strengthened the case for the King's intervention. During a long talk with Morley on 18 January Esher learnt that ministers had considered the possibility of the King refusing assent to the Home Rule Bill, but that Asquith had assured them 'all danger from that quarter was removed'.[63] Esher stressed that they were making a mistake. The man in the street was quiet because he confidently expected a compromise. The King was silent because he did not want to prejudice the discussions.

The King was informed of what Morley had said, and showed Esher his statement sent to Asquith in September which made it clear enough he would take every possible step. He was thinking of a dissolution rather than a dismissal of the government, and Esher drafted a statement which might be sent to Asquith:

> *Draft by Esher, 1 February 1914:*[64] The King thinks it right that on the eve of the opening of Parliament Mr Asquith should know frankly the King's views...
>
> The King...must not be considered to have surrendered his right of judgment, or to hand over to anyone the prerogatives

and responsibilities deliberately imposed upon him by the words of an Act of Parliament...he will consider himself bound before assenting to a measure involving great constitutional changes to feel confident that the House of Commons represents the will of the majority of his people...

The situation had so changed since the 1910 election that the King might have had to ask Asquith 'to appeal...for a national mandate to use force in Ulster'. Some compromise had to be found and 'the King relies upon Mr Asquith to find it and so remove the danger of civil war which the King is determined at all hazards to prevent'.[65] Not unexpectedly, this line of argument was not accepted by Asquith when he appeared at Windsor on 5 February, and the Prime Minister considered that rather than revive the veto, which might 'prove disastrous to the Monarchy' the King should dismiss his ministers at once, before Parliament met. The interview must have been a tense one, and Esher wrote to Asquith the same day asking him for the sake of the King's 'peace of mind' to write down that evening a demonstration that 'the Royal Veto is obsolete, and was not revived by...the Parliament Act', and that 'the King still possesses the power of dismissing his ministers', but not dissolving.[66] Bagehot, Erskine May, Sir William Anson and Balfour did not seem to agree with Asquith!

A refusal of royal assent was in any case becoming highly undesirable, since it was clear that by the time the Bill was presented for signature even the southern part of Ireland would be both organised and ready for insurrection. Nor would the loss of the whole Bill be a fair solution. Esher, personally, favoured Home Rule for the south but was equally convinced that Ulster could not be subjected to Dublin. At this point Lloyd George came to the fore as an exponent of the same solution. With Birrell he persuaded Redmond to accept the plan announced in the Commons on 9 March, which Carson called a 'sentence of death with a stay of execution for six years'. This made Ulster's ultimate exclusion from the Bill dependent on a Unionist electoral victory, and Carson would only accept present and complete exclusion. 'Give us the clean cut,' he said, 'or come and fight us.' His arrangements for a seizure of power, backed by 25,000 armed men, 100,000 constables, and the co-operation of banks, railways, etc, were in an advanced state, and were known to Bonar Law. Sir Henry Wilson, who as Director of Military Operations should have been the government's right-hand man, was actively engaged in concerting resistance in the army, Staff College and War Office to any possible use of troops against Ulster, and also in supplying Bonar Law and Milner with information.

When Carson stalked out of the Commons on 19 March it was expected that he would not wait for the passing of the Home Rule Bill before setting up his provisional government. The government countered the threat by setting up a committee on which Winston Churchill and Seely, the War Minister, were most prominent, which reported on 7 March that certain depots in Ulster might easily be rushed. Under cover of securing these by military and naval deployments the government was suspected of a design to embroil the army in a way that might cover their coercion of Ulster. Such was the position when the Curragh affair blew up. The real significance of this affair is that it awakened public opinion by presenting it with an absorbing political drama—for thanks to Wilson and Bonar Law the newspapers covered its developments day by day with a penetrating scrutiny.

It was in the newspapers that the King first read the extraordinary news of how his officers at the Curragh had been asked to consent to possible operations against Ulster or (in the case of those not actually resident in the province) be immediately dismissed. In the crisis that followed it became abundantly clear that the army could not be so used. Many like Esher had felt this all along, but it needed a crisis to demonstrate it. The question whether Sir John French, who embarrassed the government by giving a gratuitous assurance to the Curragh 'mutineers', should resign when Asquith withdrew became an opinion poll of the army, and the result was almost unanimous. Esher was anxious to show that this feeling was not confined to the officers. He wrote to *The Times* claiming that 'The deplorable trouble in the army is the outcome of a refusal on the part of the government...to give credence to what everyone who knew the army has been saying for the past two years...It is widely believed...that a movement of troops from Aldershot to Ireland was contemplated, involving the calling up of reserves, and that the place of the soldiers at Aldershot was to have been taken by embodied Territorials.'[67] Had this happened, he declared, half the officers and men would have resigned. The Curragh affair committed Asquith, who took on the War Office himself, to a purely 'law and order' policy in Ulster, but even this broke down completely when the Ulster volunteers conducted the Larne operation in

233

which 25,000 rifles were unloaded and the civil authorities remained powerless.

It was now obvious that some exclusion of Ulster was inevitable, since Asquith himself now admitted the army could not be used. But still the Liberals stuck to the form of exclusion which Carson and Bonar Law had publicly rejected. Esher had given up attending the CID because he did not wish to meet the ministers, but he was still on cordial terms with Morley from whom he heard of the cabinet's plans and reported them to Stamfordham:

> *Esher-Stamfordham, 12 May 1914:*[68] Once the Home Rule Bill is through both Houses, the government will produce an Amending Bill in the House of Lords...
>
> If the House of Lords rejects the Amending Bill we are confronted with Home Rule as it stands. If we amend the Amending Bill and make the exclusion of the six counties permanent, what will the government and Commons do? If they reject the Lords' amendments and send up the Bill again and we don't pass it, civil war is inevitable. So they throw the onus upon the House of Lords.
>
> It is a clever device, but *devilish.*

But the government was weakening. Grey thought that the exclusion of Ulster should be indefinite,[69] while Lloyd George gave Esher the impression that he wished the Lords to amend the Amending Bill in this sense while also extending the four counties to six. 'Then, although the House of Commons might re-amend, the Government would be ready to force Redmond's hand.'[70] Plainly the government had not settled their account with Redmond but were playing a game of brinkmanship with him as well as with their opponents. What if Redmond did not agree to the complete exclusion of Ulster? And so Esher 'pointed out to the King that, by amending the Bill and sending it down to the Commons, we run the risk of the Commons disagreeing with our amendments and throwing the responsibility of civil war on us'.[71]

During May and June it was quite on the cards that no Amending Bill would pass so that the Home Rule Bill, which could be neither amended nor hurried on, would be presented to the King on its own. Many Unionists wanted it to be so, and the House of Lords certainly had the power to delay the Amending Bill indefinitely. In Ireland the

234

south would break into rebellion if the Bill failed, while the north would likewise if it passed. Asquith was caught in a political as well as in a legal trap. He had set up an inexorable count-down to civil war, and there seemed nothing that he could say or do to arrest it. He took refuge in expressions of surprise that men could fight over such legal niceties or give way to such emotion. And he still seemed to imagine that some legal formula could save the situation. One such expedient, though not quite the kind Asquith envisaged, was mentioned very confidentially by the Speaker to Esher. The Veto Bill had laid down that on a third rejection by the Lords a Bill shall be endorsed by the Speaker and sent to the Sovereign. But it had been overlooked that rejected Bills were destroyed or locked in a safe. There was no means of 'forcing the House of Lords to return a rejected Bill to the Speaker', and if the Lords cared to go in for this kind of Gilbertian tactic 'a very curious and difficult situation may arise'.[72]

Inevitably the crisis dragged on, attending on the due forms of Parliament. The Commons debate on the Lords' amendments to the Amending Bill was the final crunch. The extremists on both sides wanted the Bill bounced back to the Lords, but if some final compromise on the disputed counties, Fermanagh and Tyrone, could be reached before the debate the moderates might win.[73] This was the point at which the King asked the Speaker to preside over a final conference, which met at Buckingham Palace from 21–24 July. The Conference failed to effect a compromise, but it must have convinced the cabinet that they would have to distinguish their policy from Redmond's. 'One had hoped,' writes Churchill, 'that the events of April at the Curragh and in Belfast would have shocked British public opinion, and formed a unity sufficient to impose a settlement on the Irish factions. Apparently they had been insufficient.' The cabinet met that afternoon and was about to separate without a conclusion 'when the quiet grave tones of Sir Edward Grey's voice were heard reading a document which had just been brought to him from the Foreign Office. It was the Austrian note to Serbia...The parishes of Fermanagh and Tyrone faded back into the mists and squalls of Ireland...'[74]

The King had not yet played his last card, and it was certainly not apparent that the situation had been overshadowed by the European danger for some days to come. It was still in Esher's opinion quite possible that Asquith under pressure from the Radical press, which had commented very unfavourably on the King's initiative, would still yield nothing, though he hoped the King would be saved the invidious task of approving the Home Rule Bill:

> *Esher-Stamfordham, 26 July 1914 :*[75] There is no doubt that the events of 1910 are now wiped out. No one can ever again accuse the King of weakness, or of not grasping firmly his responsibilities...
>
> If the PM desires immortal credit, he will sacrifice himself and agree at the eleventh hour to the Lords' amendments. I am sure that the *two* Bills would then pass—although he would never be forgiven by the Radicals!

But there still remained a possibility, also, that the Amending Bill would be lost and the Home Rule Bill presented to the King on its own. Morley had agreed that this would be 'most unfair' but it had never been ruled out. This was the ultimate horror with which the King was menaced.[76] And according to Asquith's constitutional doctrine, he would have no option but to sign it though it would immediately precipitate the rebellion in Ulster. On 26 July the Howth gun-running took place in broad daylight and the intervention of troops who killed three people and injured thirty-eight greatly exacerbated the situation. Both the guns and the shooting strengthened the hand of the Irish Republican Brotherhood and made it impossible for Redmond to compromise.[77] This incident made Esher very pessimistic:

> *Esher-Stamfordham, 29 July 1914:*[78] I believe that the PM will, unless unforeseen events happen, bring the Bill up to the King for signature. If he lacks the moral courage to insist upon the 'clean cut' by agreement with the Tories, and so outvote the Irish and Radicals, there would appear to be no other course open to him than to go forward with the Home Rule Bill. After what has happened it would be a monstrous thing to do, but I fear he will do it.
>
> If I were Carson, I should set up the provisional government *at once*, and thus precipitate a crisis in the higher interests of the Monarchy and the Empire.

But if Carson did not move, and if Asquith attempted the worst, what could the King do? Asquith had always been optimistic about avoiding civil war, and he had promised the King that if it seemed imminent, 'in the last moment I shall run any risk of self-sacrifice'. The moment seemed to be approaching, and the only way out was for Asquith to resign or be dismissed and for the King on his own initiative to summon some neutral statesman to form an interim government. It would have been useless to send for Bonar Law, and for the same reason futile to seek for an electoral verdict, though a referendum was another matter.

One thing is certain, that the King would not have allowed his signature to be the warrant for the outbreak of fighting. He could according to Esher dissolve if he felt that the House of Commons no longer enjoyed the confidence of the country, but a dissolution would lose the Home Rule Bill and what was wanted was an Amending Act dictated by the electorate and not by Redmond. The possibilities for a royal initiative were extremely obscure, but it seemed worthwhile to Esher to prepare evidence of a precedent for the Crown's right of initiative independent of ministerial advice. He chose the case of Disraeli in 1868, who had been reluctant to terminate his brief premiership on being defeated by Gladstone's Irish Church resolution, and had amid a great deal of parliamentary criticism thrown on to the Queen the onus of the decision to keep him in office. What reconciled the Liberal majority in the Commons to this procedure was their preference for going to the polls under the new register which was taking some months more to prepare under the terms of the 1867 Reform Act. It was hardly a convincing historical parallel, but it could be argued *legally*:

Memorandum by Esher, 26 July 1914:[79] On May 1 the government of Mr Disraeli was defeated...but when offering his resignation...he left [the Queen] to choose between two alternatives... unguided by ministerial advice. The alternatives were to accept his resignation there and then, or to appeal to the country six months later...

The leaders of the Opposition argued that the Minister was bound to offer the Sovereign definite advice...This interpretation of the constitution was, however, inconsistent with several precedents, for the Queen had...chosen on more than one occasion between accepting a dissolution and the resignation of the ministry. The new feature, however, was Mr Disraeli's open attribution to the Queen of responsibility for the final decision. The result was that by the Queen's own volition and without the direct advice of her ministers, she decided that Mr Disraeli should remain in office for another six months.

The chief purpose of this memorandum which was sent to Stamford-ham was to supply a rebuttal to Asquith's too tidy and absolute ideas about the royal Prerogative.

The government's Chief Whip wanted the debate on the Amending Bill postponed a week to allow tempers to cool, but Asquith insisted on taking it on 30 July. While he was preparing his speech that morning he received a telephone call from Bonar Law, whose motor came to collect him for an emergency conference. The argument put to him was that 'to advertise our domestic dissensions at this moment would weaken our influence in the world for peace'. That morning Grey had received from Berlin a proposal that Britain should in exchange for neutrality bargain away France's colonies and the integrity of Belgium, and British involvement in the coming war had suddenly become almost certain. This new development confronted Asquith immediately after his interview with Bonar Law. After further consultations, he announced the indefinite postponement of the Irish debate. To quote his recent biographer: 'The unsolved problem was bundled into cold storage...And when the issue was next exposed to view, at Easter, 1916, the freezing plant was shown to be disappointingly ineffective. The maggots had been hard at work.'[80]

238

Eleven

The Commitment
to France

Haldane's creation of a 'striking force' backed by a special reserve to supply its losses in the field, and further supported by the 'second line' Territorial Army, followed the requirements which the CID under Balfour had laid down with the defence of India in mind. For one thing, it envisaged a period of grace during which the Territorial Army could be embodied and receive further training. It envisaged the slow unfolding of a conflict on the north-west frontier of India in which initially the Indian Army would take the lead. Such an engagement had been declared by Balfour to be the greatest task likely to be imposed on the British Army. The launching of the expeditionary force into a military maelstrom across the English Channel had not been contemplated by the CID under Balfour and it was not a thing which Campbell-Bannerman would readily entertain. Quizzed by the pacifists and socialists below the gangway, Haldane remained seemingly averse to any suggestion that his expeditionary force should be available to fight in France or Belgium. But this pretence became more difficult to maintain as the Entente, the renewal of the Japanese treaty, and finally the agreement with Russia of 1907 rendered ever more remote the prospect of a Russian descent on India. At the same time the threat of the German naval programme assumed a new urgency as it became apparent that von Tirpitz was building not commerce-protecting cruisers but dreadnoughts of the line designed for a titanic struggle with the British navy in the North Sea. The naval scares which so embarrassed the Liberal government and spoilt Lloyd George's projects for social reform came hard upon Haldane's army reforms, and by 1914 had carried the naval estimates up to £50 million. The whole rationale which the CID under Balfour had carefully formulated became out-of-date.

It was not until the height of the Agadir crisis of 1911 which raised the question of whether and how the expeditionary force

239

might be sent to France, that Winston Churchill came to realise the vital need for speed in countering the Schlieffen plan—the essence of which was brilliantly expounded by Henry Wilson before the CID —and the important role which the British expeditionary force might play. The revelation turned Churchill the economist and opponent of dreadnoughts into Churchill the monomaniac of the Admiralty. In appointing him as First Lord Asquith knew that he would create a Naval Staff, for the express purpose of defeating the Admiralty's contention that the immediate dispatch of an expeditionary force to France was not feasible and had to wait upon their operation of clearing the seas. Asquith's decision, supported chiefly by his Foreign Secretary Grey, marks a major departure in defence policy, and one which had important corollaries for naval strategy and for the meaning of the Entente. Not only did it mark the application of Haldane's army to a new use, but also it involved the taming of the Admiralty, which under Fisher had resisted the interference of the CID or the demand for the divulging of its war plans to the politicians.

Fisher's naval strategy was well known to be that of preserving the expeditionary force from being merged, in his opinion uselessly, in the Continental mêlée and using it instead for coastal descents supported by the navy on the German flank. This remained his strategy when Churchill brought him back to the Admiralty in 1914. But was it feasible? Was the close investment of an enemy coast by battleships possible after the latest developments in the submarine, torpedo and mine? Was it still realistic to think that a military force landed in Pomerania could hold its own or be safely brought off? And if the military damage which such a combined operation might inflict were negligible, was there still any point in the Admiralty's strategy? Would it not possibly be better to blockade Germany from a distance, closing off the North Sea in which the German navy would be confined? These seemed to be questions which the CID was designed to investigate. But the Admiralty would not divulge its war plans, and would not even say whether it could protect the transports which would carry the expeditionary force.

In Esher's opinion the Liberal government allowed the political struggles over the Budget of 1909 and other issues to overshadow the crucial and unresolved decisions about defence. As the election of January 1910 approached it seemed possible that the Liberals would slide out of office leaving defence questions in chaos. It was apparent that the divergence between the War Office and the Admiralty was dangerous and nullified the CID. Fisher's successor as First Sea Lord, Arthur Knyvet Wilson, proved a disappointment and an opponent of the CID, which had gone more or less into abeyance. When Esher suggested that a standing sub-committee of the CID should sit weekly and study the details of existing plans demanding military and naval co-operation, Wilson objected that such matters should be left to the Chief of the General Staff and First Sea Lord. Haldane, who backed Esher's proposal, felt that the weakness of the defence organisation was now the Board of Admiralty with 'its want of modern ideas and its inefficient organisation'. McKenna had come to oppose the proposal, rightly suspecting that it involved a censure on his department. In this way the genuine interests of inter-service co-operation were being confused with the departmental interests of the Admiralty which seemed to be under attack. Haldane was suspected of a desire to subordinate the Admiralty and War Office to a Minister of Defence. He was also suspected of an ambition to become First Lord himself to preside over sweeping reforms. However, Esher claimed that Asquith and Grey supported the particular project of the standing sub-committee, which could so easily be regarded as a Trojan horse. He appealed to Balfour, saying that if Asquith acquiesced in Wilson's view it would strike a 'deadly blow' at the CID.[1] Balfour replied: 'From what I heard of Wilson, his attitude does not greatly surprise me...Of course there are certain technical details of joint naval and military operations which must be worked out by the Admiralty and the General Staff. But the Prime Minister and the CID must surely have some security that the plans agreed to in principle can be immediately carried into execution.'[2] Asquith seems to have been swayed, for he created the standing sub-committee which however made little progress owing to the political dissensions of the members of the government.[2]

The recalcitrance of the Admiralty remained uncurbed, and indeed received a new encouragement when King George V, a sailor with fifteen years' service and a known Beresfordian, acceded to the throne in May 1910. Although King Edward had been an enthusiastic Fisherite he had also favoured the attempt of the CID to bring the Admiralty into its purview. King George was likely to espouse the professional interests of the sailors and the traditions of the navy. Even Churchill experienced the greatest difficulties when he ran

241

counter to these, while his contretemps behind the scenes with his Sea Lords were reported to the King's private secretary by Sir Francis Hopwood. The death of King Edward was, indeed, a signal for a counter-offensive to be launched by all the opponents of the Esher 'Triumvirate', the Haldane reforms and the threat to the autonomy of the services posed by the overlordship of the CID. One manifestation of this trend was a series of articles in *The World*³ under the caption of 'The Cabal' which suggested that through the abuse of royal influence and the manipulation of the press Esher and Haldane had defeated the defence interests of the country. Haldane was attacked as an amateur, not even entitled to wear a volunteer uniform, who had gone to the War Office admitting that he had made no special study of defence. He had abolished the cadres of nine battalions of the regular army, while his special reserve consisted 'mainly of youths ...totally unfit to take the field'. As for the Territorial Army, the promised 313,000 recruits for the second line had not materialised.

Esher was attacked as a 'mysterious power'. 'Prime Ministers or First Sea Lords may come and go, but he goes on for ever.' The recommendations of the Esher committee had been formulated so precipitately that 'they suggested action upon the strength of preconceived opinions'. Now he was a permanent member of the CID with 'the special use of a room in the building which forms its headquarters'. He drew no salary and could not therefore be got at by Parliament. He retained commercial connexions, as a director of the Central London Railway Company, the Agricultural Bank of Egypt and the Grand Opera Syndicate Ltd. His official power, if rumour was correct, was 'a mere wafer compared with the weight of his influence behind the scenes. How did he get that influence? What right had he to it? What are the concrete evidences of his marvellous brain and ability which his many press friends, from Colonel Repington... to Mr Stead, ascribed to him?' He enjoyed the power of obtaining information from the heads of departments as if he were a Secretary of State, but in fact he was 'the Man outside the Constitution'. It was intolerable that someone 'wielding his power...should be beyond the reach of effective criticism at a time when such grave changes are being carried out...' Esher's position, it was suggested, should be defined in a white paper, and he should be made amenable to questioning in his place in the House of Lords. Such parliamentary scrutiny was the 'historic and well-tried antidote to abuse of power and arrogation of superior intelligence'.

The specific charges made against Haldane's conduct of the War Office came near enough to the truth to be particularly embarrassing. Esher was identified as the head of a 'section' of the CID which had 'used its influence within the precincts of the War Office in connexion with matters that do not properly come within the Committee's province'. The public might conclude from this that Haldane had used the CID to overrule the soldiers. He was also accused of bartering secrets for press support. If the Secretary of the CID, Sir George Clarke, had really given up his press connexions, it was 'somewhat difficult to account for Colonel Repington's frequent visits' to Whitehall Gardens. Repington had formerly served in the Intelligence branch of the War Office, and his continued interference there as *The Times* military correspondent was 'in the highest degree improper'. In return for privileged information Repington 'has afforded a more than generous support for the organisation schemes of the War Minister'. Esher's role *vis-à-vis* the War Office was seen as that of smoothing away problems of patronage in which he 'is understood to take so intelligent an interest', and also in defeating the opposition of leading soldiers. There was for instance the 'scandal of the Mediterranean Command', a 'crowning jobbery' designed to keep Lord Kitchener away from London. Also there was Haldane's dismissal of the Duke of Connaught from the presidency of the Selection Board, subsequently filled with his own creatures. 'Lord Esher is given credit for having assisted in rearranging the Selection Board in this way and so robbing it of its independence.' Such charges were to stick to Haldane, who by this time was openly talking of leaving the War Office.

Esher himself now completed Haldane's discomfiture by declaring publicly, as Chairman of the London County Territorial Association, that the government's target for recruitment to the Territorials would not be reached. He was also sufficiently provoked by the press criticisms to hit back, writing in the *National Review* in September, at the democratic principle that officials should be paid in order that they might be popularly controlled. Voluntary service to the state was a better ideal, he suggested, but it was on the decline. Esher's own example of the new spirit was his own experience as a Cambridge extension lecturer, when a workman in his class discovered that he was unpaid and walked out with the remark: 'Then ye are only a preacher'. The demand that MPs should be paid would be followed, he prophesied, by a similar demand in the case of the chairmen and committees of County Councils and County Associations, on the ground that as unpaid officials 'the people have no hold over them'. The same decline in the spirit of voluntary service entailed the poor enrolment in the Territorials: '...there is no sign that the 60,000 required annually...will be forthcoming...There is no steady increase, no advance. There is in many cases retrogression...It may be that the sirocco of democracy is withering in our people the spirit of sacrifice.' There was in this article more than a hint of Esher's opinion that the time had come for compulsory military service.

Haldane was scandalised by this apparent betrayal of the government by a member of the CID and managed to persuade not only Asquith, but more significantly Lord Knollys, that Esher had gone beyond proper limits. He seemed to draw attention to and glorify in his irresponsible position. When Lord Roberts had done the same thing in 1905 Balfour had forced him to resign. But Lord Roberts was then paid a salary, and Esher took the view that since he was not paid he should not be bound. He thought Haldane's remonstrance 'half pathetic, half petulant', and he did not see why his having helped to organise the Territorial Army 'disqualifies me from expressing doubts about the success of the scheme...as if I were a paid politician'.[4] This was a feeble distinction, but Esher was on much firmer ground when he argued, writing to Lord Knollys, that the CID should include men of 'independent position' 'of the type of Cromer, of Minto, of Kitchener' etc, and also 'the Defence Ministers of Canada, Australia, and South Africa'.[5] Such members could not be expected to remain silent on general political questions except when they happened to agree with the government. However, Haldane took the first opportunity to attack compulsory service, and became embroiled with Lord Roberts in a public altercation which was only made more acrimonious when Haldane joined his opponent in the House of Lords a few months later.

The attack on Haldane and Esher was thought to have been inspired by Arnold-Forster's group appealing no doubt to Beresfordians and opponents of the CID. But the timing was not fortunate, chiefly because for those interested in increasing defence expenditure the preoccupation of the moment was still the dreadnought

244

programme, of which Esher and Haldane were among the chief backers. A crisis in January 1910 had forced Asquith to agree to McKenna's minimum demand of four dreadnoughts and a battle cruiser for 1910–12, but Churchill thought this rate of building too high while at the other extreme the Imperial Maritime League called for a national loan of £100 million to stablilise the naval construction programme.[6] A party split between Liberal 'little Navy-ites' (Churchill, Lloyd George, Morley, Loreburn and Burns) and the supporters of McKenna (Asquith, Grey, and Haldane) remained a threatening possibility. Such a split would represent powerful currents of discontent and especially the exasperation among the more socialistic Liberals at the subordination of welfare legislation to defence. This was exactly the consideration which made the disappointing recruiting to the Territorials so worrying. If Haldane's scheme, the last resort of the supporters of the voluntary system, proved unsuccessful the alternative would have to be much higher army estimates or else conscription. Defence was clearly one of those great national questions, like Ireland or the House of Lords or possibly tariff reform, which split parties and which seemed only capable of solution by some kind of compact between parties. Such at least was the view taken by Lloyd George, who at the Constitutional Conference proposed a National Government to clear these distressing log jams. When this somewhat far-fetched idea dissolved, the hopes for a resolution of the dilemmas of defence centred on the CID.

Fisher, the author of the dreadnought, remained on the CID after leaving the Admiralty, pretending to be a good Liberal. Esher presided over an 'open conspiracy' to beat the German naval competition with the slogan 'two keels for one'. Before the first election of 1910 he formed the 'Islanders' who were men of position and influence in the constituencies ready to turn the scales for or against parliamentary candidates according to their stance on the naval question. The society caught on and membership soon exceeded 70,000: a huge correspondence was managed by Esher's son Maurice Brett with several assistants. W. T. Stead also thundered away in the *Review of Reviews* and made 'two keels for one' a household phrase. But the little Navy-ites were powerfully represented by H. W. Massingham of the *Nation* aided by the *Daily News* and *Manchester Guardian*. They became formidable to the government when in the summer McKenna was shaken by the Osborne Case of a wrongly-dismissed cadet. There was a chance

245

to attack him when Parliament reassembled on this and on his naval forecasts. Esher got wind of such a plot, and turned to Balfour, writing to his secretary:

Esher-J. S. Sandars, 8 August 1910:[7] I hear that McKenna is to be forced out in November over next year's estimates. That is the *mot d'ordre*. Consequently there is joy over the bungling *re* Archer-Shee. They talk of an 'inquiry' with the 'dreadnought type' and a hold-over of construction till the inquiry is over.

Winston and Lloyd George have captured Sir William White (old fool) and are belabouring McKenna with criticism...Luckily McKenna, with all his faults, is a determined fighter.

So your instincts about the navy are quite correct.

The Unionist press found it difficult to resist an opportunity of scoring against the government, and there appeared the prospect of a combination of jingoes and Radicals against the First Lord. In the opinion of J. A. Spender, a devoted follower of Asquith and friend of McKenna, the resignation of the First Lord would bring down the government. It is an interesting indication of the way Esher was now regarded as a Liberal supporter that Spender could appeal to him at this juncture to use his influence with the Tory press in order to save Asquith's government:

J. A. Spender-Esher, 10 August 1910:[8] McKenna is one of my most intimate friends, and I went step by step with him through his fight last year and was able to do a little to thwart his enemies in the final bout. So I know pretty well what to expect.

I am inclined to think that if the Conference prospers, Lloyd George will not attack naval estimates this year, for in that case he will be on a totally different line of country. But Winston is implacable, and he and Massingham and the *Daily News* and *Morning Leader* and *Manchester Guardian* group undoubtedly think that the Osborne Case gives them their chance of getting back on McKenna.

...You will see that the *Morning Post* clasps the hands of Massingham and promises him support in his campaign. If this comes off, there will be a combination of jingoes and Radicals to unship McKenna...If you have any influence with the

Morning Post, you might warn them that they are playing with fire here...no party in the cabinet can evict the First Lord on his estimates without destroying themselves and the Government.

In these circumstances Balfour launched his autumn tour with a speech at Glasgow on 19 October which reviewed the government's whole conduct of the naval programme and called it 'most lamentable and dangerous'. He raised a scare, which events proved to be unfounded, that by 1913 the Germans would have twenty-one dreadnoughts as against the British twenty-five. With the advantage of surprise a German attack might succeed. Esher was delighted with the performance. 'The whole speech is without flaw' he wrote to Balfour: 'The "chapter of accident" is a new point to people, and will do much to open their eyes to the risks we run.'[9]

In addition to prompting Balfour as the leader of the opposition, Esher was keeping him abreast of the developments in the CID. Lord Kitchener, he reported, had been nominated as a member, but had written to say he did not consider himself tied by this. Fearing that the work of the CID might be dismissed as the maunderings of a few 'harmless amateurs', Esher had been doing his best to get men like Kitchener on to it, and also to keep up the pace of the specialised work of his standing sub-committee.

Esher-Balfour, 24 October 1910:[10] The enclosed is, I think, and I hope you will agree, as good a bit of work as the CID has ever done. I want you to see the *sort* of work which the 'Standing Sub-Committee' (which I fought so hard to obtain) is doing. The composition of the sub-committee varies according to the subject of inquiry etc. But one or two of us are constant factors. Remember that this sort of thing has never been *thought of* before, much less worked out.

On the major problem of the scale and progress of German naval construction or the margin of superiority needed to offset surprise attack, the CID does not appear to have deliberated, and certainly the projected numbers publicly announced by McKenna, Churchill and Balfour continued to fluctuate within wide limits. Until the early months of 1911 Churchill continued to maintain that the British scale of building was extravagantly inflated.

I

The conversion of Churchill to the opposite view, and the conversion of the Liberal government to the principle of the Henry Wilson plan for sending the expeditionary force to France followed dramatically from the Agadir crisis. While still Home Secretary Churchill, under the supposed menace of imminent war with Germany, became nervous about the safety of the naval cordite magazines for which he was responsible. He also signed general warrants for opening mail which disclosed the German system of British paid agents. Haldane gladly afforded him the facilities of the War Office, and before long Churchill had fallen under the spell of Sir William Nicholson and Sir Henry Wilson. Wilson he describes as a man of 'extraordinary vision and faith' with 'an immense and, I expect, unequalled knowledge about the Continent' who was 'deep in the secrets of the French general staff'. In close touch with Foch and with Huguet, the French military attaché in London, Wilson plotted for years to ensure that 'we should act immediately on the side of France'.[11]

The Admiralty did not show up very well in the Agadir crisis. At one point, after Lloyd George's celebrated Mansion House speech designed to give a plain warning to Germany, a German note seemed to Grey so menacing that he asked McKenna to alert the fleet against a possible surprise attack. In spite of this alarm, the British fleets remained dispersed, their crews were given leave, and ships were immobilised by a Cardiff coal strike. Sir Arthur Wilson went off to Scotland on a shooting party. Such sang-froid naturally raised queries about the nature of the Admiralty's war plans, and the cabinet were 'shocked and amazed' to learn that no such plans could be produced in Wilson's absence, for they were 'locked in his brain'.[12] The pressing question was whether the navy's strategy allowed for the immediate dispatch of four divisions to France. In order to elicit the materials for an answer an all-day sitting of the CID was called for 23 August. The memorandum which Churchill prepared for this meeting shows him to have become a convert to the General Staff's insistent and, as was later proved, remarkably accurate prognostications demanding the immediate and elaborately timetabled dispatch of the British army following a declaration of war.[13] At the meeting Sir Henry Wilson expounded his reasons for believing that a German attack on France would come via Belgium, and the crucial importance of time. He unfolded a war game in impressive detail, using his carefully prepared map. By contrast, Sir Arthur Wilson's performance was deplorable.

His strategic assumptions were not only vague and confused, but they struck even the relatively uninformed politicians as being palpably out-of-date. He argued ineffectually for the close investment of the German coast and proposed to land a division on German soil. He was against any joint war plans between the general staff and the Admiralty, and did not think the creation of a Naval Staff necessary or feasible. He offered no prospect of being able to assist in the dispatch of the expeditionary force as required by the general staff and seemed opposed to their strategy.[14] Asquith himself did not at this stage believe in the strategy of the General Staff, but he was convinced by the First Sea Lord's performance that a Naval Staff ought to be created at once. He must have endorsed Churchill's opinion that 'No man of real power could have answered so foolishly'.[15]

The sailors claimed that the military 'conversations' with the French general staff robbed Britain of the ability to devise its own strategy. They had never agreed to the Henry Wilson timetable, but neither had they placed any alternative war plan before the CID. They now fell back on obstruction. Maurice Hankey, the Assistant Secretary of the CID and an ex-marines officer congratulated Fisher on the 'defeat of our opponents' at the CID meeting, which had dispersed without a decision.[16] Then McKenna took the line that the military conversations would encourage France to provoke Germany whereupon Britain would be morally bound to assist. Soon McKenna was threatening to resign if the military conversations were not terminated. He could expect to find support from the pacifist section of the cabinet, Crew, Morley and Harcourt, who had never been told of the conversations and who had been carefully excluded from the CID's August meeting. Asquith had to act quickly. He had, however, the unusual advantage that in this defence quarrel Churchill and Lloyd George were on the 'jingo' side. He decided to replace McKenna by Churchill at the Admiralty and force the issue of a Naval Staff.

Esher had missed the CID meeting, for he had been operated on for appendicitis and was convalescing in Scotland. He was at Balmoral early in October, however, when Asquith arrived and consulted him about getting rid of Sir Arthur Wilson, which was largely a question of finding a sailor able and willing to take his place. Asquith had recently conferred with Churchill and Haldane, both of whom aspired to McKenna's place, and decided that he could safely prefer Churchill, who had Lloyd George's support. Haldane, after all, was now a peer, and Asquith did not like his plan of sending the entire expeditionary force to France. But if Asquith imagined that his own idea of limited liability and the dispatch of only four divisions to France would obviate the commitment of the 'conversations', Esher thought otherwise. 'I reminded him,' he noted, 'that the mere fact of the War Office plan having been worked out in detail with the French General Staff...has certainly committed us to fight, whether the Cabinet likes it or not, and that the combined plan of the two General Staffs holds the field.' But it was, Esher admitted, 'certainly an extraordinary thing that our officers should have been permitted to arrange all the details, trains, landing, concentration, etc, when the cabinet have never been consulted.'[17] Esher's own personal opinion in the matter is somewhat obscure. He approved of the conversations in principle and certainly believed in supporting France in any war with Germany. At the same time he leant towards the Fisher strategy and probably preferred the retention of a large part of the army to be used in combined operations. To land the whole army in France seemed to throw away much of the advantage of naval power and to cripple British diplomacy particularly in the case of Holland and other small neighbours of Germany. When therefore Esher spoke so emphatically of the commitment to France he was thinking of the existing crisis. But unfortunately for the Fisher strategy the same plan still held the field in 1914.

Asquith asked Esher to draw up a memorandum on the proposed Naval Staff. Esher claimed no originality in the proposals he made, which had already been considered by the staff of the CID, but they certainly followed the principle of the general staff in avoiding an élite and in freely interchanging the War Staff at the Admiralty with the staff at the proposed War College. To meet the pressing dilemma of the government Esher declared that: 'General plans of operations to meet different eventualities should be worked out by the War Staff of the Admiralty, and held at the disposition of the Cabinet.'[18] Fortified by his various consultations Asquith confronted McKenna, who seems to have treated Churchill's advent as First Lord as committing Britain to the immediate and automatic defence of France. Asquith was presumably referring only to the existing crisis, which had virtually blown over, when he assured McKenna that 'he did not believe in war and that if he had thought that war were probable he would not have made the change'.[19] On the day that Churchill took over the Admiralty Esher commented:

> *Esher-Sandars, 25 October 1911:*[20] Winston has been intriguing for months to get to the Admiralty. He wants to institute great reforms there. We are to have a CID sub-committee on them at once. *This* will be highly beneficial; for the Admiralty is in a rotten state. But how he will do about estimates, heaven knows. I expect that he will spend pretty freely. *Nous verrons.*

True enough, Churchill was transformed by his new duties and his defection from the side of the naval economists turned the scales and left Lloyd George isolated and virtually powerless to curb the soaring estimates. By his own admission, Churchill ceased to be pre-occupied with social reforms, and became absorbed night and day with the fascinating and dreadful conflict which he saw approaching.

Unfortunately for the cause of naval and military co-operation the impetus given by the Agadir crisis did not last, and indeed provoked a reaction. The excluded faction of the cabinet, consisting of Morley and four others, were so alarmed at the revelation that the country might be committed to war by the joint general staffs that they denounced the Entente and the CID. The Unionist press represented by the *Morning Post* and *Standard* took up the cry that the CID was usurping the duties of the War Office and Admiralty. Churchill, also, imported an autocratic spirit into the Admiralty which did not go down well with the Board and which initially took the form of a proposal to place the new Chief of the Naval War Staff under himself and take over much of the responsibility of the CID. Asquith's idea of settling the inter-service disputes and the dangerous want of agreed war plans by knocking the heads of the two Staffs together before the CID was being lost from sight. To restore it Esher proposed a Co-ordination sub-committee to be a standing committee of the CID and hastened to muster support from Balfour and the Secretary of the CID, Sir Charles Ottley. However, before their testimony was returned Asquith had approved. 'The Prime Minister has agreed to my proposal.' Esher informed Balfour, 'not so much, between ourselves, on its merits, as for fear of certain amazing proposals of Winston's, the effect of which would have been to transfer the work of the Defence Committee to the Admiralty and to him!'[21] The purpose of the CID itself, as defined by Ottley, was to 'co-ordinate not merely the great departments of state in the UK, but the whole empire...so that when war comes the great machine passes from a peace to a war footing without friction'.[22] This was exactly the horror of the CID for pacifists like Morley.

No sooner was Churchill firmly seated in the Admiralty than he set in train one of the major changes in naval strategy of the century without any formal consultation. Faced with a new German Navy Law which by removing recruits from the High Sea Fleet virtually placed twenty-five battleships on a war footing, Churchill decided to withdraw the battleships of the Mediterranean fleet for home defence. Haldane supported him with the private observation; 'You and I must always be responsible for policy...'[23] Esher's protest had been commended by Asquith to Churchill as having 'much good sense in it', but Churchill fell back on the old departmental axiom that 'the ultimate responsibility of the First Lord must not be impaired. He cannot be expected to be responsible for faulty dispositions, or what he thinks are such! '[24] With this off-hand remark Asquith's whole policy of strengthening the CID and bringing into the open the Admiralty's strategic thinking went by the board. But Churchill overreached himself when he wrote to Grey: 'This means relying on France in the Mediterranean and certainly no exchange of system would be possible, even if desired by you.'[25] There was much to commend Churchill's policy. Austria and Italy were building dreadnoughts, and inferior ships in the Mediterranean would merely be sitting ducks. More important, as Churchill announced in introducing his naval estimates on 18 March 1912, he was obliged to step up his building programme in order to meet at any 'average' moment the enemy's surprise attack at his 'selected' moment. The strain on personnel would be greater, and it was the crews rather than the ships that he wanted nearer home.

Esher adopted a frankly patronising attitude to Churchill. 'I am strongly and irreconcilably opposed to "abandoning" the Mediterranean,' he wrote to Winston, 'but I don't want you to think that I am opposed to *you*...I have liked you since, as a child, you sat on my knee, and have admired your brilliance ever since you became a man.'[26] Churchill's parliamentary announcement of his policy of a 60 per cent margin in dreadnoughts over Germany and two keels to one for every other ship was naturally applauded by Esher, but he attributed its adoption to his own secret society, 'the 70,000 Islanders who for three years have fought all over the country for two keels to one'.[27] Now, to oppose Churchill's latest heresy, Esher was prepared to employ every official and unofficial means. The recent death of W. T. Stead robbed the navalists of their most powerful voice, but Esher still had influence with *The Times* and *Westminster Gazette*.

Churchill's policy involved the abandonment of the Mediterranean in the first weeks of a war, while a naval decision was obtained in the major theatre. If victorious the British navy would soon deal with any rival power in the Mediterranean. But the assumption that the German fleet would seek or be brought to battle was to prove incorrect. This however was not the main query raised by the CID, but rather the effect of the exposure of Malta, Cyprus and Egypt to potential enemies and the diplomatic effects of naval absence on wavering neutrals. Here again historical hindsight would have suggested a more ominous conclusion than was drawn, for the successful passage of the *Goeben* to Constantinople was one of the disasters of the coming war. Yet Churchill carried all before him. His argument with Haldane was: 'Considering you propose to send the whole British Army abroad, you ought to help me to keep the whole British Navy at home.'[28] At a conference in Malta late in May he came to an understanding with Kitchener, and *The Times* of 30 May supported his proposed withdrawal.

By this time the alternatives had crystallised into the Haldane-Churchill policy of supplementing the Entente by an agreement making France responsible for the naval defence of the Mediterranean while the British navy covered the Channel and the transports of the expeditionary force: or, alternatively, the Fisher-Esher policy of hedging on any serious military commitment to France and counting on independent diplomacy and sea supremacy. When *The Times* seemed to approve the former alternative, Esher sent a long memorandum to Repington asking him to 'see Buckle [the editor] and allow *him* to take it for a thesis'. Had he published this under his own name he would probably, as he told Balfour, have been 'kicked off the CID'.[29] The memorandum contained the very significant proposition that as a commercial and trading nation 'we should be mad to entangle ourselves in a continental strife on land'. The choices were threefold: an 'increase of naval power as will ensure sea command in the Mediterranean'; or 'the substitution of a conscript for a voluntary army'; or 'the abandonment of Egypt and Malta and the complete reversal of the traditional policy of Great Britain in regard to her trade routes and military highways to the East'. Churchill was heading for one of the last two choices. But:

> The concentration of the fleet...denudes the Mediterranean of effective ships and abandons our sea command. With this abandonment goes the power to hold against potential enemies Egypt and Malta and possibly Gibraltar. With it goes the value to Japan of the British alliance. With it comes into play a not unlikely regrouping of the Mediterranean Powers and a change in the relations of the country with Italy and Spain...The security of Egypt and the defence of Malta are based upon sea command, for no sufficient land forces under our military system can be available for these purposes without absolute sea command at the outbreak of war...
>
> [Britain] is not and never can be one of the great military Powers. She is either supreme at sea, or she is relegated to the class of secondary Powers.[30]

The theory that Britain could rely on the naval forces even of a friendly power like France was in Esher's opinion 'illusory'.

On the face of it Churchill's policy was a reasonable compromise, for it involved a stepping up of dreadnought construction, and an increase in naval forces. It looked as if the strong men in the cabinet —Lloyd George, Grey, Haldane and Asquith himself—would support Churchill and Esher feared that would mean 'an alliance with France under cover of "conversations" and conscription to cover Pussy [Haldane]'s traces at the War Office'.[31] Even Balfour and Fisher wavered, for they had initiated the concentration of the fleet. Morley, also, inclined to Churchill. Only McKenna, Lewis Harcourt and Lansdowne seemed sympathetic to Esher's strenuous arguments against the madness of concentrating everything in the North Sea. But at least the struggle was an intellectual rather than a political one, for the final decision rested with the CID and would not involve resignations. It was 'a tough fight and not a stone left unturned' culminating in an all-day session of the CID on 4 July.[32] Esher suggested a rough 'conclusion' to Asquith at lunchtime, and was delighted to find that Asquith's final resolution passed to him in a note before being put to the Committee was substantially the same. This retained a Mediter-

ranean battle fleet based on Malta and equal to a one-Power Mediterranean standard, excluding France. Churchill made a final protest,
and the resolution was accepted.[33]

The result of this, the 'hardest fought fight' for Esher in which he
had been personally engaged, was that the 60 per cent margin of
dreadnought superiority in home waters was maintained, while the
Mediterranean fleet was an extra. This had the effect of increasing the
number of capital ships, which was not however Esher's principal
idea. He thought Churchill 'deficient in imagination' and neglectful
of 'every consideration of policy, and of naval exigency, elsewhere
than in the North Sea'.[34] He also rejected the Admiralty's idea that
capital ships were the true measure of naval power. 'I should be far
happier' he wrote to Balfour 'if I could see the standard of strength
measured by 1. personnel; 2. submarines; 3. destroyers; 4. large
armoured cruisers; 5. armoured cruisers; 6. Battleships—in that
order.'[35] This proved all too true a perception. Churchill as an economist turned First Lord became caught in an escalation of capital ships
and a defensive posture. He became mesmerised by the prospect of a
short and final conflict in the 'decisive theatre' fought by battleships.
When he left the Admiralty in 1915 it remained in a mental strait-
jacket.

The adoption of a one-Power standard in the Mediterranean enabled Churchill to suggest to the French naval attaché that his
country should aim at a standard equal to Austria and Italy combined.[36] The cabinet authorised the opening of naval 'conversations'
which were concluded in a Naval Convention of February 1913. It
was futile to argue, as Churchill did, that this involved no commitment to France, and it was in vain that the Convention reserved
Britain's right to stay out of a war. For the Convention dovetailed
into the Haldane plan for sending the expeditionary force to France
and marks the acceptance of it by the Admiralty as well as the abandonment of the dreams of aggressive naval power and diplomacy
which Fisher had shared with Esher. So that when the cabinet decided
in 1914, just before news arrived of the invasion of Belgium, to try
to keep out of the war, it still was forced to decide that a German
attack on the French northern and western coasts would be for
Britain a *casus belli*. Similarly, when on the entry of Britain into the
war Asquith summoned an extraordinary War Council, the military
and naval staffs proved incapable of suggesting, much less agreeing to,

I*

any combined operations in defence of Antwerp or Zeebrugge. The CID had not considered combined operations and the necessary diplomatic preparations had been neglected. The Henry Wilson plan was the only one that had been thoroughly worked out.

It might appear strange that Esher did not follow up his successful struggle over the Mediterranean fleet with an attempt to complete the CID's hold over the Admiralty through the new Naval War Staff. Churchill's excuse was lack of time. A Naval Staff could not be so easily created. But in fact his personal relations with his new Board of Admiralty were not good. His autocratic manner was misunderstood and resented, and soon he was involved in a public dispute with Sir Francis Bridgeman, whom he had promoted rather suddenly to the position of First Sea Lord and then scarcely more than a year later had forced to retire.[37] Fisher's attitude to Churchill was decidedly ambivalent, and the disputes within the Admiralty were freely leaked to the leaders of the Opposition. Churchill therefore lacked the power and authority to coerce the Board into formulating war plans or co-operating with the CID, even had he the wish to do so. The discipline and loyalty of the naval high command was fatally rotted by the Fisher-Beresford feud and there were too many old men at the top. The impetus had to come from outside, and in Asquith's government only an international crisis or a cabinet dispute generated enough resolution to overcome the departmentalism of the Admiralty. After the Agadir war scare revealed the strength of opposition in the cabinet to war plans or commitments the course of least resistance was to leave the service departments alone. The War Office was filled by a nonentity, John Seely, and politically Churchill's separation from Lloyd George and from the criticism of naval expenditure was far too valuable to Asquith for the Prime Minister readily to risk provoking his resignation. All this must have been evident to Esher, who in any case took an increasingly hostile line to the government over Ulster and ended up by boycotting the CID. Small wonder, then, that the CID made little notable progress during the political storms of 1913 and 1914.

After the failure of the Haldane mission to Berlin to obtain any tokens of a possible 'naval holiday' or respite in the armaments race, the imminence of war was clear enough to those who could read the signs. 'A war entered upon for no other object than to restore the Germanic Empire of Charlemagne in modern form appears to me at

256

once so wicked and stupid as to be almost incredible!' commented
Balfour in March 1912 on returning some documents to Churchill:
'...imagine it being possible to talk about war as inevitable when
there is no quarrel, and nothing to fight over! We live in strange
times!'[38] One sign of the times was a book by a member of the German
general staff, General Bernhardi, which provoked Esher to a denunciation in *The Times*.[39] The book argued that Europe was not big
enough for the full moral and material development of France and
Germany, that the interests of small nations like Belgium had to be
sacrificed, that attempts to outlaw war were not only foolish but im-
moral and unworthy of humanity, and that England had to be 'beaten
at sea' by Germany. But public opinion, roused in the directions of
pacifism or jingoism by the newspapers, hardly appreciated the nature
of modern war, its totality, its devastation and horror, and the psychological forces which could will it in spite of all. The pacifists and
jingoes as represented in the vernacular of the press were equally out
of touch with the social and technological realities of the twentieth
century and imagined that war could be left to the soldiers.

Esher had done as much as anyone to popularise the principles on
which national defence and the policies of the CID rested. Now, in
1912, he devoted much of his time to the objects of the Garton
Foundation,[40] of which he was a trustee with Balfour, which was to
publish special studies of war and its social consequences. The
leitmotiv of the Foundation was Norman Angell's book, *The Great
Illusion*, which was used as the basis of a propaganda organised by
Esher's son Maurice Brett from Cambridge and from Angell's club in
London. A Cambridge man, Bernard Langdon-Davies, toured the
United States on behalf of the Foundation. Its aim as defined by
Balfour was to propagate the doctrine that 'aggressive warfare,
undertaken for the purpose of making the aggressor happier, wealthier,
more prosperous, is not only wrong but silly...under modern conditions of industry and finance civilised nations, and, most of all, the
Great Powers, have interests so intimately bound together, that the
violent disruption of friendly relations must produce disasters to all
concerned, which no indemnities, no gains in territory, no triumphal
arches, can ever compensate.'[41] This kind of message went down readily
enough in commercial cities with businessmen and civic dignitaries,
but characteristically the Foundation was confused with pacifist
groups such as the old Peace Society, while some like Rowntree refused

to join it because it supported armaments.[42] Even the theory of Norman Angell that war would be so economically disastrous that it could last only a short time tended to reinforce complacency. To counteract this Esher repeated on public platforms the message that war was entered into by men for whom prudence or respect for consequences were secondary motives, and that therefore it could only be outlawed by public understanding of its causes and public restraint upon its potential authors. 'I am here,' he told a Cambridge audience, 'because in the big affairs of mankind logic holds a subordinate place, and because inconsistency happens to be the rule of active and healthy life...men are still governed by passion and only occasionally by reason.'[43] A long period of peace had habituated people to the assumption that war would only come when there was some just quarrel and would be controlled by national interests. The idea of a deliberately planned war of aggression or a war fought with nihilistic fury had hardly impinged on public men in England trained to parliamentary government, but as Esher reminded an audience at the United Services Institution: 'The great drama of war often moved within a sphere from which men's imagination excluded all considerations of prudence.'[44]

Just as Esher advocated national armaments so long as there were nations prone to aggression, so he advocated international alliances until some real concert of all powers had been evolved. He was therefore to become a decided opponent of Woodrow Wilson's attempt to impose a supra-national system in the peace settlement, founded on rationalistic principles, on a world still governed by very irrational forces. However, in a lecture delivered to an august audience at the Sorbonne in March 1914 Esher looked forward to a time when war could be effectively controlled: '...the hope of European peace during the transition period...until the public mind is thoroughly awakened to what fratricidal European war means in the twentieth century, lies in the system or plan of alliances', which, he hoped, would finally become a 'Concert of *all* Great Powers, based upon reason and common interest, from which the uncertain element of sporadic action has been eliminated'.[45]

On the question of an alliance with France Esher now appeared to have changed his mind, and *The Times* saw him as advocating a 'New Triple Alliance'. Like Churchill he felt that Britain had incurred all the obligations of an alliance without the precise definitions. Also the deterrent value of an alliance, which would have disabused Germany of any hopes that Britain would stay out of a war, had been sacrificed to the theory that England's independent action might stop a war, and such a theory was beginning to look too optimistic. Recent events had disclosed a powerful and perhaps dominant group of ministers in favour of non-intervention, and it was reasonable to expect that in another war scare British diplomatic action would be paralysed by indecision. And it was, in the event, only the clear treaty obligation to Belgium that brought Britain into the war. The course of action was determined by the military and naval 'conversations'. Two days before the British declaration of war the cabinet agreed that German ships would not be allowed the passage of the Channel or North Sea in order to attack the coasts or shipping of France. But on the following day, 3 August, the majority of ministers were still opposed to giving France any definite assurance until the news of the violation of Belgium arrived. Esher deplored this, believing that: 'If ever a nation was bound, we are encircled by our acts and tacit promises. How I have argued this point with Asquith and Harcourt and Haldane—all these Ministers wishing to enjoy the best of both worlds—to be bound or unbound at their option, and perhaps to leave unfortunate France to be overwhelmed.'[46] Against such an uncertain political background the partial success of the CID in formulating war plans and demonstrating the importance of the military role which Britain could play on the Continent was a remarkable achievement. The Liberal party with its almost fanatical resistance to the idea of 'militarism' or involvement in land war on the Continent could be led by the nose only so far.

Twelve

The Ascendancy
of Kitchener

The CID had done its work thoroughly on the level of executive policy
and administration, to cover the immediate exigencies of the outbreak of war. Hankey's War Book effectively forestalled the commercial and financial dislocations which would have appeared failing
tight direction and control by the government, while Henry Wilson's
meticulously worked-out timetables for transporting the expeditionary force to the Meuse presented the Germans with a complete
surprise when they bumped into the British army. But on the higher
plane of war direction practically nothing existed and absolutely
nothing had been designed. This was a catastrophic oversight on the
part of the CID. It arose from a false assumption concerning the
duration of a European war and a refusal to face the prospect of
raising and deploying on a global scale the huge national army that
did emerge and for which a war directorate was indispensable. And
yet Lord Kitchener, suddenly placed at the War Office, at once proceeded to follow the opposite assumption, that the war would last for
four years and that thirty divisions would have to be raised immediately. The general staff however were allowed to leave the country at
the heels of the expeditionary force, while the CID and its secretariat
became engrossed in the task of integrating the scores of committees
that proliferated under the direction of the Prime Minister. Apart
from the cumbrous and sometimes farcical discussions of the War
Councils that were occasionally summoned by Asquith, there was no
overall direction of the war for several months until by a slow and
painful evolution the War Committee established itself.

Meanwhile the vacuum was filled by the sly and inscrutable Lord
Kitchener himself. His immense prestige was to be invaluable in
carrying the mass of the people into war and in producing hordes of
volunteers who could be seen drilling with wooden rifles and even
umbrellas. But was he a magnificent leader as well as a magnificent

poster? For some months his colleagues thought so. Asquith rated him along with Churchill and Lloyd George in the upper class of ability among his ministers. A year later his colleagues had all changed their minds. By then the unfolding of events had shown that Kitchener had lost his grip. He failed to sustain the reputation for massive sagacity and prescience which he had earned by August 1914. It is no disparagement to Kitchener to say that he failed to run the war single-handed. But it is certainly an unfavourable reflection on Asquith and on the CID's work before 1914 to observe that no consideration was given to the problem of how a war would be directed. It was left to time and chance.

The real oversight was perhaps more political than military. It was not realised that war direction requires in English conditions the kind of 'presidential' Prime Minister exemplified by William Pitt, Lloyd George or Winston Churchill backed by a small war cabinet. Asquith was supremely a reconciler and conciliator, tough and tenacious in sticking to what was right or what he thought was needed to hold his government together, but otherwise weak in enforcing a line of his own. He was orientated to principles rather than to events—as Lloyd George and Churchill were to events rather than to principles. In wartime government the Prime Minister must take events—and occasionally his colleagues—by the throat. Since a Prime Minister can hardly change his style, it is probably inevitable that a peace-time premier should be supplanted by a war leader. The decline in Asquith's prestige and the growing confidence in Lloyd George went hand in hand with public acceptance of total war. Asquith had not the temperament to direct a war, and so he failed to develop the potentiality of the CID and allowed Kitchener to absorb into his autocratic and mysterious sphere all the responsibility for the military conduct of the war—recruiting, munitions, strategic policy, and a lot else.

Kitchener was actually on his way back to Egypt when, on the day before Britain declared war, he was recalled from Dover. The demand that he should take over the War Office from Asquith who held it since the Curragh affair arose in the Northcliffe press at Repington's instigation. Haldane, as the creator of the expeditionary force, had been designated by Asquith but gave way to popular demand at once. Kitchener, who was entirely ignorant both of the organisation of European armies in general and of the Anglo-French mobilisation plans in particular, at once interfered and consequently quarrelled

261

with Henry Wilson. Before he had actually assumed the seals of office he attended the War Council which Asquith convened at Downing Street on 5 August,[1] and threw his weight into the scales against the project of sending five divisions to France which Wilson thought had been promised to the French and which Haldane supported. Only four divisions had been authorised to go when by proposing the next day (his first in office) to move a division to Edinburgh and even brigades from Aldershot to cover the supposed danger of invasion Kitchener threatened to mess up the dispatch of these.

It must be admitted that Kitchener found only confusion of counsels among the soldiers. Henry Wilson described the War Council of 5 August as: 'A historic meeting of men, mostly entirely ignorant of their subject.'[2] Even Sir John French, who was engaged in assembling his staff in London for commanding the force, suddenly 'dragged in the ridiculous proposal of going to Antwerp' which was impracticable both because the navy had not extended its screen so far, and because it involved a violation of Dutch neutrality.[3] Douglas Haig, who thought there should be a delay of two or three months (by which time in Wilson's opinion the war would be over) 'asked questions and this led to our discussing strategy like idiots'.[4] Some present thought that Liège was in Holland. The Wilson plan carried the day because it had been thoroughly worked out, but in agreeing to make Amiens the point of concentration Kitchener wanted to get confirmation from the French as to the latest developments. At the War Council of 6 August the four divisions were approved to go at once, but no more, Kitchener having become more sensitive to the danger of invasion.[5]

Esher had been following these events closely. He quickly attached himself to Kitchener, who 'glanced round the War Office for help, but could find none. Whitehall had been swept clean of soldiers of experience and talent...he found aged tired men who trembled before him and his reputation...In this novel sphere he was baffled and lost confidence in himself.'[6] His decision on 6 August to send only four divisions might reflect Esher's influence, for he noted that day 'I have always thought the strategy of tacking the small British army on to the French was arguable...By the precipitate alignment of our army...we forego the advantages of sea power.'[7] Like Hankey, Esher was concerned for the safety of the Channel ports. The belief that the Germans meant to deliver their main blow through Belgium made it even more expedient to hold a force in reserve to strike at their flank.

262

That Kitchener had already on 6 August arrived at his correct anticipation of the German plan is evident from Esher's further comment:
'It is difficult to understand the political strategy of the Germans;
their indifference to the number of enemies they provoke appears to
be madness; but there is probably a good deal of method in it...the
French are not yet sure that the passage through Belgium is the real
attack, although Lord K[itchener] is certain of it.'[8]

While Sir John French and his Chief of Staff thought the war would
last three months, Kitchener was thinking of a war of 'three years at
least' and the mobilisation of a million men.[9] He was unimpressed by
the appeals of the representatives of the Territorial troops to use
their fourteen divisions as the basis of expansion and he rejected the
offer of the use of their organisation. As chairman of the London
County Territorial Association, Esher naturally put in a plea for this
but without much conviction:

Note by Esher, 11 August 1914:[10] In a few days time, when the
London Territorial divisions move into the country, their HQ
will be empty except for a small depot in each that remains behind. This means that all over London there will be available
drill halls, room for staff, armouries, miniature ranges, clothing
stores, etc. The two Associations of the City and County of
London with their recruiting committees and their excellent staff,
together with their offices, will practically have nothing to do...
It is unfortunate that with all this valuable machinery not only
in London but all over England and Scotland, Lord Kitchener's
army should have to be raised by extemporised methods...There
seems no reason why the recruiting machinery of the TAs
throughout the kingdom should not be authorised to grind out
Lord Kitchener's army for him.

'If he persists in raising this new army,' Esher noted privately, 'I am
afraid he will destroy the morale of the Territorial force.'[11] But after a
two-hour tussle with Kitchener on 13 August the conclusion was that:
'He goes on with *his* army but he realises it will be no good for six or
eight months.'[12] Meanwhile he agreed to salvage two Territorial divisions, but only from the pick of the units at large. The rest he accepted
only as battalions, to be made up from unmarried men under thirty.
In this summary way he wiped out Haldane's work and Sir George

Clarke's dream. Esher had always regarded the 'Terriers' as a pool for the separate elements of 'expansion' and was not much disturbed. He rather admired Kitchener's panache. 'There never was such a wild elephant,' he comments: 'And yet! his instincts are true enough and he is far away from a pedant!'[13] Kitchener's army was to attract more volunteers than the conscripts that were later got by compulsion. By drawing the lines of a huge army on a national scale so early in the war in the face of prevailing opinion he rendered an incalculable service to the cause.

Kitchener's belief that the main attack was coming through Belgium was supported by Repington who published in *The Times* on 12 August a map showing the concentration of the German armies in the north. The same day some French staff officers were shepherded into Kitchener's room to listen to his warning that 'their appreciation of the military position was mistaken, and their notion of the duration of the War miscalculated'. They were impressed by the '*justesse*' of his reasoning but not convinced.[14] Nor was the British cabinet when on 19 August he told them 'the Germans would try to break through between Antwerp and Namur, and that their principal attack would be delivered there'.[15] Esher does not seem to have believed this either, for in noting it he adds: 'The best military opinion however seems to be that the principal attack will be delivered through Luxembourg south of Liège.'[16] But he was sufficiently shaken to feel that the 'myopia of the Meuse' was drawing away the British army from its 'true vocation'. 'We shall rue our folly if the Germans occupy the Channel ports.'[17] Four days later Sir John's small army after a long day's march 'bumped into the Germans' at six o'clock in the evening and fought all night and the next day at Mons. Learning that the French 5th Army on his right had decided to retreat, Sir John fell back, but on 26 August his 2nd Corps fought a rearguard at Le Cateau, losing more than a quarter of its force. Hopelessly outnumbered and suffering quite unexpected losses in men and guns, Sir John decided off his own bat to retire behind the Seine. 'The hope of making a stand behind the Somme or the Oise...had now to be abandoned owing to the shattered condition of the Army,' he explained.[18] Believing that the French had left him exposed, he refused to comply with General Joffre's order to remain on the line Compiègne-Soissons, telling Kitchener he was retiring behind Paris. When the British government queried this alarming decision Sir John explained: 'I do not see why I should be called upon to run the risk of absolute disaster in order a second time to save them.'[19]

The first shock of the news of Le Cateau with its suggestion that Kitchener's assessment was correct naturally produced regrets and in Esher's case a demand for an alternative strategy:

> *War Journals, 26 August 1914:*[20] It is an absolute disaster that we cannot without infringing the neutrality of Holland get two divisions of regulars and four divisions of territorials into Antwerp. Such a force linked up with the Belgians would inevitably bring about a retirement of the Germans all round. I cannot imagine why we do not make an attempt to send a force of this kind through Blankenberg down the canals to Bruges...
> *Ibid, 27 August*: There is a good deal of complaint at HQ of want of communication between our people and the French...I am equally sure that we should do well to retire either upon Havre or Cherbourg, and begin to create a Torres Vedras.

Any retirement on Le Havre would however have been a departure from the understanding, to which Sir John had agreed, that he would conform to French strategy. It looked as if the French armies would have to retire behind Paris and as Esher reluctantly agreed 'we shall have to go with them'. Sir John had 'shown temper' and his telegrams were 'full of inconsistencies'.[21] Such was the position when Kitchener decided to make his journey to Paris on 1 September, wearing his field marshal's uniform, to meet Sir John and persuade him to conform to the French plans. Kitchener really went as Secretary of State to transmit a decision which ministers had just approved, but in uniform and with the air of a soldier of superior rank he might have seemed to be assuming the overall direction of the campaign. Henceforward Kitchener's relations with Sir John were bedevilled by this ambiguity. Sir John gave a ready credence to the many stories which were rumoured about, one of which was that Kitchener had said to Joffre that if he could not get on with the C-in-C he could be replaced by 'an equally good soldier', namely Sir Ian Hamilton.

Of Kitchener at the War Office Esher later wrote: 'He neither argued nor discussed; he simply ignored.'[22] In his earlier career he had hated to put things in writing and relied on the initiatives of others corrected by very occasional verbal orders. Under him the War Office became more clam-like than the Admiralty had been under Fisher. And when at the end of October Churchill brought Fisher back as First Sea Lord, against the well-founded objections of the King, the scene was set for the tragic shilly-shallying that led to Gallipoli. The responsibility was Asquith's. He had consented to Kitchener though he called it a 'hazardous experiment', and now he installed Fisher aged seventy-four at the Admiralty by another 'bullying' interview with the King.[23] He expected to run the war by compartments, and by holding scratch conventions of available ministers at moments of crisis. The deficiencies in the 'supreme command' have been fully described by Hankey, who thought that the uncovering of the Channel ports, the failure to exploit the opportunities in time of landings at Ostend and reinforcements to Antwerp, and the neglect of early action against Turkey were examples of the failure of overall direction even where individual departments had done excellent preparatory work. The CID had been more or less superseded by the War Council, and became an adjunct to the cabinet concerned with specialised problems. Until Christmas 1914 it studied mainly the problem of Home Defence. It ceased to function sometimes for weeks, and was in no sense a war directorate.

In the latter part of September, after the battle of the Marne had brought stability to the allied front, Esher went over to France to do what he could to restore the personal relations of Sir John and Kitchener. In Paris he found that the British ambassador, Sir Francis Bertie, had fled to Bordeaux with his staff in the train of the French government and even the Consulate was closed. A crowd collected at the sight of his uniform as he left the Terminus hotel. Next day he was taken in an armed car to Sir John's HQ at La Fère-en-Tardenois and found the Field-Marshal in excellent health and spirits. He seemed to be getting on quite well with Joffre. The distressing feature of the visit was the appalling conditions of the wounded who were jolted on waggons on a long trek back to St Nazaire. The only motor ambulances belonged to the 'philanthropic marauders' of the American Red Cross who snatched the worst cases off to well-conducted hospitals near Paris. Esher's full and graphic account of the British hospital services produced an instant remedy from 'Lord K.' acting up to his best form. 'He gave peremptory orders that the Red Cross hospitals and all their ambulances should be sent up to Paris immediately...'[24] 'Within a few hours Sir Alfred Keogh had been recalled from France, and appointed Director-General of Medical Services at the War Office, and from that moment dates the efficiency to which the Royal Army Medical Corps attained...'[25]

The fall of Antwerp, whose forts were pounded into rubble one by one by two or three huge howitzers, the 'race to the sea' and consolidation of fixed lines of defence entirely altered the aspect of the War by the autumn. Yet as late as 11 November Sir John thought the 'campaign' could not last beyond the following summer, and that meanwhile the Germans 'will retire not upon the Rhine but upon the Meuse, and that we shall remain there face to face throughout the winter.'[26] But Esher had been converted to the Kitchener perspective. In the American Civil War, he reasoned, the South had fought on for four years though outnumbered two to one. 'It should be assumed that before Germany relinquishes the struggle she will have exhausted every possible supply of men and material.' This prospect demanded from Britain 'the husbanding of our resources, the training of every available man, the organisation of labour and of production all over the Empire', which 'will tax the administrative abilities of our people to the utmost'.[27] Few even of those who were conducting the war had any inkling of this in October 1914, and certainly not Sir John who was later to accuse Kitchener so vehemently of failing to produce unlimited quantities of ammunition. More crucially, Asquith was still very far from appraising the needs of the war correctly, or even of seeing that an appraisal needed to be made. 'We are even now very largely attempting to "muddle through",' Esher rightly observed.[28]

It is perhaps significant that Esher was not unduly worried about the monopoly of military direction which Kitchener had acquired—though he was possibly biased both by his lifelong belief in the Napoleonic ideal and by the personal consideration that he had become Kitchener's right-hand man. The opportunities which had been lost, he thought, were lost as much by inter-allied confusion as by any feebleness of direction on Britain's part. So that while he pressed hard for an inter-allied directorate he was not unduly disturbed by the condition of the 'supreme command' at home. But he did not let the faults of home government go unnoticed:

War Journals, December 1914:[29] I pointed out to Lord K. that our greatest weakness is the want of co-ordination between the naval, military and political forces of the Empire...and while the War Office has been mobilised for war, perhaps not so thoroughly as it should be, the Admiralty and Foreign Office are running, or rather crawling along, in their old peace grooves... The army of a maritime power loses half its effect when it is not employed in combination with its fleet and diplomatic service. I pointed out quite vehemently that the evil does not end here, as there is also a want of proper co-ordination between the allies...

If for the time being...power could be concentrated in the hands of a man such as Lord K. we should have better chance of success.

The War Council remained optimistic about the progress of the war until May 1915 when Sir John French's failure at Festubert and Sir Ian Hamilton's failure to extend the Gallipoli beach-heads—both operations against inferior numbers of the enemy—confirmed the minority opinion that trench warfare meant a static and protracted struggle. Before May the War Council felt that the thirty-six British divisions in France were not to be exceeded, being far more than the French had any right to expect, and the fact that Joffre and Millerand (Minister for War) were united in their 'western' policy and resistance to diversionary attacks at Zeebrugge, Salonika or the Dardanelles only confirmed the British in this belief. Kitchener's reluctance to send the 29th division to the Near East in February, and Joffre's similar refusal to help supply troops for the French '*armée de l'Orient*', which had to be raised from the reserves, both stemmed from an apprehension that the Germans might get in a quick offensive on the western front before the crushing Russian offensive expected in May was delivered. Optimists could still believe in the war being over at the end of the summer, and the War Office's projections of rifle and shell output still followed this assumption. By May the Russian army, said to consist of three million men with rifles and three million without, was in full retreat and a very different prospect, of a war of attrition requiring unlimited supplies of materials, appeared. Hence the 'shells scandal' which Sir John French and Lloyd George tried to represent as the culmination of a prolonged situation was really in its essential and political aspect a sudden reaction of disillusion and dismay. With half a million men on a 35-mile front the British had not felt unduly worried before. Only when it became plain that victory depended on the British army defeating the Germans on the western front in land

268

fighting on a 'Continental' scale, after the relative failure of the French and the Russians, did the importance of high explosive shells appear to be so transcendent.

Before the reverses of May the War Council's 'eastern' policy was inspired chiefly by a belief in the potential effectiveness of British sea power, powerfully represented by Churchill and Fisher. Fisher's plan for progressively netting in the German fleet and landing an army in Pomerania had found as its first step a project to take Heligoland in an effort to involve Denmark in seizing the Kiel Canal. This again had been put aside in favour of Spencer Ewart's plan for a combined naval and military attack on Zeebrugge which was still being discussed in the early weeks of 1915. Here the obvious snag was the formidable task of an offensive along the Flanders coastline, before which the enthusiasm of the French evaporated. Far more alluring were the projects in the Eastern Mediterranean. Lloyd George and his curiously similar Celtic counterpart, M. Briand, both favoured a landing in Salonika to assist the Serbs and encourage other Balkan states to join the allies, but Briand had cooled and there remained diplomatic difficulties in negotiations with the Greeks which were badly bungled. The other plan was simpler and seemed to maximise the advantages of naval power—an assault on the forts of the Dardanelles as a preliminary to forcing a passage into the Black Sea. Hankey, the Secretary of the CID, pressed this plan though he insisted that it depended on strong military support. It promised enormous gains. Turkey cut in two, Constantinople an easy prey, and the safe outlet of the Russian grain crops to the markets of the West to pay for the interest on the French loan, a stabilising of Russian finance and a route for the provision of munitions to arm the Russian hordes. Conversely, the failure to force the Dardanelles seemed to portend the arming of the Turks by the Central powers and enormous commitments in the defence of Egypt.

Unfortunately the War Council drifted from one plan to another, and finally opted for the Dardanelles as a 'limited liability' preference. It discussed the Zeebrugge plan on 8 and 13 January when Fisher opposed as too dangerous any purely naval action. Churchill had appealed to Sir John saying 'it was essential in the interests of the navy to capture Zeebrugge and Ostend', but Sir John looked in vain for French assistance. Churchill then turned restlessly to the Dardanelles but he was bound to quarrel even more with his First

Sea Lord over a venture that would divert into a distant theatre the capital ships and monitors and other secret equipment which Fisher was lovingly accumulating for his latest plan to attack Cuxhaven. Kitchener preferred the Salonika plan, fearing that the Germans were about to consolidate their 'door to the south' through Serbia and hoping that 'to show khaki at Belgrade would probably have a determining effect upon Romania'.[30] He had sent Esher to broach the Salonika plan to Millerand, who had returned from Bordeaux to the Ministère de la Guerre in Paris. Millerand came to London and effectively killed the plan for the immediate future by pleading that Joffre was against it. At a dinner at the French embassy on 23 January Kitchener promised 'he would not press the Serbian scheme just now'.[31] It was agreed, however, that Esher would act as a personal contact between Kitchener and Millerand in the hope that Joffre, who was an uncompromising 'westerner', would acquire broader strategic views.

A sub-committee of the CID had been deputed to study the problem of 'another theatre and objective' if the western front revealed a deadlock in the spring. For this Esher wrote a paper advocating 'violent and eccentric' attacks.[32] He believed that in May the western allies should be ready to launch two offensives in support of Russia, one in Salonika and the other along the Flanders coast to Antwerp and the Dutch frontier. The Dutch should be brought into the war by the offer of an Anglo-French force of 400,000 men and the threat of Japanese action against their colonies coupled with a declaration that if they did not join the allies Antwerp would remain permanently in German hands. Sir John still hoped for the coastal offensive, but the French chamber had rendered Joffre even less willing to co-operate by demanding an 'army of manoeuvre' ostensibly to cover Paris. To send more divisions to France would merely enable the French to denude their northern flank of more troops, and probably for this reason Kitchener preferred to keep his new divisions in England until some plan was agreed with Joffre. After two long meetings the War Council agreed on 28 January that Churchill should explain to Sir John the importance of holding troops ready for Salonika. Meanwhile Churchill got his way, at the cost of alienating Fisher, by a decision to go ahead with the attempt to force the Dardanelles by purely naval means.

Basically the lack of any clear strategic policy was the result of

French obstruction, which in turn was occasioned by an almost complete absence of any effective exchange of ideas. Esher decided to step himself into the position which ought to have been the preserve of an inter-allied council, and which was later occupied by the Supreme War Council. The creation of such a body became one of his chief preoccupations. 'I am working for a sort of *Allied Council*,' he wrote to his son at this time: 'Very small. Russia, England, France, Japan, to sit in Paris or London.'[33] After pressing this idea for many months, he got Millerand to recommend it, and it was supported by Lord Selborne in the cabinet. Even so, when Lloyd George took it up, he seemed more interested in its political advantages as a means of counteracting Haig and Robertson, than in its real strategic purposes. One might perhaps claim for the Supreme War Council under Foch and Henry Wilson much of the credit for stemming the great German offensive of 1918. But its creation was far too late, and in the meantime its absence played havoc with allied strategy.

Esher's position was, at least in his own eyes, entirely unofficial. 'I am not going to put myself out,' he writes. 'I never do. Nor am I going to "regularise" my position, which means that someone can give me orders—I never have.'[34] Nevertheless he was, with Balfour, a 'permanent' or, as he preferred to call it, an 'unofficial' member of the CID and was thereby completely *au courant* of secret affairs. He was regarded by the French as Kitchener's right arm and plenipotentiary and he soon established very intimate relations with Millerand and men in Paris like Bunau-Varilla, the proprietor of *Le Matin*,[35] on that basis. His mastery of spoken French gave him a special position which was enhanced by the freedom from any formal duties. He enjoyed the advantage which he always claimed that monarchs had over presidents, that they could receive the confidences of all on a purely social footing. Moving freely from London to Paris, from the British GHQ to the French GQG, from the lobby of the House of Lords or Buckingham Palace to the French War Ministry or Crillon Hotel, Esher was the only man of either country free to converse with the politicians and soldiers of both with a full knowledge of the latest strategic counsels. His understanding of French politics and French military purposes had to be relied upon by Kitchener and Asquith, Sir John French and Douglas Haig, for the British embassy in Paris was completely out of touch with the conduct of the war, and the

French censorship shrouded political and military matters in an impenetrable fog.

The French acted through their embassy in London, where their ambassador M. Paul Cambon was in Esher's opinion more than a match for the 'mugwumps' of the Foreign Office. They liked the normal diplomatic channels, using the amiable Sir Francis Bertie at Paris to circumvent the British GHQ and the War Office—and they still believed that Sir John had been placed under Joffre's orders. No doubt anticipating some French resistance, Esher was careful to arm himself, when he appeared in Paris in February, with a mission from Asquith to collect materials for a history of the war. He wore a general staff officer's uniform with two rows of decorations, which Bertie uncharitably called his 'fancy khaki'.[36] Esher was equally sceptical about Bertie's credentials as he viewed the interior of the embassy, Pauline Borghese's palace in the Faubourg St-Honoré, with its 'lovely rooms...I had almost forgotten them after all these years... bought very cheap by the Duke of Wellington (on the advice of my grandfather)'.[37] Bertie himself was, he thought, a representative of 'a class long since passed away' whose conversational powers were 'matured in the far-distant atmosphere of Holland House and Strawberry Hill'.[38] For some months Esher got on well enough with Bertie, but in time an emnity grew up between them as Bertie felt quite rightly that he was being supplanted.

When Esher met Sir John at Amiens on 16 February the Commander-in-Chief was 'brim full of optimism'. He thought after reviewing the numbers of German troops on all fronts that 'these cannot carry on the war beyond August...Nothing is to take place until March, when we are due to advance.'[39] He had refused French requests to extend his short front, and confidently expected a 'breakthrough'. Without any pressure to do so, Sir John had determined to attack at Neuve Chapelle. On the eve of this famous action Esher was at St Omer to confer with him:

War Journals, 9 March 1915:[40] All is prepared and Robertson, the Chief of the Staff, is confident...[Sir John] anticipates heavy losses by tomorrow night and worries over it. 5,000 killed and wounded. No-one knows of the coming fight except the divisional generals...

In this attack tomorrow at Neuve Chapelle we are said to have

3 to 1. We have 700 guns and two 15" guns. We may 'get through' —but what if we do? The French lost 14,000 men at Perthes and Beauséjour with very little result on the whole. We shall see.

The cavalry was 'massed and ready to sweep in' and the attack at first carried all before it.[41] In Paris on 11 March Esher found that the French were 'all *stupefait* at the advance' by seven brigades—they had 'never yet attacked in anything like such force'.[42] But although the enemy were got on the run, the attack petered out for three reasons which Esher enumerates as the weather, blunders, and lack of ammunition. Although the last reason was foreseeable, Sir John chose to make it the primary explanation of his failure.

The 'shells scandal' had already been prefigured in exchanges between Bonar Law and Kitchener, who was blamed not for being unaware of the need for a massive production of high explosives but for failing to set production in train months before. Lloyd George, who had chaired an ineffectual cabinet committee on munitions, was asked on 5 March by Balfour to 'take in hand the organisation of the engineering resources of the country' from the contracts department of the War Office.[43] It was well known that the French had converted the Renault works into units of mass production and had achieved a far higher output than Britain. Lloyd George's project was to mobilise the thousands of small workshops by using expert business administration. This situation was already well developed when Churchill visited Sir John on 17 March and persuaded him that he had failed for want of ammunition.[44] Three days later, when Esher spoke to Sir John at Amiens, he learnt that 'all our operations are stopped by want of ammunition, and that after a fight it takes three weeks to build up again'. Even so, Sir John contemplated another attack in April, although Churchill had warned him that 'the ammunition will not flow until August'.[45]

Strangely enough Sir John thought the war would be over by June, when the Germans would suggest *pourparlers*. And after the initial shock of disappointment Neuve Chapelle was regarded as a great success. Esher found the French GQG at Chantilly 'full of envy', while Foch praised Sir John's Chief of Staff, Sir William Robertson, as '*épassant*'.[46] Esher had to agree that the battle 'was an immense tonic; the morale of both armies is up 50 per cent. It has been what the relief of Kimberley was in 1900. Sir John is a heroic figure...'[47] Esher's own reaction had been far more pessimistic. For him the lesson had been: 'You cannot get a decision from any fight, however much it goes in your favour...It means a war of interminable length and the hugest sacrifices and consequent impoverishment.'[48] The revelation that ammunition was still months from adequate supply he thought 'most serious' and he composed a stiff letter to Kitchener which reveals his disgust with the officials under him:

> *Esher-Kitchener, 21 March 1915:*[49] If we are beaten in this war, it will be on account of shortage of ammunition. Four months ago the French showed me at Creusot, at Renault's and elsewhere, their arrangements, and were anxious to place their experience at our service...When I told you this, your people said that our arrangements were excellent...and that they had nothing to learn from the French...
>
> I raised for you 80,000 men, clothed and equipped them. I could have raised 160,000...I was discouraged and stopped by your officials...
>
> It was suggested that you, personally, should keep in close touch with [Millerand] in regard to the joint preparation for the various stages of the war...You told me that I could assist you in this...I have done my best, but without much support or encouragement...

Hankey assured Esher that Lloyd George was 'taking measures which will have good results' in the supply of ammunition, but in fact the Munitions of War Committee which was set up was 'doomed to futility' according to Lloyd George's *Memoirs* because of War Office obstruction.[50] It led to a bitter personal quarrel between Lloyd George and Kitchener in April.[51]

The dispute over munitions was the crystallisation of a wider issue between the followers of 'Squiff' or 'Squidgy' as Asquith was now being called, and the exponents of 'total war'. The latter felt that the powers of the Defence of the Realm Act (DORA) were not being thoroughly used, that the nation was not being informed of the real gravity of the war situation, and that pacifists, profiteers, strikers and shirkers were allowed too much room to flourish. In supporting Kitchener over munitions Asquith and Grey were seen as adhering to peacetime methods, exemplified also in the way the service chiefs dominated the War Council. As Balfour complained to Asquith later, referring to the War Council: 'On it...were the then First Lord of the Admiralty, and the Secretary of State for War—both very strong personalities, with very incompatible temperaments. They would not work with each other, and neither of them would have tolerated for a moment the independent examination by any member of the Committee of experts belonging to their departments. To describe that Committee as responsible for the decisions arrived at would be absurd...'[52] Departmentalism and the voluntary principle assorted ill with Kitchener's severe press censorship. As Asquith's critics pointed out, peacetime methods of running the war implied full publicity in order to get the public's co-operation. Secrecy implied conscription and direction of labour.

The Unionist opposition which stood for a much firmer direction of the war was growing restive. Attacks on Asquith for failing to deal effectively with the problem of high wages, drunkenness and absenteeism in the munitions factories appeared in the Unionist press. Lloyd George's teetotal pledge, which he persuaded the King to take, and his public denunciation of drink did not amuse Asquith, who was often well-lined with liquor.[53] The introduction of Balfour into the Munitions of War Committee was also a shrewd move on the part of Lloyd George, for the Committee was circulated with the confidential papers about munitions. On this Committee Churchill and Lloyd George became 'aggressive' towards Kitchener, who objected to the disclosure of figures he had supplied to the cabinet, and Lloyd George 'let slip in the course of the altercations some injurious and wounding innuendoes which K[itchener] will be more than human to forget'.[54] This was just prior to Asquith's well-known speech to munitions workers at Newcastle on 20 April in which he denied both the severity of the ammunition shortage and any slackness in the munitions industry. The surprise that this speech caused arose from its contradiction of Kitchener's own public statements, let alone those of his opponents. It was a counter-blast to those who criticised Asquith's general conduct of the war.

It was strongly indicative of the force of the undercurrent of opinion running against Asquith that Esher was among those who now came into the open against him. He had noticed with disapproval the mild treatment of the strikers in March:

Esher-Stamfordham, 1 April 1915:[55] The King's example will produce the best possible effect...

That clever young *Daily Mail* writer Valentine Williams who has been allowed up among the soldiers in the trenches says that he found the men very sympathetic towards the *strikers.* 'Why should they not have their bit?' 'Have they got their two bob?' 'How about champagne at the Savoy?' were the questions put to him. Surely the time has come for obligatory service all round, unless this war is to go on for years. Here, if a man refuses to work, drum head court martial and a firing company. Public opinion is so strong that if this were not done a shirker would be torn to pieces by his comrades...

...those are to blame who have not had the moral courage to explain the facts and risk the necessary action. Lloyd George got a great deal of praise in France...

After Asquith's Newcastle speech Esher contributed to the *Glasgow Herald* a strong plea for a new spirit in industry. 'Every man should be aware of the particular sacrifice demanded of him, whether it be to give his life in the trenches or his life in the factory...The contemptible phrases "business as usual" and "pleasure as usual" should never be spoken in Glasgow...'[56] This was regarded by the editor as a reproof of Asquith's speech 'with all its inopportune complacencies'. But the main argument which Esher wished to publicise was that the war was a life-or-death struggle which had to be waged totally and to the bitter end. This kind of argument was to become very familiar later, but was startling enough at this moment:

In spite of gallantry, devotion and sacrifice, no progress has been made...

There will be no general spirit of concord after this war. Put aside at once all spurious analogies between this bloody struggle and any other. We are not fighting the German Emperor or the German military caste. We are engaged in a life-or-death conflict with the German people of all sorts and classes—men who have been educated to believe, and who believe with all the fury of the rationalist, that the progress of humanity renders it necessary that Germany should stand 'above all men'. This academic passion has proved to be a mighty stimulus, and it has driven into the field of battle a people full of energy, resolution, and stoutness of heart, who so far can claim that the balance of victory and conquest is on their side.[57]

The Germans' use of poison gas at Ypres had just underlined the moral of total war, and quite apart from the munitions question a shake-up in the management of the war was widely felt to be needed.

This feeling, reflected in the letters from the front and from the industrial centres which poured into the newspaper offices but which were being scotched by the censor, encouraged Northcliffe to take up the munitions question as a stick to wield against Kitchener and his régime. He visited the front and Sir John's headquarters at the latter's invitation, he forwarded the mailbag of *The Times* and *Daily Mail* offices to Lloyd George and Bonar Law, and he located correspondents of these papers with Sir John. Sir John himself played up to the game. He nursed a grievance against Kitchener, who had re-instated officers he had sent home, and whose adverse comments on his command were carried to his ears at second-hand. In return Sir John conferred with Churchill and others about matters that really were in Kitchener's sphere, and corresponded directly with Asquith and other ministers behind Kitchener's back, regarding himself as a servant of the cabinet and not of the Secretary for War. Churchill's cousin, Frederick E. Guest MP, was one of the coterie of men near Sir John who were pulling him into politics. Another was Brinsley Fitzgerald, an old friend and relative, who had usurped the position of Sir John's military secretary, 'Billy' Lambton. These two were sent to England, immediately after Sir John's disastrous failure in the attack on the Aubers Ridge of 9 May, to lay the correspondence on munitions before Bonar Law, Balfour and Lloyd George. Sir John claimed in his memoirs that he was deliberately sacrificing his command in order to publicise the ammunition shortage which was 'doubling and trebling our losses in men'. Yet in order to make this foolish attack he had declared to Kitchener on 2 May that: 'The ammunition will be all right.'[58]

On 11 May Kitchener summoned Esher to the War Office to discuss the Aubers Ridge failure. He could not understand how 'with so large a preponderance of force we are unable to make a greater impression on the Germans'.[59] With 16,000 men per mile, or four times as many men per mile of front as the French, Sir John's attack had been beaten off by the German battalions in line without calling on any reserves. Yet Kitchener was weakening and thinking of sending Sir John more men:

> *War Journals, 11 May 1915:*[60] He told me that he was sending out one division of his new army, although he had told me before that he intended to keep these in reserve. I am sure that he is making a mistake, as Sir John has now quite as many men as he is able to handle, subject to the ammunition problem.
> The clamour for more men for the front is quite incomprehensible; the general staff out there must know that whether the ammunition problem has been dealt with well or ill, the reserves of ammunition are limited and they must be distributed between the different fields of operations. The whole of this almost fatal difficulty arises from the want of central control.

The War Council had not sat since 19 March. A meeting became unavoidable when Admiral de Robeck reported on 11 May that the army had failed to break out of its beachheads in Gallipoli, and inquired whether the naval attempt to force the Straits should be renewed. Churchill decided to send out monitors and other equipment but to recall the super-dreadnought Queen Elizabeth, which was menaced by submarines. He broke this decision to Kitchener on 13 May, and thereby renewed in an intense form the feud between his department and the War Office. Kitchener believed the withdrawal of this ship would have a disastrous effect on the army's morale and the country's prestige in the Near East. Then, on the morning of the War Council's meeting to consider these developments, *The Times* appeared with the report from Repington which forced the 'shells scandal' into prominence. The last of Asquith's War Councils, held on 14 May, witnessed the farcical quadrilateral duel between Sir John and Kitchener, Fisher and Churchill, and Churchill and Kitchener. The service chiefs were at daggers drawn with their leading subordinates, and with each other. For Fisher refused to agree to the dispatch of the monitors, and blurted out that he 'had been against the Dardanelles operations from the beginning', while Kitchener announced that he had decided not to send any of his new divisions to France.

Esher had written a paper for the CID on 12 May advocating

278

'unity of command'.[61] 'No aulic council, no cabinet, full of jarring counsels can conduct a war. You must have one brain and a single responsibility if great decisions are to be taken.' This paper was circulated to Asquith and Kitchener on the day the War Council met and must have been a wry commentary on its proceedings. The crisis that day had little to do with the 'shells scandal' or with Fisher, who had not yet resigned. It was due to the impotence of the navy and army in the Dardanelles, the failures of the allies on the eastern and western fronts, the prospect of submarine and aerial attacks and even invasion, and over and above these particular problems the manifest inability of the War Council to get a grip on events. These were what weighed on Kitchener's mind when he returned to York House to browse over the newspapers. He penned a note to Esher: 'I am deadly sick of this system of intrigue with Headquarters, and if I get an excuse I shall take it and get out of it all.'[62]

Esher went to see him after dinner. On the way an idea occurred to him—that Kitchener might be made Commander-in-Chief of the Imperial Forces of the Crown at home and oversea in addition to being War Secretary. This would clarify his position *vis-à-vis* Sir John and 'emphasise strongly in fact the belief universally entertained that Lord K. is personally responsible, not only for the administration of the army, but for the conduct of the war'.[63] This was what Esher wished as the only practicable form of unity of command. He still had faith in Kitchener's strategic wisdom. But unfortunately Kitchener was identified by his opponents—Lloyd George, Churchill and Northcliffe—with the incompetent administration of the War Office. For personal reasons, also, Lloyd George scouted the idea of Kitchener becoming a universal C-in-C and in the coming cabinet crisis the plan, although pressed by the King, finally wilted and collapsed. Kitchener was made the scapegoat for the strategic follies which had been forced upon him—the senseless offensives of Sir John, which he had wished to postpone till 1916, the premature naval assault on the Dardanelles which had stimulated the Turks into entrenching Gallipoli, and Grey's mishandling of the Greeks:

War Journals, 14 May 1915:[64] Lord K. takes a pessimistic view. In the western front there appears to be no material change... the optimistic prophesies of the general staff have not been fulfilled. The initiative which, according to them and the news-

279

paper critics in this country, had passed to the allies, seems to remain firmly in the hands of the Germans...our losses have been great and our progress nil. In the Dardanelles, after a mismanaged naval attack, which eliminated the element of surprise, we have succeeded in effecting a very brilliant landing, but at the expense of five battleships and about 30,000 men. The Russians have been heavily defeated and instead of passing into the plains of Hungary are in full retreat to the line of the San...This may free one million men for the purpose of reinforcing the line in the west. Taken together with the German attacks upon our commerce, aerial threats and possible raids, the outlook is one full of anxiety.

While Esher was conferring with Kitchener at York House, Churchill was busy that evening drafting orders at the Admiralty for naval reinforcements to go to the Dardanelles—nets, the latest type of submarine, aeroplanes and seaplanes, and a new type of monitor mounting a 15″ gun which Fisher had designed to attack Cuxhaven.[65] Fisher had absolutely no confidence in the Dardanelles venture and his nerves had been racked with anxiety over the danger to the Queen Elizabeth which was a sitting duck for torpedoes.[66] On seeing Churchill's orders which he feared would render his schemes and equipment useless he resigned the next morning (Saturday).

Fisher had threatened to leave at once for Scotland, but was tracked down in a London hotel and interviewed by Asquith on the Saturday afternoon. He remained obdurate however, although Churchill wrote persuasive letters saying that his resignation might jeopardise not only the safety of the troops at Gallipoli but also Italy's entry into the war. Meanwhile Asquith was not to be defrauded of his week-end, and left for the country. Esher was attending a review of cadets at Buckingham Palace that evening, and heard from the King the news that Fisher had resigned and that Asquith had refused to accept Churchill's sequential offer to resign. In return Esher informed the King of Kitchener's misgivings. The King thought the proposal to make Kitchener C-in-C of all forces overseas 'a practical one' and told Stamfordham to go over and discuss it with him. He declared that 'whatever happened he meant to support Lord K., even if it led to the fall of the government'.[67] By the following morning Kitchener had agreed, and Esher went over to Buckingham Palace to catch the King before he left London for the north. 'He told me,' Esher noted, 'that he had been unable to see the Prime Minister today, as he was away for the week-end playing golf', even though Fisher's resignation had now become certain. Asquith's private secretary, Bonham Carter, was given a memorandum 'explanatory of the crisis', while the King suggested what Esher called 'the solution we discussed yesterday'.[68]

Churchill had motored down to see Asquith on the Sunday afternoon with the news that although Fisher could not be persuaded to stay, Sir Arthur Wilson was willing to take his place and the Board of Admiralty could be reconstituted. But although Asquith seemed at first to endorse such a simple remedy, his private secretary later that evening 'mentioned in conversation that the situation resulting from the shell shortage disclosure and the resignation of Lord Fisher was so serious that the Prime Minister thought the Unionist leaders would have to be consulted on the steps to be taken'.[69] This would mean doom for Churchill, whom the Unionists generally disliked. Lloyd George must have realised this, and when Churchill encountered him on Monday he disclosed that 'the leaders of the Opposition were in possession of all the facts about the shell shortage and had given notice that they intended to demand a debate'.[70] The Unionists would not spare Churchill for his services in encouraging Sir John to provide his useful dossier, but would exploit the idea that he had been concerned to create a diversion from the miscarriages at the Dardanelles. He was very excited and 'jumpy' about the Dardanelles and had told Sir John he thought he would be 'ruined if the attack failed'.[71] Now his bid had been called by Fisher. As the King observed to Esher: 'Churchill is really the stumbling-block in both these critical situations.'[72]

If Asquith had not already lost the confidence of the Opposition and to a noticeable extent that of the country, and if Lloyd George had not been bent at his and Churchill's expense on ousting Kitchener, the government might have weathered the storm. If the War Council had been functioning smoothly the Unionists might have been content with more representation on it. But in the reverse of these conditions Asquith was subjected to a protracted and humiliating party wrangle over the spoils of office under the threat of public disclosures which never took place. Instead of offering some constructive solution he played the game through by a series of party compromises, with the result that Kitchener stayed, Churchill went, and the War

Committee hardly improved on the former War Council except by its judicious balance of party interests. The only constructive part of the new Coalition was the creation of a Ministry of Munitions, and this was forced on Asquith by the King.

Lloyd George's account of the reaction of Bonar Law on Monday morning stresses the shell situation as well as Fisher's resignation as points which decided the Unionists to challenge Asquith. But this may well have been his own embroidery, for the Unionists did not insist on Kitchener's removal,[73] and two days later Lloyd George was obliged to try to force the situation further by sending Asquith a letter obviously written for publication in which he refused to continue to chair the Munitions of War Committee.[74] When Bonar Law asked Esher to discuss the situation with him on Monday morning he 'felt bound not to allow Fisher's resignation' and 'spoke of a coalition government'.[75] Asquith reopened the Admiralty question on the basis of Churchill going and Fisher remaining, but Fisher's conditions for returning were so bizarre and exorbitant as to cast doubts on his soundness of mind.[76] On receipt of Fisher's reply on Wednesday Asquith announced the intended Coalition in the Commons. Churchill thought he could have vindicated his own conduct at the Admiralty, and he thought, surprisingly enough, that: 'The impressive recital of all that the War Office had achieved under Lord Kitchener would greatly have mitigated the complaints on what had been neglected.'[77]

Stamfordham returned to London on Wednesday and called on Asquith at 1 p.m., who gave as his reasons for reconstructing the government both Fisher's resignation and Repington's letter in *The Times*. Asquith pointed out that Fisher had threatened to resign several times, and that he thought his mind had become 'unhinged'. This corroborated the assessment of Fisher which the King had put to Asquith the previous October, and there was no serious attempt to save the First Sea Lord's position.[78] The day before Stamfordham had wired from Glasgow: 'King suggests Balfour for Admiralty and a minister to superintend manufacture of munitions of war.'[79] But Fisher objected as much to Balfour as to Churchill. The result of the interview was summarised as follows:

Stamfordham-King George, 19 May 1915:[80] Nothing settled: but probably Lord Chancellor, Secretary of State for Colonies and Secretary for Ireland will go, and at least two others. Unionists,

Labour and Irish invited to join, but none has yet answered and acceptance of two last very doubtful. Fisher impossible. Will not act under Balfour, but makes preposterous terms. I see no chance of his remaining. Wilson has resigned. PM considerably disturbed about War Office. I expect Churchill will go to Colonial Office, but Beauchamp tells me feeling among his colleagues is that he is primary cause of trouble and should be first to go instead of others who will lose their seats in cabinet.

Asquith evidently at this stage ignored the King's suggestion as to the creation of a Ministry of Munitions, for the next day his private secretary, Bonham-Carter, envisaged that Bonar Law might succeed Lloyd George if the latter went to the War Office.[81] Whether Asquith intended in that eventuality that Kitchener should go altogether is however doubtful. Most likely he intended to implement the proposal to make Kitchener a universal Commander-in-Chief.[82] In the Coalition government Asquith regarded his close alliance with Kitchener as the mainstay of the whole affair. It was clear that the country also was not ready to see Kitchener jettisoned, and he was marshalling a formidable case of self-justification.

As a result of the consultations on 20 May Stamfordham was able to assure the King that it was not now intended to remove Kitchener, and that he had pressed the two essential ideas which Esher had put forward—that of the C-in-C, and the detachment of munitions from the responsibility of the War Secretary:

Stamfordham-King George, 20 May 1915:[83] Latest idea is to leave Lord K. as Secretary of State, and Lloyd George to work the whole of the supply of the army from the Treasury: but whether Lord K. is to be also C-in-C Bonham Carter is not certain, but he will tell the PM your Majesty's views which remain the same as expressed in Sunday last's memorandum. I think probably the Opposition have agreed to Lloyd George being the Supply Minister as well as Chancellor of the Exchequer, or rather in his latter capacity taking charge of the Army Supply department...
    I expect that the PM will in future work in the closest touch with Kitchener and the First Lord, in fact they three would re-place the existing War Council, and Hankey would be secretary.

In this way the PM would become in spirit and in letter Defence Minister.

The idea of a 'War Cabinet'—a small group of ministers relieved of departmental preoccupations in order to meet daily to direct the strategy of the war—with a cabinet secretariat under Hankey, did not materialise under Asquith. As formulated by Stamfordham it expressed Esher's even more drastic proposal of 'Asquith acting as arbiter between Fisher, in charge of the Admiralty, and Kitchener, in charge of the War Office'.[84] Asquith's idea of a War Committee was a body which was run parallel to, and was controlled by, a large cabinet.

The King returned to London on Friday 21 May, when Asquith with some of his ministers were in conclave at Downing Street with the leaders of the opposition over the distribution of offices.[85] Asquith went to this meeting with the intention of placing Lloyd George at the War Office with charge of munitions, while Kitchener became C-in-C, but he was aware that the Unionists were championing Bonar Law in competition with Lloyd George. For the ensuing deadlock, the Asquithian solution was to give the War Office to neither, as appears from his interview with the King on Saturday:

Memorandum by Stamfordham, 22 May 1915:[86] The King saw the PM, who submitted his proposed changes in the cabinet... The King asked whether a minister should not be appointed to have special charge of the manufacture and supply of munitions of war. Mr Asquith said that this would be undertaken by the Chancellor of the Exchequer and in three months' time Mr Lloyd George ought to have the whole matter systematised and on a proper working basis after which there would not be enough work for one minister...

The King hoped Lord Kitchener would be relieved of all work and responsibility with regard to ammunition. He spoke strongly to the PM in favour of giving the fullest support to Lord K. Also with regard to friction with Headquarters...

The distribution of offices which Asquith submitted at this interview was substantially the same as that finally concluded three days later, except that Lloyd George was still Chancellor of the Exchequer and McKenna was Home Secretary. Over the week-end both Liberal and

Unionist parties boiled over in indignation at the arrangement. The Liberals could not stomach the 'cruel and absolutely groundless' vendetta against Haldane who had been dismissed as Lord Chancellor, nor the appointment of Carson as Attorney-General, which was certainly highly ironical, if not provocative. The Unionists were scandalised at the relegation of Bonar Law to the Colonial Office, for they assumed that if he were thwarted of the War Office by Lloyd George he would at least get the vacated Exchequer. By keeping Kitchener, whom neither party really wanted, Asquith prevented a tariff reformer becoming Chancellor of the Exchequer, or (had Bonar Law gone to the War Office) the capture of both service departments by Unionists, for Balfour was indispensable at the Admiralty.

These discontents expressed themselves at a long meeting on 24 May at which the Unionists made 'somewhat extraordinary demands' and 'there was much haggling and bargaining over various offices'. It was a humiliation for Asquith, and he determined 'to have no more such meetings'. It is clear that the Unionists would not accept Asquith's very questionable proposal to let Lloyd George run Munitions as Chancellor of the Exchequer. But:

Memorandum by Stamfordham, 25 May 1915:[87] The Opposition ...demanded that if Mr Lloyd George left the Treasury for the War Office as Minister of Munitions he should be succeeded by Mr Bonar Law. The PM proposed that he himself should be Chancellor of the Exchequer with Mr Montagu, who now leaves the cabinet...to assist him; but this was stoutly opposed by the Opposition on the grounds that the PM had already much to do and should superintend military and naval matters so long as the war lasted. Mr Runciman was proposed as Munitions Minister, but both sides thought the country would not regard him as of sufficient standing...The meeting broke up without arriving at any agreement.

The next morning Asquith dispatched Lloyd George to settle matters as best he could with Bonar Law, but the Unionist leader was 'very unyielding'. Bonar Law had conferred with Kitchener, who 'was no longer anxious about the advent of Mr Bonar Law to the War Office', which presumably implies that Kitchener would have been content with being C-in-C pure and simple. As for the objection that the

Unionists should not have both the fighting departments, Bonar Law repudiated Balfour and asserted that his party 'looked upon him as much more belonging to the government!'[88]

> In the end Mr Bonar Law said if the PM could not agree to his terms it might be better to give up altogether a Coalition Government. Mr Lloyd George did not seem to regard this alternative with much alarm, and had even thought of some other arrangement, by which the PM might bring into the government some non-party peers, e.g. Lords Revelstoke, Sydenham, Esher, Mr Duke MP...etc.

Asquith had arranged to see the King to report on the new ministry that evening, and he now had a last-minute discussion with Lloyd George in Stamfordham's presence of: 'A return to the *status quo ante* minus Churchill at the Admiralty plus a Munitions Minister', but the difficulty of that was that Balfour would probably decline to oblige the Liberals by joining them in isolation. Asquith regarded the position as 'critical, as he could make no further concessions' and he resolved to get a reply from Bonar Law, presumably to an offer of either of these plans, and see the King the next day.[89] Stamfordham left Downing Street in the afternoon, but by 5-15 p.m. there had been a sudden denouement and Asquith sought an interview with the King at once. Bonar Law had suddenly and unexpectedly accepted the original distribution of offices with a slight variation: Lloyd George to become Minister of Munitions and Kitchener to remain at the War Office, McKenna to replace Lloyd George at the Exchequer, and Bonar Law to accept his relegation to the Colonial Office.[90] Did Bonar Law see any important difference between Lloyd George as War Secretary with Kitchener as C-in-C, and Kitchener as War Secretary with Lloyd George as Munitions Minister? Probably his colleagues preferred half a loaf to no bread or worse, a Lloyd George ministry which would in all likelihood have emerged from a breakdown after so much drama. Asquith was lucky to be reprieved.

Asquith's style of leadership was to allow personalities and situations to play themselves out with the minimum of intervention, and to be hard and unyielding in enforcing the compacts which were ground out by the clash of interests. He could not transcend a situation by a large and solvent initiative of his own, such as Lloyd George excelled in producing. His role in the formation of the Coalition manifested the faults of his style, and his eleventh-hour rescue from disaster probably owed as much to the patriotism of Bonar Law and Lansdowne as to anything else. The Unionists still thought that Asquith, Grey and Kitchener were the best available men. But Asquith's blindness to the importance of a Ministry of Munitions or a war directorate and his reliance on political shifts and chances plainly appear in the May crisis. The *deus ex machina* of a Minister of Munitions seems to have originated in Esher's talks with the King on 15–16 May. While Asquith slighted it Lloyd George seems to have been quick to seize on its possibilities, and it saved the situation. But Esher was under no illusions as to what would emerge from the negotiations. 'It is certain that the outcome can only be a substitution of one incompetent method of carrying on a great war for another,' he noted on 18 May, '...we shall have to fall back upon an inchoate Cabinet composed of jarring elements and of men whose training and mental equipment unfit them for carrying on a struggle with the Emperor and the German Great General Staff.'[91] By the week-end he was in France at the urgent request of Sir John, leaving London before the party squabble began.

Thirteen

A Nation in Arms

Esher believed that the 'shells scandal' was engineered by the Northcliffe press in an attempt to force Lloyd George either into the premiership or the War Office. Characteristically the *Daily Mail* launched a more personal attack on Kitchener on the day of the first party discussion of the distribution of offices (21 May) which was countered by the burning of the paper on the Stock Exchange and the boycotting of the *Daily Mail* in clubs. When Esher spoke to Sir John about the munitions agitation on 23 May the latter seemed 'a very unwilling onlooker' who claimed to have 'no hand in this newspaper campaign'. But his immediate entourage seemed to have been implicated, and Esher felt obliged to warn him of the folly of 'meddling in politics'. He thought that Kitchener's position had been fortified. 'The utter miscalculation made by his possibly loyal but certainly injudicious friends is shown by the immediate reaction of public opinion against the monstrous accusations of the Harmsworth Press. Lord K. is far stronger today than he was last week." If Repington, who had quarrelled with Kitchener in August 1914 over some indiscreet press disclosures, had wished to get his own back, he had failed. And if Churchill had wanted to punish Kitchener, his plot had rebounded through the unlikely agency of Lloyd George, who was pre-eminently the man who had turned the general outcry about munitions into a personal criticism of Kitchener. He had threatened Asquith with a public exposure of his private vendetta against Kitchener on the Munitions of War Committee, and this had precipitated the Coalition and Churchill's removal from the Admiralty.

The Coalition ought to have had a dramatic effect on the direction of the war, especially in extending the opportunity to move towards conscription and the direction of labour, for the Unionists in general favoured compulsion and their parliamentary support relieved Asquith of his reliance on the Radicals and Irish Nationalists, who were strongly against it. But strangely enough the controversy over compulsion was allowed to gather momentum in the press and the labour movement rather than in the cabinet or Parliament. Being a Coalition rather than a National government, divisions on the subject within the cabinet developed on party lines, and the leakages of ministers to their respective party newspapers revealing discussions and partisanship within the cabinet reached scandalous proportions.

The need for a great national army of seventy divisions was not apparent until the summer of 1916, when the Russians were driven back behind Warsaw with enormous losses and hopes of the collaboration of Bulgaria and Greece faded. With the autumn of 1915 Asquith agreed to relieve the French by taking over more of the line, but he remained under strong pressure from Lloyd George, Curzon and others to avoid offensives on the western front. Yet the soldiers in general, and Kitchener in particular, were becoming convinced that a decision could only be had in the west, which of course implied an army which seemed beyond the resources of voluntary enlistment.

Kitchener's change of mind was heralded in his decision to commit his new divisions to France. His reluctant compliance with Sir John's importunate demands for men before they could be adequately supported by artillery had been at the root of the shells crisis. '...until the German lines were broken he felt himself obliged to keep an army in reserve...When however he was urged so strongly to reinforce Sir John...he finally consented to send out one division...and now a second division which was absolutely the last which could be supplied with ammunition.'[2] Such was the message which Esher carried. It would take many months before the supply of ammunition overtook the supply of men. But the 'westerners' foresaw this situation arising in the summer of 1916, and it implied conscription and the Somme type of offensive.

Sir John was not the man to command a huge national army, but he displayed an indecent and neurotic attachment to his position. He was haunted with the idea that Kitchener himself would come out and take over his command, and Esher had to assure him that this was not intended, that Kitchener was not against him. There was certainly no indication from Sir John that he had just sacrificed his command, or was willing to sacrifice it as later in his memoirs he claimed he had done. As he walked around the garden at Hazebrouck Sir John merely complained of a 'certain tone of coldness and lack of appreciation' in Kitchener's telegrams and letters to him. He also complained of the noise of the guns. 'It is a constant worry to Sir John,' Esher noted, 'who is continually questioning the direction and reason of this infernal noise.'³ The misunderstanding with Kitchener was patched up with a letter which Esher helped Sir John to compose, but basically Sir John could not co-operate either with Joffre (whom he cursed loudly and indiscreetly in the presence of subordinates) or with Kitchener. He did not accept either 'unity of command' or 'unity of direction'.

When the Germans occupied Warsaw in August Esher was distinctly alarmed about the danger of a separate peace. He believed the French were flagging, and that the Germans might bargain for Antwerp and compensations in the East. At home public opinion was distracted by the partisan spirit of the Harmsworth Press in calling for conscription and the equally narrow dogmatism of the anti-conscriptionists. The public did not seem to realise that a war costing three million a day with the 'untold destruction of wealth' while offering good wages and profits was a fool's paradise. The government, and even Balfour whom Esher regarded as a realist, seemed intolerably complacent, and he decided to rouse Glasgow from its apathy. Glasgow was the key to Scottish opinion, and Scottish opinion would turn the country on the compulsion question. The moment seemed opportune, as the National Register was being taken in mid-August. But while the government seemed to have abdicated their role of war leadership the sectional societies, the National Service League and No Conscription Fellowship, had the field to themselves. Esher's plea for 'equality of Sacrifice' appeared in the *Glasgow Herald* on 10 August. It attempted to bring readers to their senses by a sobering warning. It asserted that Germany was superior to the allies in respect of both the 'personal guidance of the war' and the 'concentrated purpose of her people', but hoped that if Kitchener were 'supported by the spontaneous gift to him of the supreme effort of the nation, he may even now avert defeat'. There was no time for a general political movement. Even so: 'Hundreds of capitalists are consenting still to enjoy large profits from the war which a truer reading of the facts would make them ashamed to accept. Thousands of workers are accepting abnormal increase of wages that did they realise its origin in the sufferings of their mates, their mutilation and death, they would spurn to take.' The remedy suggested to achieve equality of sacrifice was: no financial profits from the war, wages fixed by the state, and every man to agree to go where Lord K. told him.

Esher wanted Glasgow to petition the King, and aided no doubt
by his initiative the Lord Provost presided over a discussion at a
meeting on 27 August of the 'most distinguished citizens of Glasgow',
who were unanimous in approving the principles that war profits
belonged to the nation, that wartime wages should be regulated, and
that 'some form of compulsory service involving the application of
military law and discipline to the male population' was necessary.
Asquith could not have relished these resolutions, which Esher took
care to send him, along with a more direct innuendo: 'Finally it was
agreed...that it was undesirable in the interests of national unity to
continue any public debate, in a controversial spirit, of questions that
His Majesty's Government only can decide.'[4] The urgency of government action was emphasised by the protracted strike of 25,000 Welsh
miners in disregard of the Munitions Act. Yet Kitchener remained
unconvinced about conscription, and that had to precede the direction of labour. Curzon, writing to Esher, thought that the government would in the end make Kitchener their scapegoat, meanwhile
pretending that the country was not yet ready. Opinion however was
being allowed to drift or, worse, to harden into prejudice while
Asquith temporised. This was the feeling of two newspaper editors
who happened to notice Esher's appeal:

Geoffrey Robinson-Esher, 27 August 1915:[5] So far as the Radical
press is concerned this opposition has been more dishonest and
unpatriotic during the past few days than anything I can remember. On the other hand if the government who are beginning to
realise that they will have to come to it were to make up their
minds to lead, and if three men (Asquith, Kitchener and Lloyd
George) were to go out into the country in support of their
decision I believe that hardly a voice would be raised against
national service...

You have influence with Kitchener, which is very rare. Don't
you think you could make him realise the vital importance of
taking the thing in time?

J. A. Spender-Esher, 27 August 1915:[6] I needn't say I entirely
agree with you about that press...Result—to throw the whole
of organised labour into opposition; and the cabinet will presently
be splitting itself over something which one half of it could

never do without the other, and which the whole cabinet could only do if it all kept quiet till it was necessary, and then said unanimously that the time had come.

Spender believed that the voluntary system could still yield as many recruits as could be got by compulsion 'if the recruiting is carefully done'. Such was the Liberal notion of 'compulsion'.

Esher was ready to co-operate in any attempt to improve the voluntary recruitment, which needed to be systematised now that the appeal of 'Kitchener's army' had been played out. He saw Lord Derby about this question in August, and did his best to persuade the War Office to re-establish the Haldane system of local committees either for obtaining voluntary recruits or as the most palatable form of enlisting conscripts:

> *Esher-Kitchener, 27 September 1915:*[7] Whether you are forced into compulsory service by the 'facts', as Lloyd George calls them, or whether you are not, I am sure that you would do well to shift the burden of recruiting from the War Office on to the Associations, grouped in certain districts, in others not, recruiting both for the Territorial Service and *all* forces of the Crown. You could nominate one of your officers to watch the *allocation* of men…between the regular, new and territorial armies…
>
> I urged this plan upon you long ago. The War Office plan for London, to which on July 27 I gave a reluctant adhesion, has proved a complete failure; and our Territorial recruiting has gone down since that day by over 50 per cent.

It was important to decentralise recruiting and dissociate it from the 'militarism' of the War Office authorities.

Esher does not appear to have made any impression on Kitchener, but Derby was interested and asked him, when he was appointed Director-General of Recruiting, to agree to involve the TA Associations in his scheme and take charge of London and the Home District. The Derby scheme, which was to occupy the centre of the stage for the next six months, was to summon every man to an interview and ask, in the cases of those unwilling to serve, for written reasons. The interviews were to be conducted by the local branches of the Parliamentary Recruiting Committee with the aid of the

Recruiting Committee of the Trades Union Congress. The National Register had shown between 1,300,000 and 2,000,000 men of military age in the UK who could be drawn on, and Kitchener required three million men inclusive of those already enlisted: that is, an army of 1,400,000 men, another 1,200,000 men for what was somewhat euphemistically called 'wastage', and 350,00 men for home defence.

A weekly recruiting figure of 35,000 men would raise two million and over by the end of 1916 including the men just grown up. But at the cabinet on 12 October McKenna and Runciman 'demurred altogether the possibility or necessity of recruiting anything like such a rate of 35,000 a week...Lords Lansdowne and Curzon, Mr Lloyd George, Mr Long and Mr Churchill, accepting Lord Kitchener's figures, urged that on our voluntary system of recruiting' Kitchener's figure could not be attained. Asquith, Balfour and Grey, also 'accepting provisionally' Kitchener's figures, observed that 'even if Lord Derby's new organisation should fail to speed up recruiting at the required figure, it was by no means clear that any form of compulsion yet suggested (apart from the strong Labour opposition which it would encounter and difficulty of applying it to Ireland) would be found capable of producing a better result'.[8] Lord Curzon immediately undertook to produce such a scheme, but evidently Asquith was assuming lavish exemptions such as Derby was to make—only sons with dependent mothers, men running shops and businesses, etc. He could not visualise a general call-up.

Esher thought it right that Asquith should postpone the decision until 'after Eddy [Derby] has his try', but he did not wish to be associated with the Derby scheme, and later warned Eddy that he was bidding fair to become the most unpopular man in England. When Derby appealed to him to co-operate he replied:

Esher-Derby, 13 October 1915:[9] I hope you were not vexed yesterday. From our hurried talk in the morning I confess that I had not grasped the central idea of your scheme. It seems to me to be an excellent one. Do you think however that it is possible to give it a satisfactory trial if you hamper the Parliamentary Committees and the Trade Unions with people like me...

We...are as you know committed to the existing system of recruiting. We have tied ourselves up with local magnates... and with committees who would either have to be scrapped or amalgamated with the new elements that seem to be the vital essence of your scheme.

Esher feared that if he were associated with Derby and the scheme failed the Committees would blame the Associations and so prevent 'what may ultimately become the only possible solution of the problem', conscription. However, he offered that 'all those who have been associated with me will place themselves unreservedly at your disposal in a quiet and unobtrusive way'. The Derby scheme was launched on 23 October by a royal message to the nation, composed by Esher.[10] 'In ancient days the darkest moment has ever produced in men of our race the sternest resolves. I ask you, men of all classes, to come forward voluntarily.' Esher mentioned the 'highly organised enemy' but omitted to make mention of victory or an enduring peace, which the King himself added.[11]

The Derby scheme was Asquith's response to an attempt by Lloyd George, Churchill and Curzon to topple him on the compulsion question. In September there seemed every prospect that the Germans would bear down on Constantinople, buying a passage through Bulgaria by offering her Macedonia, and then mobilising the Turks with German arms and officers. Haunted by this nightmare, Lloyd George demanded the landing of an allied army in Salonika, from where it would proceed north along a single-track railway to assist the Serbs. The French had suddenly offered to send divisions for such an operation early in September, but any British force seemed unobtainable from the resources of voluntary enlistment. The general staff were against taking divisions from France. Esher assured Kitchener that the French general staff felt likewise. 'I cannot hear of any soldier who does not condemn a third European field of operations,' he wrote. 'It is a political versus the strategical view...Millerand says: "We are bound in honour to help Serbia." '[12] And so Kitchener, who had pleaded in January for the remaking of the Serbian railway without success, condemned Lloyd George's project as militarily unsound. But Churchill, whose reputation was heavily committed to the success of the Dardanelles expedition, supported Lloyd George. The result was a token force useless to assist the Serbs, and endangered when Venezelos fell and Greece's hostility threatened its rear.

The rapidly deteriorating position of the allies in the Balkans convinced Lloyd George that they were losing the war while Asquith

294

stalled on the compulsion question. He resolved in September to resign, force a general election, and so carry compulsion from which he hoped to obtain an army 'much larger' than the seventy divisions which Kitchener was aiming at, recall the 100,000 munition workers that had been enlisted, and gain 'a means of discipline of the small minority who made all the trouble in the munition works'.[13] A refusal to amend the Parliament Act would lead to an automatic general election at the end of the year, and Curzon was well positioned to persuade the Lords to throw out the Amending Bill. Churchill, like Lloyd George, wished to get rid of Kitchener and to put Lloyd George at the War Office with Haig as CIGS, and Lloyd George thought Kitchener might replace Sir John in France. Kitchener was moving towards accepting compulsion, Esher being among those who were trying to persuade him, quoting Taine's dictum that conscription was the brother of universal suffrage: 'These ideas sink into Lord K.'s virgin mind', he commented, 'but has he the power to reproduce them at critical moments?'[14] But Lloyd George's objection to Kitchener at the War Office was political. He had become Asquith's mainstay.

The questions of compulsion and Salonika were vigorously pushed by Curzon, Churchill and Lloyd George, the 'three conspirators' against Asquith early in October. As has been seen, the cabinet of 12 October split into three groups on the compulsion issue. It also split three ways over the Near East. The soldiers' plan of complete withdrawal was supported by Lord Buckmaster. The plan of switching the forces from Gallipoli to Salonika was supported by Bonar Law, Lloyd George, Walter Long and Chamberlain, and also by Carson (who tendered his resignation over the failure to aid Serbia and the general way the war was being run). The counter-plan of going all-out to win at Gallipoli was supported by Asquith, Balfour, Curzon and Churchill. The 'three conspirators' had thus been divided, the weightiest, Lloyd George, being completely at odds with the others. But this very division intensified their opposition to Asquith on the questions that united them, compulsion and the outing of Kitchener. Hence at the cabinet of 15 October Lloyd George made what Asquith called a 'blackmailing speech'. He said: 'there were two parties in the country: one which realised the seriousness of the situation, and the dangers which were being incurred, and the urgent need for action, the other who were satisfied to let things be and sit twiddling their thumbs, and expressed doubts whether it was not his duty to free himself from all reserve and go to the country to tell the people the truth.' Asquith promised to produce a 'formula' for the cabinet the following Monday which would enable him to 'state publicly our military needs and measures for securing them', but:

Memorandum by Stamfordham, 16 October 1915:[15] Some of the ministers urged that a Bill should be produced...to deal with compulsory service so that by 30 November when the results of the recruiting campaign will be known machinery will be at hand to introduce at once the necessary measures for compulsion if the numbers required have not been obtained...

The Prime Minister strongly opposed this proposal...To introduce into Parliament such a Bill would be to strangle Lord Derby's scheme in its cradle; it would arouse all the animosity of the anti-conscriptionists, every clause would be debated and even it might be finally rejected. Meanwhile the necessary number *may* have been secured; if so all the turmoil and bitterness engendered in passing and discussing the Bill would have been unnecessary. If it is found that we cannot win the war without compulsion, he will send all preconceived objections to the wind.

It was to be another case of 'wait and see', but now there were eight lined up against Asquith—the conspirators, and also Carson,[16] Bonar Law, Long, Lansdowne, and Kitchener.

Kitchener in an earlier interview with the Labour leaders had asked for 30,000 recruits a week, and had then raised his figure to 35,000. Now he had joined the compulsionists. Asquith wrote an unusual note to him on the Sunday before the crucial cabinet meeting:

Asquith-Kitchener, 17 October 1915:[17] I should like you to know that what is now going on is being engineered by men (Curzon and Lloyd George, and some others) whose real object is to oust you...they have conceived the idea of using you against me...So long as you and I stand together, we carry the whole country with us. Otherwise, the Deluge! Cannot you say that, while you aim at, and would like to obtain seventy divisions, the thing should be done gradually and with general consent...?

The same day Lloyd George, who had invited C. P. Scott of the

Manchester Guardian down to Walton Heath, told him he was wondering whether to 'bring matters to a crisis at the cabinet next day'. Churchill and F. E. Smith arrived unexpectedly to lunch, and Scott left them to discuss their action.[18] The next day Lloyd George lunched with Repington, who although a 'westerner' was so charmed by him that he told him he 'wanted him for Prime Minister, and Carson for Minister of War'.[19] Whether the conspirators still adhered to the intention of challenging Asquith that day, or whether Asquith had succeeded in arriving at a formula, must remain uncertain, for Asquith fell ill and seemed 'absolutely done'.[20] For the first time in years he spent some days in bed. The compulsion question was thus balked of an issue for the time being.

The cabinet next met with Lord Crewe presiding on 21 October, and the anti-Asquith faction seized on the opportunity to discuss and formally approve the reform of the War Committee so that it 'should be quite small and, as far as can be, non-departmental'.[21] Asquith alone seems to have prevented this reform, for the cabinet were unanimous, and even 'Bongie' his private secretary had been pressing for it. The idea, as has been seen, had been taken up by the King when he consulted with Esher in May, and thereafter the King lost no opportunity of pushing it. Asquith reorganised the war directorate in September by forming a 'War Committee' which was composed simply of the twelve members of the Dardanelles Committee—for to such inflated dimensions it had grown—and by instituting a Finance Committee of nine ministers. He also aspired to re-constitute the Imperial General Staff. These measures were a re-hash of the familiar ingredients which had overloaded the directorate with departmental and political elements. Indeed, the two committees were practically the cabinet divided in two, with Lloyd George and Churchill enjoying membership of both. In the particularly difficult period when the offensives in France and the crisis in the Near East were presenting acute problems, Kitchener had to contend with two bodies which generated chaotic cross-currents of policy. He protested, and Stamfordham approached Bonham Carter:

Stamfordham-King George, 7 October 1915:[22] I saw Mr Bonham Carter about Lord K. and the difficulties which he was experiencing in doing his work under existing conditions. Mr Bonham Carter had already heard about this and he recognised that the trouble is in a great measure due to the inordinate size of the War Committee, and has spoken to the Prime Minister on the subject urging that a small committee would do all the work in say half an hour every morning, and if any more important matters arose they would of course come before the cabinet.

He was therefore glad to get my letter yesterday (which he showed to Asquith) expressing Your Majesty's regrets that the War Committee could not be restricted to the Prime Minister, Secretary of State for Foreign Affairs, Secretary of State for War, and First Lord. He does not know what the Prime Minister will decide.

He also told me that members of the cabinet (I expect Churchill in particular) are inclined to 'heckle' Lord K., who cannot argue and defend himself like political debaters (Lord Selborne as well as Sir E. Grey complain of the waste of their time in the War Committee).

Secret He dropped hints as to possible changes of C-in-C not only in Dardanelles but in France, and rather implied that Lord K. might have to go to the latter...

But Kitchener was losing his hold on the war situation. He was fearful about evacuating Gallipoli, inactive about Salonika, and suspected of weakness in dealing with Joffre. His real fault was his incommunicativeness, so that while he never laid the intelligence telegrams that came to the War Office before the War Committee, he was also suspected of not even reading them himself. The cabinet would not have accepted him in a small directorate with Asquith, Grey and Balfour. It is therefore puzzling that the cabinet so unanimously accepted a directorate of 'not less than three or more than five' which was Asquith's formulation of their decision of 21 October, circulated a week later.[23] Did Lloyd George want a committee which would not leave him isolated among four Asquithians? What is certain is that he reacted to Asquith's plan by composing on 31 October a long tirade against Kitchener ending with the intimation that he would raise in the cabinet the next day 'the real issue' which was the removal of Kitchener. The letter was Lloyd George's familiar recital of the War Office's iniquities mixed with threats to divulge them to the public, after resigning.[24]

On receipt of Lloyd George's ultimatum Asquith called him for an interview on 1 November and said he would announce that if the 'present recruiting campaign failed "other measures" would have to be taken'.[25] But Lloyd George was now more urgently concerned with the direction of the war, and he got from Asquith in the presence of two other ministers an undertaking that Kitchener would be superseded. As soon as Asquith left the room these no doubt surprised onlookers asked each other: 'Will he do it?' and Lloyd George was somewhat doubtful himself. He thought Asquith a 'soft-nosed torpedo...he lacks the steel point'.[26] Asquith's speech the next day in the Commons gave a pledge that the unmarried men would be enlisted, if necessary by compulsion, before the married men were called on. In Lloyd George's opinion compulsion was now assured, since: 'Over a million single men had refused to attest, and the policy of recruiting them compulsorily was the inevitable sequel...all the attested married men were naturally insistent on it.'[27] But when privately questioned by C. P. Scott, Asquith 'still regarded compulsion as out of the question because it would involve conflicts which would at once ruin recruiting and instead of getting more men you would get less', and he still claimed that Kitchener agreed to this.[28]

The more formidable part of Asquith's undertaking which Lloyd George had wrung from him was set in train by Lloyd George himself, who deputed H. A. Gwynne, editor of the *Morning Post*, to go and offer Kitchener three alternatives to the War Office: to be C-in-C at home, C-in-C in France, or Viceroy of India. Kitchener said 'he would fight',[29] but rumours that he and Sir John were to be *dégommé*'d were going round. It was therefore with some relief that the cabinet, in the middle of a discussion on Salonika on 4 November, took up a suggestion which had suddenly arisen that Kitchener should go immediately to the Near East himself to report on the situation.[30] Kitchener left for Paris that very evening. On arrival there he summoned Esher for a discussion, and incidentally told him of this latest attempt to 'trip up the Prime Minister'. As for Kitchener himself: 'Nothing has been decided about his return to the War Office, which Asquith takes over temporarily. Events will decide.'[31]

Kitchener was filled with deep anxiety about the course of events in the Near East, and repeated several times: 'I cannot see light.' He had found that the new French War Minister, Gallieni, and head of the government, M. Briand, had also 'no clear ideas'. The lack of any effective liaison between the general staffs of Britain and France, or of any real concert in the political direction of the war had brought about the confusion and impotence in the counsels of the allies so manifest in the months just passed. Esher therefore readily obtained Kitchener's consent to press ahead with the scheme he had been working on since May for an Allied Council. But now the French refused to believe that there was any chance of Kitchener's return to the War Office, even though he had taken the seals with him! As Bertie had remarked, '*Qui va à la chasse, perd sa place.*'[32] Would the French now pay Esher the same respect, or regard him also as fallen from power? Letters of farewell arrived from England, and Kitchener, 'massive, inarticulate, *émotionné*', knew that his position would never be the same on his return. He was wounded by the 'unconcealed dislike' of the politicians, who in Esher's opinion no more understood him than they would an Arab sheik or a Hebrew prophet.[33]

Esher had always believed, with good reason, that the real root failure in the allied war direction was not the indecision of particular governments but the want of concert between them. This had appeared in the ill-concerted offensives of Sir John and Joffre, the strange and unexplained waverings of the French over Salonika, and the French rejection of Grey's Balkan diplomacy. At a deeper level it affected military policy. The French offensives in Champagne had been motivated by the desire for a quick decision, which was to continue in 1916, just as 'waiting for the Americans' was to motivate French strategy in 1917. British official strategy tended to lean towards attrition and 'starving rather than storming'. Yet in 1916 the British were to be hustled into the Somme offensive largely by fears that French morale might otherwise collapse. The French feared their military exhaustion and relative weakness at the peace table, and yet supported the unduly offensive strategies of Joffre and Nivelle, only to relapse in 1917 into the passive policy of Pétain after the American entry into the war and mutinies in the French army. Behind these vacillations lay political and diplomatic distrust of British intentions. It was really at the diplomatic and political level that inter-allied co-operation was most disastrously absent. Had the British and French agreed their peace objectives the dislocations in their military strategy would have been largely avoidable.

After the collapse of the allied Balkan diplomacy Esher returned to the theme of his paper of May:

CID Note by Esher, 12 October 1915:[34] I have suggested that for a war such as that in which we are engaged our system of cabinet government is unsuited...Events since the month of May have not weakened this argument...The events of the last two months, and especially of the last few weeks, are a sad commentary upon the lack of political and military directing power. The probable activities of the enemy were seen by some and not by others. There was, consequently, absence of decision and preparation. When these became necessary, the result was hurried conferences, obscured counsels, vague and conflicting purposes, followed by decisions and counter-decisions.

The remedy suggested was an inter-allied council on which military and political representatives would sit together, a 'small and efficient directing staff of the ablest French and British officers...who could so marshal and co-ordinate facts and suggestions that the inferences drawn from them would be indisputable and certain to control the executive action of the military commanders of both nations'. Esher's *Note* was taken up by Selborne in the cabinet—for the CID had now become defunct under Asquith: 'I believe that he is right, and that the absence of any striking success for the allies in this war is more due to the absence of any central control than to any other cause.'[35] As examples Selborne mentioned the French government's promise of 150,000 men to Greece without consulting us, and our promise to assist Roumania with 200,000 men without consulting them. Selborne suggested a definite scheme, which he circulated for consideration at the cabinet of 21 October, that: 'the conduct of the war be entrusted to a Council of six sitting in Paris consisting of one cabinet minister, one military and one naval officer, selected by the French and British governments respectively. The military and naval members should have adequate staffs...The two cabinet ministers would form the link with the...governments.' A concomitant of this scheme was the abolition of the existing War Committee, to be replaced by a smaller committee of six. This proposal was accepted at the cabinet of 21 October as has been seen, without any definite number specified, but Selborne suggested Curzon and Lloyd George, while Asquith's later formulation left Curzon out. The crisis over this part of Selborne's scheme eclipsed the Allied Council for a time.

Esher immediately took up what he was glad to call 'Selborne's

301

scheme' and discussed it with M. Millerand, who thought it 'excellent and workable'. But Paris was in the middle of a raging political crisis, which had already removed Delcassé and was about to remove Viviani and Millerand. Briand, the new premier, and Gallieni, the new War Minister, were regarded by Esher as more likely than their predecessors to accept a 'botched' peace. 'The French know well that one of these days they will be offered Alsace and Lorraine in exchange for the permanent occupation of Antwerp.'[36] However, Esher had seen quite a lot of Gallieni, who was a near neighbour in Paris and was less starchy than Millerand. Before Kitchener had left London Esher had reported Gallieni's favourable reception of the Allied Council idea, and had suggested to Asquith the formation of a permanent secretariat for it. He relied on Hankey to settle the British side of the business:

Esher-Hankey, 3 November 1915:[37] The work of a year approaches fruition. I think that Briand...will propose shortly a joint Conseil de Guerre of three or four from each country, with a secretariat on the exact lines of the CID. The method of working will be modelled on our CID procedure. If the members proposed from here are Briand, Gallieni, La Caze, when required...yours would follow suit.

I suggest that you should be the English head of the Secretariat, the French appointing theirs, with a French *officier de liaison* acting as the link... if a French officer deputed by M. Briand starts for London on Friday or Saturday, do not be surprised. He will bring you letters and requests for guidance and assistance.

It was extremely unfortunate that exactly at this point Kitchener was sent on his mission which the French—always better informed of English politics than conversely—immediately recognised as his downfall. Esher however continued to try to interest Asquith in the scheme and forwarded to Hankey the favourable comments of Gallieni and another minister, Léon Bourgeois, adding: 'The thing must be accomplished this week. There must be no delay.'[38] Esher also wrote to the CIGS, Sir A. Murray:

Esher-Sir A. Murray, 7 November 1915:[39] The principle of joint

consultation and action when possible between the two general
staffs has been eagerly accepted by the Minister of War here. The
two *officiers de liaison* are named. You may, and I suppose will,
appoint two. So far excellent.

But K. is most anxious that the matter should not end there,
and that *at the earliest possible date* a conference should take
place. The Minister for War here would like this conference to
be held at Calais or Amiens. The liaison officer can prepare
under your auspices and Graziani's the agenda...

For many months this closer connexion between the two
countries for carrying on the war has been steadily worked for
here...Will you show this to the PM?

Asquith was about to reform the War Committee in the absence of
Kitchener according to his agreed limit of five. It included the Prime
Minister, Balfour, Lloyd George, Bonar Law and McKenna, as
approved by the cabinet on 11 November. Churchill was excluded,
and went off to join the army in France. Just before this well-known
move Asquith seems to have adopted the Allied Council scheme with
the modification that Britain at least should have four rather than
three representatives, and they should be cabinet ministers. This
avoided any invidious choice of a substitute for Kitchener and satisfied Lloyd George's idea that the soldiers should be kept in their place.
Hankey outlined this plan in a letter to Esher of 9 November, who
replied:

Esher-Hankey, 11 November 1915:[40] The PM's plan as described by you will be perfectly satisfactory here. I gather that for
the moment the PM, Mr Balfour and Mr Lloyd George with
possibly Sir Edward Grey are the ministers who would represent
England upon an international War Council. Personally I should
be content with the PM alone...but that is not the view of parlia-
ments and democracies...

I want to impress upon you that the international War Council
can never become an effective instrument unless prior to its first
meeting...

1. ...the combined general staffs who are to be brought into
liaison by Captain Doumayrou shall have met, and...prepared
...the strategical questions military or political...

303

2. ...a competent bureau or secretariat shall have been established on the lines...of the CID.

As Esher had suggested, the Council's meetings could only be sporadic and the secretariat would ensure continuity. But a conference in Paris became so urgent, in the light of Kitchener's telegrams from the Near East, that one was hurriedly arranged for 17 November. It followed Asquith's plan and 'approved a sort of embryo constitution for future conferences'.[41] Esher was able to report optimistically on the whole proceeding when he described the scheme to the King three days later.[42]

But difficulties arose on the French side. The French War Office under Millerand had scarcely been able to control Joffre's staff at GQG, and under Gallieni it ceased even to discuss operations, becoming a mere provider. Joffre, like Kitchener, was a national symbol and no-one could gainsay him. According to Henry Wilson, who had been attached to GQG, a 'monastic silence' hung over Joffre's mess, and able and articulate generals like Berthelot or Girodon were sacked. A third force in French military policy was the Quai d'Orsay, which expected a place on any secretariat. Out of these three elements a secretariat on the French side could not be formed, and Briand vetoed it. On the British side Hankey was not over-enthusiastic, for it would have meant his relegation to Paris at the expense of an exciting political role which he had come to assume in the absence of CID duties proper. Hankey preferred *ad hoc* meetings of heads of governments. In spite of exhortations from Esher to come to Paris and solve the secretariat problem, Hankey let matters lapse. The scheme therefore failed to develop but fell back on a standing committee which meant that Hankey and Doumayrou as 'Secretary-Liaison Officers' arranged sporadic conferences and kept records of their proceedings. Two more war years were to drag out their inventory of Anglo-French suspicion and cross purposes before the Supreme War Council was constituted at Versailles.

It had been decided to relieve Kitchener of responsibility for operations, but to keep him at the War Office as a 'fixed point' of public confidence. Esher assured Asquith that the French would regard his removal even into another position as a dangerous course. More important, Lloyd George had for the time being lost interest in becoming Secretary for War, for he was now included in the small

War Committee. So long as the soldier who was to be made responsible for operations, either as CIGS or as C-in-C, had direct access to the War Committee, Kitchener's influence and power of obstruction or misrepresentation could be contained. Esher at first expected Lloyd George to replace Kitchener at the War Office, and Kitchener to be made C-in-C. On 30 November, writing to Stamfordham, he suggested that Robertson should become CIGS and positively recommended that Kitchener be C-in-C of all forces overseas, moving about 'as his own liaison officer'. Had Lloyd George wanted the War Office he could have had it.

Kitchener arrived in Paris on 29 November ready to recommend the evacuation of Gallipoli and also of Salonika, where the Anglo-French force was threatened by the Bulgarians. His ideas could not have been pleasing to Briand and Gallieni with whom he conferred. But they were supported by the cabinet, even though Kitchener threatened to resign if the troops at Salonika were not withdrawn 'at once'. A month earlier they would have accepted his resignation with alacrity. Now that they had decided to strip him of his power, they wanted his name and were content to leave him in his position.

Esher hoped that Kitchener would as C-in-C gain real powers, and he wrote to Asquith that if these were defined 'the definition of those of Gallieni would follow'.[43] Asquith shared Esher's respect for Kitchener's overall strategic insight, as did the French, whose language Kitchener could speak with a fair proficiency. Hence when a conference was hastily sought with the French over Salonika, Kitchener accompanied Asquith and Balfour, with 'a whole retinue of generals and experts', over to Calais on 5 December.[44] With Balfour's assistance Kitchener seemed to carry conviction. It was exceedingly unfortunate that for the French Salonika was a matter of honour, and that the conclusions of the Calais Conference were immediately repudiated from Paris. The first inter-allied conferences according to the new manner of proceeding were on an impossible subject. The British had to give up their decision to evacuate Salonika when the French for political reasons went back on the deliberate conclusion of the heads of state and general staffs.[45]

The decision that Kitchener should not be C-in-C came from the King, whose wishes were conveyed to Asquith by Stamfordham on 3 December. The King approved the transfer of Robertson to the position of CIGS where he would be concerned with 'strategy'.[46]

Kitchener as War Secretary would be in the same position as any other member of the War Committee to criticise Robertson's decisions, but could not interfere with his suggestions before they reached the War Committee. Kitchener it was suggested might deal especially with 'finance'. But was Kitchener never to give counsel on strategic questions? Robertson, fearing no doubt that unless this were made explicit he would find himself being interfered with and overruled in strategic decisions, drew up a written charter for himself as CIGS which was to become an important and controversial political factor later. Curiously enough he appeared in Paris with this document in Kitchener's entourage on 9 December when Kitchener and Grey were suddenly sent to deal with a new emergency arising from the allied defeat at Salonika by the Bulgarians. Kitchener was still very much the strategic overlord, and of course he would not consent to Robertson's conditions and was threatening to resign.

In this matter Esher fulfilled his usual role as a mediator. He had just executed at Asquith's request the very delicate operation of inducing the irascible Sir John French to offer to resign without being actually told to do so. He had even composed Sir John's 'excuses' for wishing to retire. Robertson as Sir John's Chief of Staff had no doubt seen enough to realise that Kitchener's subordinates needed a charter. His idea was to detach the Secretary of State and the Army Council from the general staff, and the latter would alone initiate all plans for operations laid before the War Council, even where a member of the War Council made a suggestion, and likewise execute plans as approved. Every plan or order for operations would go under the signature of the CIGS who in this field would be the 'sole adviser' of the War Council. Esher talked over this charter with Robertson at the Crillon Hotel, and then discussed it with Kitchener at length. With a proviso safeguarding the Secretary of State's responsibility Kitchener seemed disposed to accept it.[47] And so 'Wully' Robertson achieved the almost impregnable position which enabled him later to become such a thorn in the side of Lloyd George.

Robertson and Haig, who now took Sir John's place as C-in-C in France,[48] were out-and-out 'westerners', as was Henry Wilson who was relieved of his duties as Chief Liaison Officer with the French GQG and given the command of a corps. It is perhaps somewhat odd that Lloyd George did not challenge the appointment of Haig and Robertson. However, no prominent soldier at this time espoused the 'eastern' policy, which had received a severe setback. No one seemed to support Churchill's plans for remaining at Gallipoli or raiding the coasts of Asia Minor, and the divisions which were after all maintained at Salonika were there at the urgent demands of the French and the Russians.

Through Robertson the 'western' ideas of the reconstituted general staff found expression in a plea for large offensives in 1916, which the War Committee approved on 28 December. At the same time the Northcliffe press was going all out for conscription and a group of peers were still plotting to reject the amendment of the Parliament Act and force an election, if compulsion were not conceded. Asquith was himself caught by his 'pledge',[49] and was cornered when the cabinet considered Derby's recruiting drive on 28 December. He tried to compromise by proposing that the unmarried men who had not attested should be deemed to have done so if they could not satisfy a tribunal. He was supported by McKenna who thought the extra men were not needed.

But the issue now crystallised into whether fifty or seventy divisions should be the scale of the army. McKenna argued very forcibly that the country's real role in the war was to finance the allies (France was borrowing £20 million a month) and to supply them with munitions rather than raise men in excessive numbers, and Runciman at the Board of Trade emphasised the importance of the export trade in financing the war.[50] Curiously enough there were already sixty-seven divisions but Robertson only divulged this privately. Asquith on 30 December postponed the decision by referring to Kitchener and Robertson the problem of what the military needs of the army were.[51] In this way he isolated the only minister who objected to compulsion in principle, and Simon's resignation was the only loss to the Coalition when it agreed on 31 December to the immediate compulsion of the unmarried men. Asquith's surrender damaged his reputation among the Liberal pacifists. C. P. Scott called it 'a nasty trick' to keep himself in power. 'He certainly is a champion in the arts of chicane.'[52] Nor were the 'militarists and extremists' as Hankey called them[53] (for Hankey like a chameleon was as pro-Asquith as he later became pro-Lloyd George), any more pleased, when Asquith seasoned his surrender with a strong indication that he would oppose general conscription. 'Yes, we are still saddled with Squiff,' Henry Wilson wrote to Maxse, editor of the

National Review, 'and as long as we keep that cynical, callous black-guard we shall never do any good.'[54]

The compulsion of all unmarried men would naturally lead on to the calling-up of the men who had attested in very satisfactory numbers knowing they would not be summoned first. But was it fair to call on unmarried men of forty before married men of twenty? Or to exempt the Irish, whose MPs had voted so solidly against compulsion in England? Not surprisingly, a movement among the Unionists led by Carson resolved to make sure that if married men were called on the unattested would go along with the attested. The pressure for general compulsion culminated in a crisis in April in which Bonar Law found himself forced to go along with the strong feeling of his party, and throw in his lot with Lloyd George. It was the politicians rather than the soldiers who created this crisis.

Kitchener had hoped for a decisive action on the western front in 1916, where the allies still had a superiority of numbers. But five British divisions had been lured to Egypt and there was still no overall plan for 1916. Worse, the dilemma between 'a big overwhelming early offensive *versus* a husbanding of all resources with a view to a prolongation of the war for years' had been mooted but not decided.[55] It was being treated as an internal question by Britain, but what if the French could not fight on beyond 1916? The Germans evidently thought they could destroy the French will to fight on when they launched seventeen divisions against the fortress of Verdun in February and for months wasted away the French reserves. Immediately the Verdun attack was launched the French were seriously alarmed, and told Robertson: 'They expect to lose at least 200,000 men, and they are short of reserves. Their depots...are empty and any offensive on a big scale in the spring or summer will now be out of the question for them.'[56] Haig in France heard the same thing and wrote to Esher: 'They talk about having 200,000 casualties, and then whether they win or lose in that (to my mind comparatively little) fight, peace will have to be made. What I fear is at the back of their minds is the fact that their army may then cease to be the most important one in the coalition...'[57] This sudden development did not result in Haig and Robertson pressing for an immediate offensive. Rather it clarified the war outlook by making it certain that the British army would have to expand to a maximum size, and that the struggle would continue into 1917. This of course strengthened the compulsionists, for without massive military support France would not go on.

Although Kitchener had been shorn of responsibility for recruiting when Derby became Director-General, he now came forward to play a prominent role in the question of military requirements and compulsion. Yet he was not a straightforward compulsionist as Robertson was, and this no doubt encouraged the politicians to attempt to drive a wedge between him and his CIGS, and even to get rid of him abroad. A plausible proposal to the latter effect came from a Conservative MP and adviser to the Foreign Office, Colonel Sir Mark Sykes,[58] who suggested that a 'Viceroy of the Middle East' should be created to integrate the separate communications to the War Committee of the commanders in the different theatres there.[59] The title seemed carefully baited for Kitchener, whose private secretary Colonel O. A. G. FitzGerald suspected that it might play 'into the hands of those who would like to see K. out of England'. Esher considered the scheme had some merits and replied:

Esher-Colonel FitzGerald, 2 February 1916:[60] The memo. is very able and I agree with practically the whole of it. ...if the Viceroy of the Middle East is really the key to our imperial strategy K. ought to go there...

When we, you and I, discussed the future as K. was passing through Paris on his way to the Mediterranean it was agreed between us that events might so shape themselves that he would be obliged to remain in the Near East for a while in superior command. Later on when he returned the idea was modified by events which had occurred, i.e. the change in the high command in Flanders, the new responsibilities imposed upon Joffre, and the withdrawal from Gallipoli, etc etc. I then thought that K. meant to remain in England, and by means of a very small War Council and a revived general staff run the whole war from Whitehall so far as GB is concerned...

The difficulty of creating such a post from the point of view of the CIGS would be the transfer of power of military advice from the General Staff to a very great authority on their flank...

Esher referred the idea to Robertson, who was not happy about it: 'If they want to be rid of him why not move him? I imagine they dare not. Apparently I have been a disappointment, in not knocking him down, but it is no part of a CIGS's duty to intrigue against his Secretary of State. He has been all that could be desired so far as I am concerned.'[61] Another line of attack on Kitchener was through War Office expenditure, which was his responsibility and was certainly less economically controlled than that of the highly efficient Ministry of Munitions. 'There is an elaborate propaganda being worked on this head,' Esher warned FitzGerald.[62]

Kitchener shrank from compulsion largely because he had an ingrained habit of husbanding his resources for the future, and did not want a massive inflow of recruits in 1916 which would exhaust all the potential reserves of men. He also shrank from the administrative headache of handling compulsion when the data of the Registrar-General and the Derby canvass were notoriously unreliable and the legal procedure of compelling men very unsure. Esher advised him strongly not to let this buck be passed on to him. The alternative as Esher saw it was to involve the Lord-Lieutenants of the counties. He was confirmed in this belief when he witnessed the practical working of the Derby tribunals, and he advised Derby also to place the supervision of the tribunals under the County Associations. To Asquith he sent a warning that the tribunals were causing discontent in the north:

Esher-Asquith, 17 March 1916:[63] I was for four hours watching the proceedings of one of these bodies today. They all proceed on the assumption that a man's first duty is to his business, whether it is that of a farmer or an employee in any *trade* that he mainly runs...the tribunals are composed of the applicant's neighbours...In the greater number of cases...the men were 'put back' or 'temporarily relieved'...

The military representatives on the tribunals were according to Esher 'just simple folk, ministers of religion, tradesmen, etc, who...*congratulate* a man if he gets himself exempted'.[64] In one instance a Scots farmer had six shepherds, all unmarried, who were exempted because the lambs had to be brought in!

At the War Office the recruitment question was being studied by the new Adjutant-General, Sir N. Macready, whose department had no reliable figures of national manpower. Esher suspected that the supposed reservoir of a million men would not yield anything like the hoped-for numbers:

Esher-Stamfordham, 29 March 1916:[65] Meanwhile (as you know) the armies of D. Haig are 79,000 men below their establishment, and there are not out of the million men in this country 100,000 that can be sent abroad as drafts, and recruits are coming in very badly. There is no grip of the situation...I shall probably hear tomorrow what Macready has decided about sending more divisions abroad. It is criminal to send any until the whole drafting question is settled.

Yet if we could be ready in July-September with masses of reserves we might bring the war to an end this year.

The recruiting figures for January-March were disappointing. Macready thought the cabinet committee had failed in their promise, and Henry Wilson wrote to Esher to say they were a 'scandal' and that 'old Squidgy and his group must go'.[66] Esher himself thought that Kitchener should enforce a decision on the monthly quota of recruits which the government were trying to negotiate with the Labour leaders: '...if he does not slay the Amorites they will slay him.'[67]

Pursuing his notion that the Derby tribunals could be placed under the lieutenants of the counties and County Associations, Esher drove to Glasgow to see the Lord Provost on 3 April. The Lord Provost told him a very characteristic story about Asquith which was typical of the gossip going about. A deputation of leading Glasgow businessmen and officials waited by appointment on Asquith at 10 Downing Street and were ushered into the hall. There they stood for a quarter of an hour when the door of the Prime Minister's room happened to open for someone passing in or out. They caught a glimpse of Asquith 'chatting to two ladies, who were smoking cigarettes, and buttoning the glove of one of them'.[68] Gladstone, they were sure, would not have treated them in that way.

The disillusionment with Asquith now manifested itself even in Stamfordham's letters to Esher, and Kitchener was being implicated in Asquith's policy. The Unionist War Committee, chaired by Carson, demanded universal conscription. Stamfordham called the 'inimical feeling towards the government' in Glasgow 'promising, though not as to the strong man K.'.[69] The government were getting into a mess, for as Kitchener's secretary admitted: 'only about half the single men have been produced. Some tell you the other half do not exist, and that Derby's figures are all wrong. Owing to the want of organisation we have no means of finding them.'[70] As for the attested married men, many were now claiming that they were deluded into attesting on a 'distinct promise' that they would not be called up, and Walter Long stated in the Commons that such men would be at liberty to claim release! Esher was unable to persuade Derby, but he remained convinced that while the War Office authorities could not locate and drag in men, the local organisations already existing under the county lieutenants could. He warned FitzGerald of the 'criminal hiatus' in recruiting which the country would discover in the summer.[71]

The key man in the coming struggle was Robertson. Unlike 'K.' he believed in compulsion:

Henry Wilson-Esher, 13 April 1916:[72] I hope Robertson sets the pace. I would be happier if I didn't know that when talking and writing cease and we get to the real thing—the push of pike—he usually fails. This time he may, he ought to, he *must be made to* take his heart in both hands and go bald-headed for full compulsion...
...if Squiff remains in power we shall lose the war...There is a curious feeling of unrest, suspicion and loathing rising out here against the present government...and in a short time we shall see all England divided into two camps—combatants versus noncombatants. What a scandal, and all due to Squiff.

The cabinet on 14 April met to consider the report of its committee on recruiting. Lloyd George having consulted Robertson went to it resolved to resign if it did not accept general compulsion, to be announced on 18 April when Asquith's decision was expected. Balfour lunched with Repington and was told on going off to the cabinet that he was about to decide whether the war was going to be won or merely drawn. Although not persuaded himself on the need for compulsion, Balfour realised that Bonar Law would have to follow suit with Lloyd George and he himself would have to do so also. Kitchener was groomed for the meeting by Esher, who found him fit and more logical and clear than usual:

War Journals, 14 April 1916:[73] In the various papers which the Army Council have placed before the Cabinet they ask for every available man. That is the formula from which Robertson will not budge...

K. refuses to take the responsibility of making the best of the number of men he possesses, which would mean scrapping divisions at home for the purpose of sending drafts oversea...

It is calculated that there are between two and three millions of men of military age not in the army. Derby's scheme if it can be properly worked would give us 200,000 of these; but the Cabinet Council have ascertained that there are another 550,000 who could be taken for the army without affecting vital industries...

Kitchener's idea was to reserve the 550,000 who were mostly un-attested married men for 1917, fearing that 'if Robertson and Haig feel unduly strong they may embark upon enterprises that will eat up all our available reserves, and...next year when the French are exhausted we shall find ourselves in a similar dilemma'.[74] But Esher pointed out that without larger reserves he would have to break up his divisions at home for drafts. The cabinet committee's contribution to the meeting was a plan to find 'every available man' by compelling eighteen-year-olds, veterans and twice-wounded, while exempting the unattested married men and those misled into attesting. In spite of Lloyd George's strong protest, Curzon, Bonar Law and Walter Long 'finally acquiesced in the policy of the P.M.',[75] and Lloyd George left determined to compose his letter of resignation over the week-end.

Asquith remained unaware of this menace, and appeared at a special committee of soldiers and politicians the next day (Saturday) dressed for golf at Sutton Courtney.[76] Haig had come over from France to help hammer out the army's requirements, and spoke with Esher before attending. Haig's expenditure of men was obviously based on lavish estimates, even at this stage of the war, for he told Esher that if he 'employs 400,000 men, he must calculate, so he says, on losing 50 per cent in the two months that the battle might last. Under these circumstances how can he do less than ask for every man the country can produce?'[77] Significantly, Haig was at odds with Kitchener, in wanting drafts sent over rather than complete forma-tions, and Asquith prompted by Hankey seized on this difference of approach to refer the whole question back to the soldiers, evidently all too anxious to get away.

After seeing Haig, Esher had gone to the War Office where he conferred with Robertson and Macready. His concern was to create a solid front between the CIGS, the Army Council and the Secretary of State so that they would stand or fall together on the doctrine of 'every available man'. Yet, curiously enough, knowing Asquith's tenacity and his pledge against general compulsion, he still believed that Lloyd George's line was hopeless. What he wanted as second best was the modification of Derby's scheme which he had been advocating so industriously himself:

War Journals, 15 April 1916:[78] I had a long morning at the War Office. First with Robertson, and I told him frankly that the army had great faith in him, but the politicians would kill it: also that it was impossible for the Army Council to escape responsibility; that whether my Committee was right or wrong when they reorganised the War Office, the basis of the change was the responsibility of the Army Council and of every individual of which it was composed.

I then at his request had an hour with the A-G...I have since sent...to him in writing: 'Whatever the numerical product of "every available man" might be under a more drastic law, it is obscured by not knowing with any degree of exactitude what... the existing law will produce...The best way to achieve this end would be to obtain for Lord Derby a wider latitude of local support and influence...

Robertson lunched with Repington and discussed modifications of the Derby scheme. One story he told was that in January or February Kitchener had gloated over a figure of 175,000 recruits. Robertson queried it, and on examination it proved to be the number that should have come in. Only 62,000 recruits had actually appeared.[79]

That evening Lord Reading, who was the keeper of Lloyd George's conscience in moments of crisis, asked to see Stamfordham and 'clearly demonstrated' that 'a grave political crisis is imminent owing to the certain resignation of Mr Lloyd George' unless the Military Service Act were extended to 'enlist every available man within military age' (more than the soldiers were asking for). Lord

Reading also showed that Bonar Law would almost certainly have to follow because of the feeling in the Unionist party that the Coalition would break up, and that a general election would follow. This would be disastrous, for it would encourage the enemy, and scare off the USA from joining the allies! Could the King usefully interfere, not directly, but by discovering 'some means of accommodation'?[80] Clearly Lloyd George wanted to set the stage luridly before his long-rehearsed act was played.

This disclosure spoilt Stamfordham's Sunday, which he spent wrestling with the crisis while Asquith played golf seemingly with an untroubled mind. He went to see Bonar Law, who felt that Asquith ought to brave the compulsion issue and the alienation of the Labour leaders: this he thought would not divide the nation so seriously as any abandonment by himself of the Unionists' policy of compulsion. For if Lloyd George resigned and Asquith were then defeated in the Commons, no Liberals in the present government would join Lloyd George and he would be forced to dissolve on the compulsion issue in its crudest form. That would mean, said Bonar Law, government by dictatorship and martial law.[81] No doubt he accentuated this bogey to show that Asquith was really the odd man out. Yet in his compliant way Bonar Law offered to help Asquith form a broader government, presumably by shedding the anti-compulsionist Liberals. He agreed, if Asquith resigned and the King summoned him, to advise the recall of Asquith after his own inevitable failure to form a government. Asquith would then be strong enough to form a government on 'an even wider basis'.[82] The real purport of what Bonar Law was saying was that he was not prepared to ally with Lloyd George at this stage in a new Coalition at the cost of alienating the Asquithians. Some more months had to pass before this became feasible.

Lloyd George invited C. P. Scott to Walton Heath that Sunday and was also visited by one of his parliamentary secretaries, Colonel Arthur Lee. Scott thought Lloyd George would be of 'far more use outside the Cabinet than in it' and perhaps Lee's advice on the parliamentary situation did not promise any better prospect. The idea of quitting office alone did not appeal to Lloyd George, and as he sat composing his letter of resignation after lunch he fell asleep. But when he reappeared for tea he announced that 'on waking...everything had suddenly seemed clear to him...and he was resolved to take his stand and to resign if his terms were rejected'. Stamfordham had just telephoned asking to see him at 6-30 p.m., and he drove off to Downing Street 'in the greatest spirits.'[83]

Stamfordham was treated to Lloyd George's best manner of 'exuberant pugnacity'. And unlike his later self, Lloyd George professed to have every confidence in the soldiers:

> *Memorandum by Stamfordham, 16 April 1916:*[84] On my saying that from all I heard the situation appeared serious he agreed. He said the military authorities had submitted their views, which he regarded as moderate...The soldiers were the best judges, and he accepted their figures. If the government did not do so, he would resign and state to the country his reasons. We were not conducting the war with energy and determination...

The difficulties which Stamfordham mentioned—that Asquith had 'practically pledged his word' against general compulsion, the threatening attitude of the Labour leaders and the fear of opposition in the Clyde and South Wales, or the dangers of holding a general election —Lloyd George 'contemptuously brushed aside'. He did not know whether Bonar Law would follow him, nor did he seem very confident of Kitchener: His figures of men required 'go up and down—251,000 when he wants compulsion, 150,000 when not'.[85] After this interview Lloyd George dined alone with Bonar Law and found him bewildered and alarmed, for all the Unionists—even Balfour—would have to follow suit with Lloyd George and there would be a 'complete breakup' of the government.[86]

Bonar Law now followed Lloyd George in taking the verdict of the Army Council as conclusive, and wrote an ultimatum to Asquith to that effect on Monday morning.[87] But were the Army Council united? Esher found that Kitchener did not fully appreciate that the Army Council's memorandum now held the field and that if Lloyd George and others resigned because it was rejected Kitchener would have to resign also. Otherwise, as Esher warned him, his 'influence in the army would be gone', and he 'would then be no further use to the country or the army as Secretary of State'.[88] This seems to have converted Kitchener, though Asquith still thought that he had him squared. Esher then put to Kitchener the proposition that the whole Army Council would have to resign with him:

War Journals, 17 April 1916:[89] When I suggested to him that Robertson and Macready should also resign, he said this would be 'mutiny'; upon which I had to send for the Esher Committee Report and show him paragraph 7 on page 35 which clearly defines the responsibilities of the members of the Army Council. It was quite new to him, that the Chief of the General Staff stood in a similar relation to the War Office as the First Sea Lord does to the Admiralty.

Fortified by Esher's constitutional ruling the Army Council presented a united front during that day and the next, at the long discussions of War Committee and cabinet committee, of Liberal ministers and of Unionist ministers, in a frantic effort to reach some solution.

Asquith decided as a result of the conferences of 17 April that his government would not break up. At 6-30 p.m. he saw the King and reported: 'If Lloyd George goes he will be followed by Curzon and Selborne. Kitchener will not resign.'[90] Asquith also said he had decided to put off his statement till Wednesday, but: 'He does *not* accept Lloyd George's doctrine that the government are bound to accept and carry out the requirements of the military authorities.'[91] Lloyd George himself, who at that moment was staying on conferring with a rump of ministers at Downing Street, seems to have been shaken by the disappointing response of the Unionists—Curzon and Selborne were not enough to break the government.[92] He therefore decided to delay his resignation, perhaps until Carson acted.

But Asquith had not caught up with Kitchener: nor perhaps had the Unionists at their meeting, for they changed their tune the following day. Esher made sure that the King was disabused of the false idea that Kitchener would acquiesce. He saw the King after Asquith's interview, and noted: 'If the crisis becomes acute, I think that the King realises the influence he might exercise. Although he is attached to Asquith personally, and at one time would have regretted to lose him, I think his sentiments have been modified by the hopeless procrastination of the government.'[93]

MPs in the services were coming back from abroad, including Churchill who was eager for a change of ministers, and Asquith's postponed announcement meant another day of hectic politics. Esher called on Stamfordham to make sure that Kitchener's position was correctly appreciated:

> *Memorandum by Stamfordham, 17 April 1916:*[94] Lord Esher came to see me; he believed that Lord K. and Robertson may feel it incumbent upon them to resign, in which case I might perhaps think the King should intervene and prevent them doing so, though if they do not resign and the government refuse conscription they will both forfeit the confidence of the army for ever.
>
> I replied that in that case the King might have to consider whether his influence should be exerted to bring about such a fatal condition of affairs, and the question might arise as to what course taken by the Sovereign would be most in consonance with the opinion of the majority of his people. We agreed that if compulsion is now averted, it might only be putting off the evil day, as the men will have eventually to be got.

The resignation of Kitchener and Robertson on such a question would certainly have brought down the government. Bonar Law, according to Asquith's report to the King, had decided the day before 'to stick to the government and if necessary throw over his party',[95] but on 18 April the Army Council, as Esher who was watching the situation very closely observed, 'remains firm, and the Unionist members of the cabinet are stepping down on to Lloyd George's side of the fence.'[96] The emphasis now shifted to the problem of how to make compulsion palatable to the Labour party, which was holding a meeting that evening:

> *War Journals, 18 April 1916:*[97] He [Henderson] is going to lay before them two propositions. The first suggested by Lloyd George is that they should permit a compulsory bill to be passed with the reservation that it should only be put into operation by an order in council when the government are convinced of its necessity.
>
> The second proposal was suggested by Arthur Henderson himself; it is that the government should give him and the Labour members a six-weeks respite in which to appeal to their constituents and the Labour organisations to support at the expiration of that period a compulsory bill.
>
> It is not at all certain that Lloyd George would accept this

318

second proposal, but if Henderson could go to the cabinet tomorrow with the assent of the Labour party to such a course of proceeding it would undoubtedly strengthen Asquith's hand.

But the Labour party meeting unanimously rejected Lloyd George's proposal, and gave Henderson's plan only nine votes out of twenty-seven. This meant, in Esher's opinion, that they 'reject compulsion in any form'.[98]

On 19 April the cabinet was convened in the morning in order to settle the announcement to Parliament that day. Esher saw Kitchener early to discuss the Labour party's decision. Kitchener understood that 'Lloyd George and the Unionists will retire from the Government; in that case he will follow'.[99] At a three-hour session that morning the cabinet failed to agree. Lloyd George was 'still difficult' and as Asquith told the King, '*did* wish to destroy the government'.[100] Bonar Law also refused to accept Henderson's plan. Kitchener asked for 75,000 men in the six weeks of the 'conversion' of Labour. Henderson accepted that the 200,000 unattested married men had to be obtained, and made what seems a very reasonable proposal to get them. In spite of the hostile vote of his party he undertook to ask the Labour leaders to 'furnish recruits from the married unattested men at the rate of 50,000 per month, on the understanding that if in any one month 50,000 of these men were not produced, the Government would at once bring in a Compulsory Bill and he would support it.'[101] This conceded all the soldiers asked, but the politicians were uncertain. The Unionists no doubt needed a chance to accept it in conclave, and Lloyd George having worked up such a pitch of crisis in which the general conduct of the war was also in question could not have found it easy to accept one more Asquithian 'formula', of the very kind he was criticising. Asquith therefore had to announce to a very tense House of Commons that the cabinet were divided and his announcement was again postponed.[102]

Asquith now had also to adjourn the House over Easter, till Tuesday 25 April, without the cabinet having agreed its policy, but luckily on the Friday of the Easter recess it was accepted that Henderson's proposal should be submitted to Parliament in secret sessions of both Houses. The King congratulated Asquith on this 'happy agreement', but it would seem that Asquith was still fighting for his position, and that some of his ministerial colleagues still reserved their right to advocate immediate compulsion. The struggle had merely been transferred to the parliamentary arena, and MPs were dividing on the issue of confidence or no confidence in Asquith. A hundred Liberal MPs had voted a resolution supporting Asquith's leadership as a 'national necessity'—not a very reassuring number. But Lloyd George had even less of a personal following and was said to be distrusted by Liberals and Conservatives alike. The secret sessions, justified on the ground that figures of recruiting, etc., could not be divulged publicly, would incidentally reveal the strength of the Asquithian and Georgian factions.

According to Hankey, who had assumed the role of Asquith's 'trainer' for the Tuesday ordeal and collected the materials for his speech, the announcement that the cabinet were split created a 'deplorable impression'.[103] On top of this grave concern came news of the 'Easter Rising' in Dublin, where the holiday atmosphere had been shattered on Monday by an attack on Dublin Castle and the occupation of the Post Office and other buildings. Asquith heard the news before he went to bed, but it did not induce him the next day to depart from his 'brief', even though, as Esher noted: 'The news of the Sinn Fein rebellion was circulating in the lobbies' and 'absorbed the attention of every one to the exclusion of every other subject'.[104] Henderson's compromise sounded altogether too pusillanimous in the electrified atmosphere, and Asquith made the mistake of throwing in his objectionable plan of compelling the time-expired men and youths of eighteen. He was speedily obliged to withdraw, and accept immediate general compulsion.[105] Only the fact that neither Lloyd George nor Bonar Law was as yet acceptable as premier saved him from being supplanted.

It was a humiliating defeat for Asquith, whose policy had been rejected both in the cabinet and in the Commons. And yet he used the Irish rebellion as an excuse for remaining in office:

Asquith-King George, 29 April 1916:[106] After the latest intelligence from Ireland had been discussed the PM called attention to the serious situation created by the action of the House of Commons on Thursday and at the request of his colleagues stated at once his own view: namely that in the circumstances the Government have no alternative but to proceed at once with legislation for general compulsion...This view met with the assent

320

of the whole cabinet. Mr Henderson...while agreeing...warned his colleagues of serious labour troubles...

Lord Curzon and Mr Chamberlain thought that the Government ought to show more vigour in self-defence in debate and on the platform. Lord R. Cecil believed that the right course was for the government to resign or be reconstructed, but yielded to the PM's objection that in view of the troubles actual or threatened in Ireland, Mesopotamia and elsewhere, this was not the moment for such a change.

And so the Bill for National Military Service was introduced and passed by 25 May. As Hankey pointed out, those who wanted it did not want Asquith, and those who wanted Asquith didn't want the Bill. Politically the Bill led on to the problem of the direction of labour—the 'manpower' question which finally toppled Asquith in December. Militarily the case for the Bill, in Hankey's opinion, was that a 'big offensive' was wanted. Yet, he thought, being still a good Asquithian, that the big offensive was 'a plan which no member of the Cabinet and none of the regimental officers who will have to carry it out believe in, a plan conceived in the head of the red-hatted, brass-bound brigade behind'.[107] These wanted 'a regular orgy of slaughter this summer'. Perhaps he had acquired this very understandable feeling from Haig's recent demands.

But Hankey was wrong to ascribe the victory of compulsion to the soldiers. It had become the touchstone of the 'total war' faction which Lloyd George had built up, and the shibboleth of the Northcliffe press. Kitchener did not particularly want it, Robertson and Haig avoided it as a political question. As Lloyd George later admitted, he had carried the compulsion question aided only by Robertson who 'like a cunning old fox, merely stated how many men he wanted... and refused to express any opinion how they were to be found, since he regarded this as a political question. This attitude completely defeated the politicians.'[108] It was in fact Esher who supplied this winning formula,[109] and who had created the solidarity of Kitchener and the Army Council in support of it.

For Esher the real advantage of compulsion at this moment was its effect in boosting French morale, badly shaken by the continued hammering and losses at Verdun. It would convince the French that England meant to go through to the bitter end.

Fourteen

The 'Military Moloch'

The German offensive at Verdun, designed to 'bleed white' the French army which was committed to defend for patriotic reasons a salient exposed to a terrific cannonade, forestalled the planned allied offensive in the west. It also shook General Joffre's position, already undermined by well-founded criticisms in the Chamber of the manner in which Verdun had been exposed by the removal of its guns from the forts. The War Minister, Gallieni, headed the opposition to Joffre and to the Grand Quartier-Général at Chantilly which managed, or mismanaged, the 'army zone'. Although the French public did not yet realise the enormous casualties sustained by Joffre's disastrous 'plan XVII' on the eastern frontiers in August and September 1914, or his intention to abandon Paris in the subsequent retreat, and called him the victor of the Marne, his immediate associates could see his feet of clay. Like Kitchener, he was valued as a *'point fixe'*, while the command at Verdun was managed by Castelnau and Pétain. Gallieni— a soldier senior to Joffre and the real saviour of Paris who had launched its defending force at the right moment into the German flank—had come to suspect Joffre's imperturbable calm in the face of enormous losses:

War Journals, 5 May 1916:[1] General Gallieni understands that Joffre is still hankering for a big offensive this summer. Gallieni says that if this fancy is indulged it may lose us the war. The Verdun battle following upon five great attempts on the part of the French to break the German lines conclusively settles in his opinion the uselessness of an attack under present conditions; these are, the lack of large reserves of ammunition, and above all the depletion of France in men...Thirty-eight divisions have been decimated at Verdun. The Germans are holding the western front with ninety divisions in line and 30 in reserve. Together with the

322

forty-seven English divisions the French do not possess a sufficient superiority in men to justify a great offensive.

Clemenceau, then the president of the Military Committee of the Senate, was aligning himself with Gallieni and 'a large section of the army who bitterly criticise Joffre over Verdun' and who denounced an early offensive. The censorship allowed an open attack on Joffre to appear in the *Matin*, following Gallieni's denunciation of Joffre before the Council of Ministers. But Gallieni was a sick man, and when he had to resign from illness Briand replaced him by a man of straw who happened to be an intimate friend of Joffre, General Roques. Briand, as premier, upheld Joffre for political reasons, for they were twin pillars who would stand or fall together.

But Haig was easily convinced that the British could do better, and Esher heard from the liaison officers at the French GQG, Colonel Sidney Clive and Major Cavendish, that 'our people have been convinced...They have persuaded themselves that they have learned by the experience of five great failures' how to conduct a great offensive. 'It will be conducted on a wider front than anything hitherto attempted...If the German line can be pushed back ten miles, it is considered that the result would be worth large sacrifices.'[2] Joffre's histrionic performance at a conference with Haig at Beauquesne on 26 May, when he exploded with wrath at the idea of Haig waiting till August so that he could use his new 'tanks', was not really needed. Haig readily agreed to attack on 1 July on the Somme.[3]

The French politicians were embarrassed by letters from the provinces, which the censorship could not entirely suppress nor the deputies ignore, demanding to know what the English were doing. Esher found that they wanted a speedy diversion. President Poincaré told him it was needed to 'dégager' the French army at Verdun, while the Finance Minister Ribot felt that the country had to win the war before the next winter. Haig was more realistic and expected that once the offensive started it would go on for the rest of the year. As a 'westerner' he believed in wearing down the enemy rather than breaking through, and was suspicious of French hankerings after a diversion in the Balkans:

Haig-Esher, 2 June 1916:[4] It was a real pleasure to us all to see you here, so just turn up whenever you feel inclined. I got an opportunity at the Conference last Wednesday of telling Poincaré how necessary it was to have every available division in France for the coming fighting, which would probably last and ought to last till winter sets in...When the enemy's divisions become worn out, we ought to have fresh ones to put in. Concentration at the decisive point is of the first importance...

I feel sure that it is solely for political reasons that the French are anxious to press on from Salonika...Foch got a good telling-off from Briand on Wednesday. Foch had been talking and saying no offensive should take place until next year! I thought Foch's excuses lame to a degree. He struck me as shifty and unreliable. Pétain was also referred to as a thoughtless talker! and the generals were advised to keep united.

Esher was not so keen on an offensive as Haig. 'The policy of waiting until next year or even to the autumn would unquestionably suit us best,' he noted on 1 June, but it was impossible because of the pressure on Verdun. 'If *our* offensive produces great results, the spirit of France will so revive...that the war may be carried on well into 1917. If on the other hand the results of our offensive are only moderate, you must be prepared for a very difficult situation, and the fall of Joffre,' he wrote to Robertson.[5]

The internal state of France and the stability of its government was the key to military policy. The official diplomatic channels were not considered by Haig and Robertson to be at all illuminating. The ambassador Francis Bertie was an incomparable raconteur, more versed in Victorian scandals than in the military or even the political arcana of the present, and Haig complained: 'I have done my best by calling on Bertie and sending officers to see him, to get him to *play his part*, but no use! We are terribly handicapped by not knowing what the French government means or desires to do.'[6] Haig's solution was to rely on Esher, whom he asked 'to become my ambassador in Paris, until the end of the war'. Esher believed he was more in touch with what was really going on than the British embassy, and he assured Haig and Robertson that Briand's position was safe and that a British refusal to co-operate in further reinforcements to Salonika would not shake the French ministry. He knew that Briand had 'squared Clemenceau'[7] at a secret interview and: 'No-one wishes to substitute Barthou for Briand—and there is no one else available'.

Esher had an appointment to lunch with Briand on 6 June, when Briand appeared with a telegram reporting the death of Kitchener, drowned on his way to Russia. Curiously enough Macready had just posted a letter to Esher that morning, before the news had reached him at the War Office, saying that in McKenna's view Kitchener was 'more firmly seated than ever'. He had distinguished himself at the Anglo-French conference, for 'the speaking of French is not the strongest accomplishment of the cabinet'.[8] Now his death meant the almost certain succession of Lloyd George, still the exponent of the 'forward' policy at Salonika, and a further nail in Asquith's coffin.[9] Esher learnt from Bonar Law on 15 June that the latter had in concert with Lloyd George presented a kind of ultimatum to Asquith that one of them should be War Secretary, but without 'the restriction imposed by the Robertson-Kitchener agreement'. This struck Esher as 'very small and petty. What was good enough for Kitchener should be good enough for them'.[10] The crisis arrived two days later,[11] when Lloyd George composed another elaborate self-justificatory letter of resignation recounting his success at the Ministry of Munitions and threatening his usual sequel: 'The people do not realise how grave the situation is. I feel they ought to be told.'[12] Privately Lloyd George boasted that he had 'five very rich men—three Liberals and two Unionists—who were prepared to back him financially to an almost unlimited extent, to run elections and the usual party machinery.'[13] But it was difficult for him to resign on a personal question with the full *éclat* he wanted, and perhaps he realised in time (he was advised not to send his letter of resignation) that there were already four Secretaries of State in the Commons. Before Lloyd George could become Secretary for War Grey had to be shunted to the Lords.[14] Hence Asquith held the War Office for a month. Strong pressure came from the King and the Army Council and even Sir John French in favour of Asquith's retaining the War Office. In this Esher was prominent:

Esher-Robertson, 21 June 1916:[15] I suppose you are having trouble. Bonar Law told me the PM had consulted him about Lloyd George's appointment and also that Lloyd George wanted clear definitions as to the respective responsibilities of the Secretary of State and the CIGS. Bonar Law said that *he* was in agreement with Lloyd George both on the question of operations and appointments.

A reversion to the peace plan—if known—would be very unpopular in the country, although I imagine all the politicians will back each other up. The solution is for *Asquith* to keep the WO himself (as I suggested from the first) with two under-secretaries, one for the Commons, and Derby (or somebody) for the Lords.

Because there was no urgency about the succession to Kitchener, since Asquith had himself stepped into the breach, and because Ireland was occupying the attention of the public, Lloyd George's long-laid plan miscarried, and he was obliged to become Secretary for War more or less on the same footing as Kitchener.[16] Robertson still retained the soldiers' 'charter'.

Esher regarded the Somme offensive as necessary not only to relieve the pressure on Verdun, but to restore French morale and confidence. The Germans tried to sound the French about their terms for an armistice, but Joffre kept the approach secret and rejected it with extravagant conditions. In reporting this to Asquith, Esher thought there might be a strong reaction if the offensive failed, and if Briand and Joffre fell, and a Barthou government followed which had to rely on Caillaux's pacifist group. France would then become vulnerable to the divisive effect of peace offers.[17] The Germans no doubt understood the effect of peace offers on French political stability and morale, and Esher was prompted to try to remedy the feeling widespread in France that the British were doing nothing. 'You have no conception how *unpleasant* it has been,' he wrote to Robertson; 'The strain during the past two weeks when the losses at Verdun have...been particularly heavy, has been most disagreeable for an Englishman.'[18]

The communiqués from Haig's GHQ had become, as *The Times* noticed, a laughing stock for the French and Americans. One communiqué for instance related with great pomp the killing of two Germans. They were given to the French mission for transmission to the French GQG each evening, and they reached the French press via London. Esher pressed for them to go direct to Paris, where 'someone who is not a perfect fool should be speedily designated...to get in touch with the French press'.[19] The task devolved on his son Maurice, who operated a somewhat obscure office at Paris called the *Intelligence anglaise*. Haig readily agreed to take up Esher's suggestions, and his letter has the incidental curiosity of having been written on the opening day of the Somme offensive:

Haig-Esher, noon, 1 July 1916:[20] You have hardly any idea how much we in France have suffered from the want of a good man in Paris. As to the press propaganda, Charteris is writing to tell you how the matter has been tackled, and I hope you will give me the benefit of any suggestions which may strike you. In any case I hope you will give the arrangements a kindly supervision, and Charteris is to telephone you every evening through Maurice's office all information.

Our attack began at 7-30 a.m. today on a 16-mile front and has progressed well. I have a great hope of getting some measure of success. I went round all the Corps HQs yesterday and all told me the same story. The men in splendid spirit and full of confidence. Many said that they had never before been so well informed, or so instructed regarding the details of any prospected operation. For three weeks each division was exercised over a model of their particular German trenches, and on several occasions the officers of battalions and companies were withdrawn! The wire has been more thoroughly cut than ever before, and also the artillery bombardment has been methodical and continuous. Of course our French friends are already talking of the Rhine, and how soon they can be there! We have many hard fights before that objective is reached.

If the Somme was militarily a failure—and it should not be too easily assumed that that was the case—Esher meant to see to it that it was psychologically a success. Charteris arranged for the British communiqués to be posted up alongside the French ones at every post office in France. Diplomatic channels were bypassed. The Foreign Office had sent John Buchan to be attached to Haig's staff for propaganda, but his reports went back to London. Now Esher was told to make any use he liked of the reports telephoned directly to him in Paris.[21] One of his first moves was to encourage leading journalists—Gwynne, Repington, Spender, etc.—to visit Haig's headquarters. He overcame Haig's dislike of Repington, and a liberal régime was instituted by which journalists could ask anything and go anywhere so long as they submitted their final copy for inspection.[22]

Since Esher regarded the Somme battle as a trial of fighting qualities rather than an attempt at a breakthrough or even an effort to inflict higher casualties on the enemy, his comments have an air of optimism. He knew on 2 July that the French losses were far lighter than the British, but notes: 'Their attacks are unexpected. Everything is concentrated opposite *us*. Yet we have commenced brilliantly. Our losses are bound to be heavy.' Observing from the safety of an artillery observation hut at Albert he got 'a really wonderful view of the battle. The sun was just coming through the cloud, and the flashing of the guns behind us and the bursting shells on the flank of Contalmaison and the Mametz Wood made a fine spectacle. I saw a German counter-attack develop; the little grey figures coming down on the wood and the brown smoke of the shells pouring in on them.' But the following day Esher's confidence seems a little shaken, on hearing of the casualty figures of the first day's battle:

War Journals, 9 July 1916:[23] We took the Trones Wood and a post to the south yesterday with one casualty. The French took Hardecourt. A good day...

The total casualties in the first day were about 67,000 and 3,000 officers. Lawrence...asked about casualties, and quoted the above figures. I said no-one here mentioned such things, and he might say that I had told him that anyone who spoke of casualties would probably be *dégommé'*d. This is the rock ahead in London where there must be much gossip on this subject. After all, if they, soldiers and others, in London talk of casualties...comparing ours with the French, they must ask themselves: 'Whose fault is it?' The French and we started level in the way of a total inadequacy of munitions. The French are fighting the battles of Verdun and the Somme with *artillery*...Yet they do not expend *per diem* the day's output. It is miraculous, but humiliating to the greatest manufacturing country in the world...

Had we been fighting alone we might have postponed our offensive; fighting with allies our hand was forced. As, for want of munitions, for want of really first-class guns in sufficient quantities, and for want of sufficient trained gunners, we cannot use artillery as the French do, we are obliged to use *men*. Whose fault is it? The politicians, who have been slack in providing the army with the essential material, and who eight years ago when

328

they were warned reduced the artillery instead of increasing it,
have only themselves to thank...

But he took comfort in the 'slow assumption of mastery over the
enemy, [which] proves that our people are the better men. Convince Germany of that, and she is beaten.'

Although Charteris did his best to disguise the full extent of
casualties, Winston Churchill got hold of the figure of 60,000 for the
first two days of the Somme.[24] Churchill had visited France with
F. E. Smith, the Attorney-General, and according to Lord Percy (a
Staff Officer at the War Office) they had both fallen foul of Haig.
Churchill was said to bear a grudge because he had not been given
the command of anything more than a battalion, and his 'endeavours
to become familiar with Haig were consistently repelled'.[25] 'F.E.' was
arrested for travelling in the army zone without a pass, and aroused
the soldiers' dislike of the 'joy-riding' politician.[26] 'His behaviour in
France was disgraceful. He was habitually in a state of semi-intoxi-
cation, and people did not feel that his masquerading as a colonel in
the General Staff reflected much credit on the army.' He complained
to Haig, but in spite of the latter's family association with whisky he
was a Puritan in such matters and gave 'scant sympathy'. The two returned to England resolved to lay a paper before the cabinet 'to prove
that our offensive is a complete failure and that we have lost a vast
quantity of men for nothing'.[27] Churchill's memorandum, submitted
by F. E. Smith, was a clever piece of homework, though its information was such as Repington and others were also freely given at
Haig's HQ. It cannot be said that Churchill was disinterested, either.
He confessed to C. P. Scott that he 'regretted that Lloyd George had
not lifted a finger to get him appointed Minister of Munitions after
he had himself got all he wanted at the War Office'.[28] Lord Percy
seems to have detected the connexion with the *Guardian*, and he smelt
a 'dirty intrigue on foot to get Winston back and directed against our
present conduct of the war'.[29] Whatever view one takes of Haig's
merits or faults, they were certainly canvassed by the politicians for
political ends.

The French had expected a decision in the west in July and
August, or at least an indication of the way the battles were going,
but the continued deadlock threatened more divisive peace offers to
the French in September. If the Somme offensive stopped, Esher

asserted in a letter to the Queen, France would '*at once* make peace'.[30]
But at the same time he was optimistic and told Haig: 'I never felt
so absolutely sure of anything than that you will break down the
German power before the end of the autumn. From now on the
demoralisation, perhaps slow at first, should set in hard.'[31] There
seemed grave danger, whether the battles went well or ill, that
Britain's complete lack of any thoroughly considered peace objectives
would produce a catastrophe. When Lloyd George appeared in Paris
on 11 August Esher found that he had only vague ideas of what the
French were considering as their objectives. He was suspicious of
Lloyd George's interference, as War Minister, in the army's lines of
communication, where he wanted to employ African labour to relieve
starred men for return to industry, and also to economise on petrol
for the benefit of motorists at home. His manner in writing to Asquith
about the visit shows him to be still on the Prime Minister's side:

Esher-Asquith, 13 August 1916:[32] I hope your little Secretary of
State will not start off by setting himself up against the opinion of
the army here by impetuous acts and over-zeal for counsels of
perfection. He has...an exaggerated belief in 'business experts'.
Also he seems not quite to realise that 'public opinion' is as
forcibly represented by the million and a half men of all classes
out here as by what is left behind in England...

Briand is thinking a great deal of the terms of peace in case of
a sudden collapse...and you should be *au courant* of his ideas.
At present he jealously guards them.

The Caillaux group in France, whose ideas had received publicity in
England through an interview with Caillaux published by Dillon in
the *Daily Telegraph*,[33] found a counterpart in a miscellaneous English
group including Thomas Burt, Lord Courtney, Sir Edward Fry, George
Lansbury and Robert Smillie, whose views were represented in what
Esher regarded as a mischievous circular called 'a Basis for a Just
Peace'.[34] To Esher's disgust, Asquith referred the question of peace
objectives to a War Office committee which included General Maurice
and Colonel Macdonogh. He prompted this strange body, through
Robertson, to consider not territorial adjustments (in which the
French could be bought with Alsace-Lorraine at Britain's expense)
but other ways of quelling German militarism, such as 'an indem-

nity, provided it is sufficiently large, and that it is secured by a permanent hold upon German railways, etc.'[35]

Lloyd George's incursion into the military sphere seemed to Esher to be blatantly political. He brought an entourage which was known as the 'Marconi gang'[36]—headed by Lord Reading and Godfrey Isaacs, with Murray of Elibank. He breakfasted with newspaper men, posed for their cameras on dugouts eating bully beef, and turned up late for appointments with numbers of followers too large for his hosts' tables:

> *War Journals, 17 September 1916:*[37] The impressions left here by the Prime Minister...were excellent. Raymond Asquith was killed yesterday in the Guards attack. On the other hand Lloyd George made the *worst* impression and showed himself to be what he really is, a clever political adventurer seeking limelight. He came surrounded by satellites, Lord Reading who lowers the dignity, authority and status of the great office he holds by dabbling in finance and politics, Murray of Elibank, whose reputation for honest dealing is more than doubtful and lesser lights of equally questionable character. He seemed to seek the camera and the cheers of the soldiers. He was insolent and off-hand. You cannot make a silk purse out of a Welsh solicitor's ear.

Esher knew that Haig was under great strain, the 'tanks' having just proved a disappointment which frustrated his whole design. He knew of the association of Lloyd George with Churchill and F. E. Smith's attack on Haig. Then he heard how Foch on a visit to Haig recounted how Lloyd George had questioned him about the relative merits of British generals, saying 'that although we had found a large army we were still seeking a commander for them'. Foch was 'amazed' and declined to answer.[38] This story got into the hands of Gwynne of the *Morning Post* and its publication caused Lloyd George considerable embarrassment. J. A. Spender happened to be with Esher when the story appeared, and revealed some other things about the 'Marconi gang':

> *Esher-Haig, 29 September 1916:*[39] He [Spender] has been going through very stormy waters, because Lloyd George and his gang could not influence him to throw over Asquith. They bought

the *Westminster Gazette* and threatened to dislodge him, but at the last moment they funked and contented themselves with putting Murray of Elibank as chairman on the board of directors. Spender has told me some curious things about Lloyd George, and there is no sort of doubt that he and the 'Marconi gang' mean to take supreme power in their hands.

But Lloyd George was about to score a signal triumph over Haig.

Haig had refused to allow Sir Eric Geddes, Lloyd George's right-hand man at the Ministry of Munitions, to transfer his activity to the War Office by assuming the supervision of the army's lines of communication in France. But when Lloyd George saw Esher—whom he incidentally described as 'general adviser to everybody and liaison officer between everybody and anybody—a most useful kind of person' who possessed 'tact, discernment, and experience' in a 'superlative degree'[40]—Esher persuaded him that Haig would be amenable if approached personally. Lloyd George dropped his general indictment of the inefficiency of the system and proposed to Haig that Geddes should inspect and report to Haig himself. This was accepted, and Geddes got on well with Haig. After studying the railway system behind the lines for a month he was made Director of Military Railways at the War Office by Lloyd George on his return. This caused a quarrel with the Army Council and a counter move by Haig who wanted Geddes under him in France. But as Lloyd George appreciated, the massive increase in the flow of munitions and supplies behind the lines demanded a complete overhaul of the rail, road and ports system. This Geddes and his other civilian colleagues performed brilliantly, introducing light railways up to the trenches and perfecting the overall system. It was a timely and necessary reform, but Lloyd George made political capital out of it. He accused the soldiers of smug satisfaction with a system of transportation that was about to collapse.

While Geddes was carrying all before him the army's Inspector-General of Lines of Communication, Sir Frederick Clayton, was brushed aside and finally dismissed after a scandal. Esher had just placed under Clayton his former private secretary, Lawrence Burgis,[41] who occupied a 'delightful room' in Abbeville even more attractive than that occupied by Esher himself and his son Maurice at the *Intelligence anglaise* in the Place Vendôme in Paris—and when

Clayton objected to Lloyd George's project of employing African and Chinese labour behind the lines Esher cordially supported him. But Lloyd George got his way, and what had been 'Chinese slavery' in South Africa became respectable behind the lines. The 'Chinese coolies' were praised by Lloyd George for their capacity to carry four hundredweight loads, and to ignore shell-fire! Then came Clayton's downfall:

War Journals, 8 October 1916:[42] I am sure as I have been instinctively for a long time that the Germans are in full retreat for another line.

Sir Eric Geddes came to luncheon. I think he seems capable and tactful. The Rouen enquiry has gone against poor old Clayton and Marable. D[ouglas] H[aig] gave me the 'finding' to read. These two senior officers are found to have used their authority to cover the misdemeanours of a light woman whom they *knew*, and to dismiss as unfit for further service a young officer whom the court find to have acted tactlessly but in consonance with his duty...D.H. must recommend that both the IGC and Marable be relieved of their commands. Lawrence's stay at Abbeville will not be a long one, and it is lucky that we have another string in his bow in the shape of Charteris and the Intelligence.

The contrast of Geddes and Clayton did not do the army much good and presented Lloyd George with an excellent whipping post for the soldiers.

Meanwhile the Somme offensive had gone through its critical stage in September, when the tanks on which, contrary to legend, Haig in fact set great store, were first used. He had wished to delay the start of the offensive until the tanks and more heavy guns were ready. Esher gives the following impression of the hopes that were pinned on the first tank attack:

War Journals, 24 August 1916:[43] Then on 15 September we make our big surprise attack with the 80 'monsters' hidden away in a forbidden area. These machines moving at 4 m.p.h. should crash through all the German defences...If they are unexpected by the Germans nothing can stop them.

Ibid, 10 September 1916: The 'tanks' have been tried, so far as this is possible. Nothing but the German 77's can knock them out. Their crews are full of confidence. We should attack with about sixty of them, and about 200 yards apart. D.H. has eighteen divisions under Rawly [Rawlinson] and ten more under Gough. How he has scraped them up heaven knows. The coup— if the surprise comes off—may lead to the capture of the German heavy guns and perhaps two army corps. The Germans are short of petrol, and their transport is immobilised. They are building sidings for their heavy guns which looks like retreat. D.H. has taken every inch of ground he set out to take, and he kept to his timetable...

Rawly is to lead off on 15th, and Gough to come in later at Gommecourt. It is certain to my thinking that the next week must bring startling events...

According to Churchill's account, the tanks were used as 'the merest makeweight', and yet he recounts that only fifty-nine tanks reached France, only forty-nine reached the battlefield, only thirty-five reached their starting points, only thirty-one crossed the German trenches, and only nine surmounted all the obstacles.[44] The fault was surely in the design of the tanks rather than in Haig's plan for using them. That Haig appreciated the potentiality of tanks is clear from Esher's notes at his HQ:

War Journals, 17 September 1916:[45] The 'tanks' were partially successful; some worked well, others failed...One fell into a shell hole, and is in the hands of the enemy. Their engine power is too weak, and that they will be greatly improved upon is certain unless a counter to them is quickly found.

Ibid, 19 September 1916: He [Haig] has asked Bacon for flat-bottomed boats that would run up the beach with sides that let down like a flap from which the 'tanks' could walk ashore and thence over the German wire. Combined with heavy artillery from the flank and from the sea it should not be difficult to capture the Belgian coast. This would be a neat little operation for the early spring.

It was a pity that Churchill and Fisher, who might have been exercising their talents on the improvement of the tank, were engaged in political activity against Asquith's government, and Haig in the middle of the battle was distracted by the need to reply to Churchill's criticisms.

Esher certainly did a lot to protect Haig from press criticism. He had found that Haig's press officer, Colonel A. Hutton Wilson, was 'a delicate man who would not take any initiative but seems the spirit of accuracy'.[46] It was arranged that Wilson would refer to Esher his difficulties in 'ascertaining which of the numerous applicants for special privileges should receive favourable treatment'.[47] In this way Esher got in touch with the leading press tycoons that came to the front—Northcliffe, Spender, Robinson of *The Times*, Gwynne, M. Joseph Reinach, etc. He soon decided that propaganda ought to be centralised under one authority:

Esher-Haig, 24 August 1916:[48] Do you think General Charteris would consider whether the time has not come for centralising all propaganda...under some one aided by an advisory committee upon which people like Northcliffe, Buchan, etc. could have representatives...that could inspire (a) the American press, (b) the Swiss papers that have access to Germany, and (c) the Norwegian and Spanish papers.

As matters stand Mackensen can get *his* views circulated everywhere and there is no response to them. My idea is that you should have in Paris in close touch with the Maison de la Presse[49] a central authority for propaganda...under Charteris.

It was typical that the first news of Jutland to reach Paris came via the German radio. The real trouble was that propaganda was confused with intelligence, and the War Office liked to vet what was let out to the press. Esher pressed for a bold distinction between propaganda, which was 'a system of falsehood', and intelligence, which 'aims at the exact truth'. 'Both Napoleon and Bismarck understood this division of labour.'[50] Esher thought that ideally the War Office could manage the intelligence and the Foreign Office the lies.[51] Departmental jealousies, however, prevented any improvement. Esher's next suggestion was one that anticipated what would happen many months later—that the whole propaganda should be handed to Northcliffe.

In Paris he made some progress, and in January 1917 set up the *Bureau de Concorde du Concours anglais* with a committee to manage Haig's propaganda. He also set up a French branch of the Garton Foundation under his son Maurice. This was in close touch with the Round Table, and fed the War Office committee on peace objectives with French ideas about indemnities and the like.

Northcliffe had been won over, and Robinson the editor of *The Times* remained convinced that Churchill and F. E. Smith were 'wreckers', even after the apparent failure of the Somme.[52] Lloyd George was regarded as being on intimate terms with these enemies of Haig, and so he had practically no support from either press or soldiers in his attempt to curb Haig's offensive. There was however one exception, the irascible and aggrieved Viscount French, who apart from resenting Haig as his enforced successor also thought in his suspicious way that Robertson was 'trying to become C-in-C of the whole army'. He talked to Repington of resignation. Having convinced himself that Haig's casualties were intolerable, Lord French lent his aid to Lloyd George in what was presented to Asquith by Gwynne as a 'plot'. Haig was also warned of this by Lloyd George's under-secretary Lord Derby, who appeared at his HQ at Beauquesne on 6 October and revealed that Lord French was going to visit Verdun and the French lines on the Somme to report on 'the way in which the French use their artillery, and upon their infantry tactics'.[53] Naturally Haig was annoyed, but resolved to invite French to his HQ, though not to his house because he 'despised him too much'! Esher was mystified. Later he learnt from Cavendish at Chantilly that the visit had been arranged by General Yarde-Buller, who was supposed to be Haig's chief representative at the French GQG there. Consequently Esher suggested that Yarde-Buller be given an 'ornamental post' and that Colonel Sidney Clive, who was 'able and straight', should be made head of the mission. 'We shall never induce the French to believe that we are their equals until you have a mission at Chantilly as strong as theirs at GHQ,' he wrote to Haig.[54]

On his arrival in Paris Lord French pursued by reporters found time to dine publicly with the ambassador, Bertie, who incidentally had some connexion through Murray of Elibank with the 'Marconi gang'.[55] He did not take up Haig's invitation. But the timing of French's expedition was unlucky, for in November the political scene underwent a transformation which made it expedient for Lloyd George to cease castigating the soldiers. Lord French found himself unsupported, and the King sent for him 'and told him that as Head of the army' he 'would not have any one in French's position going about abusing the C-in-C in the field. It must stop.'[56] For a year Lord French remained quiescent, until a moment arrived when Lloyd George wished to use him again. Meanwhile Esher reported to Stamfordham that Haig was pleased with the reprimand, adding that he hoped after the intrigue and vilification that Haig would be made a field-marshal.[57]

Lloyd George was busily filling the key posts at the War Office with his creatures and sycophants, as his critics put it. The QMG was, like Clayton, suddenly involved in a scandal. After an alleged discovery of corruption in the clothing department it was handed over to a 'business expert', Northcliffe's brother Lord Rothermere.[58] Only Robertson, the stubborn and blunt character who was the only soldier to rise from private to field-marshal, remained openly hostile to the chief. But Robertson was wooden and inflexible and liked to hide behind concordats and fixed axioms of policy. As a 'westerner' he kept citing the early decision of the War Council that operations in the west were paramount. Lloyd George agreed to this in September, but a month later as the Germans moved on Bucharest he suddenly changed his mind and wanted eight allied divisions sent to Salonika.

The mission of Lord French was intended to demonstrate that Haig could afford to do with less men now that he was being supplied with more guns. Robertson protested, and the War Committee supported him but agreed that Joffre's opinion should be sought. Robertson sent a telegram to Joffre, but then composed a letter of resignation before the reply came back.[59] Repington was shown the letter, and advised him to have it out at the next War Committee, but Robertson hesitated. Fearing disaster, Repington went and recounted the matter to Northcliffe, who was 'much exercised'. Asquith had just sent him an appeal to support the War Secretary and government, and Northcliffe replied that he would only do so 'if the latter did not interfere with the soldiers'. He called on Robertson the next day, 11 October, and no doubt read the letter which was about to be sent to Lloyd George.[60] On leaving Robertson's room Northcliffe bumped into some of Lloyd George's secretaries in the War Office corridor and told them bluntly that if the soldiers were 'interfered with by the politicians' he would 'mobilise his press' against them.[61] This being duly reported to the Secretary of State, the latter was presented with a means of turning the tables:

> *Lloyd George-Robertson, 12 October 1916:*[62] Tonight's letter would...have caused me some surprise had not a leading newspaper proprietor given me the pith of it...He had clearly been taken into counsel by some one in your close confidence...This great journalist even threatened publication unless I withdrew immediately from the position I had taken up...
>
> I have during my short sojourn at the War Office frequently encountered this grave subversion of discipline in high places. I have found complaints against action taken by the Army Council and myself lodged with the press—even before they ever reached me...

Robertson had not in fact wanted Repington to go and see Northcliffe and still less did he expect Northcliffe's clumsy interference, but after this incident Lloyd George could accuse him of deliberate 'leaks' every time the press opposed his policy. The root of the trouble was that Lloyd George was both Secretary for War and the most active member of the War Committee. In the latter capacity he would often throw over his department's policy as agreed by the Army Council of which he was himself the head.

Strangely enough Northcliffe was about to be Lloyd George's backer for the premiership: while Robertson in November became unaccountably complacent about the 'manpower' question. The conviction had been steadily growing that Asquith was losing the war. He had seemed to have made a mess of Ireland, allowing Romania to be crushed after all the vacillations over Greece and Salonika, and failed to counter the submarine menace. By contrast Lloyd George had worked administrative wonders. Munitions were now arriving in impressive quantities—especially heavy howitzers—and Sir Eric Geddes' conspicuous success in France showed how Lloyd George knew how to pick the right man. Grudging acknowledgments came from every quarter that the little Welshman was the only man with enough dynamism to disperse the administrative log-jams that seemed to have accumulated under Asquith. Esher while being appalled by Lloyd George's ways—he thought that the famous speech that Lloyd George made at the end of September flouting American peace

338

interventions was full of 'common phraseology and braggadoccio' and the whole performance that of a 'phenomenal little cad'—had to admit that 'the little Welsh attorney possesses brilliant gifts: that he possesses political and military "flair": that he can and does get "things done", by a power of drive altogether outside administrative capacity, which he totally lacks.'[63] If the war had to be fought to a 'knock-out', as Lloyd George had put it, he was the man to direct it.

The issues of the war direction seemed to clarify themselves after Lloyd George's challenging speech, delivered in France without the consent of the government. The soldiers were demanding more 'Sommes' for 1917 and a massive 'comb-out' of the men who had avoided military service by being 'badged' in reserved occupations. Ironically, while Lloyd George had been occupied with other matters his Ministry of Munitions had 'simply shovelled out badges to any firm that had asked for them'. No less than 3,400,000 men, nominally available under the Military Service Acts, had been badged, and of these about 1,500,000 had been exempted by government offices, mainly the Ministry of Munitions.[64] The problem was now that of sifting these in some more effective way than by the easy-going tribunals. The attitude of the soldiers to this question, the dimensions of which were being unearthed at the War Office by General Auckland Geddes, the Director of Recruiting, may be seen in a representation of Esher to the CIGS:

> *Esher-Robertson, 9 November 1916:*[65] We shall be beaten in this war, if by next spring we have not *in reserve* and armed and trained 1½ millions of men, ready to come out here. Unless the French can count upon our mounting *two* Somme battles, and are thus compelled by their *amour propre* to do likewise, the growing desire that manifests itself here among the people in the towns to have done with the war will gather overwhelming force...
>
> Now we shall be late again unless you succeed in getting Mr Lloyd George...to put the whole 'combing-out' process in the hands of one man with plenary powers. All these 'Manpower' committees and tribunals, etc., are futile expedients...I am sure that Mr Lloyd George was right—'and the soldiers were wrong' —when he settled to put all the transport oversea under the sole

direction of an expert. It is not 'manpower' but 'one-man power' that is wanted.

Repington was investigating the manpower question with the freedom of access to officials which he traditionally enjoyed, and he concluded that all men under twenty-five should be given to the army, and replacements for them in industry found by compulsory national service for every man up to fifty-five. But there now emerged in the cabinet a group whose views found expression in Lansdowne's well-known memorandum of 13 November[66] raising a doubt whether the 'knock-out' policy was really worth while. The country, Lansdowne reasoned, was 'slowly but surely killing off the best of the male population' and spending £5 millions a day on the war. Shipping was being sunk faster than it was being replaced. Ought we to discourage possible German peace overtures? The peace objectives, which Esher had encouraged Asquith to refer to the government and which had now emerged from the War Office, loaded with ambitious French ideas for a huge indemnity, seemed too remote to be attainable from a Germany gorged with victories.

The question of war fought 'to a finish' versus a 'botched peace' was intimately connected with that of a *levée en masse* of the nation's manhood versus the *status quo*. The cabinet was fumbling its way towards the settlement of the 'manpower' question, and promised a drama as protracted and shilly-shallying as that over compulsion. Would the war be lost meanwhile? Such was the ethos of November. Carson, the leading critic of the government's war direction, began to draw Unionist support in his attacks on it.[67] He had criticised from his inside knowledge the War Committee of five which Asquith had instituted in November 1915, revealing how the cabinet, the inner cabinet, and the war-directing cabinet committee had been at odds and had created deadlocks and confusion.[68] He had been vindicated by events, for the new War Committee which was promised to number not more than five almost immediately swelled to seven, or nine if the CIGS and First Sea Lord are numbered. Other ministers attended occasionally. The Asquithians dominated—Asquith, Grey, McKenna, and Balfour (who was much suspected by his fellow-Unionists) were not sufficiently counteracted by Lloyd George and Bonar Law. The men with fire in their bellies—Carson, Churchill and Fisher—seemed inevitably to be rejected by the Asquithian system.

340

Bonar Law remained the prop of the government—if he withdrew, it collapsed. He had supported it since the April crisis over compulsion because he did not want a Lloyd George government and Asquith would not consent to remain as premier while Lloyd George ran the war. Lloyd George's only resource was to come to an understanding with Carson, and this he seems to have done. In the celebrated Nigerian debate, whose insignificant subject masked an important straw vote, Carson after a bitter personal attack on Bonar Law still enlisted almost half of the votes of those Unionists who thought fit to pass through the lobbies.[69] The issue of the war directorate thereby revived.

According to Lord Beaverbrook, Asquith might have saved the situation if he had come to a firm understanding with Bonar Law, whose position as Unionist leader was now seriously threatened by Carson. But Asquith had a low estimation of Bonar Law's abilities and would not dream of such a compact. The press barons moved in on the situation, demanding the solution which seemed eminently reasonable to outsiders—that Asquith should remain as Prime Minister, concerning himself with the management of the government and Parliament, while Lloyd George chaired a small War Committee. Max Aitken (Beaverbrook) himself drafted a formula on these lines which Lloyd George, Carson and Bonar Law approved at a meeting at Pembroke Lodge on 25 November, and Bonar Law took it to Asquith to consider over the weekend.[70] Asquith declined to approve the proposed composition of the new War Committee—Carson could not in his view be preferred to Balfour, Curzon or McKenna, and he feared the scheme might be used by Lloyd George to displace himself: besides, Lloyd George lacked the one thing needed for the premiership—'he does not inspire trust'.[71] The Unionist leaders whom Bonar Law consulted refused to countenance a War Committee chaired by Lloyd George—Bonar Law did not dare to mention Carson as the third member. Even so, Bonar Law resolved to back Lloyd George as chairman of a new War Committee, though he reserved his opinion as to the other members. He was not prepared to back Carson if it involved displacing Balfour from the Admiralty, which would be the signal for a split in the Unionist leadership.

The cabinet had decided on Wednesday 29 November to establish side by side with the War Committee a Committee of National Organisation dealing with the domestic problems of organising the

341

war.[72] This Asquithian 'formula' by dividing the war directorate reduced the threat of usurpation even by a War Committee composed of Lloyd George, Carson and Bonar Law.[73] Bonar Law seems to have been temporarily floored by this, and also by his Unionist colleagues' hostility the next day. When therefore Lloyd George presented Asquith on Friday 1 December with a demand that the War Secretary, First Lord, and another minister without portfolio should constitute the War Committee, accompanied by a verbal explanation that Balfour could not remain as First Lord, he was going it alone. But he knew that his case would be blazoned the next day over the front pages of the *Daily Express* and *Daily Chronicle*. Curiously, Northcliffe was not being posted on the cabinet crisis by Lloyd George.

The soldiers were solidly behind Lloyd George, just as Lansdowne was one of his chief opponents. An account of the crisis notes that: 'Lord Derby, whom Lord Stamfordham also saw, has apparently succumbed to Mr Lloyd George's influence. There was evidently a certain suspicion that the military authorities at the War Office— including Sir W. Robertson—identified themselves with the political aspects of this question.' It was reported that General Sir R. Whigham, the DCIGS, 'was actually the author of a leading article in one of the morning papers'.[74] Haig was in London on 27 November and 'was shocked by the "fluster" in political circles. Lansdowne's frame of mind he described as "dreadful". Only Lloyd George seemed to keep cool and brave. The others are crushed by the bad fortunes of Romania.'[75] Esher himself thought that Lloyd George was 'more than justified in resigning' in view of 'Lansdowne's memorandum and of the reluctance of Asquith to give a decision on manpower, food, etc.'[76]

Lloyd George was sincerely willing to serve under Asquith as premier so long as he chaired the War Committee. But Asquith refused this in his letter of 1 December, and then was persuaded to change his tune after the newspaper exposures of a 'plot' on 2 December and the ultimatum from the Unionist leaders of 3 December. Lloyd George's attitude was explained to Asquith by Edwin Montagu, who had a long tussle with the Welshman on Asquith's behalf on Saturday 2 December while the latter was away on his inviolable week-end. Lloyd George argued that with the Prime Minister's responsibilities for the House of Commons, appointments and other duties he 'should be relieved of the day-to-day work of the

War Committee, but should maintain the supreme control of the war, seeing the Chairman of the War Committee every morning before it met, receiving their reports and conferring with them' when he thought fit. The War Committee should 'sit so frequently and act with such rapidity' that the Prime Minister 'ought not to have a place on it'.[77] Montagu made it sound very reasonable, but was Lloyd George a reasonable man? The press was demanding that the three 'conspirators' should form the War Committee, and Asquith might become a mere figure-head. Who, indeed, was inspiring the press? 'I have received very bitter letters from Margot [Asquith],' Montagu added. 'She like McKenna attributes everything that has appeared in the Press to Lloyd George, notwithstanding the fact that the views in the Press are nearly all inconsistent with Lloyd George's scheme.'[78]

But the suspicion was well-founded. The next day (Sunday) Lloyd George lunched with C. P. Scott, carefully explained to him his whole plan, and sent him off to see Northcliffe, who still 'did not know e.g. whom George designated for his War Committee'. Scott found Northcliffe 'thoroughly egotistical', 'telling long stories himself all the time', and seems to have failed to get the importance of Lloyd George's carefully devised message across.[79] All the same, the incident reveals Lloyd George's methods of indirectly informing journalists.

The Unionist leaders' meeting on Sunday presents the puzzling question of why, being generally hostile to Lloyd George and certainly dead against his premiership, they nevertheless authorised Bonar Law to tender Asquith an ultimatum that unless he resigned to make possible a complete reforming of the Coalition, they would resign and so force it. They knew that Lloyd George intended to resign and probably anticipated that he might gain the premiership under the threat of forcing an election. They would even have to support him in such a contingency, for he was regarded by the country as indispensable. Asquith's inflexible position was untenable, and the Unionists' intervention forced him on Sunday evening to modify it. But Asquith would never have accepted Lloyd George's style of running the War Committee, and immediately went back on his concession.

Asquith may have hoped that Lloyd George's exorbitant terms as to the personnel of the Committee would rally the moderates after the blatant article in *The Times* of Monday, composed independently by

343

M

the editor, which seemed to revel in the conspiracy and belittle Asquith. He therefore tried to reform the ministry without resigning, but by Tuesday evening he resigned after being advised to do so on every side. He had over-estimated his importance:

Memorandum by Lord Errington:[80] He realised the very serious responsibility involved in his action. The governments of other allies were shaky. He and Lord Grey had remained as recognised representatives of the British government ever since war was declared, and he feared that his resignation might cause almost a panic in Europe and in America, in which latter country there might be serious financial results.

Bonar Law tried to form a government, but Asquith's refusal to serve under him had the effect of passing on the premiership to Lloyd George.

If Asquith hoped that Lloyd George as Prime Minister would come unstuck through his volatile enthusiasms, he was destined to be disappointed. Unexpectedly, and from extraneous causes, the whole structure of the cabinet and War Committee underwent a transformation resulting in a machine so stable and efficient that even Lloyd George's restless energy could not upset it. The emergence of the War Cabinet is, like many episodes in administrative history, a study in non-administrative factors. On Monday 4 December while Lloyd George believed that Asquith was reorganising the government on the basis of his War Committee scheme, he consulted Hankey about the adaptation of the CID secretariat, which had come to serve Asquith's War Committee, to the needs of the new model:

Memorandum by Lord Errington:[81] Mr Lloyd George held the opinion that Sir M. Hankey's office would be strengthened by further appointments and a change in the status of the Secretary of the Defence Committee. To this Sir M. Hankey objected, as he contended that such a measure would convert his office into a quasi General Staff, and bring him into possible conflict with the CIGS and First Sea Lord. This would impair the character of his post, which was that of being the machinery of the Committee. His work is pursued on the principle of carrying out the duties assigned without expressing any opinion unless requested.

It was Hankey who originally suggested the reformed War Committee to Lloyd George, and as his diary shows he had been *au fait* with the negotiations over it since 22 November. As the 'inside' man who had acted as Asquith's general factotum and who held the threads of the complicated war machine with its scores of committees, Hankey was indispensable to a premier like Lloyd George and was cultivated accordingly. When, unexpectedly and to his genuine discomfiture, the premiership came his way, Lloyd George immediately sent for him to discuss all kinds of immediate problems. Lloyd George's government had to be a large one, for he formed new Ministries or departments of Labour, Pensions, Shipping, Food and, later, National Service. He told the Labour party, which was hesitating over joining a government that seemed likely to be dominated by Unionists: 'I do not think there should be a Cabinet in the ordinary sense of the term. The War Committee should, during the continuation of the War, act as the Cabinet. When a question arises, affecting a particular Department the representatives of that Department would be called in to discuss the matter with the War Cabinet...'[82] The introduction of business men and academics into the government and its fringes, the appointment of ministers who had never sat in Parliament, the proliferation of departments and the separation of the members of the War Cabinet (of whom only Bonar Law had a portfolio as Chancellor of the Exchequer) from the departmental ministers, rendered the old system in which no cabinet records were kept impossible. Hankey's secretariat was therefore extended to the cabinet. In Hankey's own view this was 'not so novel as might at first appear. All that had happened was that a system already tested, first on a small scale at the Committee of Imperial Defence, and later on a large scale at the War Committee, had been extended to enable all the affairs of the nation to be dealt with on the same method.'[83]

So far as the direction of the war was concerned, the most glaring faults of the Asquith government had been eliminated—the tug-of-war between cabinet and War Committee, the intrusion of departmental interests, and the subordination of military to political pressures. But the new War Cabinet of Lloyd George, Bonar Law (who managed the House of Commons) Curzon, Milner and Henderson (Carson having been ungratefully dropped, ostensibly in deference to Unionist feelings) did not include any representative of the service

345

departments. There was no bridge between the soldiers and the politicians.

By coincidence the French system of war direction underwent an equally radical transformation in December. The cumbrous bureaucracy of Joffre at Chantilly had produced a shortage of rolling stock outside the army zone. Coal shortages led to popular pressure on the deputies, and during a secret session of the Chamber on 5 December it was announced that Chantilly was 'suppressed' and that Joffre would come to Paris as generalissimo to be replaced by General Nivelle as C-in-C. Lyautey, an administrator from Morocco, became Minister of War, while M. Briand in reducing the size of his ministry offended the excluded groups. The centralisation of more French military control on Paris placed much more strain on the British embassy there, where Colonel Le Roy-Lewis, the military attaché, found himself involved in weighty matters far beyond his official scope in dealings with French departments of Transport, Munitions, etc., and with the Quai d'Orsay. Lyautey failed to strip GQG and Nivelle of all strategical authority but he was nevertheless striving to set up a unified allied command under General Castelnau as CGS. He was also supposed to be working against Briand. In association with Paul Cambon and Albert Thomas (who had been Lloyd George's opposite number as Minister of Munitions and was still very intimate with him,[84] he readily used the British embassy to circumvent Haig.

Esher's relations with Bertie had deteriorated since Haig had so openly preferred Esher as his representative, and 'the Bull', as Bertie was styled after his great upward-curving moustaches, was a stock figure of ridicule among the soldiers. But Bertie could hit back. 'That silly old Bertie, who is jealous, is trying to injure me and my work', Esher wrote to Maxse in November.[85] Bertie was the doyen of the diplomatic corps and while Grey was at the Foreign Office he was safe, but now that Balfour was Foreign Secretary—he had picked his way, as it was said, like a cat across a muddy alley from Asquith to Lloyd George—something might be done. Esher criticised the way Bertie completely ignored the Russian ambassador in Paris, Isvolski, and seemed to have fallen abjectly under the influence of a banker, Baron Jacques de Gunzburg, who was associated with international pacifism and had been attacked in the senate for pro-German proclivities after acting as an intermediary between von Lancken and Caillaux in the Agadir crisis. A Berlin Jew by birth, Baron Gunzburg was naturalised a Russian at fifteen, and, Esher noted, 'joined the orthodox Greek church in order to marry a beautiful Catholic divorced by the Pope from her first husband'.[86] Esher regarded the Paris embassy as so vital to British interests that a member of the War Cabinet ought to go there as 'ambassador extraordinary and plenipotentiary' whenever there was an inter-allied crisis. He saw the allied failure in Romania as an example of the disastrous lack of contact between Bertie and Isvolski, and decided to tackle Lloyd George about it:

Esher-Lloyd George, 21 December 1916:[87] For many months neither ambassador has entered the embassy of the other. Confidential intercourse between them has been at an end. Had it not been for our military attaché, who thanks to his independence of character and position braved the displeasure of his chief, all communication on important matters between the two embassies would have ceased.

When Hardinge first returned from India I wrote and told him that his presence here as ambassador was essential, if relations between the three principal allies were to be maintained intact... I had already sufficient experience of the inner working of affairs in this capital to realise the danger of a septuagenarian ambassador who allows his private sentiments to interfere with his public duties. M. Isvolski is not a personage whose influence can be ignored...

This unfortunate state of things is complicated by the notorious and questionable intimacy between the British ambassador and an eminent financier, Baron Gunzburg...It is a matter of comment in political, financial and military circles that Lord Bertie and Baron Gunzburg are inseparable, that no matter or subject however confidential is withheld...and that his influence over the ambassador is paramount...

On reflection Esher did not send this letter, but conveyed its substance to Ian Malcolm, Balfour's private secretary, so that Lloyd George could elicit the details from Le Roy-Lewis personally, when he passed through Paris.

Lloyd George however did not remove Bertie for some time. He was too useful and indeed, unknown to Esher, he and Lloyd George were about to participate in a conspiracy with the French to get rid of Haig.[88] This was not easily suspected, because at a confrontation at Tarentum between the mysterious Sarrail (under whom the allies had now no less than twenty-two divisions futilely entangled at Salonika at immense cost in shipping) and delegations of French, English and Italian ministers, Lloyd George had resisted French demands for even more reinforcements. 'Lloyd George seems to have done well in spite of that adhesive Albert Thomas,' Esher wrote to Robertson, 'and in spite of his leaning towards the Eastern heresy.'[89] The British government were ready to back Nivelle's offensive in the west, and it would not have seemed likely that Lloyd George would choose this time to dismiss Haig. But the origin of the plot was French, and the opportunity too tempting for Lloyd George to resist.

For many months the French had been discussing the project of an 'amalgam' of the British and French armies, by which they would be mixed by brigades or battalions under a unified command. Joseph Reinach, a prominent journalist remembered from the time of the Dreyfus case, was its most persistent advocate, and he had mentioned it to Esher, claiming that Gallieni had first thought of it. Esher had turned the idea down at once, but the French continued to discuss it with the British embassy. Associated with the 'amalgam' was the project of forming a reserve army, and since the French held three-quarters of the line with hardly more numerous forces than the British, a reserve army could only be formed if Haig agreed to take over more of the line. Under the Chantilly plan agreed with Joffre, Haig was to bear the brunt of the fighting in 1917 with his long-contemplated land and sea offensive to gain the Flanders coast.

The appearance of Nivelle as C-in-C heralded a sudden abrogation by the French of that plan. Even Albert Thomas, who had seemed to Lloyd George to share his views about the impracticability of a 'breakthrough', suddenly appeared to have been converted by the persuasive ideas and successes of Nivelle. According to Lloyd George's account, at the London Conference of 26–28 December M. Ribot 'urged that we should there and then' accept the Nivelle plan to which Haig had objected. 'After a good deal of further unreasonable insistence on the part of the French delegates, I replied that I did not think that M. Ribot would ask His Majesty's government to overrule their General C-in-C without at least hearing what he had to say.'[90] But Lloyd George did in fact decide to force Haig to give up his offensive, take over more line, and conform generally to Nivelle's orders.[91] Nivelle, a persuasive speaker of English with an English mother, came to London in mid-January and convinced the War Cabinet. Haig, who was summoned to attend, reluctantly agreed to give Nivelle his chance.[92] According to Esher: 'There is no doubt that Nivelle's visit to London was the result of discussions in Paris in which all the strategical and tactical questions involved were discussed between our embassy and the French.'[93]

The military attaché found himself involved in discussions of strategical questions which had the incidental political import of circumventing Haig. One day as Esher drove to Versailles in the company of Le Roy-Lewis and Murray of Elibank they confided to him that Le Roy-Lewis had composed an appeal to Robertson asking to be relieved of the Paris post, which required, he claimed, the appointment of a more senior official. They wanted Esher to support and even to 'father' the project. Esher however thought that the extension of War Office officialdom behind Haig's lines had gone far enough, and he no doubt suspected that Murray of Elibank who was very much a Greek bearing gifts might be intending that some official more amenable to Lloyd George should replace Le Roy-Lewis, whose reasons for wishing to quit were not apparent, though they appeared later. Esher therefore wrote to Haig throwing cold water on the project:

Esher-Haig, 25 January 1917:[94] Every sort of question—supply, organisation, railways, coal, aircraft, and above all strategical and even tactical questions of first-rate importance have to be studied and dealt with by the embassy. There is not a soul except Le Roy-Lewis who is capable by training and knowledge of practical business of coping with these questions...His staff, however, is unfitted to be trusted with even knowledge of these transactions. It is recruited from casual typists, etc...

Do you or do you not object to the growth of a military authority in France in close contact with the *seat of military power* in France, that is not controlled by the C-in-C? In your place I should object, and never should have permitted as your staff has done the growth of excrescences upon the proper sphere of the C-in-C under the authority of the War Office.

Esher therefore recommended, if Le Roy-Lewis himself would not accept promotion, that the post should be filled by some 'distinguished dead-head'. The French naturally wanted to deal with Lloyd George directly through diplomatic channels. Lyautey, as Robertson later discovered to his amazement at the Calais Conference of February, did not even know who Lord Derby, the War Minister, was, though they had been officially in correspondence.

Further conversations with Le Roy-Lewis, with whom Esher spent hours strolling round the Bois, threw a new and more disquieting light on the military attaché's urgent wish to hand over to some more senior official. He told a wild story of how at a private dinner party Baroness Gunzburg had complained of maltreatment at the hands of her husband which encouraged Le Roy-Lewis to put to her a direct question about Bertie's strange dependence on him. The baroness thereupon affirmed what Le Roy-Lewis had heard from others, namely that the ambassador had been promised on retirement the chairmanship of Gunzburg's Central Mining Company. This fact, Le Roy-Lewis told Esher, had been known to the Liberal Whip, Murray of Elibank, when he came to Paris to negotiate a merger of some oil companies with Gunzburg's concern.[95] According to Le Roy-Lewis's tale, Bertie had been friendly with Murray of Elibank, who was one of Lloyd George's personal entourage, but their relations had cooled after Murray of Elibank refused to give Gunzburg concessions.[96] The latter had become interested in contracts for the War Office:

War Journals, 3 February 1917:[97] Some time ago Le Roy-Lewis being convinced that our methods of making shells was inferior to the French, endeavoured to persuade the War Office of the superiority of the bored shell. He was urged forward by the ambassador, who took a strange interest in the subject, and ultimately when a commission came out from England...the ambassador asked that Baron Gunzburg, who was a large manufacturer of the bored shell, should be allowed to give evidence. Every day the ambassador asked to see the telegrams that passed between Le Roy-Lewis and the War Office on the subject. Finally Gunzburg asked for the contract but failed to obtain it. Since then he has been more fortunate, as with the *appui* of the ambassador he has succeeded in obtaining the contract for aeroplane engines.

Almost every morning Gunzburg called at the embassy, and when he did not Bertie went round to his office. Le Roy-Lewis was worried about his own part in these transactions, and had resolved to leave the embassy if Bertie remained. He told the whole tale to Esher to protect himself in case it came out. The French police were watching Gunzburg, and Esher thought there was therefore a diminished security risk. He decided to keep quiet, though he gave the details to Haig with his judgment that there was no national peril involved, only 'national disgrace' if the allegations were known and substantiated.[98]

A week later, however, another incident occurred which raised in a disconcerting form the security aspect of Bertie's relationship with Gunzburg. Someone had asked Le Roy-Lewis what he thought of a letter from Lord Hardinge, Under-Secretary for Foreign Affairs, to the British ambassador at Petrograd, Sir George Buchanan, which had been intercepted by the Germans and broadcast over their radio. The military attaché received the intercepts of German radio broadcasts under double envelopes and secret seal but was usually too busy to read them. Bertie, on the other hand, had been 'full of curiosity about these radio telegrams, and they are sent to him'.[99] When asked for the one in question, Bertie produced a bundle from one of his boxes and handed it to Le Roy-Lewis. Under the clip that held the bundle was the visiting card of Gunzburg, with a note in his own hand, '*avec mille remerciements*'.[100] Bertie was obliged to confess that he had sent them to Gunzburg. Le Roy-Lewis had been present at dinners with Gunzburg and Caillaux, and judged that their relations were still as close as ever. Caillaux was still president of the Banque de France 'which had, and has since retained, intimate connections with Baron Gunzburg's firm'.[101] If Gunzburg was reading the secret telegrams, what use was being made of them? Esher thought it was 'out of the question to put any of Macdonogh's merry young men on to a *piste* of this kind'.[102] But, as he warned Haig: 'There is no doubt that this man has been aware of all our plans to take over the line, and where, and the reasons for doing so', and 'probably has full details of Nivelle's projected offensive as well as a glimmering idea of yours.'[103]

At the London Conference of 15–16 January Haig was persuaded to take over the line to Roye—twice the extent he first agreed to—and to replace four French by four British divisions. He also agreed to launch a great 'holding attack' as soon as possible. Nivelle greatly

351

impressed the War Cabinet, which decided to give him 'all he asked for'. In a discussion of the merits of the two C-in-C's it was concluded that: 'Haig is the best man we have, but that is not saying much, and that as between Haig and Nivelle, Lloyd George should support the latter.' Lloyd George confided to Hankey that 'he had received confidential information that Nivelle is very disturbed about Douglas Haig, whom he finds rigid, inelastic and unaccommodating' and Hankey drew the inference that his chief 'would like to get rid of Haig, but cannot find an excuse'.[104] Nivelle within a few days of his appointment had sent Haig a peremptory instruction embodying the complete change of plan, and must have been encouraged to do so by the known attitude of Lloyd George. Haig had now, perhaps unexpectedly, given way, and Lloyd George was baffled. But on the first day of the Conference in front of the French military attaché, Bertier de Sauvigny, Lloyd George had suggested that if agreement about unity of command were not reached, Haig might be instructed to conform to Nivelle's orders. It was reported to Briand: *'Sans doute, le prestige dont jouit le maréchal Haig sur le peuple et l'armée anglaise ne permettra pas probablement de le subordonner purement et simplement au commandant français; mais si le War Committee reconnaît que cette mesure est indispensable, il n'hésitera pas à donner des instructions secrètes dans ce sens au maréchal Haig.'*[105] Briand arranged for a Conference at Calais on 26–27 February to settle the matter.

According to Esher's investigation into the episode that followed, Lloyd George primed Hankey with his ideas, and Hankey 'proceeded to concoct a scheme' for subordinating Haig to Nivelle. Bertier de Sauvigny acted as intermediary. The scheme was perfected and sent to Nivelle's principal staff officer, but Nivelle's staff were not impressed by its practicability.[106] Nevertheless Paul Cambon, the French ambassador in London, writing to Briand on 23 February, insisted that Lloyd George had no confidence in Haig and desired 'that general Nivelle, in whom he had every confidence, should speak out freely and without reserve' at the coming Conference.[107] The next day he explained that Lloyd George wanted only the six principals at the meeting not only for fear of leaks but to avoid the secretaries hearing his strictures on Haig. The conclusions of the Conference would be signed 'to cut the bridges behind Douglas Haig'.[108] The unusual if not unique spectacle of a British Prime Minister thus selling his C-in-C to an allied government naturally led the French to expect that Haig was about to be replaced. Gough was tipped as his successor, and Henry Wilson as Robertson's.

The War Cabinet sanctioned the decision to place Haig under Nivelle's orders on Saturday 24 February, when Robertson was absent. No minute of this decision was circulated until after the Calais Conference, which opened the following Monday, so that neither Derby nor the King knew of it.[109] They thought, like Haig, that the Conference was going to be about transport problems. Hankey's role in the transaction was very disingenuous. He claimed, when questioned by Stamfordham by the King's command afterwards, that Robertson was given a 'very full and fair statement' on the train on Monday to the effect that Lloyd George had 'full powers'. But Hankey admitted: 'I don't remember that he [Lloyd George] said specifically that there was a prospect of General Nivelle's being given supreme command, because that point had not specifically arisen in conversation...'[110] Hankey was thus, like Lloyd George, guilty of *suppressio veri*, especially as it was his business to circulate the decisions of the War Cabinet on such a matter to Robertson.

On the French side the explanations on the train were equally conspiratorial but more honest. Lyautey boarded the train in Paris with Briand, who explained to him for the first time the background of correspondence that had passed through the embassies. To continue in Esher's words: 'Nivelle joined the train after Lyautey had gone to bed: but next morning they discussed with Briand the situation, and read Lloyd George's telegrams, etc. Lyautey then said to Nivelle that he had better think out some method of applying the principle...Thereupon Nivelle put down the heads of a "scheme" on a sheet of paper...'[111] The scheme was probably Briand's and pushed on to Nivelle. Lyautey who was not in Briand's political camp probably acquiesced.

Hankey's account of the Calais Conference tells how Haig and Nivelle unfolded their respective plans, and then Lloyd George asked Nivelle 'if he was satisfied and if not to explain quite frankly what he wanted. Nivelle got red in the face; talked generalities; and beat about the bush...So Lloyd George broke up the Conference and asked the French to put down in writing what they wanted.'[112] The *procès verbal* however shows that the dispute that arose between Haig and Nivelle was over what constituted a tactical and what a strategic decision, and that Lloyd George asked Nivelle to put down 'the rules which in his opinion ought to govern the two generals', while Briand added a plea for a 'real unity of direction' expressed in some formula which the conference could approve.[113] Haig's account states that: 'When Nivelle had finished, Lloyd George insisted that he [Nivelle] had something further to put before the meeting...he would like the French to formulate their proposals in writing...by dinner time. It was then within an hour of dinner, so I presume the paper had already been prepared.'[114] Haig learnt from Nivelle the next day that it had been drawn up in Paris and approved by Lloyd George and Briand. Nivelle had clearly refused to play the role assigned to him in spite of heavy prompting from the wings.

The *Projet d'Organisation de l'Unité de Commandement*[115] was fully fledged before dinner—for Hankey, after an hour's stroll round Calais, returned to find it in the hands of the French representatives who were already in Lloyd George's room. It was not the plan that Hankey had first devised but far more extreme. Hankey noted: 'It fairly took my breath away, as it practically demanded the placing of the British army under Nivelle: the appointment of a British "Chief of Staff" to Nivelle; who had powers practically eliminating Haig and his CGS, the scheme reducing Haig to a cypher.'[116] After dinner—Lloyd George dined alone in his room—Hankey returned with Haig and Robertson. 'Lloyd George was extraordinarily brutal to Haig,' he admits. 'When Haig objected that the "tommies" wouldn't stand being under a Frenchman Lloyd George said "Well, Field-Marshal, I know the private soldier very well. He speaks very freely to me, and there are people he criticises a good deal more strongly than General Nivelle!" He more than hinted that Haig would have to resign, if he didn't come to heel, and treated him with a good deal of contumely.'[117] Haig, who knew how to control his feelings, did not rise to the provocation. The War Cabinet had not of course approved of the full-blooded *Projet* as Hankey had to admit when questioned by Haig and Robertson after they left Lloyd George's room. The generals decided to resign rather than accept what even Hankey admitted to be the 'outrageous' French document. Robertson was too agitated to sleep that night, and Lloyd George had a bad night also. The imperturbable Haig slept soundly.

Next morning Hankey managed to persuade Lloyd George that the French scheme was too extreme to be used as a means of fighting

Haig, and produced his own scheme. This *Accord* was discussed formally.[118] Nivelle and Lyautey, although they had both disavowed responsibility for the *Projet* to Haig, still advocated the creation of a British CGS at the French Headquarters. Their understanding of what was implied by the *Accord* was not what Haig understood, as appeared later. Haig regarded the *Accord* as virtually the same as the instruction he had received from Kitchener, although there might, as he wrote to the King, still be 'something behind it'. He had to conform to Nivelle's plan and obey his strategic directions for the short period of the offensive, and there were liberal escape clauses. Everything depended on the construction placed on the vague terms of the agreement. Haig signed it, but wrote to the King offering to resign his command if the War Cabinet had lost confidence in him.[119]

The French behaved as if their *Projet* had been accepted. Esher was at Chantilly immediately after the Conference and heard that 'the "high command" was discussed at Calais, and the French say that Nivelle's supremacy was agreed to...'[120] Two days later in Paris he was told by Maurice Rothschild that at a dinner Bertie had let drop that Lloyd George had gone to Calais to supersede Haig.[121] Meanwhile Haig had received from Nivelle an extraordinary letter demanding to know his plans of operations and the orders he would give, and desiring him to send Henry Wilson as head of the British mission at Beauvais as soon as he returned from Russia. The institution of a British CGS at Beauvais had been the most objectionable feature of the *Projet*, in view of French intentions to use that officer for direct communication with London, and it had been omitted from Hankey's *Accord*.[122] Now Nivelle was not only reviving it, but dictating to Haig whom he should appoint. And indeed Henry Wilson had always been Haig's *bête noire*, in spite of Esher's tactful attempts to remove his prejudice.

Haig regarded Nivelle's letter as such that 'no gentleman could have drafted', and sent it to the War Cabinet asking if it was their wish that their C-in-C should be so addressed by a 'junior foreign commander'.[123] He also told the tale to Esher, who notes:

War Journals, 7 March 1917:[124] I cannot understand the mentality of the Prime Minister and the *military* advisers French and English who prepared that wonderful 'amalgam' document. It is our friend of that name turned up once more in 'shining armour'. I thought Bertie's tale a piece of senile malice, but it was not.

If such a scheme were forced upon them, I hope the British army would just 'walk back home'...I am glad Milner is home. I have written to him and told him how amazing it is that such a scheme should have passed any military critic who knows the two armies...The basis of the whole plan is the vanity of some Frenchmen and the gullibility of some Englishmen...Lloyd George with all his faults is bigger than Briand...I know these people, and like them. They are half *my* people. But *we* are the born leaders of nations, not they.

Milner would approve of such sentiments, but the recent Havas Agency episode (in which Haig was blamed for an indiscreet statement to some French journalists) had shown that the other members of the War Cabinet who counted were against Haig. Curzon 'showed hostility' and Bonar Law was 'weakly ineffective' in his defence.[125]

Haig had stone-walled the attempt to provoke him into resigning, and he now informed the War Cabinet that there were signs of a German attack developing on the Yser which demanded the dispatch of reinforcements to that sector at once. He was invoking the escape clause of the *Accord*. The War Cabinet sent his letter to Nivelle, who endorsed it with unfavourable comments concluding: '*Evidemment on ne peut pas compter sur lui*'.[126] The War Cabinet were thus presented with an acute dilemma. If they failed to support Haig they might incur a serious liability if Haig was right, possibly the loss of the Channel ports. If they went back on the understanding with Nivelle the French might blame them for the failure of the offensive. There is every evidence that Lloyd George would have liked to overrule Haig.[127] But by this time the feeling in the British army in France was running high against the *Projet*. Walter Long reported from the front that the plan of subordination to French command, which was being rumoured about, was 'repugnant in the highest degree to our soldiers'.[128] Esher noted:'All the army is ringing with this affair, and... there is a universal feeling of disgust.'[129]

How would Lord Northcliffe and the other press magnates react to the *Projet* if Lloyd George pressed it against the army's strong resentment? Northcliffe was now falling under Lloyd George's influence. He saw him once a fortnight, and as he wrote at this time: 'I always speak about the army.' But he was also in correspondence with Haig and Robertson. His main criticism of Haig was that he had not found time to discover and promote the brains of the nation which were now largely scattered in his ranks. He was still however on Haig's side, though he was aware that 'there is a strongly growing anti-Haig party in England'. 'It is unjust and it is wrong,' was still his view: 'Haig is paying for the blunders of his predecessors. The agitation is no longer confined to Churchill and Co., as I happen to know.'[130] Apparently Northcliffe declined to support Nivelle, and this was decisive, for Nivelle himself told Henry Wilson at the London Conference of mid-March that he thought the compromise just arrived at futile and that: 'Lloyd George would like to get rid of Haig but, for the minute, the Northcliffe press was too strong.'[131]

The Prime Minister was clearly unrepentant, and would try again later. On the eve of the London Conference which was to patch up the dispute Lloyd George had a blustering interview with the King which Stamfordham considered unsatisfactory. Since Lloyd George now saw that his position was untenable he made out that Haig had not been subordinated to Nivelle after all:

Memorandum by Stamfordham, 12 March 1917:[132] His Majesty expressed surprise and pain at so momentous a decision having been reached without either his knowledge or approval. The King reminded the Prime Minister that as head of the state and of the army he had *his* responsibilities...

The Prime Minister assured the King that there was really nothing changed from what had been agreed upon in Lord Kitchener's instructions to D. Haig...The Prime Minister's manner implied dissent from the idea of the Sovereign being head of the army.

The King told the Prime Minister that if he were an officer serving in the British army, and realised that he was under the command of a foreign general, he would most strongly resent it, and so would the whole army. If this fact too were known in the country it would be greatly condemned. The Prime Minister said that in the event of any such expression of public feeling he would go to the country and would explain matters and very soon have the whole country on his side.

But now that Lloyd George was in retreat[133] the dispute was hastily patched up on the basis of the old and vague agreement with Joffre. Even so, Haig and Esher took exception to Hankey's so-called '*procès verbal*' of the Conference, which seemed to contain a false suggestion that Haig had acted out of pique and wounded pride. So Esher composed for Haig a resounding reply which paid tribute to 'unity of command' but rejected the scheme which had been chosen to attain it: 'its inherent defects were made manifest almost immediately, and I have no expectation that the future will disclose any practical method of carrying out its intention.'[134]

The brief and in the end disastrous infatuation of Lloyd George with Nivelle displays the former's volatile political style at its worst. Unchecked by his newly-formed War Cabinet while Milner was away on his mission to Russia, he had recklessly tried to place Haig and his army of two million men under a general whom the French staff did not think any better than Micheler or Pétain and not so good as Castelnau or Foch, and who had never exercised any general command. The French politicians had grasped at the straw of Nivelle's earlier dramatic but essentially local successes, but they had also been sensible from their point of view in wanting Haig to take over more line. But the cause of 'unity of command' had been irreparably damaged, and Haig's offensive power seriously checked. The attack from the sea on the Flanders coast on which Haig set such store would now never be made. Haig had wanted to attack the enemy 'where he is bound either to fight, or to surrender some objective of strategic or political importance', and, as Hankey urged, he had a good plan prepared:

Memorandum by Hankey, 7 March 1917:[135] It is well known to the War Cabinet that Haig has for many months had an alternative plan to the Somme fully worked out…its general strategical conception is to compel the evacuation of Ostend and Zeebrugge …So much work has been done on this plan that last year, before the Somme offensive, many officers and men home on leave confidently believed the real attack was to take place in this region. There are many guns in place. Most of the communications have been prepared, and I am assured it could be 'staged' in a month. The idea, as I understand it, would be to retain the Arras-Vimy

punch, but to substitute Flanders for the Somme...On the whole
this seems to me good sense...

But the Prime Minister had succumbed to the allure of Nivelle's idea
that the German line could be broken so violently that conditions
of mobile warfare could be regained, in which the superior numbers
of the western allies in France would begin to tell. Lloyd George had
backed his hunch against all his military advisers and most of his
colleagues, and only the impossibility of getting rid of Haig prevented
him from giving *carte blanche* to the French.[136] The result was the
greatest fiasco of the war. Haig's plan was ruined with that of Nivelle,
and perversely the consequent resolve of the public to prevent further
interference by the politicians with the soldiers prevented any mean-
ingful liaison between Lloyd George and Haig during the later
Passchendaele offensive, when it was badly needed. The relationship
between the country's leading politician and leading soldier was one
of mutual contempt.

Fifteen

The American
Miasma

The Nivelle offensive was destined to be the last all-out aggressive movement that the French would make until the closing phase of the war. The conditions for its success were secrecy and a large 'army of manoeuvre' suddenly launched at an unsuspected part of the front. Nivelle himself abrogated the first condition by his unguarded and over-optimistic talk to all and sundry, so that his attack became the talking point of dinner parties in London and Paris. The second condition was abrogated by the French general staff before the Calais Conference and before the full import of the German retirement on the Somme was realised:

> *War Journals, 28 February 1917:*[1] Anyhow, the German retirement on the Somme is looked upon as a *local* re-shuffling of cards...I fancy there is an intention to shorten their line and balk our offensive. Meanwhile I gather that Nivelle's plan has been modified. Instead of the big force of three armies, or twenty-seven divisions commanded by himself, to be used as an *armée de manoeuvre* after the *bataille de rupture*, he has reduced this force to twelve battalions, sacrificing the remainder to a local attack at Rheims, and placing reserves behind Franchet d'Esperey...The French staff round Micheler are convinced that they are about to penetrate the German lines as far as Laon.

The French general staff, *troisième bureau*, had demonstrated that the proposed penetration by two armies on a 40 km. front was impossible: 'the opening was not big enough and...the supply of these armies would be impossible.' Hence Nivelle was obliged to ask that Gough should add his army to the *bataille de rupture*. Yet, as Esher relates, the whole conception was frustrated by the great German withdrawal:

War Journals, 17 March 1917:[2] Meanwhile the Germans shortened their line, with the result that D. H[aig]'s blow (Allenby) is in the air, and Franchet d'Esperey's also. Also the German reserve, owing to the shortening in the line and other changes, is increased to fifty divisions. Thus instead of three points of attack, Nivelle is reduced to one. It becomes the battle of the Somme over again in Champagne against an enemy with fifty divisions in reserve...

The objections to Nivelle's proceeding with his attack were effectively put by Pétain to the President and Council of Ministers. Moreover, before it was launched on 16 April some dramatic alterations on the international scene had effected subtle changes in the attitude and morale of the French army. The Russian Menshevik revolution by which Kerensky came to power seemed temporarily to disrupt the Russian military effort, and the USA's entry into the war further promoted the Pétain policy of the 'defensive-offensive': both developments promised massive military strength in the future, if the present could be tided over. But the American 'miasma' of millions of men, mountains of war material and stacks of dollars impinged on the war-weary *'poilus'* with a most dispiriting effect. Likewise the Russian Revolution, hailed by Lloyd George as creating a more popularly-based and more viable war effort, gave an immediate stimulus to international pacificism.[3] The day before Nivelle's offensive a Russian peace manifesto was published in Paris, and Albert Thomas had gone to Russia to 'endeavour to neutralise the socialist advances of the internationalists to the Council of workmen and soldiers at Petrograd.'[4] Rumours quickly circulated that on 16 April the soldiers west of Rheims refused to leave their trenches, saying the artillery preparation was insufficient. Nivelle's attack never got off to the whirlwind start that was planned. Within days it was seen as a complete failure.

Briand's cabinet had already been replaced by that of the elderly Ribot, who seemed to epitomise caution and prudence, and Painlevé, a mathematician and socialist, was now Minister of War. Esher found him honest and frank, in contrast with the *finesse* of Briand and the 'vanity' of Viviani.[5] Painlevé claimed to have expected the failure of the Nivelle offensive, and before the end of April Pétain was installed in Paris as his CGS. Like the Russians, the French abandoned the offensive, and while the Germans were thus freed to launch all their force against the British, the Austrians seemed willing to make a separate peace now that the Russian designs on Constantinople and the Balkans had lapsed. The Emperor Karl had in March opened a channel with the French, unknown to the Kaiser, through the Empress's brother Prince Sixte, and seemed willing to make a separate peace. Lloyd George was let into the secret on a strictly personal basis by Ribot, so that the overture did not come before the War Cabinet. When passing through Paris on 18 April Lloyd George was persuaded by Poincaré and Jules and Paul Cambon not to inform the Italians of the overture, so that a separate peace was discussed with the Italians merely as a hypothetical possibility.[6]

Esher always regarded this as one of the biggest sell-outs of the war and a sure token of the feebleness of British diplomatic influence in Paris.[7] He had attended Lloyd George's breakfast ensemble on his return through Paris and answered 'a series of questions about the French *morale* and the "shot-silk" of political issues and personalities.'[8] As a result of his persuasions Lloyd George sent for Briand, who remained favourably inclined to a peace settlement that would detach Austria from Germany, but Lloyd George was already committed. He should in Esher's view have drawn the appropriate lesson, which was to send some worthy representative to Paris. 'Cannot you send here someone…who can keep you personally in touch with the people here who matter?' he pleaded. 'You are badly served, indifferently informed, are not represented at all…It might any day prove disastrous.'[9]

The demoralisation and mutinies in the army which followed Nivelle's failure were so serious that the government hesitated to replace him, for then they would go down also.[10] Henry Wilson, who had been made Chief Liaison Officer at Beauvais at Nivelle's behest and still valued him as the only hope for an offensive policy, noted how 'all sorts of Cabinet Ministers, Members of the Chamber and others were getting passes for the Front, and going there and seeing Pétain, etc., then going back with fantastic tales'.[11] Esher and Wilson, with Haig's rather diffident support, decided to do all possible to keep Nivelle in command or at least see that Pétain's policy of quiescence did not completely triumph. Haig pleaded for a continued offensive with Painlevé, but would not meddle in questions of appointments. Henry Wilson annoyed Painlevé by criticising Pétain severely.[12] Esher was more subtle, and knowing that Ribot and

Briand still supported Nivelle, sent Repington off to interview Pétain and Henry Wilson off to London to enlist the support of Milner. Repington returned on 28 April and gave a too favourable account of Pétain to Esher and Le Roy-Lewis. The gist of his findings was sent at once to Haig:

> *Esher-Lawrence Burgis (telegram), 28 April 1917:*[13] Tell C-in-C that Repington returned here last night from Pétain...Pétain has been offered the command and has accepted. His appointment may be delayed a few days. He proposes drastic changes at Compiègne, and in all the commands. He does not suggest stoppage of your offensive but completely modifies French. He describes his tactics as 'aggressive-offensive'. The basis is to avoid losses, and to await American reinforcements. He has elaborate scheme for using Americans as drafts for French armies. This proposition has already been sent to American government... Repington thinks Pétain a Napoleon. He may however turn out to be Boulanger.

Meanwhile Henry Wilson had seen Milner on 28 April, who took a very gloomy view of affairs, especially in Russia. He saw Lloyd George the next day (Sunday) at Walton Heath, who immediately saw the significance of Nivelle's prospective dismissal for Haig's offensive and, Wilson notes, 'frightened me a little by saying that it might be best to wait till 1918 before putting in our blow'.[14] But the losses due to submarines were at their height, and only the Prime Minister, Robertson and Milner seemed to stand firm. The rest, led by Robert Cecil, were thinking in terms of an armistice.

Thanks to the intervention of Briand and others Nivelle remained in command long enough for Lloyd George to come over and settle that the western offensive would continue. In the interim, before he replaced Nivelle on 15 May, Pétain became CGS in Paris, in which position he changed Nivelle's staff from top to bottom. Pétain's policy, as he explained it to Wilson on 11 May, was to take over as little line as possible (which contravened what had just been agreed), to avoid all grand attacks and take only small offensives on narrow fronts, and to lose no men. It seemed to Wilson that Haig's operations against Zeebrugge and Ostend could not be contemplated in these conditions.[15] In deference to political pressures which had produced a constant state of crisis in the ministry, the French were opting out of the war.[16] The accounts of enormous casualties, which Nivelle claimed to be grossly exaggerated, had raised the cry that France should 'keep some men alive'.

In Esher's opinion the concert between Britain and France had never been so disintegrated. Lloyd George was preoccupied with the intractable Irish problem and then in June with the alienation of the Labour party over the Stockholm Conference. He seemed to have lost his grip on the direction of affairs, and the decisions arrived at with the French in early May were not being implemented. Lloyd George did however seem to recognise the efforts of Esher and Henry Wilson, for on 18 May Lord Derby arrived in Paris, 'excited and pessimistic over affairs in England'—food shortages, strikes, manpower difficulties—and asked Esher to consent to take Bertie's place as ambassador, while Henry Wilson would replace Le Roy-Lewis. Haig was anxious that Esher should comply, but Esher's reaction was : 'I cannot imagine anything I should detest more.'[17] He would have to demand far too drastic changes in the embassy and its organisation, which to him was synonymous with what was antiquated, ill-informed and unreliable. He wanted a cabinet minister at the embassy, and the position was later occupied by Derby himself.

While the French were paralysed by the mutinies in their army, the full scale of which was not realised by the British at the time,[18] Haig battled on along the pre-arranged lines of his programme through Vimy, Messines, and the attack on the position north of Ypres which was to introduce the joint naval and military attempt to take the coast. The wisdom of proceeding with the last project seemed extremely doubtful both to Henry Wilson and Esher:

War Journals, 25 May 1917:[19] The views from the German positions are wonderful, but the marvellous trenches and the organising power down to the cemeteries in the forest put the French efforts on similar lines into obscure shade. Bigness and imagination are the characteristics of the Boche. Everything French seems so *small*.

How are we to beat these people in the new war that is now opening? Observe: plans were laid last October. Part of these plans was a triple Russian offensive. Now Russia is out of the war, are these plans still to hold?...Have they been reconsidered? No.

Ibid, 26 May: Henry Wilson left for Bavincourt. Whether his views will please D. H[aig] is doubtful. He is fearful for the attack on Zeebrugge and Ostend. It seems a tough business and may cost 400,000 men—and fail! It is tainted by having been 'asked for' by the Admiralty. It is part of the scheme of operations decided upon last October, in combination with three large offensives by Russia, and at least one by Italy, and two by the French, all of which have fallen through.

The same scepticism was shared by Winston Churchill, who appeared in Paris on his way to visit the front and expounded his ideas to Esher in a walk around the Bois, 'at great length and with a torrent of fine language'.[20] He would abandon all offensives at Salonika, and put 120,000 of Sarrail's army on warships to make sudden descents on the Turkish coasts. He would divide the grand fleet into two, and risk one half in an attack on the German bases, and sow mines close inshore. On the western front he supported Pétain's policy, though he did not think much of Pétain himself. He wanted to wait for the Americans, but did not realise that they would not be forthcoming in great numbers until 1919![21]

Lloyd George in his elaborate self-exculpation for the tragedy of Passchendaele stresses the confident assertions of Haig and Robertson made before the War Policy Committee, which consisted of Lloyd George himself, Curzon, Milner and Smuts. The Prime Minister certainly argued strenuously against the offensive, the dangers of which were quite apparent: though in the end he had to yield his 'amateur' opinion to that of the professional advisers of the government. But the real moral of this sad tale is the complete lack of alternative plans for an offensive such as an effective war directorate would have been able to produce. The War Policy Committee was really the War Cabinet meeting informally, early or late, a coterie of grossly overburdened politicians trying to manage the whole war.[22] It was no substitute for a specialised committee, and although Churchill and Wilson made representations to it, as did Esher, such relatively unburdened outsiders were given no latitude to propose alterations of plan. Lloyd George virtually assumed the whole burden himself, and it was too much even for him. Esher had some opportunities to observe him at this phase of the war, and his comments reveal uncertainty and opportunism. Early in June he asked Murray of Elibank what Lloyd George's vision of the future really was. Murray replied that he had been told, but 'it would destroy the little PM if his views were known'.[23] He looked for 'a very moderate peace, and at an early date. A peace based upon the *status quo*, modified by concessions here and there, but "We must give the Germans one more good hammering first".'[24]

On 25 July Esher arranged a luncheon in Paris at which Lloyd George met Briand, with Waldorf Astor as interpreter. Briand developed his theory of a peace settlement at length. It would have to be an imposed settlement, and yet Russia seemed almost out of the war and the belligerents (except the USA) had already reached the limits of human endurance. If that limit was overpassed, revolution in England and France as well as Germany was certain. It was too dangerous to gamble on revolution breaking out in Germany first. Since peace could not be imposed on a united bloc of Central Powers, Austria and Turkey needed to be disengaged by tempting peace offers. 'As regards peace terms, he was emphatic upon the importance of giving Germany a free hand in Russia. Let her have the Ukraine, and develop all the resources of the Russian empire. Our compensation would be on the Rhine and in Africa.'[25] Lloyd George seemed to Esher to be impressed with this approach, and urged Briand to try and work with Painlevé. He had no better ideas to offer. Breakfasting with him the next morning, Esher thought he looked 'wonderfully well' and 'in good form', but 'still one notices a refusal to take command'.[26] He had been discussing for three days the trivial question of whether a division from Salonika should go to Syria or to Mesopotamia. Lloyd George fully realised that the real problem was what should be done if Russia went out of the war. 'No one will even look at the possibility or think of it. The time is wasted in banquets and vain talk.'[27]

The Passchendaele offensive was launched, after a titanic bombardment, on 31 July. The weather had changed the day before 'from summer to winter'. Viewing the 'inconceivable organisation of noise and material and men' from an old windmill at Schaffenberg, Esher thought 'the spectacle was wonderful in spite of the rain and clouds'.[28] Haig was in his train near Poperinghe, and Esher felt it was 'too un-

366

comfortable to go up there for a few minutes' talk'. On 1 August he noted: 'I am going home. It is too cold.'[29] The rain continued, but Haig's timetable likewise. After a fortnight a general conviction had been established that his offensive could not succeed. Esher heard from the Quartermaster-General, Sir John Cowans, that 'no one at the War Office believes that we shall defeat the enemy'. Cowans had been to Haig's GHQ and had thought the optimism there 'stupefying and ridiculous'. 'Everyone laughs at D. H[aig] and his entourage for believing that the Boche can be beaten! It is to this point that we have come,' Esher noted scornfully.[30]

There was certainly an acute shortage of drafts from England and the gun production had fallen short of what had been expected. Even more disquieting was the great divergence of opinion between Charteris, Haig's chief of intelligence, and Macdonogh, the DMI at the War Office. Macdonogh appeared in Flanders on 21 August and told Esher that the Germans had 3,600 heavy guns on the western front, who comments: 'Charteris nearly halves this number...the whole army mistrusts Charteris. The chief alone supports him.'[31] Haig's HQ was a beautifully contrived autocracy in which everyone was subject to the chief and the chief was subject to his own timetables. But interestingly enough at this critical juncture Esher found that the army commanders were almost as sanguine as Haig. In particular General Hubert Gough, who according to Lloyd George's interpretation in his *Memoirs* 'thought it so hopeless that in the middle of August he advised Sir Douglas Haig to discontinue',[32] was according to Esher's contemporary record in full accordance with Haig about going on, though less optimistic about the speed of progress:

War Journals, Blendesques 19 August 1917:[33] D. H[aig]'s optimism is invulnerable. He is well satisfied with the operations since July 31. Bad as the weather has been, he thinks it has told as heavily against the enemy as against us. In his view he will get a *decision* here before November if he can get reserves...

Gough, whom I had a long talk with this afternoon, and who commands the Fifth Army that is carrying out all these operations, is of the same opinion as regards the certainty of capturing all our objectives, but puts the final date at next spring. He thinks the delay due to bad weather has upset the timetable too far to enable the complete objectives to be won this autumn.

Ibid, Frévent 22 August 1917:[34] D. H[aig] explained again to me his plan. We have advanced 6,000 yards above Langemarck, that is on the left and centre of the position. It is on the right where Gough's Fifth Army is joined up with Plumer and the Second Army that the check has happened. It was foreseen to be the key of the battle. If we take the high ground for which the Germans are fighting most stoutly we establish a flank, we get all the observation, and there is nothing to prevent us in three more efforts getting the Passchendaele ridge. Gough thinks we shall succeed. Jacob, the best corps commander in the army, has the task and agrees with Gough.

D. H[aig] is quite confident. By September 15th we should have succeeded in rounding off this operation. Then (according to plan) the Belgians attack southward, and then the combined sea and land attack of Rawlinson and Bacon would follow.

D. H[aig] thinks that this will not happen, and that if we get Roulers the Germans will negotiate before they lose the sea coast of Belgium.

Measured against these expectations the Passchendaele offensive was a failure, relieved by some brilliant successes. But the strange feature of Passchendaele is the absence of any condemnation of it until after the fiasco of the Cambrai break-through in late November, a quite separate operation. Lloyd George like many others had grumbled about casualties, and after the Italian *débâcle* following Caporetto in late October he made a dead set at Robertson and the general staff in London. But he continued to support Haig as a field commander, and did not try to arrest the offensive in October and November.

Esher was taken ill with some internal trouble, which he attributed to old age and motoring on broken roads, and spent most of September in Biarritz. But he followed Haig's operations with keen interest and approval. The attack on the Menin road heights on 20 September he considered 'one of the best planned and executed of all his battles'.[35] The attacks on 3 and 4 October he regarded as 'perfect' and a 'monument to design, preparation, achievement'.[36] Meanwhile the French continued to postpone any supporting attack, and the Italians excused themselves also from their promised offensive. Haig was fighting the war on his own. This was the thing that was worrying Lloyd George. While the French were not calling up their 1919 class, on the grounds that the young men ought to be kept alive, Haig was consuming the available men far faster than replacements were being inducted. If Haig failed to gain a decision, and the war went on beyond 1918, there would be a very serious manpower crisis. American assistance on the western front would not become effective until late 1918 or even 1919. Russia was out of the war. The French received a peace offer in September which promised Alsace and Lorraine. Inter-allied concert had completely broken down, while the War Cabinet was bound in the strait-jacket of the Robertson-Haig combination.

Henry Wilson, who had returned to England in the summer feeling that he had become *persona non grata* at the French GQG, immediately took up the project of an inter-allied Council similar to the one that Asquith had approved in 1915: 'three prime ministers and three soldiers, to be overall CGS's and to draw up plans for the whole theatre from Nieuport to Baghdad.'[37] Lloyd George was casting about for some military body to supervise Robertson's decisions, and seemed distinctly taken with the idea. Robertson, naturally, opposed it, and the 'Bourbons' in the government—Robert Cecil, Derby, Curzon, Carson and Balfour—made it clear they would resign if 'Wully' Robertson's position were undermined. But on 11 October Lloyd George exploited a loophole which he had found in Wully's 'charter'. He boldly invited Lord French and Henry Wilson to attend the War Cabinet, excusing the incursion on the CIGS's monopoly of military advice by citing Asquith's War Councils of August 1914.[38] Lord French and Wilson were asked to write papers, but exactly on what subject is obscure.[39] According to Esher, who got his information from Haig after the latter received a letter from Robertson, the papers were to be about the military aspects of the recent German peace offers and 'the strategical situation of today'.[40] When the papers were submitted, they both recommended 'a central council, including a staff of generals in Paris, to be independent of the national General Staffs'.[41] This was undoubtedly what Lloyd George intended, and indeed he had already horrified Hankey by mentioning not only the Council but 'a permanent general staff' in Paris to Franklin Bouillon and Foch.[42] The Prime Minister was gunning for Robertson in order to gain control over war strategy, not gunning for Haig to stop Passchendaele.

The French had special reasons of their own for welcoming the displacement of Robertson and the termination of Haig's offensive.

They felt, from the recent peace offer, that the Germans were willing to buy a separate peace in the west in exchange for a free hand to carve for themselves in Poland and Russia. If Haig gained the Belgian coast, as he was absolutely set on doing, the Germans might go all out for a separate peace with England on the basis of evacuating Belgium. Would the English then fight for Alsace-Lorraine? Pétain, in a very frank exposition of his views to Repington on 7 October, wanted Haig to take over 90 km. more of line and to give up Flanders for an attack further south and east.[43] When Repington put Pétain's views to Haig's staff they were adamant against taking over more line, claiming that the numbers of enemy engaged was the true criterion, and that the Germans had to contest every foot in Flanders. Further south they might retire and throw any planned offensive into confusion. The French feared a massive attack on their attenuated defences in February or March 1918, before the ground in Flanders was dry enough for large operations, but Lieutenant-General Sir. L. E. Kiggell, Haig's Chief of Staff, thought the Flanders attack might be resumed in March 'at a pinch'. Finally Repington put it to Kiggell that it was assigning a mean role to a proud nation like the French to relegate them to a purely supporting operation.[44] On this point Haig's private opinion was that the French could not be relied on and that the British would have to win virtually alone.[45]

The French army had indeed largely recovered from the demoralisation of the mutinies of the summer, but only at the price of extended leave and political interference. Pétain admitted that his army was melting away through the withdrawal of certain classes of men for political reasons, and he was forbidden the use of the 1919 class after losing 40,000 men at Verdun. The army was now firmly controlled by the politicians, but the politicians were being swept off their feet by the moods of the Chamber. Painlevé's cabinet and war council did not keep any records, for fear that the Chamber would compel their being produced, and Hankey noticed that on his visit to England Painlevé wore an expression of frightening abstraction. He was not a success as premier, and the only man strong enough to replace him and also deal with the scandals which had come into prominence with the arrest of Bolo Pasha[46] seemed to be Clemenceau.

Esher's acquaintance Bunau-Varilla who controlled the powerful *Le Matin* newspaper was trying to effect a *rapprochement* between Clemenceau and the president, Poincaré, who had been so publicly reviled by the 'Tiger' that the proposition was very doubtful. Esher doubted whether even Clemenceau would be able to suppress the pacifists led by Caillaux and Humbert, editor of *Le Journal*. Nor did the Chamber seem disposed to swallow Clemenceau's bitter prescription for war *à l'outrance*, when it forced a reconstruction of Painlevé's ministry on 19 October. Ribot, the Foreign Minister, had to go, for suppressing a reference to the peace offer in the official record of his speech, but Painlevé survived for some more weeks. He was still in office when the Germans, aided by his pacific policy, launched the divisions which they could spare from the western front against the Italians, who were routed at Caporetto[47] with such enormous captures of men and guns that Italy seemed about to be knocked out. Her ambitions in the Trentino and Illyria, so prominent in her motives for entering the war, now vanished at a stroke.

The Italian defeat had an immediate and drastic corollary for the western front. It meant that the British had to take over more line to enable the French to help the Italians, and a switch of war material and effort. According to Esher, Lloyd George ought to have known of the impending attack on the Isonzo when he reviewed the war at the War Council of 11 October. General Mackensen was known to have gone there, and the concentration of the German army was being discussed in the Swiss newspapers.[48] The defeat certainly put Lloyd George on the spot, for such a resounding disaster on top of the apparent failure of the 'western' policy called his whole war direction into question. His response was to get the War Cabinet to agree to the creation of a Supreme War Council, and to take advantage of the Rapallo Conference to set up its first official meeting. The Italian disaster had supplied the pretext for trying conclusions with Robertson and the political interest he represented.

Lloyd George wished to stop the campaign in Flanders, but not for the reason which he stressed in his *Memoirs*.[49] His line of reasoning at this time is reflected in an interview with the King, which elaborates on the conviction also observed by Hankey, that the war would be won not in 1918 but in 1919. There were 'evident indications', he said, that the French 'do not intend to do much more fighting', while the Russians were out 'at all events for some time' and the Italians 'have come to a standstill'. Bearing in mind that Kitchener's army was of 'but little use until the second year of its life, we cannot expect much assistance from America in 1918':

Memorandum by Stamfordham, 18 October 1917:[50] It would seem probable that to us again the brunt of the fighting will fall next year, with the result that we shall sacrifice the flower of our army in a single-handed offensive...

It is his duty to ensure that whenever the climax is reached, England is at the zenith of her military strength...We must meet in conference and insist upon knowing from our allies whether or not they intend to resume a *bona fide* active offensive next year. If not, then we should consider the wisdom of contenting ourselves with remaining on the defensive in Flanders, curtailing our subsidiary campaigns, and liberating as many men as possible for employment at home in agriculture, shipbuilding, aircraft construction, etc...

British public opinion had been lulled into a passive confidence in the military authorities by the press censorship, and had little idea of the extent to which the army's numbers were being whittled away. To shake Robertson, the symbol of the nation's resolve to fight, and to subvert his policy of 'every available man' for Flanders, Lloyd George had to concert a press campaign against him. Repington noticed how 'the dead set being made at Robertson and the General Staff' began in the *Sunday Times* of 14 October, and was taken up by C. P. Scott in the *Manchester Guardian* and the London diary man in the *Evening Standard*.[51] When after the Rapallo Conference Lloyd George made another of his Paris speeches launching the Supreme War Council with a tirade against the generals, he made special arrangements for Scott to know of it in advance.[52]

Haig's attitude in this challenge was critical. If he showed solidarity with Robertson and resolved to resign with him, Lloyd George would have been checked. Hence, on his way to Rapallo, the Prime Minister met Haig by appointment in Paris to gather his views. Haig arrived at the Crillon via Pétain's HQ, where he had discussed the Wilson plan with the French C-in-C and rejected it in favour of a plan of Pétain's. This involved 'a division of the Western front into two commands, the sea to the Aisne to D. H[aig], the Aisne to the Adriatic under Pétain. It followed that the training and direction of the Italian forces would be under the aegis of the French C-in-C.'[53] This was the plan that Haig and Pétain were to implement in 1918 in despite of Henry Wilson and Versailles. However, when Haig dined at the Crillon with Esher, he was told it was 'quite impractical'. 'The Italians would rather make peace than accept such a solution,' Esher declared. Esher also dissuaded Haig from supporting Robertson. 'Robertson is to blame for the course events have taken,' he said. 'He should never have parted with his right as sole military adviser of the government. He could have made his stand at first. Now it is too late. Lloyd George has got him on the run. The French papers, inspired by Painlevé and Franklin Bouillon, are in full cry for an Allied General Staff.'[54] Haig was persuaded. Next day Haig made no trouble, but accepted it as a *fait accompli*. Robertson was abandoned,[55] Haig swallowing the unpleasant fact that Henry Wilson himself was designated as the permanent Military Member, with the Prime Minister and another minister as his political supports. Esher did not share Haig's distrust of Wilson, and the scheme seemed to him identical to that which he had promoted himself. 'So they have adopted my old scheme of November 1915,' he commented: '...It is comic, and it is tragic, for it is now too late to be of much good.'[56]

The Supreme Allied Council seemed useless to Esher unless Wilson was backed by a strong ambassador in Paris who could elicit what was going on in French political circles. He demonstrated this to Lloyd George on 12 November by telling him privately the story of the September peace *pourparlers*, which Briand supported. The Prime Minister seemed 'very angry' that this important matter had only reached Balfour at the Foreign Office in the form of a cryptic telegram.[57] Then Esher pressed hard for Milner to be sent out. Lloyd George was incensed at Bertie, a 'damned old fool', for reporting to Balfour that the French press was hostile to the Allied General Staff, and promised to bring his conduct before the War Council.[58] He could not spare Milner, but he saw at last the vital position that the ambassador occupied. Robertson, who appeared in Paris shortly before Lloyd George delivered his speech of 12 November, was still resentful, and Esher told Hankey that he feared the London general staff would starve Henry Wilson of information.

As if to emphasise the uncertainty of French politics, chance had it that the Painlevé ministry fell on the day after Lloyd George's Paris speech. This tirade against the existing system met with 'qualified approval' in Esher's opinion, the main criticism being that there could be no unity of command with two C-in-Cs. Luckily, perhaps, Lloyd George had had a private conference with Clemenceau to persuade him to support the Supreme Council on 11 November, apparently with some success. Painlevé's government fell over what Esher called his 'shifty' handling of the Bolo scandals, which Clemenceau's paper *L'Homme Enchaîné* had castigated.[59] Clemenceau's 'Victory cabinet' was formed on the 16th, with Clemenceau himself as War Minister. At first Henry Wilson thought that he would co-operate with the Supreme War Council, but in fact he almost repudiated the whole Rapallo agreement:

> *War Journals, 1 December 1917:*[60] I went to the Crillon. The Conference called for four o'clock was still in session, but I found Henry Wilson and Milner. Henry was satisfied with the first meeting of the Supreme Council. It sat at Versailles this morning ...The discussion turned mainly upon 'manpower' among the *allies*. Also Clemenceau pressed hard for the immediate taking over of more 'line'.
>
> Then Lloyd George came in and took me up to his room...He seemed satisfied with his bouts with Clemenceau...[who] tried to escape from the agreement about the Supreme Council on the ground that it was Painlevé's plan...His plan was that Pétain should have supreme command from the North Sea (as he called it) to the Adriatic. Lloyd George refused to discuss this as a practical proposition, and stuck to his 'agreement'.

Clemenceau gave way about the formal constitution of the Council, but tried to circumvent it. While Robertson remained as the British CIGS passively obstructing Lloyd George's plans, his opposite number in Paris, Foch, was completely in step with Clemenceau and able therefore to dominate Versailles through a compliant Military Member, Weygand. Wilson was forced to the conclusion that Clemenceau 'intends to direct the whole war by using Foch to work with Robertson, and then by sending Weygand to impose his [Clemenceau's] will on Versailles...'[61] The truth was that Pétain was in desperate straits for men, and Clemenceau was determined to get the British to take over more line either through Robertson or through Wilson.

To force Haig to take over the line as far as Berry au Bac would be to take away his power of offensive. Already Haig's brilliant surprise attack before Cambrai on 20 November had failed for want of supporting reserves. After the tanks had broken through all the German lines the cavalry (so often ridiculed as useless) were pushed through to the open country beyond and reached the outskirts of Cambrai. But there was no follow-up. The officers of the first division 'smoked Boche cigars, drank Boche liqueurs, and sat on their horses while the greatest opportunity of the war was ruined'. 'There was open country round them, not a German in view, no guns, nothing. They wasted time and obeyed a disastrous order to the fifty-first division...from the corps commander, Woollcombe, who was a good ten miles in rear. No army commander or any superior officers were riding with the troops; not even the following morning, when D. H[aig] himself was on the ground. Byng never showed.'[62] The immediate rap fell on the commanders, but the real failure lay in lack of reserve forces. The Germans were able to organise a regular counter-offensive against smaller numbers of British troops. When Lloyd George heard the full story from Esher at the Crillon he realised that the public would demand some scalps for the fiasco, for the censor could not hide the gain and then the loss of ground. The complaints might come to roost with the government, which had kept Haig's divisions seriously under strength. Characteristically Lloyd George lashed out at others when his own hide was at risk:

War Journals, 1 December 1917:[63] Then he launched out against 'intrigues' against him. Philip Sassoon was the delinquent conspiring with Asquith and the press. I expressed doubt and said D. H[aig] had no knowledge of such things if they existed, but Lloyd George replied that every one of the journalists etc. reported interviews and letters to him. He was kept informed of every move.

He then used most violent language about Charteris. I did my best to argue and explained the view of D. H[aig] but he was quite unconvinced. D. H[aig] had been misled, always by Charteris. He had produced arguments about German 'morale' etc. etc., all fallacious, culled from Charteris. The man was a public danger, and ruining D. H[aig]. D. H[aig]'s plans had all failed. He had promised Zeebrugge and Ostend, and then Cambrai. He had failed at a cost of 400,000 men. Now he wrote of fresh offensives and asked for men. He would get neither. He had eaten his cake in spite of warnings. Pétain had economised his.

Charteris was removed after a vendetta in the press.[64] But the policy of starving Haig of men and extending his line became folly in view of the enormous build-up of German divisions in the west and the great offensive they were expected to make in the spring.

Haig had asked in November 1916 for a margin of 1,500 men per division after they had been made up to full strength, and he had estimated that 500,000 drafts would be needed for replacements by October 1917. His divisions had remained under strength, and for the operations of 1918 he was to be allowed, according to the calculations of the Ministry of National Service, only 100,000 'A' men with a similar number of 'B' men and the usual intake of 'boys'.[65] In order to maintain nominally the same number of divisions they were reduced from twelve to nine battalions each.[66] Robertson ought, in Esher's opinion, to have made a stand against this attrition of the army, but now his authority was being undermined by a persistent press campaign while only the *Morning Post* and *Globe* seemed to defend him. *The Times* had become strangely acquiescent in the government's manpower policy since Northcliffe's American mission and viscountcy, and Repington its military correspondent found his critical articles cut about either by the Press Bureau or by the editor, Geoffrey Dawson (formerly Robinson). The climax of *The Times*'s subservience followed the controversial speech of Sir Auckland Geddes in introducing the new Manpower Bill on 14 January 1918 with its innuendoes against the generals for careless waste of life. *The Times* reported the speech in a distorted form and accompanied it with a leader which Repington called 'mendacious': whereupon Repington resigned on the ground that Dawson's 'constant deletion of whole paragraphs' of his copy prevented him from telling the country the truth. Esher's reaction to the Geddes' speech and its sequel was very similar:

Esher-Haig, 18 January 1918:[67] It was curious that *The Times* while professing to give Geddes' speech verbatim should have omitted those passages which are so misleading...I wrote to Wully [Robertson] yesterday and told him that the distortion of the truth, the concealments and tergiversations were not credit-

376

able to anyone concerned. The deduction from Geddes' speech is this: we must sit down and wait for the Americans to show a numerical superiority; then...but without 'thoughtless waste of life', meaning the *attack*, the walls of Jericho will fall...We are to achieve the millennium by rhetoric...The Germans will be content to guarantee their place in the world by fighting for it...

Repington's resignation and transfer to the *Morning Post* caused a considerable stir. On top of the attacks on Haig and Robertson in the Northcliffe press, chiefly by Lovat Fraser in the *Daily Mail*, and Repington's own demand for less secrecy, it looked like intimidation. On behalf of the King, Stamfordham asked Lloyd George what it meant:

Memorandum by Stamfordham, 22 January 1918:[68] The Prime Minister said...Repington had left *The Times* because he was against the Allied General Staff at Versailles—really personal dislike of Sir Henry Wilson. As to the Northcliffe press, he had seen Lord N[orthcliffe] and remonstrated strongly with him for the campaign against 'the generals'...

As to the Allied General Staff,...[Robertson] never said a word for or against it; yet came back to England some days before the Prime Minister, got in touch with the press, with L. Maxse, with Asquith, so that by the time Lloyd George reached London the newspapers were loudly denouncing the scheme...Robertson is *not quite straight*...

In Haig's last attack at Cambrai Pétain told him that so many French divisions would be available to bring up as a reserve; but he never even received a reply from Haig...

The War Office organisation is rotten and extravagant in men, money, material...For his recent speech in secret session in the House of Commons he was given certain figures by the staff which he quoted. Today Lord Derby...told him that they had underestimated the German strength by 700,000 men...

It was certainly true that Repington was against the Allied General Staff, but his case was not so easily dismissed. He was now unmuzzled, and with the support of Gwynne, the editor, he published an article in the *Morning Post* of 24 January 'exposing the failure of the

War Cabinet to maintain the Army'. He deliberately omitted to send the article to be passed by the Press Bureau, and was courting imprisonment.[69]

The truth was that Lloyd George himself not only inspired Northcliffe, Rothermere, C. P. Scott, Robert Donald, and other press magnates, bribing the former with peerages and ministerial offices, but his Press Propaganda Committee was a clearing house for government myths.[70] While the Prime Minister held weekly confabulations with his press minions personally or by Sutherland he objected to Robertson's far more decorous relations with Maxse and Repington. Repington was becoming a martyr in the cause of free speech, and after his defiance of the Censor he was invited by Mr Justice Darling, the First Puisne Judge, to dine at the Inner Temple, where he was showered with legal advice and offers of assistance. Censorship and official propaganda which resulted in a pillory of Robertson and Haig defeated their prime purpose, the maintenance of morale, and the manpower crisis was being deliberately concealed. The consequences were felt in the French press and were bound to undermine Robertson's position:

Esher-Hankey, 22 January 1918:[71] Today in the *Echo de Paris* there is a résumé of the attacks upon our high command coming from the Northcliffe press and from some provincial papers. The description of what is happening to Robertson is prefaced by an account of what happened to Lord K[itchener]...The fate of Lord K., his gradual depreciation in the good graces of the public, and the destruction of his authority, await Sir William Robertson. Northcliffe the king-maker follows the well-worn road...

At present therefore we stand thus. Our line is lamentably thin. We have attenuated reserves. D. H[aig] does not want to take over a foot more than the line to which he reluctantly agreed with Pétain. Clemenceau is not *really* satisfied with the Versailles compromise. So no one is pleased.

Meanwhile Sir Auckland Geddes...was allowed to make statements in the House of Commons that are '*positively untrue*' notably that in which he said our divisions were not below establishment, although he knew that these same divisions had just had their establishment lowered by three battalions apiece.

The perennial western-eastern conflict between Lloyd George and Robertson was now manifested in the former's insistence that the Supreme War Council should authorise an extension of the Syrian campaign in an offensive against Aleppo. This served the double purpose of overriding Robertson and reinsuring Lloyd George's political position in case of failure on the western front. In the desperate state of the domestic situation, with a crisis in Ireland, unrest in Lancashire, and pacifist leanings on all sides, there was a good case for heartening side-shows.

When therefore Lloyd George went over to attend the crucial meetings of the Supreme War Council at Versailles, whose staffs were now more or less complete, he pressed hard for the Aleppo offensive and the minimum reserves in France. The Aleppo foible was indulged, but only after it had been ridiculed by Clemenceau and made subject to impossible provisos. The question of 'effectives' provoked Foch to remonstrate about the weakness of his manpower policy, and Lloyd George waved him down for this intrusion into British domestic affairs. Clemenceau carried his point about a large reserve of thirty divisions in France, to be controlled by the Military Members at Versailles except that Foch, the CGS at Paris, acted instead of Weygand and presided over the Executive Board. Robertson, who fought hard to gain a place for the CIGS, personally or by deputy, on the Board, was worsted to the sincere regrets of the Americans and French. Haig was obliged to accept an extension of line twelve miles beyond Barisis, subject to agreement with Pétain.

There was little solidarity between Haig and Robertson—indeed Haig thought that Robertson ought to resign over the manpower issue. Esher argued against this. 'A year ago he might have used the threat with effect. Today he has suffered over-much from newspaper attacks. Lloyd George would in fact be delighted and would welcome Henry [Wilson] in Whitehall.'[72] Esher also thought that Wilson's position on the Executive Board which controlled the allocation of the General Reserve was a violation of the Order in Council which gave Robertson exclusive right to issue orders, and also of the statutory powers of the War Office. Robertson must surely resign, and if he did, said Esher: 'Derby will go too, and Lloyd George means to put Milner in his place.'[73]

Repington came to Paris for the Versailles meetings, and was given a full account of their transactions by Clemenceau himself. He was disgusted to find that the official account of the proceedings, written by Leo Amery (who with Lieutenant-Colonel L. Storr headed the Versailles contingent which was an extension of Hankey's secretariat) was completely uninformative as to decisions taken, a mere 'fanfaronade of a silly character, with patriotic variations'. He also noticed 'the most ludicrously false and misleading assertions' about the Supreme War Council in *The Times*.[74] Returning to London, he met his editor, Gwynne, on 9 February and learnt that 'there was a big row on here', and it was hoped 'the Army Council were all going to stand firm'. Asquith had said he would speak in the debate on the Address on Tuesday, 12 February, and Gwynne asked Repington to expose the Paris proceedings before that speech.[75] The Unionist War Committee in the Commons passed resolutions in support of the generals, and Lord Salisbury reminded Lloyd George that he depended on Unionist support.

The 'big row' was really a continuation of the furore over Sir Auckland Geddes' speech aggravated by rumours of the doings at Versailles. Geddes had himself a strong *parti pris* and presumed to criticise Derby and the War Office to the King, saying 'he considered the present position was unworkable. Sir D. Haig's being a field-marshal, Sir W. Robertson yielded on all points to him...He strongly advocated Sir W. Robertson, with Sir N. Macready as AG, to command the BEF, and Sir D. Haig to become CIGS. The War office organisation and the administration of the home army is very inefficient and ought to be at once placed on a new footing.'[76] Derby's department was still the cock-shy of indifferently-informed outsiders, and while soldiers did not enjoy the immunity of ministers from direct attacks by colleagues in office, they were nevertheless liable like other office holders to be shuffled about the board for political reasons. Lloyd George at one point shared Geddes' strange view that Robertson although useless as a strategist or administrator was good enough to command the army in the field.

It was obvious that the 'outing of Wully' was to be effected at all hazards. The Versailles meetings offered a new pretext. There, Robertson had been told he could not command the General Allied Reserve as a member of the Executive Board because he was not on the spot. But the French had then allowed Foch, although located in Paris as CGS, to sit on and indeed preside over the Board. Weygand, the Military Member for France, was a man of straw. Might not Lloyd

George follow suit with Clemenceau, who was obviously determined to keep Versailles under his thumb? By pretending that Versailles was a more important post than that of CIGS Lloyd George hoped to be able to force Wully to go there. He breakfasted daily with Derby at this time, and Derby was wobbling:

Memorandum by Stamfordham, 10 February 1918:[77] Taking into consideration what the Prime Minister said to me about Sir William Robertson on January 22, the situation as described to the King by Lord Derby last evening seems to show that the Prime Minister had achieved what evidently was in his mind on 22 January, viz. to get rid of Sir W. Robertson as CIGS and to put Sir H. Wilson in that position...

His Majesty is told that the really important post is that now occupied by Sir H. Wilson at Versailles, so the biggest man, Sir W. Robertson, *must* go there and Sir H. Wilson, deprived of the 'extraordinary' powers with which Sir W. Robertson was specially invested, will come to the War Office as CIGS and merely be an ordinary member of the Army Council...

[Robertson] is being 'got rid of' out of the most responsible position in the army, and the newly discovered 'bogey' of his abnormal powers...the tremendous responsibilities which as a member of the International Committee (NB he is *not* president or chairman) he will have to discharge with regard to the Reserve etc., is in my opinion mere 'camouflage' to which Lord Derby is unconsciously a party. A week or less ago he declared that if Sir W. Robertson left the War Office he would go also...; but is it not possible that the camouflage is being designed by which he too may follow Sir W. Robertson to France...?

In his proposed arrangement of 9 February Lloyd George had the full support of Milner and the reluctant acquiescence of Haig. Robertson was informed on the next day, and his response was to fight it. He and his friends in Lloyd George's own over-dramatised description, hoped 'to build up a Parliamentary combination drawn from all parties which would reverse the Versailles decision, supplant the Government, and substitute for it one which would make Robertson virtual dictator for the rest of the War, as Hindenburg was in Germany and by the same means'.[78]

Such was the state of play when Repington's broadside against the Versailles agreement with a supporting leader by Gwynne exploded in the *Morning Post* on 11 February. Lloyd George later wrote: 'I know nothing comparable to this betrayal in the whole of our history...[it] might, and ought to have, decided the war.'[79] Repington on the other hand claimed: '...all I had said was in the German and other foreign Press before I had said it.'[80] Was Lloyd George justified in making the momentous changes in the high command, affecting Robertson's authority and Haig's reserves, without disclosing them even in secret session of Parliament? Or were the facts about the General Reserve and passive policy on the western front commonplace to the enemy though screened from the British public? Esher's opinion was that the Downing Street camarilla (Lord Northcliffe had just been appointed Director of Propaganda in Enemy Countries and was rumoured to be moving into rooms adjoining No. 10)[81] were exercising the powers of an Inquisition. From London he wrote to Haig who returned to France early on the 11th:

Esher-Haig, 14 February 1918:[82] That the prestige of Lloyd George has received a severe shock there is no doubt. The feeling of the House of Commons is hostile to his surroundings and disgusted with the Northcliffe's, Beaverbrook's and Sutherland's (private secretary). Were it not that Asquith is faint hearted and refuses to lead an attack *à l'outrance* the government would fall...

The political crisis has submerged all other interests for the moment. Lloyd George will find it difficult to regain his lost influence. 'Everyone' says that Northcliffe has instigated the prosecution of Repington and Gwynne. The hostility to Northcliffe and Co. is widespread, but no one dares to attack openly except a few more or less insignificant MPs. The powers of the Amalgamated Press are greater than were those of the Inquisition. The King blasphemes but does not resist. He like everyone else is terrorised by Northcliffe...What an unholy gang. I am contemplating a flight to the fresh air of the Scottish hills...

Lloyd George's plan had run into snags, and Wully was still at the War Office.

Henry Wilson had been summoned from Versailles by telephone and had arrived in London on Saturday the 9th. On Monday he was shown by Derby the plan by which he would become CIGS while Robertson as Military Member at Versailles would also have a seat on the Army Council and would have to submit his advice to Wilson for approval before tendering it at Versailles. Wilson remained at his house in Eaton Place all day waiting for a summons. Esher called on him that evening, and found that he had no wish to become CIGS at the War Office where he would be ostracised as an intriguer. He preferred to remain at Versailles where, indeed, his talents for strategical planning and the organisation of 'war games' had been conspicuously to the fore. Robertson was refusing to go there, and as Esher observed: 'Until the Order in Council is revoked, only Robertson can order Robertson to take up the appointment.'

On Tuesday the government were preoccupied with the coming debate that evening. Esher observed how the War Cabinet took the whole previous day discussing a proposal to seize the machinery of the *Morning Post* and decided to do so at 6-30 p.m. Then they were informed by the Home Secretary, Sir G. Cave, that they would be beaten in the Commons on this action, and they decided at 8 p.m. not to take it.[84] Margot Asquith was acting 'as a protagonist of the attacks on Lloyd George'. 'She spends the whole day at the telephone, but her husband is not backing her.'[85] The mood of the House did not appear sympathetic when Lloyd George declined any information on the Versailles agreement on the ground that it would be informing the enemy. Nothing was said, either, about the long-expected change in the high command, for nothing had been agreed. Milner went to see Wilson that evening at 10 p.m. and confessed that the whole plan was in a mess and that Derby proposed now to retain Robertson, perhaps with curtailed powers, that Curzon was backing him and Bonar Law was 'washy', and that 'if Lloyd George does not catch hold he will be out'.[86]

The Unionists in the cabinet were seemingly apprehensive about a possible conjunction in the Commons of Asquithians and Robertsonian Unionists. The myth of Repington's 'treason' offered Lloyd George his only way out of his predicament. He appeared to be seedy and retired after the debate to his sick bed. Esher was not among those who wished to see Asquith back in office and he was a supporter of the Versailles Council and of Wilson rather than Robertson, yet he was constrained to criticise Lloyd George's weak showing:

Esher-Haig, 13 February 1918:[87] It seems that Lloyd George was much below par last night. He is said to be ill, and he is certainly not exhibiting his usual vigour of mind. Either he desires the contemplated changes or he does not. His actions show indecision...

There is much talk of a Lansdowne-Asquith combine—the former to be Prime Minister—a sort of camouflage for a peace government. Unless Lloyd George is galvanised into life again he may speedily fall. There is unrest and discontent and a widespread feeling that the war objectives are not ours but those of our allies...

For another two days while Lloyd George lay in an upstairs room in Downing Street the cabinet played out its schism with Balfour in the key position as the man who might bring together Lansdowne and Asquith.

On Wednesday morning Wilson called on Lord Derby at Derby House and offered, since Robertson still had his way about not going to Versailles, to agree to becoming CIGS in his place so that he could then be ordered to Versailles. Derby wanted to introduce Wilson on the Army Council and take away Robertson's superior position. In the afternoon Milner drafted a formula by which Wilson became Deputy CIGS and Lloyd George favoured that kind of settlement. But Wilson would not admit that Versailles could be under the CIGS and Robertson insisted that it should.

To complete the confusion at 3-15 p.m. Stamfordham arrived at Downing Street to remonstrate about Lloyd George's failure to inform the King of the appointment of Wilson as CIGS which the cabinet had agreed to but which had been thrown again into the melting pot by the turmoil of Monday and Tuesday. It was indeed a 'mess'. Stamfordham expressed the King's 'surprise to learn from the minutes of the cabinet (received that morning) that Sir W. Robertson was no longer CIGS...' Lloyd George explained that he had asked Derby to 'tell the King everything' and to show the King a copy of the new 'conditions' proposed for the posts of CIGS and Military Member at Versailles. Lord Derby surely had the document when he went to see the King the day before?

Memorandum by Stamfordham, 13 February 1918:[88] The Prime

Minister said that Robertson had been offered either Paris or to remain as CIGS. He declined either and wished to dictate to everyone...Robertson had displayed no capacity as a strategist...

I pointed out that Robertson was only asking to be in a position similar to that of General Foch, who is both CGS and member of the Executive Committee...The Prime Minister replied that there is no analogy, for Foch is on the spot in Paris... [and] it would be necessary to give orders to the Reserves at a moment's notice in cases of emergency...

Stamfordham then proceeded to Buckingham Palace and invited Derby and Robertson to come to his room and thrash out the question 'from all sides'. Derby thought Robertson 'unreasonable in his demands' and 'swollen-headed', yet he said he would have to resign with him, if he went, and so would Curzon. If on the other hand Robertson got his way, Milner and Mr Barnes would resign. Impressed by the danger of the government being brought down, Stamfordham begged Robertson 'in the King's name not to relinquish his post as CIGS, but to record his disapproval of the system, his belief that it was unworkable and might even cost us the war'. Robertson said he would think it over, and go with Derby to breakfast with Lloyd George next morning.

Robertson did not appear at the breakfast, in spite of an early morning note of encouragement from Stamfordham. But he was examined by the cabinet in the drawing room of No. 10, Lloyd George remaining in bed. At this critical interview Balfour and Curzon changed their minds. Balfour told Stamfordham that Robertson 'did not impress them', and 'revealed an evident personal dislike of Sir Henry Wilson, who would have been nominated to whichever of the two posts Sir W. Robertson refused'. The cabinet thereupon decided to reduce the post of CIGS to its former powers and to make the Versailles Member also a member of the Army Council. Balfour was deputed to offer Robertson a choice on these terms that afternoon. He failed to induce Robertson to accept either position, and reported that his objections were 'exaggerated'. Robertson insisted that only one man could give orders to the army, while under the new plan there would be two, but:

Memorandum by Stamfordham, 14 February 1918:[89] Mr Balfour would not accept this, and said that the orders would be given by the Executive Committee acting in the position of a generalissimo, that this plan had been decided upon by the Allied governments in Paris the previous week...and that the orders given by the British member to the British C-in-C were not *his* orders but those of the Committee...

Mr Balfour urged in the same way as the Prime Minister that it was impossible for the same man to be in London and theoretically at Versailles...his opinion could not be as sound and well-informed as it would be in one who day after day sat in company with the representatives of the other Allies...

Confronted with Balfour and Curzon's unfavourable verdict, Robertson tendered his resignation to Derby, who wired at 9 p.m. to General Plumer—the one general that Lloyd George approved in Haig's staff—offering him the post of CIGS. But by next evening Plumer had refused.[90]

Robertson was willing to go to Versailles if Plumer were CIGS and Derby had tried to save him. But Hankey, with Esher's encouragement, took a tough line, and wanted Lloyd George to send Robertson to India! 'His reason,' Esher noted, 'is that the incompatibility of temper between the two men and the ever-recurring quarrels depreciate L.G.'s vitality and governing power. Henry [Wilson]'s interests, personal and military, are at Versailles—if his position is regularised and defined.'[91] On Friday the 15th Hankey lunched with Asquith and Esher lunched with Lansdowne. The latter was more illuminating about their supposed combination, for Esher was able to inform Hankey that 'Lansdowne and Asquith have agreed that Lloyd George must be kept in office'.[92] Lansdowne 'sees clearly enough that there is no advantage in destroying the government, as there is no obvious successor.'[93] This reassuring news was conveyed to Lloyd George at Walton Heath that evening together with the not unwelcome news of Plumer's refusal, and Hankey, Milner and Bonar Law went down to join Lloyd George for a council of war after dinner. Lloyd George was now back in 'real fighting trim' and was free to offer Milner the War Office and Wilson the position of CIGS on the presumption that Robertson and Derby would have to resign.[94]

On Saturday Esher put in a 'Rip Van Winkle' appearance at Buckingham Palace where he made clear his view that Robertson 'having been inflated by the press into a demi-god, thinks his pre-rogatives are those of Napoleon'.[95] Robertson's resignation was now accepted and Haig had arrived to confer about Wilson's successor at Versailles. Yet when Esher phoned Wilson he had not been in-formed by Derby: not knowing whether he was CIGS he had gone down to Victoria to buy an evening paper to find out. Haig's appear-ance was in Esher's opinion regrettable, and had the strange con-sequence of keeping Derby in office. Everyone wanted Derby to go, but he lived up to his reputation for inducing others to resign while staying on at the last moment himself. After the King had told him his position was untenable he remained in deference to Haig's polite wishes.

The post at Versailles was filled at Haig's suggestion by Rawlinson, the man who in Lloyd George's view had a war career of continuous failure and continuous promotion. 'Rawly' was by habit too amenable to Haig's authority to exercise much independent in-fluence, and soon fell in with Haig's intention to send only two divi-sions to the General Reserve. Esher's support for Versailles rested on far wider considerations than military direction. He thoroughly approved of Milner as the British Minister at Versailles and hoped that in conjunction with a strong ambassador the Allied Council would develop decided peace policies. 'I am not sure whether Rawly will understand the wideness of the scope there is at Versailles for preparatory work,' he wrote to Wilson's secretary, Duncannon: 'That place *is* the nucleus of the only "League of Nations" the world is ever likely to see. But then, in order to appreciate the potential evolution of Versailles, the Irish imagination is required, or the Gaelic tem-peramental splash of colour, and I see neither in Rawly.'[96]

The importance of Versailles for Esher lay in its function of bring-ing peace objectives and inter-allied tensions into the open, which otherwise would remain in the hands of diplomats—and British diplo-mats were no match for the French or Italians. 'I entirely disapprove of the Foreign Office having committees to consider peace problems,' he adds. 'It is an office entirely out of touch with modern sentiment and modern ideas. It is perpetuating the mischievous aroma of secret diplomacy and discredited methods...the new wine requires new bottles.'[97] The new wine had a Bolshevist flavour or, equally alarming to Esher, it was tainted with the idealism of President Woodrow Wilson's entourage. He therefore pressed Hankey to set up a peace committee of men like Gilbert Murray, Jim Butler and Robert Smillie, the miners' leader, with diplomats to be employed only as 'witnesses', 'compilers of statistics' or 'geographers'.[98]

While Henry Wilson fiddled with War Office details the Versailles scheme seemed to be foundering. Was it after all merely a device to achieve the 'outing of Wully'?[99] Foch seemed impotent in the face of Haig's and Pétain's joint refusal to co-operate over the formation of the General Reserve, and Clemenceau was no more disposed to support his authority than Lloyd George. Esher who remained on the best of terms with Henry Wilson remonstrated in Wilson's own esoteric style:

Esher-Henry Wilson, 12 March 1918:[100] What has happened between Rawly and Foch? Make the Lord tell me, if it can be told. I hear rumours. But Versailles *must* develop on your old lines, hard as the task may be under inferior guidance. Otherwise the country and many reputations will suffer, because the ungodly will laugh! Ask Hankey for some notes I sent him on Versailles. *You* of all people cannot allow that infant to die of atrophy. It is your own child and the ridicule would be damaging.

The way out is to force Derby to go to Paris. The Milner project ended when you came to London. This is a very serious matter, and the sooner you get Derby out here and Milner at the War Office the better. Austen [Chamberlain] I assume is out of the running, as he seems to be the alternative Prime Minister, if by some mischance Lloyd George were to be killed by a golf-ball.

Wilson explained that Haig would resign if made to give up divisions, and that Clemenceau and Pétain were backing him. Lloyd George, to do him justice, was siding with Wilson and Foch in the interests of Versailles.

Haig was filling his extension of line towards Barisis with his reserves but even so Gough's Fifth army of fourteen divisions remained relatively weak, especially since the marshy valley of the Oise had not been thoroughly entrenched by the French. By an agreement between Haig and Pétain of February each would assist whoever was attacked by taking over line from the junction of the armies, and indeed the possibility of a German attack near the junction was viewed as one which would give the allies an advantage, for

then both French and British could become more speedily engaged
without serious logistical problems. Repington had noticed as early as
7 February the appearance of von Hutier's seventh army from Riga on
Gough's front. Von Hutier was a specialist at funnelling overwhelming masses of men on to one small sector, and as Repington observed,
the importance of Hutier's appearance 'needs no demonstration'.
Later, Gough told Repington that Pétain had been sure that Hutier's
appearance meant that Gough would be attacked, and Gough himself
had been aware of the probability for a month before the great
German onslaught of 21 March. Versailles, which had special telephone connexions with the army headquarters and accumulated every
scrap of military data from them, did not however succeed in persuading Haig to dispose his reserve divisions nearer the centre. They
were scattered mostly in the north.[101]

The story of the German onslaught on Gough's Fifth army which
was infiltrated in the mists and overwhelmed by superiority of numbers and perfection of organisation is a saga in itself. One of its morals
is that while Gough decided in accordance with his instructions to
fall back, the arrangements for reinforcing him were quite inadequate.
On the second day of the battle Haig found time to write to Esher and
had not yet foreseen a *débâcle*:

Haig-Esher, 22 March 1918:[102] And what a battle we had yesterday. It is now mid-day and all reports so far are to the effect that
the situation is the same as last night, so it is permissible to
assume that at least we have upset the Boche's plans, because all
his teaching is to go right ahead without pause or check. The
enemy's losses yesterday were large. At least thirty-seven divisions were launched against us, and of these twenty-eight were
quite fresh. Our men fought magnificently and are reported to be
in grand spirits, machine gunners, infantry and artillery all say
they never dreamed of getting such targets as they fired upon in
yesterday's battle...but we must expect the attacks to be renewed.

But two days later the situation was regarded as so grave in London
that Henry Wilson, supported by Churchill and Milner, demanded a
levée en masse, to be extended also to Ireland. By 25 March Haig
was contemplating a retirement to the Channel ports.[103] This idea was
scotched at the Doullens Conference the next day, when Foch was

given overall authority but without the power of command. Wilson blamed Haig for the lack of any effective General Reserve, but on the other hand he still expected a German attack in Italy and had not, as Haig had wanted, brought reserve divisions back which had been sent there after Caporetto. After a week of frantic activity behind the front Foch, looking like an 'old ashtray', felt he had got things under control. 'We are just, and only just, going to save the situation,' Henry Wilson wrote to Esher: 'Our Versailles war game was dreadfully prophetic.' Next day he added:

Henry Wilson-Esher, 31 March 1918:[104] Well, we *would* gamble, and now we are going to get a full value in excitement—and in downright fear. The two glaring, and to me inexcusable, mistakes are these:
1. The cabinets of all shades have refused to face the facts, and therefore have refused to get every possible man.
2. The troops we had, British and French, were very badly placed.
The first mistake was due to lack of pluck and statesmanship, the second was due to inferior generalship and lack of imagination...
The numbers of divisions, guns and aeroplanes along the British and French front on March 21 were sufficient—if properly handled (please remember our Versailles games and prophecy)—to beat back any Boche attack, or alternatively the statesmen could have given the soldiers so many men that numbers would have balanced inferior generalship...

There were obviously recriminations ahead. Gough was suspended and replaced by Rawly, but not at Haig's instigation, who thought he had 'a very big front entirely without defensive works, recently taken over from the French'. After travelling with Lloyd George in a car Haig judged he had been 'thoroughly frightened', and expected to be attacked in the Commons over withdrawing divisions. He was 'looking for a scapegoat for the retreat of the Fifth army' and seemed 'much down on Gough'. Haig was contemptuous of this kind of shuffling and regarded Lloyd George as a 'cur'.[105]

Gough on his return to England was quickly involved in the feud between soldiers and politicians. He was vindicated by Repington, and got into close touch with Leo Maxse. He regarded the criticism of himself and the Fifth army as politically inspired, aided by the 'petty jealousy of all the other army staffs in France'.[106] He pressed for an inquiry, approaching Esher among others, but Esher's advice was firmly against. 'In your place I should be as silent as the grave' he replied: 'No correspondence with any official, and not a word in public...you never forfeited the confidence of D. H[aig] or of anyone who understands the nature of war and your character...in the long run your fame will shine brightly enough, never fear.'[107] Gough however felt he had a mission not only to exculpate himself and his troops but also to expose the government's propaganda system which he thought stifled the soldiers' comments while subjecting them to an intolerable régime of denigration and gossip. He certainly had a point when he complained of the 'immense strain put on officers in war', who in addition to their military preoccupations had 'the worries and extra work incident on constantly defending themselves against their own government'. Haig was fighting the great battle in the weekly expectation of being dismissed as a scapegoat. Gough was particularly bitter against Lloyd George:

Hubert Gough-L. Maxse, 31 May 1918:[108] The government and their Press have lately taken up the cry: 'Let us alone', 'Don't harass us', 'No sniping', etc...

Ever since Lloyd George came into power he has harassed the Army Command, he has not let it alone, he has constantly and severely sniped it, using *every* means open, by intrigue and gossip and lies in London drawing rooms and through his vile press.

Maxse who was the soul and embodiment of patriotic sentiment could not understand how Northcliffe who had formerly been so staunch in support of the 'westerners' and the soldiers against the politicians had seemingly succumbed to Lloyd George's blandishments:

Maxse-Northcliffe, 13 April 1918:[109] What I have been deeply concerned about as a friend of yours is that you should have been so intimately identified with the Lloyd George government, backing it up in every single particular and treating the War Cabinet as a sort of God Almighty, whereas it contains as all the world

391

knows four or five of the biggest b—— f——'s in the country.
I feared this would happen from the moment you took charge
of the American mission, which was Lloyd George's only object
in offering it to you...

An independent Press in this country would have been even
more useful...I don't like seeing you involved in Beaverbrookism.

Northcliffe replied in a somewhat paranoiac vein: 'Whom do you suggest that I should support? *Name them...*' Oddly enough it was extremely difficult to think of 'a decent premiership instead of the present charlatanry', and Maxse could only suggest the feeble example
of Robertson. Northcliffe, or 'Beavercliffe' as he facetiously signed
himself, scored an easy win, but promised: 'When I find a dictator
who is not afraid of the politicians, I shall support him.'[110]
Esher despised Northcliffe, whom he had met once or twice. 'His
conceit is only equalled by his ignorance,' he comments about this
time.[111] But like Northcliffe Esher now supported Lloyd George in
spite of all his faults as the only leader who could keep the country
fighting in the face of disruptive influences. 'At such a moment as
this' he wrote to Milner on 13 April, 'all men's duty is plain, and it is
to back the Prime Minister for all we are worth.' Later, shortly before
the 'Maurice debate' which represented an ill-contrived attempt to defeat Lloyd George, Esher explained to Haig his rather ambivalent
reasons for supporting Lloyd George's dictatorship:

Esher-Haig, 29 April 1918:[112] After nearly four years of war,
we find ourselves nearer to internal disruption than our enemy...
'Self-determination' turns out to be a boomerang, and Lloyd
George and other demagogues, Asquith, Massingham and Co,
are all faced with a form of rebellion in Ireland that is really
Bolshevism in a green dress. If Clemenceau had to deal with this
Irish problem he would shoot both Dillon and Carson, and would
make short work of the Irish bishops...

What cannot simple 'unclever' statesmanship—such as that of
old C[ampbell]-B[annerman] in South Africa—accomplish? On
the other hand, the too-clever-by-half fellows, whether you
call them Canning or Lloyd George, land their dupes in disaster.
When the world looks back on this war, its tragedies and
comedies, they will see 'discipline' triumphant...

Indiscipline is a contagious disease. Old Wully refuses to take 'orders' in a crisis of his country's fate. Trenchard and Henderson likewise...Democracy means government by cads like North-cliffe and Rothermere. But patriotism means that gentlemen obey the cads rather than set an example of disobedience...Since the Somme battle these old gentlemen have been undoing the work of the youth of England under your command...If the Boche fails to drive you into the sea, our rulers will get another chance of making a peace of Utrecht...

Demagogy had in Esher's view created the Irish imbroglio which was distracting the country's attention from the war, while it had also thrown away chances of making a realistic peace, or would lose them in pursuit of Wilsonian idealism.

So far as Esher and Haig were concerned, the chief charge against Lloyd George was that he stopped the offensive in France and weakened Haig's offensive power by starving his ranks of 'effectives'. Although he had not supported so blatantly at Versailles the policy of waiting on America enunciated by Clemenceau, he had in effect ordained a passive-defensive policy on the western front for 1918 which his critics were now emphasising as the cause of defeat and perhaps even greater losses than an offensive policy might have incurred. Lloyd George was now trying to disguise the run-down of actual combatant troops by statements in the Commons which confused combatants with labour battalions and other support troops, which inadvertently or by a pious fraud added the British troops in Italy to the figure for Haig's army, and which juggled with figures from the DMO's and the AG's departments.[113] One may argue that Haig's army was larger in total strength in 1918 than ever before, and stronger through the addition of more specialised units, more artillery, aeroplanes, tanks, poison gas specialists, etc., but without doubt the formula of 'every available man' had been departed from, as may be seen from the numbers sent to France after the German break-through. But the DMO, General Maurice, confused military policy with politics and his exposure of the official figures, for which he was dismissed, was used for a purely political manoeuvre against Lloyd George at a very inopportune moment for the opposition. Lloyd George was attempting to apply conscription to Ireland and also pass a Home Rule Bill, each measure having the effect of pleasing and displeasing Liberals and Unionists alike. It was not the moment to attempt a new alignment of parties. But Lloyd George personally was in an extremely difficult position:

Esher-Henry Wilson, 1 May 1918:[114] The weak spot is the instability of the government. If Lloyd George falls, in consequence of his handling of Ireland, what is the alternative? Gwynne and Co are doing all they can to shake down Lloyd George. The Harmsworths have become lukewarm...Northcliffe is in high dudgeon, and both he and his brother are *frightened*. Over Trenchard the ship rocked heavily. Far more so than over Wully! There is nothing to fear so long as Asquith shrinks from office, but his last speech was menacing in tone...

What Esher was really concerned for was leadership strong enough to achieve 'a non-German peace...even though Great Britain stands alone in Europe' (that was supposing France to collapse) and 'a federal Commonwealth—*after the war*—in which Ireland takes an integral share'.[115] These aims might be attained by Lloyd George, but not in Esher's opinion by Asquith. Hence in the Maurice affair in which Esher might fairly have taken a revengeful part against Lloyd George—as might many others—he was content to stand apart. But he had his say writing to Hankey who would doubtless convey his view to the Prime Minister:

Esher-Hankey, 9 May 1918:[116] Maurice is an ass...It is inconceivable that the House of Commons should at this juncture swop horses...I am sure that given all his faults, Lloyd George can carry on with greater advantage to the country than the anaemic Asquith. That parliamentary statements of a *very* misleading kind have been made—especially Geddes's speech—is beyond question...

Certainly Lloyd George makes a great error in 'bouncing' as he does...These flowers of rhetorical optimism...nearly always followed by military reverses, have a disastrous effect on the little man's reputation. You can show him this if you like. It will do him good...

Esher had in fact lost interest in the direction of the war. He had every confidence in Versailles and Haig, Wilson and Lloyd George, Milner who was now at the War Office, and Derby who had gone to the Paris embassy to replace Bertie, now an invalid confined to a room in the Crillon. The American divisions were beginning to become operative, though they would not in spite of urgent measures become effective for some months. As the great German offensive gradually spent its force, the policy of waiting for the USA was seen to have just, but only just, proved feasible. Now Esher's great preoccupation was with peace objectives. He rejected Lloyd George's nebulous idea of 'victory' and Woodrow Wilson's 'war to end all wars' and was searching for the roots of a viable and well grounded settlement. Already he was obsessed with the idea that the peace might be lost.

Conclusion

Esher's decision to relinquish his unofficial position in Paris and return home seemed the natural thing in January 1918. In matters of inter-allied liaison and politico-military strategy the 'centre of gravity' had 'shifted to Versailles' where Henry Wilson seemed well able to look after British interests. Lord Milner, in whom Esher had every confidence as a guardian of imperial interests, looked like becoming a frequent visitor to Paris and Versailles. The men who had hitherto been entrusted with British military affairs in Paris were now stranded. General Maurice, the only British soldier in Paris at the beginning of the war who had ever since been treated by the French as the representative of the BEF, was now supplanted by a new Commandant of the Paris area. Le Roy-Lewis was cut down to the scale of an ordinary military attaché, which Esher regarded as a waste of his talents. He ought, as Esher suggested to Hankey, to be placed in charge of the propaganda to Europe, which was being mismanaged. The 'arrogance of the Boche' in the Brest-Litovsk treaty had amply appeared in the neutral press but had been strangely wanting in coverage by the British propaganda service under John Buchan. While Le Roy-Lewis knew European affairs and personalities well, Buchan knew practically nothing about them. The Paris embassy seemed also to have been abandoned, for the only person proposed as a replacement for the ailing Bertie was Lord Crewe, a suggestion which wrung from Esher the despairing comment: 'One paralytic follows another'. In these somewhat depressing circumstances Esher wound up his office, placed his private secretary Lawrence Burgis in Hankey's cabinet secretariat, and left Paris.

It was extremely unfortunate that shortly after Esher's departure from France the promising arrangement at Versailles fell victim to Lloyd George's political necessities. Henry Wilson ended up as CIGS in London with the political nonentity General Rawlinson in the key position at Versailles. When in April the amiable but ineffectual

Lord Derby arrived in Paris as ambassador the catastrophe was complete. Esher did his best to introduce Derby to the men behind the scenes in Paris who, as he had so often tried to convince Lloyd George, were the men who really mattered. If they could not be influenced at least they would provide better insights into the currents beneath the deceptive surface of French coalition politics than could be gathered from official sources. In their conception of peace objectives Britain and France were poles apart. The British plan for a European settlement adhered to the time-honoured principles of national self-determination, the economic viability of states, and the balance of power. Although the agreement with Italy of April 1915 had driven a coach-and-four through these principles by conceding to Italy the whole of Istria, a strip of the Dalmatian coast with most of the islands, and other areas with populations that were predominantly Slav, Turkish or Greek, the Foreign Office remained hopeful that there would be no enforced transfers of sovereignty. It hoped for a 'satisfactory settlement by direct friendly negotiation'.[1] The French on the other hand did not envisage a European settlement along the familiar lines preserving something like the *status quo*. By a treaty with Russia of March 1917 they granted the Russians a free hand in Poland in exchange for Alsace-Lorraine and the Saar valley and an independent Rhineland garrisoned by a French army. While the French adhered to their plans for the dismemberment of Germany and the imposition of a huge war indemnity the British government failed to evolve any official policy and was carried to and fro by the currents of public opinion.

It seemed to Esher that the ignorance and insularity of the British were being exploited by the French government and especially by the Quai d'Orsay. He always believed that the war could have been concluded in 1917 on terms no less favourable than those imposed later, though not so favourable as the French wished. Through von Lancken, the confidential agent of the Kaiser, and with the knowledge of King Albert of Belgium, the Germans in 1917 offered terms which included the restoration and indemnifying of Belgium, the withdrawal of their armies from France and the cession of Alsace-Lorraine, and concessions to Italy in the Trentino, but no proper account of this important overture reached London. The details of this affair were recounted to Esher when we lunched with Briand and Bunau-Varilla on 29 October, 1917.[2] Briand, it appeared, had given M. Ribot a long

statement in writing so that 'the whole matter should be put before
the allies, and especially Lloyd George'. Ribot merely sent a telegram
to London, drafted by Jules Cambon, 'in such a form as to preclude
any chance of the offer being considered by the English government
or any other as serious.'[3] The French meanwhile stipulated that the
German armies should retire behind their frontiers before the *pourparlers* were deemed official. The Germans as might be expected declined to negotiate on such terms. Their final refusal arrived on 24
September, and two days later the Austro-Swiss frontier was closed
and the concentration of troops for the attack on Italy began. Briand
was even threatened by innuendoes about having communications
with the enemy, and was obliged to give some account of the affair at
a secret session of the Chamber. There the reaction was so hostile to
Ribot that the fall of his government became inevitable and followed
in a few days.

Peace in 1917 would have been at the expense of Poland and
Russia, but when the Russians virtually opted out of the war it
seemed hardly feasible that the western allies should continue to
fight for some major restoration in the east. Douglas Haig certainly
did not think so, and one may surmise that his views were not much
different from those of Esher, whom he asked to support 'a more
definite and vigorous diplomacy' on returning to England:

Haig-Esher, 22 January 1918:[4] For instance: 1. Definitely
develop Austria as a counterpoise to Germany.
2. Encourage the latter to exhaust herself in northern Russia...
3. Guarantee the Turk possession of Constantinople and the
Straits, so as to prevent Bulgaria and so Germany from proceeding by that route to the East.
Our aim should be an Anglo-Saxon alliance and sea power!
Germany must be allowed to expand somewhere. Guide her into
Russia—and get her frost-bitten as much as possible *en route*.

The notion that Germany should be preserved as a bulwark against
Bolshevism was all the more acceptable in England to those who be-
lieved in the 'special relationship' with the USA and in sea sup-
remacy. But did Lloyd George, with his susceptibility to Albert
Thomas, leader of the French socialists, and his dependence upon
Lord Northcliffe?[5]

To Esher Lloyd George still appeared as an ignorant and dangerous demagogue who by his compact with Northcliffe wielded the terror of newspaper blackmail over the 'classes', and who corrupted politics by the improper distribution of offices and honours. Esher was particularly outraged by the way the King was being degraded in the process. Lloyd George had showered honours on 'all sorts of wretched people who have paid money' and Esher feared 'the King's weakness in accepting such deplorable advice will do him harm'.[6] The Prime Minister had even obtruded Sir Alfred Mond on the King as Secretary of the Office of Works, which Esher thought 'a strong order'. The King was offended, and indeed 'resented it', but did not make any objection. Rosebery had likewise been scandalised at being offered the Privy Seal without a seat in the cabinet by Lloyd George, and was too humiliated by the incident to mention it to anyone.[7] When Lloyd George appeared to be responding favourably to President Woodrow Wilson's mephitic idealism, which seemed to Esher to imply the liberation of racial minorities not only in Austro-Hungary but in India, Egypt and in all colonies, Esher wondered what had happened to the classes who had formerly supported the empire. 'They allow themselves to be eclipsed,' he decided. 'They make no show of loyalty to the institutions they should support for all they are worth. They drift aimlessly about at the bidding of anonymous writers in a corrupt press.'[8] 'The decay of Parliament, the *anonymous* press, taking the place of free and open discussion, and corruption consequential thereto, are responsible for whatever the outcome of the war may be for the British Empire.'[9] Northcliffe the 'king-maker' and other press barons were in the government, and Esher made no secret of his desire to see his head in the basket. He thought the King should 'make a final stand against Northcliffe and all the gang by refusing to retain as a minister any man who owns a newspaper'.[10] Lord Stamfordham agreed that it was 'all wrong' but dug up some saying of Lord Liverpool's to the effect that any such exclusion 'lowered the Crown and exalted the individual'.[11]

Even before the extraordinary speech which Lloyd George made, on the day after the Armistice, announcing his decision to hold an election in which the issue would be between those who stood for national rivalries and competitive armaments, and those who sought to initiate 'the reign on earth of the Prince of Peace', Esher began to oppose a Peace Congress. He did not believe that President Wilson would actually appear in Europe—that would be like Buddha walking up the War Office steps in a frock coat. He thought the personal confrontation of heads of state in another Congress of Vienna would have fatal results, and any League of Peace would be merely another Holy Alliance in a new garb. He tried to convince Henry Wilson and Hankey that a 'permanent and sound peace' could only be achieved by separate negotiations and separate agreements between the Powers concerned. He feared that in a Peace Congress: 'The idealism of Wilson and the materialism of Clemenceau will strike a bargain.' The French knew what they wanted. The British were distracted by such trivialities as whether the Kaiser should be hanged, and deeply divided over fundamentals such as whether there should be a punitive settlement with Germany, and whether massive indemnities were desirable or possible. The armistice and the political whirlwind of the 'coupon' election in which parties and issues were wildly confused produced a House of Commons hardly equipped either by mandate or by the wisdom of experience to lay down the conditions of peace. Lloyd George was himself swept off his feet. His public pronouncements became wild and inconsistent.

If Lloyd George believed that the last war had been concluded, Esher certainly did not. He thought if Italy and France could be satisfied 'we might have peace for a generation, provided we do not attempt to crush the soul of eighty millions of German people'.[12] Germany had surrendered on the basis of the Fourteen Points of President Wilson, and there was a case, supported by the British Labour movement, for the admission of the new German and Austrian democracies into the League of Nations. They were excluded, with the Soviet Union and many neutral states, while the Big Five—the victorious allies—dominated the Council of the League and confused their role as guardians of the peace with their role as the beneficiaries of a punitive treaty. The whole procedure by which the Covenant and the Peace Treaty were evolved was chaotic, a French effort to provide some systematic plan of proceedings having been brushed aside. It seemed to Esher at the time that 'intrigue, and the grouping of powers according to their pure material interests' had supplanted the original Wilsonian formula, which then made highly questionable the method of an imposed peace by one assembly. But to do the peacemakers justice, as they worked feverishly drawing innumerable new frontier lines from very imperfect information they did not know whether the

400

settlement they were completing was to be a negotiated or an imposed one, one that was permanent or merely provisional. Not least of the objections against the way in which the peace was made was the self-sufficiency and secrecy of the diplomats—the peace was an arbitrary covenant, secretly arrived at. The hostile reaction of the Labour movement both to the Covenant and to the Treaty boded ill, and this current of feeling may partly explain Lloyd George's eleventh hour attempt to mitigate the Treaty in Germany's favour. In its final form it was condemned by Beatrice Webb as 'a hard and brutal peace... Germany has gained little or nothing from her abandonment of autocracy and militarism; and Wilson's Fourteen Points, upon which Germany surrendered, have been, in the spirit and in the letter, repudiated.'[13]

Esher's verdict on the proceedings in Paris was even more damning. 'The Paris Conference,' he noted in June 1919, 'has at any rate succeeded in this, that a future war upon an even bigger scale becomes inevitable. It is something to have dispelled all doubts upon that point...not exactly what Wilson set out to do.'[14] It had been caustically remarked by Clemenceau, before Wilson appeared in Paris, that 'God was satisfied with Ten Commandments. Wilson gives us fourteen.' As his popularity in France evaporated and the optimism and goodwill with which the diplomats and heads of state had first viewed his proposals disappeared, Wilson's compromises became more sweeping. The result was that, in Esher's view, not one of the Fourteen Points was 'translated into the faintest semblance of actuality'. At the same time the idealistic haze which had blinded the war-weary populations of Europe and compelled statesmen to bow before the plausible formulations of President Wilson ensured that the normal processes of diplomacy were frustrated. Wilson had, in Esher's view, 'ruined the Peace and the hopes of Europe'.[15]

But the world in its mental, historical and political aspects with which Esher had been familiar was being rapidly transformed by the forces released by the world war. The generation which was conditioned to view international rivalries in terms of race and nationality, and world changes in terms of the dominance of Europe and competition for empire, was losing its hold on affairs. The classes who had sustained the older political ideals and conventions, conceding primacy to the patricians, cheerfully accepting the preponderance of the 'upper tenth' in Parliament, church, army and civil service, were becoming a diminishing minority. If the older ideals, represented by the 'Cliveden set' or Round Table, and the various ideologists of empire loyalism still influential in the circles of politics and the press, were by no means dead, they were subtly and fundamentally transmuted. The Empire and the 'white man's burden', the Monarchy, and the Anglo-Saxon confraternity, as the Victorians had understood them, were verging on the unintelligible and faintly ridiculous, like outdated fashions. The older nationalism tended to disappear with the dynasts and 'classes' who had represented it, while the 'national socialism' of the Milnerites and their more rabid Continental variants, the 'fascisti' and brownshirts, was a new vintage traded under older labels.

As a septuagenarian in the twenties, Lord Esher was at last able to retire into something like leisure and detachment from public affairs. Occasionally he assumed some responsibility on the periphery of politics. He was associated with Haldane's attempt to reform the machinery of government, following his Report of 1918. The idea of creating a kind of 'Defence Committee' for domestic affairs was taken up by Ramsay MacDonald in 1924. The Labour party was particularly keen on some sound base of established data and approved principles on which to found their planning. But Mr Baldwin also favoured the idea and gave it a partial implementation in the Committee of Civil Research of 1925. This conducted fourteen major inquiries by 1929, when the Labour government set up what became known as the Economic Advisory Council with the existing Committee in a subordinate role. In this manner Esher and Haldane may be claimed as the originators of what was to become the Department of Economic Affairs. Meanwhile the cabinet secretariat, with Hankey still in command, remained the fertile seedbed for innovations in the structure of government. The 'Prime Minister's department', which Esher had persuaded Balfour to create in 1904 and which Lloyd George with Hankey's aid had broadened into a more general secretariat nominally serving the cabinet but in reality serving the Prime Minister, had by the 1920s emerged as a major constitutional innovation.

In 1922–3 Esher attended an international conference on disarmament, and headed the British delegation to the Temporary Mixed Commission of the League of Nations. He developed a scheme of his own, which he thought was moderate and realistic, but he withdrew it in favour of one by Lord Robert Cecil, who was one of the few whole-hearted champions of the League ideal. Esher did not seem to attach much importance to the affair, especially as to him disarmament was a palliative and not a panacea. As for the state of international relations, he thought: 'We are back in the Europe of the 1880's—minus Bismarck.'[16]

The democracies seemed to have succumbed to the facile rationalism of the optimists or the mechanical syllogisms of the socialists. No-one appreciated better than Esher that world politics had entered a new phase, hostile to the values of imperialists like Rosebery, Milner, and himself, and quick to distort their meaning. The primacy of Europe, the ascendancy of the ruling classes and dynasties, and the whole rationale of race, nationality and culture that the Victorians and Edwardians had constructed from their view of events and the more tendentious conclusions of their historians, biologists and anthropologists was now out of vogue. The emphasis on race gave place to an emphasis on class, respect for the historical provenance of things yielded to open-minded empiricism and an insistence on economic and sociological explanations. The war itself, which for Esher represented the working out of dark natural and historical forces propelling even 'civilised' nations into rivalry and conflict, was now widely regarded as a crime perpetrated by the ruling classes. The rationalistic notion which had been popular after 1815 and became associated with Richard Cobden, that a democracy would never seek to fight a war, was now again current in the entourage of Lloyd George. It was implicit in the formulas of 'democracies *versus* autocracies' or 'a war to end all wars'. A generation which had been caught in a historical trap longed to escape from the constraints of a prescriptive destiny. But the conviction that history was 'bunk' and that by taking thought one could shake off its mental strait-jacket and dispense with landmarks and traditions seemed to Esher as dangerous and ensnaring as any of the rejected enthusiasms of the past age. That a new 'democratic' era had superseded the age of Liberalism and the 'imperialism' of the Liberals with whom Esher had associated himself, he was one of the first to proclaim. But he could not accept that the trends and impulses of the new age were better understood or better controlled than those of the times he had studied and wrestled with before the great catastrophe.

Notes

Chapter 1

1 By the Unionists in September 1903 and by the Liberals in December 1905.

2 *J & L,* 11 Oct. 1903.

3 Of Mill, Morley declared: 'He is the one living person for whom I have an absolutely unalloyed veneration and attachment, and of whose kindness I am most proud.'

4 Born 1817, second son of Rev. Joseph George Brett of Ranelagh, Chelsea. Called to bar, 1846; Q.C. 1860; MP for Helston, 1866–8; Solicitor-General, February 1868; Judge in Court of Common Pleas, August 1868; Lord Justice of Appeal and Privy Councillor, 1876; Master of the Rolls, 1882–97; Baron Esher, July 1885; Viscount Esher, November 1897. Died 1899.

5 *DNB.*

6 Born 1814, daughter of Louis Meyer, an Alsatian. Lived for a time with the Béjots of Nointel near Beaumont. Was introduced by the Gurwoods to the circle of the reputedly reclusive fourth marquess of Hertford in Paris, as well as to Parisian society at large.

7 From the day (in 1827) that the Count d'Orsay married Lord Blessington's fifteen-year-old daughter (by his first marriage) he was a social pariah. Society could tolerate an amusing *maison à trois* of d'Orsay with Lord and Lady Blessington, but not the cynical exploitation of a daughter for the malversation of an inheritance. Gore House, where d'Orsay and Lady Blessington settled after Lord Blessington's death in 1829 (and the dissolution of d'Orsay's contrived marriage) was shunned by polite society. But it became the resort of *emigrés*, authors, editors, actors and artists. 'No woman ever went there' according to Greville's *Diary* (17 Feb. 1839) 'except a few...connected with d'Orsay or Lady Blessington.'

8 Disraeli, *Coningsby*, Bk. 4, ch. 4.

9 Eugénie's comments on the post-1848 disruptions of the Paris season must have seemed gallingly *blasé* to the hard-working barrister Brett: 'Balls and parties go on, but things are worse every day. The day is coming when we shall be ruled by Reds!' (letter to Brett of Feb. 1850 quoted in Ward, *A Romance of the Nineteenth Century*, p. 265).

10 1823–92. Fellow of King's College and assistant master at Eton, 1845–72. Runner-up to Charles Kingsley for the chair of modern history at Cambridge in 1860. Took a leading part in introducing mathematics and natural science as studies at King's and ending the exclusiveness of the foundation.

11 James, *Rosebery*, p. 41.

12 Johnson considered Rosebery brilliant but indolent and passed his famous verdict on young Dalmeny when he was fifteen. In 1864, two years later, he accompanied his pupil on an Italian tour. He introduced him also to the study of Pitt, but according to legend Rosebery had already in his Eton days decided that he would marry an heiress, become Prime Minister, and win the Derby. He left Oxford rather than give up his stud of steeple-chases (Raymond, *Rosebery*, pp. 26–8).

13 Esher, *Ionicus*, pp. 219–20.

14 *Extracts from Letters and Journals of William Cory* (ed. F. Warre Cornish) p. 364: 'I am a Whig: I place some trust in written ordinances and institutions as affecting in the long run personal character...' Tories, in Johnson's view, did not believe that moral improvement could be achieved by reforms.

15 ibid., p. 350.

16 Esher, *Ionicus*. Johnson changed his name to Cory in 1872, at the time he gave up his positions at Eton and King's, in an odour of scandal. His numerous published letters and occasional pamphlets on Eton reform reveal him as a writer of delicate sensitivity and originality, and it is easy to see how his adulation of certain boys might be open to criticism or misconstruction. The public knew 'Cory' as one who composed Greek and Latin verse with consummate taste and skill. A. C. Benson went so far as to hail him as 'one of the most vigorous and commanding minds of the century'.

17 Esher, *Cloud-Capp'd Towers*, p. 37.

18 ibid., p. 51.
19 Esher, *Cloud-Capp'd Towers*, p. 50. Brett was a respected companion of the dons of Trinity, but his name does not appear on any tripos list. He matriculated in 1870, took his BA in 1874 and his MA in 1876. The historical tripos, reflecting his real interest, was instituted in 1875.
20 Gardiner, *Harcourt*, I, p. 291.
21 Hewett, *Strawberry Fair*, p. 233, describes these receptions as 'perhaps the most frequent and most frequented in fashionable life'. As a resort of political writers (Abraham Hayward, Henry Reeve, Smith of the *Quarterly*, Knowles of the *Contemporary*, and Sir Edward Strachey), Strawberry Hill had in the 1870's become the later counterpart of Gore House.
22 Esher, *Cloud-Capp'd Towers*, pp. 119–20. In spite of his criticism, Brett rarely missed a week-end there.
23 Gardiner, op. cit., I, p. 12.
24 Lady Waldegrave is said (Hewett, op. cit., p. 242) to have cultivated Hartington since his successful moving of a vote of no confidence which brought down the Derby government in 1859. At that time Hartington startled London society by his affair with 'Skittles', from whom he finally became estranged after a public scene in New York. It was after this that he began his long and equally public liaison with Louise, Comtesse d'Alten and Duchess of Manchester, whom he finally married in 1892. For Esher's impressions of 'the Duchess' see *Cloud-Capp'd Towers*, pp. 100–2.
25 *J & L*, 19 Feb. 1878.
26 *J & L*, 1 March 1904.
27 On 24 Sept. 1879 Brett married Eleanor Frances Weston, third daughter of Sylvain van de Weyer, who had died in 1874.
28 Paul H. Emden, *Behind the Throne*, p. 33.
29 *DNB*.
30 Emden, op. cit., p. 39.
31 Oliver Sylvain Baliol Brett, born 1881. Electioneered for Liberals in 1905–6. Private secretary to Morley, Secretary of State for India, 1905–10. 3rd Viscount Esher.
32 Maurice Vyner Baliol Brett, 1882–1934. ADC to Sir John French 1904–12. Lt Col. at the *Intelligence anglaise*, Paris, 1914–

16. Deputy Assistant Adjutant-General, 1916. Librarian, London Museum, 1919–34.

33 Lord Esher's collection was deposited at the British Museum by the terms of his will and is still under seal.

Chapter 2

1 Esher, *Cloud-Capp'd Towers*, p. 94.

2 ibid., p. 115.

3 When W. T. Stead assumed the editorial chair of the *Pall Mall Gazette* vacated by John Morley in 1883, with Milner as his lieutenant, Brett began to prompt Stead with Hartington's secrets, in the interests of a more vigorous imperial policy. Brett also tried to interest Rosebery in Milner, but seemingly without much success.

4 *J & L*, 5 Dec. 1878.

5 Gladstone, *Speeches in Scotland*. At Loanhead, 22 March 1880.

6 DP, Brett-Hartington, 13 Sept. 1879.

7 DP.

8 DP, Brett-Hartington, 15 Nov. 1879.

9 DP, Brett-Hartington, 2 Dec. 1879.

10 DP.

11 *J & L*, 4 Dec. 1879.

12 Esher, *Extracts from Journals, 1872–81*, II, p. 208 seq.

13 ibid., p. 212.

14 DP.

15 DP, Arnold-Hartington, 14 Dec. 1879.

16 DP, same letter.

17 Esher, *Extracts from Journals*, p. 215. Cf *J & L*, 20 Dec. 1879.

18 *J & L*, 7 April 1880.

19 DP, Brett-Hartington, 7 April 1880.

20 ibid.

21 *J & L*, 21 April 1880, wrongly given as 1st.

22 DP.

23 Eugène Leopold Selwyn Brett, born 1855: lieutenant in the Scots Guards; died on the return journey from Egypt on 8 Dec. 1882.

24 Gwynn and Tuckwell, *Dilke*, I, p. 267.

25 DP.

26 *J & L*, 29 Jan. 1884.

27 DP.

o

28 Holland, *Devonshire*, I, p. 411. Hartington-Granville, 23 Nov. 1883.

29 *Review of Reviews*, Jan. 1890.

30 *Review of Reviews*, 1912, p. 479. Esher's obituary of Stead, who had perished in the sinking of the liner *Titanic*.

31 *J & L*, 9 Feb. 1885. Brett's brother Eugène had accompanied Gordon to India in the entourage of the Viceroy, Lord Ripon, early in 1880, which may have been the occasion of Brett's first meeting Gordon.

32 Gordon's note of the interview of 18 Jan. 1884 (Holland, *Devonshire*, I, p. 418).

33 Hartington declared in the Commons on 15 Feb. 1884 '...we are not responsible for the rescue or relief of the garrisons'.

34 Elton, *Gordon*, pp. 305–6. The chaotic order of Gordon's telegrams and letters was preserved in the official blue books.

35 *J & L*, 29 Jan. 1884.

36 *J & L*, 16 Feb. 1884.

37 Holland, *Devonshire*, I, p. 428.

38 *J & L*, 16 Feb. 1884. Brett-Stead.

39 *J & L*, 19 Feb. 1884.

40 *J & L*, 1 April 1884. Brett-Hartington, quoting Gordon's letter of 3 March just received.

41 ibid. Gordon on reaching Khartoum ordered the official tax records to be burned and opened the gaols.

42 Ramm, *Correspondence of Gladstone and Granville 1876–86*, I, p. 161

43 *J & L*, 25 Feb. 1884.

44 *J & L*, n.d. but clearly early in March 1884.

45 *J & L*, Brett-Hartington, 1 April 1884.

46 ibid., same letter.

47 EP.

48 Gordon's idea seems to have been to 'hand over the negro provinces of Equatoria and Bahr-el-Ghazal, south of Khartoum, to the King of the Belgians, to be administered by Gordon himself after he had evacuated Khartoum, so that the supply of negro slaves could be cut off at its source' (note by Sir Gerald Graham, quoted in Elton, *Gordon*, p. 298). At some unspecified date in 1884 Stead went to Brussels and had a 'fierce discussion' with King Leopold. 'The King told me,' he recorded six years later,

'he was not unwilling to allow Gordon to carry out his scheme, if Mr Gladstone would give him the assurance that the provinces had ceased to belong to the Ottoman Empire.' Such an assurance would have implied British responsibility for Egypt, as Stead observed, and it was not forthcoming (*Review of Reviews*, Jan. 1890).

49 Holland, *Devonshire*, I, pp. 444–5.
50 EP.
51 ibid., same letter.
52 Ramm, op. cit., I, p. 193.
53 Gladstone in debate on motion of censure of 12–13 May, quoted in Holland, *Devonshire*, I, p. 456.
54 *J & L*, 28 May 1884.
55 EP, Brett-Stead, 9 June 1884.
56 *J & L*, 28 May 1884.
57 Ramm, op. cit., I, p. 193. Gladstone-Granville, 28 May 1884.
58 ibid., I, p. 194.
59 EP, Brett-Stead, 9 June 1884.
60 EP.
61 EP, Brett-Stead, 20 June 1884.
62 EP, Brett-Stead, 8 Nov. 1884.
63 Hugh Oakeley Arnold-Forster, 1855–1909. Son of William Delafield Arnold, director of public instruction in the Punjab. Matthew Arnold was his uncle. Accompanied W. E. Forster to Ireland in 1880 as private secretary, published anonymously in 1881 *The Truth about the Land League*. Became secretary of the Imperial Federation League in 1884 when W. E. Forster became its president. Later a Liberal Unionist and tariff reformer. Appointed chairman of the South African Land Commission by Joseph Chamberlain in 1900. Secretary of State for War, 1903–5.
64 Mary Arnold-Forster, *Arnold-Forster*, pp. 54–7.
65 ibid., 58–9 quoting Stead's narrative in *Review of Reviews*, July 1897.
66 *Pall Mall Gazette*, 29 Sept. 1884, p. 1.
67 EP.
68 *J & L*, 16 Oct. 1884.
69 *J & L*, early November 1884.
70 Gordon noted on 26 November: 'I will accept *nothing whatsoever* from Gladstone's government...I will get the King [Leopold]

to pay them [his expenses]. I will never set foot in England, but will (DV if I get out) go to Brussels and so on to the Congo (quoted in Elton, op. cit., p. 362).

71 *J & L*, 14 Nov. 1884.
72 *J & L*, 5 Feb. 1885.
73 *J & L*, loc. cit.
74 *J & L*, 11 Feb. 1885.
75 ibid., 15 April 1885.
76 ibid., 26 Feb. 1885. Lord Elton (op. cit. p. 370) describes the national response to Gordon's death: 'Gordon windows were dedicated in cathedrals and parish churches, Gordon clubs for boys sprang up in industrial towns...Pamphlets, books, and sermons on the soldier-saint poured from the press and pulpit. A national day of mourning was observed, a national subscription established the Gordon Boys' Homes...'
77 Esher, *Cloud Capp'd Towers*, pp. 125–6.
78 Esher, *Ionicus*, pp. 206–7.

Chapter 3
1 John Robert Seeley, 1834–95. Professor of modern history at Cambridge, 1869. His essay on *The Expansion of England* appeared in 1883.
2 *J & L*, 20 Sept. 1885.
3 *Pall Mall Gazette*, 29 July 1885.
4 ibid., 15 May 1885, reporting speech by Brett to his constituents at Falmouth.
5 Letter in *The Times*, 8 Aug. 1885.
6 *J & L*, Dec. 1885.
7 *J & L*, Brett-Hartington, 15 Dec. 1885.
8 *J & L*, 1 Feb. 1886.
9 *J & L*, Balfour-Brett, 4 Dec. 1885.
10 Letter in *The Times* of 2 Dec. 1885.
11 *J & L*, Oct. 1891.
12 Quoted in Lyons, *Ireland since the Famine*, p. 201.
13 Hurst, *Joseph Chamberlain and Liberal Re-union*, pp. 122–3.
14 Letter in *The Times*, 11 Jan. 1886.
15 Letter in *The Times*, 2 Dec. 1885.
16 Letter in *The Times*, 15 March 1886.
17 ibid.

18 Rosebery's comment, recorded in *J & L*, 24 Feb. 1886.

19 Milner later wrote of his association with Stead: 'We were both enthusiasts about the Race and the Empire. We were both shedding fast the old tradition of the *laissez-faire* school, and believed in the power and duty of the State to take vigorous action for the improvement of the conditions of life among the mass of the people' (*Review of Reviews* Jan.–June 1912, p. 478).

20 *J & L*, 22 Feb. 1889. Brett-Hartington relating the incident of 1886.

21 At Adelaide on 18 Jan. 1884.

22 Crewe, *Rosebery*, I, p. 219.

23 ibid., I, p. 279, 23 Dec. 1885. The idea that federal home rule, as opposed to an independent Irish state, would be conducive to the gradual federation of the self-governing countries of the empire was one shared by Stead and Cecil Rhodes, and most likely Brett also subscribed to it.

24 *J & L*, Brett-Hartington, 31 Dec. 1886.

25 DP, continuation of the same letter.

26 DP, loc. cit.

27 Brett-Chamberlain, 6 Jan. 1887, quoted in Hurst, op. cit., pp. 180–1.

28 *J & L*, 19 Feb. 1886.

29 'The Liberal Unionists and Coercion' in *Nineteenth Century*, April 1887.

30 Quoted in Michell, *Rhodes*, II, p. 47–8.

31 Sarah G. Millin, *Rhodes*, pp. 31–2, quoting from Rhodes's letters.

32 Rhodes quoted loc. cit., p. 128. Stead's imperial creed is set forth in a manifesto 'To all English Speaking Folk' which launched his *Review of Reviews* in Jan. 1890. This claims that the 'English-speaking man' already 'dominates the world' but laments the absence of any 'institution which even aspires to be to the English-speaking world what the Catholic Church in its prime was to the intelligence of Christendom'. It called for a 'fraternal union with the American Republic' and demanded that the Irish be 'compelled to manage their own affairs' in the hope that 'Home Rule will open the door by which all the Colonies may yet enter the pale of our Imperial Constitution'. Whether Rhodes inspired Stead, or Stead Rhodes, is difficult to determine on the existing evidence. The journalist H. W. Massingham thought that Stead 'invented' Rhodes, and that without Stead's

support Rhodes would have 'remained a local Colonial politician'. He credits Stead with the creation of the 'Cape-to-Cairo Imperialism' (*Review of Reviews*, 1912, p. 497).

33 *J & L*, 15 Feb. 1891. Brett was in general sympathy with Stead's ideals but not with Rhodes's methods.
34 *J & L*, 8 Jan. 1887.
35 *J & L*, 7 Nov. 1890.
36 ibid.
37 See esp. *J & L*, in March 1895.
38 For Rosebery's own narrative of this incident see Crewe, *Rosebery*, II, pp. 402–3.
39 Nevertheless the choice of Gladstone's successor by the Queen was attended with considerable drama and indeed farce. At a council of 3 March to approve the Speech proroguing Parliament Harcourt and other ministers were waiting in an ante-room when the Queen asked for Lord Kimberley to be summoned for a quite informal interview. The Lord-in-Waiting, Lord Acton, who was somewhat deaf, misheard the name and seems to have summoned Harcourt into the royal presence in a manner which may have suggested to him that he was about to be commissioned to form a government. A story to this effect gained currency, and Rosebery (who was actually absent) was substituted for Kimberley. This cruel legend, which was not dispelled when within months Rosebery appointed Lord Acton to the regius chair at Cambridge, epitomised the public's feelings about Harcourt's almost indecent desire for office. For the inflated version see Emden, *Behind the Throne*, p. 192, while the deflated story is given by Stansky, *Ambitions and Strategies*, p. 87.
40 Raymond, *Rosebery*, pp. 141–2.
41 James, *Rosebery*, p. 354.
42 ibid.
43 *J & L*, 2 June 1895.
44 Brett's daughters were Dorothy Eugénie, born 1883, later known as a friend of D. H. Lawrence, whose portrait by her is in the National Portrait Gallery: and Sylvia Leonora, (1885—1971) who married Sir Charles Vyner Brooke, Rajah of Sarawak from 1917. Sylvia Brett's childhood memories of the dancing classes at Windsor (*Listener*, 27 April 1972) are not very flattering of Queen Victoria: 'She was a very aggressive, terrifying old

woman...She sat in the middle of the dance floor with a big stick, thumping on the ground, screaming at us...She had me out in the front row because I had good legs.' Brett's daughters did not go to school, and these were the only children they met.

45 Collected under the title *Yoke of Empire*, in 1896.

46 Ponsonby, *Recollections of Three Reigns*, pp. 33–4.

47 ibid., p. 33.

48 *J & L*, 2 July 1897.

49 *J & L*, 29 Jan. 1898.

50 ibid., 20 Aug. 1891.

51 ibid., 11 July 1899.

52 Cf. Ch. I n. 1 above and Ch. 8. n. 39 below. The Viceroyalty of India was offered to Esher by Morley in November 1908, with Asquith's approval, when Minto's resignation seemed to be likely. Morley sounded Esher on accepting the War Office in Dec. 1905.

53 In succession to Sir Ralph Knox. Hicks Beach wrote to Brodrick on 3 Nov. 1900: 'I can conceive that Esher's knowledge of the Court, the world, and society might stand you in very good stead at the War Office' (quoted in Hamer, *The British Army 1885–1905*, p. 226).

54 *J & L*, 18 Dec. 1889.

55 *Fortnightly Review*, Dec. 1891, p. 777.

56 ibid., Jan. 1888, p. 8.

57 ibid., loc. cit. p. 41.

58 Hamer, op. cit. p. 93.

59 See comments of *Fortnightly Review*, Jan. 1888, p. 10.

60 *J & L*, 8 Jan. 1887.

61 *The Times*, 11 and 21 Sept. 1886.

62 Hamer, op. cit., p. 111.

63 ibid., p. 94.

64 Hansard 4 Ser. 144, p. 697. Mr Emmott quoting Dilke.

65 Hamer, op. cit., p. 181.

66 WA, E. 33–109.

67 ibid.

68 The passages Esher thought particularly relevant were II, p. 253 and III, p. 184.

69 A War Office Council existed from 1890 but was semi-defunct by 1899. The Army Board as it existed during the Boer War was a

scratch affair assembled in Sept. 1899 as a revival of the 'old confidential Mobilisation Committee' and under Lansdowne's direction it came to include five leading soldiers and two members of the civilian staff of the War Office (Cd 1789, pp. 138–9). Esher regarded such a Board as lacking independence and unduly subject to political pressure.

70 RA E33/114. Esher–Sir Arthur Bigge, 24 Nov. 1900.
71 RA E33/119.
72 *J & L*, 22 Jan. 1901.
73 *J & L*, 4 Feb. 1901.
74 *J & L*, 10 Feb. 1901.
75 *The Letters of Queen Victoria (1837–1861)*, edited by Arthur Christopher Benson and Viscount Esher, appeared in 1907, a selection in three volumes of the contents of between five and six hundred volumes of originals.
76 *J & L*, 17 Feb. 1901.
77 *J & L*, 18 and 23 April 1901. Originally Sir Frederick Ponsonby, King Edward's assistant private secretary, was asked to sort the papers of Queen Victoria, but he suggested the task was great enough to require 'a literary man aided by a clerk'. Lord Knollys was consulted, and at this point Esher stepped into the breach. 'The only thing he asked for in return was to be made Deputy Governor of Windsor Castle, which would give him some status in the Household' (Ponsonby, op. cit., pp. 70–1).
78 Esher, aided by 'a clever lady clerk' (Miss Bertha Williams), managed to get all the papers sorted during King Edward's reign, and on the accession of George V they were given into the charge of the Librarian of Windsor Castle, the Hon. John Fortescue.
79 *J & L*, 29 Oct. 1901.
80 BM, Add. MS. 49718. Esher–Balfour, 16 April 1901.
81 *J & L*, 11 June 1902.
82 FitzRoy, *Memoirs*, I, p. 98.
83 Jullian, *Edward and the Edwardians*, p. 190.
84 FitzRoy, *Memoirs*, I, p. 99.
85 ibid., p. 100.
86 ibid., loc. cit.
87 ibid., p. 101.
88 Jullian, op. cit., pp. 192–3.

Chapter 4

1 For the general origins of the Defence Committee see Johnson, *Defence by Committee*, 1960. Also PRO Cab. 37–40 No. 64 for Balfour and Lord Salisbury's initiatives in 1895.

2 PRO, Cab. 37–63 No. 145.

3 Dilke's comments are in Dilke to Arnold-Forster, 16 Oct. 1902, BM, Add. MS. 50289.

4 Selborne had asked Arnold-Forster on 18 July to help him by stating 'the leading arguments in favour of the establishment of a General Naval and Military Staff on the lines that you and I have often discussed...' (BM Add. MS. 50289).

5 loc cit., Selborne to Arnold-Forster, 15 Oct. 1902.

6 loc. cit., Selborne to Arnold-Forster, 16 Dec. 1902.

7 loc. cit.

8 RA W32/22. 21 Dec. 1902.

9 *J & L*, 14 Feb. 1903.

10 *J & L*, 14 Oct. 1902.

11 *J & L*, 29 Oct. 1902.

12 *J & L*, 1 Nov. 1902.

13 *J & L*, 27 Nov. 1902.

14 RA W38/64. Esher-Lord Knollys, 20 Jan. 1903.

15 *J & L*, 14 Feb. 1903.

16 ibid., loc. cit.

17 *J & L*, 11 March 1903.

18 *J & L*, 17 March 1903.

19 RA W38/101.

20 *J & L*, 20 March 1903.

21 RA W38/103. Memo. of 25 March 1903.

22 ibid., W38/103.

23 RA W38/105. Memo. of 30 March 1903. 'Further remarks on army reductions'.

24 Callwell, *Field Marshal Sir Henry Wilson*, I, p. 52.

25 *J & L*, 21 May 1903.

26 ibid., 9 June 1903.

27 Report of the Royal Commission on the South African War. Note by Lord Esher (Cd 1789, pp. 144–6).

28 RA W17/114. Esher-Sir Arthur Davidson, 10 Sept. 1903.

29 *J & L*, 21 Sept. 1903, Esher-Maurice Brett.

30 ibid., loc. cit.

O*

31 *J & L*, 27 Sept. 1903. Esher-King Edward.
32 *J & L*, 27 Sept. 1903. Esher-Lord Knollys.
33 RA R33/100. King Edward-Balfour, 30 Sept. 1903.
34 ibid., same letter.
35 RA R23/99. Balfour-King Edward, 1 Oct. 1903.
36 RA W38/121. Esher-Lord Knollys, 1 Oct. 1903.
37 Ponsonby, *Recollections of Three Reigns*, p. 129.
38 RA W30/10. 'A brief précis... on future naval and military policy' by Fisher, early Oct. 1903.
39 ibid., loc cit.
40 RA W38/122. Esher-Knollys, 7 Oct. 1903.
41 *J & L*, 11 and 12 Oct. 1903.
42 ibid., loc. cit.
43 BM, Add. MS. 50335. Balfour to Arnold-Forster, 4 Oct. 1903.
44 ibid., loc. cit., 5 Oct. 1903.
45 RA R24/7. Balfour-King Edward, 14 Oct. 1903.
46 RA W38/123. 10 Oct. 1903.
47 RA R24/9. King Edward-Balfour, 15 Oct. 1903.
48 RA W30/20. 31 Aug. 1903.
49 RA W30/6. 8 Oct. 1903.
50 RA W39/1a. Esher-Knollys, 8 Nov. 1903: 'The King is quite right, and although Fisher's general idea is the right one, it would be impossible to adjust the work of the War Office precisely on the lines he suggests. The following is more the sort of thing...'
51 Fisher, *Memories*, p. 166. Fisher-Esher, 19 Nov. 1903.
52 *J & L*, 27 Nov. 1903 Also PRO, Cab. 38–3 No. 71 for Balfour's 'Draft Report on the possibility of serious invasion.'
53 BM, Add. MS. 49718.
54 *J & L*, 15 Dec. 1903.
55 BM, Add. MS. 49718.
56 RA W39/4. Esher-King Edward, 29 Dec. 1903.
57 *J & L*, 30 Dec. 1903.
58 BM, Add. MS. 49718.
59 ibid., same letter.
60 *J & L*, Esher-Balfour, 16 Jan. 1904.
61 *J & L*, Esher-Maurice Brett, 26 Nov. 1903. Also RA W32/22. Esher-Knollys, 16 Jan. 1904: 'The appointments will be difficult. I agree with you—a *clean sweep.*'
62 *J & L*, Esher-Maurice Brett, 28 Nov. 1901.

63 RA W32/38. 'Observations on staff for CID' by Sir William Nicholson, 4 Feb. 1904.

64 Arnold-Forster's diary, 14 April 1905.

65 RA W32/22. 16 Jan. 1904. See also Hamer *The British Army 1885–1905*, pp. 242–4 for Fisher's jealous apprehensions of Nicholson, Kelly Kenny and the 'old gang'. Fisher reported to Sandars on 30 Jan. 1904: 'Sir George Clarke found Nicholson (DMI) closeted with Spencer Wilkinson of *Morning Post* (a pessimist of the worst type!) who is an intimate friend of Sir Charles Dilke...[who] yesterday...discredited our report in anticipation!' Sandars was asked to influence the *Morning Post* and prevent the formation of a parliamentary lobby which might muster 80 votes.

66 RA W39/23. 1 Jan. 1904.

67 There was opposition in the cabinet to the proposal that the Inspector-General should be President of the Selection Board. EP, Clarke-Esher, 30 Jan. 1904.

68 *J & L*, Esher-Maurice Brett, 9 and 11 Feb. 1904.

69 EP, Clarke-Esher, 30 Jan. 1904.

70 ibid., same letter.

71 Callwell, op. cit., I, p. 55.

72 EP, Clarke-Esher, 7 Feb. 1904.

73 PRO, Cab. 37–69 No. 38. Memo. of 4 March 1904.

74 RA W39/4. Esher-King Edward, 29 Dec. 1903.

75 BM, Add. MS. 49718. Clarke-Esher, 24 Feb. 1904.

76 RA W32/41. Memo. by Prince Louis of Battenberg, 24 Feb. 1904, saying that after 'discussing the whole scheme in detail' with the three members of the Esher committee his impression had been confirmed that 'Sir William Nicholson has entirely misunderstood the intentions of the Committee'. Also stressing the need for creating the secretariat without delay because of the danger of a change of government.

77 RA W30/67. Fisher-Knollys, 28 Feb. 1904.

78 Gordon, *The War Office*, p. 78.

79 BM, Add. MS. 49718. Sandars-Esher, 13 March 1904 and reply of 16 March (*J & L*, II, p. 45).

80 EP, Clarke-Esher, 16 March 1904.

81 ibid., same letter.

82 EP, Clarke-Esher, 14 Feb. 1904.

83 EP, Sir Edward Ward-Esher, 25 March 1904.
84 EP.
85 EP, 27 March 1904.
86 RA R24/80. Balfour-King Edward, 14 April 1904.
87 *J & L*, 1 March 1904, previously quoted at Ch. 1, n. 26.

Chapter 5
 1 BM, Add. MS. 50335. Arnold-Forster to Balfour, 5 Oct. 1903.
 2 *J & L*, 5 June 1908.
 3 BM, Add MS. 50336. Arnold-Forster to Selborne, 9 Feb. 1904.
 4 ibid., Arnold-Forster's diary, 10 Feb. 1904.
 5 ibid., loc. cit., 16 Feb. 1904.
 6 ibid., loc. cit., 25 March 1904.
 7 ibid., loc. cit., 29 March 1904.
 8 EP, Clarke-Esher, 28 March 1904.
 9 EP, Clarke-Esher, 4 April 1904.
10 EP, 7 April 1904.
11 BM, Add. MS. 50337. Arnold-Forster's diary, 14 April 1904.
12 EP.
13 BM, Add. MS. 50337. Arnold-Forster's diary, 22 April 1904.
14 ibid., loc. cit., 25 April 1904.
15 RA R24/85. Balfour-King Edward, 26 April 1904. Balfour adds:
   'A large reduction in the estimates can only be obtained by a
   reduction in the number of troops with the colours; and whether
   this can be attempted in view of our Indian responsibilities remains
   to be seen. The Defence Committee are at present engaged in an
   examination of Lord Kitchener's estimate of numbers.'
16 BM, Add. MS. 50337. Arnold-Forster's diary, 4 May 1904.
17 RA R25/5. Balfour-King Edward, 15 May 1904.
18 RA R24/88. Balfour-King Edward, 19 May 1904.
19 PRO, Cab. 37-77 No. 87.
20 BM, Add. MS. 49718. 27 March 1904.
21 EP.
22 BM, Add. MS. 49700. Clarke-Balfour, 18 June 1904.
23 *J & L*, Esher-Maurice Brett, 18 June 1904. The CID meeting
   which Balfour forgot to attend was at the Foreign Office on 29
   June (Arnold-Forster's diary).
24 *J & L*, Esher-Balfour, 17 June 1904.

25 BM, Add. MS. 50338.

26 *J & L*, Esher-Maurice Brett, 18 June 1904.

27 *J & L*, Esher-Maurice Brett, 20 June 1904.

28 PRO, Cab. 38–5 No. 64.

29 EP, 23 June 1904.

30 BM, Add. MS. 50338. Arnold-Forster's diary, 28 June 1904.

31 ibid., loc. cit., 29 June 1904.

32 PRO, Cab. 37–71 No. 90. Memo. by Arnold-Forster on 'the alteration of the army scheme'.

33 ibid., Cab. 37–71 No. 92. 'Revised proposals for army reform', 2 July 1904.

34 ibid., Cab. 37–71 No. 90.

35 BM, Add. MS. 50339.

36 RA R25/8.

37 *J & L*, Esher-Maurice Brett, 12 July 1904.

38 RA R25/12, referring to the cabinet of the previous day.

39 EP, Clarke-Esher, 15 July 1904.

40 Callwell, *Wilson*, pp. 57–8.

41 EP, L. S. Amery-Esher, 18 July 1904.

42 PRO, Cab. 37–71 No. 107. 'Army organisation. Action taken and contemplated.'

43 EP, Clarke-Esher, 11 Aug. 1904.

44 BM, Add. MS. 49718. Esher-Sandars, 27 July 1904.

45 *J & L*, 12 Oct. 1904.

Chapter 6

1 EP.

2 EP, Clarke-Esher, 11 Aug. 1904.

3 EP, same letter.

4 EP.

5 EP, Ward-Esher, 18 Oct. 1904.

6 RA W39/49.

7 EP, 7 Nov. 1904.

8 BM, Add. MS. 50341. Arnold-Forster's diary, 7 Nov. 1904.

9 RA W39/52. Memo. by Esher.

10 EP.

11 RA W39/56.

12 EP, Clarke-Esher, 29 Nov. 1904.

13 RA W39/59. Esher-Knollys, 2 Dec. 1904.

14 BM, Add. MS. 50342. Arnold-Forster's diary, 7 Dec. 1904.
15 EP, 9 Dec. 1904.
16 BM, Add. MS. 49718. Esher-Balfour, 13 Dec. 1904.
17 ibid., loc. cit. 'Note of the results of a conversation between the Adjutant-General, Lord Esher and myself at the War Office', unsigned typescript on 10 Downing Street notepaper, probably by Clarke, dated 15 Dec. 1904.
18 EP, Clarke-Esher, 15 Dec. 1904.
19 BM, Add. MS. 49718.
20 EP, Clarke-Esher, 23 Dec. 1904.
21 BM, Add. MS. 23 Dec. 1904.
22 RA W39/63. Esher-Knollys, 25 Dec. 1904.
23 RA R25/54. Balfour-King Edward, 29 Dec. 1904.
24 RA R25/57.
25 BM, Add. MS. 50343. Arnold-Forster's diary, 4 Jan. 1905.
26 EP, Clarke-Esher, 6 Jan. 1905.
27 BM, Add. MS. 49718. Esher-Sandars, 6 Jan. 1905.
28 ibid., same letter.
29 ibid., same letter.
30 BM, Add. MS. 50343.
31 Printed in PRO, Cab. 37–74 No. 10. 'Correspondence between the Prime Minister and Secretary of State…13 Jan.–27 Feb. 1905.'
32 *J & L*, Esher-Sandars, 13 Jan. 1905.
33 *J & L*.
34 BM, Add MS. 49718.
35 EP, Clarke-Esher, 18 Jan. 1905.
36 PRO, Cab. 37–74 No. 10.
37 BM, Add. MS. 50343.
38 EP, Clarke-Esher, 28 Jan. 1905.
39 EP.
40 *J & L*, Esher-Maurice Brett, 30 Jan. 1905.
41 BM, Add. MS. 50343.
42 ibid., loc cit., 31 Jan. 1905.
43 RA R25/68. Balfour-King Edward, 2 Feb. 1905.
44 RA R25/69.
45 BM, Add. MS. 50344. Arnold-Forster's diary, 1 Feb. 1905.
46 ibid., same entry.
47 ibid., entry of 2 Feb. 1905.

48 ibid.
49 Fleetwood Wilson-Esher, 4 Feb. 1905.
50 BM, Add. MS. 50344. Arnold-Forster's diary.
51 ibid., entry of 17 Feb. 1905.
52 BM, Add. MS. 49718. Esher-Sandars, 19 Feb. 1905.
53 BM, Add. MS. 50344.
54 ibid., diary entry of 6 Feb. 1905.
55 ibid.
56 EP, Clarke-Esher, 6 Feb. 1905.
57 EP, Clarke-Esher, 4, 6 and 9 Feb. 1905.
58 EP, Clarke-Esher, 4 and 20 Feb. 1905.
59 BM, Add. MS. 50344 Arnold-Forster's diary, 13 Feb. 1905.
60 EP.
61 RA W39/69.
62 BM, Add. MS. 49718. Esher-Sandars, 21 Feb. 1905.
63 ibid., loc. cit. Note by Esher, 21 Feb. 1905. Cf Cab. 38–8 No.
   14. 'Our present minimum military requirements…a reorganisation of the regular army and militia.'
64 BM, Add. MS. 50344. Arnold-Forster's diary, 23 Feb. 1905.
65 ibid., loc. cit., entry for 28 Feb. 1905.
66 ibid., 50345, entry for 1 March 1905.
67 ibid., loc. cit., 2 March 1905.
68 BM, Add. MS. 49718.
69 EP, Clarke-Esher, 12 March 1905, relating conversation with
   Balfour of 11th.
70 BM, Add. MS. 50345, diary entry of 10 March 1905.
71 RA R25/93. 10 March 1905.
72 ibid., same letter.
73 *J & L*, 7 March 1905.
74 EP, 12 March 1905.
75 RA W39/6. Esher-Knollys, 31 Dec. 1903.
76 Mrs Arnold-Forster certainly remained convinced that Esher
   was the 'villain of the piece' in her husband's unlucky tenure of
   the War Office. She eliminated Esher's name from her Life of
   Arnold-Forster for fear of 'provoking a bitter controversy'. 'The
   general public,' she wrote to Col. Raymond Marker (12 July
   1910), 'knows nothing about Lord Esher or very little. Very few
   know of his treachery' (quoted in Hamer, *The British Army,
   1885–1905*, p. 227.

Chapter 7

1 RA W34/38.
2 RA W39/26, Esher-Knollys, 23 Jan. 1904, in which Lyttelton is QMG, Stopford A-G, W. Murray DGO, and Douglas Director of Supply.
3 RA W39/31. Memo. by Esher recording King Edward's interview with Clarke. As well as objecting to the title 'commissary', the King successfully opposed Esher's proposal to re-style the War Office 'Army Office'.
4 RA W32/37. Memo. by Esher, 17 Feb. 1904.
5 RA R23/100. King Edward-Balfour, 30 Sept. 1903.
6 BM, Add. MS. 50351, diary entry of 18 Oct. 1905.
7 EP.
8 *The Times*, 12 Dec. 1904, reporting speech at Leicester.
9 EP, 12 Dec. 1904.
10 BM, Add. MS. 49718, 12 Dec. 1904.
11 ibid., same letter.
12 ibid., Add. MS. 50342. Arnold-Forster to Balfour, 12 Dec. 1904.
13 ibid., loc. cit., Lyttelton to Arnold-Forster, 16 Dec. 1904.
14 ibid., loc. cit., diary entry of 14 Dec. 1904.
15 ibid., same entry.
16 ibid., same entry.
17 ibid., Add. MS. 50347, diary entry for 15 May 1905.
18 ibid., loc. cit., diary entry of 8 May 1905.
19 ibid., entry of 10 May 1905.
20 BM, Add. MS. 49718.
21 EP.
22 Callwell, *Wilson*, I, p. 62.
23 BM, Add. MS. 50348. Arnold-Forster's diary.
24 ibid., entry for 24 June 1905.
25 ibid., entry for 26 June 1905.
26 EP., Clarke-Esher, 19 June 1905.
27 BM, Add. MS. 50349.
28 ibid., loc. cit., Arnold-Forster's diary, 10 July 1905.
29 EP, Clarke-Esher, 12 July 1905.
30 BM, Add. MS. 50349. Arnold-Forster's diary, 11 July 1905.
31 EP.
32 BM, Add. MS. 50349. Arnold-Forster's diary, 15 July 1905.
33 RA W39/84.

34 *J & L.*

35 *J & L,* 23 July 1905.

36 *J & L.*

37 EP, Repington-Esher, 18 July 1905.

38 BM, Add. MS. 50350.

39 RA R26/68.

40 BM, Add. MS. 50350. Arnold-Forster's diary, 5 Aug. 1905.

41 ibid., loc. cit., entry for 7 Aug. 1905.

42 ibid., loc. cit., entry for 9 Aug. 1905.

43 ibid., Add. MS. 50352, Nov. 1905.

44 EP, Clarke-Esher, 27 Nov. 1905.

45 *Glasgow Herald,* 25 Nov. 1919. Esher writing on the future of the general staff, comments that the 'whole of the personnel of the general staff at the War Office left for the front' and was only re-established there when Gen. Robertson returned as CIGS. It was only late in the war, Esher adds, 'that soldiers and politicians began to understand the meaning of that comprehensive term'.

46 BM, Add. MS. 49718. 'First Note' on CID by Esher, 2 Dec. 1903.

47 RA W38/103. Memo. by Fisher, 29 March 1903.

48 EP.

49 BM, Add. MS. 50350. Arnold-Forster's diary, 12 Aug. 1905: 'French is quite right in entertaining a very high opinion of Haig. I wish I could help him now, and employ him at the War Office... However, I must put him on the General Staff list without fail.'

50 EP, Clarke-Esher, 3 Dec. 1905.

51 RA W39/105.

52 *J & L,* Esher-Knollys, 2 Sept. 1905.

53 RA W39/113.

54 RA W39/118. Esher-Knollys, 16 Sept. 1905.

55 *J & L,* 16 Sept. 1905.

56 BM, Add. MS. 49718, 17 Sept. 1905.

57 *J & L,* 13 Oct. 1905.

58 BM, Add. MS. 49719.

Chapter 8

1 BM, Add. MS. 49718.

2 EP.

3 RA W39/71.

4 BM, Add. MS. 50346.

5 The Leader of the Opposition was well aware that Arnold-Forster, in attempting to make progress with his army scheme when presenting his estimates in April 1905, was being opposed by his own front bench. Campbell-Bannerman commented, writing to Haliburton (2 April 1905): 'All he said from first to last rarely evoked a cheer: his colleagues gave him no support. His metallic voice, sour visage, and dogmatic egotism bored when it did not irritate...It is quite understood that his scheme is dead' (quoted in Hamer, *The British Army, 1885–1905*, p. 256).

6 EP.

7 BM, Add. MS. 49718. Esher-Balfour, 18 June 1905.

8 PRO, Cab. 37–78 Nos. 106–9.

9 RA R26/41. 23 June 1905.

10 EP.

11 EP.

12 BM, Add. MS. 50349. Arnold-Forster's diary, 4 July 1905.

13 EP, Clarke-Esher.

14 RA W 39/82.

15 BM, Add. MS. 50349. Arnold-Forster's diary, 6 July 1905.

16 ibid., loc. cit., same entry, referring to statement of Lyttelton's of 5 Aug. 1904.

17 EP, Clarke-Esher, 10 July 1905.

18 BM, Add. MS. 49701.

19 EP, Clarke-Esher, 13 July 1905.

20 EP, Clarke-Esher, 23 July 1905.

21 BM, Add. MS 49701. Clarke-Balfour, 11 July 1905. The plan was discussed, further discussed on 13th and approved on 20 July.

22 RA W32/91 and 92, 26 July 1905.

23 BM, Add. MS. 41719.

24 *J & L*, Esher-Balfour, 16 Sept. 1905.

25 RA W39/118. Cf above, Ch. 7, n. 54.

26 *J & L*, Esher-Maurice Brett, 17 Sept. 1905.

27 *J & L*, Esher-Balfour, 5 Oct. 1905.

28 ibid., same letter.

29 BM, Add. MS. 49719. Haldane's Machiavellian plot is spelt out quite explicitly in his letter to Asquith of 6 Oct. 1905. It was to arrange for the King to summon Campbell-Bannerman to Sandringham in November when he had returned from abroad in order

to suggest to him that only 'a young man can be both Prime Minister and Leader in the House of Commons with the increasing business. This leaves it open to Campbell-Bannerman to think that Lord Spencer may be sent for...' (NL of S, HP 5906). Lord Spencer was in fact too ill to preside over a Liberal ministry as Leader in the House of Lords, and the idea was to frighten Campbell-Bannerman into accepting a peerage so that Asquith could lead in the Commons. Indeed Haldane and Asquith went so far as to concert with Knollys a complete distribution of offices behind the back of the Liberal leader who was to receive the King's commission (ibid., loc. cit., Haldane-Asquith, 9 Oct., Haldane's undated letter to Knollys *c.* 15 Oct., and Knollys's reply of 17 Oct. which asserted that King Edward 'thinks that all the proposed arrangements in it with respect to the distribution of offices are good...' except for Herbert Gladstone at the Admiralty). But Campbell-Bannerman's firmness later cheated Asquith of the Treasury and Haldane of the Woolsack. Esher is described by Haldane as 'very much consulted' at Balmoral, but Haldane told Asquith 'I gave him of course no hint of our attitude or the correspondence...' Esher nevertheless knew of these things.

30 ibid., loc. cit.
31 ibid., loc. cit., Esher-Clarke, 10 Oct. 1905.
32 ibid., same letter.
33 RA W32/99. Lord Roberts-Balfour, 28 Aug. 1905.
34 *J & L,* 5 Nov. 1905
35 i.e. 7 Nov. 1905.
36 RA W32/97 (printed copy).
37 The announcement was agreed on 1 Dec., and Balfour resigned on the 4th.
38 *J & L,* 1 Dec. 1905.
39 ibid., same entry.
40 *J & L,* 11 Oct. 1903.
41 *J & L,* 6 Dec. 1905.
42 *J & L,* 5 Dec. 1905.
43 *J & L,* 7 Dec. 1905. See Asquith-Haldane 7 Dec. 1905 (NL of S, HP 5906 f. 243) informing Haldane that 'an offer of the War office will soon be on its way' and explaining that 'from our talk the other day' Asquith had gathered that this would be Haldane's wish in preference to the Home Office. Asquith's 'endeavours, carried

on ceaselessly for two days', had failed to persuade Campbell-Bannerman to quit the Commons. Accordingly, Grey was at this point resolved not to accept office, but Asquith had decided to give way, fearing that if the imperialist Liberals stood aloof: 'It would be said that we were at issue about Home Rule, the Colonies, the Empire, etc.,' and people might look instead to Rosebery. 'The *tertius gaudens* at Dalmeny would look on with complacency.' According to his wife, Asquith was 'shattered' by the defeat, but the Court had got what it wanted and Esher wrote to Haldane: 'After our talks at Balmoral, you can imagine the pleasure with which personally I see the idea, which germinated there, come to fruition. The King is *delighted*' (ibid., loc. cit., f.527: 9 Dec. 1905).

44 *J & L*, 10 Dec. 1905.
45 EP.
46 *J & L*, 11 Dec. 1905.
47 *J & L*, 6 Dec. 1905.
48 *J & L*, Esher-Kitchener, 21 Dec. 1905.
49 Repington, *First World War*, I, p. 2.
50 Monger, *End of Isolation*, p. 236. Other accounts of the initiation of the 'conversations' are in Williamson, *Politics of Grand Strategy*, and Robbins, *Grey*.
51 Quoted in Monger, op. cit., pp. 239–40. Clemenceau lunched with Esher on 13th and spoke of the immediate necessity 'to arrange very secretly what military and naval action should be taken in the *first week*' of a war.
52 Cab. 38–11 No. 4. Notes on Conferences to discuss naval and military action in the event of war with Germany, 9 pp.
53 Repington, op. cit., I. p. 3.
54 ibid., p. 4.
55 Quoted in Monger, op. cit., p. 242.
56 Cab. 38–11 No. 4. The text of the questionnaire and the French replies are printed in Repington, op. cit., pp. 6–10.
57 ibid.
58 Repington (op. cit., pp. 11–12) describes how Clarke told him on 14 January that Fisher was 'not prepared to guarantee the passage of our Army across the Channel', and he learnt 'that Sir John French was for the Fisher plan, and at this time opposed union with the French on French soil'.

Chapter 9

1 PRO, Cab. 37–86 No. 9.
2 Maurice, *Haldane*, I, p. 169.
3 *J & L*, 19 Dec. 1905.
4 EP.
5 PRO, Cab. 38–11 No. 3.
6 RA W40/4.
7 ibid., same letter.
8 ibid., same letter.
9 On receipt of Esher's long exposition Haldane replied: 'Our ideas seem to be running on the same lines...You have correctly summed up the chief points which I have suggested...I feel we are progressing towards definiteness, but most of the road has yet to be travelled.' In this odd way Haldane appropriated his plagiarisms to himself (NL of S, HP 5907 f. 28).
10 Cooper, *Haig*, I, 105. Esher-Haig, n.d. It is clear that Esher was behind Haig's appointment to 'the most important Directorate in the General Staff', that of Military Training, which covered War Organisation and Home Defence. See Esher-Haldane 6 Jan. 1906 and Haldane's reply of 9 Feb.: 'You will be glad to hear that I have practically settled things for Douglas Haig...' (NL of S, HP 5907, ff. 5, 30).
11 *J & L*, n.d. (*c.* June 1906).
12 *J & L*, Esher-Maurice Brett, 22 May 1906.
13 *J & L*, Esher-King Edward, n.d. (*c.* June 1906).
14 Maurice, op. cit., I, pp. 185–6.
15 RA W40/38.
16 RA W40/34.
17 *J & L*.
18 *J & L*, 30 Sept. 1906.
19 *J & L*.
20 William Waldorf Astor, 1848–1919. Born in New York, where with his cousin John Jacob Astor he built the Astoria and Waldorf hotels. Settled in England in 1889 and became naturalised. Gave Cliveden to his son as a wedding present in 1906. Baron 1916, Viscount 1917.
21 EP, 30 Sept. 1906.
22 EP.

23 *J & L*, 18 Dec. 1906. For report of sub-committee see PRO, Cab. 38–12 No. 5.

24 *J & L*, Esher-Maurice Brett, 19 Dec. 1906.

25 *Westminster Gazette*, 10 April 1907.

26 EP, Clarke-Esher, 26 Jan. 1907.

27 Issue of 23 March 1907: 'Let the Militia then make known their wishes, and there is no fear whatever of the Secretary of State being found unwilling to make concessions.'

28 BM, Add. MS. 49719.

29 *Standard*, 19 March 1907, leader, p. 6.

30 *Westminster Gazette*, 18 June 1907, which also explains: 'The acceptance of Mr Arnold-Forster's amendment meant that the Militia, with few exceptions, would not come under the authority of the new County Associations...These will be third battalions, and they will do their usual annual training, and be available as a Special Reserve, and as drafts for the Regulars. All these battalions will belong to the Regular Army instead of to the Territorial Army; thus the Militia will be in the first line instead of the second.'

31 BM, Add. MS. 50832. Clarke-Sir Valentine Chirol (director of the foreign dept. of *The Times*) 6 Dec. 1907.

32 ibid., loc. cit., Clarke-Chirol, 11 Nov. 1907.

33 Clarke had fallen foul of Fisher, as of Haldane. Hence he disliked C. P. Scott, Fisher's protégé, as he disliked Repington, who was Haldane's. 'Scott is a swell-headed little bounder, who has profited overmuch by advertisement and by Fisher's patronage' he wrote to Chirol, 11 Nov. 1907 (ibid., loc. cit.).

34 Lloyd George, *War Memoirs*, I, p. 6.

35 For the Hague Conference see Halévy, *Hist. of Eng. People, Epilogue*, II, pp. 220–4. Oddly enough W. T. Stead edited the *Courrier de la Conférence* at his own expense and played the role of opposing a naval scare, the opposite of his role in 1884.

36 *The Times*, 6 Feb. 1908, p. 15a. letter from Esher dated 22 Jan.

37 *J & L*, II, p. 283, dated Berlin, 14 Feb. Esher had of course given up his position at the Office of Works before 1903.

38 *J & L*, 19 Feb. 1908.

39 *The Times* of 6 March, which carried Repington's article 'Under Which King?' did not in fact give the text of the Kaiser's letter.

40 *J & L*, 26 June 1908.

41 *J & L*, Esher-Knollys, 26 June 1908.
42 RA W41/12 Esher-Knollys, 5 Dec. 1907.
43 *J & L*, 12 Nov. 1908.
44 RA W41/22. Esher-King Edward, 27 Jan. 1908.
45 RA W41/23. Esher-King Edward, 5 July 1908.
46 Announced by Asquith on 29 July 1908 in the Commons.
47 RA W41/79. Esher-King Edward, 2 Nov. 1908.
48 S. McKenna, *McKenna*, p. 71. McKenna-Grey, 30 Dec. 1908.
49 ibid., p. 73. McKenna-Asquith, 3 Jan. 1909.
50 ibid., same letter.
51 BM, Add. MS. 49719.
52 *J & L*, 3 March 1909.
53 *J & L*, Esher-Maurice Brett, 12 March 1909.
54 BM, Add. MS. 49719, letter of 24 April 1909.
55 ibid., same letter.
56 ibid., loc. cit.
57 *J & L*, 15 March 1909.
58 *J & L*, 26 Feb. 1909.
59 *J & L*, 3 March 1909. Esher adds: 'I kissed his hand, after this, when he said goodbye.'

Chapter 10

1 Spender, *Asquith*, I, p. 255.
2 *J & L*, 12 Sept. 1909.
3 *J & L*, 26 Sept. 1909.
4 *J & L*, 4 Oct. 1909.
5 *J & L*, 8 Oct. 1909.
6 BM, Add. MS. 49719.
7 *J & L*, 17 Nov. 1909.
8 *J & L*, Esher-Knollys, 1 Dec. 1909.
9 ibid., same letter.
10 *The Times*, 6 Dec. 1909 etc., reprinted in Esher, *The Influence of King Edward*, pp. 61–80.
11 i.e. Esher.
12 Spender, op. cit., I, pp. 261–2. Knollys-Vaughan Nash, 15 Dec. 1909.
13 *J & L*, 9 Jan. 1910.
14 *J & L*, Esher-Balfour, 24 Jan. 1910.
15 *J & L*, Esher-Balfour, 23 Jan. 1910.

16 *J & L*, Esher-Maurice Brett, 25 Jan. 1910.
17 *J & L*, Esher-Maurice Brett, 30 Jan. 1910.
18 *J & L*, Esher-King Edward, 10 April 1910.
19 Spender, op. cit., I p. 279.
20 *J & L* 27 April 1910. memo. of a conference at Lambeth.
21 *J & L*, 16 Oct. 1910.
22 *J & L*, 9 Nov. 1910.
23 ibid., same entry.
24 Mentioned in *J & L*, Esher-Stamfordham, 28 Dec. 1913, which may refer to the memo. in BM, Add. MS. 49719 dated Oct. 1910.
25 Nicolson, *George V*, p. 182.
26 ibid., p. 187.
27 ibid., p. 188.
28 Jenkins (*Asquith*, p. 243) distinguishes guarantees for the existing Parliament, and guarantees taken during it for action in the next.
29 Nicolson, op. cit., pp. 190–1. Jenkins (op. cit., p. 247) fails to see much significance in the condition of secrecy and claims that an open pledge would have suited the government much better.
30 *J & L*.
31 *J & L*, 19 Nov. 1910.
32 Nicolson, op. cit., p. 191.
33 ibid., pp. 207–8.
34 ibid., p. 189.
35 *J & L*, 19 Nov. 1910.
36 ibid., same entry.
37 *J & L*.
38 *J & L*, 10 Jan. 1911. Memo. of a conversation at the Marlborough Club.
39 Balfour-Stamfordham, 9 Aug. 1911, quoted in Young, *Balfour*, 302.
40 Knollys-Balfour, 8 Sept. 1911 (ibid., p. 304).
42 Balfour-Stamfordham, 9 Aug. 1911 (ibid., p. 302).
42 *J & L*.
43 BM, Add. MS. 49767, diary of Parliament Bill.
44 ibid., loc. cit.
45 *J & L*, 11 Aug. 1911.
46 *J & L*, Esher-Fisher, 27 April 1911.
47 BM, Add. MS. 49719.

48 *The World*, 21 June–16 Aug. 1910.

49 *J & L*, 14 Feb. 1913.

50 ibid., same entry.

51 Actually Stamfordham, King George's private secretary, was in touch with a political middle group led by Cromer and St Loe Strachey (editor of the *Spectator*) which seemed to support a congenial policy *vis-à-vis* the House of Lords and the Monarchy. Strachey wrote to Stamfordham on 4 March 1913: 'To my mind everything centres on the question of an election before the third time of asking. We must make everything lead up to that' (BL, SP, S/13/15/7) By Sept. 1913 *The Times* was running a correspondence on the King's right to dissolve Parliament before the Home Rule Bill was assented to.

52 *J & L*, 10 Sept. 1913. Sir William Anson wrote to *The Times* the same day expressing his opinion that the King could call on other ministers who supported his view, if he could find them. It was observed that the Home Rule Bill would not be killed if a dissolution came before the beginning of its third session which was 1914. A. V. Dicey agreed with Anson.

53 *J & L*, 11 Sept. 1913. Asquith, having just presented the King with a memo. on 'what are, and what are not, the functions of a constitutional sovereign', warned Churchill: 'You will find the Royal mind obsessed; and the Royal tongue exceptionally fluid and voluble.' Nevertheless, Asquith was ready to accept a 'round table' on the Ulster problem, and Churchill admitted to Stamfordham (17 Sept.): 'If Ireland has the right to claim separate government from England, Ulster cannot be refused similar exemption from government by an Irish Parliament.' (R. Churchill, *Churchill*, II. pp. 474–6).

54 *J & L*, 11 Sept. 1913.

55 ibid., 13 Sept. 1913.

56 ibid., same entry. While wishing to prevent the King from making any overt move, Esher like Stamfordham was in touch with the Cromer group and encouraged Strachey's sympathetic editorials. See e.g. Esher-Strachey, 18 Aug. 1913 complimenting him on his 'brilliant' editorial 'exposing the tactics of those who want to use the King as a stalking horse, and jeopardise (if not destroy) the Monarchy...You should know of the really formidable intrigue on the part of those cowardly members of the House

of Lords and others, who, too timid to stand shoulder to shoulder with Carson and his merry men, want to skulk behind King George' (BL, SP, S/6/1/9).

57 Nicolson, op. cit., pp. 302–7.
58 ibid., loc. cit.
59 *J & L*, 3 Dec. 1913.
60 ibid., 28 Dec. 1913.
61 EP.
62 EP.
63 *J & L*, 19 Jan. 1914.
64 EP.
65 EP, same draft.
66 *J & L*, 5 Feb. 1914.
67 *The Times*, 25 March 1914.
68 EP.
69 *J & L*, 22 May 1914.
70 *J & L*, 23 May 1914.
71 ibid., same entry.
72 *J & L*, Esher-King George, 23 May 1914.
73 Asquith found Redmond and Dillon 'decidedly impractical' on 13 July and foresaw 'great difficulties in the coming week which will practically decide whether we can come to an agreement'. Two days later he warned Bonar Law that 'failure to settle would mean a general election with a very difficult situation at the end of it whoever was victorious'. The King had carried his point, and on 16 July the cabinet decided that Asquith should advise 'the King to interfere with the object of securing a pacific accommodation' (Asquith, *Memoirs & Reflections*, II. pp. 6–7).
74 W. Churchill, *World Crisis*, I, p. 155.
75 EP.
76 Unfortunately for the King, the basis for appealing to some neutral group, which might rally moderate opinion in the country, had seemed to have collapsed when Strachey reported to Stamfordham that with the concurrence of the Archbishop of Canterbury the Cromer group had changed its mind. Strachey told Stamfordham (17 July) that he had decided his old view was right, that the risk would be too great for the King to refuse assent to the Home Rule Bill even if there were no Amending Bill accompanying it. It would, he wrote, have been a different

432

matter if the Duke of Devonshire still lived, but 'unfortunately we have got no one who commands the neutral opinion in the country in the way he did, and to justify such action it would be necessary to obtain beforehand the command of neutral opinion.' (BL, SP, S/13/15/13).

77 Lyons, *Ireland since the Famine*, p. 309.
78 EP.
79 EP.
80 Jenkins, op. cit. p. 361.

Chapter 11

1 *J & L*, 24 Dec. 1909.
2 BM, Add. MS. 49719. Balfour-Esher, 28 Dec. 1909. For the work of the standing sub-committee as chaired by various ministers see Cab. 38–16 No. 1, 7, 9, 19, 21, and Cab. 38–25 No. 34.
3 *The World*, 21 June–16 Aug. 1910. Cf. above Ch. 10, n. 49.
4 *J & L*, Esher-Maurice Brett, 8 Sept. 1910.
5 ibid. *J & L*, 10 Sept. 1910.
6 Marder, *Dreadnought to Scapa Flow*, I, p. 214.
7 BM, Add. MS. 49719.
8 ibid., loc. cit.
9 ibid.. loc. cit., 21 Oct. 1910.
10 ibid., loc. cit.
11 W. Churchill, *World Crisis*, I, p. 36.
12 Marder, op. cit., p. 241 seq.
13 W. Churchill, op. cit., I, 42–6. Memo. of 13 Aug. 1910.
14 Marder, loc. cit.
15 R. Churchill, *Churchill*, 11, p. 532.
16 Marder, op. cit., p. 392.
17 *J & L*, 4 Oct. 1911.
18 *J & L*, Esher-Asquith, 6 Oct. 1911.
19 Marder, op. cit., p. 250.
20 BM, Add. MS. 49719.
21 ibid., loc. cit., 2 Jan. 1912.
22 ibid., loc. cit., Ottley-Esher, 6 Jan. 1912.
23 R. Churchill, op. cit., II, p. 582. 24 Jan. 1912.
24 ibid., II, p. 581.
25 ibid., II, p. 561. 31 Jan. 1912.
26 ibid., II, p. 595. 1 July 1912.

27 *J & L*, Esher-Fisher, 29 March 1912.

28 R. Churchill, op. cit., II, p. 588.

29 BM, Add. MS. 49719. 30 May 1912.

30 ibid., same memo.

31 *J & L*, Esher-Maurice Brett, 2 July 1912.

32 *J & L*, 5 July 1912.

33 ibid., same entry.

34 ibid., same entry.

35 *J & L*, 23 July 1912.

36 R. Churchill, op. cit., II, p. 596.

37 ibid., II, p. 629 seq.

38 ibid., II, p. 571.

39 *The Times*, 30 March 1912.

40 Formed by Sir Richard Garton, with himself, Balfour and Esher as trustees, the Foundation originally promoted studies of 'international polity'. During the First World War it developed an interest in reconstruction and especially education. Esher claimed that one of its publications on industry was the root of the Whitley Councils.

41 BM, Add. MS. 49719. Balfour-Esher, 12 Oct. 1912.

42 ibid., loc. cit., Esher-Balfour, 10 Sept. 1913.

43 Esher, *Influence of King Edward*, p. 213.

44 *The Times*, 21 March 1912.

45 *The Times*, 28 March 1914.

46 *J & L*, 3 Aug. 1914. For policies and decisions leading to Britain's entry into the war see Cab. 38–28 No. 51.

Chapter 12

1 Asquith decided on 5 Aug. 'to give up the War Office and install Kitchener there as an emergency man until the War comes to an end'. That Asquith was thinking in terms of a short war is also indicated by his offer to keep Kitchener's 'place at Cairo open so that he can return to it' (*Memories and Reflections*, II. p. 30).

2 Callwell, *Wilson*, I, p. 159.

3 A Foreign Office paper of 25 May 1915 (Cab. 24–1 No. 78) reveals the confusion of British policies with regard to Holland. England believed in 1914 that it was in Germany's interest to keep Holland neutral, wrongly assuming that 'German trade carried in neutral bottoms would be free to enter neutral ports'. It

was thought the Germans would attack Holland, however, if the Dutch closed the Scheldt to their trade. The Germans were not expected to invade Belgium, of course, but it was assumed that if they did they would attack Holland also and form a naval base at Antwerp, which could not be used without violating Dutch territorial waters.

4 Caldwell, op. cit., I, p. 158.
5 The CID official history of the first months of the war reveals a real fear of invasion and also a fear of civil disturbances which might have required the presence of a substantial military force (Cab. 38–28 No. 51).
6 Esher, *The Tragedy of Lord Kitchener*, p. 30.
7 *J & L*, 6 Aug. 1914.
8 EP, WJ, 6 Aug. 1914.
9 Haig also foretold a war of 'several years', as Kitchener but none of the politicians did. See Terraine, *Haig*, pp. 73–4. Haig noted at the same time (5 Aug.): 'I mentioned one million men as the number to aim at immediately, remarking that that was the strength originally proposed for the Territorial Force by Lord Haldane...I urged that a considerable proportion of officers and NCOs should be withdrawn forthwith from the Expeditionary Force...'
10 EP, prepared for Kitchener.
11 *J & L*, 12 Aug. 1914.
12 ibid., 13 Aug. 1914.
13 ibid., same entry.
14 Esher, *Kitchener*, p. 32.
15 EP, WJ, 20 Aug. 1914.
16 EP, same entry.
17 *J & L*, 19 Aug. 1914.
18 French, *1914*, p. 79.
19 Hankey, *Supreme Command*, I, p. 190.
20 EP.
21 *J & L*, 2 and 3 Sept. 1914.
22 Esher, *Kitchener*, p. 63.
23 Jenkins, *Asquith*, p. 382. Stamfordham recorded that on 27 Oct. the King saw Churchill about Battenberg's retirement as First Sea Lord after his nerves were affected by a movement against him on account of his name and parentage expressed in

anonymous letters and personal attacks. The King declined to accept Fisher and proposed Sir Heathcote Meux. Next day Asquith took up Fisher's case with the King, who maintained his objection to Fisher on account of his being distrusted and changing his opinions 'from day to day'. Asquith replied that he had not heard this before, and in spite of a written objection from the King, carried his point on the 30th. On being overruled, the King asked to record his 'protest', whereupon Asquith suggested that 'a less severe term', 'misgivings', might be used (RA GV Q1079/41. Memo's of 27, 28 and 30 Oct. 1914.) Cf. account in Gilbert, *Churchill*, III, pp. 149–53.

24 *J & L*, 30 Sept. 1914.
25 Esher, *Kitchener*, p. 60.
26 EP, WJ, 11 Nov. 1914.
27 RA GV Q724/20. Esher-Stamfordham, 9 Oct. 1914.
28 ibid., same letter.
29 *J & L*.
30 *J & L*, 22 Jan. 1915.
31 *J & L*, 24 Jan. 1915.
32 PRO, Cab. 24–1 No. 64. 'After Six Months', 29 Jan. 1915: '...the military initiative still remains with Germany...France was not as well prepared in August last as the highest military opinion in this country considered her to be. The CID had been told over and over again...that there would be no question of an immediate invasion on a large scale of French territory, and...that if the assistance of Great Britain was immediately forthcoming France would not be invaded at all.'
33 *J & L*, Esher-Maurice Brett, 30 Jan. 1915.
34 *J & L*, Esher-Maurice Brett, 1 Feb. 1915.
35 Maurice Bunau-Varilla, 1856–1944. Collaborator in 1940.
36 Bertie, *Diary*, I, p. 111.
37 EP, WJ, 12 Feb. 1915.
38 Esher, *Kitchener*, p. 97.
39 EP, WJ, 16 Feb. 1915.
40 EP.
41 EP, WJ, 15 March 1915.
42 EP, WJ, 11 March 1915.
43 Lloyd George, *War Memoirs*, I, p. 103.
44 Churchill's visit to the suggestible Sir John caught him discom-

fited by the *coup manqué* of Neuve Chapelle and suspicious of Kitchener who had been invited to a conference with Joffre and Millerand and was seemingly about to be persuaded to divert further ammunition from the western front to the Dardanelles. Instead of blaming Churchill for the Near East operations, Sir John 'sent him to the cabinet with an ultimatum about Lord K.'s visit' (EP, WJ, 18 March). When Churchill had left, Sir John summoned Esher by telephone to a week-end consultation, and conveyed Churchill's information about the 'most serious' state of the ammunition supply (EP, WJ, 20 March). For criticisms of Churchill's visits to France and to GHQ see Gilbert, op. cit., III, p. 348 etc.

45 EP, WJ, 20 March 1915.
46 EP, WJ, 21 and 22 March 1915.
47 EP, WJ, 24 March
48 *J & L*, 15 March 1915.
49 *J & L*.
50 Lloyd George, op. cit. I, p. 111.
51 Asquith, op. cit., II, p. 83 describes the origin of the quarrel at the end of March, seemingly over the restive attitude of the Tory press, which was afraid to attack Kitchener directly and was threatening to blame Lloyd George for the ineffectiveness of his Committee.
52 Spender, *Asquith*, II, p. 187, c. Sept. 1915.
53 See R. Churchill, *Churchill*, II, p. 344 for an occasion in 1911 when Asquith could hardly speak when on the front bench, and it was observed 'only the persistent free-masonry of the House of Commons prevents a scandal'. Stamfordham resented the way Lloyd George 'practically hustled the King into giving up any drink in his establishment on the ground that the government were going to compel the country to do the same' (BL, SP, Stamfordham-Strachey, 12 Feb. 1917. S/13/15/31).
54 Spender, op. cit., II, p. 139, 16 April 1915.
55 RA GV Q724/24.
56 *Glasgow Herald*, 28 April 1915, p. 8. 'Lord Esher and the War'.
57 ibid., 28 April 1915.
58 Hankey, op. cit., I, p. 312.
59 *J & L*, 11 May 1915.
60 EP.

61 PRO, Cab. 37–128 No. 11, calling on Asquith either to take 'the sole direction of the war into his own hands', or delegate its direction to Kitchener: and to suspend further 'the custom that sanctifies Cabinet meetings and responsibility'.

62 *J & L*, 14 May 1915.

63 ibid., same entry.

64 EP.

65 W. Churchill, op. cit., II, pp. 788–9 for a list of the reinforcements.

66 Gilbert, op. cit., III. p. 419, mentions a suggestion that Fisher's mind was overwrought by having to manage the Admiralty while Churchill was in Paris, for he waylaid Mrs Churchill in a corridor and to her astonishment said: 'You are a foolish woman. All the time you think Winston's with Sir John French he is in Paris with his mistress.'

67 EP, WJ, 15 May 1915.

68 EP, WJ, 16 May 1915. The idea that Kitchener might be made C-in-C of all forces overseas was to play a vital part in the ensuing crisis even though in the end it was dropped. Another idea, the establishment of a Ministry of Munitions, seems to have originated in the discussions between King George, Esher and Stamfordham on 15–16 May. Taken together, the two proposals solved the political problem of how to relieve Kitchener of responsibility for munitions without placing Lloyd George over him at the War Office.

69 W. Churchill, op. cit., II, p. 797.

70 ibid., pp. 797–8. Gilbert, op. cit., III, pp. 446–7, suggests as a reason why Asquith gave way to Lloyd George his failure of nerve after his affair with Venetia Stanley was unexpectedly terminated.

71 EP, WJ, 20 March 1915. For the suspicion among Liberal MPs that Churchill was 'privy to the intrigue which resulted in the Repington disclosures' see Gilbert, op. cit., III, p. 460. W. M. R. Pringle-Asquith, 20 May.

72 *J & L*, 16 May 1915.

73 Blake (*The Unknown Prime Minister: Bonar Law*, p. 249) mentions that Asquith told Bonar Law he was 'getting rid of Kitchener' when he consulted him about a Coalition government. But Asquith in reporting this development to the King the same

day (17 May) expressly stated that 'the questions which have
arisen as to Fisher and Kitchener can stand over' (RA GV
K 770/1). What Asquith wanted was a replacement for Churchill,
and Kitchener's translation from War Office administration to
overseas strategy.

74 Lloyd George, op. cit., I, p. 121.

75 *J & L*, 17 May 1915. In a cabinet circular to his colleagues
Asquith explained that he had been contemplating a Coalition
for some time, and that it was necessary to avoid a disturbance in
Parliament over either shells or Fisher's resignation which might
discourage Italy from joining the allies. (PRO, Cab. 37–128.
No. 19, dated 17 May 1915).

76 W. Churchill, op. cit., II, p. 805, quotes Fisher's letter. Actually
Fisher greatly modified his terms and tone the next day, but too
late.

77 ibid., p. 804.

78 Except by Churchill himself, who offered Fisher his post again
with a seat in the cabinet on Wednesday evening (19 May).
Fisher rejected these 'thirty pieces of silver' and disclosed the
overture to Bonar Law. (Gilbert, op. cit., 111, p. 456).

79 RA GV K770/2.

80 RA GV K770/4.

81 RA GV K770/6.

82 See e.g. RA GV K770/8, where Stamfordham in reporting to the
King on 20 May the events of the day envisaged that a new
Secretary for War would still have to work closely with Kitchener,
although he admitted: 'I can detect a certain want of faith in
Kitchener on both sides. The Prime Minister is I know favourable
to Lloyd George's going to the War Office. I am aware that he
and Lord K. have differed but the latter never bears ill will.
I expect Lloyd George would do better with contractors etc. than
perhaps Bonar Law.'

83 RA GV K770/7.

84 *J & L*, 18 May 1915.

85 This was the real height of the crisis, and the day chosen for the
attack by the Harmsworth press on Kitchener. Lady Cynthia
Asquith (*Diaries*, p. 25) describes how she 'lunched at Downing
Street, where a tremendous atmosphere of tension and distress
prevails...I have never before seen him [Asquith] look either

tired, worried, busy, or preoccupied, but this time he looked really shattered with a sort of bruised look in his eyes...'

86 RA GV K770/11.
87 RA GV K770/12.
88 ibid., same memorandum.
89 ibid., same memorandum.
90 ibid., same memorandum. The basis for the final settlement may have been an understanding that Lloyd George's tenure of the new Ministry of Munitions should be brief, for an undated 'formula' in Asquith's papers reads: 'Mr Lloyd George has undertaken the formation and temporary direction of this Department and during his tenure of office as Minister of Munitions will vacate the office of Chancellor of the Exchequer' (Bod. L, AP, 27, f. 208).
91 *J & L.*

Chapter 13
1 EP, WJ, 22 May 1915.
2 EP, WJ, 21 May 1915.
3 EP, WJ, 22 May 1915. Sir John's frayed nerves were also manifested in 'violent language about Joffre before casual guests and servants' (EP, WJ, 4 April 1915).
4 *J & L,* 28 Aug. 1915.
5 RA GV Q724/43. Robinson (later Dawson) of *The Times* no doubt approved the attack on the government in the issue of 1 September, which described it as designed to keep political peace at home rather than to wage war abroad. *The Times* demanded 'a far smaller cabinet, capable of being assembled at any moment, and meeting daily as a matter of course'.
6 RA GV Q724/44.
7 EP.
8 RA GV R252. Asquith-King George, 12 Oct. 1915.
9 EP.
10 EP, draft by Esher of 15 Oct. 1915.
11 EP, Stamfordham-Esher, 22 Oct. 1915.
12 *J & L,* 7 Oct. 1915.
13 Wilson, *Political Diaries of C. P. Scott*, p. 135.
14 *J & L,* 17 Sept. 1915.
15 RA GV K869/1.

16 Carson resigned on 12 Oct. 1915.
17 Quoted in Jenkins, *Asquith*, p. 423.
18 Wilson, *Political Diaries of C. P. Scott*, pp. 146–7.
19 Repington, *First World War*, I, p. 54.
20 Jenkins, op. cit., p. 421.
21 ibid., p. 423. 'Non-departmental' had implications for Kitchener, and indeed the War Committee members stayed behind after the cabinet meeting and decided that Kitchener would have to go. (Gilbert, *Churchill*, III, pp. 558–9)
22 RA GV K873/2.
23 Lloyd George, *War Memoirs*, I, p. 306.
24 ibid., I, pp. 307–9.
25 Wilson, *Political Diaries of C. P. Scott*, p. 153.
26 ibid., p. 153.
27 Lloyd George, op. cit., I, p. 436.
28 Wilson, *Political Diaries of C. P. Scott*, p. 155.
29 Callwell, *Field-Marshal Sir Henry Wilson*, I. p. 260.
30 *J & L*, 5 Nov. 1915.
31 ibid., same entry.
32 *J & L*, 7 and 10 Nov. 1915.
33 *J & L*, 6 Nov. 1915.
34 EP.
35 EP, cabinet print by Selborne, 18 Oct. 1915.
36 EP, Esher-Hankey, 24 Oct. 1915.
37 EP.
38 EP, Esher-Hankey, 7 Nov. 1915.
39 EP.
40 EP.
41 Hankey, *Supreme Command*, II, p. 451. The conference at the Elysée Palace on 17 Nov. approved a joint Standing Committee of allied premiers, ministers and experts, whose meetings were to be 'preceded by an interchange of views between the General Staffs, the Marine Staffs, and other departments'. The Standing Committee was to have a permanent secretariat. (PRO, Cab. 24–1 No. 40).
42 *J & L*, 9 Nov. 1917, recalling an interview with the King on 20 Nov. 1915.
43 *J & L*, 29 Nov. 1915.
44 Spender, *Asquith*, II, p. 200.

45 Hankey, op. cit., II, pp. 453–4.

46 RA GV Q838/46. The King 'deprecated' the proposal that Kitchener should be C-in-C of all forces overseas *except* those in France.

47 *J & L*, 9 and 10 Dec. 1915. 'War Council' remained the formal way of referring to the War Committee.

48 The decision to replace Sir John French was taken in principle by Asquith in October. He squarely blamed Sir John for withholding the reserve from Haig until too late. Writing to Selborne on 26 Oct. 1915 Asquith had no doubt that the reserve was 'late in being ordered up, that through bad staff work some of the units took the wrong road, that the new troops were tired and hungry when they reached the scene of action, and that a number of them ran away.' For this the 'main responsibility rests with Sir J. French, and a very serious one it is...before long Haig will have to take his place' (Bod. L, Sel. P, pp. 80–64).

49 Sir Francis Hopwood, Stamfordham's 'private eye' at the Admiralty, reported to him on 20 Dec: 'The Prime Minister must honour his pledges or go under...It is hardly for any cabinet to lose its Lord Chancellor and Chancellor of Exchequer and survive. Then what of Mr Balfour? Only a few days ago he told me he was quite unconverted to any form of compulsion' (RA GV K869/2).

50 S. McKenna, *McKenna*, p. 254.

51 Cynthia Asquith, *Diaries*, p. 118: 'apparently nearly all the principal cabinet ministers are now agreed on the small army. It was Kitchener who, quite arbitrarily, pledged the seventy divisions to the French Government.'

52 Wilson, *Political Diaries of C. P. Scott*, p. 166.

53 S. McKenna, op. cit., p. 258.

54 MP, 3 Jan. 1916.

55 RA GV Q724/66. Esher-Stamfordham, 25 Jan. 1916. The dilemma was also sometimes referred to as 'starving or storming'.

56 EP, WJ, 23 Feb. 1916.

57 EP, Haig-Esher, 22 Feb. 1916.

58 For an appreciation of Mark Sykes see Nicolson, *Peacemaking*, p. 263.

59 EP, Memo. of 30 Jan. 1916.

60 EP.
61 EP, Robertson-Esher, 4 Feb. 1916.
62 EP, 3 Feb. 1916.
63 EP.
64 EP, Esher-Derby, 19 March 1916.
65 EP.
66 EP, 5 April 1916.
67 EP, Esher-Macready, 2 April 1916.
68 EP, WJ, 3 April 1916.
69 EP, Stamfordham-Esher, 6 April 1916.
70 EP, O. A. G. FitzGerald-Esher, Sat. [15?] April 1916.
71 EP, 10 April 1916.
72 EP.
73 EP.
74 *J & L*, 14 April 1916.
75 EP, WJ, 15 April 1916.
76 Roskill, *Hankey*, p. 264. Asquith's casual manner belied his
   anxieties. See e.g. Cynthia Asquith, *Diaries*, p. 154. Lunching at
   10 Downing Street that Saturday she found 'Margot was very
   hysterical and saying they would never be in Downing Street
   again after the following Tuesday'.
77 EP, WJ, 15 April 1916.
78 EP.
79 Repington, op. cit., I, p. 186.
80 RA GV K951/1. Memo. by Stamfordham, 15 April 1916.
81 RA GV K951/2. 'If the Unionists were returned with a mandate
   for general compulsion, government would have to be by a dictatorship. Strikes, resistance to enlisting would follow and have to be
   put down by force and martial law.'
82 ibid., same memo.
83 Wilson, *Political Diaries of C. P. Scott*, p. 198.
84 RA GV K951/3.
85 ibid., same memo. Cf. Nicolson, *George V*, pp. 362–3.
86 Wilson, op. cit., p. 199.
87 Blake, *The Unknown Prime Minister: Bonar Law*, p. 284.
88 *J & L*, 17 April 1916.
89 EP.
90 RA GV K951/5. Memo. by Stamfordham, 17 April.
91 ibid., same memo.

92 Wilson, *Political Diaries of C. P. Scott*, p. 199. Stevenson (*Diary* pp. 105–7) confirms that Lloyd George meant to resign with the members of the Army Council (entry for 17 April) and mentions a new cabinet committee without McKenna formed on the 18th to confer with them. Lloyd George is said in this account to have been working to avoid a smash on that day (entry for 18 April).

93 EP, WJ, 17 April 1916.

94 RA GV K951/5.

95 ibid., same memo.

96 *J & L*, 18 April 1916.

97 EP.

98 *J & L*, 19 April 1916.

99 ibid., same entry.

100 RA GV K951/7. Memo. by Stamfordham, 19 April 1916.

101 *J & L*, 19 April 1916.

102 Frances Stevenson, (*Diary* p. 107, 19 April) tells how at the cabinet that morning Lloyd George sent a note across to Robertson demanding 50,000 men in the first month. The cabinet decided that Henderson should confer with the Army Council that afternoon. The next day Cynthia Asquith, lunching with Harold Baker, a War Office official, learnt that: 'The political corner—I suppose the sharpest—has been safely rounded, and a secret session (without precedent) has been decided on.' Asquith however was not out of the wood, and at this juncture Henry Wilson made his characteristic remark to Milner: 'We hope that you and Carson and LG have, at last, got him by the throat. No mercy please' (Gollin, *Milner*, p. 342).

103 Hankey, op. cit., II, p. 475.

104 EP, WJ, 28 April 1916, referring to the secret session of 25 April, which he describes as a 'ridiculous farce', since Lord Crewe's speech said nothing that could not have been said in an open House.

105 Asquith's compromise Bill was introduced on 27 April but withdrawn on Carson's attack. A Bill for full compulsion was brought in on 2 May. Ireland was however not included, ostensibly because the Derby canvass had not been extended there, in reality because of the difficulties of applying compulsion to it.

106 RA GV R284.

107 Roskill, *Hankey*, I. p. 266.

108 Repington, op. cit., I, p. 285.

109 The formula which Kitchener took in to the cabinet of 19 April was written for him that morning by Esher in these terms: 'The Army Council in a memo. circulated to the cabinet have explained that in their opinion every available man is required... They have declined to define the methods by which every available man should be determined and obtained, this being in their opinion the function of the government. Impressed by the danger of uncertainty and delay, they must...decline to express themselves as satisfied with the methods now proposed' (EP, WJ, 19 April).

Chapter 14

1 EP.

2 EP, WJ, 6 May 1916.

3 As early as 18 May Esher knew the joint offensive would take place 'about the end of June'. 'To postpone an offensive till next year or even till autumn means a depletion of the French armies that they are unable to face with equanimity' (EP, WJ).

4 EP.

5 EP, 18 June 1916.

6 EP, Haig-Esher, 20 May 1916. A month later Haig comments: 'Bertie lives a life apart from the active world.'

7 EP, Esher-Robertson, 18 June 1916.

8 EP, Macready-Esher, 6 June 1916.

9 On the day after Kitchener's death was announced, Churchill went to see Lloyd George at the War Office, and encountered Northcliffe coming out of his room, who said jokingly: 'I suppose you have come after LG's job.' This was too near the mark for Winston to think it funny (Gilbert, *Churchill*, III, p. 783). Churchill applied to succeed Lloyd George at the Ministry of Munitions via Lord Reading on 13 June. Since January Churchill had been plotting for an alternative government to Asquith's 'wait and see' affair (Gilbert, op. cit., p. 697).

10 *J & P*, 15 June 1916.

11 On 13 June Asquith had 'a very long interview' with Lloyd George which was inconclusive. On 16th Asquith told Stamfordham that Lloyd George wanted the War Office with 'its former plenary powers restored', but seems to have also conveyed the

objections: for Stamfordham added that this 'is impossible as Robertson's present position would be compromised. Best solution is for PM to remain at WO. Whole Army Council want this ...LG's proposals go beyond what a unanimous cabinet would sanction' (RA GV K951/16 and 17).

12 Lloyd George, *War Memoirs*, I, p. 459.

13 Wilson, *The Political Diaries of C. P. Scott*, p. 220.

14 Jenkins, *Asquith*, p. 460.

15 EP.

16 Churchill commented: 'Meanwhile Asquith reigns supine, sodden and supreme. LG made a half-hearted fight about munitions. He is very much alone...' (Gilbert, op. cit., p. 788).

17 *J & L*, 23 June 1916.

18 EP, 27 June 1916.

19 EP, Esher-Hankey, 28 June 1916.

20 EP.

21 EP, Gen. Charteris-Esher, 1 July 1916.

22 Esher took Northcliffe to see the army's lines of communication and converted him to the idea that thanks to Haig's efficiency the Somme was the first 'scientific' offensive of the war (EP, Esher-Haig, 2 Aug. 1916).

23 EP.

24 W. Churchill, *World Crisis*, II, p. 1085, memo. of 1 Aug.

25 MP, Lord Percy-Maxse, 5 Aug. 1916. Sir John French had pressed a brigade on Churchill, which Esher had thought 'a great mistake'. Asquith, who had agreed to the appointment, later vetoed it, which made Churchill feel 'every tie severed' with Asquith (Gilbert, op. cit., pp. 609–11). When Haig succeeded French he gave Churchill the command of a battalion but failed to give him the expected promotion later. The incident was important in cementing Churchill's friendship with Sir John French, who was to become a politician's catspaw.

26 F. E. Smith's military arrest in January 1916 was particularly humiliating since he was Attorney-General at the time and technically the overseer of the military courts.

27 MP, Lord Percy-Maxse, 2 Aug. 1916.

28 Wilson, *Political Diaries of C. P. Scott*, p. 224.

29 MP, Lord Percy-Maxse, 2 Aug. 1916.

30 EP, Esher-Queen Mary, 4 Aug. 1916.

31 EP, Esher-Haig, 7 Aug. 1916.
32 EP.
33 *Daily Telegraph*, 8 Aug. 1916, p. 6.
34 EP, Esher-Robertson, 19 Aug. 1916.
35 EP, Esher-Robertson, 21 Aug. 1916.
36 Even Sir Thomas Hughes, Lloyd George's assistant, admitted some months later that he 'had been surrounded too long by a poisonous crew, whom practically everyone at Westminster knew all about...' (Thomas Jones *Whitehall Diary*, I. p. 20).
37 EP.
38 EP, WJ, 18 Sept. 1916.
39 EP. Lord Cowdray had the controlling interest in the *Westminster Gazette*, and Spender later wrote an appreciative biography of him. But the other shareholders, Aberconway, Elibank, Mond and Alec Murray were probably those whom Spencer feared. When Lloyd George became Prime Minister the hostile shareholders would not permit criticisms of his régime, and as Spencer complained to Asquith (4 Oct. 1917) threatened to sell or wind up the paper while Lloyd George himself 'declared open war by starting a libel action...for a news paragraph...' This led Lord Crewe to complain that 'the one mouthpiece of educated Liberalism' was in danger of becoming 'a mere semaphore for Lloyd George' (Bod. L, AP, 18 ff. 17, 18).
40 Lloyd George, *War Memoirs*, I, p. 472 seq.
41 Lawrence Franklin Burgis, born 1892, private secretary to Esher, 1909–13. Capt. serving in France from Jan. 1917. Principal and Assistant Secretary in Cabinet Office, 1921–45.
42 EP.
43 EP.
44 W. Churchill, op. cit., II, p. 1083.
45 EP.
46 EP, WJ, 30 July 1916.
47 EP, same entry. Haig's propaganda by 1918 was centralised under a Major Roberts at Chateau de Traincourt, where journalists and politicians were shown films, pamphlets, exhibits, etc., and given excursions to the front (RL, FDRP, Large Box 8, Hist. of Office of U.S. Naval attaché in Paris).
48 EP.
49 The Maison de la Presse was instituted after the war began for

P*

propaganda to neutral and allied countries. It organised *L'Union des Grandes Associations Françaises contre la Propagand Ennemie*, and kept in touch with the Paris representatives of the foreign press.

50 *J & L*, 17 Oct. 1916.
51 The Foreign Office did not believe in propaganda, arguing that it was self-defeating. See e.g. 'British Propaganda in Allied and Neutral Countries' (PRO, Cab. 24–3 No. 101, 1916) which admits that while Germany spent 'fabulous sums' on propaganda in the USA, Britain spent nothing on 'offensive' propaganda since Lord Robert Cecil, the Under-Secretary for Foreign Affairs, felt strongly that it was a waste of money. The News Dept. of the Foreign Office did however run an information service using the Naval Attaché in Washington (Capt. Gaunt), and bureaux in Petrograd and Italy. There was no such bureau in France where the vital importance of sustaining French morale by publicising the British war effort seems to have been overlooked. This task fell by default to Haig's Intelligence Officer, Charteris. Later, in 1917, Haig's propaganda agent, John Buchan, and Lord North-cliffe were appointed to propagandise enemy countries, but only after resistance from the Foreign Office (Cab. 24–6 No. 26).
52 EP, WJ, 8 Oct. 1916.
53 EP, WJ, 7 Oct. 1916.
54 EP, 11 Oct. 1916.
55 Bertie, *Diary*, II, pp. 42–3.
56 EP, WJ, 29 Nov. 1916.
57 RA GV Q724/84. Esher-Stamfordham, 1 Dec. 1916. Haig was gazetted Field-Marshal on New Year's Day 'as a gesture against Lloyd George' (A. J. P. Taylor, *English History*, p. 74n).
58 Wilson, *Political Diaries of C. P. Scott*, p. 237.
59 Repington, *The First World War*, I, p. 358 *seq.*
60 Bod. L, AP, 30 f. 255.
61 *J & L*, 26 Oct. 1916.
62 Bod. L, AP, 30 f., 257.
63 EP, WJ, 29 Sept. 1916.
64 Repington, op. cit., I, pp. 361 and 364.
65 EP.
66 Text in Asquith, *Memories and Reflections*, II, pp. 165–75. The crux was: '...if the additional year, or two years, or three years,

finds us still unable to dictate terms, the war with its nameless horrors will have been needlessly prolonged...'

67 Carson had over 150 MPs associated with his Unionist War Committee, set up early in 1916, and was almost as hostile to Bonar Law as to Asquith. He wanted state control of shipping, food, coal, etc.

68 Hankey, *Supreme Command*, II, pp. 440–1.

69 i.e. of the Conservatives who divided, 65 went with Carson and 71 with the government, and as Gilbert (op. cit., III, p. 815) observes: 'Had Carson been supported by only four more Tories, Bonar Law, under the pledge he had given the Conservatives on joining the Government in May 1915, would have had to resign, and the Coalition would have collapsed.'

70 Blake, *The Unknown Prime Minister, Bonar Law*, p. 305.

71 ibid., p. 307.

72 RA GV R310 Asquith-King George, 30 Nov. 1916.

73 It satisfied Crewe, who wrote to Asquith on 4 Dec: '...no meeting for some time past has been of any service to the country or the government. If it is possible to substitute two small boards of three each, with you as President of both, business ought to be promptly done' (quoted by Peter Lowe in *Lloyd George*, ed. A. J. P. Taylor, p. 126).

74 RA GV K1048a/2. Memo. on fall of Asquith administration by Lord Errington, Dec. 1916.

75 EP, WJ, 29 Nov. 1916.

76 *J & L*, 4 Dec. 1916. Esher had heard from Murray of Elibank that 'people at home' expected to find the men needed to maintain Haig's army by a 'comb out' from 'the army itself'. Robertson seemed in Esher's view to have accepted this plan, which to Esher meant 'absolute and deadly failure to produce men *in time*' (EP, Esher-Haig, 2 Dec. 1916).

77 Bod. L, AP, 31 f., 8. Montagu-Asquith, 2 Dec. 1916. Parts of this letter are quoted in Spender, *Asquith*, II, p. 254.

78 ibid., same letter.

79 Wilson, *Political Diaries of C. P. Scott*, p. 244. According to Frances Stevenson (*Diary*, p. 125) Northcliffe told Max Aitken he was out to 'destroy LG' after Lloyd George's criticisms of the army's lines of communication, which Northcliffe had praised. However, on 1 Dec. (ibid., p. 130) Northcliffe 'turned

up again, grovelling, and trying to be friends with David again
...if there is anything big happening Northcliffe would hate to
be out of the know...' This would seem to be the overture that
prompted the errand of C. P. Scott. It is claimed on scant evidence
(Pound, *Northcliffe*, p. 513) that Lloyd George himself saw
Northcliffe on 3 Dec.

80 RA GV K1048a/2. Having resigned at 7-30 p.m. on 5 Dec.,
Asquith at dinner looked 'rubicund, serene, puffing a guinea
cigar...and talking of going to Honolulu'. He had however remarked that Lloyd George might fail to form a government
at all: 'The Tories—in urging him to resign—had predicted such
a failure' (Cynthia Asquith, *Diaries*, p. 241).

81 RA, same memo.

82 Lloyd George, *War Memoirs*, I, p. 628. The War Cabinet idea
was pressed on Lloyd George by the Unionists and especially
Austen Chamberlain.

83 Hankey, op. cit., II, p. 580. The mechanisation of War Cabinet
business through Hankey's extended secretariat and Lloyd
George's personal secretariat (the 'garden suburb')—both dominated by Milne's bureaucratically-minded disciples—made possible
a large extension of government departments and functions.

84 M. Thomas's cousin was Lloyd George's French interpreter.

85 MP, Esher-Maxse, 7 Nov. 1916.

86 EP, WJ, 27 Dec. 1916.

87 EP.

88 Esher knew that Albert Thomas when in London had asked that
Haig be *ordered* to take over more of the French line, which he
thought was 'pretty cool...these political upstarts. They are a
dirty lot' (EP, WJ, 2 Jan. 1917).

89 EP.

90 Lloyd George, op. cit., I p. 887.

91 L. S. Amery, who became with Mark Sykes a joint political
secretary to the War Cabinet, claims to have given a new direction to British war policy by a memo. of Jan. 1917 advocating
tighter control over overseas operations. 'We could then ration
France were such troops as we considered might be required
for the defence of her territory...' No doubt this was the kind of
thinking behind Lloyd George's decision to master Haig (L. S.
Amery, *My Political Life*, II, p. 92).

92 RA GV Q1079/1. Memo. by Stamfordham, 16 Jan. 1917. Haig agreed to take over more line, and co-operate in an early attack.

93 EP, Esher-Robertson, 24 Jan. 1917. Esher was 'very doubtful' about Nivelle's optimism, 'so vehemently expressed'. If there were a check to his operations 'the reaction will be violent, and the French will descend into the depths of depression' (EP, Esher-Robertson, 2 Feb. 1917). Robertson replied (6 Feb.): 'He talked far too much when in London about the certainty of succeeding.'

94 EP.

95 EP, WJ, 3 Feb. 1917. Murray of Elibank was in charge of the Oil Dept. of the Mexican Eagle Company owned by Lord Cowdray and was engaged in prospecting outside Mexico in areas including France, Algeria and Morocco. Cowdray's construction company, S. Pearson & Son, had among its wartime enterprises contracted for the munitions town of Gretna (J. A. Spender, *Cowdray*, 208–9). Elibank's firm had just made 'a large Algerian development contract' with the French government which was before the Chamber (NL of S., M of EP 8804 f. 67. Elibank-Asquith, 29 Nov. 1916).

96 Just before the British entry into the war Elibank had introduced Lloyd George to Baron Gunzburg, inviting him to stay at the Baron's 'delightful house on the links' at Dieppe. He added: 'I must wire to Baron de Gunzburg this morning, so that he may let Bertie know.' Gunzburg, he explained, was 'the head of one of the biggest finance Houses in Paris', had an 'extraordinary know-ledge of European conditions', and was 'a great personal friend of Bertie's' (BL, LGP. C/6/5/18. Elibank-Lloyd George, 31 July 1914). There is a letter from Gunzburg to Mr Moir in French from Gunzburg's Paris address, 47 rue Cambon, dated 17 Sept. 1915, in which he claims to manage at Paris *des affaires qui concernent le gouvernement russe* and asks for a British munitions expert to visit his works at Montbard with Le Roy-Lewis (BL, LGP, D18/2/9). Gunzburg seems to have acted in liaison with the president of the International Bank of Petrograd.

97 EP.

98 EP, Esher-Haig, 5 Feb. 1917.

99 EP, WJ, 11 Feb 1917. The French had broken the code used by the Germans between Spain and Germany, and gave the texts of the intercepts to the American naval attaché later after the USA

had entered the war. Presumably Le Roy-Lewis enjoyed the same facilities. These radio messages were mostly to Germany with information derived from France and even Great Britain but also included instructions to submarines, and Commander Sayles, the American attaché in question, first heard of the landing of American troops in Le Havre from this source. How the Germans got information from France to Spain so quickly 'baffled the efforts of some of the best Intelligence Officers of all the allied Services' (RL, FDRP, Large box 8. History of Office of US Naval Attaché, 1914–18, pp. 197–201).

100 EP, WJ, 11 Feb. 1917.
101 EP, same entry.
102 EP, Esher-Haig, 12 Feb. 1917.
103 EP, same letter.
104 Roskill, *Hankey*, p. 361.
105 'Without doubt the prestige which Marshal Haig enjoys among the British people and army would probably not allow him to be completely subordinated to the French command; but, if the War Committee recognised that this measure is essential, it will not hesitate to give secret instructions to this effect to Marshal Haig.' (Suarez, *Briand*, IV, p. 150)
106 EP, WJ, 25 March 1917.
107 Suarez, op. cit., IV, p. 151.
108 ibid. Also *Poincaré, Au service de la France*, IX, p. 67 seq.
109 RA GV Q1079/17. Hankey-Stamfordham, 4 March 1917.
110 RA same letter.
111 Esher-Haig, 1 March 1917, quoted in Blake, *Haig*, 206.
112 Roskill, op. cit., p. 362.
113 Suarez, op. cit., IV. pp. 161–3.
114 Blake, *Haig*, pp. 203–4.
115 Text in Suarez, IV, pp. 163–5.
116 Roskill, op. cit. p. 363.
117 ibid., p. 363. According to Frances Stevenson (*Diary*, pp. 146–7), Lloyd George was prepared to threaten resignation if Haig refused to sign the Agreement.
118 Text in Suarez, IV, pp. 170–2.
119 Blake, *Haig*, p. 203.
120 EP, WJ, 28 Feb. 1917.
121 EP, WJ, 2 March 1917.

122 Suarez, op. cit., IV, p. 175.

123 Blake, *Haig*, p. 203.

124 EP.

125 EP, WJ, 22 Feb. 1917.

126 EP, WJ, 8 March 1917.

127 A revealing document which Hankey drew up for Lloyd George on 7 March shows that even at that late date the War Cabinet did not accept Haig's prognostication that the Germans were about to shorten their line. On 21 Feb. Haig had shown Esher aerial photographs of the new German lines from Cambrai to St Quentin. The French GQG dismissed the prospect of a German withdrawal to the new line as a 'local reshuffling of the cards' but to Esher it meant 'an intention to shorten their line and balk our offensive' (EP, WJ 21 and 28 Feb.). Hankey also agreed with Haig, and warned Lloyd George: 'We shall consequently expend a vast amount of effort, huge stores of ammunition, and involve much wear and tear to guns in bombarding and assaulting an empty shell...My belief is that Haig is right and Nivelle is wrong... If the plan is changed we should absolutely insist on tackling the Belgian coast and we should take no denial...' (PRO, Cab. 63–19, memo., by Hankey for Lloyd George, 7 March 1917). Lloyd George had hoped that Hankey would advise the dismissal of Haig for obstructing the Nivelle plan.

128 RA GV Q1079/41. Undated memo.

129 EP, WJ, 13 March 1917. Esher began to lose faith in Robertson after this incident. 'I am surprised that you indicate that I am "resolved to let the French assume control of our armies".' Robertson wrote to him (EP, 14 March), explaining rather feebly that he was tired of hearing stories of the 'wicked French', and resolving characteristically: 'In future soldiers will avoid conferences as I have always done.'

130 MP, Northcliffe-Maxse, 20 Feb. 1917.

131 Wilson, *Political Diaries of C. P. Scott*, I. p. 326

132 RA GV Q1079/35.

133 Frances Stevenson, *Diary*, p. 148 (16 March): '...the whole business was a source of worry to D[avid].'

134 EP, WJ, 23 March 1917.

135 PRO, Cab. 63–19.

136 ibid., same memo., where Lloyd George's misgivings about Haig

were said to be based partly on 'instinct' but 'more on his excessive optimism'. Lloyd George's grievances against Haig in March 1917 were chiefly his misuse of the tanks, his reluctance to accept railway experts, his failure to economise on tonnage at the expense of fodder, and failure to encourage new ideas in subordinates. Nevertheless, Haig was still supported by Curzon and Milner, as Hankey found on making discreet soundings, while Bonar Law alone in the War Cabinet would have sanctioned Haig's dismissal, though without conviction, and Hankey added the warning: 'Personally I believe that, if Haig resigned, the Government would very likely be defeated...the late Prime Minister would, I believe, on this issue rally to him his old followers, and many waverers; they would be joined, from sheer mischief, by the dis-united Irish, by the pacifists, and possibly by some of the Tories...'

Chapter 15

1 EP.

2 EP.

3 See Alan Bullock, *Ernest Bevin*, I, pp. 74–7 for impact of the overthrow of the Tsarist state on the British Labour movement.

4 EP, WJ, 17 April 1917. The Soviet of Workers' and Soldiers' Deputies acted in 'contemptuous independence' of the Russian Provisional Government, which was obliged in May to adopt the Soviet's demand for a policy of negotiated peace with no annexations or indemnities (Bullock, loc. cit.). Albert Thomas, a socialist disciple of Jaurès, appears to have addressed the Petrograd Soviet on 21 May declaring that French socialists were also 'fighting capitalism and imperialism' (Zeman, *A Diplomatic History of the First World War*, p. 289).

5 EP, WJ, 19 April 1917.

6 For the incident see Lloyd George, *War Memoirs*, II, p. 1186 and Poincaré, op. cit., IX, p. 70. According to Gordon Wright (*Poincaré*, pp. 171–3), Poincaré had stood out for French annexation of all territories on the left bank of the Rhine. When, at the insistence of Ribot and Lloyd George, the general proposition of a separate peace with Austria was put before the Italians at the Conference of St Jean-de-Maurienne on 19 April, Sonnino

naturally rejected it as incompatible with Italy's ambitious territorial designs in the Adriatic.

7 *J & L*, 13 April and 5 May 1918.

8 EP, WJ, 20 April 1917.

9 *J & L*, Esher-Lloyd George, 25 April 1917.

10 A torrent of defeatist literature, said to be directed or subtly influenced by a powerful German propaganda machine centred on Switzerland, was in full spate before the Russian revolution or the failure of Nivelle. Indeed, Nivelle himself complained on 28 Feb. of pamphlets and pacifist newspapers circulating among the troops, naming the most flagrant propagandists. The supine if not positively treasonable régime of the Minister of the Interior, M. Malvy, found expression in refusal to prosecute, even to the extent of quarrelling with the Police department. Malvy's régime was epitomised by the case of Sébastien Faure, the leading disseminator of anarchist propaganda, who was arrested for 'abnormal sexual intercourse with a small boy in a public park' but released and the charge quashed by direct order of the Prefect of Police (RL, FDRP, RG 10 Box 31. Report of Arrival of US troops in France. Capt. W. R. Sayles—Director of Naval Intelligence, 13 May 1919, p. 5).

11 Callwell, *Field Marshal Sir Henry Wilson*, I, p. 340.

12 Painlevé, then War Minister, wanted with the aid of the Radical socialists to replace Nivelle by Pétain, if necessary overthrowing Ribot in the process (Bertie-Stamfordham, RA GV Q1079/45 27 April 1917). Pétain was already identified with the policy of 'waiting for the Americans' which for Esher spelt doom in the spring of 1918 when the Germans would bring their full strength over to the west.

13 EP.

14 Callwell, op. cit., I, p. 344.

15 ibid., I, p. 354 (Wilson's diary of 20 May). Esher, who was acting in close concert with Wilson at this point, notes: 'Derby says that *if* the French refuse or shirk, D. H[aig] will be *forbidden* to carry out his plans. Lloyd George will manage somehow to clear up the situation. As Clemenceau said of him: *"Il ne sait rien, il ne veut rien savoir, mais il se tirera d'affaires"*' (EP, WJ, 20 May 1917).

16 The psychological reaction of the French to the American entry

into the war, as judged by the US Naval attaché in Paris, was one of despondency rather than elation. It took Nivelle's defeat and the Joffre mission to produce the first US convoy, which landed on 27 June. It was believed in Paris that the USA had entered the war to effect a compromise peace, and that submarines would prevent the transport of any substantial American army to Europe. Hence the naval attaché believed that 'if the first convoy had not arrived safely and when it did, France would have speedily been reduced to the same condition of chaos, confusion, and anarchy to which the German Intelligence Departments had brought Russia' (RL, FDRP, RG 10 Box 31. Report on Arrival of US troops in France, p. 6).

17 *J & L*, 19 May 1917.

18 Esher certainly knew of the mutinies, and notes, e.g. (EP, WJ, 8 June) that 'the other day...the 20th Corps, that famous Corps, was in a state of mutiny' and that the situation in Paris on 2 June was so serious that the troops were confined to barracks. It is possible that the British GHQ did not wish to emphasise the weakness of the French army in case Haig's Flanders campaign should be called off. Thus L. S. Amery (*My Political Life*, II, p. 122) accuses Haig and Robertson of concealing the full extent of demoralisation in the French army from the War Cabinet. Henry Wilson also seems to have misled the War Cabinet, for the minutes of its meeting of 8 June record: '[he] did not confirm the rumours which had reached the War Cabinet that an incident had occurred in the French army amounting almost to a mutiny, but he said there was a good deal of unrest...' (Cab. 23–16. WC 159a).

19 EP.

20 EP, WJ, 29 May 1917.

21 EP, same entry.

22 Hankey, *Supreme Command*, II, pp. 672–3.

23 EP, WJ, 6 June 1917.

24 EP, same entry.

25 EP, WJ, 25 July 1917. On 6 July Erzberger made his speech in the Reichstag against annexations and for a negotiated peace, and Paris seemed to catch the same mood with expressions of opinion hostile to annexing the provinces west of the Rhine. Esher noted on 22 July that the subsidised newspapers were be-

ginning to clamour for a revision of the Constitution in favour of open diplomacy. On 28 July the new German Chancellor, Michaelis, gave to the press details of the secret Franco-Russian treaty and the debates upon it in the secret session of the Chamber in early June. Ribot was exposed as a liar and Briand came in for much obloquy. Albert Thomas and the socialists were mortally offended, and the *union sacrée* shattered.

26 EP, WJ, 27 July 1917.

27 EP, same entry.

28 EP, WJ, 31 July 1917.

29 EP, WJ.

30 EP, WJ, 18 Aug. 1917.

31 EP, WJ, 22 Aug. 1917.

32 EP, WJ, 22 Sept. 1917.

33 EP.

34 EP.

35 EP, 22 Sept. 1917.

36 EP. WJ, 8 Oct. 1917.

37 Callwell, op. cit., II, p. 10. See also Amery, op. cit., II, p. 125, where Wilson is described as plotting with Milner and Amery, his 'old confederate', to produce a plan for 'strategic and political unity of action' and also for 'providing Lloyd George with authoritative military advice...independent of Robertson'.

38 ibid., II, p. 16.

39 Roskill, *Hankey*, p. 446.

40 EP, WJ, 15 Oct. 1917.

41 Hankey, op. cit., II, p. 715.

42 ibid., II, p. 714.

43 Repington, *The First World War*, II, pp. 79–84.

44 ibid., II, p. 103. Esher summed up the results of the Pétain interview after discussing it with Repington on 8 Oct. as: the abandonment of the Flanders attack in 1918 in favour of an attack further south and east; the two allied armies to attack side by side; a fair division of the line for the coming winter; and the French to have two armies in reserve.

45 Blake, *Haig*, p. 233: '...Great Britain must take the necessary steps to win the war by herself, because our French allies had already shown that they lacked both the moral qualities and the means for gaining the victory.'

46 For the scandals of *l'année troublée* see Adam, *Treason and Tragedy*. The murder of Miguel Almeyreda, an anarchist who organised a gang of Corsican bravos to protect Mme Caillaux in 1914 during her trial for shooting the editor of *Figaro*, was perhaps the most squalid. Almeyreda was strangled in gaol, and as Esher commented (EP, Esher-Stamfordham, 17 Aug.) it was as if Lloyd George had given orders to kill Ramsay MacDonald after having used him for nefarious purposes. Malvy had subsidised Almereyda's *Bonnet Rouge*, and his head of the *Sûrété Général*, M. Leymarie, had shielded Duval, who imported German money to corrupt the French press. Malvy resigned, and in the ensuing witch-hunt of the German-subsidised press Bolo Pasha emerged as the archetype of the treasonable conspirators of the Left. A Frenchman who got his title from the deposed khedive of Egypt with whom he acted as a German agent, Bolo doublecrossed both and, visiting New York in 1916, got a further subsidy from the Germans to subvert *Le Temps* and *Figaro*. Malvy's game was probably to keep these obscure and relatively innocuous persons in play. The witch-hunt was promoted by Clemenceau and the Right as a means of striking at Caillaux and 'Caillautism'. The British agent Mrs Kathleen Roseo informed Steel-Maitland writing on 4 Sept. 1917 that it was the British who uncovered the Bolo Pasha affair: 'I have known of it *for months*.' She suspected that Caillaux, 'an animal with many tentacles', was behind Bolo as well as Duval, for 'His activities in *Geneva* never cease' (SRO. S–MP, 173–1).

47 23 and 24 October.

48 EP, WJ, 29 Oct. 1917.

49 Lloyd George, op. cit., II, p. 1311 seq., especially p. 1315 where it is suggested that he would have liked to dismiss Haig. The disappointment of the Flanders campaign was manifest in early October even to the optimistic Charteris, whose diary reads: '8 Oct.: ...unless we have a very great success tomorrow it is the end for this year so far as Flanders is concerned...With a great success tomorrow, and good weather for a few more weeks, we may still clear the coast and win the war before Christmas... 10 Oct.: I was out all yesterday at the attack. It was the saddest day of this year...the mud...prevented us from doing better...

there is no purpose in it now...' (quoted in Terraine, *Haig*, pp. 367–8).

50 RA GV K1340/1.

51 Repington, op. cit., II, p. 127, entry of 3 Nov.

52 Wilson, *Political Diaries of C. P. Scott*, p. 311.

53 EP, WJ, 3 Nov. 1917.

54 EP, same entry.

55 See Terraine, *Haig*, p. 364 for Haig's annoyance with Robertson for approving at the Boulogne Conference (25 Sept.) of the British taking over more line, when Haig was not present.

56 *J & L*, 5 Nov. 1917. Frances Stevenson (*Diary*, pp. 164–5) confirms the suspicion that for Lloyd George the Wilson scheme was primarily 'an ingenious device for depriving Robertson of his power'.

57 EP, WJ, 12 Nov. 1917. See also Conclusion n. 3.

58 EP, WJ, 12 Nov. 1917.

59 On becoming premier Clemenceau changed the title of his paper back to *l'Homme Libre*, and adopted an easygoing attitude to the socialist and *défaitiste* press.

60 EP. For the way Henry Wilson and Amery ensconced themselves at Versailles see Amery, op. cit., II, p. 128.

61 Callwell, op. cit., II, p. 38. Weygand is described by Amery (op. cit., II, p. 126) as 'Foch's personal staff officer and *alter ego*'.

62 EP, WJ, 27 Nov. 1917.

63 EP.

64 Esher thought Charteris 'dangerously optimistic' and observed (EP, WJ, Oct. 16): 'He is considered a "national danger" by all the army commanders, and goes by the name of the "U-boat".' But Charteris had 'never let D. H[aig] down once on military facts of vital importance', and he became in large measure a scapegoat.

65 Hankey, op. cit., II, p. 740.

66 Repington, op. cit., II, p. 180 and p. 186.

67 EP.

68 RA GV F1259/4.

69 Repington, op. cit., II, p. 197.

70 The 'irresponsible controllers of the press' denounced by Philip Keer at this time were Northcliffe, Rothermere, Hulton and Bottomley. The Astors were angry at the way Lloyd George 'used Astor and Philip Kerr as virtuous window dressers, while

in the background he works through Sutherland, Northcliffe, and Co.' (Jones, *Whitehall Diary*, I, pp. 39–40). A. J. P. Taylor (*Eng. Hist.*, 28n) adds Riddell (*News of the World*), Dalziel (*Reynolds News*) and Robertson Nicholl (*British Weekly*) to the list of Lloyd George's 'close friends and advisers'. For a protest by the Unionist War Committee at Lloyd George's press relations see Beaverbrook, *Men and Power*, p. 383.

71 EP.

72 *J & L*, 28 Jan. 1918.

73 *J & L*, 2 Feb. 1918.

74 Repington, op. cit., II, p. 213 and p. 225.

75 ibid., II, p. 228. Esher, incidentally, thought Gwynne a 'thick fellow' and was aware of Repington's impulsiveness. 'As he allows his views to be coloured by his personal likes and dislikes, one cannot pay much attention to the stories he tells of "intrigues" and so on. Some I know to be false' (Esher-Haig, 28 Sept. 1917 NL of S, HP).

76 RA GV F1259/4. Memo. by Stamfordham. 23 Jan. 1918.

77 RA GV F1259/14.

78 Lloyd George, op. cit., II, p. 1673.

79 ibid., II, p. 1676.

80 Repington, op. cit., II, p. 233.

81 Beaverbrook was made the first Minister of Propaganda and Chancellor of the Duchy of Lancaster on 10 Feb. 1918. He installed Northcliffe as Director of Propaganda in Enemy Countries, but Northcliffe insisted on being under the direct control of the Prime Minister. Northcliffe remained critical of Lloyd George, whom he called at this time 'a vitaliser, not an organiser'. But his faith in Haig had been shaken by the way tanks were ordered into the mud of Passchendaele and by remarks of his brother Rothermere's son when fatally wounded to the effect that as well as being wounded three times he had been 'muddled' three times. Reporting his impressions from speaking to soldiers at the front Northcliffe wrote to Rosebery (17 Feb. 1918) : 'All say that they are ordered to do the impossible, and that, with the exception of a division under Sir Montagu Harper, and Plumer's Army, our losses from sheer ignorance on the part of those who issue orders are appalling' (NL of S, RP., Gen. Corresp. 85).

82 EP.

83 *J & L,* 11 Feb. 1918.

84 EP, Esher-Haig, 13 Feb. 1918. See also Cab. 23–5, WC Mins. 342–44. The political row concerned two questions—Robertson's retention as CIGS, and the Versailles scheme of the Executive Board controlling the Reserve, which the public did not know about until Repington defied the Censor. Macdonogh, the DMI told the War Cabinet on 11 Feb. that he could not swear on oath that Repington's disclosures were 'likely to be of any great use to the enemy'. The soldiers were accusing Lloyd George of using the censorship for political ends.

85 EP, Esher-Haig, 13–14 Feb. 1918. Beatrice Webb's acid comment on Margot Asquith at this time was: 'a scatter-brained and some-what vulgar but vital little woman—acquainted with the mentality of great personages but wholly unversed in great affairs—and with the social creed of the commonplace plutocrat.' (LSE, PP, Beatrice Webb's diary, 31 Jan. 1918).

86 Callwell, op. cit., II, p. 59.

87 EP.

88 RA GV F1259/32.

89 ibid.

90 RA GV F1259/26.

91 *J & L,* 14 Feb. 1918.

92 Roskill, *Hankey,* p. 479.

93 *J & L,* 15 Feb. 1918.

94 Callwell, op. cit., II, p. 61.

95 *J & L,* 16 Feb. 1918. The revulsion of feeling against Robertson and his supporters was apparent in the Commons debate the next week, when Lloyd George was cheered on his entrance and Asquith was received 'in absolute silence'. In reporting this to Selborne, Lord Salisbury commented (21 Feb. 1918): '...the history of the crisis has given the Prime Minister a moral ascendancy in military matters which he never possessed before' (Bod. L. Sel. P. 7–1).

96 EP, Esher-Lord Duncannon, 7 March 1918.

97 EP, same letter.

98 EP, Esher-Hankey, 7 March 1918.

99 EP, Esher-Henry Wilson, 22 March 1918: 'Either the plan was "drafted in serious trust"...or it was a mere manoeuvre to get rid of Wully.' When Wilson visited GHQ in France early in March

he was received well by Haig, in spite of the fact that he left his motor running under Haig's window while Haig was performing his Müller breathing exercises with his characteristic adherence to timetable. But Wilson left the impression that now he was CIGS 'his one object is to reduce Versailles to a wash-out' (EP Philip Sassoon-Esher, 2 March 1918).

100 EP.

101 For a map showing the disposition of divisions on 21 March see Wright, *At the Supreme War Council*, (App.). According to Amery the 'war game' was played at Versailles for Haig's benefit, but he appeared 'frankly bored' and twiddled his moustache impatiently in spite of results which proved all too accurate. It was as late as March that Foch discovered that Pétain and Haig had misled him about the reserves, whereupon Lloyd George debated with Milner whether Haig should be 'dismissed out of hand for deliberate insubordination' (Amery, op. cit., II, pp. 138–9 and p. 145).

102 EP. By 8 p.m. on the 22nd Haig had received a telephone message from Gough: 'Parties of all arms of the enemy are through our reserve line' (Terraine, op. cit., p. 417).

103 Lloyd George, op. cit., II, pp. 1738–9, for text of Haig's order of 25 March.

104 EP.

105 Blake, *Haig*, p. 301.

106 MP, Gough-Maxse, 12 April 1918.

107 *J & L*, 1 May 1918.

108 MP.

109 MP.

110 MP, Northcliffe-Maxse, 16 April answering Maxse of 15th.

111 EP, Esher-Sir B. G. Faussett, n.d. (Feb. 1918).

112 EP.

113 For a recent discussion of the Maurice debate see Stephen Roskill in *The Times* (Sat. Review), 4 April 1970.

114 EP.

115 EP, same letter.

116 EP. Ninety-eight Liberals out of 268 opposed Lloyd George in the Maurice division. No Unionists supported Asquith, and even Carson voted with the government. 'On 9 May 1918 the historic

Liberal party committed suicide...' (Taylor, op. cit., pp. 74n., 105). 105).

Conclusion

1 PRO, Cab. 24–1 No. 78. 'Suggested Basis for a Territorial Settlement in Europe' by Sir Ralph Paget and Sir William Tyrell, 7 Aug. 1916, and ibid., No. 81, 'Conditions of an Armistice, by Earl of Crawford and Balcarres', 17 Sept. 1916. The stumbling block of British policy was Austria-Hungary, the dismemberment of which was being advocated in the Foreign Office by Lewis Namier, Wickham Steed and R. W. Seton-Watson. A separate peace might have preserved Austria-Hungary.

2 *J & L*, 30 Oct. 1917. Cf. Poincaré, *Au service de la France*, IX, p. 299 and Ribot, *Journal*, p. 216.

3 EP, WJ, 30 Oct. 1917. Frances Stevenson (*Diary*, pp. 162–3) comments: 'Probably the suggestion would not have been accepted by the allies, but D[avid] thinks he [Ribot] should have communicated it to the British government.' A. J. P. Taylor (*Eng. Hist.*, 162n.) dismisses the Briand-Lancken negotiations as of 'no real importance' and von Lancken as 'unofficial'. Esher's account makes it clear that the approach, although tentative, was genuine. Balfour only reported the Cambon communication to the War Cabinet on 24 Sept. when it was too late, adding 'M. Cambon had expressed the apprehension that, if once it became known in France that the cession of Alsace–Lorraine was included in the offer, it would be very difficult to keep France in the war'. Balfour complained that his information was 'absolutely vague' but he was nevertheless 'quite confident that it constituted a genuine offer' (Cab. 23–16 WC 16a 24 Sept. 1917).

4 EP.

5 One of Lloyd George's closest advisers on foreign affairs was Thomas Jones, once professor of economics at Belfast and friend and adviser to the Welsh millionaire David Davies. 'T.J.' was brought into the War Cabinet secretariat by Lloyd George as 'keeper of his democratic conscience' and immediately began to counteract the influence of Milner, Amery and the 'Junker' party in the government. When Milner chaired a cabinet committee on the territorial terms of peace in March 1918 Thomas Jones, secretary to the committee, gave an alarming account to Beatrice Webb

of 'a vivid movement...to prepare for another war'. 'This gang of Power worshippers are running down the Russian revolution and minimising the entry of the USA...They are bent on maintaining a ruling caste of a ruling race: they fear and despise democracy (LSE, PP, Beatrice Webb's diary, 18 March 1918). According to this source Lloyd George was encouraged to believe that the war had become one between democracies and autocracies, and that: 'The USA...is bent on destroying the Hohenzollerns and has no fear of revolution in European countries—rather welcomes it' (ibid.. 10 May 1917).

6 Esher believed that Beaverbrook's peerage was earned not only by his services in detaching Bonar Law from Asquith but also by paying £30,000 'to get F. E. Smith out of a scrape' (EP, WJ, 2 Jan. 1917).

7 EP, WJ, 16 Jan. 1917.

8 EP, Esher-Sir Byam G. Godfrey-Fausett, n.d. (Feb. 1918).

9 EP, Esher-Haig, 18 Jan. 1918.

10 EP, Esher-Sir B. G. Godfrey-Fausett, cited above.

11 EP, Stamfordham-Esher, 26 Feb. 1918.

12 *J & L*, 12 Nov. 1918.

13 Beatrice Webb, *Diaries*, 1912–24 (ed. Margaret Cole) pp. 159–60.

14 *J & L*, 16 June 1919.

15 'A Great Ambassador' by Esher, *Quarterly Review*, April 1923.

16 *J & L*, 15 Oct. 1922.

Bibliography

UNPUBLISHED SOURCES
1. *Manuscript collections*

Asquith papers. Bodleian Library, Oxford.

Arnold-Forster papers. British Museum, Add. MS. 50289, and esp. Add. MSS. 50335–53, diary and letters concerning departmental and political affairs kept by Arnold-Forster while Secretary for War.

Austen Chamberlain papers, Birmingham University Library.

Balfour papers. British Museum, esp. Add. MSS. 49684–752. Esher's letters to Balfour are in Add. MSS. 49718–9.

Bonar Law papers. Beaverbrook Library, London.

Devonshire papers. Chatsworth. Esher's letters to Devonshire are in MSS. 340/799–2631.

Dilke papers. British Museum, Add. MSS. 43877–922, and 49610.

Esher papers. Formerly at Watlington, now at Churchill College, Cambridge.

H.A.L. Fisher papers. Bodleian Library, Oxford.

Gladstone papers. British Museum.

Gordon papers. British Museum, Add. MSS. 56444–53.

Haig papers. National Library of Scotland, and Scottish Record Office, Edinburgh.

Haldane papers. National Library of Scotland.

Kitchener papers. Public Record Office.

Lloyd George papers. Beaverbrook Library, London.

Lothian papers. Scottish Record Office.

Maxse papers. West Sussex Record Office.

Milner papers. Bodleian Library, Oxford.

Murray of Elibank papers. National Library of Scotland.

Passfield papers. British Library of Political and Economic Science, London.

Roosevelt papers. Franklin D. Roosevelt Library, Hyde Park, New York State.

Rosebery papers. National Library of Scotland.

465

Royal Archives. Windsor Castle. Esher's correspondence with King Edward and King George V, and also with Lord Knollys and Lord Stamfordham. Prime Ministers' letters, and files concerning the army, navy, and Committee of Imperial Defence.

St. Loe Strachey papers. Beaverbrook Library, London.

Selborne papers. Bodleian Library, Oxford.

Steel-Maitland papers. Scottish Record Office.

Sydenham papers. British Museum, Add. MSS. 50305, 50832–6.

2. *Official and secret papers prepared for the Cabinet or CID.* The asterisked items are fairly complete collections available on standard microfilm.

Cab.	1	(Miscellaneous records) is largely repeated in Cab. 37 but has important military papers of 1917–19.
Cab.	2—18	contain the records of the CID from its inception in the Colonial Defence Committee down to 1939.
Cab.	19	covers the Dardanelles and Mesopotamia Special Commissions.
Cab.	21,	23 and 24 cover the cabinet's registered files minutes and memoranda respectively between 1916 and 1939.
Cab.	25	contains the records of the Supreme War Council at Versailles, 1917–19.
Cab.	26	and 27 cover cabinet committees between 1915 and 1939.
Cab.	28—32	cover allied, international and imperial conferences between 1915 and 1937.
Cab.	34	and 36 cover CID sub-committees from 1920.
*Cab.	37	Photographic copies of papers submitted to the cabinet by ministers between 1880 and 1916, listed in Public Record Office Handbook No. 4 (1964).
*Cab.	38	Photographic copies of the most important records of the CID down to 1914, taken from Cab. 1—Cab. 18, listed in the Public Record Office Handbook No. 6 (1964).
*Cab.	41	Photographic copies of the reports of cabinet decisions submitted to the Sovereign between 1868 and 1916.
*Cab.	42	Photographic copies of the records of the War Council, Dardanelles Committee and War Committee in 1915 and 1916, listed in PRO Handbook No. 9 (1966).
Cab.	63	contains papers and correspondence collected by Lord Hankey, chiefly memoranda prepared for the CID and War Cabinet with related correspondence.

3. *Theses*
    d'Ombrain, J. 'The Military Departments and the CID. 1902–14.' D. Phil., Oxford 1968.
    Lydgate, J. E. 'Curzon, Kitchener and the Problems of Indian Army Administration, 1899–1909.' Ph.D., London 1965.
    Mon, Howard R. 'The Invasion of the UK: Public Controversy and Official Planning, 1888–1918.' Ph.D., London 1968.
    Summerton. Neil W. 'The Development of British Military Planning for War against Germany. 1904–1914.' Ph.D., London 1970.
    Schurman, D. M. 'Imperial Defence, 1868–1887.' Ph.D., Cambridge 1955.

PUBLISHED SOURCES (Place of publication in London unless otherwise indicated).

1. *Contemporary diaries and letters*
    Asquith, Lady Cynthia. *Diaries, 1915–18.* 1968.
    Benson, A. C. and Viscount Esher (ed.) *The Letters of Queen Victoria.* 3 vols., 1907.
    Blake, Robert (ed.) *The Private Papers of Douglas Haig.* 1952.
    Blunt. W. S. *My Diaries, Part 2 (1900–14).* 1920.
    Chamberlain, Sir Austen. *Politics from Inside.* 1936.
    Cornish, F. W. (ed.) *Extracts from the Letters...of William Johnson Cory.* 1897.
    Esher, Reginald Baliol Brett Viscount. *Journals and Letters.* (ed. M. V. Brett) vols. 1 (1870–1903) and 2 (1903–10); (ed. Oliver Visc. Esher) vols. 3 (1910–15), and 4 (1916–30). London, 1934, 1938.
    Esher, *Extracts from Journals, 1872–1881.* 2 vols., Cambridge, 1908, 1914.
    FitzRoy, Sir Almeric. *Memoirs.* 2 vols., 1927.
    French, Lord. *Some War Diaries.* (ed. the Hon. Gerald French) 1937.
    Gallieni, Joseph Simon (ed.) *Les garnets de Gallieni.* Paris, 1932.
    Jones, Thomas. *Whitehall Diary.* (ed. Keith Middlemas) vol. 1 (1916–25). 1969.
    Kemp, P. K. (ed.) *The Papers of Admiral Sir John Fisher.* 1964.
    Lennox, Lady Algernon Gordon (ed.) *The Diary of Lord Bertie of Thame, 1914–1918.* 2 vols., 1924.
    Poincaré, Raymond. *Au service de la France.* 10 vols., Paris, 1926–33.
    Raikes, Thomas. *A Portion of the Journal of Thomas Raikes.* 4 vols., 1856–7.

Ramm, Agatha (ed.) *The Political Correspondence of Mr Gladstone and Lord Granville, 1876–1886,* 2 vols. Oxford, 1962.

Reeve, Henry (ed.) *The Greville Memoirs.* 8 vols., 1874–87.

Repington, Col. Charles à Court. *The First World War.* 2 vols., 1920.

Ribot, Alexandre. *Journal...et correspondence inédites.* Paris, 1936.

Roskill, Stephen (ed.) *Hankey: Man of Secrets.* 1970.

Stevenson, Frances. *Lloyd George. A Diary.* (ed. A. J. P. Taylor). 1971.

Suarez, Georges. *Briand,...avec son journal et...documents in édits.* Paris, 6 vols. 1938–52.

Webb, Beatrice. *Diaries.* (ed. Margaret Cole) 2 vols., 1952, 1956.

Wilson, Trevor (ed.) *The Political Diaries of C. P. Scott, 1911–28.* 1970.

2.   *Autobiographies and Biographies*

Amery, L. S. *My Political Life.* 2 vols., 1953.

Arnold-Forster, Mary. *Hugh Oakeley Arnold-Forster.* 1910.

Asquith, Earl of Oxford and. *Memories and Reflections.* 2 vols., 1926.

Beaverbrook, Lord. *Politicians and the War.* 1928.

— *Men and Power.* 1956.

Blake, Robert. *The Unknown Prime Minister: Bonar Law.* 1955.

Buchan, John. *Comments and Characters.* 1940.

Bullock, Alan. *Ernest Bevin.* 1960.

Callwell, Maj-Gen. Sir C. E. *Field-Marshal Sir Henry Wilson.* 2 vols., 1927.

Churchill, Lord Randolph. *Winston Churchill.* 1966

Churchill, Winston. *The World Crisis.* 2 vols., 1938.

Collier, Basil. *Brasshat: Field-Marshal Sir Henry Wilson.* 1961.

Cooper, Duff. *Haig.* 2 vols., 1936.

Crewe, Lord. *Rosebery.* 2 vols., 1931.

Dugdale, Blanche E. C. *Balfour.* 2 vols., 1936.

Elton, Godfrey Elton, Lord. *General Gordon.* 1954.

Fisher, Lord. *Memories.* 1919.

— *Records.* 1919.

French, Lord. *1914.* 1919.

Gardiner, A. G. *Harcourt.* 2 vols., 1923.

Gilbert, Martin. *Winston Churchill.* vol. 3 (1914–16). 1971.

Gollin, Alfred M. *Proconsul in Politics, Milner.* 1964.

Gwynn, S. L., and Tuckwell, G. M. *Dilke.* 2 vols., 1917.

Haldane, Lord. *An Autobiography.* 1929.

Harris, Henry Wilson. *J. A. Spender.* 1946.
Holland, Bernard. *Devonshire.* 2 vols., 1911.
James, Robert Rhodes. *Rosebery.* 1963.
Jenkins, Roy. *Asquith.* 1967.
Lloyd George, David. *War Memoirs.* 2 vols., 1938.
Magnus, Sir Philip. *King Edward VII.* 1964.
Maurice, Sir Frederick. *Haldane.* 2 vols., 1937.
Michell, Sir Lewis. *Rhodes.* 2 vols., 1910.
Morley, John. *Gladstone.* 3 vols., 1903.
McKenna, Stephen. *Reginald McKenna.* 1948.
MacKenzie, Faith C. *William Cory.* 1950.
Nicolson, Sir Harold. *Curzon.* 1934.
—*King George V.* 1967.
Ponsonby, Sir Frederick. *Recollections of Three Reigns.* 1951.
Pound, Reginald, and Harmsworth, G. *Northcliffe.* 1959.
Raymond, E. T. (pseud. of E. R. Thompson) *Rosebery.* 1923.
Robbins, Keith. *Sir Edward Grey.* 1971.
Spender, J. A. *Asquith.* 2 vols., 1932.
—*Weetman Pearson, Viscount Cowdray.* 1930.
—*Life, Journalism and Politics.* 1927.
Sydenham of Combe, Lord. *My Working Life.* 1927.
Terraine, John A. *Douglas Haig.* 1963.
Ward, Charles H. Dudley. *A Romance of the Nineteenth Century*
1923.
Wrench, John Evelyn. *Geoffrey Dawson and our Times.* 1955.
Young, Kenneth. *Balfour.* 1963.

3.   *General*
a.   *Books*

Adam, George. *Treason and Tragedy, French War Trials.* 1929.
Allard, Paul. *Les dessous de la guerre révlés par les comités*
secrets. Paris, 1932.
Amery, L. S. *The Problem of the Army.* 1903.
Anon. *As They Are: French Political Portraits.* New York, 1923.
Arnold-Forster, H. O. *The War Office, the Army and the Empire.*
1900.
—*The Army in 1906.* 1906.
—*Military Needs and Military Policy.* 1909.
Berger, Marcel, and Allard, Paul. *Les secrets de la censure pendant*
la guerre. Paris, 1932.
Bernhardi, Gen. Friedrich von. *Germany and the Next War.* (trans.
H. Powles). 1913.

Biddulph, Sir Robert. *Lord Cardwell at the War Office.* 1904.

Binion, Rudolph. *Defeated Leader: the Political Fate of Caillaux, Jouvenel and Tardieu.* New York, 1960.

Boraston, J. H. (ed.) *Sir Douglas Haig's Despatches.* 1920.

Charteris, John. *At GHQ.* 1931.

Churchill, Winston S. *Mr Brodrick's Army.* 1903.

Clarke, Sir George Sydenham. *Imperial Defence.* 1897.

Collins, Doreen. *Aspects of British Politics, 1904–1919.* 1965.

Dilks, David. *Curzon in India.* 2 vols., 1969, 1970.

Disraeli, Benjamin. *Coningsby.*

Douglas, Roy. *The History of the Liberal Party, 1895–1970.* 1971.

Dunlop, Col. John K. *Development of the British Army 1899–1914.* 1938.

Ehrman, John. *Cabinet Government and War 1890–1940.* Cambridge, 1958.

Emden, Paul Herman. *Behind the Throne.* 1934.

Esher, Reginald Baliol Brett, Viscount. *Footprints of Statesmen during the Eighteenth Century.* 1892.

—*Yoke of Empire.* 1896.

—*The Influence of King Edward and Other Essays.* 1914.

—*After the War.* 1918.

—*The Tragedy of Lord Kitchener.* 1921.

—*Ionicus.* 1923.

—*Cloud-Capp'd Towers.* 1927.

Fairlie, John A. *British War Administration.* Oxford, 1919.

Falls, Cyril. *The First World War.* 1960.

Fergusson, James. *The Curragh Incident.* 1964.

Fischer, Fritz. *Germany's Aims in the First World War.* 1967.

Flournoy, F. R. *Parliament and the War.* 1927.

Gibbs, N. H. *The Origins of Imperial Defence.* 1955.

Gladstone, W. E. *Speeches in Scotland.* 2 vols., 1880.

Gordon, Hampden. *The War Office.* 1935.

Gottlieb, W. W. *Studies in Secret Diplomacy during the First World War.* 1957.

Guinn, Paul. *British Strategy and Politics, 1914–1918.* Oxford, 1965.

Haldane, Lord. *Before the War.* 1920.

—*Army Reform and Other Addresses.* 1907.

Halévy, Elie. *History of the English People. Epilogue Vol. II.* 1934.

Hamer, W. S. *The British Army: Civil-Military Relations, 1885–1905.* Oxford, 1970.

Hamilton, Sir Ian. *Compulsory Service.* 1911.

Hankey, Lord. *Government Control in War.* Cambridge, 1945.
—*The Supreme Command, 1914–1918.* 2 vols., 1961.
—*The Supreme Control at the Paris Peace Conference, 1919.* 1963.
Hardie, Frank M. *The Political Influence of the British Monarchy, 1868–1952.* 1970.
Hazlehurst, Cameron. *Politicians at War.* 1971.
Hewett, Osbert H. *Strawberry Fair.* 1956.
Howard, Michael (ed.) *Soldiers and Governments.* 1957.
Huguet, Gen. *L'Intervention militaire britannique en 1914.* Paris, 1928.
Hurst, Michael. *Joseph Chamberlain and Liberal Reunion.* Toronto, 1967.
Hurwitz, Samuel J. *State Intervention in Great Britain, 1914–1919.* 1949.
Johnson, A. F. *Defence by Committee.* 1960.
Judd, Denis. *Balfour and the British Empire.* 1968.
Jullian, Philippe. *Edward and the Edwardians.* 1967.
Lloyd, E. M. H. *Experiment in State Control at the War Office and Ministry of Food.* 1924.
Luvaas, J. *The Education of an Army: British Military Thought.* Chicago, 1964.
Lyons, F. S. L. *Ireland since the Famine.* 1971.
McCallum, R. B. *Public Opinion and the Last Peace.* 1944.
Marcellin, Léopold. *Politique et politiciens pendant la guerre.* 4 vols., Paris, 1922–4.
Marder, Arthur J. *From Dreadnought to Scapa Flow.* Vol. 1, 1961.
—*British Naval Policy, 1880–1905.* 1940.
Miller, Kenneth E. *Socialism and Foreign Policy.* The Hague, 1967.
Monger, G. W. *The End of Isolation, 1900–1907.* 1967.
Nicolson, Sir Harold. *Peacemaking.* 1919.
Pedoya, Jean Marie Gustav. *La commission de l'armée pendant la grande guerre.* Paris, 1921.
Pedroncini, Guy. *Les mutineries de 1917.* Paris, 1967.
—*Les négociations secrètes pendant la grande guerre.* Paris, 1969.
Pingaud, Albert. *Histoire diplomatique de la France pendant la grande guerre.* 2 vols., Paris, 1938.
Preston, Adrian (ed.) *In Relief of Gordon: Lord Wolseley's Campaign Journal...1884–5.* 1967.
Preston, R. A. *Canada and Imperial Defence.* Durham NC. 1966.
Reinach, Joseph. *La guerre sur le front occidental.* Paris, 1916.
Renouvin, Pierre. *Les formes du gouvernement de guerre.* 1925.

Q

Rothwell, H. V. *British War Aims and Peace Diplomacy 1914–1918*. Oxford, 1971.

Roux, Marie de. *Le défaitisme et les manoeuvres pro-allemandes*. Paris, 1918.

Ryan, A. P. *Mutiny at the Curragh*. 1956.

Samuel, René. *Le parlement et la guerre, 1914–1915*. Paris, 1918.

Searle, G. R. *The Quest for National Efficiency: a Study in British Politics and Political Thought, 1899–1914*. Oxford, 1971.

Seeley, John Robert. *The Expansion of England*. 1883.

Spears, Edward L. *Prelude to Victory*. 1939.

Stansky, Peter. *Ambitions and Strategies*. 1964.

Stead, W. T. *Coming Men on Coming Questions*. 1905.

Taylor, A. J. P. *English History 1914–1945*. Oxford, 1965.

—(ed.) *Lloyd George: Twelve Essays*. 1971.

—*Politics in Wartime and Other Essays*. 1964.

Tyler, J. E. *The British Army and the Continent, 1904–1914*. 1938.

—*The Struggle for Imperial Unity, 1868–1895*. 1938.

Vergnet, Paul. *L'affaire Caillaux*. Paris, 1920.

Wheeler, Owen. *The War Office, Past and Present*. 1914.

Wilkinson, Henry Spenser. *The Brain of an Army*. 1890.

Williamson, Samuel R. *The Politics of Grand Strategy...1904–1914*. Harvard, 1969.

Wilson, Sir Guy Fleetwood. *Letters to Somebody*. 1922.

Woodward, Sir Llewellyn. *Great Britain and the War of 1914–1918*. 1967.

—*Great Britain and the German Navy*. 1935.

Wright, Gordon. *Raymond Poincaré and the French Presidency*. New York, 1967.

Wright, Peter E. *At the Supreme War Council*. 1921.

Zeman, Z. A. B. *A Diplomatic History of the First World War*. 1971.

b. *Articles*

Bedford, Duke of. 'The Collapse of the Special Infantry Reserve.' *Nineteenth Century and After*, LXXII (Jan. 1913).

Bliss, Tasker H. 'The Evolution of the Unified Command.' *Foreign Affairs*, I (Dec. 1922).

Bond, Brian. 'R. B. Haldane at the War Office.' *Army Quarterly and Defence Journal*, vol. 86 (April, 1963).

Boyle, T. 'The Formation of Campbell-Bannerman's Government...a Memorandum by J. A. Spender.' *Bulletin of the Institute of Historical Research*, XLV No. 112 (Nov. 1972).

Douglas, Roy. 'Voluntary Enlistment in the First World War.' *Journal of Modern History*, 42 No. 4 (Dec. 1970).

Ellison, Gen. Sir G. F. 'Reminiscences.' *Lancashire Lad*, 1935–6.

Esher, Reginald Viscount. 'Liberal Unionists and Coercion.' *Nineteenth Century*, April 1887.

—'What are the Ideals of the Masses?' *Nineteenth Century*. October 1890.

—'National Strategy.' (pamphlet) 1904.

—'A Great Ambassador.' *Quarterly Review*. April 1923.

Fest, W. B. 'British War Aims and German Peace Feelers... (December 1916–November 1918).' *Historical Journal* XV, 2 (1972).

Gollin, Alfred M. 'Asquith. A New View.' in *Century of Conflict* (ed. Martin Gilbert), 1966.

Hazlehurst, Cameron. 'Asquith as Prime Minister.' *English Historical Review*, LXXV (1970).

Kennedy, P. M. 'Imperial Cable Communications and Strategy, 1870–1914.' *English Historical Review* LXXVI (1971).

Lockwood, P. A. 'Milner's Entry into the War Cabinet, December 1916.' *Historical Journal* VII, No. 1, (1964).

McGill, Barry. 'Asquith's Predicament, 1914–18.' *Journal of Modern History*, 39 No. 3 (Sept. 1967).

Mackintosh, John P. 'The Role of the Committee of Imperial Defence before 1914.' *English Historical Review*, LXXVII (1962).

Morris, A. J. A. 'Haldane's Army Reforms, 1906–8: the Deception of the Radicals.' *History*, 56 (1971).

—'The English Radicals' Campaign for Disarmament and the Hague Conference of 1907.' *Journal of Modern History* 43 No. 3 (Sept. 1971).

Renouvin, P. 'Les buts de guerre du gouvernement français.' *Review Historique* (1966).

Taylor, A. J. P. 'The War Aims of the Allies in the First World War.' in *Essays Presented to Sir Lewis Namier*, eds. R. Pares and A. J. P. Taylor, 1956.

Trainor, Luke. 'The Liberals and the Formation of Imperial Defence Policy. 1892–5.' *Bulletin of the Institute of Historical Research*, XLII (Nov. 1969).

Tucker, Albert. 'The Issue of Army Reform in the Unionist Government, 1903–5.' *Historical Journal*, IX, No. 1 (1966).

Warman, Roberta M. 'The Erosion of Foreign Office Influence in the Making of Foreign Policy, 1916–1918.' *Historical Journal*, XV No. 1 (1972).

c. *Periodicals*
   British Parliamentary Papers:
   Report of the [Hartington] Royal Commission...into the civil and professional administration of the naval and military departments and the relation of those departments to each other and to the Treasury. (C. 5979, 1890).
   Report of the [Dawkins] Committee on War Office Reorganisation. (1901, Cd. 580) XL.
      „   „   „   Minutes of evidence (Cd. 581, 1901) XL.
   Report of the [Elgin] Commission to inquire into the military preparations, and other matters connected with the war in South Africa. (Cd. 1789, 1903) XL, 1904.
      „   „   „   Minutes of evidence, 2 vols. (Cd. 1790–1. 1903) XL, 1904.
      „   „   „   Appendices. (Cd. 1792, 1903) XLII, 1904.
   Report of the Royal Commission on the militia and the volunteers. (Cd. 2061, 1904) XXX.
      „   Minutes of evidence, 2 vols. and appendices. (Cd. 2062–3–4. 1904) XXX, XXXI.
   Report of the [Esher] Committee on the reconstitution of the War Office. (Cd. 1932, 1904) VIII
                        (Cd. 1968, 1904) VIII
                        (Cd. 2002, 1904) VIII
   Army: Particulars regarding the proposed army organisation scheme. (Cd. 1910, 1904) LI.
   Order in Council defining the duties of the Army Council. (Cd. 2251, 1904) XLVI, 1905.
   Order in Council defining the duties of the Inspector General of the Forces. (Cd. 2252, 1904) XLVI, 1905.
   Report of the Committees on sales and refunds to contractors in South Africa. (Cd. 2435, 1905).
   Army: memorandum by the Secretary of State for War on army reorganisation. 30 July 1906. (Cd. 2993, 1906) LXVII.

Daily Telegraph
Dictionary of National Biography
Fortnightly Review
Glasgow Herald
Hansard
Le Matin
Liberal Magazine
Listener
New Statesman

Bibliography

Pall Mall Gazette
Qui Etes Vous? (Paris)
Review of Reviews
Spectator
Standard
The Times
The World
Westminster Gazette
Who's Who

d.   *Bibliographical*
     Higham, Robin (ed.) *A Guide to the Sources of British Military
     History*. 1972.

Abbreviations:

AP	=	Asquith Papers
BL	=	Beaverbrook Library
Bod L	=	Bodleian Library
BM	=	British Museum
Cd	=	Command Paper
CID	=	Committee of Imperial Defence
DNB	=	*Dictionary of National Biography*
DP	=	Devonshire Papers
EP	=	Esher Papers
FDRP	=	Franklin D. Roosevelt Papers
HP	=	Haldane Papers
J and L	=	*Journals and Letters of Viscount Esher*
LGP	=	Lloyd George Papers
LSE	=	London School of Economics and Political Science
MEP	=	Murray of Elibank Papers
MP	=	Maxse Papers
NLS	=	National Library of Scotland
PP	=	Passfield Papers
PRO	=	Public Record Office
RA	=	Royal Archives, Windsor Castle
RL	=	Roosevelt Library
RP	=	Rosebery Papers
Sel P	=	Selborne Papers
SMP	=	Steel-Maitland Papers
SP	=	St Loe Strachey Papers
SRO	=	Scottish Record Office
WJ	=	War Journals

Index

Q*

480

Index

C-in-C of Army, 124–7, 147, 162–3; and General Staff, 151, 154–6; friendship with Haig, 157–9; and Haldane's army reforms, 180, 190–1, 193, 196, 202; and success of Esher's territorial recruiting drive, 205–206; and Esher's indiscretions over navy estimates, 200; and Lloyd George's budget of 1909, 208–209; and 'guarantees' to Asquith, 212–13; death of, 214–15, 242

Egerton, Lady Louisa, 29

Egypt, 3, 6, 55, 102, 399; and evacuation of the Sudan, 42–3; appointment of General Gordon in Sudan, 42–4; and Gladstone's policy over Sudan, 45–9; relief expedition to Khartoum, 46, 53–4; fall of Khartoum, 53–4, Rosebery's policies in, 62–3, 65; and Churchill's Mediterranean policy, 253–4; in First World War, 261, 269, 308.

Elgin Commission on South African War, 79, 87–8, 91; Report of, 90, 92–3, 95, 174

Eliot, George, 9, 32

Elliot, Arthur, 91

Ellis, Tom, 68

Ellison, Colonel Sir Gerald, 21, 120, 134, 180, 182–3, 191

Englishman's Home, An, 205

Entente, between Britain and France, 110, 181, 239, 240, 251, 253

Errington, Lord, 344

Esher, 2nd Viscount (formerly Reginald Brett), 1–2; association with Sir Ernest Cassel, 1, 81, 87; parents, 2; historical writings, 2, 17, 69, 71; and CID, 1, 4, 14, 20–4, 28, 79, 85, 88–9, 123, 144, 166–74, and role in national defence policy, 2–3, 19–20, 106–107, 146–7, *and see* CID, Esher Committee, Secret Esher Committee; military and constitutional adviser to Edward VII, 5–6, 13–15, 17–20, 80–3, 87–91, 106, 122, 124–7, 162–3; education, 7–11; private secretary to Lord Hartington, 12, 31–8, 55–6; early political career as inter-party mediator, 12–13; MP for Penryn and Falmouth, 13, 36, 38–9, 66; and Esher Committee, 13–14, 21, 78–9,

90, 92–108, 111, 122, 124, 149; marriage to Eleanor van de Weyer, 15–16, 32; and Queen Victoria, 16–17, 68–70; Secretary of Office of Works and Deputy Governor of Windsor Castle, 17–18, 68–71; 80–3; on Elgin Commission, 19, 79, 87–8, 91, 174; and contacts with the press, 21, 27, 40, 44, 46, 48, 50–3, 56, 61, 75, 227, 233, 242–3, 245, 276–7, 290, *see also* Northcliffe, Lord, and Stead, W. T.; and Ulster problem, 24–5, 215, 233; as unofficial adviser to Kitchener, 25–7, 262–5, 267, 270, 277, 299, 312–13, 316–17; on the Duchess of Manchester, 29–30; and events in Egypt, 39, 43–50, 53–4; and issue of rebuilding the Navy, 51–3; views on social conditions, 56; and alliance with Radical Liberals, 1885, 56–8; and Irish Home Rule, 56–9, 64, 215, 253; candidate in 1885 election, 56; and Round Table Conference, 59, 63–4; and Unionist Liberals, 61–2; relationship with Rosebery, 66, 68–9; offered Under-Secretaryship of State for the Colonies by Chamberlain, 71; association with War Office, 72–3, 91–2, 100–107, 122, 136, 153, 162–3, 175, 179, 196; and reform of War Department under Balfour, 77–9, 87–91, 92–3, *and see* Esher Committee; awarded KCVO, 79; relations with Lord Northcliffe, 81, 382, 392–3, 399; and opposition to Arnold-Forster's schemes for army reform, 110, 112, 115–17, 120–1, 124–31, 166; and secret Esher Committee, 131–47, 151, 154; and creation of 'general staff', 100, 148–62, 186; and promotion of Douglas Haig, 157–9; and changes in government on Balfour's resignation, 179–81; and Anglo-French military conversations, 173, 182–4, 190, 250; conception of role of Militia and Haldane's army policies, 186–96: and conscription, 192–4, 205, 244, 294–5, 312–14, 318–19, 321; and committees to inquire into territorial aspects of Haldane's army reforms, 190–2;

483

Index

487

Index

Round Table Conference, 63–4; diffidence of, 63, 66; defence policy, 78, 88; and Gladstone, 60–1; offered Privy Seal by Lloyd George, 399
Rothermere, Lord, 337, 378, 393, 394
Rothschild, Alfred, 30, 224
Rothschild, Leopold de, 30
Rothschild, Mrs Leopold de, 30
Rothschild, Maurice, 355
Rothschild, Nathaniel de, 30
Roumania, 270, 301, 338, 342, 347
Round Table Conference, *see* Liberal Party
Rowntree, Joseph, 257–8
Royal Army Medical Corps, 267
Runciman, Walter, 285, 293, 307
Ruskin, John, 8
Russell, Lord John, 5
Russia, 30, 110, 114, 146, 271, 325; and Constantinople, 12, 74–5, 362; Russo-Japanese War, 100, 149, 181, 190; British Agreement of 1907, 239; defeat of army early in First World War, 268–9, 280; and Churchill's Dardanelles policy, 269–70; defeats of 1916, 289; and Salonika, 307; Revolution in, 361, 363; out of the war, 364–6, 371, 398; German ambitions in, 370; French Treaty with, 1917, 397

St Aldwyn, Lord, *see* Hicks Beach
Salisbury, Lord, 7, 32–3, 80, 214, 380; as Prime Minister, 59, 74, 85; and Boer War, 76–7; and Defence Committee, 78, 84; schemes for army reform, 110, 112–13
Salonika, 268–70, 294–5, 298, 300, 305–307, 324–5, 337–8, 348, 365–6
Sandars, J. S., private secretary to Balfour, 4, 94, 111, 125, 136, 159, 164, 246, 251; delegation of authority to by Balfour, 21, 106, 122, 128, 146, 166, 171–2; and Esher Committees, 104, 163; and Arnold-Forster's army reforms, 121, 130–4, 139, 141–2, 144, 156, 158, 170; and Sir Neville Lyttleton, 152–3; and CID, 166, 171, 176, 178, 180; and issue of naval rebuilding, 203–205; and constitutional crisis after 1909 Budget, 208–209, 224–5

Sarrail, Maurice, 348, 365
Sassoon, Mrs Arthur, 30
Sassoon, Philip, 375
Schlieffen plan, 240
Schnadhorst, Francis, 61, 64–5
Scott, C. P., 299, 307, 329; and Lloyd George's use of press, 296–7, 315, 343, 372, 378
Scott-Montagu, Hon. J. W. E. D., 113
Sedan, battle of, 75
Seeley, J. R., 2, 55
Seely, J. E. B., 113, 233, 256
Selborne, Lord, 3, 37; as First Lord of the Admiralty, 85–8, 92, 94, 98, 103, 108; and Militia, 110–11, 140, 142; supports plan for Allied council, 271, 301–302; and conscription, 317
Serbia, 235, 270, 294–5
Seymour, Beauchamp, 51
'Shells scandal', 268–9, 273–5, 277–9, 281–2, 289; and Northcliffe press, 288; and Somme casualties, 328–9
Shute, Lt.-Col. H. G. D., 116
Sidgwick, Henry, 9
Simon, Sir J., 307
Sinclair, Captain, 21, 180
Sixte, Prince, 362
Smillie, Robert, 330, 388
Smith, F. E., 297, 329, 331, 336
Smuts, General J. C., 77, 365
Smythe, George, 7
Socialism, 63, 65, 147, 208, 239
Somme offensive, 26, 289, 300, 323, 326–7, 393; casualties, 328–9; German retirement on Somme, 360–1
South Africa, 6, 65, 71–2, 244; Jameson Raid, 13; South African War (Boer War), 13, 18–19, 50, 72–3, 76–7, 79, 90, 110, 121, 160; Elgin Commission on war, 79, 87–8, 90–3, 95; coolie labour in, 333
Soveral, Portuguese Ambassador to London, 83
Spain, 254
Spectator, 21, 35
Spencer, Lord, 60, 66–7, 117, 120
Spender, J. A., 21, 123, 179–80, 246–7, 291–2; visits Haig's HQ, 327; and Lloyd George, 331–2; and war propaganda, 335
Stamfordham, Lord, *see* Sir Arthur Bigge

El